CAPITALISM AND NATIONALISM AT THE END OF EMPIRE

T0314196

CAPITALISM AND NATIONALISM
AT THE END OF EMPIRE

STATE AND BUSINESS IN DECOLONIZING
EGYPT, NIGERIA, AND KENYA, 1945–1963

Robert L. Tignor

PRINCETON UNIVERSITY PRESS   PRINCETON, NEW JERSEY

Copyright © 1998 by Princeton University Press
Published by Princeton University Press, 41 William Street,
Princeton, New Jersey 08540
In the United Kingdom: Princeton University Press, Chichester, West Sussex
All Rights Reserved

Library of Congress Cataloging-in-Publication Data
Tignor, Robert L.
Capitalism and nationalism at the end of empire : state and business in
decolonizing Egypt, Nigeria, and Kenya, 1945–1963 / Robert L. Tignor.
p.   cm.
Includes bibliographical references and index.
ISBN 0-691-01584-8 (cloth : alk. paper)
1. Africa—Economic conditions—1945–1960.   2. Capital—Africa—
History.   3. Africa—Colonial influence.   4. Industrial policy—Africa—
History.   5. Nationalism—Africa.   I. Title.
HC800.T52   1998
330.96′032—dc21   97-13796   CIP

This book has been composed in Times Roman expanded 105%

Princeton University Press books are printed on acid-free paper
and meet the guidelines for permanence and durability of the
Committee on Production Guidelines for Book Longevity of the
Council on Library Resources

Printed in the United States of America

1   3   5   7   9   10   8   6   4   2

Contents

Acknowledgments

IT IS A distinct pleasure to pay tribute to the people and organizations who helped me at various stages in this project. This work would not have seen the light of day without the assistance I received from the many individuals who administer the extraordinary archival collections around the world dealing with the colonial experience. I am indebted to the staffs of the National Archives of the United States; the National Archives of Kenya; and the Colonial Research Project Archives at Rhodes House, Oxford University. Anyone who has had the pleasure of studying in those facilities knows how agreeable the staff make the work of the researcher.

Much of the primary source documentation for this study comes from the Public Record Office in London, where I was a frequent visitor. The staff there were especially encouraging during the dark and discouraging winter months several years ago when the archive was forced to shut down because of an air-conditioning problem. My spirits sank. I envisaged a whole research trip wiped out. My friends at the Kew building kept me informed about the prospects for reopening and encouraged me not to lose hope. We all enjoyed a private champagne toast when the facility finally reopened. I am grateful to them for support. I also want to acknowledge the archivists and others connected with the Ford Motor Company, Shell Oil, Cadburys, Mobil Oil, Barclays Bank, DCO, Unilever, Calico Printers, and Bradford Dyers, all of whom made using business records an exciting and worthwhile experience. It would be nearly impossible for me to offer a tribute to the individual librarians in all of the collections where I did research, but I would be unforgivably remiss if I did not record my gratitude to the staff at the Firestone Library of Princeton University, my own institution. They did yeoman's work in informing me about Princeton's resources and borrowing whatever Princeton did not possess from other institutions.

Comparative work can be daunting. Because one can hardly expect to be an expert on everything that one compares, I tried to ensure that I got good advice from experts who knew more about individual parts of the story than I did and could, so that I did not lose sight of the historical reality I was trying to describe. Of course, those friendly advisers are in no way accountable for the arguments advanced here. They will quickly see where I have relied on their cautions and where I have not. In particular, I wish to thank L. Carl Brown, Frederick Cooper, Michael Doran, David Gordon, Jeffrey Herbst, Zachary Lockman, Gyan Prakash, Heather

Sharkey, Robert Shell, Robert Vitalis, and John Waterbury for having read part or all of the manuscript for this book. Arno Mayer and Stanley Stein have been intellectual comrades throughout my career at Princeton and constant commentators on my work. I dedicate this study to them.

AG   Action Group
AWAM   Association of West African Merchants
B of E   Bank of England
BOT   Board of Trade
Cab   Cabinet
CO   Colonial Office
COR   Calabar, Ogoja, and Rivers
CRO   Commonwealth Relations Office
DCO   Dominions, Colonies, and Overseas
DO   Dominions Office
EC   Egypt Committee
FO   Foreign Office
IBRD   International Bank for Reconstruction and Development
Kadu   Kenya African Democratic Union
Kanu   Kenya African National Union
KAU   Kenya African Union
KC   Kenya Coalition
KCA   Kikuyu Central Association
KKM   Kikuyu Kia Muingi
KLFA   Kenya Land Freedom Army
KNA   Kenya National Archives
KNFA   Kenya National Farmers Association
£   Pound sterling
£E   Egyptian pound
MCI   Ministry of Commerce and Industry
NCNC   National Council of Nigeria and the Cameroons
NEPU   Northern Elements Progressive Union
NIP   National Independence Party
NKP   New Kenya Party
NPC   Northern People's Congress
PREM   Premier's Office
PRO   Public Record Office
RCC   Revolutionary Command Council
UAC   United Africa Company
USNA   United States National Archives

CAPITALISM AND NATIONALISM AT THE END OF EMPIRE

Perspectives on Decolonization

AT THE END of the fifteenth century the European states embarked upon a quest for global dominance that saw little pause until the close of World War II. Each century seemed only to deepen and intensify Europe's involvement in non-European affairs until, in the late nineteenth century, in conjunction with the partition of Africa, the European powers had established their formal colonial rule over the African and Asian continents. Although Asians and Africans were active agents in this reorientation of world power, as either facilitators or resisters, it was not until 1945 and after that the men and women in most colonial and semicolonial regions of the world succeeded in rolling back the many layers of European dominance. The decade and a half after World War II, known generally as the decolonizing years, started with a transfer of power from Britain to Indian nationalists in 1947, and thereafter a movement of political liberation rampaged through the Asian continent and spread into the Middle East and North Africa. This groundswell reached into Africa south of the Sahara only a decade later.

The ending of the great European empires in Asia and Africa must count as one of the watershed events in world history. Delhi, Cairo, Beijing, and Jakarta became new centers of power, taking their place alongside London, Paris, Washington, and Moscow as the locations of decisions affecting millions around the world. Yet just how much had changed and how much remained when the flags of the new nations were substituted for those of the old imperial powers? In a gloomy moment, black Africa's most visible anticolonial nationalist and the first prime minister of an independent tropical African state, Kwame Nkrumah, opined that independence had merely witnessed an exchange of one set of masters for another. Multinational executives and agents of international organizations replaced colonial administrators in the seats of power on the continent. Formal colonialism gave way to neocolonialism.

To date, the political aspects of decolonization have received more attention than the economic features, perhaps in recognition that Nkrumah was right when he asserted that the quest for political independence ought to precede other matters. Nonetheless, this emphasis is surprising and misplaced since colonial officials and African nationalists alike regarded the economic ties that bound metropole and periphery as more

vital to that relationship than the political connections. This study empha-
sizes Euro-African economic institutions and economic relationships in
the crucial era of power transfer, seeking to evaluate Nkrumah's complaint that Africans succeeded in ridding themselves only of the accoutre-
ments of formal power while remaining in profound economic subordination to the developed world.

In *Africa and the Victorians* Ronald Robinson and John Gallagher laid
out a research technique for understanding power transfers in imperial
settings.[1] They proposed that the most feasible way to answer the vexed
question of why Britain, or any other modern expansionist power, embarked on colonial conquest was to examine the ministerial decisions that
were made to commit troops and to take on colonial responsibilities. Their
research breakthrough yielded impressive, though not unchallenged results, and now has emboldened a new generation of Robinson and Gallagher enthusiasts to apply the same approach to that other major moment
of power transfer—the conferring of political independence. Yet the pit-
falls of this approach become even more obvious for the later decisions,
when Europe was no longer the hegemon. Decisions could not be made in
isolation from Washington or from thoughts about the Soviet Union. The
power equation between Europe and Africa had changed so that the imperial powers could no longer be certain of their ability to intimidate their
nationalist opponents. In addition, decolonization decisions were not
purely political matters—whether to leave and when. They also entailed a
complex set of nonpolitical issues and inevitably involved numerous nongovernmental groups. Many of the most crucial and controversial issues
of power transfer were related to economics; they were concerned with
how much of the old colonial economic structure the departing powers
could persuade the new nationalist challengers to leave in place and how
much would have to be sacrificed on the altar of political necessity.

In colonial conquest, the overriding issue was whether to send troops.
In colonial withdrawal, the removal of troops and the ending of formal
political controls were often subordinated to the economic and cultural
arrangements that could continue to be imposed between metropole and
former colony. Yet the colonial officials were compelled to be interested
in much more than preserving the metropolitan economic stake in Africa.
They realized that African economic growth was a key to future political
stability and ongoing amicable relations with the metropole. For those
officials and the rising African nationalists the crucial question of the
period was how best to promote the kind of economic development that
could be sustained after independence. The political elites as well as

[1] Ronald Robinson and John Gallagher, with Alice Denny, *Africa and the Victorians: The
Climax of Imperialism* (London, 1961).

groups outside the formal political arena debated how large the role of the state should be and what encouragement, if any, should be given to the private sector, which had previously been dominated by foreign capital but in many decolonizing territories possessed a new and rising indigenous business class.

The decolonizing winds blew across the whole of the African continent, and though, with a few exceptions in the southern, white-dominated parts of Africa, it brought political independence by the mid-1960s, not every new polity at independence looked the same, especially if economic matters are placed at the center of the analysis. Indeed, three countries of vital interest to the British empire, albeit in manifestly different ways, traversed divergent and in some ways surprising economic pathways to their independence and had markedly different economic systems at the end of the era of decolonization.

Those three countries—Egypt, Nigeria, and Kenya—were crucial to the well-being and smooth functioning of the British empire in Africa. British influences, economic and political, were of a high order in each country in 1945. Yet by the early 1960s their economies and their ties with Britain were quite dissimilar. Egypt had all but dismantled its corporate business sector, a surprising development given the strength of Egypt's business community in 1945. The Egyptian military leaders claimed to have created a new brand of third-world socialism. In contrast, Kenya's private sector weathered the storm of the Mau Mau conflict and the conferral of political power on Jomo Kenyatta, the man whom the British held responsible for the spread of anti-Europeanist sentiment. In spite of these political and military shocks the private sector had been well insulated from the nationalist struggle and was poised, under an independent though largely conciliatory and pro-Western regime, to take advantage of the relative health and vigor of its business groups. As for the Nigerian private sector, after showing early promise, it had fallen into disarray. It was deeply infected with the corruption that was engulfing the political arena, and it had been drawn into the maelstrom of competing ethnic nationalisms.

Analysts of decolonization agree that three factors are crucial in explaining decolonization, although they disagree sharply about how much weight to attach to each factor generally and in specific cases. The factors are rising nationalism, changes in the international balance of power, and shifts in the attitudes of groups within the metropole toward empire.[2] One

---

[2] For useful summary statements on the general factors leading to the transfer of power in Asia and Africa, see, in particular, the article by William Roger Louis and Ronald Robinson, "The United States and the Liquidation of the British Empire in Tropical Africa, 1941–1951," in Prosser Gifford and William Roger Louis, eds., *The Transfer of Power in Africa: Decolonization, 1940–1960* (New Haven, Conn., 1982). There is an immense scholarly

of the purposes of this study is to evaluate the importance of each of these forces in the three countries investigated here.

To preview some of the findings of this study in light of the three elements involved in decolonization, let us begin by considering the role of nationalism in bringing an end to empire in Africa. No scholar would question the decisive importance of nationalist movements in the toppling of the British, French, and Dutch empires in Asia. There is, however, little consensus on the significance of nationalism in ending the European empires in Africa. Historians whom one might identify as from the imperial school, given their preference for working in imperial archives and according primacy to imperial forces, deny that African nationalism compelled the European withdrawal. To them, Europe's ruling classes were the critical actors from the beginning of empire to its close. They terminated their formal rule in Africa for reasons of their own choosing and not because they faced an overpowering challenge from African nationalist movements. To be sure, in some cases these officials mistook protest movements for the kind of coherent nationalist activity that had proved so decisive in Asia. But, in reality, to the historians of the "official mind," African protests did not emanate from deep-seated nationalist sentiments. On the contrary, they were atomized and instrumentalist expressions that stemmed from specific grievances, usually of an economic nature. Rarely did the protesters articulate long-range nationalist goals. For the imperial school, especially historians of the British empire, tropical Africa never succeeded in being anything more than an adjunct to Asia. Acquired for defensive and strategic reasons in relationship to Britain's more compelling economic and cultural interests in Asia, its independence was foreordained once Asia had seized its political freedom.[3]

---

literature on decolonization, but I found the following works most helpful. John Darwin, *Britain and Decolonisation: The Retreat from Empire in the Post-War World* (London, 1988); R. F. Holland, *European Decolonisation, 1918–1981: An Introductory Survey* (New York, 1985); Miles Kahler, *Decolonization in Britain and France: The Domestic Consequences of International Relations* (Princeton, N.J., 1984); Henry Grimal, *Decolonisation: The British, French, Dutch, and Belgian Empires, 1919–1963*, tr. Stephen de Vos (Boulder, Colo., 1978); Colin Cross, *The Fall of the British Empire, 1918–1968* (London, 1968); Crawford Young, "Decolonization in Africa," in Peter Duignan and L. H. Gann, eds., *Colonialism in Africa, 1870–1960* (Cambridge, 1970), vol. 2; Rudolf von Albertini, *Decolonization: The Administration and Future of the Colonies, 1919–1960* (New York, 1971); David Goldsworthy, *Colonial Issues in British Politics, 1945–1961: From Colonial Development to Winds of Change* (Oxford, 1971); Tony Smith, *The Patterns of Imperialism: The United States, Great Britain, and the Late-Industrializing World since 1815* (Cambridge, 1981); Franz Ansprenger, *Auflösung der Kolonialreiche* (Munich, 1966); and the other works cited throughout the footnotes.

[3] Here the work of Ronald Robinson is of great significance, especially his oft-cited article on Andrew Cohen. Ronald Robinson, "Andrew Cohen and the Transfer of Power in Tropical Africa, 1940–1951," in W. H. Morris-Jones and Georges Fischer, eds., *Decolonisa-*

Another group of historians of empire, who might be called nationalist historians, bristle at this demeaning view of African nationalism. The transfer of power in Africa, according to these analysts, was driven at every stage by a surging challenge from African nationalists. In Nigeria, according to J. F. Ade Ajayi and A. E. Ekoko, Nnamdi Azikiwe's demands for a fifteen-year timetable of independence in 1943 and the NCNC (National Council of Nigeria and the Cameroons) challenges to the Richards constitution were the key initiatives that placed Nigeria on the pathway to independence.[4] By the same token, Kenyan nationalist historians stress the many challenges originating from African groups. They depict decolonization as a tumultuous set of events rather than an orderly process of gradual transfer of power to African leaders. E. S. Atieno-Odhiambo claims that the imperial school "sanitizes struggle, eliminates contradictions, and smuggles a plan—God's or empire's, it does not matter—into Kenya's history."[5]

The sharp differences over African nationalism prove, however, on closer examination, to be less pronounced than they seem at first glance. If one remembers that the British empire was an integrated whole, particularly in matters of garrisoning and policing, it becomes clear that the forces of opposition needed to challenge the British in Africa had to be less substantial than those required to topple the British empire in Asia. Britain's primary imperial military force was stationed in India where the British not only had a large army of occupation but also relied on an even more substantial Indian army, constituted from Indian recruits who were commanded by British officers seconded from the British army. Although the main duty of those forces was to preserve internal order and defend India's northern frontiers, the troops were available for emergency use elsewhere in the British empire. Indian troops were detached to Egypt when the Egyptian army invaded the Sudan in 1898. A second major imperial base existed in Egypt, where the British also had their own army of occupation, albeit a much smaller one than in India. Nonetheless, during World War II the British constructed their largest overseas military base alongside the Suez Canal, and it became the linchpin of imperial military strategy after the end of the war. Although an Anglo-Egyptian treaty negotiated in 1936 restricted the size of British ground forces sta-

---

tion and After: The British and French Experience (London, 1980). But one finds echoes of this thought in the work of many of the authors cited in the previous note and also in the writings of Robert Pearce and David Fieldhouse, cited later in this chapter.

[4] J. F. Ade Ajayi and A. E. Ekoko, "The Transfer of Power in Nigeria: Its Origins and Consequences," in Prosser Gifford and William Roger Louis, *Decolonization and African Independence: The Transfer of Power, 1960–1980* (New Haven, Conn., 1988).

[5] E. S. Atieno-Odhiambo, "The Formative Years, 1945–55," in B. A. Ogot and W. R. Ochieng, eds., *Decolonization and Independence in Kenya, 1940–93* (London, 1995), p. 26.

tioned in the Suez Canal base to 10,000, except in times of war, in fact the canal base was capable of supporting upwards of 100,000 men and did so during the troubled Anglo-Egyptian period of the early 1950s. This force, as well, could be dispatched to troubled areas of the empire, as it was during the Mau Mau disturbances in Kenya.

In contrast to India and Egypt, the British imperial establishment did not provide large military forces for colonial Africa. Its officials expected the African colonies to garrison and police themselves and to do so on the cheap with relatively small forces. After India achieved its independence and the British withdrew their soldiers from Egypt, imperial strategists elected not to establish a strong British military presence in Africa. Here, they continued to require colonial officials to administer territories with the same minimal coercive capacities that had existed before the imperial army had been shorn of its strongest military redoubts elsewhere. As a consequence, African nationalists did not have to measure their political organizations against powerful occupying armies, as the Indian and Egyptian nationalists did, or even for that matter against large British-officered indigenous military and police forces. It was not surprising, then, that when military and civilian colonial officials in Africa were queried about their capability to deal with rising nationalist challenges, as they were repeatedly in Nigeria and Kenya, they usually responded skeptically, because of their admittedly understaffed and light coercive capacities. Britain did dispatch substantial military forces to crush the Mau Mau uprising, but that intervention sealed the fate of the recalcitrant white settlers and made the enfranchisement of Africans inevitable.

Africa's postcolonial experience has emboldened the imperial school to question the validity of African nationalist impulses. The continent's record of coups d'etat, ethnic violence, and civil war suggests the long-term failure of African nationalist leaders to establish grassroots support and mass-based, disciplined political organizations. But the political divisiveness and lack of direction in the postcolonial era did not arise because anticolonial sentiments were not widespread or because African protesters had no vision of a continent without European overrulers. Quite the contrary, late colonial Africa suffered from a cacophony of voices and protest activities. It produced many moments of heightened agitation against colonial suzerainty and projected numerous visions of a postcolonial world, albeit often contradictory ones. Workers, students, peasant farmers, and the urban unemployed were not passive bystanders, only occasionally involved in challenging colonial authority and easily manipulated by colonial officials and nationalist elite groups.

In Nigeria and Kenya early demands for power sharing arose from ethnically based, elitist political parties and from the landed and industrial wealthy in Egypt. But have-not elements, like the Mau Mau disaffected, labor agitators in the main cities of Nigeria and Kenya, cocoa farmers and small merchants in southwestern Nigeria, and workers, students, and Muslim Brothers in Egypt shifted the political initiative away from these elite organizations and leaders at critical moments and put the colonial authorities under pressure to devise new, more populist policies. The growing intensity of nationalist discontent that emerges in each of the case studies bears witness to the role of subalterns in undermining the gradualist programs of the colonial officials and their elitist collaborators and in bringing about reformist agendas. The decolonizing period in Africa was far from consensual. It did not entail a smooth transfer of power in which the British accomplished most of what they wanted to do. It was instead a tumultuous era, one that was full of conflict and that continuously challenged the formulas colonial officials tried to impose on local populations.[6]

The second variable invoked to explain decolonization is the shift in metropolitan attitudes toward empire. Here too, the existing scholarly literature is fractious, and detailed case studies can make a contribution. Practitioners of the imperial school have argued that a change in the mentality of the European ruling classes occurred shortly after the close of World War II, led by the British, who had no expectation that empire would be everlasting. Unencumbered by ideas of assimilation and paternalism, the British had an easier time comprehending the nationalist assertions and arranging for orderly transfers of power.[7] The chief architects within those British circles concerned with Africa are held to be Governors Alan Burns and Bernard Bourdillon of the Gold Coast and Nigeria respectively and Andrew Cohen in the Colonial Office. These men set the stage for an accelerated devolution of power, first by repudiating Lord Hailey's strategy of ruling through traditional chiefs and then by bringing the new African-educated elites within the orbit of political authority. For Robert Pearce, British officialdom reached a psychological "point of no return" somewhere between 1938 and 1948. By the end of that crucial decade, "the door to rapid decolonization was unlocked."[8] For nearly all

---

[6] I cite the literature that catalogues subaltern and elite protest in the chapters on Egypt, Nigeria, and Kenya, but here I want to mention the introductory chapter of Florencia Mallon's study *Peasant Nation: The Making of Colonial Mexico and Peru* (Berkeley, Calif., 1995), p. 2, for its attentiveness to the many divergent discourses on nationalism other than the "dominant visions of nationalism as an ideology created by the bourgeoisie," which has garnered most of the work of scholars of nationalism.

[7] See, in particular, Dennis Austin, "The Transfer of Power: Why and How," in Morris-Jones and Fischer, eds., *Decolonisation and After*, and Kahler, *Decolonization in Britain and France*.

[8] R. D. Pearce, *The Turning Point in Africa: British Colonial Policy, 1938–48* (London, 1982), p. 204.

of the scholars of the official mind, the Accra riots of 1948 in the Gold Coast were a decisive event in persuading British colonial policy makers that African nationalism had, indeed, emerged and independence was only a short distance away.[9]

In reality, Egypt, Nigeria, and Kenya traveled a much less rationalized and coherent road to their political freedom—one that never fully achieved a point of no return in the minds of the African nationalists or the British colonial authorities. How else to explain the British decision to invade Egypt, which as a political and military exercise sought not only to topple President Nasser (a monumental task in itself) but also anticipated the creation of the kind of "veiled protectorate" over Egypt that Lord Cromer had erected in the halcyon days of imperial control. Nor was Kenya ever an integral part of British official thinking about the appropriate timetable for African independence. Its powerful white settler population entitled it to a different framework for power transfer, or so the colonial officials and the European settlers thought. This exclusion of Kenya from the wind of colonial change persisted in London right up until the fateful Lancaster Conference in 1960. Even in Nigeria, which in most imperial histories moves in lockstep with the Gold Coast, the British colonial bureaucracy engaged in a robust debate as late as 1956 about whether to withdraw promises for regional self-government and halt constitutional reform programs until the Nigerian politicians had demonstrated a greater capacity for "good government."

Historians of the official mind have concentrated on the political elite and have focused on crucial political debates and decisions. On the rare occasions when they have looked at the economic side of the debate, they have divided sharply over the importance of economic questions and especially of the influence of large-scale foreign businesses in decolonization. A first perspective, well represented in the studies of David Fieldhouse, argues that the emphasis on political issues by imperial historians has been well justified by the events themselves. Business groups, even powerful multinationals, were never more than subordinate actors. For Fieldhouse, decolonization "was primarily a political rather than an economic phenomenon as far as British officials and businessmen were concerned."[10] In his view, the business community did not think aggressively about decolonization. It was content to defer to political agents. Indeed, as Fieldhouse's detailed treatment of the United Africa Company in West Africa contends, UAC officials there and in London were always on the defensive, afraid of being depicted as the source of West Africa's

[9] The Accra riots are crucial to Pearce, *The Turning Point in Africa*, and to Ronald Robinson, "Andrew Cohen and the Transfer of Power."

[10] D. K. Fieldhouse, *Black Africa, 1945–80: Economic Decolonization and Arrested Development* (London, 1986), p. 12.

economic and political woes. They sought to curry favor with the rising nationalist elites and tried to win the support of the nationalist press. The UAC erred in the era of decolonization, and beyond, in Fieldhouse's opinion, because its officials believed naively "in the honesty and impartiality of the colonial state" and were passive in dealing with state bureaucrats.[11]

Fieldhouse's work and that of like-minded business historians provide a useful corrective to the all too common tendency of many commentators to view the large British-based business entities as the arbiters of decolonization, much as Gary Wasserman did in his analysis of Kenya and Kwame Nkrumah did in his polemic on all of Africa.[12] But in their haste to be revisionist, they understate the power of large-scale businesses, the intense interest that business groups took in decolonization, business's understanding of what was occurring, and its ability to intervene at critical moments. In Egypt, where the international business community had always deferred to British political and military leaders, the arson, rioting, and murder in Cairo on black Saturday, January 26, 1952, shocked foreign merchants and industrialists into action. Led by those British business organizations possessing large investments in Egypt, corporate delegations, individually and collectively, met with British officials to argue, presciently, albeit unsuccessfully, that Britain's continuous military presence in a country inflamed with nationalist sensibilities was a detriment to Britain's long-term economic and cultural stake in that country. They predicted that a failure to withdraw the British armed forces promptly would radicalize the Egyptian nationalist movement and embolden its leaders to demand the extinguishing of all Western influence.

Similarly, in Kenya, Mau Mau caused such an outflow of investment funds that British officials were compelled to involve the large British banking houses and agribusinesses working in Kenya in the ongoing discussions over power sharing and the eventual transfer of authority. Although the British business groups failed to achieve a consensus, their insistence that the Kenyan nationalists, not the settler factions, were the key to political negotiations and future economic and political stability was a meaningful intervention.

A second perspective on the economic dimensions of decolonization exists—one that argues for the decisive importance of foreign, large-

---

[11] D. K. Fieldhouse, *Merchant Capital and Economic Decolonization: The United Africa Company, 1929–1987* (Oxford, 1994), pp. 279–80. Certainly the work by Josephine Milburn, *British Business and Ghanaian Independence* (London, 1977), ought to be mentioned in any account of works dealing with the role of business groups in colonial Africa.

[12] Gary Wasserman, *Politics of Decolonization: Kenya Europeans and the Land Issue, 1960–1965* (Cambridge, 1976); Kwame Nkrumah, *Neo-Colonialism: The Last Stage of Imperialism* (New York, 1965).

scale capital throughout this period. This point of view found expression in a number of early studies of decolonization, including those of Wasserman and Leys on Kenya, Nkrumah's essay on neocolonialism, and an article written by Catherine Coquery-Vidrovitch claiming that colonialism was the avatar of imperialism.[13] It has enjoyed a spirited restatement in a recent overview of British imperialism authored by P. J. Cain and A. G. Hopkins.[14] Just as metropolitan capital brought about the partition of Africa, using the colonial era to implant a capitalist ethos, free-market institutions, and a collaborating elite on a continent relatively isolated from the effects of the world economy, so, according to these commentators, the still powerful and purposeful capitalist forces withdrew from the continent once the ties that bound Africa to the capitalist centers had been tightly lashed.

For P. J. Cain and A. G. Hopkins the truly dynamic sectors of British capital were its financial and service branches, which had progressively merged with landed wealth in the nineteenth century to create an effective and expansive gentlemanly capitalism. Far from being in decline in the twentieth century, the financial and service sectors enjoyed prosperity in the interwar years and then orchestrated the end of empire in Asia and Africa in ways that supported their interests. Cain and Hopkins's gentlemanly capitalists favored empire down to World War II, used imperial possessions to prosecute the war against the Axis powers, reconstructed Britain with the support of these possessions after the war, and conceded independence only when the empire offered fewer economic inducements than investments in the rest of the world. The arrival of African decolonization in 1960, according to these scholars, just two years after sterling had achieved full convertibility, was hardly coincidental. By then, "the policy-makers calculated that the City and invisible earnings generally had more to gain from emerging opportunities in the wider world than from remaining penned in the sterling area. . . . The gentlemanly interests . . . *sustained the empire down to World War II (and) also managed and to some extent planned its demise.*"[15]

Such a thoroughly rationalized and economistic view must, of course, arouse suspicion. Its ability to explain developments in the three countries dealt with here proved to be limited. Like so much of the work of

---

[13] Colin Leys, *Underdevelopment in Kenya: The Political Economy of Neo-Colonialism* (Berkeley, 1974); Catherine Coquery-Vidrovitch, "De l'impérialisme ancien a l'impérialisme moderne: l'avatar colonial," in J. Bouvier and J. Girault, eds., *L'impérialisme française d'avant 1914* (Paris, 1976).

[14] P. J. Cain and A. G. Hopkins, *British Imperialism: Innovation and Expansion, 1688–1914* (London, 1993); P. J. Cain and A. G. Hopkins, *British Imperialism: Crisis and Deconstruction, 1914–1990* (London, 1993).

[15] Cain and Hopkins, *British Imperialism: Crisis and Deconstruction*, pp. 265–66.

the imperial school, its rootedness in metropolitan affairs did not serve its practitioners well in assessing the actions and initiatives occurring in the colonial periphery. To be sure, this perspective does call attention to the central role of the financial sector in colonial affairs, manifested throughout the decolonizing events in the heightened influence of banks and insurance companies. It also highlights the importance of Britain's commitment to sterling, the domain of influence of bankers and insurers, even when policies to protect sterling entailed sacrificing vital political and economic interests, as they did when the British invaded Egypt. But Cain and Hopkins allow little room for noneconomic factors, and they erase from the historical record local, non-British-based capital. In reality, by the end of World War II in Egypt and Kenya, and to a lesser extent in Nigeria, locally based business groups were becoming a political and economic force. Among their ranks were dynamic economic and political leaders who were determined to exercise influence over the arrangements for power sharing.

The third factor most frequently cited in explaining post–World War II Asian and African decolonization is the change in the international balance of power.[16] Certainly no commentator would deny the influence of the United States, the Soviet Union, and the Cold War in Egyptian developments under Nasser. Elsewhere, however, such as in Anglophone Africa, the American role in decolonization appears muted. American business groups were almost entirely absent from the Kenyan and Nigerian discussions. It is difficult to argue on the basis of this decolonizing record that American foreign policy in this period, at least in Africa, was driven by the expansive needs of American capital.[17] The only occasions when American business agitated energetically and as a group in Egypt occurred after Nasser nationalized the Suez Canal Company and provoked the American oil companies operating in the region to file protests at the State Department. Oil executives were fearful that the Egyptian action would serve as a dangerous precedent to like-minded nationalist leaders

---

[16] On the American influence on decolonization, one should consult the following overviews, most of which review the bibliography in the field. Carey Fraser, "Understanding American Policy toward the Decolonization of European Empires, 1945–64," *Diplomacy and Statecraft* 3, no. 1 (1992), pp. 105–25; William Roger Louis, *Imperialism at Bay: The United States and the Decolonization of the British Empire, 1941–1945* (New York, 1978); William Roger Louis and Ronald Robinson, "The United States and the Liquidation of the British Empire in Tropical Africa, 1941–51," in Gifford and Louis, eds., *The Transfer of Power in Africa*; William Roger Louis, "American Anti-colonialism and the Dissolution of the British Empire," *International Affairs* 61, no. 3 (1985), pp. 395–420; and Miles Kahler, "The United States and the Third World: Decolonization and After," in *Centerstage: American Diplomacy since World War II*, ed. L. Carl Brown (New York, 1990).

[17] The classic statement of this point of view is Gabriel Kolko, *The Politics of War* (New York, 1986).

in the region and beyond. Again in 1957 Egyptian legislation nationalizing a large number of foreign companies threatened American trading firms. The American companies intervened and succeeded in modifying the law. Otherwise, American corporations were largely silent in this era, preferring to withdraw their businesses to Beirut as Nasser's socialist inclinations became clearer.

In Anglophone Africa the American business presence was even more tenuous. It was so distant that it does not appear in this narrative. The British efforts to protect sterling from dollar incursions, employing a mixture of import, licensing, and currency regulations, proved successful. Britain kept American capital at bay in tropical Africa. Ironically, the only concerted protests came from American diplomats and local capitalists rather than from American corporate executives. One energetic American diplomat in Kenya complained that the British measures to defend sterling violated free-trade promises that the British had made to the Americans. His protest was shelved in Washington. Also unanswered by American business groups and American diplomats was a spate of requests from local Asian business persons in Kenya eager to become agents of American capital in East Africa. In Nigeria British officials reacted hostilely and with suspicion to a World Bank recommendation that Nigeria establish a central bank. The British suspected that American capitalist groups had sponsored the recommendation. In fact, no great influx of American capital followed the establishment of the Nigerian central bank.

The ideological influence of American anticolonial sentiment in accelerating decolonization cannot be discounted, but it played a subordinate role at best. It is undoubtedly true that the British initiated constitutional and economic reforms in Africa toward the end of World War II with a view to countering likely American criticism of the British empire.[18] In the postwar era, however, under the impact of the Cold War, official American interest in speeding the transfer of power in Nigeria and Kenya was minimal. American diplomats in Kenya and Nigeria were as pessimistic (and as racist) about the political future of an independent Africa as their British colleagues. More difficult to evaluate but certainly a factor were the ties between African nationalists and nonofficial groups in the United States. Many Nigerian nationalists, especially those educated in the United States, sought to use their contacts with American groups to pressure the British and legitimize their organizations. Nigerians made cultural, political, and economic trips to the United States. These contacts worried British officials, more because they might embolden the nationalists in Nigeria than because they might result in official American demands for an accelerated timetable for independence.

[18] See Louis, *Imperialism at Bay*.

Egypt occupied an entirely different status in official American circles. Its location, of strategic importance to both the United States and the Soviet Union, gave it a high prominence in Cold War strategizing and enabled a young, ambitious nationalist like Nasser to insert himself into international politics on behalf of his country. By the early 1950s American diplomats had come to the conclusion that the British were maladroit in dealing with Egyptian nationalist sensibilities. They were eager to substitute American influence for that of the old imperial hegemon.

One of the purposes of this study is to identify and weigh the factors that led to decolonization in Africa. Another is to assess the influence of organized business on ending empire. By altering the lens of our analytical focus from politics to economics, we immediately catch sight of the large-scale business firm as a primary actor in colonial capitalism and a force in the private sector. Certainly, by the end of World War II, although African private sectors were varied and housed many different organizational forms, big European-based firms had planted themselves firmly in the African economic landscape—so much so that they had created local imitators. These firms were accustomed to being consulted on all matters, political as well as economic, and were determined to influence the outcome of decolonization. As Western- and Asian-run businesses saw empire coming to an end, they took defensive steps to protect their interests. Rising African business leaders also endeavored to forge a place for themselves in the private sector. They employed nationalist rhetoric to attract local capital and government favor.

In the political arena, nationalist elites and colonial bureaucrats tried to evaluate the contribution that business, indigenous and foreign, could make to economic progress. These officials, who had the power to arrange the African political economies of independence, vehemently debated what kinds of relationships they wanted to create between the state and private business organizations as well as the boundary lines they proposed to draw to separate public and private arenas.

The role of the modern corporation in the economic transformation of Western Europe and North America is undisputed. Whether these firms, particularly in their multinational form, have been agents of economic progress or economic immiseration in the third world is, however, much less agreed upon. Supporters attribute the economic breakthroughs in the Pacific rim countries to large business organizations; critics contend that multinationals have drained the human and material resources out of much of the world for the enrichment of the West, leaving the areas in which they operate incapable of sustained economic progress.

This study does not attempt to resolve this debate. The short time span of roughly fifteen years and the often turbulent political conditions of the decolonizing era make the period unsatisfactory for assessing the economic impact of foreign investment. Rather, this study addresses two other important and highly controversial questions: the influence of the large-scale firm on decolonization and the success or failure of local nationalist elites in establishing national control over these organizations.

The modern corporation came into existence in the last third of the nineteenth century as a result of a managerial revolution involving the rise of salaried managers and the separation of management and ownership functions within the firm. The resulting transformation in production and distribution that accompanied the rise of a management elite produced economies of scale and scope never before achieved and catapulted the United States, Germany, and Britain into world economic leadership. Even as late as the outbreak of World War II, firms in these three countries accounted for no less than two-thirds of the manufacturing output of the world economy and an even greater share of foreign direct investment.[19]

The definition of multinational employed here is any enterprise "that controls operations or income-generating assets in more than one country."[20] This is a spare definition. It is preferable in this study to definitions that insist that multinationals must have a large capitalization and involvement in many countries. In reality, the private sectors of Egypt, Nigeria, and Kenya were populated by a large number of firms of different sizes and capitalization and had many small but politically powerful firms who were heard in the deliberations over the private sector.[21] In addition to multinational enterprises large and small, local joint stock companies, family firms, partnerships, and single-owner businesses all participated prominently in the debates over the transfer of power. Largely outside the framework of power, however, were small intermediary business persons, small money lenders, and "bulkers and breakers" of local and international trade, although they sporadically organized and made their positions known to colonial officials, nationalist elites, and large-scale business organizations and occasionally erupted in protest action.

A first set of questions then arises for investigating the influence of the

[19] See Alfred D. Chandler, Jr., *Scale and Scope: The Dynamics of Industrial Capitalism* (Cambridge, Mass., 1990), p. 3; and Geoffrey Jones, *British Multinational Banking, 1830–1990* (Oxford, 1993).

[20] Geoffrey Jones, *The Evolution of International Business: An Introduction* (London, 1996), p. 4. See also a similar definition by Mira Wilkins that also downplays size, capitalization, and involvement in a large number of foreign countries. Mira Wilkins, "History of European Multinationals: A New Look," *Journal of European Economic History* 15, pp. 483–510.

[21] Raymond Vernon, *Sovereignty at Bay: The Multinational Spread of U.S. Enterprise* (New York, 1971); Raymond Vernon, *Storm over Multinationals: The Real Issue* (Cambridge, Mass., 1977); and Christopher Tugendhat, *The Multinationals* (London, 1971), stress size and geographical dispersion in their definition of a multinational enterprise.

business communities on decolonization. How well did they comprehend the events that were unfolding around them? How interventionist were they? Were their interventions timely and effective? Until recently, the scholarly consensus, admittedly based on impressionistic evidence rather than detailed case studies, is that the business community, especially the multinational enterprises, was powerful and influential in the political arena.

The ability of multinationals to work through the colonial bureaucracy was thought to be unchallenged. Stephen Hymer has singled out multinationals as the advance guard of a new global world order, far ahead of governments and labor organizations in creating cosmopolitan units of production and establishing a hierarchical division of labor among the geographical regions of the world.[22] Robert Gilpin and Raymond Vernon identify American multinational enterprises as the most powerful actors in the international environment, able to overshadow national states, even the most powerful ones in Western Europe and North America, to say nothing of the fledgling polities of Asia and Africa.[23]

Recently, a few scholarly works have taken a skeptical position on the dominance of European- and American-based multinational enterprises, even in those parts of the world lacking strong nation-state organizations. In this study I also conclude that the capacity of the multinational enterprise to dominate the decolonization debate was limited. I also stress the independence of local capitalists and the autonomy of colonial bureaucrats and rising nationalist elites. At no time in the two decades of decolonization in Egypt, Nigeria, and Kenya did foreign capital, local capital, and the state form the kind of firm alliance that scholars have identified in other parts of the developing world.[24]

Since local capital played such an important role in the discussion over the private sector, it is well to note at the outset that Africa's rising business classes were new elements in the colonial political economy of that continent. They did not descend from precolonial commercial and entrepreneurial traditions, which had been dealt a devastating blow by the forces of colonial capital in the nineteenth century. Before the colonial era Egypt and Nigeria had impressive merchant cadres—individuals and groups that moved long-distance trade, including, for Nigeria, the Atlantic and Saharan slave trades. Although Kenya's involvement in long-distance trade was not

[22] Stephen Hymer, "The Multinational Corporation and the Law of Uneven Development," in *Economics and World Order from the 1970s to the 1990s*, ed. Jagdish N. Bhagwati (London, 1972).

[23] Vernon, *Sovereignty at Bay*; Vernon, *Storm over Multinationals*; and Robert Gilpin, *U.S. Power and the Multinational Corporation: The Political Economy of Foreign Direct Investment* (New York, 1975).

[24] See, in particular, Peter Evans, *Dependent Development: The Alliance of Multinational, State, and Local Capital in Brazil* (Princeton, N.J., 1979).

as highly developed, it too had a mercantile tradition. Groups, like the Kamba in the Central Highlands and the Swahili peoples along the coast, had acquired a considerable experience in commercial matters.

Africa's precolonial merchants were rudely handled during the incorporation of their regions into European colonial empires. In truth, Muhammad Ali's state-dominated modernizing programs had already challenged local merchants, and the dismantling of the ruler's state monopolies in the 1840s proved far more of a boon to foreign merchants than to local business persons. The Egyptian cotton boom of the mid-century and the country's judicial privileges for foreigners, the Capitulations, attracted foreign investors and traders. The British occupation merely solidified the privileged place that foreign business had created for itself in Egypt. Yet by the end of World War II, largely as a result of a small but energetic band of local entrepreneurs, a cadre of Egyptian business persons had become a crucial element in Egypt's private sector.

In Nigeria and Kenya the colonial rupture proved even more decisive. The details for Kenya are not as well known, but in Nigeria the colonial intrusion entailed far more than military conquests and political take-overs. In league with their military forces, British administrators carried out campaigns to rid the area of its most powerful merchant-princes. These local notables were ousted in order to permit ambitious British merchants, like George Goldie of the Royal Niger Company, to break out of their confinement at the coast and trade directly with the Nigerian peoples of the interior. Although the British justified the capture, trial, and exile of these individuals on the grounds of preventing domestic slavery and the internal slave trade, the end result was a clearing of the mercantile infrastructure for British penetration. For every Dantata, a Hausa mercantile family who weathered the colonial takeover storm and remained an important commercial actor right through the colonial period, many more like Nana Olomu of the Itsekiri, Jaja of Opobo, and the Aro mercantile community saw their commercial networks torn asunder by British power.[25] The reality of the era of colonial conquest was that African peoples witnessed the destruction of their merchant elites and the assumption of a dominant economic position within their societies by large-scale European trading and financial firms, supported by a plethora of Syrian, Lebanese, Indian, and Mediterranean middlemen. Local capitalists were compelled to fight their way back economically within a

[25] See especially J. C. Anene, *Southern Nigeria in Transition, 1885–1906* (Cambridge, 1966); Obaro Ikime, *Merchant Prince of the Niger Delta: The Rise and Fall of Nano Olomu, Last Governor of the Benin River* (London, 1968); K. Onwuka Dike, *Trade and Politics in the Niger Delta, 1830–1885* (Oxford, 1956); and Sylvanus Cookey, *King Jaja of the Niger Delta: His Life and Times, 1821–1891* (New York, 1971).

colonial framework that favored non-African groups. They did so only gradually and with difficulty. In Nigeria they were beginning to reestablish themselves at precisely the moment when the British were contemplating their departure from the country.

This is a work in comparative history. It draws inspiration from Marc Bloch and other comparativists who insist that the comparative method provides the only sure safeguard against antiquarianism and the only certain way to identify commonalities and differences in historical experience.[26] Like most of the comparative work done by historians, this study uses the case method rather than focusing on key variables. Instead of specifying a few predetermined variables for study, it employs a set of three cases, much as Barrington Moore did in his analysis of democracy and dictatorship and as Crane Brinton did in his taxonomy of revolutions.[27]

The cases used in comparative study must, of course, be selected purposefully rather than "haphazardly from a large pool of equally plausible selections."[28] The three territories examined here are purposeful in the sense that they were integral parts of the British empire (even though Egypt had been theoretically independent since 1922 or at least 1936). They all achieved full formal political independence in the 1950s or early 1960s and thus were part of the first wave of African independence movements. They are useful, then, as exemplars of the decolonization processes that swept through Asia and Africa in the first two decades after World War II and can highlight the commonalities of this experience.

They have another relevancy for comparative purposes in that they displayed marked variations in their decolonizing experiences, especially in the economic sphere. To be sure, in many respects Egypt must be differentiated from Nigeria and Kenya because of its political autonomy. Although Egyptian nationalists would never have regarded their country as independent as long as British soldiers remained on Egyptian soil (hence the validity of including Egypt in a comparative work on decolonization), in reality the 1922 proclamation of independence and the 1936 Anglo-Egyptian treaty elevated Egypt to a semicolonial status. Egyptians participated in elections, formed parliaments, passed laws not subject to

---

[26] Marc Bloch, "A Contribution towards a Comparative History of European Societies," in *Land and Work in Medieval Europe: Selected Papers by Marc Bloch*, trans. J. E. Anderson (London, 1966).

[27] Barrington Moore, *Social Origins of Dictatorship and Democracy: Lord and Peasant in the Making of the Modern World* (Boston, 1966); Crane Brinton, *The Anatomy of Revolution* (New York, 1938).

[28] Charles C. Ragin, "Introduction: The Problem of Balancing Discussion on Cases and Variables in Comparative Social Science," in Charles C. Ragin, *Issues and Alternatives in Comparative Social Research* (London, 1991), p. 1.

the veto of the British crown, and most important, selected their own rulers. Thus, in spite of the large British army of occupation stationed in the Suez Canal base, the Egyptians could have a coup d'etat and could see a group of young, radical officers seize power from the old landed elite. The Egyptian experience in the 1950s reveals that a significant degree of political autonomy afforded ruling groups the opportunity to launch an all-out assault on capitalist institutions.

Other country variations are relevant for this study. Egypt was strategically the most important territory for Britain overseas because of the Suez Canal base and the canal as an international waterway. Kenya was an area of European settlement even though the European population living there numbered no more than 60,000, small by comparison with other areas of European settlement in Africa. Nonetheless, its political and economic evolution was supposed to follow a different model from the rest of tropical Africa, more like South Africa and Southern Rhodesia (later Zimbabwe), if not Canada, Australia, and New Zealand. Nigeria had always been a primary British trade and investment area, even before the colonial era. Although its poverty was widely recognized, its potential for economic development and West African political leadership made it the most important of Britain's West African possessions—a territory in which Britain wished to retain cultural and economic ties. One of the purposes of this study is to determine how important these different imperial purposes and legacies were in the decolonization settlements.

BRITISH THINKING ABOUT AFRICAN ECONOMIES
AFTER WORLD WAR II

At the close of the war no person in the colonial service or in nationalist opposition believed it possible that colonial African states would achieve their independence in the late 1950s and early 1960s. Yet everyone realized that political and economic changes in the relationship between Britain and Africa were in the offing. With the prospect of African independence looming on the horizon, those colonial officers involved in economic affairs—the economic experts at the Colonial Office; the governors; and the colonial financial secretaries, later called ministers of finance—realized that they too must prepare the territories economically for independence. Most of those individuals saw that African economies would have to become more self-reliant. Those who hoped that the old economic arrangements could be maintained after independence soon learned from the nationalist speeches and slogans that African leaders expected meaningful economic changes. From every corner of the continent came statements that political independence without economic autonomy would be a sham liberation. Before long there was a consensus on the main economic goals toward which African states should aspire, though much dispute over methods and timing. A consensus developed around the notion that Africa must be more diversified economically, that it must become more industrial, that it must have more control over its finances, and that it must be less dependent on external trade, especially the proceeds from a few export commodities. The nationalist economic experts added to this perspective a concern for the creation of an indigenous entrepreneurial elite and demanded greater African control over the continent's monetary and banking institutions.

World War II had already laid foundations for a more self-reliant African economy. Cut off from Europe and thrown back on their own resources, even the most dependent and export-oriented colonies of tropical Africa had to force an industrial sector into being. The need to husband scarce local economic and financial resources also produced planning measures.

Sydney Caine was the economic counterpart to Andrew Cohen at the Colonial Office. While Cohen was delineating the blueprints of African constitutional advance, Caine was sketching out the economic guidelines. By World War II Caine had become the "[Colonial] Office's leading economic expert, . . . the one most able to maintain personal as well as professional links with economists such as Robbins, Keynes, and Henderson."[29] During his tenure at the Colonial Office he helped to energize economic thinking on overseas possessions. No important colonial economic document escaped his attention.

Caine's most important statement on African economic policy was contained in a terse 3,000-word memorandum circulated in August 1943. This memo stressed the need for urgency on economic matters, the advantages of centralized planning, and the desirability of fostering contacts with non–United Kingdom financial interests. Unlike many others in high office, Caine was acutely aware that Britain would emerge from the war in a weakened economic condition. Although the United Kingdom needed colonies for its own economic health, Caine also believed that Britain would be able to contribute to colonial economic progress through economic planning. Extolling the Tennessee Valley Authority project in America and Russia's five-year plans, he pressed the Colonial Office to devise schemes that would enhance living standards in Africa and foster the autonomous economic development of that continent.

Caine's vision fit well the nationalization efforts that were beginning to gain expression in British politics at the time and that would be put into

---

[29] J. M. Lee and Martin Petter, *The Colonial Office, War, and Development Policy: Organization and the Planning of a Metropolitan Initiative, 1939–1945* (London, 1982), p. 168.

effect once the war ended. It also drew upon previous planning experiments in the colonies, most notably Governor Guggisberg's projects for the Gold Coast just after World War I and the goals of Britain's two Colonial Development and Welfare Acts. The first, enacted in 1929, was scarcely implemented because of the onset of the Depression. During its lifetime the British government had spent a mere £6.5 million. The British government, however, intended more from the 1940 legislation, and at the conclusion of the war the newly installed Labour Party set about drawing up plans for the expenditure of £120,000,000 on colonial development projects over a ten-year period.[30] The fascination the officials had with the public sector did not mean, however, that they minimized the contribution of the private sector, only that they spoke less about it, regarded private capital as less problematic, and took its contributions more for granted.

Nonetheless, Caine's aspirations for the centralized planning of African economic development encountered numerous problems. Britain was chronically short of sterling and was forced to look to its colonial areas to save on dollars and protect sterling. Colonial interests were so regularly sacrificed to metropolitan concerns that much of Caine's vision could not be implemented. Nor were the colonial governors and their financial secretaries eager to concede their autonomy to a central planning bureau. The outspoken governor of Kenya, Philip Mitchell, scoffed at Caine and his colleague, Gerard Clauson, calling the two of them "ignorant schoolboys," talking "childish nonsense" with "incredible naivete."[31] Within the Labour Party itself, other than the colonial secretary, Arthur Creech Jones, known for his dedication to colonial issues and his desire to promote liberalizing reforms, the high-ranking members of the party viewed empire "with indifference, horror, or as an essentially economic concern. . . ."[32] Foreign Secretary Ernest Bevin and fellow cabinet minister Herbert Morrison regarded the empire primarily as a prop for the British economy. They were prepared to subordinate colonies to the financial and economic needs of the metropole.[33]

In spite of these difficulties, a rough consensus did exist at the close of World War II in favor of some form of centralized economic planning in the colonies and the need for industrialization. Moreover, colonial offi-

---

[30] David Meredith, "The British Government and Colonial Economic Policy, 1919–1939," *Economic History Review*, 2d ser., 28, no. 3 (1975); David Goldsworthy, *Colonial Issues in British Politics, 1945–1961: From Colonial Development to Wind of Change* (Oxford, 1971), p. 11.

[31] Pearce, *The Turning Point in Africa*, p. 179.

[32] Ibid., p. 97.

[33] Mike Cowen, "Early Years of the Colonial Development Corporation: British State Enterprise Overseas during Late Colonialism," *African Affairs* 83, no. 330 (January 1984), pp. 63–75.

cials found support for their programs from the newly emerging field of development economics, and they were able to employ the new economic specialists as consultants on their economic projects.[34] Thus, the decade after 1945 was marked by heated debates over the value of governmental economic intervention, the extent of economic diversification, and the need for industrialization. In their discussions officials met with representatives of private business to consider the limits to planning, the contribution that could be expected from private business, and the pace of diversification and industrialization. Much of the ensuing narrative deals with the bodies that elaborated and implemented the programs of economic development, the pressures that they came under, and the role that those programs gave to private business organizations.

Political economies, like all human constructions, emerge through the visions of usually powerfully placed individuals. They are invariably contested. In decolonizing Africa the primary decision makers were state officials and spokespersons representing business firms. But those elites were not unencumbered in their actions. Their proposals for creating an enabling environment for economic growth ignited crucial debates in the Parliaments and the press of decolonizing states. They also reverberated among the so-called subalterns—urban workers, peasants, and the like—who did not enter the halls of parliament or participate in official debates but were nevertheless always in the consciousness of the elites and on numerous occasions made their influence felt through overt political activity.

This study focuses on the institutional and juridical ingredients of private sector health—the so-called enabling environment—and thus pays much less attention to the numerous important noninstitutional factors, such as education levels, population growth rates, and divergent levels of economic development that are so often emphasized in studies on comparative economic development and that are clearly significant in accounting for varying outcomes. This comparative inquiry focuses primarily on the ideations of economic development—the plans, thoughts, and visions of those responsible for making and implementing economic policy.

In the immediate aftermath of World War II there existed a coalescing, if still contested vision of the appropriate methods for bringing about economic development in countries about to emerge from colonialism. Despite different political and economic circumstances, the dominant elites in Egypt, Nigeria, and Kenya in 1945 shared much of this vision. They agreed on the need for more industrialization, based primarily on import substitution (though not exclusively so in Egypt) and on an en-

[34] Osvaldo Sunkel, "The Development of Development Thinking," in *Transnational Capitalism and National Development: New Perspectives on Dependence*, ed. Jose J. Villamil (Hassocks, Sussex, 1979), pp. 19–30.

hanced role for the state as a planner of economic change and marshaller of resources. Although the political elites did not stress the value of the private sector as much as they did the role of the state in accelerating economic growth, they assumed that private enterprise would be an important vehicle of economic transformation. Only as nationalist outbursts, labor discontent, Cold War tensions, and political infighting among the dominant elites set the different countries on divergent decolonizing paths did the economic experiences of the three countries cease to resemble each other. The outcomes were hardly predictable, and yet the economic processes of decolonization revealed both the underlying factors at work in all three countries as well as the forces that produced different outcomes.

Only by means of comparative study, albeit one organized by country and not sharply focused on one or two variables, can one hope to identify the factors that led one regime to take over big business (Egypt), another to blur the boundaries between business and the state bureaucracy (Nigeria), and the third to give a wide degree of autonomy to business entities (Kenya).

Part One

EGYPT

CHAPTER 1

Egypt, 1945–1952

PART A
THE PRIVATE SECTOR AND
A NEOCOLONIAL VISION UNREALIZED

Egypt, more advanced economically than the other two British-dominated territories featured in this study, was juridically independent and even enjoyed representation at the United Nations in 1945; nonetheless it was occupied by a large British military force. Despite the country's many barriers to economic development, not least of which was a limited resource base of land and raw materials and a dangerously high rate of population growth, the Egyptian economy was more diverse and Egypt had a stronger and more autonomous set of economic institutions and pressure groups than did Kenya and Nigeria. Not only did it have a small but extremely talented cadre of entrepreneurs, possessing considerable experience in administering large-scale limited-liability joint stock companies, but it enjoyed a plethora of private, politically active pressure groups, like the Egyptian Federation of Industries and numerous chambers of commerce and industry. In addition, its legal system had been altered over the years to support the activities of joint stock companies and the private sector. It was difficult to imagine in 1945 that this powerful private sector would be in total disarray by the early 1960s, yet the preconditions for its dispossession were being established in those crucial postwar years.

In 1943 and 1944, Britain's irrepressible ambassador, Lord Killearn, contemplated the future of Egypt and the evolution of Anglo-Egyptian relations as the war was drawing to a close. Mindful of the power of Egyptian nationalism, with which he had contended since his arrival in Egypt, he knew that the leading politicians would call for full-fledged independence for their country once the war was over. *Al-Istiqlal al-Tamm* (complete independence) had been Egypt's political slogan ever since the 1919 revolution. But Killearn believed that new, more subtle bases of control other than military might could bind Egypt to Britain. He had, in fact, been meeting with Ahmad Abbud, one of Egypt's most dynamic and visionary entrepreneurs. Abbud had outlined a series of economic projects, including a takeover of the Misr economic empire, that would make him the veritable economic czar of Egypt and that, in Abbud's exposition, would rely on large infusions of British capital and technical expertise. These schemes intrigued the British ambassador. They would simultaneously line the pocket of British capitalists and shareholders, serve as a spur to the British postwar economy, and anchor the Egyptian political economy in Britain's orbit. If Britain were forced to cut back on its military position in Egypt because of nationalist sensitivities (and Killearn was not certain that this would be necessary), Egypt would remain linked to Britain through powerful and mutually beneficial cultural and economic ties.[1]

By the time the war ended and Killearn had retired from the scene, British officialdom in Egypt was focused on two major economic projects that they hoped would attach the Egyptian economy to Britain. The first entailed the use of Egypt's large sterling reserves accumulated in Britain during the war to engineer the postwar development of the country and to ensure that these efforts occurred under British business auspices. The second was a scheme to develop the full irrigation potential of the Nile basin and to do so under British hydraulic, electricity, and construction companies, as had occurred in the past. In short, British officials believed that a large expansion of Egypt's private sector was not only essential for Egyptian social harmony but also possible. They were determined that it would occur through British investment. As events unfolded in the years immediately following the conclusion of the war, these projects faltered, and in the process they poisoned the economic and financial relations between the two countries; in particular, some Egyptian nationalists began contemplating the reduction of foreign business influence in the country and even thought about nationalization schemes.

Few countries within the ambit of the British empire had such a confusing relationship to the suzerain. Enjoying many of the trappings of formal independence, including, after 1936, membership in the League of Nations, Egypt was occupied by the largest British military contingent on the African continent. In the halcyon days of Lord Cromer the force numbered 5,000. It was located in Cairo and Alexandria and made regular forays through the heavily populated Egyptian delta. Incidents involving Egyptian civilians were not uncommon. According to the 1936 treaty, the British agreed to keep no more than 10,400 forces in Egypt and to garrison them in the Suez Canal area, once a base to accommodate that force had been constructed. In this way, the British soldiers, such an obvious symbol of Egypt's subject status, would be removed from the

[1] Telegram no. 265 (hereafter referred to by number only), Lord Killearn to Foreign Office, August 6, 1943, PRO FO 371/35586.

country's main population centers and would seem to concern themselves exclusively with matters of imperial communication. Unfortunately, even before the Suez Canal base had been completed, World War II broke out, and Egypt became a major military theater. Up until 1947, when the British reduced the size of their forces and confined them to the Suez Canal base, more than 100,000 British soldiers had been garrisoned in Alexandria and Cairo as well as the Suez Canal base.[2] In the heightened nationalist environment of the postwar era the soldiers were repeatedly engaged in incidents with the local population.

THE EGYPTIAN ECONOMY IN 1945

Unfortunately for those who dreamed of a dynamic private sector, infused with foreign capital, spearheading economic development, Egypt's twentieth-century record was not promising. The economy had not enjoyed a high economic growth rate up through 1945, and many observers of Egypt feared that the private sector would need to be dramatically transformed if the country were to avoid a social explosion.

Egypt was, in fact, in a state of considerable social and economic tension, though whether it was on the verge of social revolution is hard to determine.[3] For years, Egyptian political and business leaders had worried about the potential in the country for social chaos and had promulgated programs of economic development designed to prevent such an occurrence. Certainly by the end of the war the fear of social revolution gripped many members of the ruling elite. They believed time to be running against them, for their schemes had yet to yield the kind of economic growth that the country so desperately needed.

With the advantage of hindsight, we know that these perceptions of an economic slowdown and resulting social and economic tensions were valid. The Egyptian economy had stagnated and even declined from the turn of the century until 1945. Per capita income may have been 20 percent lower in 1945 than in 1900; half of the decline had occurred during World War II.[4] Nearly all of the leaders who worried about the Egyptian economy concluded that industrial development was the main

---

[2] Peter L. Hahn, *The United States, Great Britain, and Egypt: 1945–1956: Strategy and Diplomacy in the Early Cold War* (Chapel Hill, N.C., 1991), p. 40.

[3] For an informed and provocative discussion of whether Egypt was in fact on the verge of a revolution in this period, one should consult Robert Vitalis, *When Capitalists Collide: Business Conflict and the End of Empire in Egypt* (Berkeley, Calif., 1995).

[4] Bent Hansen and Girgis A. Marzouk, *Development and Economic Policy in the UAR (Egypt)* (Amsterdam, 1965), p. 5; Bent Hansen, *The Political Economy of Growth: Egypt and Turkey* (Oxford, 1991), pp. 96–98 and 104–8.

hope for securing rising standards of living. The population was expanding at more than 1 percent per year and agricultural development was not keeping pace. The cropped area, which had been 0.64 per person in 1910–1914, had declined to 0.44 feddans in 1950–54 (a feddan is an Egyptian unit of area equal to 1.038 acres).[5]

Unfortunately, industrial development had not yet provided the economic spark that its advocates hoped for. Egyptian industrial progress had been hostage to the world economy. Up until 1930, Egypt's legal injunction against altering its tariff barriers, the result of international treaty obligations, had restrained investors interested in industrial projects. When tariff freedom finally arrived in 1930, the world was mired in depression. Abundant investment funds for industries never arrived. Industry accounted for only 13 percent of Egypt's gross domestic product in 1947, while agriculture accounted for 38 percent. The service sector was slightly more important to the gross domestic product (14 percent in 1947) and grew at a faster rate than industry between 1947 and 1952.[6]

Egypt's economic stagnation increased the levels of poverty in the country and heightened disparities of income. In the countryside, landlessness had become increasingly apparent. Thirty-eight percent of the rural population was without land in 1939, up from 24 percent in 1929. That figure grew to 44 percent in 1950. In contrast, a small number of individual families (a few more than 2,000) held estates of 200 feddans or more and accounted for 35 percent of the cultivated area.[7]

Changing Views of the Private Sector and the Rise of Dissident Voices

Not only had the private sector failed to be a powerful engine of economic development, but in the period leading up to the military coup in 1952 it came under intense scrutiny from many segments of Egyptian society. Virtually every group held marked opinions about the value of the private sector to Egypt's future. Even those who continued to look to private capital as the major stimulant for economic growth realized that the state would need to be more interventionist and socially conscious.

[5] Robert Mabro and Patrick O'Brien, "Structural Changes in the Egyptian Economy," in *Studies in the Economic History of the Middle East from the Rise of Islam to the Present*, ed. M. A. Cook (London, 1970), p. 412.

[6] Bent Hansen and Karim Nashashibi, *Foreign Trade Regimes and Economic Development: Egypt* (New York, 1975), p. 12.

[7] Mahmoud Abdel Fadil, *Development, Income Distribution, and Social Change in Rural Egypt (1952–1970): A Study in the Political Economy of Agrarian Transition* (Cambridge, 1975), p. 3.

Critics of capitalism, however, considered the private sector the very source of Egyptian backwardness.

Even the established political parties realized that the old free-market, laissez-faire economic orientation would have to give way to more socially conscious reform programs. But the most determined and powerful attack on the private sector came from extraparliamentary and antiparliamentary groups that had risen to prominence in Egypt in the 1930s. They kept up a steady stream of complaints about the abuses and inequities inherent in capitalism and Egypt's need for new social and economic institutions. The left wing of the Muslim Brotherhood, best symbolized by Sayyid Qutb and Muhammad al-Ghazalli, stressed the social and egalitarian aspects of Islam and was critical of capitalism as excessively individualistic and exploitative of people.[8] Ahmad Husayn's Socialist Party, though it had a much smaller following, had completely changed its interwar orientation and become unabashedly socialist,[9] while the communist movement, though small and fragmented, rallied some of Egypt's burgeoning industrial working elements, especially textile laborers from the factories in the Shubra al-Khaima area, against capitalism.[10]

A final discontented element in the Egyptian post–World War II equation were segments of the Egyptian army. Right up to the moment of the coup the army was seen as a force linked to the status quo because its higher ranks were populated by appointees of the king and the leading parties. Under British influence, the army had not been intended as a fighting force, at least not since the reconquest of the Sudan. It was no more than an instrument for maintaining internal order. Not surprisingly, its younger meritocratic officers resented its inferior status, all the more so when it was sent, largely unprepared, into the Palestinian war in 1948 and suffered defeat. The military men blamed the civilian leadership for their humiliations on the battlefield and complained about their inferior weaponry.

Even before the 1948 fiasco, Egypt's younger officers had become, in Kamal al-Din Rif'at's apt phrase, politicians in military clothing.[11] The

---

[8] Richard P. Mitchell, *The Society of the Muslim Brothers* (London, 1969); see *al-Ahram*, September 20, 1946, for one of Qutb's critiques of capitalism.

[9] *al-Ahram*, March 2, 1950, carries a report of a meeting of the Socialist Party and speeches by Ahmad Husayn and other party leaders. See also James P. Jankowski, *Egypt's Young Rebels: "Young Egypt," 1933–1952* (Stanford, Calif., 1975), pp. 88 ff.

[10] See Joel Beinin and Zachary Lockman, *Workers on the Nile: Nationalism, Communism, Islam, and the Egyptian Working Class, 1882–1954* (Princeton, N.J., 1987); Ellis Goldberg, *Tinker, Tailor, and Textile Workers: Class and Politics in Egypt, 1930–1952* (Berkeley, Calif., 1986); and Selma Botman, *The Rise of Egyptian Communism, 1939–1970* (Syracuse, N.Y., 1988).

[11] Mudhakkirat Kamal al-Din Rif'at, *Harb al-Tahrir al-Wataniya bayn alugha Ma'ahada 1936 wa alugha Ittifaqiya 1954* (Cairo, 1968), p. 52.

British military intervention of February 4, 1942, reminded these men of the fraudulence of Egypt's nominal independence and alienated them from the nationalist Wafd party and the other established parties. As the most politicized officers began to cohere around Gamal Abdel Nasser and to establish a secret, politically conscious organization within the military, they embraced many of the extraparliamentary, anti-British, anticapitalist, and terrorist ideals being circulated among the Muslim Brothers, Young Egypt, and socialist- and communist-inspired intellectuals. Yet those conspirators retained their own autonomy and refused to become the handmaidens of any particular ideology or organized political group.[12]

The debate over social questions elevated certain words to almost liturgical prominence. Established politicians as well as extreme elements of the religious right and the socialist and communist left agreed that Egypt was afflicted with three great ills: *faqr* (poverty), *marad* (sickness), and *jahl* (ignorance).[13] Education, health services, wealth redistribution, and economic development were the keys to a just and happy society. Two other words figured prominently in the political vocabulary: *islah* (reform) and *ishtirakiya* (socialism). Although true socialists were in a small minority, even the politicians of the established parties were fond of characterizing themselves as socialists. They were quick to argue that socialism was not to be confused with communism, an unacceptable system for organizing the political economy. For the main-line politicians socialism meant no more than increased government regulation of a predominantly capitalist economy. Many left-leaning politicians, however, were impressed with experiments in social democracy taking place in Europe in the postwar period, most notably the nationalizations occurring in Britain under the Labour government.

The Egyptian Private Sector

The Egyptian private sector was one of the most rooted and well developed on the African continent in 1945. Certainly in comparison with private sectors in sub-Saharan Africa, except for South Africa, it had a brilliant past, having moved, largely through its own initiatives and with little government assistance, from total reliance on foreign trade to a more diversified, increasingly industrialized economy. While elsewhere in Africa business corporations were a novelty, having been established

---

[12] Joel Gordon, *Nasser's Blessed Movement: Egypt's Free Officers and the July Revolution* (New York, 1992), pp. 39 ff.; Kirk Beattie, *Egypt during the Nasser Years: Ideology, Politics, and Civil Society* (Boulder, Colo., 1994).

[13] See *al-Ahram*, June 16, 1946.

entirely as foreign affiliates, the limited-liability firm had a long and estimable history in Egypt. And all of the most successful firms did not owe their achievements to foreign capital and foreign managers. Egypt had an enviable record of local entrepreneurship.

The political and business elites of Egypt hoped that the country was entering a new stage in its capitalist evolution when simple import-substitution and consumer goods industries would give way to a capital goods industry. The capstone of the new industrial push was to be found in an iron and steel complex, long favored by leading politicians of all of Egypt's political parties. Publicists for the scheme portrayed iron and steel as the anchor of an Egyptian capital goods industry, capable of facilitating the move from consumer goods industries to capital-intensive factories.[14]

Yet textiles were still at the heart of Egyptian manufacturing. They accounted for 43 percent of value added in manufacturing in 1947 and experienced an explosive growth in investment and capital reserves after the war.[15] Five firms predominated: Misr Spinning and Weaving Company at al-Mahalla al-Kubra; Filature Nationale d'Egypte; Société Egyptienne des Industries Textiles; Misr Fine Spinning and Weaving Company; and Beida Dyers. They were responsible for 80 percent of the total yarn output in postwar Egypt and 50 percent of the weaving production.[16]

Next in importance to textiles were beverage, tobacco, and food processing companies. Unquestionably, Egypt's most powerful food processing firm was the Egyptian Sugar Company. From its inception during the reign of Khedive Ismail the Egyptian Sugar Company had grown steadily by increasing its share capital, which was overwhelmingly French. By the late 1920s, the Egyptian Sugar Company had the capacity to supply almost all of the internal market, although its prices were still not competitive with world prices and its finances were precarious.

Oil was the key to Egyptian industrialization, having replaced coal as the primary energy source during World War II. Fortunately, Egypt had substantial domestic oil reserves, and much exploration work in the eastern and western deserts, in Sinai, and off the Red Sea coast remained to be undertaken. Also, Egypt had first-rate refining and distributing capacities—an arena in which British and American capital was dominant. All of the British oil companies operating in Egypt were affiliates of the British-Dutch conglomerate, the Royal Dutch Shell Company. In Egypt,

---

[14] Officer in Charge, American Embassy, to Secretary of State, March 21, 1949, USNA 883.6511/3–2149.

[15] Robert Mabro and Samir Radwan, *The Industrialization of Egypt, 1939–1973: Policy and Performance* (Oxford, 1976), p. 101.

[16] A. A. I. el-Gritly, "The Structure of Modern Industry in Egypt," *L'Egypte contemporaine*, nos. 241–42, November–December 1947, p. 506.

Shell Oil's most important affiliate was Anglo-Egyptian Oil, the capitalization of which, in nominal terms, was £1,808,000 in 1946.[17] Anglo-Egyptian Oil prospected for oil, removed the oil from below the surface, refined the oil at its Suez refinery, and distributed its oil products in Egypt through another of the parent's affiliates, the Shell Company of Egypt. Among the American oil companies involved in Egypt, Standard Oil of Egypt and Caltex sold their products in the local market, but the major American firm operating there was Socony-Vacuum (later Mobil Oil).

In Egypt's transportation sector the Suez Canal Company dwarfed all others. Company officials and interested foreign governments argued in favor of the company's unique corporate status as an international public utility, buttressed by statutes that had been internationally negotiated.[18] Yet juridically, the Suez Canal Company was an Egyptian firm, registered in Egypt, even though its capital and managers were entirely foreign. Of the 800,000 shares outstanding in 1956 when the company was nationalized, Egyptians held a mere .2 percent. Individual French investors were the primary shareholding group, owning 45 percent of the shares; next was the British government with 44 percent, the result of Disraeli's purchase of Egyptian shares in the company in 1875; the Swiss held 6 percent; and individual British shareholders held 2 percent.[19] The company itself was run formally by a thirty-two-member Parisian-based board of directors, of whom in the immediate postwar period eighteen were French, ten were British (three were designated by the British government to represent its interests as the largest single shareholder), two were Egyptian (the result of a 1936 agreement between the Egyptian government and the company), one was Dutch, and one was American. Each board member served an eight-year term, and the board met monthly.

The Parisian board was activist and interventionist. It took a close interest in the affairs of the company. Detailed oversight was exercised, however, by the nine-member, Paris-based Comité de Direction whose members were drawn from the board. In Egypt the company was run by its agent supérieur, based at Ismailia. Ever since the 1936 accord, the Egyptian government had designated a special commissioner to represent Egyptian matters to the French agent supérieur.[20]

Egyptian participation in the affairs of a company that so powerfully affected the economy and polity of Egypt was still at a rudimentary level. Indeed, virtually all of the Egyptian involvement in the company—its right to have two board members and its Commissionaire Spéciale, plus a

[17] Memorandum, Egypt, n.d., but sometime in December 1948, PRO FO 371/69242.
[18] Hankey to Clutton, August 25, 1948, PRO FO 371/69241.
[19] Jean Ducruet, *Les capitaux Européens au Proche Orient* (Paris, 1964), p. 144.
[20] E. Ford to P. F. Kinna, April 26, 1950, PRO FO 371/80526.

guaranteed annual payment to the government and promises to hire more Egyptian workers, including pilots—had come about only as a result of negotiations in 1936.

Egypt's diverse and dynamic banking sector had been subject to widespread nationalist complaint for many years. Even the founding of Bank Misr in 1920 did not keep Egyptian patriots from protesting that foreign influence in this sector was excessive and that banks were too little committed to Egypt's development needs. Although the banks had become impressive attractors of deposits and accumulators of Egyptian investments in the 1930s, they still retained most of their funds overseas. As they had done in the nineteenth century, the foreign banks spearheaded the economic interests of their nationals in Egypt. Barclays Bank, DCO; Crédit Lyonnais and Comptoir Nationale d'Escompte; and Banque Belge et Internationale en Egypte seemed to their critics insufficiently concerned with the economic and social problems that beset the country.

There were numerous other branches of the private sector, many of which had increasing influence in the country. Foreign automotive firms, mainly Ford and General Motors, were already contemplating the establishment of assembly plants in Egypt because of the potential that the Middle East market held for cars and the seeming centrality and attractiveness of Egypt as the location for supplying that market. A whole range of insurance companies, mainly though not exclusively foreign, had been formed in Egypt. They tended to model their behavior after the foreign banks, attracting policies and investment from local subscribers but keeping most of their funds in the metropole.

The thicket of private business firms, many of them public limited-liability corporations, that dotted the Egyptian business landscape in 1945 did not prevent the private sector from experiencing its most acute political crisis in modern times. Attacked on the left and right by Muslim Brothers and communists and upbraided by main-line politicians for not contributing more mightily to economic progress, the private sector was also beset by internal cleavages. These were numerous and glaring. Many within the landed classes resented the rising business community, and tension still existed between the foreign and domestic wings of the business community, although there had been a steady mixing of the capital streams. Perhaps more important, disagreements existed among capitalists seeking to promote Egypt's export orientation and those striving for a more self-contained and industrialized country. In addition, the different branches of the haute bourgeoisie competed for the favor of the state. Even while representatives of the private sector were extolling the benefits of the free market, they were also looking to the state to support their own specific interests, even in dramatically interventionist ways. Many professional Egyptians and members of the lower and lower-middle orders complained that they felt like strangers in their own country, so overweening was the foreign presence. The foreign business group felt intensely besieged, as the Egyptian ruling groups used a combination of legislative enactments, especially the company law of 1947, and shareholding acquisition to increase Egyptian participation in the business sector.

Few would deny the brilliance of those Egyptian entrepreneurs who had emerged in the twentieth century and provided Egyptians with a credible threat to the foreigners in the corporate world. Tal'at Harb had led the way for a generation of astute business executives: Abd al-Rahman Hamada, the new Misr textile giant; Hafiz Afifi, too easily dismissed as a politician, but an astute business personage who was ably assisted in the Misr complex of companies by Abd al-Maqsud Ahmad; Ahmad Abbud, a business dynamo involved in every aspect of Egypt's economy; and the Alexandrine cotton merchants and exporters Ahmad Farghali and the Yahya family. By 1948 the Egyptian business presence had resulted in Egyptian nationals' owning 39 percent of the share capital of companies operating in the country; in 1900, in contrast, they had held a minuscule 9 percent.[21]

BRITAIN'S NEOCOLONIAL PLANS FOR EGYPT

The first of the large-scale economic projects by which the British intended to link Egypt to Britain revolved around the disbursement of the £425 million that Britain owed to Egypt as a consequence of World War II expenditures. Egypt, Britain's third largest creditor, nonetheless was a much lesser concern to the British than India, to whom the British owed £1,177 million.[22] Even had the British negotiators wanted to be helpful to the Egyptians, they did not want to set precedents that Indians and other creditors would invoke. This concern became all the more pronounced after Egypt left the sterling area in July 1947 and Britain imposed nonconvertibility on sterling in August of that same year.[23] Yet Foreign Office officials, supported by military men who were eager to use any device to win Egyptian approval of the British military base, were also eager to be

[21] Robert L. Tignor, *Egyptian Textiles and British Capital, 1930–1956* (Cairo, 1989), table on p. 128.

[22] Albert E. Hinds, "Sterling and Imperial Policy, 1945–51," *Journal of Imperial and Commonwealth History* 2 (January 1987), pp. 148–69.

[23] C. B. S. Newton, "The Sterling Crisis of 1947 and the British Response to the Marshall Plan," *Economic History Review*, 2d ser., 37, no. 3 (August 1984), pp. 391–408; Scott Newton, "The 1949 Sterling Crisis and British Policy towards European Integration," *Review of International Studies* 11, no. 3 (July 1985), pp. 169–82.

generous with the Egyptians. So were business persons with economic interests in Egypt. They met a stone wall of resistance from the Treasury and the Bank of England, however.[24]

All of the economic negotiations that occurred in these years—those that were of far-reaching significance to the Egyptian and British economies, like the disposal of sterling surpluses and the hydraulic schemes in the Upper Nile regions, as well as lesser fiscal and economic matters—occurred within an overheated political climate. They could never be judged entirely on their own terms but were always subject to critical evaluation by deeply sensitive Egyptian nationalists. Indeed, the period leading up to the 1952 military takeover was intensely political and nationalist, featuring the Egyptian efforts to revise the 1936 political treaty between Egypt and Britain, rule by minority regimes until the Wafd won the last election before the military takeover in 1950, increasing tension in the canal zone between the British military and Egyptian guerrilla bands, and the Wafdists' promises to renounce the 1936 treaty if they were returned to power and could not achieve a political settlement with the British.

In 1947, after strenuous and often acrimonious bargaining, the British and Egyptian governments finally reached a provisional agreement on how the large sterling balances from World War II were to be disposed of. Although a final agreement was not reached for several more years, parts of the first accord governed the use of the balances throughout the postwar era, until the funds were finally exhausted in the early 1960s. The essence of the agreement was a decision to divide the balances into two separate accounts. Egypt was to be permitted immediate access to the funds placed in the number one account (though its purchase of other currencies, like dollars, was subject to British government approval). The Egyptian government would retain the right to the number two account, subject to further negotiations with the British government on just when and how much of these funds could be released into the number one account. The accord thus obligated the British and Egyptian governments to undertake yearly negotiations on any further releases from the number two to the number one account and made likely additional bitter exchanges between representatives of the two governments.

Since these financial discussions occurred in a climate of intense Egyptian nationalism, and since the British often consciously linked them to

---

[24] In the opening round of interoffice British discussions on Egypt's sterling balances, the Treasury suggested that the Egyptian government cancel £170 million of the debt. Their officials argued that the debt Britain accumulated while defending Egypt from invasion was excessively large because of inflation in the Egyptian economy. The Foreign Office refused to put this proposal before the Egyptian delegation. W. J. Johnson, Note, August 8, 1945, PRO FO 141/1049.

Britain's political and military agenda in Egypt, they were explosive politically as well as financially. On occasion, the British negotiators threatened to withhold release of sterling in order to force Egyptian politicians to be more accommodating in the military negotiations over the Suez base; at other times, employing the reverse logic, they released funds more quickly than usual, hoping that a magnanimous gesture would soften the Egyptian military bargainers.

According to the 1947 agreement, the number one account consisted of Egypt's current and deposit accounts with banks in the United Kingdom as well as U.K. Treasury bills and sterling assets held as cover for the note issue of the National Bank of Egypt. Although it is difficult to determine the exact size of these funds, they probably fluctuated between £150 and £175 million. But however large they may have seemed to the interested parties, the funds were designated for quite specific purposes. They could not be used in discretionary ways. The remainder, about £250 million in discretionary monies, went immediately into the number two account and was not available to the Egyptians without the approval of the British government.[25]

The agreement of 1947 deflated the hopes of the Egyptian government, the British business community in Egypt, and British firms with trading ties with Egypt. And their disappointment gave way to anger when, within six weeks of signing the agreement, the British suspended convertibility of sterling. The Egyptians had counted on being able gradually to exchange some of the £150 to £175 million in the number one account for other currencies and gold. Business groups were equally dismayed as they saw their hopes for a large infusion of capital dashed. The British business community had hoped to use sterling releases to reestablish Britain as Egypt's primary trading partner. And Egyptian officials, who were eager to use the balances to jolt the economy into growth, were also dissatisfied. Furthermore, the agreement contained no promises of later transfers into the number one account. Thus, British merchants and manufacturers dealing with Egypt and Egyptian economic planners were deterred from making long-range projections that relied on these funds.

Subsequent negotiations over sterling releases, especially those undertaken in 1950, were equally bitter. The previous summer Britain had devalued the pound. At a stroke, Britain reduced the dollar value of Egypt's sterling holdings (still nearly £250 million) by almost 30 percent. Moreover, the British chancellor of the exchequer made it clear that Egypt would not be permitted to increase its purchase of dollars from the ster-

[25] Great Britain, *Financial Agreement between the Government of the United Kingdom and the Egyptian Government, London, June 30, 1947, House of Commons Sessional Papers*, cmd. 7163, vol. 26, 1946–47.

ling already in the number one account despite the devaluation.[26] The British ambassador in Egypt, Ronald Campbell, noting the rising anger and sense of betrayal among the members of the Egyptian negotiating team, feared a complete breakdown in the financial discussions and thought it possible that the Egyptians might launch a campaign of economic and financial warfare against Britain.[27]

As the sterling balance negotiations dragged on in 1950, the British financial experts began to consider the possibility of "full economic warfare" and how such would affect British economic interests at home and in Egypt. Thus, well before the 1956 Suez invasion—indeed, steadily and throughout Anglo-Egyptian discussions over a whole range of issues, including the continuation of the base as well as the release of sterling—British planners had considered the economic consequences of a break with Egypt. The consensus of the discussions was well summarized in a Foreign Office memorandum prepared in March 1950. The Foreign Office drafters concluded that Egypt "may well be able to survive without undue discomfort the economic consequences of the worst that we can do to them," while many British interests, including Britain's vast business empire in Egypt, could be held hostage in the event of a diplomatic rupture.[28]

The military men, however, were not impressed with the worries of the Foreign Office. They were quite prepared to subordinate financial interests to political and military goals, and, at least at that stage of the bargaining with Egypt, they had the support of some key diplomatic figures.

The same tendency to subordinate economic matters to political concerns was evident on the Egyptian side of the financial negotiations. Egypt's chief negotiator, Galil al-Imari, admitted that the releases were far more important to Egypt symbolically and psychologically than financially. Britain had accumulated its debts during the war on the understanding that payment would be made in a timely fashion and in full at the conclusion of the war. No upstanding Egyptian politician, Imari pointed out, could go before the Egyptian Parliament and the intensely nationalist press with an agreement bringing Egypt anything less.[29] When British negotiators pointed out to Imari that Egypt was already running a large sterling balance with Britain, mainly the result of the £13 to £15 million annual military charges at the Suez Canal base, and would be

[26] Roger Makins, Note, February 9, 1950, PRO FO 371/80409.

[27] No. 135, Campbell to Foreign Office, February 8, 1950; no. 266, Foreign Office to Cairo, February 10, 1950, PRO FO 371/80409.

[28] J. F. Naysmith, Foreign Office Minute, March 7, 1950, PRO FO 371/80411.

[29] No. 1, Leonard Wraight, British Middle East Organization, to Foreign Office, January 3, 1949, PRO FO 371/73518.

unable to use any additional sterling releases effectively, Imari countered that any scaling down of Britain's debts or slowing of the releases would be interpreted in Egypt as a bargaining defeat and treated as a blow to national pride.

The inability of negotiators to achieve a long-term financial accord in 1950 intensified the pressures from the interested business groups. The British business community in Egypt, feeling its economic foothold in that country grow weaker as trade and investment declined and as Egypt turned to other nations for trade, pleaded with the British Embassy in Cairo and the Foreign Office in the metropole to pursue a more liberal stance. Frederick Leith-Ross, a top British official working at the National Bank of Egypt and a strong advocate relying on economic and cultural ties rather than military controls in Egypt, composed a scathing critique of British policy. His letter, widely circulated at Whitehall, argued that the general policy of freezing sterling balances in the United Kingdom was forcing Egypt to look elsewhere for economic assistance and was bringing about the gradual dismantlement of a once lucrative and widespread British financial presence.[30] Wraight at the Treasury, in reply, conceded only a small part of the Leith-Ross critique. He asserted that the British government had a task much larger than supporting British trade and investment in Egypt: the metropolitan government must protect the integrity and overall strength of sterling as an international currency. Allowing Egypt free convertibility and easy access to its sterling balances, Wraith argued, would be a first and irreversible step toward the general conversion of all sterling assets into dollars. It would probably spell the end of sterling.[31]

The constant hidden partner in the financial negotiations was the British military establishment, preoccupied with securing Egyptian recognition of Britain's base along the Suez Canal. The progress of the military negotiations always determined the military's advice to the negotiators. In 1950–51, when military talks were not faring well, the generals were opposed to treating Egyptian requests favorably except "as a tactical move in securing a satisfactory defense arrangement."[32]

Given the low priority that the negotiating teams of Britain and Egypt were allowed to give to financial and trade concerns, it is hardly surprising that a comprehensive accord on sterling holdings was not achieved until July 1951—a full six years after the end of the war. Nor did the

[30] Leith-Ross, Note, National Bank of Egypt, Sterling Balances, June 19, 1950, in Stevenson to Wright, July 1, 1950, PRO FO 371/80413.

[31] Leonard Wraight, Sterling Balances: A Note on the Memorandum submitted by Sir Frederick Leith-Ross, July 10, 1950, PRO FO 371/80413.

[32] P. Ramsbotham, Foreign Office Minute, Egypt, Financial Negotiations, January 2, 1951, PRO FO 371/90166.

agreement strengthen Egypt's already declining trading and investment links with Britain, though it did have the virtue of making clear the sterling sums that would henceforth be available to Egypt each year until they were exhausted. According to the final agreement, Britain would release £150 million of the £230 million from the number two to the number one account over a ten-year period. Twenty-five million pounds were to be released immediately, of which £14 million could be converted into dollars. On January 1 of each succeeding year for the next nine years, beginning in January 1, 1952, an additional £10 million would be released. An additional £5 million, up to £35 million, would be made available whenever the total of Egypt's sterling balance in the number one account fell below £45 million. The remaining £80 million, still in the untouchable number two account, would be the subject of further discussions before the expiration of the agreement in 1961.[33]

As before, the releases were modest amounts. They did not cover even Britain's continuing military expenditures in Egypt, and they constituted only a small percentage of the total value of Egypt's import bill. Clearly the sterling balances that had seemed such a powerful lever of financial and political control to Killearn at the end of World War II had not proved to be so. Nor could they have been, given the financial exhaustion of Britain at war's end, the decision to turn first to economic reconstruction at home, and the desire to maintain sterling as an international currency. Yet the intense and often bitter financial negotiations between the two countries over the holdings and the different attitudes with which the negotiating teams approached their talks marred British-Egyptian relations and made it difficult for either side to envision a new era of Anglo-Egyptian relations based largely on the mutuality of financial and economic interests. The slowness with which sterling was released also put at risk the economic interests of Britain in Egypt and compelled the Egyptian government to seek new economic partners. Killearn's vision of neocolonial economic ties binding together Egypt and Britain was far from realized in the financial area.

British officials were optimistic, however, that some of the sterling releases could be used for Nile water development and that British engineers and contractors would dominate those projects, as they had dominated them in the past. Ever since the occupation of Egypt in 1882, the Egyptian government had looked to hydraulic engineers like William Garstin, Colin Scott Moncrieff, and William Willcocks to lay out Nile hydraulic schemes and had turned to British engineering and construction firms to carry out the projects. Even though the irrigation department had

---

[33] No. 168, Chapman Andrews to Foreign Office, March 12, 1951, PRO FO 371/90166.

been steadily Egyptianized during the interwar years, there was no reason for British officials to believe any lessening of British influence would occur on the big development projects planned for the Nile waters in the postwar years.

As far as British irrigation experts were concerned, large-scale projects all along the Nile were the order of the day. Ever since William Garstin had made his original survey of the upper reaches of the Nile after the conquest of the Sudan, the British hydraulic personnel had been enamored of coordinated Nile waters development. In particular, the British hoped to establish a dam, water storage area, and hydroelectric power station somewhere near the source of the White Nile, a bypass canal at Jonglei in the Sudd area in the southern Sudan where much water was lost through evaporation; they also hoped to make water flow improvements from Lake Tana into the Blue Nile in Ethiopia.[34] Britain had many advantages for assuming control over these projects, most notably its imperial power over most of the territories through which the Nile passed. Its diplomats and colonial officials would be the ones to negotiate the requisite water-sharing and other agreements that a comprehensive Nile river development scheme required.

A preliminary postwar document on water use appeared in December 1945. Its author, R. M. MacGregor, expressed disappointment at how little had been accomplished outside of Egypt since 1914 and reinvoked the old ideas of Garstin for the fuller utilization of all of the water of the Nile for irrigation and hydroelectricity.[35] This document was followed by a major publication from the Egyptian Ministry of Public Works, written by H. E. Hurst, R. P. Black, and Y. M. Simaika and published in 1946. Volume seven of this monumental study was entitled *The Future Conservation of the Nile*, and it restated the old ideas of Garstin and other hydraulic engineers for the storage of Nile waters in the equatorial lakes of Africa. Hurst was the primary architect, and he labeled his idea "century storage" because the goal of the series of dams and other water works in the interior of Africa was to ensure a predictable supply of water from one year to the next despite the vagaries of annual rainfall.[36]

Not until 1948 and 1949, however, did the schemes for developing the upper regions of the White Nile begin to come to fruition. The most immediate plan was for a large-scale storage area on the upper White Nile, originally sited at Lake Albert, with a dam at Nimule. This scheme

[34] For a discussion of these projects, see John Waterbury, *Hydropolitics of the Nile Valley* (Syracuse, N.Y., 1979); and Robert O. Collins, *The Waters of the Nile: Hydropolitics and the Jonglei Canal, 1900–1988* (Oxford, 1990).

[35] R. M. Macgregor, Upper Nile Irrigation Projects, December 10, 1945, PRO FO 141/1100.

[36] Collins, *The Waters of the Nile*, pp. 198–246.

would increase the water available for irrigation downstream in the Sudan and Egypt, but it would also require a difficult set of negotiations for the redivision of the Nile water. The dam at Nimule would provide cheap hydroelectric power for Uganda, envisioned by the British as the industrial hub of East Africa.[37] The Egyptians supported the project, but when the scheme was opposed by the governments of Uganda and the Belgian Congo, they and the British experts turned their attention to a dam at Lake Victoria.

Victoria had a number of distinct advantages. A dam at Owen Falls could generate the cheap electricity that Uganda was counting on and thereby enable the city of Jinja to become an important industrial center. In addition, even an extremely large dam would raise the level of a huge lake like Victoria only a few inches and would cause many fewer problems of resettlement than the scheme for Nimule. The one disadvantage was that the states abutting the lake or near it (Uganda, Kenya, Tanganyika, the Belgian Congo, Rwanda, and Burundi) would need to give their consent and would have a claim on compensation if any resettlement of people were involved.

Despite the obvious negotiating difficulties, the British hydraulic and economic officials were enthusiastic about the Owen Falls dam. Always mindful of the need to strengthen sterling, officials at the Foreign Office suggested that the integrated economic development of the Nile river basin, under British auspices, would further reduce Britain's dependence on American dollars and would serve as "an excellent means of perpetuating wholesome Western influence in the Middle East."[38] But the considerable financial outlays worried the British planners. In the middle of 1949 the British estimated that the total expenditure on the dam at Owen Falls, the hydroelectric project, and the Jonglei canal would reach £83,850,000.[39] Within a month the estimate had grown to £150,000,000, and although the government of Egypt was expected to contribute almost £70,000,000, the British financial experts wondered where Britain would find its share of the funds.[40]

From the outset, the International Bank for Reconstruction and Development (IBRD—more commonly known as the World Bank) had taken an interest in the discussions and had indicated a willingness to provide funding. The British hesitated. On the one hand, IBRD funding would reduce the British obligation. But British officials were reluctant to cede

---

[37] M. J. Davies to McDermott, March 4, 1949, PRO FO 371/69231.

[38] D. J. D. Maitland, Note on the Nile Waters, April 29, 1949, PRO FO 371/73623.

[39] Hugh-Jones, Note, July 14, 1949, PRO FO 371/73623.

[40] E. A. Bayne, Loan Officer, Loan Department, International Bank for Reconstruction and Development, Memorandum on the Equatorial Nile Scheme, August 9, 1949, PRO FO 371/73623.

preeminence to the United Nations and saw American hydraulic, engineering, and construction interests looming in the background. D. J. D. Maitland at the Foreign Office questioned "the altruism of the Bank's motives." He concluded his assessment of the bank's interest with the statement that "to a certain extent therefore Mr. Bayne's proposal represents long-term competition between British and American industry."[41]

Not surprisingly, given the myriad of countries and interests that needed accommodating, no comprehensive agreement was reached. Under pressure from the British governor of Uganda, John Hall, who was eager to move ahead with Uganda's industrialization schemes, an Owen Falls hydroelectric agreement was signed at the end of May 1949. The Egyptian government agreed to pay £E4.5 million to resettle people living in areas around the lake whose properties would be submerged. The agreement fell far short of what the British had set out to achieve, however. The interests were too conflicting, and the governments involved had to settle for only a small part of the larger scheme.[42]

Nationalistically minded Egyptians with an interest in hydraulic issues had always been suspicious of Nile water development schemes carried on outside their country. They did not want another power determining the amount of irrigation water available to Egypt. They were also apprehensive that irrigation water provided to other countries would turn these states into competitors in the world cotton market, as the Sennar dam had done in the Gezira region of the Sudan.

Even while the Nile water projects were being negotiated with the governments of Egypt, the Sudan, and Uganda, voices of nationalist protest were raised in Egypt. By 1949 two projects with Egypt as their primary focus had crystallized as alternatives to schemes for the overall development of the Nile. At first the Wadi el-Rayan scheme commanded the most support. It would store water in a large trough five miles southwest of Fayyum and would have the obvious advantage of allowing Egypt to retain within its own borders all of the waters it needed for irrigation purposes.[43] A second scheme, however, quickly captured the attention of the Egyptian leadership. It was put forward by a Greek hydraulic engineer, Adrian Daninos, and called for the construction of a massive dam just south of the existing Aswan Dam. The obvious technical and construction difficulties involved in building what would be the largest dam in the world and the resettlement problems involved once a huge lake had been created behind the dam at first dissuaded experts. But

[41] D. J. D. Maitland, Foreign Office Minute, July 8, 1949, PRO FO 371/73623.

[42] Collins, *The Waters of the Nile*, p. 217.

[43] Chancery to Foreign Office, March 16, 1949, PRO FO 371/73614; *al-Misri*, March 6, 1949; *al-Muqattam*, March 18, 1949; *al-Musawwar*, May 27, 1949; Maclean to Clutton, June 2, 1949, PRO FO 371/73618.

with the passing of time, the high dam at Aswan seemed to offer Egypt the best answer to the panoply of British proposals for Nile control, all of which would occur outside of Egypt and render Egypt vulnerable to external pressures.

In the seven-year period from the end of World War II until the military coup d'etat of July 1952, most of the British hopes to strengthen the economic ties between Egypt and Britain were dashed. Sterling could not be released in a timely fashion, and the negotiations between British and Egyptian financial experts spilled over into the political arena and inflamed Egyptian sentiment against the British. Only a small fraction of the Nile river development project came to fruition, mainly in Uganda. In the meantime, Egyptian engineers came forward with their own development schemes designed to store water within Egypt. The British business community saw its position eroded, largely because of Egypt's failure to gain access to sterling and the desire of Egyptian financial officials to create dollar reserves. In short, the weakening of British capital made it difficult for Britain to use its previously strong economic position in Egypt to good effect. Moreover, the determination of Britain to maintain its military position in Egypt so alienated the Egyptian populace that it threatened the economic interests and even on occasion the lives of the British business community.

PART B
IMPERILING THE PRIVATE SECTOR: MILITARY TALKS, 1945–1952

If the negotiations over the sterling balances and the Nile waters prevented the British from strengthening the position of British capital in Egypt and even raised the wrath of Egyptian negotiators and nationalists, the efforts of the British to maintain their military presence within the country through the Suez Canal base antagonized even larger segments of the Egyptian population against the British. Although on the surface the dispute revolved around military and political matters, in fact the spillover effect in the economic arena, and specifically the place of foreign capital in the country, was profound. If one is to understand how such an important and deeply entrenched foreign business presence in Egypt was put at risk and came to be seen by many nationalists as a detriment to Egypt's economic progress, and if one is to understand how Egypt's political elites could contemplate and then bring about the difficult uprooting of this foreign presence, one must look first at the bitter political-military negotiations over the Suez base. Those discussions, like those on sterling releases and irrigation schemes on the Upper Nile, further embittered Anglo-Egyptian relations. Indeed, the prehistory of the nationalizations and expropriations of foreign businesses following the British-French-Israeli invasion cannot be understood without entering the military and political conference and bargaining rooms.

For decades, Britain had used its political and military predominance in Egypt to strengthen its economic and financial hold over the country. Then, in the period immediately after World War II, when Britain found itself less able to dominate Egypt's economy, its political and military position also began to be challenged. Yet because of Egypt's strategic importance to Britain, ever increasing as the contours of Cold War politics became clear and Britain's military base in the Suez Canal region became more vital, Britain's efforts to retain political-military predominance in Egypt began to threaten its economic interests. Violent confrontations between British forces and Egyptian guerrilla nationalists, which increased in intensity following the Wafdist repudiation of the Anglo-Egyptian treaty in October 1951 and culminated in death and property destruction in Cairo on January 26, 1952, finally persuaded the foreign business community in Egypt to play a more active role in British affairs. Its members began to pressure the British government to be more accommodating to nationalist demands.

Ordinarily, representatives of the private sector left the details of political and military discussions to the diplomats and generals. But the Suez base had become the centerpiece of Anglo-Egyptian conflict in the postwar years. The British political establishment viewed it as the foundation of its military power in the Mediterranean and beyond, while the Egyptian nationalists saw it as a clear and unacceptable infringement of Egyptian sovereignty. As negotiations dragged on year after year with no resolution in sight, and nationalist sentiments became inflamed against all aspects of Western influence, the business community was drawn into the controversy. Details of the negotiations took on decisive, indeed life-threatening, importance to its members and were seen, accurately, as influencing the long-term status of foreign and even local investors in Egypt.

Juridically, the British military base in the Suez Canal area existed because of the Anglo-Egyptian treaty of alliance of 1936. By that agreement Britain undertook to remove its troops from Cairo, Alexandria, and the delta area and to relocate them in the region of the Suez Canal. In all, the British were limited to a force of 10,000 soldiers, 400 air force pilots, and an unspecified number of auxiliary personnel. The treaty was to run for twenty years; if no new treaty had been concluded by the expiration date, Egypt and the United Kingdom agreed to place Anglo-Egyptian military relations before the League of Nations.

Situating a base along the Suez Canal was in keeping with the reasons Britain had justified its continued military presence in Egypt when it proclaimed the country's independence in 1922. The base defended imperial communications and served (in theory, though not as effectively as the military bases in Cairo and Alexandria had) as a protector of foreign interests in the country itself. World War II altered the base in profound ways. It was expanded and became Britain's primary military staging arena for the whole of the Middle East. At a cost of £500 million, the base had required three and a half years of feverish construction activity during the war to bring it to its final stage. Equipped with workshops for the repair of military equipment, communication power stations, and hospitals, it housed 700,000 tons of ammunition and 14,000 vehicles in the early 1950s. It also had numerous airfields and could accommodate a force in excess of 100,000 troops.[44] It was, in fact, the largest British military base in the world, 120 miles long and thirty miles wide at its widest point.[45] Clearly, the 1945 base was a far cry from the modest establishment that the military negotiators had envisioned in 1936. After the war, the growing tension between the Western powers and their former wartime ally, the Soviet Union, enhanced the strategic and military purposes of this new and enlarged base to the British and their American allies.

Nonetheless, at war's end, the British electorate replaced Winston Churchill and his Conservative Party with the Labour Party of Clement Attlee. Although the electorate was concerned primarily with domestic issues of reconstruction and wealth redistribution, Labour brought a new vision of foreign and colonial affairs. Ernest Bevin as Attlee's new secretary of state for foreign affairs was under no illusions about the vital importance of the Middle East to Britain, especially because of its oil resources. Egypt held particular significance to Bevin as one of Britain's primary cotton suppliers and as the location for "an irreplaceable offensive base."[46] Yet Bevin believed that Britain must enter a new era of cooperation with formally colonial and quasi-colonial possessions like Egypt, forswearing the old ties of domination. He sought to negotiate a new treaty based on mutual economic and military interests.[47] He was acutely aware, as some of his successors chose not to be, that a military base in a country turned hostile toward Britain by nationalist venom would be unusable.[48] Even so, at the time that Bevin was negotiating a

---

[44] Ministry of Defense to BJSM, Washington, December 19, 1952, PRO FO 371/96980.

[45] Dodds-Parker, Foreign Office Minute, June 2, 1954, PRO FO 371/108450 JE 1193/108.

[46] Alan Bullock, *Ernest Bevin: Foreign Secretary, 1945–1951* (Oxford, 1985), p. 113.

[47] Cabinet Discussions, April 24, 1946, PRO Cab 128/5 37(46)1.

[48] Revision of Anglo-Egyptian Treaty Memorandum by Secretary of State for Foreign Affairs, June 5, 1946, PRO Cab 129/10 CP 46 (219). This memorandum stated that "the implementation of any defense scheme maintained in peace time on Egyptian territory and by Egyptian personnel depends on the good will of the Egyptian government and the Egyp-

new relationship with Egypt (1946), the Cold War had not fully gripped the minds of Western statesmen. In addition, the British still believed it possible that if they were unable to obtain Egyptian approval to maintain the British base there, the military could turn elsewhere, perhaps to Palestine or Cyprus, or to Cyrenaica in Libya.

In Ismail Sidqi, Bevin found an ideal negotiating partner. A political pragmatist, a devotee of the West, and a critic of extreme expressions of nationalist sentiment, Sidqi, too, sought new bases of political accommodation between Britain and Egypt. Perhaps Sidqi would even have permitted Britain to maintain its Suez base on a smaller scale, but nationalist attacks, led in particular by the Wafd, precluded such a compromise. In late 1946 Sidqi and Bevin seemed to have achieved an understanding: British forces would be withdrawn from Cairo and Alexandria in 1947 and from Egypt in its entirety in September 1949. And the British were not to be granted any automatic right of reoccupation in the event of warfare; they would have to secure such permission in discussions with the Egyptians.[49]

It is futile to speculate on how postwar Anglo-Egyptian relations would have been altered had this treaty come into being. The treaty failed over the Sudan, over which the negotiators were vague. In subsequent clarifications, the British stated that they had no intention of abandoning the Sudan to Egyptian suzerainty; in reply the Egyptians reaffirmed their commitment to the unity of the Nile valley.

In the meantime, even as the Sidqi-Bevin negotiations were under way, the Suez base was growing in military importance to Britain. In the first place, it provided the West with air bases from which to bomb vital Russian oil supplies in Baku and the Caucasus and even to strike Moscow in the event of war.[50] British military planners were certain that, should war occur, Soviet forces would launch early strikes against the Middle East, not only because of the proximity of the Egyptian base to Soviet oil reserves but also because the Middle East held Western Europe's major oil supplies. In an effort to develop the airfields in the Suez complex and make them indispensable to the American strategic air command the British undertook to modernize the largest of the bases there,

---

tian people." Most of the military did not accept this position, arguing that in the event of war Britain would require full military facilities in Egypt and that in peacetime the base needed to be maintained by British personnel. June 7, 1946, PRO Cab 129/10 CP 46 (224).

[49] For a discussion of the treaty, see William Roger Louis, *The British Empire in the Middle East, 1945–1951: Arab Nationalism, the United States, and Post-War Imperialism* (Oxford, 1984).

[50] See Peter L. Hahn, *The United States, Great Britain, and Egypt, 1945–56: Strategy and Diplomacy in the Early Cold War* (Chapel Hill, N.C., 1991), pp. 39 ff.

Abu Sueir. An extended runway would enable it to handle American long-range B-29 bombers and thereby increase the Soviet targets reachable from Egypt.[51]

The British regarded the limitation on military personnel in the Suez base as grossly inadequate in the changed military environment of the Cold War. According to their assessment of the minimal requirements to maintain the base in peacetime, the British needed to station 25,000 troops there. If it were to function as the regional military headquarters for the Middle East and possess adequate air defense capabilities, the base required a covering force of a reinforced brigade group.[52] In addition, even in peacetime, it depended upon a large number of Egyptian workers. The British estimated that they needed 7,900 skilled workmen and 19,050 unskilled laborers and that they would have to hire an additional 23,000 workers, mainly artisans, to make the base fully operational in wartime.[53]

During the Bevin-Sidqi negotiations the British believed that another base or series of smaller bases could be established in the Middle East. The creation of the state of Israel in 1948 removed one possibility from consideration. Tensions on the island of Cyprus made that area less promising. Cyrenaica and Gaza continued to have their backers, but increasingly, the British planners were forced to conclude that "Egypt is the only possible base in wartime for the defense of the Middle East."[54] Its array of training grounds, recreational areas, ammunition storage depots, and air bases could not be duplicated elsewhere even if the British were able to identify another geographic region and willing government. The British and the Egyptians continued to engage in military conversations following the failure of the Sidqi-Bevin talks, though the desiderata of the two countries had become so different by then as to virtually preclude agreement. The Cold War had persuaded most British political and military officials of the high strategic value of Egypt, even if stationing troops in the country ran the risk of arousing Egyptian resentment. The Egyptian ruling elite, though, could no longer tolerate a British military presence there.

The failure of the many political and military discussions over the base and the specter of social revolution predisposed the British to contemplate a new direction in their policy toward Egypt. As so often in the past

[51] Ministry of Defense, London, to General Headquarters, Middle East Land Forces, April 22, 1949, PRO FO 371/73552.

[52] Foreign Office Minute, Brief for the Chief of the Imperial General Staff for the Meeting with King Farouk, November 1949, by Stewart, October 29, 1949, PRO FO 371/73563.

[53] Allen, Foreign Office Minute, Labor Situation in the Canal Zone, December 21, 1951, PRO FO 371/97068.

[54] M. R. Wright to Stevenson, October 20, 1950, PRO FO 371/80456.

when the British could not have their way dealing with usually pliant minority political leaders, they looked to Egypt's majority nationalist party, the Wafd, to come to their rescue. They had done so in 1936 and obtained the Anglo-Egyptian treaty of that year. They had also brought the Wafd into power through military intervention in 1942. Once again, they saw the Wafd as a possible solution, probably their only hope.

In spite of its checkered past and its well-established penchant for venality, the Wafd was like a hydra, able to grow a new head whenever the old one was lopped off. It had survived the death of its founder, Sa'd Zaghlul, in 1927, the defection of two of its most influential leaders in the 1930s (Ahmad Mahir and Nuqrashi), the revelations of party malfeasance by one of its disaffected spokesmen, Makram Ubayd, at the end of the war, and the growing loss of energy of its most visible leader, Mustafa al-Nahhas. By the postwar period, it had a new constellation of leaders, who despite their many differences in social background and ideology appeared ready to submerge these differences to work together for social reform and national independence. On the left, dynamic young professionals were deeply influenced by socialist thought. Among the most articulate was Muhammad Mandur, editor of the left-leaning Wafdist newspaper, *al-Wafd al-Misri*, which he and his colleagues used to publicize the ideals of wealth redistribution and economic growth through planning. Gathering up the reins of power was Fuad Serag al-Din, who, while appealing to party old-timers as a large landowner and a man of great wealth, had impressive ties with student and labor groups. His skillful manipulation of nationalist ideology, especially anti-British propaganda, and his use of the socialist ideology that had become so widespread in Egyptian society in the immediate postwar era, made him an especially formidable adversary for the British.

British officialdom should have been more concerned about the Wafd's return to power in 1950 than it was. The British lack of urgency stemmed from a number of plausible assumptions that, however, rested on one major miscalculation—the strength of nationalist sentiment even among the most privileged classes. One of the themes running through the British assessment of the Egyptian political scene was that, although the country seethed with social discontent and numerous discontented groups, some of a highly secret nature and favoring violent confrontations with the British military, were in existence, the prospects of fundamental change were minimal. In the opinion of British experts, the groups of the extreme right or the extreme left—the Muslim Brothers, the Communists, the students, and parts of organized labor—were not well organized and were unlikely to seize power. Moreover, the king and his clients, the British believed, had placed conservative and pro-British elements in the top positions in the civil bureaucracy, the religious establishment, and most important, the military.

Ambassador Ralph Stevenson put this position well, noting that "opposition elements are weak and divided and leadership seems to be entirely lacking. There is no apparent alternative to the Wafd. . . . Trouble from students can probably be suppressed without too much difficulty. . . . The expected trouble from the army can probably be dealt with by throwing to the wolves a sufficient number of officers and others involved in arms scandals and by purging the higher ranks of the armed forces."[55]

The first extended discussion of the possibility of a military coup d'etat did not take place in British circles until 1949.[56] The prospects did not alarm most officials, who depicted the army as a conservative institution where the interests of crown and landlords would be strongly represented. Thus, in the British view, should the Egyptian political scene become deeply disturbed, a military coup backed by the king would restore order to the country and provide powerful safeguards for Western interests.

A minority school of British thought had a completely different perspective on Egypt, yet reached similar policy conclusions. This group of officials talked about the near inevitability of a social revolution. They wrote about plots against the king and leading politicians and foresaw a period of considerable political instability. They saw the Wafd, however, as the most effective barrier to revolution. M. R. Wright summed up this segment of Foreign Office opinion: "The Wafd are certainly the party best equipped to introduce social reform. . . . If a serious social disturbance or revolution should come in Egypt, the Wafd would be the obvious party to take charge unless there were a military dictatorship."[57] Thus, from differing premises, British officials came to the conclusion that a changeover to Wafdist rule, even with the expected surge of nationalist sentiments, was inevitable, possibly beneficial, and unlikely to be deleterious to the wide range of British interests that they were obligated to defend.

One other factor emboldened the British to face the prospect of a Wafdist return to office. Having concluded in 1947 that evacuation "because of the international situation is out of the question," the War Office and Foreign Office began to engage in a more determined examination of Egypt's ability to drive the British military forces out of the Suez Canal base.[58] The consensus was that the Egyptian nationalists could not make the British position "untenable."[59] If necessary, Britain could seal off much of the canal zone from the rest of Egypt and establish British military rule over the canal area.

---

[55] No. 718, Stevenson to Foreign Office, October 16, 1950, PRO FO 371/80456.

[56] G. L. Clutton, commenting on a note by R. W. Barley at the Foreign Office, January 29, 1949, attached to Chapman Andrews to Clutton, January 21, 1949, PRO FO 371/73463.

[57] W. R. Wright, Note, February 7, 1949, PRO FO 371/73463.

[58] G. L. Clutton, Foreign Office Note, September 7, 1949, PRO FO 371/73504.

[59] Allen, Foreign Office Minute, July 4, 1951, PRO FO 371/90134.

To be sure, the British could no longer intervene militarily to put the Wafd in power as they had in 1942. But they could still manipulate Egyptian politics from behind the scenes. Using their influence, they persuaded the king to prorogue Parliament and to call for new elections. Here, too, the British made known their preference for free elections. In the ensuing elections the Wafd won an overwhelming victory, capturing 226 seats of a total of 329 in the Parliament.[60] Participation rates in the cities, where the Wafdist proportion of the vote was the highest, were not large, suggesting that the electorate no longer placed faith in the democratic process or the mission of the Wafd.

The new Wafdist Ministry reflected the different tendencies of the party. Nahhas became prime minister. The all-important post of minister of the interior was turned over to Fuad Serag al-Din. But idealistic, socially conscious, and professional elements were well represented by the so-called doctors' contingent. Dr. Ahmad Husayn, darling of the American social engineers, went to the Ministry of Social Affairs. Dr. Taha Husayn took over the Ministry of Education, and Dr. Zaki Abd al-Mut'al became minister of finance. All of these men were protégés of Nagib al-Hilali, one of the Wafdists most committed to social reforms.[61]

The Wafd occupied office for two full years, from January 1950 until the end of January 1952. Its tenure in power was marked by a steady decline in the influence of the social reformers in the Ministry and by an intensification of oppositional relations with the British.[62] In the January 1950 speech from the throne the new government promised a panoply of social legislation and pledged to renounce the Anglo-Egyptian treaty if negotiations with the British continued to be stalemated.[63] In that speech and subsequent statements the Wafd promised to press ahead on the big irrigation projects, to electrify the Aswan Dam and the Helwan railway, to promote new housing projects, to reclaim land among the poor, and to introduce filtered water throughout the countryside.[64] One of the Wafd's showiest items was a social insurance scheme that was to begin on a small scale by providing allowances to the aged, the widowed, and poor children. Later it was to be extended to provide protection against illness, old age, and unemployment generally.[65] The Wafdist newspaper, al-Misri,

[60] Azzah Wahbi, 'Tajarib al-Dimuqratiya al-Libraliya fi Misr,' master's thesis, Cairo University, 1978, p. 75; al-Ahram, January 12, 1950.

[61] Joel Gordon, Nasser's Blessed Movement: Egypt's Free Officers and the July Revolution (New York, 1992), pp. 23–25; al-Ahram, January 12, 1950.

[62] Also, the opposition joined ranks against the Wafd. See, for instance, their intention to oppose as reflected in al-Ahram, March 18, 1950, and the leftist critique of Wafdist policy as pure capitalism in al-Ishtirakiya, August 26, 1951.

[63] For the speech from the throne and press opinion, see al-Misri, January 13, 1950; and al-Ahram, January 14, 16, and 18, 1950.

[64] See Majlis al-Nuwwab, Majmu'at Madabat, November 16, 1950, pp. 6 ff.

[65] See National Bank of Egypt, Economic Bulletin 3, no. 2 (1950), pp. 70–72; and an inter-

greeted the speech from the throne with the headline "Socialist Policy of the Government,"[66] and Rashid al-Barrawi, one of the most economically sophisticated and left-leaning social observers of the period, had only words of praise for the intentions of the new government.[67]

One by one, however, the social reformers were dropped or marginalized as Fuad Serag al-Din became the Wafdist strongman. First to go was Zaki Abd al-Mut'al, the minister of finance. Not surprisingly, this vital office was taken over by Serag al-Din himself.[68] Many outside observers, especially the American diplomats, who had begun to take an intense interest in domestic Egyptian affairs and were convinced that Egypt required far-reaching social reform, regarded the resignation of Ahmad Husayn, the minister of social affairs, as the coup de grace to the Wafd's social energy.[69] In fact, Ahmad Husayn, though well connected through family relations, had never enjoyed great influence within the Wafdist leadership. His appointment had been as much a way to appease the Americans as it had been an indication of Wafdist seriousness to press ahead with social reform.

As soon as the Wafd entered office, the British opened negotiations on the 1936 agreement.[70] Although the Egyptian government entered into the discussions, few on the British side were optimistic about the outcome. Ambassador Stevenson believed that only King Faruq and Egypt's entrepreneur-politician, Ahmad Abbud, were truly amenable to a negotiated treaty and a continued British military presence in Egypt.[71] The British negotiators concluded that their most effective bargaining chip was arms supplies. Yet their room for maneuver was limited. The British army had first to be supplied, and the backbenchers of the Labour Party and the Conservative Party at large were likely to oppose military assistance to Egypt at that juncture. As the political tensions mounted, the British added to the strength of the British force in the base.[72]

Finally, with its social idealism spent, the Wafd sought to energize its followers with the one item it had left in its bag of campaign promises.

---

view with Ahmad Husayn on the social insurance scheme in *al-Misri*, January 18, 1950.

[66] *al-Misri*, January 13, 1950.

[67] *al-Ahram*, January 16, 1950.

[68] Still, as late as September 9, 1951, Serag al-Din claimed that he was a socialist and that his party did not represent capitalist elements. See *al-Ahram*, September 9, 1951. On the replacement of Zaki Abd al-Mut'al as minister of finance, one should consult no. 501, Stevenson to Bevin, November 23, 1950, PRO FO 371/80349.

[69] No. 28, Stevenson to Morrison, July 31, 1951, PRO FO 371/90115.

[70] G. L. Clutton, Foreign Office Minute, Anglo-Egyptian Treaty Negotiations, March 23, 1950. Preparations for the negotiations had been going on for months before the elections themselves. See G. L. Clutton, Note, June 24, 1949; and no. 3159, Foreign Office to United Kingdom Delegation to the United Nations, September 28, 1949, PRO FO 371/73464.

[71] No. 288, Stevenson to Younger, July 7, 1952, PRO FO 371/80382.

[72] Captain Butler to Stewart, July 26, 1950, PRO FO 371/80451.

On October 16, 1951, the Wafdist minister of foreign affairs announced the abrogation of the 1936 treaty. Immediately clashes began to occur in the canal zone. The Egyptian nationalist movement headed on a collision course with the British military. The resolve of the British to hang on in the canal zone was to be tested. Inexorably, private foreign economic interests were dragged into the dispute, and the primacy of politics revealed itself. Both sides were prepared to sacrifice economic well-being for political gains. Economic and financial concerns were assigned second place.

The Egyptian decision to abrogate the treaty led to four immediate consequences, each having economic side effects: the entrance of liberation squads into the canal area to carry out acts of violence and intimidation against British soldiers and Egyptian collaborators; the introduction, albeit in a modified form, of a long-worked-out British plan for sealing off the canal from the rest of Egypt; the use of the oil weapon to pressure the Egyptian government to modify its policies; and the forceful intervention of American diplomats to pressure both sides into an agreement.

As the moment when treaty negotiations seemed likely to break down approached, the many small, secret guerrilla groups intensified their preparations for a campaign of violence. According to British intelligence, the Muslim Brothers, the Socialist Party of Ahmad Husayn, the Watanists, and the National Pact Committee all had opened up training areas where young persons were schooled in the use of violence.[73] These quasi-military training areas were dotted around Egypt. The Socialist Party operated a large center at al-Abbasiya.[74] Many small camps were located in the Sharqiya province, often on the estates of large landowners.[75] As had been the case in 1946 and 1947 when clashes occurred in Alexandria and elsewhere between civilian groups and the British, the liberation squads enjoyed the secret support of the more nationalistically minded Egyptian army officers. The young military men trained the squads and supplied them with small arms.[76]

The liberation groups operated in a highly individualistic way. Their numbers may not have exceeded 1,000, but they were remarkably successful. They kept up a steady campaign of terror all along the far-flung lines of the British base. By the end of 1951 the British military reported 154 incidents of sniping, 41 bomb attacks, 18 acts of sabotage against

[73] Wardle Smith to Allen, November 9, 1951, enclosing note by B. Morris, Extremist Groups in Egypt, November 7, 1951, PRO FO 371/90119.

[74] See al-Ahram, November 2 and 5, 1951.

[75] Kamil al-Sharif, al-Muqawama al-Sirriya fi Qana al-Suwis (Beirut, 1957), pp. 30 ff.

[76] Kamal al-Din Rif'at, Mudhakkirat Kamal al-Din Rif'at: Harb al-Tahrir (Cairo, 1968), pp. 71 ff; Abd al-Latif al-Baghdadi, Mudhakkirat Abd al-Latif al-Baghdadi (Cairo, 1977), vol. 1, p. 37; and Kamil al-Sharif, al-Muqawama, pp. 30 ff.

water supplies and 11 against the railway, 86 cable cuttings, 27 thefts of arms, 8 assaults on British soldiers, 18 murders, and 12 woundings.[77]

A major goal of the nationalist movement was to withdraw Egyptian labor from the base, thereby rendering the base inoperative. The British thought it unlikely that such a boycott campaign could succeed because of the massive problem of unemployment in the canal zone.[78] But the Wafdist Ministry enacted legislation prohibiting Egyptian workers from engaging in employment on the base and promised support for those who honored the boycott. The liberation teams backed up this legislation by retaliating against individuals who sought to break the boycott. To their astonishment and dismay the British were forced to concede that the withdrawal of Egyptian labor had been effective.

Violent confrontations between liberation groups and British forces intensified nationalist feelings in the country and deepened anti-British and anti-European resentment. Perhaps the most important long-term contribution of these squads to Anglo-Egyptian, indeed Euro-Egyptian, relations was the flourishing of a pamphlet literature extolling nationalism, sanctioning violence, and even demanding the rooting out of all forms of European domination, economic as well as political and military.

In the Suez Canal zone the British set in motion the plans that they had prepared for sealing off the area and placing it under de facto military rule. The more extreme military plans to establish a de jure military government were not invoked; they were, however, held in abeyance in case political conditions worsened. In early November 1951 the British army issued orders forbidding the Egyptian army to enter or leave the canal zone. They divided the area into seven regions, each under its own military commander.[79]

Although the British planners had thought it impossible for the Egyptians to render the British military position in Egypt unfavorable, that is precisely what the liberation squads and nationalist propaganda did. By December 1951, the British military men at the base conceded that the boycott was so successful that "the former fully operative base still exists but it is no longer operative and no more than maintained."[80] The stiff resistance and continued acts of violence compelled the British military to tighten its administration of vital parts of the canal region. These acts in turn led to more violent confrontations and heightened sensitivity to the British presence in the country. In early December 1951, responding

[77] G. F. Rodgers, British Middle East Organization, to Foreign Office, January 2, 1952, PRO FO 371/96859.

[78] No. 244, Stevenson to Morrison, July 6, 1951, PRO FO 371/90134.

[79] al-Ahram, November 2, 1951.

[80] Joint British American Embassy Estimate of the Current Political Situation in Egypt, December 4, 1951, PRO FO 371/90150.

to acts of sabotage against their water supply in the region of Suez city, the British established a military presence around the waterworks plant. In the process, the army demolished 107 structures that had housed 350 people.[81] In addition, the British military established checkpoints along the main access roads into the canal and regulated movement into and out of the region.[82]

The endemic violence in the area was punctuated by larger flare-ups bringing considerable loss of life. Those incidents added to the outrage of the Egyptians. On November 17 and 18 British tanks and armored cars assaulted the city of Ismailia, and British forces disarmed the Egyptian police for having aided the liberation groups.[83] Another set of incidents occurred at Suez city on December 3 and 4, followed by more serious disturbances exactly one month later. Temporarily, the British military banned all movement on the Cairo-Suez road and railway.[84] Nonetheless, terrorist attacks continued apace. Sorties were carried out against the large military establishment at Tel el-Kebir. This area was one of the most important parts of the Suez military complex and one of the most exposed. Located further inland from the canal than the rest of the military base, the Tel el-Kebir extension contained machinery and plants capable of effecting every kind of repair on armored vehicles and guns. The Tel el-Kebir area itself covered 35,000 acres and had a perimeter that stretched over 17 1/2 miles.[85] Confrontations at Tel el-Kebir on January 12, 1952, led to a British military order restricting movement in that area between 10:00 AM and 3:00 PM.[86] But these efforts to control movement in the area were hardly a success. On January 16, 1952, 100 Egyptian civilians, supported by thirty to forty Egyptian auxiliary police, attacked British forces at Tel el-Kebir. In retaliation, the British carried out clearing operations at el-Hamada, near Tel el-Kebir, where they captured and interrogated 120 heavily armed police.[87]

To counter the nationalist challenge, the British turned to their most powerful economic weapon: the interdiction of oil supplies from the Suez area. Because Egypt was heavily dependent on various types of oil for different purposes, the British embargo of supplies could affect different

[81] No. 128, Rapp, British Middle East Organization, Fayid, to Foreign Office, December 16, 1951, PRO FO 371/90122.

[82] Roger Allen, Foreign Office Minute, Control of Movement in the Canal Zone, January 18, 1952, PRO FO 371/96859.

[83] No. 1036, Stevenson to Foreign Office, November 20, 1951, PRO FO 371/90119.

[84] No. 605/CCL, General Headquarters, Middle East Land Forces, to Ministry of Defense, January 15, 1952, PRO FO 371/96859.

[85] Dodds-Parker, Foreign Office Minute, June 2, 1954, PRO FO 371/108450 JE 1193/108.

[86] Roger Allen, Foreign Office Minute, Control of Movement in the Canal Zone, January 18, 1952, PRO FO 371/96859.

[87] No. 606/CCL, General Headquarters, Middle East Land Forces, to Ministry of Defense, January 16, 1952; no. 93, Stevenson to Foreign Office, January 17, 1952, PRO FO 371/90172.

sectors of the economy and the population. Black or industrial oil was the fuel of Egypt's industrial and transportation economy. It was transported by train from the Anglo-Egyptian Oil Company refinery at Suez city. Its interdiction could bring the whole of the Egyptian economy to a halt.[88] White oil was used in ordinary households for cooking, lighting, and heating. It reached the population centers partly by rail and road and partly through the Agrud to Cairo pipeline, which was constructed during World War II with lend-lease funds and was still owned by the British War Office. Thus the British military was in a position to turn off Egypt's access to oil simply by restricting the movement of oil from the Anglo-Egyptian refinery at Suez.[89] Anglo-Egyptian Oil's refinery produced 2 million tons of refined oil per year, sufficient to supply two-thirds of Egypt's needs. The Egyptian government ran a much smaller refinery at Alexandria, which was not in a position to replace the Suez oil supplies if they were cut off.

The British planners engaged in intense debates about the efficacy of using the oil weapon and the likely Egyptian responses. On balance, the military men favored a boycott. Some wanted to cut off all oil supplies so as to put "a stranglehold on the Egyptian economy and deprive the population of Cairo and the delta of power on which sewage disposal among other things depends [as well as] of kerosene and petrol."[90] Such tough economic measures, they conceded, were likely to expose British economic interests to intense criticism and even retaliation. They feared that BOAC and Anglo-Egyptian Oil would be likely targets. But to the mind of the military men, Egypt was valuable to the British above all else for its geomilitary significance. Lieutenant Colonel B. Collins at the War Office summed up this point of view when he stressed that the primary British goal must be "a base in Egypt, functioning in peace from which we can support our forces in the event of Russian aggression and unrestricted use of the Suez Canal to all shipping."[91]

Much of the Foreign Office and the Board of Trade did not agree. They opposed the policy on the grounds that it was too provocative and would intensify conflict between Britain and Egypt. An uneasy compromise was reached.[92] The military was permitted to apply intermittent restrictions on oil supplies in hopes that Egyptian politicians would amelio-

[88] D. H. Crofton, minister of fuel and power, to Allen, Foreign Office, November 2, 1951, PRO FO 371/90172.

[89] Foreign Office Note, Cairo/Agrud and Fanara / Abu Sueir Pipeline, Mackworth-Young, March 31, 1952, PRO FO 371/97032.

[90] No. 539/CCL, General Headquarters, Middle East Land Forces, to Ministry of Defense, October 27, 1951, PRO FO 371/90145.

[91] Lt. Col. B. Collins, War Office, to R. Allen, November 6, 1951, PRO FO 371/90172.

[92] R. J. W. Stacy, Board of Trade, to Bowker, Foreign Office, October 20, 1951, PRO FO 371/90172.

rate their behavior and assert control over the liberation squads.[93] Although the policy was in effect for too short a time to determine its efficacy, evidence suggests that the policy was not successful. The Wafd never had control of the terrorist groups, and the cutting off of oil supplies further alienated the extremist elements in the nationalist movement. More ominously, it called attention to the economic powers that foreign firms could employ against the nationalist cause.

Embargoing oil brought Britain's economic power in Egypt squarely into the purview of the nationalists, who chose not to distinguish between British military policy and the stance of British firms. To them, the cutting off of supplies from Anglo-Egyptian Oil's refinery at Suez city demonstrated collusion between British business and the British military. The nationalist distaste for foreign capital was heightened.

In reality, Anglo-Egyptian Oil had disagreed with official British policy.[94] In a series of meetings and correspondence between top Shell Oil officials and the Foreign Office, the directors of Shell Oil made clear their misgivings about the oil embargo. Even as early as October 31, 1951, just two weeks after the Wafd had renounced the Anglo-Egyptian treaty, Stephens, a director of Shell, called at the Foreign Office to protest plans to interdict oil supplies. He warned that such harsh measures would put pressure on the government of Egypt to nationalize the production, refining, and distribution of oil.[95]

Shell stepped up its expressions of concern in early 1952, following the January 26 disturbances in Cairo. Director Taitt wrote to the Foreign Office to argue that too much attention was being paid to the "military aspects of the problem. . . . The fact seems to be that because of this military emphasis the fate of British affairs in Egypt, the success or total failure of our trading interests there, the real friendship for England of a majority of thinking Egyptians, and indeed the very lives of some 40,000 to 50,000 British subjects are in the hands and depend almost exclusively on the actions of a group of generals whose primary responsibility is bound to the safety of their troops and the preservation of their military position." Barring "a quick and generous gesture" to Egyptian nationalism, Taitt feared that the British community would "be lucky if it gets out [of Egypt] with its skins intact."[96]

Just before the Ismailia confrontation the Foreign Office conducted another debate on their policy options in Egypt. They concluded that they could not accommodate the Egyptian negotiators on the issue of the

[93] No. 1490, Foreign Office to Cairo, November 24, 1951, PRO FO 371/90148.

[94] No. 894, Stevenson to Foreign Office, November 1, 1951, PRO FO 371/90145.

[95] E. A. Berthoud, Foreign Office Minute, October 31, 1951, PRO FO 371/90145.

[96] Geoffrey S. Taitt, Shell Oil, to Robert Scott, Foreign Office, February 2, 1952, PRO FO 371/96923.

Sudan. To do so would violate promises made to Sudanese leaders and set off waves of violence there. Instead, they opted to sit it out in Egypt, hoping to prolong the negotiations with the Egyptians. As for employing a range of economic sanctions against Egypt, they concluded that such action would lead to economic and political chaos, "the loss of all British commercial interests and the loss of British lives in riots and disturbances, immense administrative commitment at any rate temporarily in Alexandria and Cairo, lasting resentment of Egyptians, American horror, Arab fury, and probably liberal repudiation throughout the world."[97] A more prescient assessment of the impact of their later invasion of Suez could hardly be imagined. Yet their decision to wait out events in the canal base provoked more of a nationalist response than the Foreign Office anticipated.

The confrontations in the canal zone culminated on January 25, 1952, when British forces clashed with Egyptian police and auxiliaries. In what was nothing less than a battle, though between unequal forces, forty-two Egyptians were killed, fifty-eight wounded, and 800 detained for interrogation. On the British side three soldiers were killed and thirteen wounded. When news of the events at Ismailia spread to Cairo, violent rioting erupted. According to British accounts, some of the rioting was the handiwork of well-organized squads numbering between twenty and fifty members each. The British believed that most of those groups were under the control of Ahmad Husayn's Socialist Party, although some Muslim Brotherhood cells also participated.[98] The terrorist elements were joined by an undisciplined mob interested in looting. The British attached much blame to Serag al-Din for providing arms, money, and incendiary equipment to the groups in the early stages of the rioting. They also held the acting Wafdist minister of war, Abd al-Fattah Hasan, responsible since he had jurisdiction over the training and conduct of the liberation units and, like Serag al-Din, had encouraged their actions in the early stages.[99] The nationalist and anti-British agitation began to spill over into the economic sphere. Cairene protesters made foreign businesses primary targets, setting fires to the Turf Club, cinemas, restaurants, cafes, department stores, and many other foreign-owned business establishments. The hardest-hit British firms were BOAC, Barclays Bank, the tourist department of Thomas Cook, William Smith and Sons, and the Rivoli Cinema.

---

[97] R. Allen, Foreign Office, Notes on Possible Policies in Egypt, January 23, 1952, PRO FO 371/96920.

[98] Chancery to Foreign Office, January 31, 1952, PRO FO 371/96871.

[99] Chancery to Foreign Office, February 18, 1952, PRO FO 371/96872. Egyptian accounts of this critical moment may be found in Muhammad Anis, *Hariq al-Qahira* (Cairo, 1982); Jamal al-Sharqawi, *Asrar Hariq al-Qahira* (Cairo, 1985); and Tariq al-Bishri, *al-Haraka al-Siyasiya fi Misr, 1945–1952* (Beirut, 1983).

In addition, ten British subjects lost their lives, and the damage to British property was substantial.[100]

The January riots awakened the British business community to its declining, even perilous, situation in Egypt. Never in their wildest dreams had the business leaders living in Cairo imagined that 70,000 British troops would sit by in the Suez Canal base while British property burned to the ground and British lives were lost. In fact, the British generals had calculated that they would encounter stiff resistance from the Egyptian army if they tried to march on Cairo. In addition, they feared that the forces remaining behind would not be strong enough to defend the base from the Egyptian military.[101]

British business groups began to criticize British policy and to call for timely political and military concessions to Egyptian nationalism, even the evacuation of the base. In early February, for instance, a high-powered delegation of British businessmen representing Anglo-Egyptian Oil, Eastern Tobacco, Imperial Chemical Industries, and BOAC arranged a special meeting with Ambassador Stevenson to stress the vulnerability of their position in Egypt.[102] In London, Alexander Keown-Boyd, once an important official in the British Embassy in Egypt and then in the 1930s and early 1940s a British businessman in Egypt, met with Foreign Minister Selwyn Lloyd to press the Foreign Office in favor of military evacuation and recognition of Faruq as king of Egypt and the Sudan.[103] In the same vein, E. T. Peel of the important Peel and Company cotton exporting firm—a family and a firm with Egyptian economic connections dating back to the nineteenth century—wrote to Walter Monckton, minister of labour and national service, that "security and British interests generally in the Middle East are being jeopardized for an unattainable objective—a secure base on the canal."[104] Peel's worry was legitimate. He was one of the many Britishers expelled from the country in the wake of the 1956 invasion.

Of the three countries considered here, Egypt commenced the postwar years with the most solidly rooted private sector. It had an array of impressive entrepreneurs and a well-organized business community. The government looked to its leaders to spur the country's economic progress. Yet, on the eve of the military coup d'etat, its political future was being

---

[100] No. 48, Stevenson to Eden, February 29, 1952, PRO FO 371/96872.

[101] General Robertson, commander in chief, to General Brownjohn, January 30, 1952, PRO FO 371/96870; no. 48092/MIL, General Headquarters, Middle East Land Forces, to Ministry of Defense, February 11, 1952, PRO FO 371/96985.

[102] Stevenson to Bowker, February 6, 1952, PRO FO 371/96872.

[103] Selwyn Lloyd, Foreign Office Minute, March 26, 1952, PRO FO 371/96926.

[104] E. T. Peel of Peel and Company to W. Monckton, April 3, 1952, PRO FO 371/96929.

questioned. Critics complained that private capital was unable to address Egypt's severe social problems. But British policies on the release of sterling and on the preservation of their military base in the canal zone fueled a special resentment against foreign capital. As yet, no groundswell of nationalist opinion had insisted on ridding the country of foreign capital. But such voices could be heard, and the worry expressed by foreign business persons to their diplomatic agents that the country was courting an attack on all foreign influence was not misplaced.

CHAPTER 2

Contradictions in a Mixed Economy, 1952–1956

THE FOUR YEARS leading from the military coup d'etat to the nationalization of the Suez Canal Company witnessed confused political and economic probings and reflected the uncertainty of the new military leaders in economic affairs. Seeking to consolidate power and to appeal to as large a spectrum of groups as possible, the military regime delivered contradictory messages to the ruling elements as well as the rank and file. Its populism and identification with the poor tilted the regime toward social transformation, most obviously in the land reform and redistribution program and labor legislation. But the government counterbalanced this leftist orientation by cultivating business leaders and relying on Western-trained and procapitalist technicians from the old regime for crucial financial advice. The result was the establishment of an institutional and juridical environment, which, while seeming to resemble conventional mixed economies of the Western European variety, lacked a clearcut economic ethos and obfuscated the boundary lines between the private and public domains.

SEIZURE OF POWER AND APPEASEMENT OF
THE PRIVATE SECTOR IN 1952

Toward the end of July 1952 a small group of middle-level military officers seized power. Not surprisingly, they were young, raw in administrative matters, and not nearly as well educated as their civilian counterparts. The average age of the first Revolutionary Command Council (RCC) was thirty-three, even counting the fifty-one-year-old Muhammad Neguib, who was not one of the original conspirators. Only three of its members had higher education beyond the military college: Nasser, who had spent five months in the Egyptian Law School in 1936–37; Muhammad Neguib, holder of a law degree; and Khalid Muhi al-Din, a bachelor of science in commerce.[1]

Internal events had compelled these men to seize power before they were yet ready to rule; thus they came to office without a clear agenda.

[1] P. J. Vatikiotis, *The Egyptian Army in Politics: Pattern for New Nations* (Bloomington, Ind., 1961), pp. 48–49.

To be sure, the free officers had enunciated their six principles just before seizing office: the destruction of colonialism, the destruction of feudalism, the ending of monopolies and the control of the state by capital, the establishment of social justice, the construction of a strong national army, and the creation of sound democratic life. But these principles were vague and elastic. And the military men did not believe that all of their laudable goals could be realized quickly. Moreover, the six principles bore the imprint of leftist thinking within the free officers movement—an influence that did not accurately reflect the opinions of the coup makers.[2]

The free officers were probably no more than ninety to a hundred men within an officer corps that numbered 5,500.[3] Although many had served on the staff of the war college between 1945 and 1948 and felt the sting of military humiliation during the Palestine campaign in 1948, they did not form a cohesive group until late in 1949.[4] Bridging nearly all of the different branches of the military, the men had been deeply infused with the radical extraparliamentarianism of the 1930s. Individual members had ties with the Muslim Brothers, Young Egypt, the Watanists, the Wafdist Vanguard, and the communists—in short all of the radical and discontented groups in Egyptian society. They accepted much of the prevailing critique of the corruptibility and failure of Egyptian civilian, parliamentary society of these groups. They believed that big business exploited the Egyptian masses. And, even as their alienation from palace and parliament intensified, they also limited their ties with these groups. As they contemplated political action, they affirmed their primary loyalty to the army as an autonomous and efficient institution. They worried that a military takeover would fail to transform Egypt if the military men lost their solidarity with one another. They feared becoming the handmaidens of some other group's ideology, as they believed had been the case in Syria.[5]

The secretive ideological pronouncements issued before July 1952 proved to be no sure guide to the early actions of the military men. In the aftermath of seizing power the new rulers were preoccupied with only a few overarching goals. They needed to deal with their archenemy, King Faruq, and strip away the power of the landowning elite. The rest of their

[2] Ahmad Hamrush, *Qissa Thawra 23 Yulio* (Cairo, 1974), vol. 1, p. 149; P. J. Vatikiotis, *Nasser and His Generation* (London, 1978), pp. 47–66 and 101–12.

[3] Joel Gordon, *Nasser's Blessed Movement: Egypt's Free Officers and the July Revolution* (New York, 1992), p. 48; Kirk Beattie, *Egypt during the Nasser Years: Ideology, Politics, and Civil Society* (Boulder, Colo., 1994), p. 67.

[4] Vatikiotis, *The Egyptian Army in Politics*, p. 45; Tariq al-Bishri, *al-Dimuqratiya wa-l-Nizam 23 Yulio, 1952–70* (Beirut, 1987), pp. 50–66. A recent and authoritative account of the early organizing efforts of the disgruntled Egyptian army officers and the scholar's difficulties in establishing the numbers involved at any stage of their organizing is available in Beattie, *Egypt during the Nasser Years*, p. 85 and throughout.

[5] Gordon, *Nasser's Blessed Movement*, p. 53.

program, especially their relationship with the business community, evolved slowly, often in response to specific challenges. Moreover, the military junta had to proceed cautiously because of deep cleavages within its own ranks. Not only was the inner group of ten to fifteen prime conspirators often bitterly divided, but the larger military establishment created frequent challenges to the ruling clique. In 1953 and then again in 1954 opposition to the Revolutionary Command Council solidified in the prestigious artillery and cavalry units and threatened Nasser and his collaborators with a loss of office.

Within days of taking power the military deposed King Faruq. An entirely predictable action, the removal of a monarch who symbolized what was unconscionable in the old order was widely applauded. But the military retained the monarchy by establishing a regency for Faruq's infant son.

A much more decisive first test of the military's position on labor and business was its handling of a severe workers' strike at the Kafr al-Dawwar textile works, a major textile complex located a short distance from Alexandria. The workers there were in a state of high excitement after the coup, as was organized labor all around the country; they expected much from the new government. Indeed, within weeks of the takeover, workers at the Delta Light Railways Company dispatched a delegation to the Ministry of Communications to complain of the company's inertia and to protest the practice of discharging employees without paying back wages. At the time, the company was in the hands of a government-appointed sequestrator and owed the government £E400,000.[6] A week later, on August 7, 1952, a second deputation of workers from the Heliopolis Electric Railways Company, a lucrative Belgian-run public utility, laid claim to part of the dividend of that company, on the assumption that profit sharing would occur in the new Egypt.[7]

That the first serious labor challenge arose in the textile industry was entirely consistent with the highly routinized, almost mind-numbing work regimens in that sector, its mediocre wage scales, and the abundant opportunities for employees to organize and conspire. Many textile workers had imbibed socialist and communist teachings in their trade unions. The hotbed of radical discontent was the Shubra al-Khayma locale outside Cairo.[8] Three large textile plants existed near Alexandria, including the

<hr>

[6] *L'Observateur*, July 30, 1952.

[7] Ibid., August 7, 1952.

[8] Ellis Goldberg, *Tinker, Tailor, Textile Workers: Class and Politics in Egypt, 1930–1952* (Berkeley, Calif., 1986), pp. 139–72. There are excellent accounts of the Kafr al-Dawwar dispute in Joel Beinin and Zachary Lockman, *Workers on the Nile: Nationalism, Communism, Islam, and the Egyptian Working Class, 1882–1954* (Princeton, N.J., 1987), pp. 421–

two most efficient and profitable of Egypt's textile companies, Beida Dyers and the Misr Fine Spinning and Weaving Company. Up until 1952 those two firms had succeeded in avoiding the severe problems of over-production and declining profitability that had beset the rest of the indus-try, largely because they dominated the internal market for textiles and realized profits from exports.

Labor-management relations in the factories were extremely hostile, however. Management sought to stymie the efforts to organize the work force, paid inferior wages while earning high profits and paying out large dividends, and circumvented much of the labor legislation against dis-charging workers. The firms were notorious for the glaring disparities in income and social amenities between workers and managers. The original stimulus for labor protest occurred at the Beida factory. There, workers had finally established an effective labor union. The resignation of the all-powerful managing director, Elias Andraus, under government pres-sure, emboldened the union leaders to demand, with success, the removal of five unpopular factory managers. Those victories spurred other la-borers in the area to believe that the climate of opinion was shifting in favor of the work force. At the Misr Fine Spinning and Weaving plant, workers also began to organize and to call for far-reaching changes. A dispute escalated there into violent confrontation with the police on Au-gust 12 and 13, 1952, and the military was finally forced to intervene.[9]

Pro-labor accounts asserted that the management had engaged in pro-vocative actions with a view to bringing about the confrontation.[10] But the labor attaché in the British Embassy, M. T. Audsley, insisted that commu-nists had infiltrated the textile unions in the area and that Ahmad Taha Ahmad, a communist labor organizer, was secretly running an important trade union committee there.[11] Whatever the case, the protesters made clear their grievances against management. They destroyed the buildings occupied by plant guards who had responsibility for searching workers as

26; and Selma Botman, *The Rise of Egyptian Communism, 1939–1970* (Syracuse, N.Y., 1988), pp. 125–31. I have also tried to develop an interpretation of the events from source materials.

[9] The first report of the disturbances appeared in *al-Ahram* on August 14, 1952. The most detailed reporting from the time that I have seen came from Paul S. Lunt, labor attaché to the U.S. embassy, who arrived on the scene the day after the riots. British officials regarded this aggressive reporting as "tactless," but the result was that their otherwise excellent discussions were compiled at a much later date. See report by Paul Lunt, August 25, 1952, USNA 874.06, reel 16; and the British comment on the American actions in no. 210, Stevenson to Eden, September 19, 1952, PRO FO 371/96882.

[10] See Botman, *The Rise of Egyptian Communism*, pp. 125–31, whose account draws heavily on interviews with participants.

[11] No. 210, Stevenson to Eden, September 19, 1952, PRO FO 371/96882.

they left the plant. Workers' personnel files were spilled out on the floor and burned. Strikers ravaged the medical clinic, believing that the firm used medical pretexts to discharge employees.

Confronted with an unexpected and unwanted challenge, the military leaders rapidly aligned themselves with management and against labor. After dispatching troops to the area, they arrested 545 workers and eventually placed twenty-nine of those deemed the ringleaders on trial. To be sure, they questioned Amin Afifi, son of Hafiz Afifi and chief accountant of the Misr plant, as well as Muhammad Husayn al-Jamal, the manager of the plant. Both were released without charges. A military tribunal was hastily assembled in the clubhouse of the Misr factory for the purpose of taking evidence. On August 18 the tribunal issued, in dramatic fashion, its first round of verdicts. Before 1,000 workers, transported to the area from textile factories in the vicinity and lined up along three sides of a soccer field facing a long line of armed soldiers, with a tank stationed at the far corner of the field, the chairman of the tribunal read the indictments and sentences over a loudspeaker. These included a death sentence for Mustafa Khamis. Then followed a message from General Neguib, declaring that the government would purge Egypt of troublemakers.[12] A similar public announcement took place approximately three weeks later in front of assembled workers. The second sentences included an order of execution against Muhammad Hasan al-Baqari, deemed a key agitator.[13]

The swift response to worker unrest reflected the military's deep-seated fear of public disorder rather than a clear preference for a capitalist ethos. Having already received reports stressing radical elements within the workers' movement, and fearful that violence would prompt the British to intervene, the military junta demanded that labor remain politically quiescent.[14] In subsequent meetings with labor leaders around the country, military speakers stressed the same theme. To groups of labor delegates the military men emphasized that the present moment, while the British still remained in military occupation of Egypt and might at any time unleash their troops on the delta, was not propitious for labor agitation. Any workers who wished to take bold action were exhorted to join the special squads being assembled in the canal area.[15]

Members of the Revolutionary Command Council also met with busi-

[12] See the detailed accounts in *al-Ahram* and the *Egyptian Gazette* for August 18 and 19, 1952.

[13] *al-Ahram*, September 6, 1952; *Egyptian Gazette*, September 7, 1952.

[14] For a description of the excitable mood of the military junta, see Hamrush, *Qissa*, vol. 4, pp. 431–32.

[15] See an example of this approach in the meeting organized with the workers of Alexandria by Hasan Ibrahim and Zakariya Muhi al-Din in the *Egyptian Gazette*, April 21, 1954.

ness personages. The tone of the meetings was hardly confrontational, yet the new praetorians pled for conciliation of the labor movement. Immediately after suppressing the workers at Kafr al-Dawwar, Neguib and his colleagues stressed the obligation of the business community to consider the welfare of their workers and to ensure that strikes and lingering disputes no longer occurred.[16] As they sought to ameliorate tension between labor and capital, they made clear their often unarticulated but strong preference for corporatist arrangements. Their message was that labor and management must work together, subordinated to the state.[17] Seeking to silence labor discontent and respond to union complaints, the military also passed new labor laws, which, while rendering strike activity illegal, tightened restrictions against discharging employees and imposed more stringent health and social requirements on employers.

Once the turmoil let loose at Kafr al-Dawwar had quieted, the military turned to its second most pressing concern following the removal of Faruq: land reform—a concern that had obvious implications for the private sector. In the estimation of the rulers, land redistribution was called for not only on the grounds of social justice and the elimination of glaring income disparities but also as part of an overall program to refocus investment and business energy away from agriculture toward industry.

As it had with so many other postwar issues, the civilian government had discussed land reforms but failed to make meaningful changes. The new government's attempt to introduce a scheme brought forth the first confrontation with advocates of the private sector. Prime Minister Ali Mahir resigned in protest in early August 1952, only to be replaced by General Neguib. Although the new land law did not go as far as some of its proponents wanted, its restriction of individual land holdings to 200 feddans and family estates to 300 feddans was a bitter pill for many of the wealthy to swallow. The military men and their technical experts argued that the effect of the law would be to spur industrial investment, but most of Egypt's leading industrialists, at least those of Egyptian nationality, had large estates and would suffer a financial loss. The new law itself passed only after a long and stormy cabinet meeting, lasting from 6:00 in the evening until 3:30 in the morning.[18] Even before its enactment, and no doubt as a protective measure, the government arrested forty-six prominent leaders. Most were important politicians, like Fuad Serag al-Din and Nagib al-Hilali, who were well connected with the landed magnates and whom the military feared would rally opposition.

[16] *Egyptian Gazette*, August 15, 1952.

[17] See meetings involving the military leadership and business representatives as reported in *al-Ahram* on August 4 and October 29, 1952, and in the *Egyptian Gazette*, October 12, 1952.

[18] No. 1335, Stevenson to Foreign Office, September 9, 1952, PRO FO 371/96881.

But the regime also put labor and business on notice. It arrested Abbas Halim, a member of the royal family with close ties to the labor movement, and Hafiz Afifi, a businessman-politician who ran many of the Misr companies.[19]

The members of the Revolutionary Command Council lacked economic training or sophistication. Although Khalid Muhi al-Din held a bachelor's degree in commerce, his leftist views on economic issues aroused the suspicion of his colleagues. Hasan Ibrahim had had some experience in managing military supplies and was often deputed by his colleagues to represent the RCC with external financial and economic groups.[20] Recognizing their technical deficiencies in economics, the new governors at first delegated the management of the economy to civilian officials. Many of the first wave of economic technocrats were men who had served in earlier governments. The RCC's first minister of finance and economy was Abd al-Galil al-Imari, who held a degree in commerce from Leeds University and had served in earlier administrations. Similarly, its first minister of commerce and industry was a proven bureaucrat. Imari admitted that he enjoyed a free hand at his ministry, despite the perilous state of Egyptian finances at the time of the seizure of power. He did not meet a single one of the officers until mid-August, and only then because the military men objected to Imari's proposal to increase taxes on cigarettes and tobacco. Imari favored the tax increases because the state desperately needed more money, and the taxes would generate £E5 million in revenue. Neguib, Nasser, Abdal-Latif al-Baghdadi, and Gamil Salim vetoed the increase on the grounds that tobacco was a popular and even essential commodity and that the new government could not initiate its rule with such an unwelcome tax.[21]

Although the military men steered clear of technical economic concerns at the outset, they did endeavor to recruit financial and economic experts who were not tied to the previous governments and were likely to be sympathetic to their six principles. While continuing to favor an important role for the private sector, the new recruits were expected to favor programs of social justice and income distribution and to support an interventionist role for the state.

One of the first of the new technicians was Rashid al-Barrawi. A professor in the School of Commerce at Cairo University, his newspaper articles on land reform, industrialization, and government intervention

---

[19] *al-Ahram*, September 8, 1952; no. 1326, Stevenson to Foreign Office, September 7, 1952, PRO FO 371/96881.

[20] Interview with Hasan Ibrahim, September 10, 1989, Cairo, Egypt.

[21] Abd al-Jalil al-Imari, *Dhikrayat Iqtisadiya w-Islah al-Masar al-Iqtisadi* (Cairo, 1986), p. 25.

in the economy had caught the eye of the free officers even before the coup.[22] Barrawi was brought onto the new National Production Council. Shortly thereafter he became head of the Industrial Bank. A person with strong socialist credentials, he wanted the state to be active in economic affairs. At the same time he favored the liberalization of the company laws of 1947 and 1948, particularly the mining and quarrying law, the restrictiveness of which he believed retarded the development of Egypt's oil resources. Oil prospecting and mining companies, he believed, needed licenses of long duration and guarantees against possible confiscation if they were to invest the large sums needed to develop Egypt's oil areas.[23]

The military cultivated another gifted economist, Aziz Sidqi, destined to be Egypt's first minister of industry and ultimately the chief architect of the burgeoning public sector. His frequent press commentaries on economic matters brought him to the attention of the RCC. There he extolled the virtues of state planning as the best method for coordinating and maximizing scarce resources. Sidqi held a 1951 Ph.D. in regional planning from Harvard University and was a professor in Egypt in 1952.[24]

Within the military establishment itself the engineering corps yielded a few individuals conversant with economic affairs. Mahmud Yunis and Samir Hilmi, the outstanding examples, were elevated to the boards of numerous state economic organizations. Indeed, an economic meeting held in November 1953 to discuss a fertilizer project at Aswan offered a good picture of the emerging economic decision-making elite. It included government bureaucrats Abd al-Galil al-Imari and Ibrahim Bagumi Madkur, who was vice president of the National Production Council; rising economists Ali al-Giritli and Rashid al-Barrawi; engineer Samir Hilmi; and sympathetic business leaders, usually drawn from the Misr cluster of companies.[25]

Lacking economic talent within their own ranks, the military also sought to enlist experts from the private sector. At the outset, certain individuals were ruled out because of their close involvement with the palace and the old political parties. Elias Andraus and Hafiz Afifi were two of Egypt's most powerful business personages from the pre-1952 era. Both had led important companies and served on the boards of numerous firms. But the fact that they had been members of King Faruq's royal

[22] Hamrush, *Qissa*, vol. 1, p. 255.

[23] *Egyptian Gazette*, November 27, 1953.

[24] See one of his early articles on planning in *al-Ahram*, January 26, 1953. His Harvard thesis bore the revealing title, "Industrialization of Egypt and a Case Study of the Iron and Steel Industry."

[25] *al-Ahram*, November 24, 1953. An important discussion of the rising engineer group within the Egyptian government can be found in Clement Henry Moore, *Images of Development: Egyptian Engineers in Search of Industry* (Cambridge, Mass., 1980).

cabinet disqualified them. Andraus was removed as head of Bank Misr and Beida Dyers shortly after the military coup, and Hafiz Afifi was among the first group of old regime leaders whom the military arrested.[26] The military courted the favor of others, however. It was particularly eager to win the allegiance of the leaders of the Misr empire. For the fertilizer project scheduled to be constructed at Aswan and to draw upon the cheap and abundant supplies of electricity generated there, the government turned to Abd al-Rahman Hamada, head of the Egyptian Federation of Industries and the Misr Spinning and Weaving Company at al-Mahalla al-Kubra, and Ahmad Inan, head of the Misr Insurance Company.[27]

This first effort to associate important businessmen with the development plans of the new government included frequent meetings with large business delegations that often involved foreign businessmen. The purpose was to win their approval of the government's economic and social programs. On August 4, 1952, just days after the change in government, the new prime minister, Ali Mahir, called a press conference to reassure foreign capitalists about the security of their investments in the country.[28] Neguib himself held a special meeting with more than 500 leading business persons on August 15 to discuss the implications of the Kafr al-Dawwar outburst and to emphasize the government's strong commitment to business interests.[29] No doubt Ali Mahir's resignation in early September and the enactment of a land reform bill were deeply unsettling to the business community. Yet on October 11, 1952, at the instigation of Abd al-Magid al-Rimali, long-time secretary of the Egyptian Chamber of Commerce, Neguib met with members of the chamber. At the meeting, attended by numerous government officials and heads of industrial companies and banks, foreign as well as Egyptian, Neguib endeavored to explain the government's economic policies. The overall policy, he asserted, was based on three elements: a strong commitment to economic stability, with government intervention occurring only where absolutely required; encouragement of all capitalist enterprises; and respect for the autonomy of business decisions, as long as business firms promoted the welfare of their workers.[30] Shortly after the meeting, the Ministry of Commerce and Industry issued a statement that Egypt was not interested in nationalizing the Suez Canal Company.[31]

Seeking to offer immediate evidence of its support of business, the

---

[26] *al-Ahram*, September 10, 1952; no. 1335, Stevenson to Foreign Office, September 9, 1952, PRO FO 371/96881.

[27] *al-Ahram*, November 24, 1953.

[28] Ibid., August 4, 1952.

[29] Ibid., August 15, 1952.

[30] Ibid., October 11, 1952; *Egyptian Gazette*, October 12, 1952.

[31] *Egyptian Gazette* and *al-Ahram*, October 16 and 17, 1952.

Revolutionary Command Council reformed the company law of 1947 to allow foreigners to own up to 51 percent of the capital of companies and even as much as 100 percent under certain circumstances.[32] The government also declared its readiness to expedite the process of obtaining visas and residence permits and promised to ease restrictions on the holding of long-term visas.[33] On several occasions, to demonstrate the seriousness of their commitment to encouraging foreign investment and their desire to deal with the constant complaints about visas and residence permits, Neguib and Nasser appeared at government offices to distribute these documents to members of the foreign community.

Given the flattering statements the RCC made about foreign capital, it is hardly surprising that the main public organs of foreign and domestic capital rallied to the side of the RCC. The *Journal of the British Chamber of Commerce* lauded the military for effecting a bloodless change in regime and for having reinvigorated Egyptian society without disrupting the business sector.[34] After the government had altered the company legislation, the Egyptian Federation of Industries called the new legislation "a turning point" in Egypt's political economy.[35] This endorsement was all the more significant coming as it did after the federation had criticized the state for failing to attract foreign capital and had complained that its early company legislative reform was timid.[36]

Although the Egyptian business community had no reason to complain about the first fiscal and economic measures of the new government, it also agitated for a more aggressive procapitalist approach. The annual report of the Egyptian Federation of Industries for 1952 catalogued the full measure of economic encouragement that it hoped for. In it the barons of industry argued that Egypt's poverty, its expanding population, and low savings and investments rates made it dependent on foreign capital. The foreign investor, however, had other attractive investment opportunities and would be drawn to Egypt only if the corporate laws were made more flexible and if the labor legislation were modified.

Specifically, the authors of the 1952 document complained that Egypt's heavy burden of taxation on companies and persons of wealth discouraged foreign capital, and they called for "a complete revision" of the taxation code.[37] As for labor legislation, the report complained about the indemnification payments made to workers when they were discharged, the provisions for medical assistance in factories, and the injunction pro-

---

[32] *Egyptian Gazette*, July 31, 1952; *al-Ahram*, March 4 and 24, 1953.

[33] *Egyptian Gazette*, August 6, 1952.

[34] British Chamber of Commerce of Egypt, *Journal*, August 1952, pp. 215–16.

[35] *L'Egypte Industrielle* 29, no. 4 (April 1953), p. 21.

[36] Ibid., no. 2 (February 1953).

[37] Ittihad al-Sina'at al-Misriya, *al-Kitab al-Sanawi*, 1952–53, p. 20.

hibiting lockouts. While recognizing that the new regime could hardly afford to change all of this legislation at once, especially while it was still settling into power, it asked that the laws be "toned down" and take better account of how the economic and political settings of Egypt differed from those of Europe and North America.[38] No doubt this report, issued by the most powerful organ of industrial opinion, disappointed the military men. It demanded of them far more than they could reasonably be expected to grant and indicated some of the areas of tension that were likely to trouble military-business relations.

The encouragement that the state gave to business did not prevent government officials from attending to the public sector. From the outset, the RCC proclaimed its intention to build an equally dynamic public sector. The new military leaders were eager to push forward, by means of public initiative and public funds, a number of large-scale development projects that had been under discussion for years. They took up the pre-1952 interest in a massive hydraulic scheme within the borders of Egypt, eventually designating the Aswan High Dam as their developmental centerpiece. The dam was to contain a hydroelectric component, and the regime reopened discussions for creating a massive fertilizer complex in Upper Egypt. Although the actual division of duties between public and private sectors had yet to be determined, the military men did not contemplate placing the whole of such a vital part of Egypt's future infrastructure in the hands of private entrepreneurs.[39]

Industrialization, another priority of the military regime, also received considerable attention. Within the first few months of taking power, the military announced its commitment to an iron and steel complex, depicted as the core of Egypt's industrialization effort, and exhorted private business persons to join with the state in implementing this long-standing Egyptian dream. The state was prepared to contribute funds and mobilize technical expertise, and it also promised to guarantee the profitability of the enterprise in order to attract private investors.[40] To this end, a special committee consisting of Hasan Fahmi Rahman, Mahmud Yunis, and Dr. Muhammad Ali Salih submitted a preliminary report to the Council of Ministers in late 1952. The document argued that iron and steel production was feasible in Egypt, despite the doubts raised by foreign experts, and claimed that the iron and steel factory would move Egypt to a new stage of industrial progress, beyond consumer goods manufacturing into heavy industrialization.[41]

Late in 1952 the Egyptian government created the National Production

[38] Ibid., p. 23.
[39] Vatikiotis, *Nasser and His Generation*, pp. 209–11.
[40] *al-Ahram*, October 26, 1952.
[41] Ibid., December 28, 1952.

Council (NPC). Described as a successor to the old and largely moribund Economic Council, the NPC was to advise the government on general economic policy and to draw together expertise from private and public sectors. Its overarching purpose was to promote a mixed economy.[42] It possessed authority to participate financially and administratively in the creation of companies. In keeping with its status as a bridge between the public and private sectors, its fourteen-member administrative committee included military men, professional economists, and representatives of the private sector. Among the first group of recruits were Husayn Fahmi, its head, a former minister of finance and general manager of the Egyptian Salt and Soda Company; the ever-present Rashid al-Barrawi; Abd al-Rahman Hamada, head of the Misr Spinning and Weaving Company; the engineer Muhammad Ali Husayn, who was Ahmad Abbud's son-in-law; Ali Giritli, a professional economist and frequent government consultant to the military; and Yahya al-Alaili, an agricultural engineer and manager of the Kom Ombo land committee.[43]

Soon after removing the king and enacting land reform, the military turned its attention to the all-important issue of ousting the British military from the Suez base. No demand was more crucial to Egyptian nationalists, and discussions on no other topic were more likely to inflame public sentiment. As before, the military negotiations threatened a renewal of violent conflicts with the British forces, increased the potential for a British military intervention in Cairo and the delta, and put at risk all of Britain's interests in the country. The prospects of open warfare, whether confined to the Suez Canal area or spreading out to Cairo and the delta, compelled the military rulers, as it had their civilian predecessors, to draw up a political, economic, and fiscal plan that they could implement against British interests in Egypt if the worst were to happen. By the same token, the deteriorating state of Anglo-Egyptian political relations heightened the fears of the representatives of foreign and domestic capital, who could no longer forget the extreme exposure that they had experienced in early 1952. Even though more British military and political officials were realizing the strength of the Egyptian nationalist movement and the valuelessness of a base in a country hostile to its existence, several new factors militated against the conclusion of an Anglo-Egyptian accord in 1953.[44] In Britain rejectionist groups, albeit a minority in the Parliament, claimed some influential policy makers, not the

---

[42] Ibid., September 17 and 29, 1952, and February 21, 1953; National Bank of Egypt, *Economic Bulletin* 6, no. 1 (1953), pp. 44–46.

[43] *al-Ahram*, December 22, 1952; no. 1253, Robert McClintock, Chargé d'Affaires, United States Embassy, to Department of State, December 27, 1952, USNA 774.13, reel 7.

[44] Chiefs of Staff (52), 119th meeting, Minute, British Personnel To Be Left in Egypt, August 26, 1952, PRO FO 371/96977.

least of whom was Winston Churchill, who returned as prime minister following the election of 1951. Churchill remained intransigent in the face of the nationalist pressures, arguing against any thought of evacuation before 1956 and offering evacuation after 1956 only if the Egyptians proposed terms satisfactory to British interests.[45]

Churchill's obdurate attitude owed much to the emergence in 1953 of the Suez group that made concessions to Egyptian nationalists problematic in British domestic politics. This pressure group had originated in January 1953 through a chance meeting between Captain Charles Waterhouse and Julian Amery in Cape Town, South Africa.[46] Fearing what they believed would be the precipitous dissolution of the British empire and believing that Egypt and the Suez Canal were decisive for Britain's continuing imperial mission, these men recruited such eminent conservative politicians as Enoch Powell, Lord Hankey, Lord Killearn, Lord Cromer, John Morrison, and Fitzroy Maclean to their cause. Throughout the negotiations of 1953 and 1954 the Suez group kept a close watch on the government and fulminated against any proposal to withdraw British troops from Egypt.[47] According to one of their most intemperate members, Lord Hankey, the canal would be rendered impassable within a year of the departure of the British forces.[48] Although the Foreign Office regarded these criticisms as unenlightened and called their opponents "rebels," they recognized their ability to stir influential groups inside and outside Parliament against the government.[49] The Suez group remained in existence even after the signature of the Anglo-Egyptian treaty in 1954. Its steady drumbeat of complaints against a weak-willed government spurred the Tory cabinet to be unyielding to Nasser in 1956.

Anglo-Egyptian negotiations resumed in February 1953, were broken off in early March, and then started again in May. They went badly from the British point of view, and as the negotiations floundered, political tension intensified and the prospects of violent clashes in the Suez Canal zone increased.[50]

Although the wholesale sequestration and subsequent Egyptianization

---

[45] Churchill to Selwyn Lloyd, August 7, 1952, PRO CO 371/96977.

[46] Julian Amery, "The Suez Group: A Retrospective on Suez," in *The Suez-Sinai Crisis, 1956: Retrospective and Reappraisal*, ed. Selwyn Ilan Troen and Moshe Shemesh (London, 1990), p. 110.

[47] J. Amery to Churchill, October 7, 1953, PRO FO 371/102766; J. Amery to Eden, March 18, 1953, PRO FO 371/102807.

[48] Lord Hankey and the Suez Canal, Foreign Office Minute, July 22, 1953, PRO FO 371/102766.

[49] Foreign Office Minute, December 12, 1953, PRO FO 371/102766.

[50] Foreign Office Minute, June 11, 1953, Anglo-Egyptian Negotiations: a Note for the Prime Minister on Cases A and B, PRO FO 371/102810; Holmes, United States Embassy, London, to Churchill, June 11, 1953, PRO FO 371/102811; *al-Ahram*, April 23, 1953.

and nationalization of British and French property following the Suez invasion of 1956 surprised the European powers, it should not have. The increasing levels of violence between Britain and the Egyptian population during the sputtering negotiations in 1953 and again in 1954 conditioned both sides to think about the consequences of overt military confrontation and to consider the economic weapons that could be employed against adversaries. On the British side, detailed contingency planning focused on how the British might harm Egypt economically and militarily if the negotiations collapsed and the Egyptian population resorted to violence. By the same token, the Egyptian government was aware of the extensive and exposed British economic interests in Egypt and was prepared to retaliate if the British employed trade and financial sanctions against Egypt. Indeed, British planners were aware that open warfare would put the British business empire in Egypt in jeopardy. Yet they believed that their ultimate military superiority in any showdown would enable them to reverse any radical actions taken against British interests in Egypt.

We know much less of the Egyptian side of the equation because we do not have access to the confidential discussions of the RCC and the Council of Ministers. But we do know that Egyptian intelligence was proficient. The Egyptian government had obtained the British contingency plans for occupying Cairo and the delta (Operation Rodeo), and thus it is reasonable to assume that the Egyptian leaders had prepared countermeasures, including economic actions, to deal with any British effort to occupy the population centers of the country.[51] The counterpart to the British projects to cut off oil supplies from the Suez Canal area, to block sterling releases in London, and even to implement a full-scale trade boycott of Egyptian products must surely have included plans to sequester British businesses in Egypt. Thus, the gestation period for the sequestration acts of November 1956 occurred in the buildup of tension and the occasional moments of confrontation themselves, stretching out between late 1951 and the signature of the Anglo-Egyptian treaty in 1954.

Even though the repercussions of provocative action against the British military establishment at Suez constantly threatened the Egyptian rulers with British retaliation, the Egyptian military leaders attached such an overriding importance to expelling the British from their military redoubts at Suez that they did not hesitate to use terror and intimidation to demonstrate to the British how valueless their military might was. They did so artfully, intensifying guerrilla incursions when the negotiations dragged and ameliorating relations when the British showed themselves accommodating. The goal was to demonstrate the Egyptian government's

[51] Roger Allen, Note, Operation Rodeo Flail, January 31, 1953, PRO FO 371/102912.

control over the contestation and to remove any doubt the British might have that guerrilla activities would subside of their own accord. The canal zone itself was thrown into a veritable state of chaos. Chronically short of food and labor supplies, the British maintained the base only by bringing food and laborers from the outside. In May 1953, when the first round of military conversations was coming to an unsuccessful close, the Egyptian army moved its forces to block any British military intervention into the delta. Armed units were stationed along the main roads between the canal zone and Cairo, interdicting British movement beyond the base.[52] Subsequently, the Egyptian government dispatched 4,000 auxiliary police from Cairo to the canal area. They were joined by some 1,000 Muslim Brotherhood members, organized into guerrilla bands of forty to fifty persons.[53]

Unlike its civilian predecessors, the RCC succeeded in maintaining a high degree of oversight over the violent confrontations with the British military forces in the canal. Keeping its larger political agenda in view, the RCC sought always to channel the rage of the Egyptian populace so as to prevent the kind of mass fury that had undone the Wafd in 1952.[54] It was not entirely successful, however. The British found evidence of Muslim Brotherhood bands operating under their own military discipline, not controlled by Nasser's forces.[55] Nonetheless, a group of military officials, including Kamal Rifat, Abd al-Fattah Abu al-Fadil, Fuad Hillal, and Amr Lutfi, all working under the direction of Zakariya Muhi al-Din, the Egyptian minister of the interior, a free officer and member of the Revolutionary Command Council, trained the liberation squads. In no fewer than twenty-eight training camps batches of 100 men were prepared for guerrilla warfare and then dispatched into the canal in squads of three to five men.[56] In addition, the soldiers themselves participated in sabotage raids, entering the canal zone dressed as workmen in *galabias* (long, loose garments with full sleeves and hoods), the standard clothing of unskilled workers.[57]

Even while confronting the British in the canal zone the military men let loose a barrage of propaganda against the British. The most extreme of these statements made no distinctions between British political, cul-

---

[52] Roger Allen, Minute, Action in Egypt in the Event of Trouble, May 5, 1953, PRO FO 371/102813.

[53] Minutes of Defense Committee, May 13, 1953, PRO FO 371/102765.

[54] Abd al-Latif al-Baghdadi, *Mudhakkirat* (Cairo, 1977), vol. 1, pp. 75 ff.

[55] P. G. Oates to Duff, Foreign Office, April 22, 1953, enclosing note prepared jointly by GS (I), General Headquarters, Middle East Land Forces, GS (I), Headquarters, British Troops in Egypt, PRO FO 371/102807.

[56] Hamrush, *Qissa*, vol. 2, pp. 26 ff.

[57] No. 698, Stevenson to Foreign Office, April 27, 1953, PRO FO 371/102847.

tural, and economic influence. They excoriated all as equally opposed to Egyptian aspirations. No doubt the remarks attributed to Group Captain Hasan Ibrahim and Lieutenant Colonel Zakariya Muhi al-Din that the British were "using Egyptians as their tools and making use also of corruption, slavery, oppression, and theft" was profoundly disquieting to the British business community.[58] No more reassuring was a speech made by Major Salah Salim in which he accused the British of blocking the economic progress of the country.[59]

As negotiations faltered in mid-May 1953, the British anticipated outbursts of violence on a scale larger than the rioting of January 26, 1952. The British ambassador, Ralph Stevenson, called together leaders of the British community in Cairo and warned all of those without essential duties there to leave the country.[60] At the same time, the British military stockpiled food in the canal zone and revived plans to sever the canal area administratively and economically from the rest of Egypt and to place it under military jurisdiction.[61] At the Foreign Office, Roger Allen thought the likelihood of guerrilla activity in the canal area considerable if the military talks failed. He indicated that the British armed forces would again need to cut off oil supplies to the delta, demolish houses in the canal zone to enhance their defensive capabilities, and disarm Egyptian police and military forces in the vicinity.[62] Those acts of warfare (though they were often not recognized as such by the British officials) would compel the British government to decide whether to pursue a policy of armed intervention in the delta, where Allen was certain disturbances would occur. If the British did intervene beyond the canal, Allen believed that the Egyptians would be prepared to dismantle the British economic position in the country.[63]

The British plans for intervening in Egypt were nothing less than acts of war. Egyptian and British officials alike were aware that they could have the most profound economic and social consequences. Operation Rodeo Flail (the name was changed and the plan modified when the British learned that the Nasser government had obtained a copy of it) called for a seaborne assault and an air drop on Alexandria, in addition to a forced military march on Cairo.[64] The revised plan provided for the movement of a brigade group from Cairo, once it was occupied, to Alex-

[58] *Egyptian Gazette*, April 21, 1954.

[59] Ibid., April 14, 1953.

[60] Roger Allen, Foreign Office Minute, May 13, 1953, PRO FO 371/102765.

[61] Measures to Maintain our Position in Egypt, Report by Chiefs of Staff to First Sea Lord, January 17, 1953, PRO FO 371/102761.

[62] Roger Allen, Foreign Office Minute, May 13, 1953, PRO FO 371/102765.

[63] Ibid., Action in Egypt in the Event of Trouble, May 5, 1953, PRO FO 371/102813.

[64] Roger Allen, Note, Operation Rodeo Flail, January 31, 1953, PRO FO 371/102912; Creswell to Allen, March 30, 1953, PRO FO 371/102803.

andria. One of the reasons that the British were reluctant to bring Rodeo into operation was that their forces were unlikely to arrive in Alexandria in time to protect the very British lives and property that the forces had been sent to rescue.[65] Still, the hawkish element within the British government continued to favor a forward military policy.

In February 1953, Churchill recommended that British forces secure the surrender of the Egyptian army on the east bank of the canal if the Egyptian government delivered an ultimatum to the British. General Brian Robertson in Egypt opposed Churchill's proposal. He saw any action against the Egyptian military as likely to imperil British lives. Rodeo, Robertson opined, would become inevitable, and Britain would have to destroy the Egyptian army, which was "the only element of comparable stability in the country . . . [thus] engendering a state of chaos which could lead to an indefinite occupation." Preferring vigilance in the canal to a military incursion into Egypt's population centers, Robertson was willing to intervene in the delta only if British lives were threatened.[66]

The British judged the 15,000-man Egyptian army as "badly led, badly trained, and poorly equipped." Their opinion was based largely on their assessment of the Egyptian military during the war in Palestine. Yet they were aware that the rank-and-file Egyptian soldiers had fought courageously in Palestine even after being deserted by their officers. They were sure that these men would give an even better accounting of themselves when defending their homeland.[67]

The British military's neglect of the economic implications of their stalled negotiations could hardly have come at a worse time for the British business interests operating in Egypt. As British trade and investment in Egypt declined, Britain saw its capacity to sweep Egypt into a neocolonial relationship through economic ties disappear. And no other power was able to insert itself into the Egyptian economy to achieve the economic hegemony that Britain had enjoyed in Egypt in the early twentieth century. The erosion of British economic power also intensified pressures for the Egyptian state to be more assertive in economic affairs. Anglo-Egyptian trading and financial ties reached a nadir in 1952 and 1953; 1952 had, in fact, been the worst in Anglo-Egyptian trading history, and as the year drew to a close, British diplomats and business persons frantically sought to reverse the trends that, if unchecked, seemed certain to eradicate the entire British business presence in the country.

[65] No. 96, British Middle East Organization to Foreign Office, February 11, 1953, PRO FO 371/102912.
[66] T. C. Rapp, British Middle East Organization, to Bowker, February 25, 1953, PRO FO 371/102801.
[67] Chiefs of Staff, Note, March 2, 1953, PRO FO 371/102801.

The trading decline flowed first from the paucity of sterling available in Egypt, to which was added a precipitous decrease in the British demand for Egyptian cotton. Not only had the cotton collusion crises of 1950 and 1951 left the Egyptian government with a vast quantity of overpriced cotton, but simultaneously British cotton buyers were experiencing a decline in their orders and were not placing orders for Egyptian cotton. Moreover, of the small stock of sterling available in Egypt, much of it had to be used to purchase non-British imports, primarily tea from Ceylon and India and crude oil from the Middle East. As British trade plummeted, the British commercial officer attached to the embassy in Cairo sounded the alarm: Britain was "in danger of losing one of our most lucrative overseas markets . . . [and] the market once lost, will be difficult to regain."[68]

The Egyptian government response to the sterling shortages, which was entirely predictable and justifiable in spite of the further damage it did to trade relations between the countries, was to impose severe restrictions on all imports from sterling countries. The restricted list was all-encompassing, little less than a dagger pointed at the heart of the British commercial establishment based in Egypt. It included such staples of Anglo-Egyptian trade as soap, cotton piece goods, apparel, radios, electrical apparatuses, and cars. The British Board of Trade filed a formal protest, claiming that the restrictions, if allowed to remain in effect for the full year (which they ultimately were), would cost British traders £11,400,000.[69] Far from ameliorating its position, the Egyptian government tightened the noose around the sterling traders by introducing formal import licensing controls for all merchants importing and exporting to sterling areas.[70]

On top of worries about their own physical safety and the destruction of their property, so energetically articulated following the January 26, 1952, violence in Cairo, British business persons began to fear that Anglo-Egyptian trade had no future. In January 1953 the Anglo-Egyptian Chamber of Commerce, based in London, dispatched a trade delegation to Egypt to meet with British and Egyptian officials there and to present arguments in favor of a trade stimulus. The trade delegation drew its representation from the British firms most deeply affected by the contraction in trade: Barclays Bank; Hewat Bridson and Newby, chartered accountants; Peel and Company, cotton exporters; Imperial Chemical Industries; and Anglo-Egyptian Oil.[71] Simultaneously, representatives of the

[68] Cumberbatch, British Embassy, Cairo, to A. H. More, Board of Trade, January 13, 1953, Bank of England (hereafter B of E), OV 43/54.
[69] No. 246, Foreign Office to Stevenson, July 29, 1952, PRO FO 371/96958.
[70] D. R. Serpell to Saleh Kubba, July 30, 1953, PRO FO 371/102787.
[71] Frank B. Anderson, President of the Anglo-Egyptian Chamber of Commerce, to H. R.

Anglo-Egyptian Chamber of Commerce, as well as representatives of different British Chambers of Commerce in Egypt, held meetings with British government officials in London.[72] The British Chamber of Commerce in Egypt submitted a pamphlet entitled "Anglo-Egyptian Trade Relations," while Taitt of Anglo-Egyptian Oil argued that British policy had been so inflexible as to offer the Egyptians little incentive to improve trading relations.[73] A few days later, Archibald Boyd, managing director of Metropolitan-Camwell Carriage and Wagon Company, traditionally one of Egypt's primary suppliers of railway equipment, called at the Foreign Office to seek support for his firm. He pointed out that his company, already in a deep financial crisis, had made the lowest tender for a large contract in Egypt but could not receive the contract because of Egypt's shortage of sterling.[74] A similar petition was submitted six months later, in June 1953, when a delegation of British automobile manufacturers complained that they were in danger of losing the whole of the Egyptian automobile market to foreign competition because of sterling shortages.[75]

Whenever British business delegates met with Foreign Office or Board of Trade representatives, the discussion turned automatically to the Egyptian sterling deposits held in London. The business persons begged that these funds be released in a timely fashion, and if possible that sums larger than those agreed to in 1951 be turned over to the Egyptian government as a spur to trade. They also insisted that the releases be coupled with guarantees that the funds would be used to purchase British goods and services. Invariably, they found ready assent from the Board of Trade, hesitancy from the Treasury, and ambivalence from Foreign Office officials. The Treasury, in particular, worried that any large and accelerated release of sterling, like the £25 million being proposed by one of the business delegations, would depress the value of sterling worldwide.[76] The Foreign Office, predictably, wished to tie sterling releases to the political and military negotiations and to make these releases conditional on Egypt's acceptance of the British stance in the treaty negotiations.[77]

The declining presence of British capital in Egypt gave the new regime additional reasons to promote a larger role for the state in economic affairs. The business community awaited with anticipation Minister of Fi-

---

MacKeson, Board of Trade, December 19, 1952; no. 9, Stevenson to Foreign Office, January 13, 1953, PRO FO 371/102788.

[72] Brief for the Secretary for Overseas Trade, January 20, 1953, PRO FO 371/102788.

[73] B of E, OV 43/54.

[74] R. Bowker, Foreign Office Minute, January 26, 1953, PRO FO 371/102788.

[75] L. M. Minford, British Embassy, Cairo, to N. H. A. Whitford, Board of Trade, June 29, 1953, PRO FO 371/102790.

[76] Wright, Foreign Office Minute, September 19, 1952, PRO FO 371/96952.

[77] Record of Meeting at the Foreign Office, January 26, 1953; P. Ramsbotham, Foreign Office Minutes, March 19 and April 17, 1953, PRO FO 371/102789.

nance Imari's budget statement of 1953, marking the new regime's first comprehensive budget analysis. Bowing to the heightened powers of the RCC, Imari presented his budget first to the RCC before taking it before the Council of Ministers. Imari found the military men still unfocused economically and distinctly unconcerned about budgetary details. Nasser did speak to the minister about the government's need to adhere to a comprehensive economic policy and cautioned about the dangers of jumping from one model to another. He held up India as an effective mixed economy where the boundary lines between the public and private sectors had been clearly demarcated. But, other than this homely advice, the military men made few comments.[78]

The budget contained something for most groups while stressing Egypt's commitment to a mixed economy. It began with a cautionary note on private sector excesses under the old regime. Imari revealed for the first time how parlous the Egyptian economy was at the time of the coup d'etat. Its foreign reserves had been so dangerously low that the state teetered on the verge of bankruptcy.[79] Brought to "the shadow of catastrophe" through the nefarious cotton-buying intrigues between wealthy cotton merchants and a compliant government, the new government had restored fiscal order only at the last minute.[80] The abolition of the cotton futures market had revived cotton sales while the tightening of exchange controls and import licensing had reduced the outflow of hard currencies.

The cornerstone of the new budget was an institutional innovation involving the separation of regular expenditures from development outlays. This reform, by then standard in many countries, even those under formal colonial authority, was designed to segregate those projects intended to accelerate economic development and needing special nurturing from the regular and recurrent programs of the budget. The plan laid out a vast array of development programs that Imari divided into two categories. One category included the programs to be financed, sponsored, and administered by the Egyptian government itself. Most of these were connected with traditional public sector activities in hydraulics and included the Aswan High Dam, hydroelectric and fertilizer plants at Aswan, power stations in Cairo and elsewhere in the delta, and land reclamation schemes. The second category of enterprises included those that the government would sponsor and even help finance but that it expected financial and managerial help with from private enterprise: steel, tires, batteries, paper, spare parts, jute, milk, pesticides, and hotels.

Illustrative of the public-private initiatives was the National Cement Company, which had come into being in March 1953. Of its initial cap-

[78] Imari, *Dhikrayat*, p. 30.
[79] *Egyptian Gazette*, July 1, 1953.
[80] *al-Ahram*, July 1, 1953.

italization of £E1.2 million, £E700,000 came from al-Tahrir province administration, £E100,000 from the National Production Council, £E100,000 from the Industrial Bank, £E100,000 from civil service insurance and savings fund administration, £E200,000 from Bank Misr, £E90,000 from the Misr Insurance Company, and £E20,000 from the iron and steel company. The remaining £E500,000 was to be raised in a public subscription scheduled for the second half of 1953.[81] This mix of parastatal organizations, like the NPC and the Industrial Bank, with private firms deeply enmeshed in the public sector, like the Misr Insurance Company and Bank Misr, was typical of the new projects. It reflected a government expectation that the private sector would be enthusiastic about the regime's projects. In each succeeding year, this instrumentalist orientation toward the private sector became more pronounced.

Because the Egyptian government looked to the private sector to be a powerful force for economic change, the bureaucrats in the government's economic ministries also wanted to establish a more favorable environment for business. Changes in company legislation were again discussed. Business persons had been only partly appeased by the changes in the company law that the military had introduced after seizing power. They continued to insist on a more comprehensive review of company and investment laws. This they received. During the course of 1953 the military men and their economic advisers, working in close consultation with the leaders of the business community, revised the legislation. The secretary of the Egyptian Federation of Industries was a frequent visitor to the Egyptian Ministry of Commerce and Industry, the body responsible for redrafting the legislation. To facilitate contacts, the government established a liaison committee with the business world that counted among its members Egyptian Chamber of Commerce secretary Abd al-Rahman al-Rimali; Ali Yahya; and Ahmad Inan, managing director of the Misr Insurance Company.[82]

Two major pieces of legislation flowed from these discussions. In January 1954, a complete redrafting of Egypt's company legislation was promulgated. A new set of regulations clarified the juridical distinctions separating the different business organizations: private enterprises, joint stock companies possessing limited liability, limited partnerships, and joint stock companies limited by shares.[83] Of more immediate interest to the business community, however, was a law passed in April 1953 that liberalized the repatriation of profits, permitting a company to repatriate up to 10 percent of its invested capital each fiscal year. The law also

---

[81] *Egyptian Gazette*, March 9, 1953.

[82] *al-Ahram*, June 26, 1953; British Chamber of Commerce of Egypt, *Journal*, December 1953, pp. 349–50.

[83] *al-Ahram*, January 21, 1954.

allowed a firm to begin repatriation of its original capital after it had remained in Egypt for five years at the rate of one-fifth of the registered capital per year.[84]

The immediate reception to the new legislation was undiluted enthusiasm. The journal of the Egyptian Federation of Industries claimed that the investment law marked "a turning point in the political economy of the country."[85] In the opinion of the editors of the journal, it was a vast improvement on previously restrictive legislation that had failed to attract foreign investment. But the business community grew discontented upon discovering that this law was not a first step, as it had been led to believe, but the military regime's final effort. The Egyptian Federation of Industries, the organ of domestic and foreign capital invested in Egypt, complained that the law applied only to new capital. It did not offer enough to companies already in place in Egypt. The organs representing foreign investment turned openly hostile. At the British Chamber of Commerce, the chief editor, S. Nathan, pointed out that the law, while "a step in the right direction," did not go far enough.[86] After consulting widely with business groups, Ambassador Stevenson concluded that the new law was unlikely to make Egypt attractive to foreign investors.[87]

The Egyptian government was stunned by these negative responses to laws about which it had consulted widely. Indeed, its agents believed that it had made generous, and in some instances risky concessions to appease foreign and domestic investors. Although the debate was a somewhat arcane and technical one, carried out behind the scenes in specialized publications, it constituted a first and in many ways decisive rupture between the business community and the new regime.

1954: THE TRIUMPH OF NASSER

In 1954 Gamal Abdel Nasser emerged, unchallenged, as the voice of the Egyptian revolution. Yet in defeating his rivals he accumulated numerous debts, not least of which was an obligation to reward those in Egyptian society—especially workers and bureaucrats—who had supported him in the crisis and would favor an expansion of the public sector.

In the three decolonizing countries compared here, the lower classes challenged the prevailing developmentalist vision in the early 1950s. The response of the ruling elites to the subaltern challenge was crucial for the private sector and the business community. In Egypt, unlike in Nigeria and Kenya, that challenge had been a concerted one ever since the end of

---

[84] Ibid., March 4 and 24 and April 2, 1953; *Egyptian Gazette*, April 2, 1953.

[85] *L'Egypte Industrielle* 29, no. 4 (April 1953), p. 21.

[86] British Chamber of Commerce of Egypt, *Journal*, May 1953, pp. 135–36.

[87] No. 116(E), Stevenson to Churchill, May 16, 1953, PRO FO 371/102837.

World War II. And two years into their rule the new Egyptian military rulers still had not articulated a full-fledged developmental strategy. But perhaps the moment when the challenge from below posed the most severe threat to the rulers and caused them to reflect on economic issues as well as political ones was in the early months of 1954 when Neguib and Nasser struggled for political preeminence. The outcome of that dispute had implications not only for the establishment of a democratic system in Egypt but also for the relationship of the state to private capital.

The political crisis of early 1954 began when General Neguib resigned from the government, charging the RCC with failing to include him in its most important discussions. The RCC accepted Neguib's resignation, glad to be rid of a man who had not participated in the original rebellion but who had won much favor with the Egyptian populace. The military men were unprepared, however, for the outpouring of sentiment, inside and outside the army, in favor of Neguib.[88] The old parties, though dissolved, still aspired to power. In particular, the Wafd retained a considerable following among the people. In addition, the extraparliamentary groups were not satisfied with the growing rigidity of the military government. The Muslim Brothers, workers, and students applauded Neguib's challenge to Nasser and left the RCC with no alternative but to return their antagonist to office.

The month of March was one of maneuvering that seemed to culminate in further triumphs for Neguib's supporters. On March 24, 1954, the Egyptian leader announced the imminent creation of political parties and promised direct and free elections to a constitutional conference as well as the dissolution of the RCC.[89] These actions proved, however, to be the high-water mark for the groups aligned around a prodemocracy cause. Although, at various times, Neguib, Nasser, Anwar al-Sadat, Abd al-Hakim Amr, Khalid Muhi al-Din, and Yusuf Sadiq had espoused a democratic rhetoric, the commitment of some of them was often self-serving. It did not stand up well against that group of free officers who rarely wavered in their antipathy to the ballot box and parliamentary life—the Salim brothers, Baghdadi, Hasan Ibrahim, Abd al-Munim Amin, and two other officers whose sympathies lay with the Muslim Brotherhood, Kamal al-Din Husayn and Husayn al-Shafi'i.[90]

Although Nasser had extolled the virtues of democracy on many occa-

---

[88] No. 68, Stevenson to Eden, March 15, 1954, PRO FO 371/108316 JE1015/12. For discussions of tensions within the military at this time, one should consult Sayyid Mari, *Awraq Siyasiya* (Cairo, 1979), vol. 2, pp. 266 ff.; Baghdadi, *Mudhakkirat*, vol. 1, pp. 177 ff.; and Hamrush, *Qissa*, vol. 1, pp. 328 ff.

[89] *al-Ahram*, March 24, 1954; Hamrush, *Qissa*, vol. 1, pp. 341 ff.

[90] Baghdadi, *Mudhakkirat*, vol. 1, pp. 95 ff. and 177 ff.; Mari, *Awraq*, vol. 2, pp. 266 ff.; see especially Khalid Muhi al-Din, *W-al-An Atakallam*, who claims throughout this revealing memoir that only he among the free officers had an abiding commitment to democratic institutions.

sions, he did not believe that Egypt was yet prepared for a restoration of parliamentary life. The political arena had not been purged of its corrupt, old-regime elements, and Nasser distrusted Neguib's political ambitions. Rallying elements in the army to his cause and aligning himself with important labor leaders in the transportation, banking, oil, and public utilities sectors, Nasser inspired a series of strike actions, commencing in late March 1954.[91] Those work stoppages threatened to bring the country's economy to a halt. On March 29, with transport, commercial, tobacco, oil, cinema, banking, and textile workers already on strike, and electricity, gas, and water workers prepared to join the work stoppage the next day, Neguib was forced to abrogate his announcement of March 24. Although Neguib stayed on as president of the Council of Ministers for some months, Nasser and his loyalists stripped him of power.

The March dispute had massive repercussions for Egypt's private sector. Nasser owed a huge debt to critical labor groups. He did not intend to share power with labor, but he sought to reward its followers by providing them with jobs and accelerating the state's control of the economy. During the crisis Nasser strengthened his ties with key trade union leaders. Ibrahim al-Tahawi, the assistant general secretary of the Liberation Rally, and Ahmad Tuayma, director of the trade union section of the Liberation Rally, worked in close alignment with the president of the Union of Commercial Workmen and Employees, the president of the Transport Workers (Anwar Salama), and the president of the Eastern Tobacco Workers (Fathi Kamil).[92] Strike plans were prepared in concert with the president of the Socony–Vacuum Oil Company Union, the Oil Workers Federation, and Eastern Tobacco Workers. Moreover, the strike enjoyed widespread support at Beida Dyers, Filature Nationale des Textiles, and the Eastern Tobacco Company.

The March troubles enabled the new Nasser-dominated government to consolidate its hold on power and to root out opposition. Disloyal cavalry officers were put in prison while prodemocracy elements in the rest of the army were carefully monitored. Even though the army did not emerge unified from this grueling test, no one, not even from the inner core of ruling officers, was any longer prepared to challenge Nasser's autocracy. Toward civil society Nasser was no less domineering. Shortly after the March crisis had ended, the Nasser government enacted a decree that forbade anyone who held high office between February 1942 and July 1952 from exercising political power.[93] The state also dissolved the Council of Journalists' Syndicate on the grounds that it had become a breeding ground of opposition to RCC rule. It fined a number of opposition news-

[91] C. Marshall, British Embassy, Cairo, to A. Greenhough, Ministry of Labour, April 3, 1954, PRO FO 371/108583 JE2187/9.

[92] Marshall to Greenhough, April 5, 1954, PRO FO 371/108583.

[93] Hamrush, *Qissa*, vol. 1, p. 350.

papers for having printed articles condemning the regime. The two newspapers most critical of Nasser, *al-Misri* and *al-Jumhur al-Misri*, had to pay stiff fines—so massive in fact that *al-Jumhur al-Misri* was forced out of existence. The owners of *al-Misri* were tried in absentia for treason.[94]

The attack on the journalists' syndicate was but the first governmental assault on independent professional organizations. During the next few years the regime took similar overt and covert actions against the professional organization of lawyers, the different business pressure groups, including the Egyptian Federation of Industries, and the many, formerly powerful and relatively autonomous chambers of commerce.[95] The once lively and insightful journals and publications of these groups became little more than organs for the dissemination of business decrees and government publicity. They were devoid of meaningful editorial comment, none of which was critical of state policy.

On April 17, 1954, Nasser rid the Council of Ministers of many of its more independent-minded probusiness members, replacing them with military men and civilian technicians, who were less likely to oppose the more statist orientation that the government planned for its economic policies. While naming himself as president of the new ministry in which Neguib was permitted to remain only as president of the republic, Nasser removed Imari and Giritli from the Ministry of Finance and Economy in favor of Abd al-Hamid al-Sharif and Abd al-Munaim Qaysuni.[96] To the business world, these changes were worrisome. Imari was considered a sound and conservative fiscalist who had prevented a socialist drift in Egyptian policy.[97] Also removed from the government were Hilmi Bahagat Badawi, the minister of commerce and industry; and Hasan Baghdadi, Abbas Ammar, and William Salim Hanna, all of whom were independent-minded civilian technicians greatly respected by Western diplomats. The Council of Ministers was left with eight RCC men—the closest fusing of these two instruments of power that Egypt had experienced to that point. Indeed, the only RCC persons missing from the Council of Ministers were Abd al-Hakim Amr, commander in chief of the Egyptian Armed Forces, and Anwar al-Sadat.[98]

A mere five months after neutralizing dissidence within the officer corps, Nasser accomplished the overarching goal of all Egyptian nationalists. In September 1954, British and Egyptian negotiators concluded a treaty by which the British pledged to remove all of their forces from the

[94] Gordon, *Nasser's Blessed Movement*, p. 140.

[95] No. 1284, Caffery to Department of State, January 3, 1955, USNA RG 84, Cairo Embassy, General Records, 1955, box 263.

[96] *al-Ahram*, April 18, 1954.

[97] No. 101, Donald Edgar, American Consul General, to Department of State, April 10, 1954; no. 1322, Caffery to Department of State, April 18, 1954, USNA 774.13, reel 8.

[98] Hamrush, *Qissa*, vol. 1, p. 350.

country within the span of eighteen months. In return, the Egyptians agreed to allow British forces to reactivate the base in the event of an international war. The base was to be maintained in a state of war preparedness by 1,200 British technicians and a group of British civilian contracting companies. While there could be no doubt that the British had retreated a long distance from their original maximalist position (with its insistence on a permanent British military force of 7,000), so had the Egyptians. Their allowing an ongoing British civilian and business presence in the Suez Canal area provoked alarm and suspicion among many segments of Egyptian society. The Muslim Brotherhood, still an effective organ of dissent, marshalled the discontents in protests that culminated in an attempt on Nasser's life. The Egyptian president exacted his revenge on the Muslim Brothers, imprisoning their leaders and effectively limiting their influence for the next decade. But these draconian measures could not alter the fact that Nasser had made significant concessions in order to secure the removal of British troops from Egypt.

By the end of 1954 the shape of Egypt's mixed economy had become clearer. In February the state initialed three important agreements for an iron and steel works, a fertilizer factory, and an international hotel in Cairo. In all three projects public finance predominated but did not preclude important roles for private capital. The government signed an agreement with the German firm of Demag to erect an iron and steel company at Helwan. Of the original capitalization of £E2.1 million, the government contributed £E2 million in kind (land and construction materials) and the National Production Council £E40,000, the Industrial Bank £E10,000, the Misr Group £E40,000, and Demag £E10,000. A critical increase in the equity of the program occurred in September 1954 and involved payments of £E900,000 from the NPC, £E240,000 from the Industrial Bank, and £E960,000 from the Misr Group. By the end of 1955 the capital of the iron and steel works had grown to £E6,260,000.[99]

On the same day that the iron and steel program was signed, the Egyptian government announced the creation of a fertilizer plant at Aswan—a project expected to cost £E22 million and to produce 370,000 metric tons of fertilizer a year when operating at full capacity. Much the same combination of local private and public enterprises was employed to provide the start-up capital. Egypt continued to look to the West for technical and managerial guidance. No fewer than nine Western chemical-fertilizer conglomerates submitted bids for the construction of the plant.[100]

Finally, in the same month, the Egyptian government declared its intention to bring together public and private funding, including American

[99] *al-Ahram*, February 9, 1954; *Egyptian Gazette*, November 22, 1955; no. 573, John Fitzgerald to Department of State, November 22, 1955, USNA 874.331/11–2255.

[100] *al-Ahram*, February 9, 1954; no. 2748, John Fitzgerald to Department of State, May 22, 1954, USNA 874.3972, reel 29.

investment from the Hilton complex of firms, to construct a luxury hotel in the center of Cairo. Contributing equity on the Egyptian side was the usual lineup of government agencies and a number of large private companies, especially those of the Misr empire. The Hilton corporation undertook to oversee the construction and management of the hotel once it was functioning. Its equity contribution was small, however.[101]

These mixed enterprises demonstrated the government's approach to development programs that required large outlays of capital and much managerial and technical talent. Both Barrawi and Nasser extolled mixed enterprises as the bedrock of Egypt's industrialization effort.[102] Nasser continued to assert that the National Production Council would be used to vet new endeavors and would facilitate the bringing together of private and public capital and technical skills.[103] Yet from time to time the state technocrats expressed their disappointment with private sector initiatives and chided private firms for failing to introduce the projects most needed in Egypt. In August 1954 the National Production Council referred openly to the fiscal conservatism of the business community. An NPC study of Egypt's economic problems pinpointed rapid population growth as the largest obstacle to economic growth. But the NPC claimed that far too much private capital was finding its way into land acquisitions and overseas trade when what the Egyptian economy required was industrial progress.[104] Not much different was a speech from Nasser upbraiding the business elite for contributing little to the country's economic growth.[105] These criticisms added to the growing uncertainty in the minds of business leaders, who were much shaken by the March crisis and the overtures to labor.

1955 AND 1956: PRELUDE TO THE NATIONALIZATION OF THE SUEZ CANAL COMPANY

The most dramatic political developments of 1955 included Nasser's journey to a gathering of third-world leaders in Bandung, Indonesia, where he espoused a strong neutralist stance in international relations, and the Czech arms deal of September 1955. They had their economic counterpart, however, in an increasing reliance on public enterprise, an extolling of parastatal bodies like the NPC, and a growing litany of criticism of the private sector for its failure to contribute to Egyptian development.

---

[101] *al-Ahram*, June 15, 1954.
[102] A Barrawi speech was reported in *al-Ahram*, February 12, 1954.
[103] *al-Ahram*, September 1, 1954.
[104] Ibid., August 13, 1954.
[105] Ibid., September 1, 1954.

It was at this propitious moment that the Soviet Union began to intrude decisively into the Egyptian narrative. The Soviet Union, of course, had never been far absent in the calculations of Western politicians or, for that matter, Egyptian leaders, even during the civilian regimes. Given Egypt's strategic location, the Western powers had always been apprehensive of Soviet overtures and had tried to tie Egypt up in a Western military alliance. By the same token, even the Egyptian civilian ministers had seen the benefits that accrued to them if they pursued trading ties with East bloc countries. But it was not until September 1955, when Egypt consummated its arms deal with the Czech government, that the Soviet Union became a full-fledged actor in Egypt's diplomatic relations. Naturally, the political and military implications of the Soviet entry have received the greatest scholarly attention. But economically, the Soviet rapprochement had large implications, not the least of which was a more state-centered and less capitalist orientation toward economic change.

Once again, if we place Egypt in a comparative framework with Kenya and Nigeria, what stands out is that the Egyptian leadership had the freedom to negotiate arrangements with any state in the world. Egypt was juridically sovereign and had its own government. The treaty of 1954 with the British had started the withdrawal of British forces. Yet the withdrawal was not completed when the Egyptians made their arms deal with the Czechs, and no Egyptian leader could be completely sanguine that the British would honor the treaty, given the strong right-wing sentiment in Britain against evacuating the troops. Nigeria and Kenya were prevented from forming overt ties with communist bloc countries by their British colonial overlord (though it was rumored that the Kenyan nationalist Oginga Odinga was accepting money from the Soviets in the late 1950s). Not only did the Cold War, then, increase the maneuverability of the Egyptian elite, but it opened up seductive alternative views of economic development—ones that extolled the capabilities of the state to accelerate economic growth and overcome barriers to development.

Whether the Israeli raid into Gaza in February 1955 was the military engagement that pushed Egypt into the arms of the Soviets or merely a pretext, certainly the killing of thirty-four Egyptian soldiers and the revelation of the shockingly poor state of preparedness of the Egyptian army galvanized Nasser's concern about arms supplies. The Egyptian army was seen at that crucial moment to have only six serviceable planes and only enough tank ammunition for a one-hour battle.[106] Alarmed that the Soviet Union would prey on Egyptian panic, the American Embassy in Cairo warned Washington that Soviet Ambassador "Shepilov had brought

---

[106] Keith Kyle, *Suez* (London, 1991), p. 65; no. 2159, H. A. Byroade to Secretary of State, May 20, 1955, USNA RG 84, Cairo Embassy, General Records, box 265.

word [that] Russia [was] prepared to go all out in assisting Egypt."[107] When American and British military assistance did not materialize, Egypt did turn to the Soviet bloc, signing an arms deal with Czechoslovakia. At the same moment, Shepilov dropped a hint that the Soviets were interested in providing more than military help. According to Nasser, the Soviets had informed Egyptian officials that they might finance Nasser's favorite project, the high dam, and provide general economic assistance.

In 1955, well before the Suez invasion, Nasser also began shifting the balance between the private and public sectors. Expressing concern over the sluggishness of the Egyptian economy and characterizing Egyptian society as in the grip of monopolists and feudalists, the Egyptian president divulged the new economic and social emphases of his government in a secret and provocative speech to armed forces officers at the end of March. As the contents of the speech began to be disseminated to the outside, it became clear that Nasser had dilated on the still unrealized economic implications of the revolution. He excoriated business executives for their excessive political influence and lack of social conscience and raised the possibility of nationalizing Egypt's major industries.[108] When in a subsequent speech Nasser portrayed Egypt as thoroughly dominated by captains of industry and then placed Abu Nusayr at the head of the Ministry of Commerce and Industry, business confidence fell to a low point.[109] Though he was a former Bank Misr official and married to the daughter of a cotton merchant, Abu Nusayr was best known in the business world for his advocacy of bilateral trade arrangements and devotion to a highly regulated business sector.[110]

No piece of legislation was more disturbing to the business persons in this period than the reform of the company law, enacted in March 1955.[111] Though a brief decree, the enactment contained several clauses that angered the old business elite. In contrast to previous business legislation, which the government had adopted only after full consultation with business groups, this act appeared without any forewarning or advance discussion.[112] The most controversial clauses in the decree dealt with directors of companies. The law required directors to retire at age sixty rather

---

[107] No. 234, Byroade to Secretary of State, August 15, 1955, USNA RG 84, Cairo Embassy, General Records, 1955, box 263.

[108] Detailed accounts of this important address were carried in no. 1884, Perry Ellis to Department of State, April 1, 1955, USNA 874.00/4–155; and no. 69, Stevenson to Macmillan, April 15, 1955, PRO FO 371/113578 JE1015/16.

[109] No. 2208, Byroade to Secretary of State, June 1, 1955, USNA RG 84, Cairo Embassy, General Records, 1955, box 263.

[110] No. 597, James N. Cortada to Secretary of State, November 29, 1955, USNA RG 84, Cairo Embassy, General Records, 1955, box 264.

[111] The text of the law is to be found in *al-Ahram*, March 20, 1955.

[112] *al-Ahram*, March 18, 1955.

than seventy. It also stipulated that only the Egyptian Council of Ministers could grant exceptions, and for only one year at a time. Previously, the law had permitted shareholders to make retirement exceptions, and they had almost always done so. Another clause obligated public utilities to obtain the approval of the Council of Ministers for all of their board nominees.

Rashid al-Barrawi defended the decree on the grounds that it would bring younger, more dynamic business persons into the private sector. Nasser argued that the legislation derived from the social goals of the revolution. It reflected the regime's opposition to monopolies and its desire to free the government from capitalist domination.[113] At a stroke, the law removed no fewer than 200 directors who were older than sixty or served on the boards of public utilities. In order to respond to the numerous requests for exceptions, the government had to create a special office. The National Bank of Egypt lost eight of its directors, including Ali Shamsi and Imari, and Bank Misr had to find replacements for seven of its twelve directors.[114] That the law was designed, in the words of the British ambassador, Ralph Stevenson, "to break the financial stranglehold exercised by a limited group over the industrial activities of the various Misr companies," was indisputable given the fact that the government refused all of the bank's requests to exempt its overage directors.[115] So dispirited was Abd al-Maqsud Ahmad, longtime director of many of the Misr companies, that he tendered his resignation and was replaced by Abd al-Hamid al-Sharif, a former minister of finance who in turn resigned before the end of 1955 in favor of Muhammad Rushdi.[116] Although Rushdi was described as "a firm believer in private enterprise," the blow dealt to private sector confidence can hardly be overestimated.[117]

The law did indeed target the old Egyptian business elite, whom Nasser and others believed had failed the new government. Almost none of the Egyptian requests for exemptions was accepted, though nearly all of those from the predominantly foreign-run companies were. Of even greater concern to the Egyptian business elite was the government's contention that banks, like the National Bank of Egypt and Bank Misr, were to be treated as public utilities. This meant that all of their directors had to be approved by the Council of Ministers. At the National Bank the

---

[113] Ibid., March 29 and 30, 1955.

[114] Stevenson to Eden, March 26, 1955, PRO FO 371/113646 JE1103/11.

[115] Chancery, Cairo, to African Department, Foreign Office, December 7, 1955, PRO FO 371/113646 JE1103/23.

[116] No. 1896, Perry Ellis to Department of State, April 4, 1955, USNA RG 84, Cairo Embassy, General Records, 1955, box 266.

[117] No. 650, James H. Cortada to Secretary of State, December 14, 1955, USNA RG 84, Cairo Embassy, General Records, 1955, box 266.

government also carried out a campaign to eliminate foreigners from the firm's top administrative posts.[118]

Even while it assaulted the private sector in highly publicized speeches and enacted laws that business representatives claimed were inimical to their interests, the state intensified its pressure on those same firms to contribute capital and managerial talents to the country's mixed enterprises. The iron and steel company, after raising £E6,200,000 in equity capital, decided it needed an additional £E2 million so that it could commence production in 1957 with an output of 220,000 tons, approximately two-thirds of the country's requirement.[119] It expected big business to help raise the needed funds. The first goal that the state set for the company was to produce sheet steel, building materials, steel rails, railway carriages, and ingots. The state's longer-term aim, for which it needed an additional £E16 million of equity, was to become a steel exporter. Although the government sought a public subscription, it demanded that big firms garnish the wages of their workers and staff members for the project.[120] The shares being oversubscribed by about £E3 million, the government employed all of the capital to increase the company's equity from £E6,200,000 to £E11,360,000.[121]

Similarly, the government accepted the offer of a German-French chemical conglomerate (composed of the four companies Uda, Badsche Anilin, Schneider et Kuhlman, and Colman Creusot) to run the much-heralded fertilizer factory at Aswan.[122] The cost to Egypt was estimated at £E12,277,000, of which the National Production Council agreed to subscribe £E2 million. The new company, called the Egyptian Chemical Industries Company, had an initial capital of £E8 million, subscribed by the usual alliance of public enterprises and private firms: the NPC, the Insurance and Savings Fund, the Ministry of Waqfs (religious endowments), the Industrial Bank, the Misr Insurance Company, and the Agricultural and Cooperative Credit Bank.[123]

Dragooned into supporting many of these public sector programs, the private sector feared that it was becoming a subordinate of the state. The two national production loans of 1956 did little to alleviate its worries. The loans were intended to provide the state with equity capital for additional development projects, and they were oversubscribed. But the apparent ease with which the funds were raised belied the massive and much-resented pressures that the state applied to business groups in order

[118] No. 1876, Perry Ellis to Secretary of State, March 31, 1955, USNA RG 84, Cairo Embassy, General Records, 1955, box 266.

[119] *Egyptian Gazette*, November 22, 1955.

[120] Ibid., December 16, 1955.

[121] No. 799, John Fitzgerald to Department of State, January 21, 1956, USNA 874.33/1–2156.

[122] *Egyptian Gazette*, February 9, 1956.

[123] No. 864, John Fitzgerald to Department of State, February 10, 1956, USNA 874.3972/2–1056.

to make the subscriptions a success. Banks contributed £E7 million; £E3 million came from commercial and shipping companies; £E1.5 million from industrial companies; and £E9 million came from insurance companies and savings banks. For the first time ever, the Suez Canal Company subscribed to a domestic project, but only under relentless state pressure.[124] The Misr companies, always under government scrutiny, contributed £E5 million. Shell Oil, conscious of its large investments in Egypt and its exposed political position, subscribed £E250,000. The government had suggested £E1 million, and Shell Oil had offered £E150,000.[125]

Next in this avalanche of statist and interventionist acts came the new constitution on January 16, 1956—a document that crystallized the social and economic themes sounded so regularly in presidential speeches. The document stressed the eradication of capitalist monopolies and the control of capitalist influences over the government. It also contained a strong emphasis on public welfare.

The new aggressive stance toward capital could easily be exaggerated and probably was among the hypersensitive agents of foreign business operating in Egypt. Cooler heads in the British and American Embassies discounted much of the rhetoric in the constitution, in which they saw little that they believed should alarm the business groups of Egypt. British ambassador Humphrey Trevelyan described the Egyptian political economy, as delineated in the constitution, as "the type of mixed economy with which Western Europe, and the United Kingdom, in particular, is familiar." He noted that the constitution expressly forbade the expropriation of private property except for purposes of public welfare and guaranteed the right of private property holders. Trevelyan believed that the government of Egypt was fully committed to investing "in key industrial projects established within the framework of private enterprise and [intended] to leave the remainder of the economy, including commerce, the distributive trades, and the ownership of non-agricultural real estate in private hands."[126] The American view was no different. American intelligence described the constitution as reflecting "the eclecticism and ambivalence which characterizes the younger, Western educated group throughout the Arab world today."[127] Both embassies considered the document a blow to Egyptian leftists because it contained not a single reference to the doctrine of socialism.

Yet, just before the nationalization of the Suez Canal Company, the

---

[124] *Egyptian Gazette*, April 1, 4, 11, and 12, 1956.

[125] No. 1059, James N. Cortada to Department of State, April 17, 1956, USNA 874.10/4–1756; no. 65E, H. Trevelyan to Selwyn Lloyd, May 3, 1956, PRO FO 371/118941 JE1116/1.

[126] No. 144, H. Trevelyan to Selwyn Lloyd, February 2, 1956, PRO FO 371/118832 JE1015/9.

[127] United States Department of State Intelligence Report, February 29, 1956, PRO FO 371/118832.

Egyptian government took an important step indicative of its intention to direct Egypt's industrial development. It divided the Ministry of Commerce and Industry into two separate ministries and named Aziz Sidqi as the first minister of industry. Sidqi was well known as Egypt's most energetic advocate of state planning and public sector involvement in industrialization. Also added to the cabinet was Dr. Mustafa Khalil, a graduate of the Cairo University faculty of engineering and an employee of the Egyptian state railway administration. Like Sidqi, Khalil was American-trained, having obtained a doctorate from the University of Illinois in 1951. During his apprenticeship in the United States, Khalil had worked for four years with the Chicago–St. Louis Railway Company. Upon returning to Egypt, he had become a professor of railway and road engineering at Ein Shams before moving to Cairo University.[128]

The new appointments in crucial economic and financial ministries, involving not merely Sidqi and Khalil at the Ministry of Industry but earlier Qaysuni as Imari's replacement as minister of finance, marked a major departure in Egypt's political economy. Seen in a comparative context in relationship to Kenya, where a powerful minister of finance (Ernest Vasey) held onto power throughout the Mau Mau era, and Nigeria, where the British minister of finance in the central government (Eric Himsworth) was forced out of office, it demonstrated that the military men, notably Nasser, were in charge of economic affairs as well as political matters. No longer would the chief economic and financial experts in the government be given a free hand as Imari was in the early days of military authority. It also meant that the subordination of economic concerns to political issues would continue apace. Although Qaysuni, Sidqi, and Khalil's appointments were well received among the business elite largely because they had a solid grounding in neoclassical economics and ties to the West, the reality was that they were put in office because they would not oppose the wishes of the RCC. Nonetheless, the Western embassies were far from apprehensive. One foreign report described the two new men at the Ministry of Industry as "moderate civilian technicians of predominantly Western connections and training."[129] At the same time that they were being added to the cabinet, a number of RCC officers serving in the Council of Ministers were removed. This change, too, was greeted with approval in the private sector, since it seemed to suggest a heightened sensitivity to the fears being expressed in the business world.

Between 1952 and 1956, then, the Egyptian government failed to give a clear and decisive message to the business community. At first, leading government officials consulted widely with business groups and removed

---

[128] No. 1142, H. Trevelyan to Foreign Office, June 30, 1956, PRO FO 371/118832 JE1015/29.

[129] J. H. A. Watson, Foreign Office Note, July 4, 1956, PRO FO 371/118832 JE1015/34.

many of the complaints the local and foreign capitalists had against earlier nationalist legislation. But with the passing of time and the unwillingness of the business groups to display ardor for the military's most cherished economic projects, the junta grew disenchanted. The concern these men had about the lack of economic progress, their dissatisfaction with the contribution of business firms to industrialization, and their opening to the Soviet Union put the business world on the defensive. Already, business leaders were complaining that they were no longer consulted on key economic programs and that overtly anticapitalist legislation was beginning to be enacted. Still, at the midpoint in 1956, there was little on the political and economic horizon to suggest that within five years almost the whole of Egypt's large-scale business sector would have passed into state hands.

CHAPTER 3

Prelude to the Nationalizations:
Case Studies of Business-Military
Tensions, 1952–1956

THE EGYPTIAN MILITARY elite had no certain economic policy as the fateful year of 1956 began. It judged its efforts to mollify foreign capital and enlist domestic capital in the country's development efforts as only partially successful. Within the inner counsels of the military, opinion was deeply divided on the role that private capital should play. A circle of advisers, best exemplified by Wing Commander Gamal Salim and the oil government technician Abu Zayd, resented the powerful position of foreign capital and wanted the regime to enlarge the powers of the state. These individuals made their anticapitalist and antiforeign-capital attitudes clear in the increasingly difficult negotiations between the state and the big foreign oil conglomerates operating in the country. By the same token, another group within the officer corps believed that a country lacking capital and many technical and managerial skills must turn to foreign capital and make the country attractive to foreign investors.

Not surprisingly, a dramatic event pushed Egypt off its indeterminate course and began a process that witnessed the dissolution of the Egyptian private sector over the next five years. Of the many riveting events in the middle of 1956, the Egyptian government's decision to nationalize the Suez Canal Company, although stemming from a complex web of interconnected economic and noneconomic events, proved decisive for the business community in Egypt.

That the military junta would quarrel with the directors of the Suez Canal Company was nearly inevitable. That such a quarrel would lead to the nationalization of the company, the British-French-Israeli invasion of the country, and the dissolution of much of the private sector was far from certain, however. Here domestic politics, the tensions of the Cold War, and the ideological preferences and personal ambitions of the ruling elite, as well as Egypt's long history of resenting foreign economic dominance, came into play.

Although the military men and the company directors shared many traits—their secretiveness and their vaunting ambition, to mention the most obvious—they represented the clash of imperial and nationalist mentalities in an extreme form. The company directors scorned Egyptian administrative capacity. They were persuaded (and persuaded others as well) that the Egyptians were incapable of running the Suez Canal should the Egyptian government elect to do without the company after the concession expired in 1968. For their part, the Egyptian military bristled at these derogations of Egyptian capability. They also embraced the view, widely articulated within Egyptian society at the time, that the canal company had exploited Egypt ruthlessly for its own enrichment and that it constituted a veritable state within a state—an impediment to Egypt's political and economic independence.

In all other ways the individuals who were to emerge at the center of the canal company dispute could not have been more dissimilar. The inner core of French directors were older men who were well connected in French, European, and even North American financial circles. They had grown up in the classical imperial era and were uncomfortable with the thought of independent power centers around the world. They were intensely conservative in their political beliefs and actions, many of them having supported the Vichy government during the war. While they sought to expunge this association from the historical record of the company, they were disinclined to accept into their midst any individual who had been, or for that matter continued to be, strongly against the Pétain political legacy.[1]

Ranged against these exemplars of the old financial and political order were Egypt's young military autocrats, hypersensitive to imperial slights against Egypt's national honor, real or imagined. These men had suffered personally at the hands of an overweening foreign presence in Egypt. They were determined, even at great personal risk, to assert Egyptian dignity in the face of these oppressive foreign influences. As a group, they overflowed with resentment against British military influence and condescending foreign residents. No organization brought its nationalist assertiveness to a more heightened state than the Suez Canal Company.

Not only were the mentalities of these two protagonists antithetical to accommodation, so were the policies elaborated by the Suez Canal Company executives in the decade leading up to nationalization. The directors placed the company and the military regime on a collision course. The company directors might have averted the collision had they accepted the inevitability of the termination of the concession—a position taken by virtually every group in Egyptian society, regardless of political persuasion—and worked with the Egyptian government to effect a smooth

[1] Revealing correspondence on this subject occurred in 1953 over the appointment of a new French director. The discussions over qualifications of the candidates made clear the continuing reactionary convictions of the French directorate. See Meiklereid to Allen, September 15, 1953, PRO FO 371/102906.

transfer of power. They would have had to accelerate the Egyptianization of the company's personnel, the equalization of benefits provided to Egyptian and expatriate staff, and the investment of a reasonable proportion of the firm's increasing profits and reserve funds in Egypt.[2] But such policy departures were beyond the ken of even the most liberal directors, including the representatives of the British government, let alone the inner core of intensely conservative French financiers. All of the directors were thoroughly imbued with a belief in the irreplaceability of the company and eager to have this profit-making juggernaut continue to exist after 1968. They approached the Egyptians as adversaries rather than potential partners.[3]

The Suez Canal Company had been constituted in such a way that more liberal, less imperialist, and more accommodationist perspectives had little chance of being heard. The board of directors had little input into the all-powerful Comité de Direction, a body that administered the affairs of the company with little advice from outside forces. A director from outside this inner circle admitted that neither he nor most of his colleagues on the board understood the company's finances or knew the true rate of profit or the exact size of the various reserves.[4] From the beginning of the enterprise, during the management of Ferdinand de Lesseps, critical decisions were made by inner cabals, rarely in the formal meetings where hard-to-digest reports and statistics received cursory oversight. Secrecy had been a hallmark of the early days of de Lesseps's administration and remained so in the financially buoyant era after World War II. Although the British government ultimately purchased the Egyptian government's 44 percent share of the original equity capital, this purchase brought the government only three places on a board of thirty-two. Because the Suez shareholders were never solicited for funds after 1866 and the company's capitalization grew almost effortlessly through self-financing and the issuance of bonds, a few individuals could easily dominate its affairs. The Suez Canal Company was an autonomous business entity that enjoyed far-reaching political influence in Egypt, France, and beyond.[5]

When, after World War II, the huge growth in oil traffic through the canal had produced large increases in earnings, the company officials defended their financial policies from critics by pointing out that the company had to prepare for its ultimate liquidation in 1968. At that point, it would need to have reserve funds to compensate its shareholders and to indemnify or provide pensions to its employees. Yet the ever-increasing

---

[2] Hubert Bonin, *Suez: du canal à la finance, 1858–1987* (Paris, 1987), p. 146.
[3] Ibid., p. 163.
[4] H. Trevelyan to T. E. Bromley, October 20, 1955, PRO FO 371/113747 JE1424/128.
[5] Bonin, *Suez*, pp. 61 ff.

reserves tempted the directors to see themselves as a financial corporation. More and more frequently they referred to the company as an investment firm and less as a maritime facility. To play such a role, the company would need to funnel its funds out of Egypt for investment in the most lucrative markets in the world. Such activity was well under way in the late 1940s and early 1950s but was also seen as a likely point of contention with Egyptian nationalists.

One of the most effective propaganda efforts by the company was its campaign to persuade observers that the canal company alone was capable of managing this vital international waterway. Guided visits by distinguished visitors through the workshops and offices of the company in Egypt produced gratifying results. A British director, Francis Wylie, after returning from a visit to the canal, concluded that "what is too often forgotten is the fact that the European superior technical staff now at Ismailia, Port Said, and Port Tewfik—say 200 individuals in all—is the only group of men anywhere in the world competent to run the Suez Canal and to keep at the same time the confidence of the international shipping community which uses it and uses it every year in increasing numbers."[6] Employing the same argument, the canal officials put pressure on the British military negotiators to secure an extension of Britain's right to occupy the canal base, fearing that once the British forces were withdrawn the Egyptian government would attempt to take over the canal.

In reality, the Suez Canal was a relatively easy waterway to operate, as one anonymous observer pointed out in a critique laid before the British Foreign Office. This note should have alerted British and French officials to the likelihood of nationalization and to the exaggerated propaganda flowing out of the company's offices. But it did not. Pointing out that the Suez Canal, unlike its counterpart, the Panama canal, had no locks, that a straight run lay from the Red Sea to the Mediterranean, and that internal depressions formed lakes where ships could be held in waiting while those proceeding in an opposite direction passed, the observer asserted that, if necessary, the ships' pilots themselves could navigate the canal if the company's pilots were withdrawn. "It would demand," he wrote, "a quite unusual degree of incompetence to create a traffic muddle and . . . the canal would run at a pinch without traffic control at all." The writer questioned the company's high fees and suggested that a large proportion of the earnings went to support its extravagant offices in Paris and the high fees paid to its politically well-connected directors and supporters.[7]

Many issues troubled company-government relations in the period

---

[6] Wylie to Allen, March 12, 1953, PRO FO 371/102888.
[7] E. Monroe to D. W. G. Wass, Treasury, September 17, 1953, PRO FO 371/102893.

leading up to the nationalization. A constant backdrop to the disputes was the specter of nationalization itself. Despite repeated assertions that the Suez Canal Company was an international firm and that its relations with the government of Egypt were different from those enjoyed by other firms by virtue of the international treaties signed between the company and the Egyptian government, legal experts in Egypt and abroad conceded that the Suez Canal Company was an Egyptian joint stock company, registered with the Egyptian government and hence subject to Egyptian law. Like any such firm it was capable of being nationalized. The nationalization issue was aired frequently in the Egyptian press and in political statements.

When the military came to power, the talk of nationalization did not end. One of the government's first acts was the creation of a special government administrative organ to deal with canal affairs. The Egyptian government argued that it needed this parallel department operating in the shadow of the company so as to prepare for the day when the concession would expire.[8] But the existence of this body, developing capacities to administer the canal, haunted the company.

Even more troubling were the writings and speeches of a young Egyptian nationalist, originally a Wafdist supporter, who quickly aligned himself with the new military men. In Paris, Mustafa al-Hifnawi had written a thesis on the history of the canal. He had even been given access to confidential company records, having persuaded influential board members that his thesis would extol the contributions the company had made to Egyptian economic progress. In fact, when published, the thesis excoriated the company as one of the chief reasons for Egypt's impoverished and colonial status. Within four months of the regime change, Hifnawi was delivering a public lecture on the canal. General Neguib was in the chair for the lecture, and the audience, numbering more than 300, contained a large number of important military men. Also in attendance was a company agent sent to take detailed notes on the lecture. He reported that Hifnawi had gone through his familiar historical litany, recounting the onerous financial, labor, and land contributions that Egypt had made to the construction of the canal, Disraeli's purchase of the canal shares, and Egypt's subsequent minuscule return on its mammoth early contributions. Hifnawi concluded his speech by calling on the government to prepare itself for 1968. It would be easy to read into his remarks a demand that the government strike a better financial and managerial bargain with the company or perhaps even take the decisive step of assuming full control over the company.[9]

Few companies contemplate their imminent liquidation with equanimity. A firm as extravagantly successful as the Suez Canal Company

[8] *al-Ahram*, October 16, 1952.
[9] Wylie to Allen, November 26, 1952, PRO FO 371/97015.

cast about for ways to remain in existence beyond 1968. Its directors worked on two fronts, which were not mutually incompatible: securing for the firm a continued role in managing the canal and transforming the company into an investment firm. First, in the late 1940s and the early 1950s, the company directors led an effort to persuade the major international shipping countries—their chief diplomats and shipping magnates—to support a company effort to have the company designated as the permanent manager of the canal. Company directors approached British and French officials in secrecy, for fear of arousing Egyptian antagonism, and the British and French delegates then met in 1952 and agreed to approach U.S. State Department officials.[10]

Far more promising was the concept of transforming the company into an investment firm. This effort had progressed significantly by 1956 and became the company's salvation after nationalization. As early as 1952, the matter was raised in a board meeting. The canal company would found, as an auxiliary but separate entity under its overall administration, an investment trust, utilizing the large reserves at its disposal for investment wherever profitable financial opportunities presented themselves. Advocates of the plan argued that the company would only be doing what many of the most profitable enterprises routinely did. The example of Anglo-Iranian Oil was cited. More important, they contended that by channeling funds into an investment body, the company's assets would be less easily expropriated by the government of Egypt should it decide to move against the company and its reserves.[11] The opponents of the scheme, led by Edgar Bonnet among the board members, argued that the funds were already well managed and that the action proposed was likely to arouse the suspicion of the Egyptian government and the company's shareholders.[12]

A crucial development in this debate occurred when Jacques Georges-Picot was appointed director general of the company. Historically, the director general was the dominant force in the company. The appointment of Georges-Picot sealed the company's fate as an investment trust, for Georges-Picot's chief talent lay in international finance and investment rather than canal management. At the time of his appointment Georges-Picot was head of the Groupe du Crédit Industriel et Commercial, which had large investments in North America. In addition, he was vice president of the Crédit Nantes and administrator of the Société Bordelaise de Crédit Industriel et Commercial as well as a board member of many other companies.[13]

Under Georges-Picot's prodding, the directors were brought around to

[10] R. Allen, Foreign Office Note, August 2, 1952, PRO FO 371/97011.
[11] F. Wylie to Allen, December 23, 1952, PRO FO 371/102887.
[12] Ibid., January 3, 1953, PRO FO 371/102887.
[13] Wylie to Boothby, December 3, 1953, PRO FO 371/102906.

the idea of creating a separate Suez investment firm.[14] His clinching argument was that, far from tempting the government of Egypt to take over the canal company, the investment trust would deter the Egyptians.[15] Even the British board members, who had been suspicious of this scheme, were convinced of its merits, and in mid-1955 the new organ came into being, affiliated with the Suez Canal Company. Its accounts were credited with most of the large reserves that the parent company had accumulated.

At the heart of the problem facing the Suez Canal Company in the postwar decade were its mounting surpluses. These stemmed from the dramatic rise in the tonnage moving through the canal and the explosion in earnings. By 1953 the company's profits were running at £14 million per year, and the gross foreign exchange earned by the company averaged about £26 million a year.[16] There were, however, different ways of viewing the surpluses. Most of the board members argued for the need to accumulate large reserves for the approaching end of the concession. Within official British circles, however, a different view prevailed, most forcefully articulated by D. R. Serpell at the British Treasury. Fearing that the growing reserves would tempt the Egyptian government to seize the company and desiring that the company be seen as a public utility devoted to the efficient and inexpensive management of a vital communications link rather than a profit-oriented business firm, Serpell argued that the company should reduce its dues and limit its earnings and profits.[17] He convinced the Foreign Office of this vision, and the Foreign Office instructed the three British government representatives on the board to place the policy before the full board. The British delegates raised the issue at board meetings between March and June 1953, but the other directors soundly rejected the proposal that the dividend stay the same while the dues were reduced.[18]

THE ASWAN HIGH DAM AND PRIVATE INTERESTS

There were many other areas of tension between the government and large-scale business. The textile sector was under state pressure to produce more, to sell more at cheaper prices, and to provide more employment. Many in the ruling circle regarded the major oil conglomerates operating in Egypt—Anglo-Egyptian Oil and Socony-Vacuum in particu-

[14] Draft Letter from Treasury to F. Wylie, July 29, 1955, PRO FO 371/113746 JE1424/95.
[15] Note of a Meeting Held at the Treasury on July 25, 1955, PRO FO 371/113746 JE1424/96.
[16] D. Serpell to Morris, Ministry of Trade, February 19, 1953, PRO FO 371/102888.
[17] D. R. Serpell to Allen, January 6, 1953, PRO FO 371/102887.
[18] Meiklereid to Serpell, May 5, 1953, PRO FO 371/102889.

lar—as excessively powerful and able to make unseemly profits for their shareholders. The state's negotiations with these firms over pricing policies and stabilization funds were highly conflictual and never satisfactorily resolved. Yet the issue that finally led to a rupturing of relations was the construction of a new high dam at Aswan. The project negotiations soured Egyptian relations with the West, and had they been resolved differently, so that Western construction and electrification firms had gained the lucrative contracts for the work on the dam, the history of private-public sector relations in Egypt might have been altered.

The Revolutionary Command Council announced its commitment to the Aswan High Dam soon after seizing power. Within the span of a few years the dam became the leading development project of the new government. The Aswan scheme had natural appeal to Egyptian nationalists. It would store all of Egypt's vital irrigation waters within the boundaries of the country and would accelerate industrial development by providing cheap electrical power. Within a year of taking office the military released preliminary studies on the dam. These estimated the cost of the project at £E200 million, including the construction work on the dam itself, a power station, a fertilizer plant, power lines, and associated irrigation projects for bringing new areas under cultivation. The government predicted a 50 percent increase in the country's natural wealth from irrigation and drainage improvements, a large increase in arable land, and the provision of cheap and abundant power supplies.[19]

The preparation of the final construction plans, on which tenders would be sought, required a full year of work by a large number of expert officials, including Dr. Muhammad Ahmad Salim, secretary of the National Production Council; the engineer Samir Hilmi, also a member of the National Production Council; Dr. Hasan Zaki from the Ministry of Public Works; and the engineer Ahmad Ali Kamal, technical expert to the Ministry of Public Works and secretary to the High Committee for the High Dam. These men were subsequently dispatched to Europe to engage in technical and business discussions with the leading construction, irrigation, and electrical firms likely to have an interest in bidding on the Aswan High Dam contracts.[20]

If the technical planning required long hours of painstaking work and involved numerous individuals and committees, the negotiations and bargaining for the actual construction of the dam were even more difficult and intricate. They were carried out between mid-1954 and mid-1956 and provided the Nasser government with crucial lessons in playing foreign powers, even superpowers, off against one another. Interest in the con-

[19] *al-Ahram*, June 8, 1953.
[20] Ibid., June 27, 1954.

struction of the dam, with its many lucrative business contracts, was widespread among Western business firms. The first to come forward was a European conglomerate, involving as its principals the German firm, Hochtief, and the British electrical giant, English Electric. In its preliminary discussions with Egyptian officials, the consortium accepted the Egyptian estimate that the cost of the first phase of the project was likely to be £E200 million, of which £E80 million would be found in local currency; the remaining £E120 million would be needed in hard currency. The Egyptian government indicated that it would be able to provide £E30 million of the hard currency requirement; the consortium would need to make up the remaining £E90 million. Some consideration was given to employing the resources of the International Bank for Reconstruction and Development (IBRD) for a loan of $300 million.[21]

Hochtief was a German engineering company based in Essen. It had the financial backing of two large German firms, Siemens and AEG. At English Electric, the prime mover for the project was Douglas Betts.[22] For many decades, English Electric's proposals to heighten and electrify the old Aswan Dam had foundered on nationalist sensitivities about allowing a British firm to have such far-reaching influence over the Egyptian economy. Now, for the first time in more than a decade, a new government enjoying popular support seemed on the verge of awarding a contract of great magnitude to a British company.

The Egyptian government turned to European private business groups for obvious reasons. The Egyptian leaders preferred a mix of European business interests to the overpowering influence of a business group from a single national state. More important, they were eager to exclude American and World Bank capital for fear that American financial involvement (or that of the World Bank, which the Egyptian leaders regarded as a proxy for U.S. interests) would lead to American domination of the Egyptian economy.[23] In addition, the Egyptian government was delighted by the prospect of dealing with European construction and electrical firms rather than agents of foreign governments. That attractive feature quickly disappeared when the firms indicated that they would be unwilling to undertake such a massive economic project without the backing of their respective governments. English Electric took the lead, insisting that the British government give it full financial guarantees in the event of an Egyptian default.

Despite the many obstacles that plagued the negotiations between the

---

[21] Foreign Office Note, February 7, 1955, PRO FO 371/113730 JE1423/10.

[22] R. W. Jackling, British Embassy, Bonn, to K. E. Mackenzie, Board of Trade, April 19, 1955, PRO FO 371/113732 JE1423/54.

[23] Arrangements for Financing the Construction of the Aswan High Dam, Record of a Meeting Held in the Board of Trade, April 10 and 22, 1955, PRO FO 371/113733 JE1423/67.

Egyptian government and the consortium, including opposition from the U.S. government and the World Bank, the two parties were close to reaching an accord. The Egyptian government was prepared to sign a letter of intent with the consortium, only to have Betts of English Electric, apparently concerned about the large financial obligations that his firm would be accepting in the Aswan project, break ranks with his colleagues by insisting on the inclusion of the World Bank in the accord. At that juncture the British government also hesitated. Treasury officials believed that relying exclusively on the consortium would present "financial risks of astronomical dimensions" because of Egypt's likely inability to meet its share of the foreign exchange costs. An agreement with the consortium, backed by the British government, "would seem to involve Her Majesty's Government in nothing less than an open-ended commitment to underwrite the whole of the Egyptian economy."[24]

Had the consortium scheme somehow materialized it would surely have had a large effect on Egypt's business sector. The European firms eager to build the dam would have swelled the size and strength of the private sector and placed in Egypt some of the most energetic and politically powerful multinationals of the era. On the British side, in addition to English Electric, were George Wimpey and Company and British Insulated Callendar's Cables Ltd, both of which were also involved in maintaining the Suez Canal base. The French and German firms were equally powerful financially and politically. It is conceivable that these firms might have been interested in participating in other parts of Egypt's development effort.

The contract was not signed, however, and from mid-1955 the World Bank and its dynamic director, Eugene Black, assumed the lead role for Western interests. Although the consortium remained active, Western negotiations passed through World Bank offices. Black brought a cautious and suspicious attitude to the discussions. In his view, the chief development officials of the Egyptian government lacked fiscal and economic realism—traits that Black believed the World Bank could offer Egypt.[25] Although Black and the bank's technical experts regarded the project as "a thoroughly sound engineering proposition but also a pretty promising economic proposition provided that Egypt is prepared to apply to herself the discipline and austerity that will be necessary if it is to be carried out efficiently and without galloping inflation," they also stressed its vast scope[26] To the British, the bank officials said that "Saad el-Aali is the

[24] Draft Cabinet Paper, Note by the Chancellor of the Exchequer, Aswan Dam, November 1, 1955, PRO FO 371/113737 JE1423/184.

[25] M. T. Flett, British Embassy, Washington, to A. K. Potter, May 18, 1955, PRO FO 371/113733 JE1423/86.

[26] M. T. Flett to Armstrong, July 28, 1955, PRO FO 371/113735 JE1423/18.

largest single project ever to be undertaken in Egypt. It is the largest single project which the Bank has ever been asked to consider. It ranks among the major development projects in the world."[27] Black estimated that the final price tag would be at least double the Egyptian estimate of £E200 million. The first stage, he believed, would cost at least £330 while the whole project was unlikely to cost less than £470 million.[28] Black's trepidation was that an overambitious and inexperienced Egyptian government would attempt too many things at once. It would rearm itself at a high level of readiness and undertake the dam. Inflation would overwhelm the country, bringing great suffering to the people.

Bold political departures in September 1955 caused American and British diplomats as well as World Bank officials to suppress their reservations. Not only did the Egyptians sign an arms agreement with the Czechs in September of that year, but they also intimated that the Soviets were interested in aiding the Aswan project and promoting the general economic development of Egypt.[29] In Britain, Prime Minister Anthony Eden fixated on the Aswan dam project as the key to stemming the advance of communism into Africa.[30] Despite continuing skepticism about Egypt's creditworthiness and doubts about the willingness of the Egyptians to strengthen their ties with the West, the Americans, the British, and the World Bank agreed in December 1955 to approach the Egyptian government with a proposal for financing the construction of the dam.

According to the terms of the proposal, the United Kingdom would contribute £5.5 million as well as sterling releases of £5 million in 1955, £10 million per year from 1956 to 1962, and the balance in 1963. The United States would contribute $54.6 million. All funds for the project were to come to the Egyptian government through the World Bank in the form of a $200 million loan. The agreement was contingent on the government of Egypt's accepting a letter of intent that would impose economic restraints on the Egyptian government. The Egyptians would be required to give economic priority to the dam project, ensuring that hard currency was always available for the prompt repayment of the loan and allowing the bank to determine what additional development expenditures the Egyptian government could undertake.[31] For a new, inherently resentful nationalist government, having just recently negotiated the

[27] M. T. Flett to Armstrong, July 28, 1955, PRO FO 371/113735 JE1423/18.

[28] Minutes of Meeting at the Board of Trade between Mackenzie and D. Betts, September 16, 1955, PRO FO 371/113735 JE1423/139.

[29] H. Trevelyan to T. E. Bromley, October 13, 1955, PRO FO 371/113736 JE1423/152.

[30] Shuckburgh, Foreign Office Note, November 28, 1955, PRO FO 371/113738 JE1423/253; C. B. Reynolds, Board of Trade, to T. E. Bromley, Foreign Office, November 25, 1955, PRO FO 371/113739 JE 1423/268.

[31] No. 1139, Dulles to U.S. Embassy, Cairo, December 2, 1955, USNA 874.2614/11-3055; no. 3116, R. Makins to Foreign Office, December 17, 1955, PRO FO 371/113741 JE1423/337.

evacuation of an army of occupation and ever vigilant to preserve its national integrity, these arrangements implied a new form of imperial subordination.[32]

No encounter was more fateful to the Aswan dam scheme and Western-Egyptian relations than Black's meeting with Nasser on January 28, 1956. Black was mindful of Egyptian nationalist sensitivities and sought to modify the letter of intent. He agreed to allow the Egyptian government a free hand in managing its economy. The bank loan itself, as distinct from the U.S. and British government loans, would come on line only when and if needed. As long as the bank's financing was not required, the bank would exercise no supervision of the Egyptian economy. Although this was a substantial concession, it did not impress the Egyptian president. As he later recounted, he could not remove from his mind the image of Ferdinand de Lesseps, who in Nasser's opinion, had spoliated the Egyptians by extracting a one-sided concession for the construction of the Suez Canal. Nasser could not dispel the thought that an agreement with the World Bank would bring about the recolonization of his country at the hands of Western financial groups. Nor could Nasser forget the Egyptian historical record, recalling how dual British-French control over the Egyptian Ministries of Finance and Public Works in the 1870s had been the prelude to the British occupation. Imperialist memories were altogether too fresh to enable Nasser to believe that a new era of changed relationships was finally in the offing.

By March 1956 British and American diplomats had also changed their minds about the high dam. They had decided against the financing, though they had not yet determined whether to inform the Egyptians of their decision or simply to allow the discussions to come to a slow and inconclusive end. The British were increasingly angered at the vitriolic, anti-British propaganda spewing forth from Voice of the Arabs radio and the Egyptian press. To Anthony Eden the climactic moment arrived when King Husayn of Jordan dismissed Glubb Pasha as commanding general of the Arab Legion. In Eden's mind the dismissal stemmed directly from Nasser's propagandistic outburst against the Jordanian ruling elite and his avowal of pan-Arab, anti-imperialist feelings in Jordan and indeed throughout the entire Arab world.[33] Although the United States did not consult with Britain on the final decision to withdraw Western aid for the high dam, the two countries had been in step at every stage up to the final moment.

[32] See Ambassador Byroade's description of the mood of the Egyptian leadership at this time in no. 1214, Byroade to Secretary of State, December 29, 1955, USNA 874.2614/12–2955; see also no. 2, H. Trevelyan to Foreign Office, January 1, 1956, PRO FO 371/119046 JE1422/3.

[33] Anthony Nutting, *No End of a Lesson: The Story of Suez* (London, 1967), pp. 17 and 32–35.

The U.S. reversal on Aswan was a longer and more complex affair. The Americans grew increasingly disenchanted with Nasser's espousal of neutralism, which, to the mind of many in the State Department, was little more than alignment with the Soviet Union. Nasser's recognition of Red China irked the Americans. Egyptian opposition to the Baghdad pact (a defensive military alliance of Britain, Iran, Iraq, Pakistan, and Turkey), which, in the absence of an Egypt-centered defensive alliance in the Middle East, became the linch-pin of Western containment of Soviet expansionism in the area, was a constant irritant to the Americans. Project Alpha, a secret and unsuccessful effort to bring about an Egyptian-Israeli accommodation, involved exchanging land for Egyptian recognition of the state of Israel. And American diplomats could not disregard more practical concerns, as well. By 1956, with the pro-Israeli and cotton lobbies lined up against Egypt, the prospect of obtaining the necessary funds from the U.S. Congress was dimming.[34] American technical experts continued to be skeptical of Egypt's financial capacity to achieve the full dam program and warned the political officers in the State Department that an increasingly impoverished and discontented Egyptian population would blame the West for its unhappiness. All of these factors converged to persuade Secretary of State John Foster Dulles and his staff at the State Department to rule against Western participation.

In a memorandum entitled Omega, Dulles presented the new policy to President Dwight D. Eisenhower on March 28, 1956. According to the memorandum, the goal of U.S. policy was "to let Col. Nasser realize that he cannot cooperate as he is doing with the Soviet Union and at the same time enjoy most favored nation treatment with the United States." Yet the Americans did not want an open breach with Nasser that would throw Egypt into "a Soviet satellite status." They preferred to leave "a bridge" back to good relations with the West.[35]

At first the Americans and the British (who had made a similar decision at a cabinet meeting on March 21) made no formal statement of a change in policy. But when Dulles learned that Egypt's ambassador to Washington, Ahmad Husayn, would be arriving with instructions from Nasser to accept all of the Western conditions, as outlined in the earlier aide-mémoire and letter of intent, he decided to forgo the policy of dissimulation and to announce that the West was no longer willing to finance the dam. In the meeting between Dulles and Ahmad Husayn, the U.S. secretary of state claimed that the West was withdrawing its offer because it had concluded that the project was too big for the Egyptians.

[34] William J. Burns, *Economic Aid and American Policy toward Egypt, 1955–1981* (Albany, N.Y., 1985), p. 78.

[35] Dulles, Memorandum for the President, March 28, 1956, Dulles Papers in the Eisenhower Library, Subject Series, box 10, file: Israeli Relations (3).

Privately, Dulles had decided to make an example of the Egyptians and to show others the heavy price to be paid for moving too close to the Soviet Union.[36]

Just what was on the mind of Nasser when he dispatched his ambassador with instructions to accept the Western offer has never been entirely clear. Before Ahmad Husayn's departure a headline in *al-Ahram* announced that the Western powers had agreed to finance the high dam.[37] Gamal Salim, the free officer who had worked the most ardently for the deal, believed that a compromise was in the offing.[38] In later accounts, however, Nasser claimed to have known in advance of the U.S. decision to withdraw the offer and instructed his ambassador to accept the terms.[39] At the least, the Egyptian leader must have wanted closure on the West's interest in the Aswan High Dam, because the project had been in a state of preparation for four years. Also likely was Nasser's conclusion, given his close consultation with Western diplomats in Cairo, that a chilling of the West toward his country was occurring.

No doubt Nasser had given thought to what actions Egypt might take if Western assistance were not forthcoming. Given that the entire four years of Egyptian military rule had been fraught with near ultimatums and contingency plans, the Egyptian ruler was not facing a new dilemma. But he could hardly have anticipated (unless his intelligence network was far more proficient than anyone has realized) that Dulles would provide him with such a decisive rupture. Previously the Americans and the British had used a variety of delaying tactics, insisting that there must be a prior Nile waters agreement with the Sudan or citing parliamentary and congressional difficulties.

Even while Nasser was preparing his dramatic riposte to the Western rejection (which was intended as a humiliation to Egypt and was seen as such), the Western diplomats readied themselves for the Egyptian response. In Britain, where Anthony Eden was receiving secret MI6 reports of Nasser's growing subservience to the Russians and the rise of dissident elements in the army, covert plans to unseat Nasser were going forward.[40] The Americans believed that Nasser might retaliate by expelling the Point Four mission that provided technical assistance to Egypt. The French

---

[36] G. V. Allen, Memorandum, July 19, 1956, USNA 874.2614/7–1956.

[37] *al-Ahram*, July 18, 1956.

[38] No. 63, Byroade to Secretary of State, July 12, 1956, USNA 874.2614/7–1056.

[39] See, in particular, Mohamed Heikal, *The Cairo Documents: The Inside Story of Nasser and His Relationship with World Leaders, Rebels, and Statesmen* (London, 1973), pp. 64–69.

[40] A. D. M. Ross, Foreign Office, July 21, 1956 PRO FO 371/119058 JE1422/291; Keith Kyle, "Britain and the Crisis, 1955–56," in *Suez 1956: The Crisis and Its Consequences*, ed. William Roger Louis and Roger Owen (Oxford, 1989), p. 109; and W. Scott Lucas, *Divided We Stand: Britain, the United States, and the Suez Crisis* (London, 1991), pp. 101–3.

ambassador in Washington opined that Nasser was likely to make life difficult for the foreign business community operating in Egypt.[41] What was surprising was that none of these observers anticipated Nasser's next move—the nationalization of the Suez Canal Company—despite the fact that this action had been a constant subject of concern in British, French, and U.S. diplomatic and business discussions since the end of World War II.

AHMAD ABBUD AND THE SEQUESTRATION WEAPON

The Egyptian government had thus far used sequestration sparingly, other than during the two world wars when it had been used against enemy properties. It was to be used to great effect, however, following the British-French and Israeli invasion in 1956 and often after that. There were some ominous harbingers of this tactic before 1956, however. The military first sequestered a business firm in August 1952 when the government took over the defunct and bankrupt Egyptian Delta Light Railways Company.[42] Subsequently, various bus and transportation companies were threatened with sequestration unless they improved the quality of their services.[43] But it was the sequestration of Ahmad Abbud's Egyptian Sugar Company, one of the most heavily capitalized and long-standing firms in the private sector and a company connected to powerful, mostly French foreign financial interests, that seemed to mark a dramatic departure from previous practice in Egypt. To many in the business community, the government's explanations notwithstanding, the action was viewed as a threat to business autonomy.

Not surprisingly, the local businessman with whom the military had the most conflictual relationship was Ahmad Abbud. Abbud's streak of independence and his favor with Western business and political groups often grated on Egypt's military autocrats. His buoyant self-confidence and belief that he could be the master of any political situation aroused the antagonism of those military men who were by nature and early training suspicious of the arrogance of the business community. Though Abbud never stated so openly, in private he informed Western friends that he was in full control of the new military regime and had appointed many of its members secretly to his boards. His larger-than-life behavior in Egypt and his insinuation that the Egyptian rulers desperately needed his entrepreneurial skills intensified resentment against him.

[41] Memorandum of Conversation on Aswan Dam, July 25, 1956, USNA 874.2614/7–2556.

[42] *al-Ahram*, February 28, and March 7, 1953, and March 1, 1954.

[43] Commercial Secretary, Cairo, to Africa Department, January 23, 1954, PRO FO 371/108509.

Abbud's cluster of companies in the 1950s included the Egyptian Sugar Company, the Egyptian Fertilizer Company at Suez, the Khedivial Mail Line, and the Nouzha Spinning and Weaving Company. In addition, he sat on the boards of numerous other firms, including the Suez Canal Company, albeit briefly, and Bank Misr. Unlike the Misr firms, which were financially involved in the support of many mixed enterprises, the Abbud firms made few financial contributions to the major development projects sponsored by the military regime. The weak link in the Abbud business empire, however, was the Sugar Company, which since the end of World War II had been engaged in ongoing disputes with the Egyptian government. Their differences arose over the back payment of taxes and the division of wartime profits between the firm and the state. In the latter days of civilian rule the government had pressed the Sugar Company for payments totaling £E5 million; the military regime did the same.[44]

Abbud's economic empire was a tightly connected and interwoven structure. It was well known that profits appeared on the balance sheets of the companies most closely administered by Abbud himself, while firms whose stock was widely dispersed, like the Sugar Company's, showed few profits and made meager dividend payments.[45] Few outsiders were able to gain detailed knowledge of the Abbud companies, but several business experts believed that action against any one enterprise would threaten the entire structure. The U.S. consul general at Alexandria believed that Abbud's "corporate pyramid . . . is so delicately balanced an affair that it cannot withstand any severe shock." For this reason the ongoing dispute with the government was not merely a danger to the Sugar Company but a "threat to the entire business structure, even, in fact, jeopardizing Abbud's ability to raise external loans for new enterprises."[46] And the Egyptian government was not Abbud's only critic. Some of the shareholders of the Egyptian Sugar Company, many of whom resided in Egypt and attended the annual shareholder meetings, began to criticize his handling of company affairs. At annual meetings in 1953 and 1954 they took the unusual step of articulating their grievances publicly, claiming that in spite of a large and increasing production and growing sales the company's profits were minuscule and the dividends derisory.[47]

In 1955 the firm and the government agreed to submit their dispute to arbitration. When the company refused to carry out the arbiter's finding to pay the government £E5 million plus interest and to increase dividend

---

[44] *al-Ahram*, August 23 and October 8, 1952.

[45] No. 1011/62/52G, Chancery to Foreign Office, July 7, 1952, PRO FO 371/90876.

[46] Donald Edgar, Consul General at Alexandria, to Robert M. Carr, Counselor for Economic Affairs, August 18, 1955, USNA RG84, Cairo Embassy, General Records, box 266.

[47] *al-Ahram*, February 28 and March 7, 1953, and March 1, 1954.

payments to its shareholders, the government felt justified in intervening. It placed the company under sequestration.[48]

To reassure the business world, the government explained that its action was calculated to strengthen the private sector rather than undermine it and even to preserve Abbud's economic activities rather than diminish them. Given the fact that Abbud's economic structure was tightly interwoven, that some shareholders of the firm were disgruntled and even openly rebellious, and that the arbitration ruling, if carried out, would have an impact on all of Abbud's holdings, the government's decision to remove this apparent albatross from Abbud's neck could easily be regarded as Abbud's salvation. Just a month after the sequestration the Egyptian government endorsed Abbud's request for a $6 million loan from the Export-Import Bank to finance the purchase of American equipment for a new paper factory.[49]

Government spokespersons continued to claim that its sequestration order had been a specific response to unusual circumstances and did not constitute a precedent.[50] Arguing that the company had forfeited the faith of the public as well as its shareholders, the government agents pointed to the company's inefficient administrative record and its failure to hold shareholder meetings for two years. The government both assured the Egyptian investing public that it had intervened to buttress the rest of Egypt's private sector and insisted that the company would soon be returned to private hands. Within months of the sequestration, the government compensated the company's foreign investors and those local investors who opted for compensation. It reissued stock to Egyptian shareholders who wished to retain their investment in the reorganized company. To be sure, the government had rid the company of all of its foreign investors and, in the process, had become the firm's majority shareholder. Yet like many other business organizations in Egypt in 1956, the Sugar Company was a mixed public and private enterprise.

Most observers seeking to explain the 1956 nationalizations and Egyptianizations have stressed the regime's disappointment at the scant sums of new foreign capital that were being invested in the Egyptian economy during the four years following the military takeover. Certainly, the military men had reason to be disappointed by the tepid response of foreign investors to their efforts to amend the laws pertaining to joint stock companies and their open appeals to foreign firms to favor the Egyptian economy with their funds. But the lack of high levels of investment was only the most visible irritant between foreign capital and the Egyptian state.

[48] *Egyptian Gazette*, August 26, 1955.

[49] No. 267, Fitzgerald to Department of State, September 6, 1955, USNA 874.053/9–655.

[50] This also was the editorial opinion of *al-Ahram*, August 26, 1955.

The day-to-day relationships between the most powerful foreign firms and the Egyptian government bureaucrats produced countless examples of distrust and mutual recrimination.

The reality was that the firms and the state had completely different perspectives on the role of business in Egypt. The business concerns used the traditional criteria of profitability and safety to decide on their investments. They naturally shied away from many of the large-scale projects that were close to the heart of the Egyptian rulers. In contrast, the military men were not merely enamored of large projects for themselves and for the legitimacy they might bring to the ruling faction. They felt a desperate urge, motivated by their desire to stay in power, to jolt the Egyptian economy into forward motion. They believed that this could be accomplished only through profound structural change. They concluded that if the business community was unwilling to play a lead role in this effort then the state must. These tensions were in the foreground when Dulles decided to withdraw Western financial support for the high dam project. Nasser countered by nationalizing the Suez Canal Company. That these dramatic and provocative actions would produce profound repercussions throughout the private sector went without saying. That they would result in the dismantling of British, French, and Jewish capital, however, stemmed directly from the British, French, and Israeli invasion of Egypt.

CHAPTER 4

The Rupture, 1956–1961

THE SUEZ WAR of 1956 is an oft-told story. A legion of scholars has pored over the newly opened British and U.S. diplomatic archives, leaving, so it would seem, little to add.[1] Yet, the economic dimensions of the story have received scant attention despite the fact that for Anglo-Egyptian relations and especially the evolution of the Egyptian private sector the consequences were profound. The Suez invasion turned the regime's ambivalence toward British and French capital into enmity and led to the expulsion from Egypt of large numbers of British and French nationals and Jews, whose involvement in private business was indispensable at the time. In addition, this action had an even more profound impact than anyone at the time could have anticipated, for it set in motion an anticapitalist thrust that led inexorably to the expropriation of Egyptian capital.

The events and decisions that occurred in Egypt in the relatively short span of three months from November 1956 to the end of January 1957 proved altogether decisive in the evolution of the Egyptian private sector. The Egyptian business community never recovered from the blows administered during these months. This is not to suggest an *histoire événementielle* explanation for the vast differences that ultimately separated the private sectors of Egypt, Nigeria, and Kenya in 1960. Quite the contrary, this short period saw the eruption of long-pent-up aspirations and the working out of national and imperial logics. The Egyptians saw the invasion as proof that colonialism was not in retreat and that the British were prepared to use all of their instruments of power, economic as well as military, to reassert themselves in the Middle East. The British countenanced the invasion in order to reassert imperial greatness, spurred on by a conservative right wing and a small cabal of ministers who allowed themselves to lose touch with national and international realities.

Recent scholarly accounts have paid insufficient attention to the Egyp-

[1] It is impossible to list all of the books and articles that have dealt with the British-French-Israeli invasion of Egypt, or for that matter to identify those that have been most important in my thinking about the topic. On the international aspects of the Suez crisis one might consult Peter Hahn, *The United States, Great Britain, and Egypt, 1945–1956: Strategy and Diplomacy in the Early Cold War* (Chapel Hill, N.C., 1991); Diane B. Kunz, *The Economic Diplomacy of the Suez Crisis* (Chapel Hill, N.C., 1991); and William Roger Louis and Roger Owen, eds., *Suez 1956: The Crisis and Its Consequences* (Oxford, 1989).

tian side of the story. To be sure, Egyptian archives remain sealed; hence the Egyptian perspective lacks immediacy, derived, as it is, from less intimate, more tailored memoirs and public statements. But a different narrative emerges if one places economics and Egypt at the center of the account.

Whether Nasser had planned for some time to nationalize the Suez Canal Company or had responded in a fit of anger to Dulles's challenge may never be known.[2] Nasser took few individuals into his confidence. Only days before the announcement did he begin to consult. What was clear throughout, however, was his purposeful, shrewd, and cautious approach to peril. Nasser offered no provocation to his antagonists after the nationalization. The announcement itself, made in a flamboyant and sometimes demagogic speech at Alexandria on July 26, was nonetheless exquisitely timed. Although he gave the speech on the fourth anniversary of the military takeover, thus suggesting a preoccupation with politics, Nasser chose the correct financial moment. Just the day before, Egypt had collected £E2.5 million from the Suez Canal Company in taxes and royalties, and a few days earlier it had deposited in the National Bank of Egypt the company's check for £E10 million as a first installment on the agreement of May 30, 1956.[3]

Nasser knew that the nationalization decree would outrage Western business and diplomatic circles. He expected the French to agitate for a military confrontation and the British to be tempted. He counted on the Americans to exercise restraint. The maximum danger period, in his view, was the first few weeks, while Western opinion was most excited. If Egypt could survive those weeks, he expected cooler heads to prevail and the chances for a peaceful resolution to increase. He did not foresee hostilities occurring after two months, by which time he was confident that the military option would have been discarded. The Egyptian president was enormously cheered when Egyptian military intelligence accurately informed him that the British had no large naval and landing forces in the eastern Mediterranean and would therefore need a full two months to mount an invasion of the country. Nasser discounted the possibility that the British and the French would join with Israel to attack Egypt, given the opprobrium that such an alliance would bring on them throughout the Middle East.

The Israelis, on the other hand, might launch their own preemptive military strike. Nasser believed that the Egyptian army could defend the

---

[2] In an article in *Akhir Sa'a*, August 15, 1956, Muhammad Hasanayn Haykal claimed that Egypt had been planning to nationalize the Suez Canal Company for some time and that the Egyptian government had learned of efforts on the part of the British government and the oil conglomerates to force a twenty-year extension of the concession on Egypt.

[3] Francis Wylie to J. H. A. Watson, May 17, 1957, PRO FO 371/125531 JE 1425/95.

country.[4] Even moments before the invasion Nasser continued to rule out a British-French-Israeli attack. He refused to believe reports from Egyptian military attachés in Paris and Ankara warning of an impending attack—despite the fact that the information from Paris had a high probability of accuracy since members of an active Jewish community residing there had obtained it secretly through their access to French military circles.[5]

Although Nasser thought military action unlikely, he expected economic warfare of savage intensity. He took steps to prepare Egypt. Days before the nationalization, he instructed his minister of economy and finance to move government assets out of American-, British-, and French-controlled banks and into banks of other countries.[6] Unfortunately, not all of these transactions had been consummated by July 26. Realizing that the Suez Canal Company would offer a stiff challenge and was likely to withdraw its non-Egyptian employees from the country, the nationalization act stipulated that the former employees of the Suez Canal Company automatically became employees of the new Egyptian Canal Authority. If they failed to obey its rulings, they were subject to imprisonment and could be stripped of their jobs and pensions.[7] The Egyptian government also prohibited the export of merchandise, including cotton, to Britain and France once the British and French governments had frozen Egyptian accounts in their countries. Thus, the economic warfare that had been so often threatened between Egypt and Britain, and even occasionally waged between 1951 and 1956, had finally become a reality.

On July 30, 1956, the Egyptian government took a census of British and French companies in the country—a census that demonstrated what earlier studies indicated: that Britain and France had far more to lose financially than Egypt in an economic contest.[8] The census should have alerted British and French officials to the possibility that the Egyptian government might, at any moment, retaliate against its economic adversaries by expropriating their enterprises.

The final element of Nasser's strategy was a demonstration of Egyptian competence in the handling of canal affairs. To this end, the Egyptian leaders selected a skilled team of Egyptian officials to administer the new Egyptian Canal Authority. Muhammad Hilmi Bahgat Badawi, former minister of commerce and industry, occupied the top executive position.

---

[4] The best account of Nasser's thinking in this period is to be found in Mohamed H. Heikal, *The Cairo Documents: The Inside Story of Nasser and His Relationship with World Leaders, Rebels, and Statesmen* (London, 1973), pp. 64–69.

[5] Ahmad Hamrush, *Qissa Thawra 23 Yulio* (Cairo, 1974), vol. 4, p. 164, and vol. 5, pp. 39–40.

[6] Abd al-Latif al-Baghdadi, *Mudhakkirat* (Cairo, 1977), vol. 1, pp. 31 ff.

[7] K. J. Hurd to A. Greenhough, July 31, 1956, PRO FO 371/119093 JE 14211/445.

[8] *L'Observateur*, July 30, 1956.

He had been an Egyptian government director of the old Suez Canal Company and was respected in Western business circles. The general manager of the authority was Muhammad Yunis, a military engineer and general economic troubleshooter for the Revolutionary Command Council. Outside observers considered Yunis "Westernized and competent." The remaining directors were equally noted for their abilities and the orthodoxy of their economic ideas. The only troubling appointment was Mustafa al-Hifnawi, whom the British described as "the self-appointed tormentor of the Canal Company."[9]

Nasser instructed this able team of administrators to be conciliatory in dealing with shippers. Although Egypt had nationalized the Suez Canal Company for the purpose of capturing its revenues, the Egyptian Canal Authority permitted shippers, if they chose, to make toll payments in London and Paris rather than Egypt. Between July 26 and October 30, approximately 60 percent of the transit dues were paid into the accounts of the old Suez Canal Company outside of Egypt, and the Egyptian government made no formal complaint about the payments.[10] Finally, from the outset, the Egyptian government indicated its intention to compensate the company's shareholders. Its first proposals, though far from satisfactory, were clearly intended to open the negotiating process. While agreeing that shareholders should be compensated at the value of the shares on July 26, worth £70 million at that time, the government pointed out that the company had liquid reserves of £62 million. Thus, in the view of the Egyptian government, the shareholders were owed a mere £8 million.[11]

As Nasser anticipated, Western censure of the nationalization was immediate and vociferous. In the House of Commons, Hugh Gaitskell of the opposition Labour Party demanded that the Conservative Party develop plans to force Nasser to rescind his nationalization decree. Chancellor of the Exchequer Harold Macmillan underscored Britain's alarm when he told Dulles in a meeting on August 1 that if Britain let Nasser's action stand "Britain would be finished as a world power. . . . [The nationalization] jeopardized Britain's entire position in the Middle East."[12] Within a day of the decree, Anthony Eden, the prime minister, established a small steering committee of leading cabinet members, called the Egypt Committee, to develop policy for the crisis. The Egypt Committee, consisting of the prime minister, the lord president, the chancellor of the exchequer, the foreign secretary, the commonwealth secretary, and the minister of defense, was to meet in secrecy. The secretaries of the committee were Norman Brook and H. O. Hooper, and other interested officials were to

---

[9] Chancery to Foreign Office, August 6, 1956, PRO FO 371/119103 JE14211/729.
[10] Note of a Tripartite Meeting, August 24, 1956, PRO FO 371/118946 JE1119/83.
[11] al-Ahram, July 28, 1956; Egyptian Gazette, July 28, 1956.
[12] Memorandum of Conversation, August 1, 1956, USNA 974.7301.

be invited to attend when needed. It was expected that the first lord of the admiralty and the secretary of state for air would be brought into the meetings on a regular basis. The Egypt Committee immediately began to evaluate military options.[13]

French officials made immediate contact with the British and expressed their interest in coordinating a policy to undermine Nasser. The Egyptian leader had become a thorn in the side of French diplomats and statesmen who held Nasser responsible for inciting the Algerian revolt. On July 30, the French ambassador in London indicated to the British that the French "were ready to go all the way with us. They were prepared to put French forces under British command if this were necessary, and they contemplated making land and air forces available as well as naval forces."[14] The ambassador's position was precisely that of the French foreign secretary, Christian Pineau, who the day before had informed Selwyn Lloyd that the French government was ready to go with Britain "to the end in dealing with Nasser. The question for them was not only of the Middle East but also of Algeria. They would associate fully with the United Kingdom in all measures including the military."[15]

Although Britain and France contemplated a military response from the start, the Americans, as Nasser predicted, adopted a more cautious approach. Their officials expressed grave reservations about the use of force. Completely opposed to the military option was the American ambassador in Cairo, Henry Byroade, well known for his sympathies toward Nasser. He immediately cabled, advising against any participation in British military planning. He predicted that even tacitly condoning an armed response would be "heavily counterproductive to United States long-term and immediate interests throughout Arab countries or Near East."[16] Byroade opposed even the use of economic sanctions against Egypt, having embraced Nasser's argument that Egypt was legally entitled to nationalize the Suez Canal Company.

At home, the U.S. government did not reject the policies of its major allies as forcefully as Byroade wished. Yet on August 1, while emotions were running high, Eisenhower counseled his British colleagues to be moderate. In a personal letter to Eden, he favored exhausting other possibilities before employing force. Coercion should not be used, he insisted, "merely to protect national or individual investors."[17] Eden's reply left little doubt that Britain's policy toward Egypt would have less to do with the Suez Canal than with Nasser. "The primary object [of British pol-

[13] Cabinet Office Document, July 28, 1956, Norman Brook, PRO PREM 11/1089 13.

[14] Foreign Office Minute, July 30, 1956, PRO FO 371/19078 JE14211/36.

[15] Record of Conversation between Secretary of State and M. Pineau, July 29, 1956, PRO FO 371/119081 JE14211/124.

[16] No. 157, Byroade to Secretary of State, July 27, 1956, USNA 974.7301.

[17] No. 3479, Eisenhower to Eden, August 1, 1956 PRO FO 371/119083 JE14211/196.

icy]," he wrote, "was to undercut what Nasser has done and to set up an international regime in the canal. But this is not all. Nasser has embarked on a course which is unpleasantly familiar. His seizure of the canal was undoubtedly designed to impress opinion not only in Egypt but in the Arab world and in all Africa too. The removal of Nasser and the installation in Egypt of a regime less hostile to the West must therefore rank high among our objectives."[18]

Nasser's belief that Egypt would face heavy economic and financial pressure from Western governments and Western business interests was entirely correct. Most of the business pressure came from expected sources, notably the Suez Canal Company and the oil firms with interests in the Middle East. Other firms and business pressure groups bided their time, awaiting the outcome of government-to-government negotiations. As Nasser anticipated, the nationalized Suez Canal Company used all of its vast political influence to counteract its seizure. Company spokespersons argued that the nationalization decree was not valid because the company was not an Egyptian firm but enjoyed an international status. In addition, its representatives pointed out that the concession had another twelve years to run. The latter arguments, though frequently heard in public debate, were given little credence in the confidential British, French, and American diplomatic discussions, where the legality of the Egyptian takeover was conceded. Western diplomats did, however, question the willingness and capacity of the Egyptian government to ensure free access to the canal for shippers of all nationalities as guaranteed by the Constantinople Convention of 1888.

But the Suez Canal Company sought nothing less than total economic warfare and welcomed the prospect of full-scale military conflict. At the first full board meeting following the nationalization, the French directors took a hard line. Recognizing the likelihood that "whatever the outcome of the dispute with Egypt might be, nothing can be the same as before," the French directors sought confrontation with the Nasser regime.[19] The immediate repatriation of the company's non-Egyptian staff, they believed, would so severely disrupt canal traffic that it would compel the European powers to intervene militarily. To their consternation, the French directors failed to win the support of the other members of the board. The British government required its officials to oppose the plan and pressured other board members to do the same.[20] At this crucial meeting, the Suez Canal Company board decided to instruct its non-Egyptian personnel to obey the orders of the Egyptian government while registering their loyalty to the company with their consular representa-

[18] Eden to Eisenhower, August 1, 1956, PRO FO 371/119083 JE13211/196.

[19] F. Wylie to J. H. A. Watson, August 7, 1956, PRO FO 371/119099 JE14211/604.

[20] C. W. Ramsden, Foreign Office Minute, August 4, 1956, PRO FO 371/119099 JE14211/601.

tives. They were also expected to indicate their ultimate intention to leave Egypt if the dispute were not resolved.[21] The French directors were so incensed at this action that they insisted that their opposition be noted in the Foreign Office record.[22]

The company believed that its most potent weapon was its capacity to create chaos at the canal by withdrawing its non-Egyptian employees. In everyone's view, the crucial employees were the pilots who guided ships through the canal. According to an August 15 estimate, of the 160 pilots, seventy were British and French. They were expected to leave if asked to do so by the company.[23] By mid-September the Canal Authority had increased the number of non-British and non-French pilots only to ninety-seven, most of whom were Egyptian nationals. Yet fifty-three of these men were still in training. Only three of the forty-four experienced pilots were qualified to take large tankers through the canal. The company directors believed that the Canal Authority would be unable to handle more than forty ships a day if the non-Egyptian pilots left, and even at that reduced number, serious traffic problems could not be averted.[24] The total number of foreign employees in the service of the Canal Authority was 352, of whom 159 were French, 105 British, 37 German, 9 Italian, 8 Yugoslav, 8 Dutch, 5 Lebanese, 5 Norwegian, 3 Danish, 2 Swiss, 2 American, 1 Swedish, 1 Belgian, 1 Polish, and 6 of other nationalities. Of this group 169 were housed at Port Said and Port Fuad, 140 at Ismailia, 39 at Port Tewfiq, and 4 in Cairo.[25] The consensus, save among Egyptian authorities, was that without these employees the canal would cease to function and economic dislocations would occur in Europe as the states there experienced shortages of vital raw materials. The Suez Canal Company agreed to postpone its withdrawal of foreign personnel in order to allow Robert Menzies, prime minister of Australia, time to conduct negotiations with Nasser in Cairo. But it made clear that if the Menzies mission failed it would be free to withdraw its personnel. In anticipation of the failure, the company advised its employees to prepare for departure on or before September 15. As inducement, it promised to pay employees indemnities and pensions. If they remained, however, the company would strike their names from the firm's books.[26] Not surprisingly, a large number of employees left Egypt on or shortly after September 15. Yet, to the

[21] G. Jebb to Foreign Office, August 4, 1956, PRO FO 371/119086 JE14211/22.

[22] C. W. Ramsden, Foreign Office Minute, August 4, 1956, PRO FO 371/119099 JE14211/601.

[23] No. 34, Consul, Ismailia, to Foreign Office, August 15, 1956, PRO FO 371/119108 JE14211/833.

[24] Ibid., September 14, 1956, PRO FO 371/119137 JE14211/1628.

[25] No. 327, G. Jebb to Foreign Office, August 29, 1956, PRO FO 371/119120 JE14211/1177.

[26] No. 49, Consul, Ismailia, to Foreign Office, September 2, 1956, PRO FO 371/119123 JE14211/1250.

astonishment of outside observers, the new Canal Authority weathered the storm. During the first week after the departure of the non-Egyptian employees the authority handled a full complement of ships. As the staff of the Canal Authority gained experience and recruited more pilots, the danger of serious mishaps diminished.

The only other significant business group to respond aggressively to Nasser's nationalization were the oil companies possessing economic interests in the Middle East. They viewed Nasser's *démarche*, coming as it did a mere five years after the largely unsuccessful but still troublesome nationalization of the Anglo-Iranian Oil Company, as a harbinger of other anticapitalist actions in the region. They took up cudgels against Nasser and became self-appointed representatives of the larger business world. John Case of Socony Mobil, James T. Duse and Harold Minor of Aramco, and Howard Page of Standard Oil were active on the American side, and they were ably seconded in Britain by J. H. Loudon and Rodney Searight of Shell Oil. The oil companies viewed the nationalization decree with a dread approaching mania, certain were they that this unprincipled grab would endanger all Western businesses in the region. Their eagerness to stymie Nasser included support for the military option.

On August 1, just four days after the nationalization edict, Socony-Vacuum dispatched a high-powered delegation consisting of John Case, a vice president; Austin Foster, general counsel; and Rear Admiral (ret.) Thomas Kelly to the Department of State. They sought advice on where to pay canal transit tolls and indicated their displeasure with any recognition of the nationalization. Case worried about "the irresponsible governments who believed that they could nationalize at will. He complained about the nationalization of Anglo-Iranian Oil and argued that a stop must be put to this trend." The Department of State countered with the remark that little could be done at this juncture because Nasser had violated no law.[27] At a follow-up meeting a week later, Case continued to warn about "a whole series of adverse developments affecting Western interests in the Middle East and elsewhere."[28] On the same day, Aramco representatives meeting at the State Department expressed concern about "possible violence to the Persian Gulf area" spilling over from Egypt.[29]

The first full-scale meeting of oil officials at the British Foreign Office did not occur until August 20. On that occasion Rodney Searight and J. P. Berkin of Shell argued that recognition of the nationalization "would enormously increase the dangers to which notably the oil and pipeline concessionary companies of the Middle East are already exposed in their

---

[27] Memorandum of Conversation on Nationalization of the Suez Canal Company, August 1, 1956, USNA 974.7301.

[28] Memorandum of Conversation on Suez Canal, August 9, 1956, USNA 947.7301.

[29] Ibid.

arrangements as commercial utilities . . . confronted by sovereign states." The oil men proposed the creation of an international body to acquire the Suez Canal Company's assets and to administer the canal.[30] Searight and Berkin were supported by George Parker of Esso, Howard Page of Standard Oil, and J. H. Loudon of Shell; these grandees of the oil conglomerates claimed to be speaking on behalf of shipping and importing firms and to be profoundly troubled by the imminent prospect of an interruption of canal traffic.[31] With military action no longer an option, they reoriented their thinking toward a massive buyout of the Egyptian government. Loudon, for one, believed that the Egyptian government could be induced "to forgo the political fruits of nationalization in return for substantial benefits both immediate and long-term."[32] The oil and shipping barons were convinced that a payment of £150 to £175 million would tempt Nasser to abrogate the nationalization act and create an international authority to run the canal.[33] The British government cooled on the proposal once it realized that the Western governments and the World Bank would have to write the check.

Seeking to seize the initiative from Western business firms like the Suez Canal Company and the oil companies, whom the government officials distrusted, the British and French governments employed a range of economic measures against Egypt in an effort to force Egypt to abrogate the nationalization decree. But they were reluctant to open the pressure gauge full throttle for fear of irreparably damaging their own trading interests. On July 28, the British and French governments froze the assets of the Suez Canal Company, primarily to prevent the Egyptian government from laying its hands on the funds. This action, however, also had the effect of preventing the company from making use of the assets. Then Britain placed Egypt outside the transferable sterling account area, thereby prohibiting Egypt from selling its sterling holdings for other currencies. The British government blocked the transfer of sterling to Egypt and subjected all transactions from Egyptian accounts in Britain to exchange controls. No payments to and from Egyptian accounts in the

[30] D. A. H. Wright, Foreign Office Minute, Recognition of the Nationalization of the Suez Canal, August 20, 1956, PRO FO 371/119117 JE14211/1095.

[31] Memorandum of Conversation with Representatives of Rubber Manufacturers, August 8, 1956, USNA 974.7301; Memorandum of Conversation with George M. Parker, President, Esso Export Corporation, August 21, 1956, USNA 974.7301; D. A. H. Wright, Foreign Office Minute on Recognition of Nationalization of Suez Canal, August 20, 1956, PRO FO 371/119117 JE14211/1095; D. A. H. Wright, Memorandum on Suez Canal, August 29, 1956, PRO FO 371/119122 JE14211/1233; and R. Makins to Foreign Office, October 4, 1956, PRO FO 371/119151 JE14211/2031.

[32] J. H. Loudon, Shell Oil, to Harold Caccia, Foreign Office, August 23, 1956, PRO FO 371/119124 JE14211/1278.

[33] D. A. H. Wright, Memorandum, August 23, 1956, PRO FO 371/119124 JE14211/1279.

United Kingdom were to be allowed without reference to the Bank of England.[34] The bank was not required to maintain a total embargo, but was to be guided at all times by a concern for maintaining the integrity and value of sterling.[35]

The French had fewer financial ties with Egypt. Nonetheless, they too imposed banking and currency restrictions. Under British and French pressure the U.S. government also froze the accounts of the Suez Canal Company as well as official Egyptian banking accounts.[36] The other European states, despite siding with Britain and France, did not follow their lead. They maintained traditional trading and financial ties with Egypt. The majority of shippers from European states, other than Britain and France, elected to pay transit dues directly to the new Egyptian Canal Authority.[37]

For half a decade British officials had discussed a variety of economic measures that could be used to alter Egyptian behavior toward Britain. At this moment of acute crisis, the British discovered the limitations of their economic power in Egypt. To begin with, the British elected not to impose a trade embargo. Financial experts at the Board of Trade and the Treasury concluded that a trade boycott would be difficult to enforce against countries that were sympathetic to Egypt and would serve as willing trading conduits for British exports destined to Egypt. More important, the British were reluctant to extinguish a trade that had finally risen to £28 million in 1955.[38] Having already experienced the fury of discontented British business groups involved in the Egyptian trade, the bureaucrats sought to avoid the outcry that a full trade embargo would certainly provoke within that group.

Ambassador Byroade, in an early estimate of the impact of economic sanctions on Egypt, had predicted that they would produce economic dislocation and considerable personal suffering in the country. He feared that embargoes would undermine the middle classes, the very group the West wanted to favor, and drive the country in radical, anti-Western directions.[39] Byroade overestimated the bite of the financial sanctions, and he did not take account of Britain's reluctance to apply the economic weapon at full pressure. Economic compulsion did not bring Nasser to the negotiating table. Nor did opposition groups in Egypt rise against the

---

[34] No. 3370, Foreign Office to Washington, July 28, 1956, PRO FO 371/119078 JE14211/19.

[35] Chancellor of the Exchequer, Minute, Financial Question, EC(56)2, Cabinet, Egypt Committee, July 27, 1956, PRO Cab 134/1217.

[36] R. Makins to Foreign Office, August 1, 1956, PRO FO 371/118946 JE14211/134.

[37] Note of a Tripartite Meeting, August 24, 1956, PRO FO 371/118946 JE1l19/83.

[38] Chancellor of the Exchequer, Note, EC(56)3, Cabinet, Egypt Committee, July 30, 1956, PRO Cab 134/127.

[39] No. 486, Byroade to Secretary of State, August 28, 1956, USNA 974.7301.

regime. Quite the contrary, the embargoes took a grievous toll on British and French interests. British trade plummeted once again after its brief revival, and the Suez Canal Company found itself in a veritable financial paralysis without the use of its frozen funds in Britain, France, America, and Egypt. With the economic weapon sputtering, the British and French intensified their military planning.

Even as the Western diplomats and business leaders discussed economic responses to Nasser's nationalization, the Egypt Committee of the British government weighed a variety of breathtaking military options. The military program that the committee considered involved nothing less than completely reversing the processes of decolonization unfolding all over the British empire at that time. Such a decision, whether it involved an attack on Alexandria followed by an advance on the Suez Canal via Cairo, or more limited operations on Port Said, would be certain to meet with formidable opposition from the Egyptian army and would result in many Egyptian civilian casualties. In the Alexandria landing the British military men were prepared to make available the whole of the second infantry division based in Germany as support for the third infantry division from Britain itself. The French pledged 17,000 men and 200 tanks, with backup support to be dispatched when and as needed.[40]

While the military plans were pored over and developed in painstaking detail, the long-term economic and political aspects of the invasion were dealt with cursorily and unrealistically. In keeping with the pattern of diplomatic relations established between Egypt and Britain since the end of World War II (and of course before), the political and military strategists gave little thought to the British and French economic interests in Egypt and how they would fare in the aftermath of an invasion. Only once, in the third meeting of a committee subordinate to the Egypt Committee, was the issue of British investment in Egypt discussed. The consensus of that abbreviated discussion was that those interests would have to be sacrificed on the altar of political necessity. C. G. Thorley of the Treasury expressed "some concern about the damages which might be suffered by British commercial interests in Egypt in the disorder and the administrative chaos which would arise if the Egyptian government machine collapsed."[41] British officials expected Nasser to nationalize British firms and concluded that nationalization might have to be accepted and compensation sought. Perplexing was just how quickly the issue of nationalization was passed over in light of the origins of the dispute over the Suez Canal Company. Equally short was a discussion of the future of

---

[40] André Beaufre, *The Suez Expedition, 1956*, tr. Richard Barry (London, 1969), p. 36.

[41] Minutes of the Third Meeting of Egypt Committee, August 30, 1956, PRO Cab 134/1225.

the British community in Egypt. The Egypt Committee estimated its numbers at 17,500 but thought that no more than 6,750 would be at risk because of their close ties to the United Kingdom. They would need to be evacuated. The committee recommended such action, without, however, noting that British and French nationals formed part of the core of Egypt's private sector and that their departure would surely bring economic dislocation.[42]

Equally unrealistic was British thinking about the political future of Egypt and Anglo-Egyptian relations, assuming that the military operation succeeded. The goal for all three of the invading powers was "a well disposed Egyptian government in Cairo."[43] The British believed that a corps of independent-minded politicians and disaffected officers existed and that those individuals would make themselves available to rule Egypt in a more accommodating spirit. The British were also aware that Nasser and his colleagues had plans for conducting guerrilla warfare should the invasion succeed. Nasser had informed the British ambassador that his regime had created bases outside of Cairo and had established a chain of command in case any of them were killed or imprisoned.[44] Nasser had already chosen Tanta as his headquarters, from where he would lead the opposition if he were expelled from Cairo.[45]

The British military and political plans were full of obvious contradictions. The operation depended for its ultimate success on a compliant, pro-Western regime in Egypt, one that Britain had been unable to fashion ever since the end of World War II. For this reason, British plans were doomed even if the Americans and the Soviets had not forced an early halt to the military part of the enterprise. The military campaign, whether via Alexandria or Port Said, called for a brief foray into the delta and Cairo, at most a few days, where it was understood that the risk of bloodshed and heavy military and even civilian casualties was at its highest and where international public opinion was likely to be the most incensed.[46] Yet the political changes that the invasion was designed to produce could never have been achieved in a few days of fighting, however violent they might be. In order to ensure the future of a new, pro-Western regime, the military believed that it would need to eliminate Egyptian army intelligence, the Liberation Rally organization (the political party

[42] Secretary of the Cabinet, Note, Evacuation of British Subjects, EC(56)20, Cabinet, Egypt Committee, August 14, 1956, PRO Cab 134/1217.

[43] Minutes of Fourth Meeting of Egypt Committee, September 11, 1956, PRO Cab 134/1225.

[44] H. Trevelyan to A. D. M. Ross, September 16, 1956, PRO FO 371/118999 JE11927/2.

[45] Heikal, *Cairo Documents*, p. 110.

[46] Foreign Secretary, Memorandum, Egyptian Military Planning, EC(56)28, Cabinet, Egypt Committee, August 20, 1956, PRO Cab 134/1217.

that the military was creating as a support group), and the National Guard.[47] If the Nasser government were not overthrown, "it may be found necessary . . . to capture the headquarters of this resistance which will be in Cairo and to depose the government which it directs."[48]

After the invading army had brought a new regime to power in Cairo, it was to establish itself in the Suez Canal area and create an agency there to administer the canal. Ironically, no thought was given to restoring the old Suez Canal Company. The British hoped that their forces could be withdrawn quickly from the Suez Canal area, but they recognized that they might need to stay on in order to enhance political stability in the country and to support the new regime. The military forces were to take with them a political adviser who would be the liaison person with the new Egyptian government. The British also anticipated a large British staff, working as advisers with the Egyptian government.[49] The scheme could not have borne more similarities with the British occupation of Egypt in 1882 if the British officials had ransacked their own archives for the guidelines. On that occasion a large British force was sent to destroy a nationalist government and to install a pro-Western regime. The occupation was expected to be brief, and British influence was to be exercised behind the scenes through informal advising mechanisms.

Much of the British-French strategy was based on the assumption that the Egyptian regime was divided and cowardly and that an invasion would strike terror in the hearts of its members, rendering them easy targets for opponents. British intelligence stressed the deep divisions that it knew existed within the Revolutionary Command Council.[50] The Israelis even predicted that the Egyptian leaders would fall out and begin to kill one another.[51] And, in fact, the invasion did go some way toward realizing the goal of frightening the Egyptian rulers and sowing discord in their ranks. Hakim Amr, the commander of the armed forces, who was increasingly critical of Nasser's policies and resentful at not being fully consulted before the decision to nationalize the Suez Canal Company, balked at Nasser's order to remove Egyptian forces from the Sinai while the Israeli invasion was in full swing. Before long, he was in a state of full panic and could not be relied on to give Nasser unswerving

[47] Minutes of First Meeting of Egypt Committee, August 24, 1956, PRO Cab 134/1225.

[48] Minutes of Fourth Meeting of Egypt Committee, September 11, 1956, PRO Cab 134/1225.

[49] Minutes of First Meeting of Egypt Committee, August 24, 1956, PRO Cab 134/1225; and Foreign Secretary, Memorandum, Egyptian Military Planning, EC(56)28, Cabinet, Egypt Committee, August 20, 1956, PRO Cab 134/1217.

[50] W. Scott Lucas, *Divided We Stand: Britain, the United States, and the Suez Crisis* (London, 1991), pp. 101–3.

[51] I. Kirkpatrick, Foreign Office Minute, November 3, 1956, PRO FO 371/118904 JE1094/35.

support.[52] Salah Salim was also prepared to desert the Egyptian president. He advised Nasser to go directly to the British Embassy and surrender himself so that Egypt could be spared devastation. Salim instinctively knew against whom the invasion was directed.[53] At the cabinet meeting called to discuss the British-French ultimatum, there was at first only stunned silence. Nasser turned first to his foreign minister, Mahmud Fawzi, and asked what should be done. No answer forthcoming, he broke the silence and insisted on resistance. Nasser's resolve carried the day; talk about capitulation ceased.[54]

On October 29, Israeli troops crossed the border into Egypt and launched an invasion of Sinai. A few hours later, Britain and France, having colluded with the Israelis, called upon the Israelis and Egyptians to withdraw from the Suez Canal area and threatened to land troops if the combatants failed to do so. The British-French ultimatum was patently unfair, calling on Egyptian forces to withdraw from their own territory in the Sinai while permitting the Israeli army to continue its push through Sinai to the canal area. After aerial bombardment, British and French paratroopers descended on Port Said on November 5, the advance guard for an assault on the Suez Canal area. But even before the British and French forces had reached the midway point in the canal zone, they halted their advance under the combined pressure of the United States, the Soviet Union, and world opinion. Acrimonious discussions with the Americans and the United Nations ensued, finally resulting in the withdrawal of the British and French armies on December 22. In all, the ground fighting of the British and French, other than occasional attacks on soldiers in place, had lasted only a week, and British and French forces had occupied Egyptian territory for less than two months.

These military events, measurable in hours rather than months, nonetheless set in motion a train of measures that ultimately dissolved the financial, economic, and cultural links that had bound Britain and France to Egypt. Important population migrations occurred. Large numbers of foreigners residing in Egypt up to that moment left the country; not all of them were British, French, and Jewish, but all foresaw bleak economic prospects for themselves if they stayed. A Swedish businessman noted at the height of the crisis that every plane leaving the Cairo international airport was completely full.[55] More significant, the vast commercial, financial, agricultural, and industrial assets that British and French nationals and Jews of various nationalities had accumulated over the course

[52] Mohamed H. Heikal, *Cutting the Lion's Tail: Suez through Egyptian Eyes* (London, 1986), pp. 110–11.

[53] Hamrush, *Qissa*, vol. 4, p. 188 (testimony of Salih Nasr).

[54] Sayyid Mari, *Awraq Siyasiya* (Cairo, 1979), vol. 2, pp. 357 ff.

[55] Letter from businessman, November 30, 1956, PRO FO 371/125411 JE1015/22.

of a century were sequestered. Many of their properties were subsequently Egyptianized and later transferred to the Egyptian public sector. The process of disentangling the holdings and arranging compensation took almost three years of arduous diplomacy and left deep feelings of resentment.

The dissolution of the British and French economic presence in Egypt unfolded in conjunction with the invasion. At first the Egyptian actions were taken as wartime measures; only later were they made permanent through regular governmental decrees. By viewing the evolution of the government's relationship toward foreign capital during this period of acute strain, it is possible to see how the regime, so conflicted on the issue of foreign capital and the private sector, took its first decisive steps to undercut the power of foreign capital.

The crucial beginning in the assault on British-French economic predominance in Egypt began with Egyptian military proclamations numbers 4 and 5, issued on November 1, 1956. Proclamation 4 established a regime to administer the property of persons interned or under surveillance. Proclamation 5 created a custodian general to administer the assets of all British and French nationals as well as British- and French-owned companies.[56] So far-reaching were the ordinances that nearly every individual connected with the British and French communities in Egypt and every British and French economic interest was involved. Many wealthy Jewish families were also sequestered.[57]

Given the speed and overall efficiency with which the Egyptian government carried out the sequestration operation, it is difficult to believe that the Egyptian government had not prepared the sequestration plans well in advance. No doubt the strained political and economic relations that had troubled Anglo-Egyptian relations from the end of World War II onward had compelled the different governments to develop measures to respond to economic pressure and military action. Certainly the British and French diplomatic corps believed that the Egyptian rulers had laid their plans ahead of time.[58]

Nasser's economic elite, most notably Abd al-Munaim Qaysuni, Ali al-Giritli, and Hasan Mari, were given the task of drawing up the sequestration plans and selecting the sequestrators.[59] The administration of all the properties was centralized under a sequestrator general, who was aided by two deputies, one for British property and a second for French property. Each large property had its own sequestrator. The smaller properties were loosely grouped under single administrators. The sequestrators were

[56] *al-Ahram*, November 3, 1956.
[57] T. W. Garvey, Note, December 20, 1956, PRO FO 371/25568 JE1461/1.
[58] T. S. Tull, Foreign Office Minute, November 26, 1956, PRO FO 371/118834 JE1015/77.
[59] *al-Ahram*, November 3, 1956.

businessmen, lawyers, professors, and others drawn from the professional ranks of Egypt. By November 30, 1956, Egypt had appointed 208 sequestrators for 371 firms.[60]

British and French diplomats were thunderstruck by the audacity and size of the Egyptian sequestration effort. From the outset they feared that the sequestrations would not be reversed and would spell the end of British and French business in Egypt. The French directly contested the legality of the Egyptian action, claiming that because a state of war had never existed between the two countries Egypt had no right to seize property. Even if a state of war were conceded, French officials claimed that the Egyptians had no right to carry out the sequestration orders once the fighting had stopped, as it had on November 7. Moreover, the French diplomats argued that as soon as hostilities had ended, the Egyptian government was obligated to withdraw the order and restore properties to rightful owners. The French claimed that the most systematic execution of the ordinances had, in fact, occurred well after November 7.[61]

British diplomats complained less about legalities and more about the way in which the acts were carried out. Their officials conceded that Egypt and Britain were in a state of hostilities, at least until the last of the British troops left Egyptian soil in late December. In their opinion, then, the Egyptian government was entitled to sequester the property that belonged to the nationals of its enemies. It was not, however, entitled to deal with the property as if it belonged to the state of Egypt. Officials at the Foreign Office complained that the sequestration orders went well beyond the requirements of war. They noted that many of the individual acts of sequestration involved "other nationals, e.g. Dutch, Danes, and Belgians," and asserted that "he [Nasser] is also seizing the opportunity offered by the present crisis to continue the process of breaking the economic power of the present upper classes in Egypt and continuing nationalization wherever possible."[62]

In the view of T. W. Garvey of the Foreign Office, sequestration was legitimate only when used to deny an enemy power advantage from its economic assets. "It is clear," he added, "that the Egyptian measures constitute nothing of the sort. They are measures carried out with the political purpose of liquidating the British and French (and to a lesser extent, the Jewish) communities in Egypt."[63]

Far more devastating to the future of the private sector than the sequestration decrees (which were justified as wartime measures and quite possibly reversible at the conclusion of hostilities) was the government's treatment of

[60] *Egyptian Gazette*, November 30, 1956.
[61] W. Godfrey, Note, December 20, 1956, PRO FO 371/125508 JE1461/2.
[62] T. S. Tull, Foreign Office Minute, November 26, 1956, PRO FO 371/118834 JE1015/77.
[63] T. W. Garvey, Note, December 20, 1956, PRO FO 371/125508 JE1461/1.

members of the British, French, and Jewish populations residing in Egypt. The expulsion orders visited on them gave a clear signal that large-scale changes in Egypt's private sector were intended. One of the obvious strengths of the Egyptian private sector was its abundance of entrepreneurial and managerial talent, much of which, however, was drawn from foreign populations living in the country. The future of these groups and with it the vitality of the private sector was put in question when nationals of the two invading countries received orders to leave the country. Under criticism from interested international groups, most notably organizations alarmed at the harsh treatment of the Egyptian Jewish community, Nasser and other high-ranking Egyptian government officials denied the issuance of expulsion demands. But although not every British, French, and Jewish foreign national received a visit from the Egyptian police, most did. Those born in Europe were contacted without exception.[64]

Once again, much of the information about who made the decision to expel foreigners is indirect and comes from the treatment of foreigners and some of the interactions between Egyptian officialdom and those being expelled. This admittedly spotty record suggests that the decision to expel was made at the highest levels, in the Revolutionary Command Council (though precisely who in that group favored the action and who was opposed is not known); and though the decision had considerable popular support it was not wholeheartedly endorsed by other members of the ruling classes. Indeed, it was made against the wishes of the police who favored interning the foreign nationals during the hostilities and then permitting the interned to return to their customary activities after the war.[65] It also does not appear to have enjoyed wide acclaim in high administrative circles. The governor of Alexandria, for instance, allowed the foreigners whom he was obligated to deport to know of his distaste for the policy.[66]

The exact number of British and French residents in Egypt in late October 1956 is not known. According to the last census (1947), there were 28,246 Britons, of whom 19,754 were recorded as being English. Certainly not all of them were metropolitan Britons, for many came from Malta and other parts of the Middle East. Many had acquired British nationality while residing in Egypt. Of the 9,717 Frenchmen, 7,622 were said to be native-born French and the rest came from Middle East locales.[67] These numbers were in decline in the early 1950s. The U.S. Em-

[64] See file JE1015/22, PRO FO 371/125411.

[65] J. E. Killick, British Embassy, Addis Ababa, to T. F. Buckley, Foreign Office, February 1, 1957, PRO FO 371/125412 JE1015/44.

[66] George Middleton, British Embassy, Beirut, to A. D. Ross, Foreign Office, December 17, 1956, PRO FO 371/125411 JE1015/11.

[67] Egypt, Ministry of Finance, Statistical Department, *Population Census of Egypt* (1947), pp. 410–11.

bassy estimated that about 13,500 British subjects were living in Egypt before the invasion, of whom 6,500 were Maltese, 4,500 Cypriots, and 1,500 of U.K. origin.[68]

During the months of November and December expulsions occurred at the rate of 200 to 250 per day, and an early U.S. estimate was that most of the metropolitan British and French nationals had departed by the end of 1956.[69] A more careful U.S. calculation in January 1957 suggested that about 10,000 of the estimated 13,500 British subjects were still residing in Egypt at that time. Of those 10,000, 4,500 were Maltese, 4,500 Cypriots, and 500 to 800 were of U.K. origin.[70]

The devastating impact of the expulsion effort was indisputable. The census of 1960 gave no separate listing of British and French nationals, so small were their numbers.[71] More important, the British and French business communities had ceased to exist. In late 1960, the British Embassy in Cairo reported that there were only a half-dozen British businessmen resident in Cairo and a few more in Alexandria—a far cry from the heady days of interwar Egypt when Egypt counted among its most wealthy individuals such Britishers as the Peels, the Barkers, the Finneys, and the Rolos. Despite prospects for a renewal of trading ties between the countries and encouraging prospects for investment in the late 1950s, few British business persons had an interest in living in the country. Almost none of the individuals who had been expelled in 1956 and 1957 was willing to return.[72]

A closer look at the actual expulsions, as recorded by British and French diplomats at various listening posts when they interviewed the deportees, indicates even more clearly how divided the Egyptians were on this crucial moment in the country's modern history, as one would expect them to be given the long history of many of those foreign families in Egypt. Some departing foreigners were dealt with cruelly and made to suffer humiliations. Others experienced the comical side of a bumbling and uncertain bureaucracy, and still others left amidst much sorrow and pathos. No doubt certain Egyptian officials wanted British and French nationals and Jews to feel the sting of their nationalist fury, to know how Egypt had suffered under foreign rule and privilege, and to understand the country's rage over the military invasion and the resulting loss of life. A number of deportees complained of being stripped and physically searched before departing. One recounted being under house

---

[68] No. 3567, Aldrich, London, to Secretary of State, January 4, 1957, USNA 874.411.

[69] No. 2023, Hare to Department of State, December 26, 1956, USNA 874.411.

[70] No. 3567, Aldrich, London, to Secretary of State, January 4, 1957, USNA 874.411.

[71] United Arab Republic, Maslaha al-Ihsa w-al-Ta'dad, *al-Ta'dad al-Amm lil-Sukkan* (Cairo, 1963), vol. 2, pp. 46–47.

[72] J. R. Wraight to E. S. Taylor, Federation of British Industries, September 22, 1960, PRO FO 371/150955 VG1151/95.

arrest and allowed to go outdoors for only one hour a day.[73] The Peel family, longtime residents of Alexandria and owners of a major cotton exporting firm, Peel and Company, were expelled with nothing save the clothes they were wearing and £20 in their pockets.[74]

H. Alwyn Barker, a British merchant who resided in Alexandria where he was head of Barker and Company, was expelled and his firm sequestered. He mentioned that all of the passports of deportees bore the stamp "never to return to Egypt," but his contained the addendum "for the time being." Barker attributed this gesture to the influence of the Egyptian sequestrator appointed to take charge of the affairs of the firm and the family—an individual known to the Barker family. The Barkers were permitted to take with them £100, of which only £5 was to be in sterling and the rest in Egyptian pounds, which had little exchange value outside Egypt. The family had to turn over the keys to houses and business premises to agents of the Egyptian government. Barker took his leave of the governor of Alexandria, an old friend, who had to be circumspect in conversation because of the presence of a military officer. The governor reassured the British businessman that the present difficulties would soon pass and that he expected to see Barker in Alexandria in three or four months.[75]

The more comical side of the story generally revealed a bureaucracy rendered inept by the sheer size of its duties. Edward B. A. Pisani, senior partner in B. A. Pisani and Company of Alexandria, an importer of printing machinery, was placed under house arrest in early November and served with an expulsion order on December 8, well after the hostilities had ceased. He ignored the notice and was allowed to go about his business, largely, he thought, because he was well connected in Alexandria. On January 19, 1957, he received a reminder. This, too, he disregarded. His firm was finally sequestered on January 21, and he left Egypt on January 31.[76]

Max Rolo and Josephine Finney, the widow of Oswald Finney, both of them aging and wealthy Britishers who were well connected in Alexandrian society, paid no heed to the law. Finney defied the authorities by driving ostentatiously through the streets in her Rolls Royce and living in luxurious fashion. Apparently the Egyptian authorities tolerated the defiance of the aged.[77]

[73] See the files in JE1015 in PRO FO 371/125411.

[74] Charles Pryor to Col. J. Harwood Harrison, January 2, 1957, PRO FO 371/125568 JE1461/20.

[75] George Middleton, British Embassy, Beirut, to A. D. Ross, Foreign Office, December 17, 1956, PRO FO 371/125411 JE1015/11.

[76] Interview with E. B. A. Pisani, February, 1957, PRO FO 371/125412 JE1015/44.

[77] Report by Brigadier H. V. Fraser, February 12, 1957, PRO FO 371/125413 JE1015/67.

The treatment accorded P. C. Palmer of the Egyptian Export-Import Agency offers a final example of a hard-pressed bureaucratic machine, some of whose members were indifferent to the government's policies. In November the police advised Palmer to leave the country. This advice he ignored, as he did a request from the Egyptian sequestrator of his property to hand over his car to the authorities. The government then lost track of him for three months, when it finally sequestered his business. Palmer got on well with his sequestrator. He reported that he went to his office every day even though there was no work to do. The sequestrator appeared twice a month to write out checks—£E50 to compensate himself for his work and £E75 for Palmer's living expenses.[78]

Although expulsions and sequestrations had this occasional gentle and inefficient side, their overall effect was catastrophic for the foreign community. The Egyptian government had full records of the prominent foreigners living in Egypt and managed to contact all of the British and French nationals of means. Those who had metropolitan origins could expect to receive a visit from the police, and though they might prolong their stay in Egypt, almost all of them were ultimately compelled to leave. The awkward and vulnerable position of the Jewish population of Egypt subjected many of its members to nightmarish experiences as the government applied expulsion orders to some of its members. Ever since Egyptian nationalists had been drawn into the Palestinian question, first during the Wailing Wall incident in 1929 and then decisively when the Egyptian army intervened to oppose the creation of the state of Israel in 1948, the government and the public had viewed the political sympathies of Egyptian Jewry with suspicion. Jewish opinion was torn on the question of Zionism and the state of Israel. Some members of the Jewish community, even individuals of wealth and privilege, were known to have Zionist loyalties. Others had distanced themselves from Zionist propaganda and supported the Egyptian nationalist cause. Probably the vast majority had insulated themselves from politics and gave little thought to Zionism and Israel.[79] Nonetheless, the period leading up to Suez was tumultuous for the whole community. Especially troublesome was the November 2 anniversary date of the signing of the Balfour Declaration that had promised Zionists a national home in Palestine, when Egyptian nationalist zealots sometimes attacked Jewish property and threatened Jewish lives.

The Jewish population had declined, though only gradually in the twentieth century, and not as rapidly as the foreign populations in general. This slower rate of decline stemmed from the deep historical roots

[78] T. F. Brenchley, Note, September 15, 1958. PRO FO 371/133991 VG1461/20.
[79] See Gudrun Krämer, *The Jews in Modern Egypt, 1914–1952* (Seattle, Wash., 1989), pp. 167–204.

of the Jewish community in the valley of the Nile. Although many eastern Mediterranean and European Jews emigrated to Egypt during the era of economic expansion and relative political tranquillity in the nineteenth and twentieth centuries, they joined an already deeply rooted community. Jewish business and religious leaders had firm ties in Egyptian ruling circles. Although the numbers in the community declined between the census of 1947 and the invasion, probably quite precipitously immediately after the Palestine War in 1948, the Suez War signaled a death knell for these people. According to the 1960 census, only 8,561 Jews were then living in Egypt.[80]

The Egyptian government's handling of Egyptian Jewry during the Suez War became a subject of hot controversy and criticism at the time. International groups, not all of them Jewish, accused the Egyptian authorities of trying to drive the Jewish population out of the country. Under heavy criticism, including protests from the Red Cross and the American Embassy, President Nasser asserted that Jews were not being persecuted and that only those who were British or French nationals or who had overtly aided Israel were being required to leave.

The archival record, while spotty and mixed, suggests otherwise. To begin with, the American diplomats noted that sequestration orders had been filed against 539 Jews by name and 105 Jewish firms, in addition to Jews covered in the sequestration orders filed against British and French nationals. They also had information that many more Jews than the Egyptian government admitted had been placed in detention camps as Israeli sympathizers.[81] In the opinion of the Americans, the Jewish population en masse was subject to the same campaign of harassment that beset British and French nationals. They too suffered midnight police raids, loss of employment, sequestration, and the freezing of bank assets. The conclusion of the American diplomats was that an "expulsion operation has appearance of well-designed plan of long-standing, prepared in anticipation of an opportunity such as one presented by Anglo-French-Israeli action. Responsible opinion confidentially expects same treatment to be eventually accorded other foreign non-Moslem elements with ultimate objective of eliminating all foreign influence."[82] Drawing on reports from their embassies and consulates outside of Egypt, the British Foreign Office came to much the same conclusion, claiming that action against Egyptian Jewry was carried out "ruthlessly and efficiently."[83]

[80] United Arab Republic, Maslaha al-Ihsa' w-al-Ta'dad, *al-Ta'dad al-'Amm lil-Sukkan*, vol. 2, p. 13.

[81] No. 1752, Hare to Secretary of State, December 2, 1956; no. 1777, Hare to Secretary of State, December 4, 1956; both in USNA 874.411.

[82] No. 312, Washburn, Alexandria, to Secretary of State, December 20, 1956, USNA 874.411.

[83] George Middleton, British Embassy, Beirut, to A. D. Ross, Foreign Office, December 17, 1956, PRO FO 371/125411 JE1015/11.

The vast majority of Egyptian Jews suffered a grave disability in an intensely nationalistic Egyptian polity. They had no recognized national status, or at least no national status that a suspicious Egyptian government was willing to accord them. They were in effect stateless. The Red Cross claimed that of the 60,000 Jews living in Egypt in mid-1956 only 4,000 actually held Egyptian passports or could make valid claims to Egyptian citizenship. Another 16,000 held passports from other countries, but a full 40,000 were stateless.[84] The Egyptian government, far from alleviating the distress of the community, increased its vulnerability by enacting a new, more restrictive nationality law in November 1956. The law made the acquisition of Egyptian nationality more difficult than before (essentially restricting the status to children of an Egyptian father). It also empowered the state to strip any individual of Egyptian national status if that person had engaged in Zionist activity.[85]

Under pressure, Jews emigrated at a rapid rate in 1956 and 1957. Italy agreed to accept a large number of Jewish refugees, as did other European states. The Americans estimated that of the 45,000 Jews they believed to be living in Egypt at the beginning of 1956 (an estimate 15,000 less than that of the Red Cross) only 20,000 to 25,000 remained at the end of October 1956. And there was no appreciable slowing of the emigrations after hostilities ceased in November or after the withdrawal of foreign troops in late December. Jews continued to leave at a rate of 500 per month, and pressure was still being applied on individuals, albeit "sporadically." The Ministry of the Interior continued to issue notices in July 1957, depriving Jews of their Egyptian citizenship because of "Zionist inclination and activity," and the sequestrators of British and French firms removed Jewish employees from their companies.[86] All of these actions lent credence to the British and American charges that the campaign against the Jews was far more than a wartime and defensive measure or an outpouring of resentful nationalist sentiment but reflected part of a government scheme to eradicate the most powerful and most deeply rooted blocs of foreign economic authority from the country.

The treatment of the Jewish community was a lesson not lost on the other foreign communities still living in Egypt. Their plight, too, was a hard one, and their options narrow. The Greeks, Italians, and Syrians, like Egyptian Jewry, had large poor and politically powerless populations who had nowhere to flee. The rich had more havens, but they would forfeit their assets if they left. The Egyptian elite made no effort to calm the dread of these foreign communities during the height of the crisis, as it had often done in the past. Not until mid-1957 did President

[84] George L. Warren, Note, Movement of Jews from Cairo, December 31, 1956, USNA 874.411.

[85] *Egyptian Gazette*, November 30, 1956.

[86] No. 48, Robert W. Stookey to Department of State, July 20, 1957, USNA 814.411.

Nasser offer encouraging words to leaders of the Greek community, stating that the measures directed against the British and the French had been necessitated by the state of war and did not reflect any lessening of a commitment to foreign capital or the presence of foreign populations in Egypt.[87]

As the French and British officials pointed out, sequestration did not involve a final determination of the economic and financial assets of their nationals. Any lingering hope that properties might be restored to their owners was removed on January 15, 1957, less than a month after the British and French forces had withdrawn, when the Egyptian government enacted four ordinances that asserted Egypt's intention to control key economic sectors once dominated by the British and French. Ordinance number 22 stipulated that all banks operating in Egypt were to have only Egyptian shareholders and Egyptian directors. Banks not under sequestration had five years to conform to the law. Sequestered banks were transformed immediately into Egyptian banks. Thus, at a stroke, the core of the old British and French economic establishments was dissolved and placed in Egypt's hands. Barclays Bank, the Ottoman Bank, and the Ionian Bank had previously held the deposits of British business persons as well as those of the British Embassy and military. Similarly, the French banks in Egypt, Crédit Lyonnais and Comptoir Nationale d'Escompte de Paris, branches of large banking houses in France and central to French business in Egypt, were Egyptianized.[88]

A second law, patterned after the banking ordinance, imposed similar restrictions on insurance companies. Firms not under sequestration were also given five years to turn themselves into Egyptian companies with only Egyptian stockholders and directors. The sequestered British and French insurance companies, like their banking counterparts, were turned directly into wholly Egyptian-owned and -managed companies.

In justifying these decisive changes, Qaysuni, the minister of finance, argued that foreign banks and insurance companies had been draining money from the country for years, spurring economic progress in Europe and North America and retarding development in Egypt. The British and French banks, he asserted, had never raised their equity capital beyond £E2 million, most of which in any case they retained with their parent firms in the metropole. Despite this derisory amount of equity capital, the banks attracted massive deposits of £E70 to £E100 million, little of which they kept in Egypt. The same situation, Qaysuni stated, existed with the insurance companies, which, despite bringing little equity capital

---

[87] *Egyptian Gazette*, May 26, 1957.
[88] Comte Philippe de Liedekerke, Chargé d'Affaires de Belgique à Caire, à Henri Fayat, Ministre du Commerce Extérieur, May 25, 1957, PRO FO 371/125575 JE1463/121.

to Egypt, carried out a vast insurance business that enriched European and North American shareholders at the expense of the Egyptian economy.[89]

Law number 20, the third of the ordinances, created the Egyptian Economic Organization (al-Mu'assasa al-Iqtisadiya), destined to be the primary instrument of public sector expansion. Established primarily to oversee all of the British and French companies sequestered in November 1956, but not Egyptianized in the ordinances of January 15, 1957, the Economic Organization also assumed administrative responsibility for all state-run enterprises, including the newly created Iron and Steel Corporation and the Egyptian Fertilizer Company. At the time of its creation Qaysuni soothed the anxieties of business persons by pledging the return of the firms that had been placed under the jurisdiction of the Economic Organization to the private sector, either to their former owners or by selling them to Egyptian entrepreneurs. Qaysuni's message at the time was that Egypt sought only Egyptianization in the private sector, not nationalization. Still, no one would gainsay the commanding position that the Economic Organization occupied atop the Egyptian economy. Even a partial list of the firms that it administered reveals how its existence had shifted the balance of authority from private to public hands. Among its affiliates were the National Bank of Egypt, the former British and French banks and insurance companies, the Crédit Foncier Egyptien, the Tractor and Engineering Company, Misrair, Beida Dyers, the Misr Insurance Company, the Helwan Portland Cement Company, the Egyptian Sugar Company, and the Eastern Company. All of these latter firms had come under the jurisdiction of the Economic Organization because they had some significant amount of British or French capital, though not in every case a majority of the firm's equity. All told, the firms under its jurisdiction had a paid-in capitalization of £E17,000,000.[90]

The fourth of the laws, dealing with commercial agencies, had the greatest potential for Egyptianizing the economy and undercutting the presence of foreign capital. It was, however, vaguely and hastily drafted and did not stand up to the pressure of the representatives of foreign business remaining in the country. The law obligated all commercial agents and commercial agencies, if they were the sole distributors of a product, to turn themselves into Egyptian companies and to conform to Egyptian company legislation. The intentions of the law drafters were unclear. Exponents described it as the logical extension of the laws on banking and insurance companies and part of a general campaign to

[89] al-Ahram, January 16, 1957; Egyptian Gazette, January 16, 1957.
[90] al-Ahram, January 16, 1957; L'Observateur, January 16, 1957; Egyptian Gazette, January 24, 1957; no. 865, Philip E. Haring to Department of State, March 1, 1958, USNA 714.13.

Egyptianize the economy. Others justified the ordinance on the grounds that it would not expel foreign capital en masse but instead compel foreign importing and distributing agencies to diversify their activities and invest in manufacturing. The four ordinances marked as sharp a break with the past as any of the other more celebrated events of the first decade of Egyptian military rule. Most historians have focused on the Czech arms deal, the withdrawal of Western aid for the Aswan High Dam, and the tripartite aggression. The general accounts of these years have ignored the enactments of the laws affecting non-Egyptian businesses. Perhaps this oversight occurred because the Egyptian legislators themselves minimized the importance of the laws, seeking to portray them as temporary measures. But they rattled the private sector and began the march toward public sector dominance. Unfortunately, the historian struggling to pierce the wall of secrecy surrounding the inner workings of the Egyptian elite learns little of how and why these decisions were made and what the intentions of the decision makers were at the time. Egyptian rulers have been more forthcoming in discussing the most noteworthy political events of this era, but they have remained silent on their economic actions. We are thus left to piece together an interpretation from the bits and fragments left behind.

What we do know of the decision making is that the Egyptian economic elite at the time—Abd al-Munaim Qaysuni, Aziz Sidqi, Abu Nusayr, Sayyid Mari, and Kamal Ramzi—were involved in all of the important economic decisions from the outset. Their military superiors ordered them first to organize the Egyptian economy so that Egypt could withstand the British, French, and American financial pressure that Nasser and his colleagues knew would follow the nationalization of the Suez Canal Company. Subsequently, they had to place the economy on a war footing.[91] The January 15 decision about how much property to Egyptianize (banks, insurance companies, and commercial agencies) and how much to leave in the hands of the sequestrators for future determination marked an apparent triumph for the economic moderates, the Sidqi-Qaysuni faction, who wanted to preserve a significant role for private capital. Aligned against them were the public sector advocates, led by Abu Nusayr.[92] Qaysuni later asserted that the whole of the Egyptian ruling elite, fiscal conservatives as well as radical socialists, was determined to seize control of the financial institutions operating in Egypt because of the uncooperative and even demeaning attitudes of the foreign bankers to Egypt's war effort. But he also contended that he and his supporters wanted to limit the takeover to those commanding financial heights.

[91] *al-Ahram*, January 8, 1957.
[92] On the rise of Sidqi and Abu Nusayr, see the discussion in chapter 2.

The only substantial account of these matters arises from an interview that Qaysuni gave to Abdul Aziz Sarek of the *Egyptian Gazette* in July 1961. It is worth following in detail. According to Qaysuni the idea of nationalizing the banks and creating a large Egyptian economic entity first arose because the banks in Egypt "began playing tricks and started to reject the idea of financing [the cotton crop]" at the time of the invasion. Three or four days after the banks had been sequestered in early November, Qaysuni met with their heads and requested their support. He was shocked and dismayed by their attitudes. "They were a strange collection. One of them was a Count; another was a Marquis. They were the remnants which the French Revolution did not destroy. A company of men of the same mentality used to run the Suez Canal before the nationalization. I noticed during the meeting that they were listening but hardly uttered a word. And if one spoke it would be after he had weighed his words. There was great reserve and caution." Qaysuni's dealings with these local bankers led him to conclude that they were taking their instructions directly from the metropolitan firms and that their intention was to bring the Egyptian economy to a standstill. He surmised that there "was a local plan to bring about a collapse of cotton prices. There was another plan, a foreign plan. . . . Surely it was a conspiracy planned in London and Paris. Their plan was that the agents of colonialism in the banks and insurance companies were to act soon after the institution of the economic blockade in the hope of destroying the Egyptian economy." The banks were instructed, according to Qaysuni, to transfer liquid funds to foreign companies, to abstain from financing the cotton crop, and to create "chaos." Qaysuni claimed that the same was true of the insurance sector where foreign insurers raised the rates for goods passing through the canal. In Qaysuni's opinion the banks and insurance companies, at this moment of crisis, demonstrated that they operated in Egypt for "their own personal benefit and not for the national benefit." In his view Egypt could no longer tolerate the arrogant independence of business persons occupying positions critical to the country's development plans.[93]

The British and American archives do not provide any confirmation of Qaysuni's charges, and in fact seem to suggest that any raising of insurance rates and any caution in lending to Egyptian merchants and cotton cultivators was a consequence of the unsettled political circumstances and the need to be fiscally prudent. Barclays was a special target of the Egyptian nationalists because it played such a crucial role in the export of cotton. According to Egyptian critics, it refused to make its usual resources available to merchants and farmers during the crisis. But the Barclays correspondence with the Foreign Office at the time of the crisis,

---

[93] *Egyptian Gazette*, July 13, 1961.

when its officials were aware of the buildup of opposition to their policies in Egypt, indicates that they held funds back, not to subvert the Egyptian economy but to maintain a strong liquidity position at a time of extraordinary financial and political uncertainty.[94]

The way in which the Egyptian government dealt with the storm of protest against the fourth of their January 1957 decrees offers further proof of how sharply divided the elite still was over the role that the private sector would be expected to play in the future. The ordinance dealing with commercial agencies threatened a larger and more diverse group of foreign firms than did the banking and insurance decrees, because foreign firms tended still to be congregated in the importing and distributing sectors. This law alarmed American, Greek, Italian, Lebanese, and Syrian capitalists because so much of their investment was in trading activities. Numerous American corporations had established themselves in Egypt after World War II, primarily to distribute their manufactures. They included some of the most heavily capitalized firms with overseas interests: Otis Elevator, United States Rubber International, Firestone Tire and Rubber Company, Singer Sewing Machine, National Cash Register, and Kodak. They received support from the big three American automotive firms: Ford, General Motors, and Chrysler. The auto firms feared that the new commercial law would apply to them despite the fact that they had established automobile assembly operations in Egypt. Similarly concerned were the American oil companies. They too worried that an increasingly nationalist Egyptian government might argue that the oil companies were purely commercial agencies, involved in the distribution of a single product.[95]

The Lebanese, Greek, and Italian business representatives joined the Americans in protest.[96] But the businessmen were not content to rely on diplomatic complaints. The more bold among them defied the law, no one more openly than Henry Rabbath, a nationalized Egyptian of Lebanese descent. Rabbath ran the heavily capitalized Delta Trading Company, which had a significant equity position in the Iron and Steel Company and the Tractor and Engineering Company. Rabbath refused to comply with the law requiring him to register his Delta Trading Company with the minister of commerce. He threatened to close down the firm and discharge all its employees if the Egyptian government endeavored to force the law on his company.[97] Similarly, American companies began to prepare plans for liquidating their businesses in Egypt and moving the

---

[94] P. G. A. Wakefield to K. E. MacKenzie, Board of Trade, August 24, 1956, PRO FO 371/119024 JE1332/6.

[95] No. 2362, Hart to Secretary of State, January 23, 1957, USNA 874.19.

[96] No. 49, Barr V. Washburn to Department of State, January 30, 1957, USNA 874.19.

[97] No. 2751, Hare to Secretary of State, February 28, 1957, USNA 874.19.

seat of their Middle East operations to Beirut, which was viewed as more hospitable to foreign capital than Egypt.

The outpouring of protest took its toll on Egyptian resolve. Wishing to prevent a mass exodus of American and other commercial firms, Abu Nusayr, the minister of commerce and a keen advocate of state-controlled economic development, engineered a fast retreat. He employed a series of press conferences and press releases to reinterpret the scope of the law. In responding to requests for clarification, Abu Nusayr said that the law referred only to firms and individuals who were the sole importers and agents of a single product. Agencies that sold a variety of lines or that engaged in market competition with other firms, domestic and foreign, were exempt.[98] When officials of the Kodak Corporation inquired whether their firm would be required to Egyptianize because it imported only cameras and films, Abu Nusayr replied that because the firm was not the sole importer of these products the law did not apply.[99] In short, this ordinance, once so worrisome, was rendered a dead letter within months of its issuance.

Another indication of just how uncertain and divided the Egyptian elite was over its economic directions came as it tried to decide how to deal with the British and French business firms that still remained sequestered. The government repeatedly made decisions about these companies at the last minute. First, in late May 1957, one day before the Egyptian government was to begin financial discussions with the British about restoring cultural, political, and financial relations between the two countries, the Egyptian government took a further step to diminish British and French economic influence in Egypt. The timing of the action indicated that the disposition of these firms had produced lively debate right up until the enactment of the ordinance.

On May 23, the Egyptian government expropriated British and French shareholding in nine large firms previously sequestered. These were the Eastern Tobacco Company, a subsidiary of British American Tobacco; Helwan Portland Cement, a subsidiary of Tunnel Cement; Beida Dyers, partly owned by Bradford Dyers; the Nile Textile and Yarn Company; the Egyptian Dyeing Company; Sinai Minerals; Metal Casting; United Mines; and Egyptian Phosphates.[100]

This "second round of Egyptianization" brought a storm of protest from British officials, who were outraged as much at the Egyptian failure to consult with owners as with the expropriations themselves.[101] Officials

[98] al-Ahram, February 28, 1957.

[99] No. 2750, Hare to Secretary of State, February 28, 1957, USNA 874.19.

[100] J. H. A. Watson, Note, May 23, 1957, PRO FO 371/125461 JE1102/4.

[101] T. F. Brenchley, Foreign Office, to M. E. Johnston, Treasury, June 24, 1957, PRO FO 371/125461 JE1102/10.

at the British Foreign Office learned the details of the action only through Associated Press bulletins and a Belgian diplomatic dispatch.[102] British American Tobacco lodged a strong protest at the Foreign Office, unable to do so in Cairo because the firm had no representation there and no access to its local subsidiary. The company held 75 percent of the shares of the Eastern Company which, at £17 million, was one of Egypt's most heavily capitalized firms. Directors of British American Tobacco expressed their eagerness to resume business in Egypt, not least because the Eastern Company was an important revenue earner for the parent company, remitting on average £1 million in profits each year. The British directors indicated that they would be willing to offer the Egyptian government a large block of shares in the Eastern Company if the state would rescind the nationalization order.[103]

The May expropriations were the first of a series of sell-offs of British and French property. Others followed, with alarming and chilling regularity, in June and July 1957, even as financial discussions among Britain, France, and Egypt were under way. The firms expropriated remained under the jurisdiction of the Egyptian Economic Organization, the spokespersons for which offered their usual promises that the companies would ultimately be transferred to the private sector.

Egypt's financial negotiations with Britain and France, which were designed to restore diplomatic and economic relations among the countries, revealed in great detail the vast business treasure that British and French military and political leaders had so foolishly put at risk. British and French diplomats had made earlier estimates on the basis of incomplete information. The new calculations were based on data submitted by the firms and individuals themselves and were far higher than the officials had originally believed possible.

In October 1956, with the invasion less than three weeks away, the Foreign Office took its first sounding of the worth of British property in Egypt. It concluded that the major British enterprises, excluding the four Shell companies (worth £55 million) and British holdings in the Suez Canal Company (worth £31 million), had a value of £48.8 million. If secondary enterprises were included, the figure was £55 to £60 million, and this number took no account of the value of War Office property held in the canal zone.[104] This estimate of corporate assets in Egypt proved not

[102] A. J. Wilton, Foreign Office, to K. E. MacKenzie, Board of Trade, June 20, 1957, PRO FO 371/12557 JE1463/123.

[103] A. D. McCormack, Secretary, British American Tobacco, to Permanent Under Secretary of State, Foreign Office, May 24, 1957, PRO FO 371/125461 JE1102/6.

[104] C. G. Thorley, Treasury, to J. B. Flux, Foreign Office, October 9, 1956, PRO FO 371/118935 JE11016/1.

far wrong, for later more exact calculations of the total value of the major British firms Egyptianized during 1957 came to £47 million, again excluding the Shell companies and the Suez Canal Company.[105]

In all, the Egyptian government had sequestered 106 concerns, of which ten had a valuation of more than £1 million.[106] If this figure were not alarming enough, the British officials learned to their horror that they had grossly underestimated the value of smaller British properties in Egypt. These assets, which also had been sequestered in November 1956, were worth no less than £63 million and included personal checking accounts, urban real estate holdings, small business agencies, and land holdings.[107] Virtually every British national who had been living in Egypt at the time of the invasion had a claim. By mid-1957, British officials in the metropole were aware that the total worth of British property in Egypt was probably not less than £165 million. To be sure, this amount represented the owners' own estimations, for which there was no way for the British government to obtain independent verification. Even discounting for exaggeration, the total was enormous. And the British were not in a strong bargaining position with the Egyptians as the two sides began discussing compensation payments for the losses. If the financial negotiations with Egypt were to fail for any reason, the British believed that the Egyptian government would seize all of their assets. Egypt's assets still frozen in Britain had a market value of approximately £78 million at the end of 1957, considerably less than the £165 million that the British negotiators were trying to reclaim.

French diplomats were similarly stunned at the immensity of their losses. To be sure, French business persons and investors had not been as active as the British in twentieth-century Egypt. Very little French capital had found its way into the industrial sector, the one noteworthy exception being the Egyptian Sugar Company, which the Egyptian government had sequestered and then Egyptianized before the Suez invasion. Most French capital, not counting the Suez Canal Company, was located in banks (£E10 million), insurance companies (£E3 million), and public utility firms—a total of £E15.6 million. An even greater amount of the French imperial treasure was contained in French cultural, scientific, and educational establishments, many of which dated back to the nineteenth cen-

---

[105] Foreign Office Note to Mr. de Zulueta by R. J. Langridge, December 2, 1957, PRO FO 371/125578 JE1463/197.

[106] British Property in Egypt Section, Memorandum, January 29, 1959, PRO FO 371/138189 JEP4/11.

[107] Brief for the Anglo-Egyptian Talks in Rome, starting October 9, 1957, PRO FO 371/125477 JE1158/10; copy of Minute to the Prime Minister attaching Treasury Report on Negotiating Tactics at Resumed Rome Discussions, October 3, 1957, PRO FO 371/125476 JE1156/92; R. J. Langridge, Foreign Office Note to Mr. de Zulueta, December 2, 1957, PRO FO 371/125578 JE1463/197.

tury. In all, the French appraised the value of their sequestered or Egyptianized property at just a little less than £E50 million, again excluding the Suez Canal Company.[108] Like the British, the French were in a weak bargaining position because they had far more resources in Egypt than Egypt had in France.

THE PROBLEMS OF ECONOMIC DELINKING

From the outset of the wave of nationalizations, Egyptianizations, and sequestrations, the Egyptian government asserted its intention to compensate owners for their seized property. At no time did the rulers of Egypt adopt a radical stance and suggest repudiating the claims that British and French investors had on Egypt. When the government took over the Suez Canal Company, it promised to compensate the shareholders and duly noted the price of the shares on the day before the nationalization decree. Similarly, when the state sold British and French banks and insurance companies to the Egyptian sector, it agreed to reimburse on the basis of the share prices of the firms. Nasser's preference for neutralism disposed him to restore Egyptian relations with the West, and he knew he could do so only by coming to terms with business concerns that the state had seized. The Egyptian leader also realized that Egypt's need for financial assistance would require continuing overtures to Western countries and that these were unlikely to be welcomed until he had healed the deep wound stemming from the Suez War.

Nonetheless, the financial negotiations among Britain, France, and Egypt proved how difficult it was to separate economies that had been so tightly linked for more than a century. The negotiations that took place over the next three years left much ill will on all sides and again revealed splits within the Egyptian elite. Moreover, disentangling the British and French component from Egyptian sources of wealth became an accounting nightmare; determining just compensation was equally arduous. The final settlements left the private sector in Egypt in an amputated condition and prepared the way for the further takeovers of commercial and industrial property.

Franco-Egyptian negotiations proceeded more swiftly than the Anglo-Egyptian discussions. French interest groups, led by textile manufacturers, pressured the French government to be accommodating and to recognize the weakness of its bargaining position. Even before the first round of the negotiations commenced in Geneva in September 1957, the French had lifted their full embargo on financial dealings with Egypt and

---

[108] Jean Ducruet, *Les Capitaux Européens au Proche-Orient* (Paris, 1964), p. 320.

agreed to barter wheat, flour, and fertilizers for Egyptian cotton.[109] French trade had run at around £E33 million before the breach, a not insignificant figure, and the French manufacturing and trading interests demanded a resumption of this trade. In April 1958, at a crucial moment in the stalled negotiations, the textile industrialists complained to the French Foreign Affairs Ministry that they had only six weeks of Egyptian long-staple cotton in their warehouses and that without a resupply they would have to close down factories and discharge workers.[110]

The opening rounds of discussion did not go well, however. Each side offered a one-sided view of the war, on which it based its claims. Still affirming the legitimacy of their military action and the invalidity of the nationalization decree, the French bargainers argued that the total amount of French property Egyptianized or sequestered, worth £100 million according to their calculations, should be fully compensated or the property returned to the original owners. Without at first challenging this inflated figure, the Egyptians replied that they themselves were seeking £170 million in war damages.[111] As the sides moderated their positions, the Egyptians employed a terror tactic that they would use to good effect later against the British. They sold off a large French-owned department store in Cairo, Orosdi Bac—a move that frightened the French into thinking that a failure to be accommodating would result in further Egyptian takeovers of French property.[112]

The French negotiating team gave way on point after point. The final agreement, concluded on August 22, 1958, reestablished cultural, economic, and financial relations between the two countries, permitted French citizens to return to Egypt if they wished to do so, and provided compensation to the owners of property that had been sold. The Bank of France abandoned a claim to £E6.2 million held in Egypt since Suez, and France granted substantial trade credits to Egypt. Part of the proceeds from the sale of Egyptian cotton to French importers was to be used to cover the transfer to Egypt of funds held by Egyptians in French banks but frozen during the Suez War.[113]

According to official French estimates, made public at the time of the agreement, the Egyptian government had sequestered assets worth £50 million. The Egyptian government agreed to pay £12 million as compen-

[109] J. A. Ford, Note for the Record, August 27, 1957, French Financial Negotiations with Egypt, PRO FO 371/125467 JE11317/3.

[110] C. M. Maclehose to R. Arculus, April 12, 1958, PRO FO 371/125467 JE11317/13.

[111] C. M. Maclehose to T. F. Brenchley, Foreign Office, November 6, 1957, PRO FO 371/125467 JE11317/15.

[112] Ibid., December 9, 1957, PRO FO 371/125467 JE11317/20; C. M. Maclehose to J. H. A. Watson, February 7, 1958, PRO FO 371/131353 JE11317/4.

[113] *Journal Officiel de la République Française*, August 22, 1958, pp. 7919–27; no. 408, G. Young, Paris, to Foreign Office, August 14, 1958, PRO FO 371/131354 JE11317/24.

sation for the property it had sold off to Egyptian businesses or the public sector and to desequester the rest.[114] Though dressed up in language flattering to the French and avoiding any admission of wrongdoing on the French side, the final agreement, in financial terms, clearly favored the Egyptians and reflected the advantages that the Egyptian negotiators had exploited from the beginning of the discussions.[115]

Simultaneous with the Franco-Egyptian talks, discussions took place between the government of Egypt and representatives of the old Suez Canal Company. The larger Franco-Egyptian talks were contingent on a successful outcome to these negotiations, which were concluded on April 29, 1958, four months before the end of the Franco-Egyptian talks. In the opinion of Jacques Georges-Picot, chief negotiator for the old Suez Canal Company (and its former president), the Egyptians deprived the shareholders of the canal company of fair compensation.

The tensions between Egyptian and French negotiators ran deep from the beginning to the end of these talks, reflecting the long-standing antagonisms between these two ancient adversaries. The Egyptian negotiating team was unwilling to accord official status to Georges-Picot; they were willing to talk to him only in his capacity as an unelected agent of a no longer existing Egyptian joint stock company. Georges-Picot, for his part, insisted on his status as the president of the Suez Canal Company and continued to challenge the legitimacy of the nationalization decree.[116]

To strengthen his bargaining position and to prevent Egypt from attempting to seize the assets of the Suez Canal Company outside Egypt, Georges-Picot persuaded the French National Assembly, in May 1957, to confirm the juridical status of the Suez Canal Company.[117] He had an additional reason for obtaining French parliamentary recognition for his company. After concluding the compensation discussion with the Egyptian government, he wanted the company to begin a new existence as an investment trust.[118] To this end, he changed the firm's name to Compagnie Financière de Suez (Suez Financial Company); reduced the number of board members from thirty-two to twelve, thus rendering the direction of the firm less cumbersome; and did away with the founders' shares. In order to effect these changes the company directors had to call no fewer than six extraor-

[114] *al-Ahram*, September 19, 1958; *Middle East Economic Digest* 2, no. 19 (August 29, 1958), p. 227.

[115] C. T. Crowe, Note, Anglo-Egyptian Relations, September 13, 1958, PRO FO 371/133980 VG1151/213.

[116] Francis Wylie to J. H. A. Watson, March 15, 1957, PRO FO 371/125529 JE1425/43.

[117] Jacques Georges-Picot, *The Real Suez Crisis: The End of a Great Nineteenth-Century Work*, tr. W. G. Rogers (New York, 1975), p. 116.

[118] In addition, the liquidation of the company would result in heavy taxation on the final distribution to shareholders. Future of Suez Canal Company, J. A. Ford, Treasury, April 26, 1957, PRO FO 371/125530 JE1425/73.

dinary shareholders' meetings in 1957 and 1958. By the end of 1958, Georges-Picot boasted that the changes he had wrought in the structure of the old Suez Canal Company had expunged "the original Egyptian connection" of the firm and given it an "exclusively French" nature.[119]

The chasm between the two sides seemed unbridgeable when negotiations opened in January 1957. Not only did officials of the former canal company seek compensation for the value of the company at the time of nationalization, as determined by its share price, but they demanded payment for the profits forgone for the years 1956 to 1968. They did not mention a figure, knowing full well that the mammoth sum that they had in mind (£200 million to £240 million) would incense the Egyptian bargainers and also alarm European shippers, who were aware that they would ultimately underwrite the compensation settlement by paying increased transit dues.[120] They did inform the Egyptian team that the company's representatives had a large sum in mind.[121]

The Egyptian government held a different view of the matter. Reiterating its contention that Egypt had broken no law, and implying that the company had for years made abundant profits and did not need to be compensated for forgone earnings, the Egyptian delegation adhered to Nasser's original promise to compensate the company at its share price on the day before nationalization. The company's shares had been worth £70 million on July 25, 1956, but the Egyptian delegation contended that the firm had assets outside Egypt valued at £55 million. In addition, the Egyptian delegation claimed that the company had contracted debts in Egypt amounting to £10 million and had caused Egypt to lose another £10 million through transit dues paid outside the country. The Egyptian government claimed that the company owed Egypt £5 million.[122]

As was the case in the Franco-Egyptian discussions, fierce bargaining delayed a final settlement and produced a difficult and, to many, unhappy compromise. Georges-Picot, after having hinted at a total compensation demand of £200 million, reduced the company's claim to £70 million. The Egyptians adopted a different strategy. They made a final, take-it-or-leave-it offer of £23 million that "shocked" Georges-Picot but was accepted under heavy pressure from Eugene Black at the World Bank and representatives of the British and French governments. He did so with regret and resignation. In a later impassioned account, Georges-Picot

---

[119] Georges-Picot, *The Real Suez Crisis*, p. 118.

[120] Suez Canal Company Draft, Indemnisation de la Compagnie, January 15, 1957, PRO FO 371/125528 JE1425/12; H. Beeley, Foreign Office Note, Discussion with the Quai d'Orsay and the Suez Canal Company, February 13, 1957, PRO FO 371/125528 JE1425/12.

[121] J. A. Ford, Foreign Office Note, Suez Canal Company and the Anglo-Egyptian Talks in Rome, May 20, 1957, PRO FO 371/125531 JE1425/98.

[122] F. Wylie to J. H. A. Watson, June 15, PRO FO 371/125532 JE1425/117.

characterized the final settlement as "a wretched document as far as indemnification went" and asserted that had it not been for the external
pressures he would not have signed.[123] What irked the French businessman was that the French delegation had dropped its demands a full £130
million over the course of the bargaining sessions, while the Egyptians
had raised their compensation offer a mere £12 million and refused to go
any further. In the view of British observers, the company maintained its
old mentality toward Egypt up to the end. "The Company felt that if they
were going to legalize robbery they would need to get a better price for
doing so."[124]

The agreement was far from one-sided, however. British officials were
not wrong in concluding that the terms were fair and that the company's
claim to the forgone profits was "a pretty forlorn hope." The final arrangement enabled the new Suez Financial Company to come into being,
with acknowledgment from the Egyptian government, and to take over
all the assets that the old Suez Canal Company held outside of Egypt,
even including the tolls that shippers had paid in London and Paris after
the nationalization decree. In return for a cash payment amounting to
nearly 70 percent of the real value of the company's assets in Egypt, the
Egyptian government, in its turn, took over all of the old Suez Canal
Company's properties in Egypt.[125]

The agreement proved to be an entirely pragmatic document, reflecting
the realities of power rather than law or morality. Egypt was allowed to
keep the properties that it had seized in Egypt and that economic pressure
and military invasion had not forced it to disgorge. The new Suez Financial Company took over all the properties outside of Egypt. For a cash
payment of a mere £E23 million Egypt gained control of the canal and
acceptance of the nationalization decree.

Parallel negotiations took place in Rome in 1957 and 1958 between
Egyptian and British negotiators. Because of the large financial amounts
at stake, the bargaining sessions were even more strained. Each side had
substantial assets with which to threaten the other, though in the final
analysis, the Egyptians had the stronger bargaining position. The final
agreement concluded in March 1959 laid the groundwork for a full restoration of relations between the countries.

Before the discussion got under way, the Foreign Office engaged in
conversations with agents from Barclays, Shell, the Egyptianized insurance companies, the Federation of British Industries, the Association of
British Chambers of Commerce, the British Chamber of Commerce in

[123] Georges-Picot, *The Real Suez Crisis*, p. 148.

[124] F. Hoyer-Miller, Note, April 15, 1958, PRO FO 371/31384 JE1425/60.

[125] A. D. M. Ross, Foreign Office Minute, Suez Canal Company, April 15, 1958; A.
Clarke, Rome, to Foreign Office, April 4, 1958; both in PRO FO 371/131382 JE1425/51.

Egypt, and the Suez Canal London Association. These meetings revealed the divided opinion on whether firms were interested in returning to Egypt if the Foreign Office were able to negotiate a rollback of the Egyptianization decrees.[126] Most firms, like Barclays, would give no opinion until they were allowed back into the country to inspect their properties and examine their books. Barclays agents had been told that the government of Egypt had collected large amounts of taxes from the firm. The Ottoman Bank said that it had yet to obtain a copy of the contract outlining the sale of its assets to the Jumhuriya Bank.[127]

A few companies were adamantly opposed to returning and pressed the Foreign Office to exact full compensation from the Egyptian government. Imperial Chemical Industries, Egypt, had information that the Egyptian sequestrator had run down its properties. Its officials were also certain that the Egyptian business climate would remain unattractive for many years to come.[128] Determined not to reinvolve his firm in Egypt was David Ades, who ran an exporting business valued at £E1,469,457. The firm had been sequestered but had remained in the hands of the sequestrator general. In the view of the Ades family, their whole internal network of commercial agents, many of whom were Jewish merchants, had been removed after the invasion. Because of the exodus of foreign populations the Adeses were dubious that they could reestablish themselves in the country.[129] But some firms were eager to return. BOAC; Lloyds; and Cook's, Egypt, resented the opportunities afforded to their chief rivals to enhance their position in the region's major tourist center and the hub of air routes between Europe, Asia, and Africa.[130]

The issue of rolling back the Egyptianization measures never came up in the financial discussions. At the first round of negotiations in late May 1957, the Egyptian diplomats announced that the state would not rescind the Egyptianization decrees and was only willing to discuss compensation for the Egyptianized companies.[131] In spite of this discouraging news, the British endeavored to be accommodating. They came under pressure

[126] M. E. Johnston, Treasury, Draft Minute to D. Rickett, Anglo-Egyptian Talks, Consultation with British Commercial Interests, July 8, 1957, PRO FO 371/125475 JE1156/78.

[127] Record of Meeting with Representatives of British Banks and Insurance Companies with Interest in Egypt, August 8, 1957, PRO FO 371/125578 JE1463/160.

[128] K. E. MacKenzie, Board of Trade, Note, ICI Interests in Egypt, July 11, 1957, PRO FO 371/125577 JE1463/138; K. E. MacKenzie, Board of Trade, Note, ICI and Egypt, November 28, 1957, PRO FO 371/125578 JE1463/196.

[129] Position of David Ades and Son, Cairo, n.d., September 1957, PRO FO 371/125578 JE1463/181.

[130] Walter Barrie, Chairman of Lloyds, to Dennis Rickett, Treasury, October 10, 1957 JE1463/179; S. Adams of Cook's to Colonel Abdel K. Hatem, Egyptian Embassy, London, October 21, 1957, JE1463/180; both in PRO FO 371/125578.

[131] *al-Ahram*, June 27, 1957.

to reach some kind of agreement from numerous firms that were eager to be desequestered or compensated, especially manufacturing and trading companies with an interest in resuming contacts with Egypt, and the diplomatic corps, which was alarmed at growing Soviet influence in the region.[132] The sequestered firms had a special sense of urgency because the Egyptian sequestrator general was charging firms 10 percent of working capital per year for administering the companies.[133] But the group that came to symbolize the interests of those working for a speedy settlement were the so-called Egyptian refugees—those 600 to 800 Britishers expelled from Egypt with few resources and compelled to live in parlous circumstances in a few houses established for them in England.[134]

By late 1958, the British and Egyptian sides had narrowed their differences on compensation to £10 million. The British were willing to halve the amount, but the Egyptians refused.[135] Again, the Egyptian government abruptly nationalized an important British property—David Ades and Company—which created the specter of a full-scale expropriation of British properties.[136] In March 1959 the two sides finally achieved an agreement. The British removed all controls on blocked sterling in the number one account and released the accounts in the United Kingdom belonging to Egyptian banks, companies, and individuals. In return, the Egyptian government terminated the measures of sequestration on British property. The British estimated that 351 firms and some 4,000 individual properties were desequestered, the net value of which was an estimated £130 million. British citizens were permitted to return to Egypt to take possession of their desequestered assets. If they chose not to, they could claim compensation, though no property owner was permitted to remit more than £5,000 overseas. Excluded from the desequestration order were the companies that had been Egyptianized between October 30, 1956, and August 2, 1958. Those firms, valued at £47 million, were to be compensated with the payment of £27.5 million. In deciding how to divide the £27.5 million among the claimants, the British government adopted the principle that smaller firms and individuals were to receive full compensation, where possible, and larger companies and wealthy individuals were to obtain a portion of their net worth.[137]

[132] H. Macmillan, Personal Minute, February 14, 1959, PRO FO 371/142029 VG1461/33.

[133] T. F. Brenchley, Note, September 15, 1958, PRO FO 371/133991 VG1461/120.

[134] C. T. Crowe, Note, Anglo-Egyptian Relations, September 13, 1958, PRO FO 371/133980 VG1151/213.

[135] No. 608, Hohler, Rome, to Foreign Office, September 3, 1958, PRO FO 371/133979 VG1151/196.

[136] No. 205, W. Montagu-Pollock, Swiss Embassy in Berne, to Foreign Office, November 22, 1958, PRO FO 371/133991 VG1461/128; no. 80, United Kingdom Delegation to Financial Talks in Cairo to Foreign Office, February 17, 1959, PRO FO 371/141969 VG1151/80.

[137] The agreement can be found in Great Britain, *House of Commons Sessional Papers,*

Although the Egyptianization measures had targeted the heart of the British business empire there (Barclays, Beida, Calico, British American Tobacco), some British-run firms had not been Egyptianized and had remained sequestered. They were returned to their original owners. Among the desequestered firms were BOAC, Mitchell Cotts, Thomas Cook, Unilever, and the four Shell Companies, including Anglo-Egyptian Oil. In short, the British business connection with Egypt was not completely severed although, save for the Shell Companies, the assets of which stood at £55 million, the remaining desequestered firms, though large in worldwide capitalization, had relatively modest investments in Egypt.

The Shell Company had been encouraged by the Foreign Office to pursue its own negotiations with the Egyptian government.[138] Its four affiliated companies (Anglo-Egyptian Oil; Shell Distributing Company, Egypt; British Petroleum, Egypt; and Shell Company of Egypt) constituted the second-largest cluster of business properties in Egypt, behind only the Suez Canal Company. Had the Egyptian government Egyptianized these properties, the bill for compensation would have soared and jeopardized a viable financial settlement. No doubt that fact influenced the Egyptian government, but the companies' centrality to the Egyptian oil sector and the unpreparedness of the Egyptian government, at that point, to take responsibility for the multiple functions that the Shell companies fulfilled, restrained the Egyptians as well. Anglo-Egyptian Oil was the most substantial producer of local crude oil and ran Egypt's largest refinery at Suez; its distributional network in Egypt was efficient and widespread as well. Resisting the temptation to take over these operations, the Egyptian government signed a separate accord with Shell Oil on April 21, 1959. All four companies were desequestered and returned to Shell control.[139]

Difficult to explain was Shell's willingness to return to Egypt. Its executives adduced numerous arguments against the step. In the first place, the Shell companies had quarreled with the Egyptian government over pricing and profit issues right up to the Suez invasion. And the parent company did not have any reason to believe that its operation would be profitable or that it would be able to remit profits to Britain if they were made. Reports from Egypt indicated that the first Egyptian sequestrator, Ibrahim Lutfi, had made large payments from the Shell coffers to the state to extinguish previously disputed tax bills. Lutfi had also systematically removed good technicians from Anglo-Egyptian Oil, particularly those who were Jewish, and saddled the firm with a large and inefficient labor force.[140]

1958–59, vol. 34, cmd. 639. There is a good summary and commentary in the *Middle East Economic Digest* 3, no. 9 (March 6, 1959), pp. 106–7.

[138] J. A. Ford, Foreign Office Note, August 26, 1958, PRO FO 371/33980 VG1151/219.

[139] R. Arculus, Note, Agreement between Shell and Egypt, January 1, 1959, PRO FO 371/142045 VG15321/1; *al-Ahram*, April 22, 1959.

[140] J. A. Ford, Foreign Office Note, August 26, 1958, PRO FO 371/33980 VG1151/219.

Although the Egyptianization measures had targeted the heart of the British business empire there (Barclays, Beida, Calico, British American Tobacco), some British-run firms had not been Egyptianized and had remained sequestered. They were returned to their original owners. Among the desequestered firms were BOAC, Mitchell Cotts, Thomas Cook, Unilever, and the four Shell Companies, including Anglo-Egyptian Oil. In short, the British business connection with Egypt was not completely severed although, save for the Shell Companies, the assets of which stood at £55 million, the remaining desequestered firms, though large in worldwide capitalization, had relatively modest investments in Egypt.

The Shell Company had been encouraged by the Foreign Office to pursue its own negotiations with the Egyptian government.[138] Its four affiliated companies (Anglo-Egyptian Oil; Shell Distributing Company, Egypt; British Petroleum, Egypt; and Shell Company of Egypt) constituted the second-largest cluster of business properties in Egypt, behind only the Suez Canal Company. Had the Egyptian government Egyptianized these properties, the bill for compensation would have soared and jeopardized a viable financial settlement. No doubt that fact influenced the Egyptian government, but the companies' centrality to the Egyptian oil sector and the unpreparedness of the Egyptian government, at that point, to take responsibility for the multiple functions that the Shell companies fulfilled, restrained the Egyptians as well. Anglo-Egyptian Oil was the most substantial producer of local crude oil and ran Egypt's largest refinery at Suez; its distributional network in Egypt was efficient and widespread as well. Resisting the temptation to take over these operations, the Egyptian government signed a separate accord with Shell Oil on April 21, 1959. All four companies were desequestered and returned to Shell control.[139]

Difficult to explain was Shell's willingness to return to Egypt. Its executives adduced numerous arguments against the step. In the first place, the Shell companies had quarreled with the Egyptian government over pricing and profit issues right up to the Suez invasion. And the parent company did not have any reason to believe that its operation would be profitable or that it would be able to remit profits to Britain if they were made. Reports from Egypt indicated that the first Egyptian sequestrator, Ibrahim Lutfi, had made large payments from the Shell coffers to the state to extinguish previously disputed tax bills. Lutfi had also systematically removed good technicians from Anglo-Egyptian Oil, particularly those who were Jewish, and saddled the firm with a large and inefficient labor force.[140]

1958–59, vol. 34, cmd. 639. There is a good summary and commentary in the *Middle East Economic Digest* 3, no. 9 (March 6, 1959), pp. 106–7.

[138] J. A. Ford, Foreign Office Note, August 26, 1958, PRO FO 371/33980 VG1151/219.

[139] R. Arculus, Note, Agreement between Shell and Egypt, January 1, 1959, PRO FO 371/142045 VG15321/1; *al-Ahram*, April 22, 1959.

[140] J. A. Ford, Foreign Office Note, August 26, 1958, PRO FO 371/33980 VG1151/219.

Yet these considerations were not decisive. From the beginning of the Suez crisis, the bogeyman for the Shell directors in London was nationalization. Having failed to induce Nasser to rescind the decree nationalizing the Suez Canal Company, the Shell officials became determined to prevent him from nationalizing their enterprises.[141] Egyptian negotiators, sensing the Shell strategy, dealt harshly with the Shell negotiating team. Aziz Sidqi would not budge on critical financial issues even when Shell officials predicted that their implementation would lead to bankruptcy. Sidqi merely shrugged his shoulders, opining to Frank McFadzean, the chief negotiator for Shell, that Egypt was "not prepared to see a substantial proportion of the oil industry in Egypt in the hands of foreign firms which can be subjected to political pressure from their governments in the event of any further troubles in the Middle East."[142]

The final agreement may not have been an unmitigated negotiating disaster for Shell—after all, Egypt returned the sequestered firms to Shell hands—but it fully reflected the weakness of the Shell bargaining position. The firm was compelled to capitulate on one essential demand after another, starting with its longest-standing grievance with the Egyptian government—the sixty-one prospecting licenses ostensibly promised in 1954—and moving on to the oil price stabilization fund. Indeed, it remitted £500,000 to persuade the Egyptian government to desequester the companies.[143] The chairman of the Shell board, J. H. Loudon, put the best face on the accord, arguing that "it was very much in the interests not only of the oil companies that the Shell Company should get back into Egypt as soon as possible."[144]

When Shell finally returned to Egypt, it found the oil sector greatly transformed. German, American, and Italian competitors were firmly in place, and the Egyptian government had used the three-year hiatus to establish an oversight agency for the oil sector, called the General Petroleum Authority. The authority's reach extended into every corner of the oil sector. It engaged in prospecting and mining itself, often in alliance with foreign capital, and operated an oil refinery at Suez, which by 1959 was able to refine nearly as much oil as Anglo-Egyptian Oil. More important, it was the only body permitted to import crude oil and to distribute oil products in Egypt as a wholesaler. These changes gave the Egyp-

---

[141] There had been frequent rumors of impending nationalization of the oil companies. See, for instance, *al-Ahram*, November 2, 1956.

[142] Frank McFadzean, Shell Oil, to D. Rickett, Treasury, August 19, 1958, PRO FO 371/133980 VG1151/220.

[143] R. Arculus, Note, Agreement between Shell and Egypt, January 1, 1959, PRO FO 371/142045 VG1532/1.

[144] F. Hoyer Miller, Memorandum, Foreign Office, February 12, 1959, PRO FO 371/142045 VG1532/3.

tian government a power it had sought for decades—the authority to set the wholesale price of Egyptian oil products and to subordinate foreign oil conglomerates to state power. The new power structure in the oil sector forbade Anglo-Egyptian Oil, for instance, from bypassing the authority even when it wished to sell its refined oil to its own affiliates, the Shell Company of Egypt and the Shell Chemicals Distributing Company of Egypt.[145]

Shell officials were appalled at the physical and financial condition of their companies when they returned to Egypt. Loudon complained that the desequestration settlement notwithstanding, Anglo-Egyptian Oil was still owed money by the government of Egypt. He considered the condition of the price stabilization fund lamentable and worried that the three-man expatriate staff at Anglo-Egyptian Oil, which was tiny in comparison with the forty-person staff of 1956, would not be able to gain control over the affairs of the company.[146]

Delinking has been a favorite watchword of economic nationalists in the third world. The Egyptian experience underscores just how difficult it was to disentangle economies so closely tied over more than a century. Yet it also reveals that the Egyptians, exploiting the strength of their economic position and the desire of the British and French to reach agreements, were able to arrive at bargains that were financially advantageous to them.

BELGIAN CAPITAL

The Egyptian campaign to root out long-established and powerful foreign national investors had one last target: the Belgians, owners of the third largest national economic empire in Egypt. Though less visible than British and French capital, Belgian investments also dated from the turn of the twentieth century and drew their resources from the most highly placed segments of the domestic Belgian haute bourgeoisie, including the Société Général de la Belgique and the Empain family.

As usual, the Egyptian government employed political differences as the pretext for dispossessing this community. Political turmoil in the newly independent Congo in late 1960 had seen the struggling Kasavubu government throw its lot in with the West and expunge Soviet influence. The Congolese government also closed the Egyptian Embassy in the

[145] Anglo-Egyptian Oil, File Note, September 10, 1959, Shell Archives, GHC/EG4/B6/1.

[146] Roger Stevens, Memo of Conversation with John Loudon of Shell after his return from a tour of the Middle East, March 15, 1960, PRO FO 371/150977 VG1153/2; J. B. B. Richmond, British Property Commission, to C. T. Crowe, Foreign Office, July 14, 1959, PRO FO 371/138888 JEP3/147.

Congo, accusing Egyptian diplomats of meddling in the internal affairs of the country.[147] The Nasser government replied in early December with a series of orders to sequester and nationalize Belgian properties in Egypt. Later, Egypt broke diplomatic relations with Belgium and required the small Belgian community residing in Egypt to leave the country.

The first measures applied against Belgian property occurred on December 2, 1960. Nasser cited Belgium's neoimperialist activities in the Congo, but the careful planning of the operation, coupled with Nasser's private remarks, left even less doubt this time that Egypt's plans had been devised well in advance.[148] The first decrees were directed at the heart of the Belgian business empire, notably the Banque Belge et Internationale en Egypt (with nominal capitalization of £E2,625,000) and the Heliopolis Oases and Tram Company, an important utility concessionaire founded by Baron Empain at the turn of the century.[149] The Heliopolis Oases and Tram Company, one of Egypt's most heavily capitalized firms, was subject to a barrage of nationalist complaint when it was taken over by the Ministry of Municipal and Rural Affairs, where Abu Nusayr was carrying out a nationalizing campaign against a large number of foreign-owned public utilities. Nusayr excoriated the Heliopolis Company for a poor record of public service, contended that the firm's transportation equipment was out of date and in poor repair, and criticized the company's foreign managers for their flamboyant lifestyles.[150] One of the firm's foreign directors, he claimed, had at his disposal a fleet of six expensive automobiles. In much the same vein, after the state had taken over the Belgian-financed and -run Shepheards and Semiramis Hotels, Abu Nusayr leaked the information that the management of Semiramis had set aside a whole wing of the hotel for the firm's chief accountant, who was paid an extravagant salary.[151]

So intense was the campaign against Belgian business interests that it brought a formal severing of diplomatic relations, followed by further sequestrations as well as a decree expelling Belgian citizens. Among the firms sequestered in February 1961 was the Jacques Rolin group of companies that had been founded at the turn of the century.[152]

By mid-1961, as a result of two powerful Egyptianization and nationalization campaigns, first from January 1957 to August 1957, and second from December 1960 to March 1961, the British, French, and Belgians ceded their economic predominance in Egypt. The net worth of foreign

---

[147] *al-Ahram*, December 2, 1960.
[148] No. 940, Crowe to Foreign Office, December 2, 1960, PRO FO 371/151007 VG1462/11.
[149] *Egyptian Gazette*, December 2, 1960; *al-Ahram*, December 3, 1960.
[150] *Egyptian Gazette*, December 2, 1960.
[151] *al-Ahram*, December 4, 1960.
[152] Ibid., February 27 and 28, 1961.

businesses taken into the Egyptian private and public sectors was not less than £140 million—a figure that takes no account of the substantial assets ultimately desequestered and put back into British, French, and Belgian hands but which the original owners elected not to accept in favor of the small compensation allowed to them. Indeed, the total foreign assets Egyptianized, nationalized, and sequestered during this period could not have been less than £300 million.[153]

Nasser's Egyptianization campaign realized a goal that had animated but eluded the Egyptian population at all levels for many decades: a dominant Egyptian presence in the local economy. The Egyptian press, Egyptian intellectuals, and Egyptian socialist and communist groups had all attacked foreign capital as one of the chief impediments to Egypt's autonomy and its capacity to develop. An Egyptian-run economy and an end to foreign economic preeminence were not merely the vision of leftist groups and the working classes in Egypt. The Egyptian middle and upper classes had also agitated for more independence, no one more aggressively than Tal'at Harb and, on occasion, Ahmad Abbud, both of whom believed that the Egyptian middle class was capable of spearheading economic development. In the Nasser era, Qaysuni and Sidqi continued this Egyptianizing impulse.

Although the Egyptianizing campaign may seem to have been the logical culmination of nearly all of the strands of Egyptian nationalism, elite as well as mass, the actual decisions to dismantle foreign capital were made by a small inner circle of military men and their subordinate economic advisers and produced considerable opposition. The incredible folly of the British and French military planners allowed the Egyptian military men to respond in ways that must have seemed out of reach at the time. Yet Nasser's break with Britain and France raised alarm, most of which was lodged within the upper segments of Egyptian society.

Elements of the bureaucracy, fearful of their loss of power at the hands of the military men, and most of the Egyptian business community recoiled from the new policies even though they were justified on the grounds of elevating Egyptians into the businesses of the old European captains of industry, commerce, and finance. Indeed, the Egyptian business elite viewed Egyptianization as nothing less than a death sentence. Ever since Tal'at Harb's experiment in establishing wholly owned Egyptian companies foundered in the 1930s, many members of the Egyptian

---

[153] The figure of £140 million consists of £47 million in British business properties; £71 million, the share value of the Suez Canal Company; £12 million in French assets; and £10 million in Belgian properties. To this must be added, in order to reach the figure of £300 million, £120 million in British property and £38 million in French property sequestered in 1956–57 but eventually returned to owners. A fuller discussion of the total public sector takeover may be found in the next chapter.

capitalist class had made their peace with foreign capital, content to work in alliance with overseas business groups. Nasser's expropriation of foreign capital frightened Egyptian entrepreneurs, who saw themselves as the next likely targets of the government's nationalizing energies. Nasser, Qaysuni, Sidqi, and Nusayr exhorted Egyptian businessmen to take the lead in industrializing, even when they themselves were journeying to Moscow and imbibing the ideology and practice of state planning. The local bourgeoisie, reeling from the land reform measures, the Egyptianization of foreign capital, and the establishment of the Economic Organization, parried the state's overtures and were notably reluctant to risk capital on those projects most cherished by the government leaders. Egyptian businessmen awaited in terror and paralysis the inevitable assault on the remaining sources of independent capital, their own firms. And the public sector did not disappoint them. In 1960 and 1961 the state completed the dismantling of private business activity, begun in earnest with the sequestration proclamations of November 1, 1956.

The revolutionary changes in the private sector that took place between November 1956 and mid-1957 were massively event-driven. They stemmed from the British-French-Israeli invasion, which in turn followed Nasser's nationalization of the Suez Canal Company. Although the nationalization of the Suez Canal Company had been part of nearly every Egyptian nationalist's agenda, it would be difficult to argue that the dismantling of large-scale British and French capital in Egypt was also an inevitability in the same way. The military regime lost little time, however, in seizing the opportunity to dissolve the powerful foreign presence and sending its foreign communities out of the country. No doubt the ever-present political and military tensions between Egypt and Britain between 1952 and 1954 had forced Egyptian government officials to prepare economic plans to deal with hostile acts from the British. The government, then, was in a position to carry out those plans when the invasion occurred. Still, within the ruling circles differences of opinion existed over the most beneficial role that private capital could play in Egypt's development plan. These issues were to be debated in the next half-decade and resulted in the dismantling of domestic capital.

Enlarging the Public Sector, 1956–1961

IF UNFORESEEN EVENTS enabled an opportunistic regime to engineer the first, and in many ways most decisive takeovers of the private sector in 1956–57, deep-seated ideological drives and political ambition became dominant in the final destruction of private initiative and the rise of the omnipresent state. To be sure, circumstance still played a role. The regime shaped its ideology in a growing disillusionment at the performance of the private sector. The breakup of the United Arab Republic in September 1961 offered another opportunity for the military junta in Cairo to rage against real and imagined opponents and to blame the business community. But while it would have been difficult in 1952 to visualize Egypt without an autonomous bourgeoisie, once the position of foreign business had been undercut, an Egyptian economy under state domination was no longer unthinkable.

Analysts of Nasser's Egypt have warred over the question of Egypt's move to a state-centered economy in the 1950s. Some have stressed the political imperative. They have emphasized Nasser's aggrandizing spirit, portraying him as a ruler who feared all rivals and who, having rid himself of large landowners and foreign capitalists, was in a position to destroy that last bastion of independent, ancien regime power, the Egyptian bourgeoisie.[1] Others have stressed economic inexorability. The regime's commitment to economic development led it to repudiate the private sector for egregious failures and to make the state responsible for economic progress. Some have seen the tensions and conflicts of the 1950s and 1960s as part of Egypt's failed effort to move from import-substitution industrialization to heavier industrialization.[2] More recently, variations on these themes have stressed Egypt as a "stalled society" and have noted the incompatibilities of a political economy requiring popular participa-

[1] There are numerous Nasser-centered studies of this period, starting with the first biographies of Nasser, particularly those by Jean Lacouture, Robert Stephens, and Hrair Dekmejian. A later work stressing political dynamics and the worldview of the young military officers is P. J. Vatikiotis, *Nasser and His Generation* (London, 1978).

[2] Books that place economic factors closer to the center of the analysis include all of the works of Bent Hansen; Robert Mabro, *The Egyptian Economy, 1952–1972* (Oxford, 1974); Patrick O'Brien, *The Revolution in Egypt's Economic System: From Private Enterprise to Socialism, 1952–1966* (London, 1966); and John Waterbury, *The Egypt of Nasser and Sadat: The Political Economy of Two Regimes* (Princeton, N.J., 1983).

tion and an autocratic government.[3] Scholars have not neglected explanations that stress political opportunism or drift or the influence of regional and international politics, though these factors have usually not been claimed to be the predominant ones.

What now should be clear is that the removal of the foreign bourgeoisie, or at least its most powerful segment, following the tripartite invasion, changed the political and economic calculus in Egypt. It brought local business persons face to face with the state. From 1957, when the critical decisions were made not to allow most large foreign firms back into Egypt until 1961, when the Egyptian government began its campaign against the remaining local capitalist centers and organizations, the Egyptian regime was compelled to work out its relationship with the private sector. By the end of this period, a combination of ideological, personalistic, sheer opportunistic, and economic motives had driven the government to dismantle almost the whole of the large-scale private sector.

Following the takeover of foreign businesses, publicists for the Egyptian regime claimed that Egyptianization had strengthened the private sector and enlarged its Egyptian component. British and French banks and insurance companies became Egyptian joint stock companies. Although law number 20 of January 15, 1957, created the Economic Organization, this body was meant to have a brief life span. As late as 1958, Qaysuni, Sidqi, Higazi, and Giritli insisted that the Economic Organization was a pump-primer, prepared to sell off its treasure to deserving entrepreneurs.[4]

The Economic Organization did not wither away, however. Quite the contrary, it spearheaded the state's absorption of private business activity. From the outset, the Economic Organization's administrative purview was so wide-ranging as to include the railway administration, the General Administration of Petroleum, the Industrial Bank, the Egyptian Sugar Company, the Iron and Steel Company, and the Egyptian Chemical Industries, as well as a growing list of British and French firms that the government elected not to desequester. These included Beida Dyers, Filature Nationale des Textiles, and Société Egyptienne des Industries Textiles in the textile sphere and various other manufacturing enterprises. Although the French and British banks and insurance companies had become Egyptian joint stock companies when they were seized, the Eco-

---

[3] See especially Hamied Ansari, *Egypt: The Stalled Society* (Albany, N.Y., 1986); and Beattie, *Egypt during the Nasser Years: Ideology, Politics, and Civil Society* (Boulder, Colo., 1994).

[4] *Egyptian Gazette*, January 24, 1957, provides a good example of the arguments made at the time the Economic Organization was established and repeated with regularity for several years.

nomic Organization held most of their share capital and therefore was primarily responsible for their administration.

The law establishing the Economic Organization gave it the authority to raise internal and external loans, to create its own firms, and to join with private capital in mixed enterprises. Moreover, wherever the Economic Organization possessed 25 percent or more of the equity of a company, it was entitled to nominate at least three board members and to designate the chairman or the managing director. In no case was its representation on the board to be less proportionate than its share of the equity capital.[5]

Far from privatizing its holdings, as promised, the Economic Organization increased its economic sway. At the time of its founding, in January 1957, its equity capital totaled £E17 million. But once the Egyptianization drive picked up momentum the equity capital skyrocketed, increasing from £E26 million at the end of 1957 to £E58 million by the end of 1958 and to £E63 million at the end of 1959.[6] By 1960 the Economic Organization intruded into every sector of the economy, overseeing companies that had at their disposal capital resources totaling £E506 million.[7]

As the public sector grew, the private sector shrank into a defensive shell. Even before this unhealthy cycle finally culminated in the socialist laws of July 1961, big business had been rendered catatonic from a series of blows too numerous to catalogue. As each new measure cowed the business classes, the governing clique grew in its certainty that only the state could generate economic growth.

At first, government impatience with private investors was muted. It expressed itself in occasional legislative acts, more frequently in complaints about the timidity of local entrepreneurs. Conflict between the two forces was truly joined in late 1958 and early 1959, however, when the government revised the company law in ways that profoundly distressed the business elite. The first controversial decree restricted the number of board positions that an individual could hold to two and the number of managing directorships to one.[8] A later act limited a director's compensation to £E2,500, except for the salary paid to a managing director.[9] More controversial and resented was a regulation that obligated companies to set aside 5 percent of their profits for the purchase of government bonds. This law also stipulated that dividends were not to exceed 10 percent of

[5] Nazih N. M. Ayubi, *Bureaucracy and Politics in Contemporary Egypt* (London, 1980), p. 215.

[6] *al-Ahram*, February 16, 1959, and July 2, 1960; *Egyptian Gazette*, January 14, 1960; no. 865, Philip Haring to Department of State, March 1, 1958, USNA 714.13.

[7] *al-Ahram*, July 2, 1960.

[8] Ibid., October 9, 1958.

[9] Ibid., November 7, 1958.

those that had been distributed in the previous year. Only the Ministry of the Economy could make exceptions.[10]

This legislation, with its curtailment of dividends and emoluments and its garnishing of profits for the state, loosened the tongues of the business community. For the first time, business representatives spoke of the deepening despair of the investing community and its inability to lead the industrialization effort. The government relented under the barrage of criticism, but only a little. It allowed companies to increase dividends to 20 percent of those paid out in the previous year, and it granted exceptions to the dividend rule to the first three applications it received.[11] But because the applicants were firms that had always enjoyed state favor (the Egyptian Salt and Soda Company, the Misr Spinning and Weaving Company, and the Misr Fine Spinning and Weaving Company), the exemptions did little to reassure the rest of the business community.[12]

These concessions notwithstanding, the state organs continued to thunder against the blinkered views of most business leaders. Government spokespersons argued that firms had only themselves to blame for the new laws. Hassan Zaki Abbas, the minister of economy, claimed that boards of directors were inflating stock prices by distributing excessive dividends and failing to build up reserve funds. In the minister's opinion, this practice restrained the capacity of firms to expand and innovate— strictures that had merit because the tradition in Egypt was to pay out large dividends and skimp on reserves. The inflated stock prices had the effect, the minister pointed out, of creating an informal, black market stock exchange where shares traded at a sharp discount among persons knowledgeable about the true value of companies.[13]

A second move against the private sector presaged the final assault in the socialist laws of July 1961. In February 1960 the government issued a decree nationalizing Egypt's two most powerful, yet still privately run banks: the National Bank of Egypt and Bank Misr. In justifying the takeover of the National Bank, the minister of finance, Qaysuni, argued that the National Bank had become Egypt's central bank, and since it therefore held the deposits of the government, served as a bank of issue, fixed the primary interest rates, and maintained the reserves of Egypt's commercial banks, it should not, he asserted, be run by private shareholders. Nor should a central bank's policies be dictated by a quest for profits. Rather, a central bank should be a state-administered organ, albeit protected from government interference by a special charter.[14]

[10] Ibid., January 13, 1959; *Egyptian Gazette*, January 12 and 13, 1959.
[11] *al-Ahram*, January 15, 1959.
[12] Ibid., January 19, 1959.
[13] *Egyptian Gazette*, January 26, 1960.
[14] *al-Ahram*, February 20, 1960.

A few raised questions about terminating the private status of the National Bank of Egypt, but questions about the nationalization of Bank Misr abounded. Bank Misr had been the most active instrument of Egyptian capital since its founding in 1920. Although its equity capital was a modest £E2 million, its deposits, totaling £E100 million, represented one-third of the deposits in Egypt's commercial banking sector. The bank's investments of £E19.3 million consisted of £E7.8 million in government securities, £E7.9 million in the stock of Misr companies, and £E3.6 million in other securities. Since its creation it had served as a vehicle for launching a broad range of commercial and industrial firms—some twenty-seven by 1960—which had a nominal capital of £E20 million and were involved in all sectors of the economy of Egypt. The Misr companies had a commanding presence in the textile sector, where the Misr Spinning and Weaving Company and the Misr Fine Spinning and Weaving Company accounted for half of Egypt's output of cotton piece goods. The bank was also no dupe of foreign capital. It continued to adhere to its original charter of having only Egyptian stockholders and directors.[15]

Qaysuni's defense of the seizure was transparently false. He argued, as was his wont, that the government had sought to protect the larger interests of the private sector. He observed that Bank Misr held a substantial amount of the stock of its affiliated Misr companies. If it were to dispose of those shares on the stock market, which according to Egyptian law it was obligated to do, the damage to share prices would be catastrophic. He added that the government had provided the bank with a substantial loan, which, if called, would place the bank in a precarious financial position. He concluded his justification by pointing out that although the bank was being nationalized, the affiliated Misr companies were not. According to his argument, their position as private entities would grow stronger because all government shareholding in the firms would cease. In 1957 the Economic Organization had acquired the British shares in a large number of these companies, including Misr Air, the Misr Insurance Company, and the Misr Fine Spinning and Weaving Company. It was now compelled to transfer those shares to a new, privately run company called the Misr Organization.

Anyone with a rudimentary knowledge of the history of Bank Misr could refute Qaysuni's rendering of Egypt's recent economic history. To be sure, had the bank sold off the holdings of its affiliates, the stock market would have been rocked. But since the early 1940s the state had exempted the bank from any obligation to do so. The same was true of the government loan to the bank, which had been extended in 1941 to

[15] Ibid., February 12, 1960; National Bank of Egypt, *Economic Bulletin* 13, no. 1 (1960), p. 33; Bank Misr, *al-Yubil al-Dhahabi, 1920–1970* (Cairo, 197?), pp. 101–20.

keep the bank liquid. The government had never demanded repayment. Nor were the bank and its affiliated companies bastions of independent action. Even before the bank crisis of 1939–1941, Bank officials had worked in close alignment with the state. The Misr firms were generous to a fault in supporting Nasser's economic projects. Their boards contributed funds to all of the favorite schemes of the military men, and in proportions that often proved embarrassing to other segments of the private sector. The most plausible explanation for the takeover was that the government could not resist the temptation to seize the bank's massive assets so that they could be employed fully in the development effort.[16]

The buildup to the socialist laws was so determined and so widely publicized in 1960 and 1961 that nationalization legislation in July 1961 did not come as a surprise. In his speeches, Nasser had begun to single out what he called monopoly capital as the barrier to Egyptian development. Yet the sweeping socialist laws went far beyond what the press and public predicted. The laws targeted nearly all of Egypt's joint stock companies and dealt with them in draconian ways. A first law, number 117, authorized the state to take all of the share capital of 149 firms, including all of the banks and insurance companies; even the British and French banks and insurance companies that had been Egyptianized in January 1957 and were extolled as the core of a newly invigorated Egyptian private sector were not exempt. The firms completely nationalized included companies in the cement, steel, fertilizer, and hotels sectors. If any principle could be discerned, it was that those firms likely to compete with major state-run enterprises, like the Iron and Steel Company and the KIMA Fertilizer Company, were expunged of all private sector influences. By a second law, number 118, another group of companies, ninety-one in all, was obligated to sell 50 percent of its shares to the public sector. Although private shareholding remained juridically at 50 percent, the state's dominant managerial position in the firms was never in doubt. Finally, law number 119 was applied to 159 companies representing firms of long duration in the Egyptian economy, including many of its industrial behemoths (the Misr Fine Spinning and Weaving Company, the Misr Company for Silk Weaving, Nestor Giannaclis, the Egyptian Sugar Company, the Salt and Soda Company, the Egyptian Fertilizer and Chemical Industries, the Misr Rayon Company, and Beida Dyers). It prohibited any investor, individual or corporate, from owning more than £E10,000 worth of the shares of these firms. Any shares held in excess of that amount had to be sold to the state.[17]

---

[16] There were reports that officials at Bank Misr were not in sympathy with Egypt's development plans and were threatening to erect obstacles to its implementation. For a discussion of these matters, see no. 15, C. T. Crowe to Lloyd, March 25, 1960, PRO FO 371/150953 VGll13/6.

[17] *Egyptian Gazette* and *al-Ahram*, July 21, 1961.

The socialist laws left the power of the state virtually unchallenged in the corporate sector. To take but a few examples, shipping, where several indigenous firms under Egypt's most dynamic entrepreneurs had competed for state and private contracts, now came under the jurisdiction of a general public entity for maritime shipping. Similarly, the four main cotton pressing companies were placed under the overall direction of the General Organization for the Pressing of Cotton. In justifying these changes, state officials spoke of the advantages of centralized planning and the value of coordinating scarce resources. The state showered itself with paeans while disparaging unregulated competition and free-market mechanisms. It portrayed privately run firms as large and arrogant entities that were constantly colluding to fix prices and curtail services. Additional socialist legislation required companies to appoint two workers to their governing boards and to limit public salaries to £E5,000 per year.

One of the firms in which the government acquired a 50 percent equity position was Anglo-Egyptian Oil. That which the Shell directors in London had struggled to prevent had ultimately come to pass. The new firm renamed itself al-Nasr Oilfields.[18]

The Egyptian political elite portrayed the socialist laws as the logical culmination of the original principles of the revolution epitomizing the socialist, democratic, and cooperative ethos that Nasser and colleagues had been stressing since the end of 1957. Ali Sabri, underscoring those themes, argued that monopoly capitalism had finally given way to popular control of economic institutions. He claimed that the takeovers would not only increase industrial productivity but would make Egypt a more just society.[19] In editorials, Muhammad Hasanayn Haykal asserted that Egypt had struck an irreversible blow against income disparities and that economic exploitation could not thrive because the state, rather than a small clique of wealthy business captains, owned the major business enterprises. The state, in Haykal's view, was an instrument of the people.[20]

Although the July laws destroyed the Egyptian business classes, they galvanized the latent opposition of the Syrian bourgeoisie and its political allies. In February 1958, Nasser had been persuaded to merge Syria and Egypt as the United Arab Republic. Although he believed the time unpropitious, a group of Syrian politicians convinced him that a union with Egypt would prevent Syria from slipping into communism and chaos. At first the Egyptian rulers exercised restraint in their dealings with Syria, recognizing the wide differences between the two countries. But as Nasser's commitment to an enlarged public sector intensified, and his assault

[18] Foreign Office Note by P. A. R. Blaker, Anglo-Egyptian Oilfields, July 24, 1961, PRO FO 371/158856 VG1531/10; H. Muller, Shell, Cairo, to H. P. deBoer, Shell, London, March 26, 1962, PRO FO 371/165425 VG1531/11.

[19] al-Ahram, July 11, 1961.

[20] See Haykal's editorials in al-Ahram, July 14, August 4, and August 11, 1961.

on capital became more determined, he no longer limited his purview to Egypt. First came a Syrian land reform scheme, then the nationalization of several large banks, and finally selective nationalizations of important Syrian industrial firms. The July laws as applied in Syria, though a pale imitation of their Egyptian model, awoke the anti-Egyptian, anti-Nasser, and antisocialist forces that were already gaining strength in Syria. On September 28, 1961, elements of the Syrian army, under Lieutenant Colonel Haydar al-Kuzbari, seized power in Damascus and proclaimed an end to the federation. They argued that the heavy-handedness of Egyptian authority and the subordination of Syria to Egypt had inspired their opposition. They criticized the Nasser government for enacting legislation that threatened to emasculate the Syrian bourgeoisie as it had the Egyptian business classes.

The Syrian banking, industrial, commercial, and landowning elements were politically more vigorous and autonomous than their Egyptian counterparts. And their ties with foreign business groups had not been severed. Anticipating an assault similar to the destruction of the Egyptian bourgeoisie, they turned to the military, which had chafed under the autocratic and insensitive policies of Abd al-Hakim Amr, Nasser's special representative in Egypt and the head of the northern region in the federation.[21]

Nasser attributed the September 1961 Syrian military coup to reactionary forces who were threatened by the revolutionary energies that Egypt had let loose in Syria. Still, the dissolution of the United Arab Republic marked the first palpable setback for the Egyptian regime. Although Nasser had regarded the union as premature, he responded to its breakup with rage and defiance. Rejecting charges of Egyptian arrogance, Nasser asserted that the military plotters were financed by monopolist capitalists, imperialist agents, Zionists, and the state of Israel and were encouraged by the feudal monarchs of Jordan and Iran. In excoriating the Syrian capitalist classes, he singled out the Khumasiya Company for meddling in political affairs. Nasser described this heavily capitalized export-import firm and textile manufacturer as the source of Syria's "dictatorship of capital."[22] Nasser pointed out that one of the six primary rebels, Lieutenant Colonel Haydar al-Kuzbari, was a relative of the person installed as president of the new government and intimately connected with the Khumasiya Company.[23]

Nasser had good reason to fulminate against the Syrian middle classes. His contention that the Egyptian middle classes were also positioning

---

[21] See Tabitha Petran, *Syria* (London, 1972), pp. 106–48; and Malcolm Kerr, *The Arab Cold War: Gamal abd al-Nasir and His Rivals, 1958–1970* (New York, 1971), pp. 1–33.

[22] *al-Ahram*, September 30, 1961.

[23] Ibid., October 3, 1961.

themselves to do damage to his government, however, was unfounded, since the Egyptian business and professional groups were by then a spent force. Yet, using the Syrian rupture to vent his anger on the remnants of the bourgeoisie in Egypt, Nasser employed the well-worked mechanism of sequestrations to deprive more members of the Egyptian owning classes of their assets. New properties were added to the bounty of the Egyptian bureaucracy and military. Sequestrations took place between 1961 and 1964 and constituted the final mopping up of Egypt's independent business elements.

As a first step, the government arrested thirty-seven individuals and accused them of plotting to overthrow the regime. The thirty-seven represented three different strains of the old regime: politicians; remnants of the old landed elite like the Badrawi Ashur family; and a mixed group of merchants and industrialists, a few of Egyptian nationality and many more of foreign descent. The old politicians of the Wafd, still seen as a possible touchstone of opposition, were returned to prison.[24] The business persons detained represented a veritable who's who of corporate Egypt: Jean-Pierre and Joseph Matossian, the tobacco entrepreneurs; members of the Wahba and Habashi families, who had sat on the boards of numerous limited-liability companies; Abd al-Maqsud Ahmad of Bank Misr; the merchant Joseph Sidnawi; Elias Andraus, former confidant of King Faruq and ex–managing director of Beida Dyers; Elias Smouha, large landholder and investor; British exporter and cotton merchant David Ades; Ahmad Farghali, the leading Alexandrian cotton exporter; the textile industrialist François Taghir; Ahmad Abbud; and Khalil Sursock, an important business executive. Simultaneously, the press published the names of persons with holdings of more than £E10,000 in Egyptian joint stock companies as a portrait of the monopolistic and capitalist domination of ancien regime Egypt. Although the lists of arrested individuals often included no explanations, it was assumed that these men and women of wealth were accountable for Egypt's deplorable economic condition. Occasionally the local press took a strongly nativist position by commenting that most of those being detained had non-Egyptian names.[25] The arrests crushed the old non-Egyptian business elite. The once resplendent cosmopolitan Alexandrine bourgeoisie suffered its final indignity.[26]

[24] Ibid., October 22, 1961; *Egyptian Gazette*, October 22, 1961.

[25] See the issues of *al-Ahram* for late October and November 1961.

[26] Chancery, Cairo, to Foreign Office, November 21, 1961, PRO FO 371/155852 VG1461/61; G. A. Crossley, British Embassy, Berne, to R. S. Scrivener, Foreign Office, December 14, 1961, PRO FO 371/158855 VG1461/129. Crossley was writing on behalf of Harry Rofe, who complained that he had been out of the country for some time, had Swiss as well as British nationality, and was not guilty of any business improprieties. His protests were to no avail, however.

Thus, by the end of 1961 the public sector had supplanted the private sector throughout Egypt. Although individuals were entitled to own rural and urban property, no agricultural estate could exceed 100 feddans. Wholly autonomous large-scale companies, other than those belonging to corporations owned by Americans and a few other nationalities, had ceased to exist. To be sure, many of the same personnel stayed on to manage the public sector enterprises. Now, however, these individuals reported to high-ranking Egyptian bureaucrats, not boards of directors; and their performances were judged on the basis of job creation and production targets attained rather than profitability and dividend payouts.

Between 1952 and 1961 the Egyptian government seized a vast total of assets from the private sector. Yet because the takeovers occurred over a full decade rather than at one cataclysmic moment, the task of estimating their value has never been an easy one. Rough assessments have varied from £E500,000,000 to £E2 billion.[27] My own calculation, as detailed in the accompanying table, allows a higher valuation for the land than most have made and concludes that the Egyptian government seized assets to the value of nearly £850,000,000. Of this total, the state eventually desequestered £166 million while retaining £681 million in the public sector.

However one values the properties seized by the government of Egypt, there can be no gainsaying that it paid a minimal price for its acquisitions—a paltry £321 million, according to my calculations, and enjoyed, thereby, a windfall of £360 million. The bulk of the gain for the state came at the expense of the landowning class, especially the royal family, which received no compensation for its seized properties. Its holdings of close to 180,000 feddans were worth £E72 million at 1951 land prices.

The above totals take no account of the substantial British and French assets (some £158.8 million) that were officially desequestered in 1958 and 1959. Much of this property was never taken back by the original owners. Those who chose not to take over their assets were entitled to compensation but could repatriate no more than £5,000. If a person elected not to reclaim his or her property, the state took it over after the compensation sum had been agreed upon. A large number of British and French citizens had no desire to return to Egypt and thus lost most of the wealth that they had accrued over many years. But just how many and how much their assets were worth we have no way of determining. In

---

[27] In a speech in December 1961, Nasser claimed that the full amount of property taken by the state was £E500,000,000. In a careful and persuasive analysis, Mahmud Mutawalli, in *al-Asul al-Tarikhiya lil Rasmaliya al-Misriya wa Tatawwuraha* (Cairo, 1974), arrived at the figure of £E453,894,225 (p. 310). John Waterbury, *The Egypt of Nasser and Sadat*, p. 75, proposed £E700 million; and Faruq Juwayda, *Amwal Misr: Kayf Da'at* (Cairo, 1976), p. 39, suggested a figure of £E2 billion.

Value of Properties Taken Over by the Egyptian Government, 1952–1961
(in £000,000)

	Properties Taken Over	Desequestered	Retained Public Sector	Price Paid	Gain to Government of Egypt
Land Reform Measures, 1952–1961[a]	320	—	320[g]	124	196
British Poperty[b]	165	118	47	27.5	19.5
French Property[c]	63.4	47.8	15.6	15.6	—
Belgian Property[d]	8	—	8	8	—
Suez Canal Company[e]	32	—	32	23	9
Socialist Laws of 1961[f]	258	—	258	122.5	135.5
TOTAL	846.4	165.8	680.6	320.6	360

[a] There is little agreement on exactly how much land was taken over in the various land reform acts between 1952 and 1961. I have taken the figure of 800,000 feddans from Mahmoud Abdel-Fadel. *Development, Income Distribution, and Social Challenge in rural Egypt* (Cambridge, 1975), p. 10. A feddan of land was worth about £400 in 1951, and owners were compensated at about half that amount.

[b] The value of British property comes from the British archives and is mainly a self-valuation.

[c] Jean Ducret, *Les capitaux Européens en Proche Orient*, pp. 319–21. I have not used the French or Belgian archives for arriving at this figure and believe that Ducret's estimates of the Belgian and French property sequestered are accurate for the company assets but seriously underestimate the large amount of property held privately by French nationals.

[d] Ibid., pp. 323–24.

[e] These figures come from Hubert Bonin, *Suez: du canal à la finance, 1858–1987* (Paris, 1987), p. 178.

[f] These figures come from *al-Ahram* issues for February 9 and March 2 and 3, 1962. They have also been analyzed in Charles Issawi, *Egypt in Revolution: An Economic Analysis* (New York, 1963), p. 60.

[g] These lands were held privately.

addition, many individuals whose shares were sequestered in the socialist laws of July 1961 were not compensated because they were not entitled to receive payments on their sequestered assets.

That the government of Egypt acquired a vast economic empire at bargain basement prices is undeniable. Even so, the payments the state was compelled to make to those whom it dispossessed imposed a heavy burden on the local exchequer. Compensation payments to Britain, France, Belgium, and the Suez Canal Company were far from modest at £74.1 million, though they were stretched out over a number of years. They proved to be the equivalent of 21 percent of the balance-of-payments deficit Egypt ran between 1959 and 1962, or 61 percent of the deficit on current payments. In addition, the figure of £74.1 million takes no account of the individual payments made to British and French nationals which, though limited to £E5,000 per applicant, must have been substantial. Moreover, although the land reform scheme was supposed to be self-financing and thus cost-free to the state, the new owners were not able to keep up their payments to the state, and much of their debt had to be written off.

Paying for the nationalized properties was less than half the battle. More difficult by far was the sheer problem of running all of the companies that the state had brought into the public sector. Anecdotal information from the mid-1950s indicated that some enterprises, like the new Suez Canal Authority, were exceedingly well run. The canal authority was allocated Egypt's most skilled administrators. Some European businessmen, upon returning to inspect their nationalized properties, were pleased to discover, as the directors of Bradford Dyers did when they visited their old Beida Dyers plant, that the government of Egypt had not disturbed the Egyptian management team and that those individuals had done a competent job without British oversight.[28] But other firms suffered grievously from mismanagement. Whatever the case, the state's penchant for treating firms as sources of employment caused an obvious deterioration in economic performance.

To administer this vast new economic empire, the Egyptian bureaucracy expanded at a rate unprecedented even in a country known from earliest times for its centralizing and bureaucratic tendencies. The number of ministries grew from 16 to 22 between 1952 and 1960, and the number of state employees went from 350,000 in 1951–52 to 770,000 in 1962–63 and then to 1,200,000 in 1969–70. By 1969, Egypt had 29 ministries, 50 public authorities, 46 public organizations, 381 public companies, and 6 independent bodies. The public bureaucracy at that time employed 60 percent of the nation's university graduates and had become an employer of last resort for all university graduates.[29]

EXPLANATIONS

How had an economy in which private enterprises had been so securely anchored moved with such rapidity and seeming ease to public sector domination? Certainly events themselves and the geopolitical setting of Egypt in the Cold War played a paramount role. No event loomed larger than the Suez War, without which the Egyptian government would have found it infinitely more difficult to move against the great firms. Egypt's strategic significance in the Cold War enabled the Egyptian leadership to

---

[28] See letter from Geoffrey Bird to J. H. E. Allison, February 18, 1992. This letter was sent to me by Mr. Allison and is in my possession.

[29] Ayubi, *Bureaucracy and Politics in Contemporary Egypt*, pp. 213 and 243.

play the West against the Soviets and also provided Egyptians with an attractive alternative model of development to the capitalist emphasis championed by Western officials. But deep-seated domestic factors were just as decisive in compelling the Egyptian ruling elements to expand the public arena. Five were predominant: ideology, political ambition, bureaucratic competition, economic necessity, and a planning vision.

Ideology

The military men, stepping prematurely into office without a clear economic perspective in view, confined themselves at first to ridding the country of regressive forces, identified at the time as the British army and the landed magnates. The business classes were not yet viewed as antagonists. Yet the new political rulers had faith in centralized economic planning. Echoing the standard ideas of development economists of this period, the military men portrayed unregulated capitalism as a luxurious form of economic development, not well suited to the limited resources and the shortened time horizon of their country's goals. These men were also committed to development schemes on a grand scale, and they had concluded that numerous projects were beyond the unaided capacities of the private sector. Early in their tenure the young officers surrounded themselves with men like Sidqi, Nusayr, and Barrawi, who were equally enamored of planning and thought that the state, rather than free markets, would forge economic progress.

Soon after seizing power, Nasser and his colleagues made clear their desire for economic planning. The creation of the National Production Council and the separation of the Ministries of Commerce and Industry underscored Egypt's intention to enlarge the state's economic role. A growing political and military rapprochement with the Soviet Union brought Egyptian bureaucrats into close contact with Soviet officials. At the time that the Egyptian technocrats were developing the country's first five-year plan (in early 1957) Egypt was also solidifying its political and military alliance with the Soviet Union. Not only did the Egyptians accept a large Soviet loan in support of their development projects, but Egyptian economic experts began to travel to the Soviet Union for advice on the five-year plans.

The emphasis on state-sponsored development led inexorably to suspicions of the private sector. The military men were wary of big business from the outset, although they manifested their caution only indirectly through the occasional hostile remark about the insensitivity of business groups toward the regime. But the animus grew as the regime came to believe that the private sector was lagging in its contribution to economic transformation and was insufficiently enthusiastic about big development schemes. Toward the end of 1957 the government's ideological pronouncements took on a sharp antibusiness and anticapitalist edge. In a speech in December 1957, President Nasser enunciated for the first time his vision of Egypt as a democratic, socialist, and cooperative society.[30] Increasingly, Nasser criticized the capitalist pathway toward economic growth. To be sure, his severest attack was reserved for the so-called monopoly capitalists. Yet most wealthy business persons and directors of heavily capitalized joint stock companies believed that the president's strictures were directed against them. Even in those sectors of the Egyptian economy where competition was most pronounced, like shipping; textiles; and cotton ginning, pressing, and exporting, the government complained about price collusion, cartelization agreements, excessive profits, high dividend payments, and excessive executive perquisites.

The government's pronouncements also had a social and ethical dimension. Government officials complained that the private sector was not merely wasteful of limited resources and incapable of mobilizing the large amounts of capital required for Egyptian development projects. It also produced gross disparities in income. Capitalism created a small elite of super-wealthy whose life styles were an affront to the rest of society while impoverishing the great mass.[31] In the years leading up to the socialist laws, Nasser claimed that a state-led form of economic development would put an end to hyperexploitation, eradicate income inequities, and establish popular control over the instruments of economic power. The key words of the late 1950s—socialism, democracy, and cooperativism—were accompanied by claims that Egypt would be both productive and just in the economic sphere.

To dismiss ideology as camouflage for material interests requires overlooking the fact that the military men were the first generation of rulers to spring from the rank and file of Egyptian society. Earlier nationalists had cast themselves as true Egyptians, but the military men had a more valid claim to represent the suffering, economic misery, and marginalized status of the vast majority. Scholars have discounted the programmatic explanations issued by Nasser, Haykal, and the publicists of the regime for the move from a political revolution to one with more social content in late 1957 and early 1958. Equally, they downplay the ideological em-

---

[30] *al-Ahram*, December 6, 1957; Minute by A. P. Parsons, Nasser's Internal Policy, June 23, 1960, PRO FO 371/150902 VG1016/11.

[31] See, as an example of the concern about equity issues, the introductory comments of Baghdadi to the first five-year plan. Baghdadi wrote that although Egypt was poor it still had mammoth disparities in wealth and income, which would only widen under an unregulated free-market form of economic development. United Arab Republic, Lajnat al-Takhit al-Qawmi, *Cadre du Plan Quinquennal Général* (Cairo, 1960), p. 8.

phasis in Nasser's speeches in 1960–61 and Haykal's editorials in the columns of *al-Ahram* at that time as rationalizations. The National Charter promulgated in 1962 is often given short shrift for the same reasons. But even though Egypt's route to its peculiar brand of socialism and its enlarged public sector was marked by historical accident and considerable opportunism, it also reflected the yearnings of the new ruling stratum. These men possessed a powerful sense of their Egyptianness; their sense of mission toward the poorer segments of Egyptian society, particularly the peasantry, cannot be minimized.

Haykal's writings in *al-Ahram* undoubtedly encapsulated the philosophy of the ruling elite as it unfolded in the late 1950s and early 1960s.[32] In columns penned at the time of the socialist laws, Haykal claimed that Egypt was forging a new pathway toward economic development—neither capitalist nor communist. In his view, the route traversed by Western capitalism was no longer available to late developers like Egypt. Nor was it morally acceptable. The West had accumulated its capital, he claimed, through the exploitation of the rest of the world, first under plantation slavery in the new world and subsequently under colonial domination. But in an anti-imperial era, states were no longer permitted to extract the wealth of other peoples to enrich themselves. The communist experiment of the Soviet Union was not to be emulated either. Stalinism had brought economic progress through a ruthless squeezing of the peasantry, a formula that the Egyptian leaders, claiming to spring from peasant roots, could not embrace. The third pathway, that chosen by the Egyptians, was state-controlled economic progress, based on rigorous planning, state ownership of the vital sectors of production, and an attentiveness to the welfare of the entire population. The Egyptian brand of socialism, according to Haykal, reflected Egyptian circumstances and Egyptian character. It permitted private property but forbade exploitation. It paid fair compensation for the private property it took over, and it gave a greater role to the individual than was permitted in Soviet-style communism.

The National Charter, presented by President Nasser at the inaugural session of the National Congress of the Powers of the People on May 21, 1962, formalized these same themes. Although divided into ten chapters, the charter developed its primary ideological thrust in chapter 8, entitled "On the Inevitability of the Socialist Solution." The document condemned capitalism for "its unruly tendencies" and argued that "capital in its natural development is no longer able to lead the economic drive." Egypt, the charter affirmed, was to achieve its economic progress by means of a blending of private and public initiatives. The socialist route "does not

---

[32] See especially the editorials of July 14 and August 4 and 11, 1961, in *al-Ahram*. The themes enunciated there found a strong echo in the National Charter of the next year.

necessitate the nationalization of all means of production," but a country seeking economic growth needs "a capable public sector that would lead progress in all domains and bear the main responsibility of the development plan." Private businesses can also participate "without exploitation."[33]

Only occasionally in Egyptian economic matters is it possible to move beyond the official statements and to identify the actual individuals and groups agitating in favor of certain policies. One such opportunity was in late 1961 when a well-regarded British economist, Elizabeth Penrose, visited Cairo and engaged in discussion with some of Egypt's leading economists and bureaucrats. Her visit coincided with the application of the socialist laws and was an occasion for her to question many knowledgeable and influential Egyptians about the events leading up to these decrees. Penrose concluded that the older group of economists, as represented by Zaki al-Shafi'i, dean of the Faculty of Economics at Cairo University, and Dr. Nabil Naggar, were critical of the government's economic programs and skeptical of the government's economic pronouncements. But the younger economists at Cairo University were enthusiastic Nasserite socialists and accepted the view that big capital had to be rooted out in order to promote a more just society. Most of the government economists, Penrose discovered, were from this younger generation of graduates, and it was they, she believed, who had promoted the July laws. Her own view of these men and women was that they were grossly inexperienced in administration and wildly optimistic about what state regulation and planning could accomplish. Moreover, she surmised that there had been little planning before the laws were announced. She concluded from her interviews, "The planners have not yet even become aware of the problems of planning to run a nationalized industrial sector in its entirety, especially with respect to the volume of financing in relation to prices and output of goods and the payment of incomes to the people." She failed to identify the individual architects of the nationalization laws except to determine that they constituted a small group of advisers around the president.[34] Egypt's planned economy also owed inspiration to a group of dedicated, and in some cases internationally renowned, development economists, many from foreign countries, such as the Swede Jan Tinberger and Ragnar Nurske from Holland, who worked inside the Egyptian government.

Like other worldviews, the ideology of the Egyptian ruling group was rooted in personal experience. It was tinged with deep feelings of resentment. Max Sheler has suggested that feelings of impotence, rage, and desire for revenge manifest themselves most intensely among displaced and marginalized classes. In his view the resentful groups in any society

[33] United Arab Republic, *The National Charter* (Cairo, 1962), pp. 49–58.
[34] Elizabeth Penrose, Report on Discussion in Cairo, September 17–21, 1961, PRO FO 371/158824 VG1103/12.

come from the lower-middle artisans and small official classes—in short, the petite bourgeoisie—those whose status has declined and who are driven by impulses to strike out at those whom they must serve and who control their destinies.[35] It is, of course, always dangerous to transpose constructs derived from the Western experience to other parts of the world, but Sheler's idea of resentment seems especially helpful for understanding the behavior and worldview of the Egyptian military and its closest civilian collaborators. What requires revision is his view that the resentful classes are marginalized and falling. Quite the contrary often occurs in a colonial setting where those who feel the most intense rage tend to come from a rising-middle or lower-middle stratum; they are the sons and daughters of the poorer and middle urban and rural strata, who are destined to displace the old colonial elites. Although the rich indigenes in colonial areas bristled at racial and religious biases, their resentment was tempered by the benefits that they and their offspring gained from colonial affiliation. Not so the middle and lower-middle elements, like the young Egyptian military officers, the young civil servants, the middle peasantry, and the unskilled workers in Egypt's modern industrial sector. They saw their career aspirations blocked by colonial authority; they felt the sting of colonial privilege and colonial humiliation. Even those from relatively privileged backgrounds, like the two military officers, Zakariya and Khalid Muhi al-Din, still must have felt the frustration of being treated as lesser persons in their own country.

Egypt was a territory, despite its confused imperial status, where colonial power sat heavily and crudely on local populations and where the middle and lower-middle classes were constantly confronting colonial symbols. The country was saddled with a large and omnipresent army of occupation that until the late 1940s moved freely through the major cities, populated rural areas, and paid little attention to Egyptian national amour propre. Contributing to the rising anger were the special laws that protected foreigners (the Capitulations); the special courts for foreign nationals, known as the Mixed Tribunals; and the large foreign populations living luxuriously in Egypt's prime cities, yet always near the mass of urban Egyptians and even not far from the rural populations. Even so well established a nationalist politician and intellectual as Muhammad Hasan Haykal could rage against Egypt's colonial subordination and assert that Egyptians were forced to live as foreigners in their own country. But it was the new military rulers and the civilians they brought into government who lifted these feelings onto the stage of history and achieved the revenge that fermented in the minds of so many others.

It is hardly surprising that the military leaders had ties with such exem-

[35] Max Sheler, *Resentment*, edited and with an Introduction by Lewis A. Coser (New York, 1972).

plars of a resentful brand of nationalism as Hasan al-Banna, founder of the Muslim Brotherhood, and Ahmad Husayn of the Young Egypt movement. Many of the military men came from the same social and cultural strata, or if they did not, they had experienced the same disabling discrimination that those movements so vehemently resented. Hasan al-Banna's radical and antiforeign Islamism was forged in a city of colonial privilege and disparity—Ismailia, where the Suez Canal Company was created and where European privilege was writ large.

Evidence for a resentful nationalism in the Nasser years comes from the rhetoric of the military elite, which was so condemnatory of British military and political power in Egypt at first and then later of capitalist domination and exploitation.[36] The language of Egyptian nationalism could be flamboyantly antiforeign. It depicted foreign influences as the evil source of Egyptian woes. Even clearer evidence comes from the treatment of foreign groups during moments of acute crisis. British and French nationals and Jews were expelled from Egypt unceremoniously as if they, rather than the politicians and military men in London, Paris, and Tel Aviv, had planned the invasion of Egypt. Similarly, the small Belgian community was treated in a humiliating fashion when it was forced to leave in 1961. The wealthy classes in Egypt were subject to harsh sequestration decrees and even more condemnatory language in the early 1960s, as if they alone were responsible for Egypt's dismal record of economic and social progress in the twentieth century. This resentful brand of nationalism made it difficult for the ruling cadres to differentiate between the political and economic spheres and to allow economic need and rationality to take precedence over political desire and political emotion.

Although the Egyptian nationalist and socialist ideology was deeply rooted in Egyptian experience, there can be no question that the Egyptian leaders, especially Nasser, drew support for their radical political and economic initiatives from other decolonizing polities. Nasser cultivated the friendship of Nehru, Sukarno, and Tito; his sense of being part of a new third force in international affairs was solidified during his attendance at the Bandung conference.

Political Ambition

The Egyptian rulers, as Nasser so often remarked, were first and foremost military conspirators. They were animated by a powerful instinct for po-

---

[36] The writings of Nasser and Sadat are full of suppressed anger and hostility toward their antagonists. See especially Anwar el-Sadat, *In Search of Identity: An Autobiography* (New York, 1978), in which, despite protestations about spirituality and belief in the power of love, his rage at the British and the wealthier classes is poorly muffled.

litical survival, and this instinct became a second, potent cause of public sector growth. The first four years of the Revolutionary Command Council were marked by repeated internal and external challenges to authority. The contest for supremacy within the council was not resolved until March 1954, and later that year an assassination attempt was made on Nasser. The British, French, and Israelis invaded Egypt to unseat Nasser and establish a more compliant regime. The growth of the public sector was linked inextricably to the ruling elite's campaign to eliminate other centers of power and to fill the government institutions with their own supporters. First to be eliminated were the old-style politicians and the landed magnates. Next came the foreign business elites, linked in the minds of the military junta with the British-French-Israeli effort to remove the military leaders from power. The shock of the breakup of the United Arab Republic led to reprisals against the wealthy in Egypt, who were thought to have been involved with the Syrian middle classes. Not only were wealthy individuals removed from positions of power but their assets were incorporated into the public sector and made available to appointees and loyalists of the military regime.

Nasser's rise to preeminence was steady, almost inexorable; at each stage of his ascent his powers of patronage grew. In January 1953, with the dissolution of the old political parties, Nasser became vice president of the country. Egypt's status as a republic was announced in June 1953, simultaneous with Nasser's becoming minister of the interior and his loyal junta members' taking cabinet positions. By the end of 1954, Nasser had beaten back the challenges of Neguib, the advocates of democracy, and the Muslim Brothers, and his political supremacy was no longer in doubt. Next to feel his aggrandizing ambitions were the wielders of independent economic power. Nasser's critics often charged him with a desire to make Egypt a bureaucratic state, dependent on his whim. As an inveterate conspirator, he saw independent institutions as potential havens for political opponents and felt secure only when large numbers looked to him for their livelihoods.[37]

Bureaucratic Competition

The public sector grew through a bureaucratic imperative. Ideology set the tone, but once a large and expansive public sector had come into being it generated its own momentum. Bureaucratic factions and groups competed to profit from the expanding employment opportunities. Politi-

[37] This well-known story has been developed in many of the standard accounts of the Nasser years. I am particularly indebted to the study of Tariq al-Bishri, *al-Dimuqratiya wa-Nizam 23 Yulio, 1952–70* (Beirut, 1987).

cal blocs used the public sector to magnify their power. On August 24, 1961, for instance, just after the socialist laws were enacted, the government issued a decree appointing more than 1,500 managing directors, presidents of the boards of nationalized companies, and members of boards to the more than 350 banks, insurance companies, and other firms involved in the takeovers of the previous month.[38] The newly appointed officers had many opportunities to use their powers to make additional appointments and to create small bureaucratic fiefdoms. Much of the chaos and inefficiency that marked the Egyptian public sector in the later Nasser years stemmed from the uncoordinated and disorganized way in which competing factions endeavored to build up strength at the expense of antagonists.

Clear-cut factions and cliques were difficult to discern. Alliances were constantly made and unmade. Battles occurred behind the scenes. Individual aspirants moved from one group to another as the fortunes of the blocs waxed and waned. Factionalism began at the top of the political pyramid. Nasser's favor was always decisive, but his circle of close allies was in motion. The changing political alignments at the top were shrouded in secrecy, only visible during moments of crisis when individuals were banished from the inner circle and new persons brought to the fore. Because alliances were unstable, so were the blocs and factions that drew their legitimacy from the men at the top.

During the first decade of military rule the public sector was dominated by several overarching organizations whose jurisdiction was often overlapping and unclear. Competition among these entities fueled expansion in the public sector. The most powerful, in order of their coming into being, were the military industries, the High Dam Authority, the Ministry of Industry, the Economic Organization, the Authority for the Five-Year Industrial Plan, the Nasr Organization, the Misr Organization, and the Authority for the Five-Year Plan. The High Dam Authority, the Nasr Organization, and the Misr Organization represented only slices of the whole economy, whereas the Ministry of Industry, at first, and the Authority for the Five-Year Plan, later, made claims to oversight of the whole economy. By the early 1960s, Aziz Sidqi, head of the Ministry of Industry and apostle of centralized planning, was at the storm center of all of these institutional struggles. To be sure, the minister of economy and finance should have exercised economic oversight, but the office tended to rotate among technocrats who were chosen for their high standing in Western financial circles. Qaysuni, minister of finance in the 1950s, was much less dynamic than Sidqi and did not enjoy Nasser's confidence.

Following the 1954 conflict, the Egyptian political elite was a one-man

---

[38] *al-Ahram,* August 25, 1961.

operation in which Nasser was consulted on every major decision and a bewildering array of minor matters.[39] He, in turn, relied on Abd al-Hakim Amr; Ali Sabri, the minister for presidential affairs; and Muhammad Hasanayn Haykal, a confidant and intellectual spokesman for the president. In the 1960s Abd al-Hakim Amr created his own power bloc, independent of Nasser and based on his position as commander in chief of the Egyptian armed forces.[40] Below these individuals came Zakariya Muhi al-Din, the long-time minister of the interior; Abd al-Latif al-Baghdadi, general troubleshooter of the Nasser governments of the 1950s, and as minister for economic planning during much of that era the military man most intimately concerned with economic questions; and finally Kimal al-Din Husayn, minister of education.

The creation of the Ministry of Industry in June 1956 gave the public sector a new center of gravity. Aziz Sidqi extended the sway of his ministry throughout the Egyptian economy. In a bureaucratic dispute in January 1957 he bested his chief adversary, Abu Nusayr, head of the Ministry of Commerce, by engineering the takeover of the British and French banks and insurance companies and founding the Economic Organization. Using the support of the minister of finance, Qaysuni, he prevented Abu Nusayr, Rashid Barrawi, Ahmad Fuad of Bank Misr, and Colonels Sidqi Sulayman and Samir Hilmi of the National Production Council from enacting more far-reaching nationalizations.[41]

At the Ministry of Industry, Sidqi moved from triumph to triumph, enlarging his circle of supporters and his scope for action. By mid-1957 he had established a general office for industrial progress within the ministry, headed up by Yahya Sabr al-Malla. Also, Sidqi brought the Authority for the Five-Year Industrial Plan into being. Sidqi himself chaired this body and appointed to its board Amin Hilmi Kamil and Ahmad Fuad, Abu Nusayr's former ally.[42]

Sidqi had helped to found the Economic Organization, but in time it became an independent center of bureaucratic power under the guidance of the military officer Hasan Ibrahim. Although Sidqi had also been responsible for establishing the large industrial holding company called the Nasr Organization, which encompassed the automotive industry and a large proportion of Egyptian investments in the oil sector, it too became an independent entity under the leadership of Muhammad Abd Allah

[39] No. 16, C. T. Crowe, Cairo, to Selwyn Lloyd, April 19, 1960, PRO FO 371/150902 VG1016/4.

[40] Of the many accounts of Amr's rise, see Sadat, *In Search of Identity*, pp. 160–61.

[41] No. 2335, Hare to Secretary of State, January 20, 1957, USNA 874.19; no. 445, James N. Cortada to Department of State, January 3, 1957, USNA 774.1.

[42] *al-Ahram*, July 1, 1957; Commercial Department, Cairo, to Foreign Office, April 1961, PRO FO 371/1588818 VG1102/5.

Marzapan. Similarly, the Misr Organization, the holding company for all of the affiliated Misr commercial and industrial companies, evolved into a large and independently powerful economic empire.

Economic Necessity

Many accounts of these years argue that the action against the private sector was necessitated by the failure of business to play a dynamic role in Egyptian development.[43] Scholars cite a decline in the growth of capitalization of joint stock companies throughout the 1950s and sluggish rates of industrial progress. They also refer to comments made by members of the ruling elite about the timidity of Egyptian capital for new and vital projects and the preference of private investment for urban properties. Yet the economic record of the private sector was far from clear. Not all of the economic results impelled Egypt's rulers to prefer the public sector over private initiatives, although some did.

The statistical information available to the ruling elite was incomplete and hard to read. Many of the figures cited by economic analysts to demonstrate a lack of vigor on the part of private investors and a slowing of industrial growth rates were not available before crucial decisions were made. Economic data came from various research organizations, like those established by the National Bank of Egypt and Bank Misr as well as the National Planning Council. They yielded an equivocal portrait of Egyptian economic growth in the 1950s. An annual growth rate in equity capital of approximately 3 percent was far from outstanding but could easily be rationalized on the basis of the rude shocks the Egyptian economy and private investors had been forced to absorb in the land reform of 1952 and the Egyptianization of British and French businesses in 1957.[44] And the statements of the Egyptian rulers were not particluarly hostile to the private sector. The most critical remarks were invariably made after the old business empires had been dismantled and seem to have been later justifications.

Nonetheless, certain factors did militate in favor of increased government involvement in economic affairs. Notably, 1960 was a difficult and disappointing year economically, especially in the financial markets. Even the least sophisticated in economic matters could not ignore the

[43] Representative of these studies are Bent Hansen and Girgis A. Marzouk, *Development and Economic Policy in the UAR (Egypt)* (Amsterdam, Netherlands, 1965); and, from the political science perspective, Waterbury, *The Egypt of Nasser and Sadat*, esp. pp. 57–82.

[44] Central Bank of Egypt, *Economic Review* 1, no. 2 (1961), pp. 221–30. In the documentation that follows I have tried to cite data that were widely available to the Egyptian rulers at the time and likely to have influenced their thinking on economic issues.

implications of the warning signals. Growth rates of the gross national product and industrial productivity dipped precipitously in that year and were well below the targets established by the planners. The amount of new equity capital mobilized in joint stock companies grew by an anemic 2 percent.[45] The average price of shares on the Egyptian stock exchange, after surging in 1958 and part of 1959 in reaction to the signing of financial accords with Britain and France, went into a tailspin. The value of industrial shares on the stock exchange fell a full 25 percent in the course of the year.[46] Having just published its new and ambitious five-year plan in 1960, the Egyptian regime became fearful that the private sector would be unable and unwilling to carry out the large and important tasks assigned to it in the plan. Committed as it was to achieving the plan's goals, the state felt obligated to take the place of private capital.[47]

Crises in balance-of-trade and balance-of-payments accounts further forced the state to be more interventionist. In no single year since the end of World War II had Egypt achieved a favorable trade balance. It had seen its currency reserves, once at a seemingly unassailable level, fall from 65 percent of gross national product in 1946 to zero by the end of 1962.[48] The dire currency condition had compelled the government to devalue the currency in 1962.[49] Investment and productivity figures were never clear and were subject to varying interpretations, but the size of foreign currency holdings had a concreteness that other figures did not. Egypt was moving rapidly and ominously into financial deficit, and although the Nasser government was prepared to spend more than it earned during these years devoted to creating the economic conditions for a growth takeoff, it was wary of the perils of indebtedness and insolvency not only from its bitter nineteenth-century historical experience but also from the constant lectures it received from Western statesmen and economic experts. Between 1955 and 1963, Egypt's cumulative deficit on current payments was £E348.8 million.[50] During those years the country had expended the remainder of its sterling balances and had begun to use Soviet loans and American wheat shipments to close the deficit on its balance of payments.

Payments crises do not necessarily require governments to dismantle private enterprises. Control mechanisms, like currency exchange regulations, import and export licensing, and tariff regulations, can correct trade

---

[45] Ibid.

[46] National Bank of Egypt, *Economic Bulletin* 14, no. 2 (1961), p. 266.

[47] Ismail Sabri Abd Allah, *Tanzim al-Qita' al-Amm* (Cairo, 1979), pp. 260 ff.

[48] Hansen and Marzouk, *Development and Economic Policy*, pp. 186–87.

[49] On the devaluation, see Bent Hansen and Karim Nashashibi, *Foreign Trade Regimes and Economic Development: Egypt* (New York, 1975), pp. 89–106.

[50] Hansen and Marzouk, *Development and Economic Policy*, p. 14.

and payment deficiencies. But the Egyptian government had little faith in the cooperation of private business groups and became convinced that private enterprises were subverting its efforts. It concluded that the only way Egypt could deal with its financial problems was through a full take-over of firms, primarily importing and exporting companies, but also commercial and industrial companies engaged in international trade.

Finally, the state's dissatisfaction with Egyptian industry's treatment of labor disposed it to bring companies into the public sector. Egyptian in-dustrialists, foreign and native-born, had a well-deserved reputation for treating labor harshly and paying low wages. Despite the regime's efforts to ameliorate working conditions by guaranteeing paid holidays and im-proving health insurance, labor benefited less from the productivity gains of the 1950s than did capital. The government despaired of the business classes' ever developing a social conscience. Later economic analyses revealed that only one-third of the gross value added in industry went to wage earners, while two-thirds accrued to profits. Moreover, labor's por-tion was falling in the 1950s while management, instead of plowing its growing earnings back into the firms, distributed them in the form of increased dividend payments to shareholders. Although the regime did not have these details at hand, it could see that the material conditions of the working classes had not ameliorated in the 1950s. According to a later economic analysis of labor conditions, "One can hardly think of anything more deserving of the epithet 'exploitation' than the earlier con-ditions of work in Egyptian factories and the rise in profits experienced by Egyptian industry during the last 25 years."[51]

Planning

Finally, the Egyptian ruling classes, like all of those in the less-developed countries in this era, believed in the efficacy of centralized economic planning. At first, planning meant little more than state oversight of the economy and the establishment of investment and production targets, to be realized in large measure by private initiative. But within a few years, as the Soviet Union became the most important foreign ally of Egypt, the state itself became the primary economic agency, relying on its parasta-tals to achieve production goals. A five-year plan to promote industrial development was announced in January 1957, shortly after the creation of the Ministry of Industry. The plan called for the expenditure of £E248 million over the full five years and was intended to bring self-sufficiency to Egypt in a large number of industrial products. Though short on spe-

[51] Ibid., p. 169.

cifics, it stressed iron and steel, engineering, chemicals, textiles, and foodstuffs. It did not differentiate between the responsibilities of the private and public sectors, although it expected the government to participate in the caustic soda, pencil, and paper industries. Of the £E248 million, £E16.5 million would be allocated to general programs, £E21 million to mining, and £E25 million for the expansion of the petroleum industry. The Egyptian government would raise £E96.5 million of the investment capital, and the rest would come from local sources or foreign assistance.[52]

Under Soviet pressure the planning effort became a more serious and state-driven activity. In 1957 the Soviet Union announced that it would contribute £E62 million in economic aid.[53] The announcement followed Abd al-Hakim Amr's twenty-day negotiating visit to Moscow, during which the Egyptian and Soviet teams discussed economic and military matters together. It revealed that the Egyptian-Soviet alliance was more than a military partnership, and it brought economic planning and state control over the economy to the forefront in Egypt. In their economic discussions Amr's delegation had emphasized Egypt's dire need for industrial development to offset the country's growing population and deepening poverty.

Qaysuni and Sidqi took up the baton passed to them by Amr. They assembled a delegation to work out the details of the preliminary agreement that Amr had concluded with the Soviets. The Egyptian team sent to Moscow included persons with specialized knowledge of the engineering and mining industries, chemicals, textiles, and petroleum.[54] Sidqi announced that Egypt's industrial effort would concentrate on the petroleum sector, the manufacture of mining equipment, and what he called the transformation industries, especially automobiles. Among the specific proposals that the Egyptian delegation placed before the Soviets was a design for a mammoth sugar refinery, to be erected in Edfu at a cost of £E20 million and capable of producing 16 million tons of sugar per year; a drydock, able to produce 50,000-ton ships and costing £E9 million; and an automobile industry, manufacturing at the outset 2,500 trucks per year and costing £E7.5 million.[55]

The result of these negotiations was the announcement of Egypt's five-year industrial plan of 1957. The plan envisioned the establishment of 129 new factories, most of them to be state-run. The Soviet Union was to assist in the creation of sixty-eight of these plants, many of which were simply to

[52] *al-Ahram*, June 1, 1957; no. 817, First Quarter 1957, Economic Report, April 29, 1957, USNA 874.00.

[53] *al-Ahram*, November 2, 1945.

[54] Ibid., November 22 and 27, 1957.

[55] Ibid., December 3, 1957.

be disassembled in the Soviet Union and reassembled in Egypt. West Germany was to provide twenty plants, and Japan fifteen. Twenty-five programs were to be executed locally. The only project not clearly allocated was the automobile program, a key project that the Egyptian government had not yet brought to the stage at which it could solicit bids.[56]

Impatience characterized Egypt's planning effort. Just as the Soviets had exceeded their planning goals in the interwar years, so the Egyptians were counseled to believe that they could do the same. Nasser was completely won to this perspective, and he took up the idea of planning with an excitement verging on mania, pressuring his planning staff ruthlessly to set higher and higher target figures and insisting always that goals be revised upward.[57] In a speech delivered on August 1, 1959, he pointed out that the average income per person in Egypt was £E40 per year; in Europe it was £E200 to £E250 and in the United States £E600. Planning and state-led industrialization, Nasser predicted, would bring Egypt to a par with Europe in twenty years.[58]

Each succeeding year, as goal after goal was said to be achieved on or ahead of schedule, Nasser lifted the planning expectations. By 1958 he claimed that Egypt would reach its full five-year industrial plan by 1960, two years ahead of schedule, and would then be ready for a comprehensive five-year plan involving all sectors of the economy.[59] Even as the technocrats were gathering data for the new plan, Nasser raised the preliminary goal from doubling national income in twenty years to doubling it in ten years. The new target obligated Egypt to sustain an improbably high annual rate of economic growth of 7.2 percent, rather than the more manageable rate of 3.4 percent.[60]

The top levels of the polity, especially the Office of the President, expressed boundless faith in the possibilities of planning and a growing public sector. Hindsight was to indicate that the planning effort put the public sector under excessive pressure; haste and poor preparation were the result. Goals were rarely met. Yet spokespersons were pressured into announcing they had reached their targets. Projects did not succeed one another in a logical and timely order. They arose pell-mell, often in response to Nasser's desire to proclaim new successes. While the industrial plan was in full swing in 1959, Sidqi boasted that the country was establishing a new factory every week, that Egypt would soon be able to

---

[56] Ibid., September 18, 1958.
[57] Ibid., September 14, 1958.
[58] Ibid., August 2, 1959.
[59] Ibid., September 14, 1958.
[60] There are many useful studies of the plan. See Charles Issawi, *Egypt in Revolution: An Economic Analysis* (London, 1963), pp. 66 ff; and Hansen and Marzouk, *Development and Economic Policy*, pp. 295 ff.

produce armored cars and tanks, and that its processed foodstuffs and industrial equipment met the highest international standards.[61] Egypt's controlled press added to the unrealism of these years, regularly featuring articles and editorials on the economic advances. None was more flattering or misleading than an *al-Ahram* editorial boasting of "the coming prosperity."[62]

By 1960, the minister of industry was claiming that the industrial plan had already achieved its goals and had infused the economy with £E330 million in investment funds. Aziz Sidqi boasted that its two most capital-intensive schemes, the iron and steel company, which had an equity capital of £E27.5 million in 1960, and the KIMA fertilizer complex at Aswan, with nominal capitalization of £E29.9 million, had laid the foundation for a new capital goods industry. He also pointed out that of the £E330 million in investment capital no less than £E250 million had originated in the public sector.[63]

In July 1960 the Ministry of Planning launched Egypt's first comprehensive five-year plan, intended to raise national income from £E100 million to £E184 million. Even more grandiose than its industrial predecessor, the total investment price tag was £E1,577 million, of which £E439 was earmarked for industrial projects. The emphasis remained on petroleum, which was allocated £E104.7 million in the plan, and heavy industrialization, where the iron and steel works, shipbuilding, mining, and new consumer industries, including automobiles, were expected to receive most of the funds.[64]

The plan represented the aspirations of the Egyptian elite as its members took stock of the economy in July 1960. While it anticipated sizable contributions from the private sector, the plan stressed state involvement. The main aims were to create balanced economic growth, expand employment, achieve social justice, and correct Egypt's unfavorable trade balance. Overall, the architects of the plan laid maximum emphasis on the gains to be achieved through planning itself, described as the "most rapid and favorable means for accelerating economic growth and social progress," and through industrialization, held to be "the cornerstone of

[61] *al-Ahram*, August 2, 1959.

[62] Ibid., September 18, 1958.

[63] The material in this paragraph is taken from several Egyptian booklets that described the industrial projects of the first and second five-year plans and were analyzed in the British Foreign Office. Crowe to Earl of Home, December 21, 1960, PRO FO 371/150950 VG1103/42.

[64] One can consult the United Arab Republic, Presidency of the Republic, National Planning Committee, Southern Region, Egypt, *General Frame of the Five-Year Plan for Economic and Social Development, July 1960–June 1965* (Cairo, 1960), especially tables on pp. 25 and 29, but equally revealing is the exposition laid out in *al-Ahram*, December 15, 1959.

the development plan." In particular, Egypt's emphasis on the establishment of a capital goods industry would provide "a way that will ensure the transition from being a high-consumption economy to being a high-production economy." Although the plan anticipated a large contribution from foreign investment (38 percent of the total) and from privately raised funds, it also contained strong words of criticism for a purely capitalist approach to economic development.[65]

Yet the announcements of targets achieved and even the plans themselves, with which the regime filled the press and the radio, were publicity statements and propaganda moments far more than revelations of economic realities. Like the pre-Nasser governments, the Egyptian bureaucracy was unable to execute its most ambitious programs in a timely way. Each year the development budget was left with large amounts of money unspent. Nasser and his colleagues had come to power determined to produce a better economic record than their predecessors'. Their efforts fell short of aspirations. Contrary to their claims, the first five-year industrial plan had not been completed in 1960. Many contracts remained to be let, and more than two-thirds of the projects were still being worked on when the government declared the plan fully implemented. The first comprehensive five-year plan began, then, under the shadow of a backlog of schemes from the industrial plan and large sums of investment funds yet to be expended.[66]

BUSINESS AND THE PUBLIC SECTOR

By 1961 it seemed as if the entire Egyptian economy, except for agricultural lands, urban properties, and small-scale enterprises, lay in the public sector. The socialist laws of July 1961 had established the state's juridical authority over most of Egypt's business enterprises. Even those firms in which the government did not hold all or 50 percent of the shares had been forced to concede a powerful shareholding and managerial position to the state. Only the informal sector was left as an area where private business persons could create their own enterprises. Here, however, the lesson of 1960 and 1961 was that any firms that became large and successful would be likely targets for state takeover.

Looked at juridically and structurally, then, the state either monopolized or held a dominant position in Egypt's financial services, foreign trade, "strategic" industries, medium and heavy industries, textiles, sugar

---

[65] The quotations in this paragraph come from an earlier and more unguarded English version of the plan. They are drawn from the first five pages.

[66] See a full and exceedingly critical analysis of the five-year industrial plan and an assessment of the prospects of success for the first comprehensive five-year plan in C. T. Crowe to Home, December 21, 1960, PRO FO 371/150950 VG1103/42.

refining, food processing, transportation, public utilities, information services, reclaimed and redistributed land, construction, the high dam, and the Suez Canal.[67] Yet such a view, which is drawn from legal documents and represents a taxonomy of public sector organizations, gives more coherence to the public sector than it warrants. Public enterprise was a creation of historical forces and often of historical accident. Its ad hoc quality was always apparent. Juridically, as late as 1961, it was regulated by only two decrees: law number 20 of 1957, which established the Economic Organization, and a law in 1960 that extended the characteristics of the Economic Organization to the Misr and Nasr Organizations. Only later in the 1960s did the state pass a comprehensive set of laws laying out the different functions and responsibilities of the many public organizations that had come into existence during the nationalizing decade.[68] Egypt's public bodies bore various names—public organizations, public authorities, public companies, and so forth—each of which was intended to highlight different functions. Often the names bore little relationship to what the organizations actually did. If instead of looking at the organizational structure of the public sector, one tries to determine where real decision-making power resided, it becomes clear how truly mixed and hybrid Egypt's economy still was. The Egyptian economy, as it entered the decade of the 1960s, could be characterized, in a nutshell, as having a small but highly regulated private sector and a large but relatively decentralized public sector.[69]

A disaggregated analysis of the public sector shows that state power predominated in financial services, iron and steel, the high dam, textiles, and transportation, while private interests retained considerable autonomy in pharmaceuticals, automobiles, and petroleum.

Iron and Steel

The keystone of Egyptian development planning was heavy industrialization and the construction of the Aswan High Dam. From the outset, the Nasser regime viewed private capital in those two areas with suspicion and eventually monopolized their activities. The iron and steel industry was seen as the heart of Egypt's heavy industrialization program, the vehicle for initiating a capital goods industry. Even in the first two years of military rule, when the Revolutionary Command Council sought accommodation with private capital, even foreign capital, it retained control of the Iron and Steel Company. Its early equity partners included various Misr companies that were not yet absorbed into the public arena but

---

[67] See the list in Waterbury, *The Egypt of Nasser and Sadat*, p. 76.
[68] Ismail Sabri Abd Allah, *Tanzim al-Qita' al-Amm*, pp. 346 ff.
[69] Hansen and Marzouk, *Development and Economic Policy*, p. 276.

obedient to the wishes of the military elite. The German firm, Demag, was brought into the enterprise for its technical capacities rather than its equity contribution. The state held the majority of the shares and was the predominant influence on the board.

Over time, state capitalization increased and private interests receded. In response to Qaysuni and Sidqi's urging, the Iron and Steel Company was promised £E23.8 million in equity capital in the first five-year industrial plan and another £E30 million in the first comprehensive five-year plan. By 1960, at the end of the five-year industrial plan, Egypt was producing 225,000 tons of steel per year, mainly in the form of sheets, ingots, and rails.

The Aswan High Dam

Although the state had established a special agency, the High Dam Authority, to oversee this project, no final decision on the specific form of financing and construction of the dam was reached until October 1958. In that month, the Soviet government agreed to provide machinery, equipment, and a line of credit of up to 400 million rubles (£37.5 million) and announced that it would assume primary responsibility for the first stage of the dam.[70] Repayment was to commence only after the completion of the first stage. The announcement, coming just after Eugene Black and other World Bank officials had concluded a visit to Cairo, disappointed Western financial groups that had maintained an active interest in the project.[71] The construction of the dam was to take place in three stages. Stage one, which the Soviets had agreed to aid, involved the digging of a diversion canal for the Nile and the construction of two coffer dams. The second stage entailed the construction of the dam itself, part of the power station, and the electrical transmission lines. The third stage involved the completion of the power station. Work was to begin on the second stage in 1962. The main part of the project was to be completed in 1968, and the power station was scheduled to be opened in 1970. The total cost of all three stages was estimated at £400 million. The first Soviet offer of £37.5 million did not, therefore, cover the costs of even the first stage of the program.[72]

Unfortunately for Western business groups, their interest in the Aswan project came to naught. The Egyptians preferred to act in concert with their Soviet advisers, even though a great deal of the work was put out for competitive bids. For the extensive groundwork in the first stage of

[70] *al-Ahram*, October 24, 1958.

[71] Foreign Office Minute, unsigned, October 30, 1958, PRO FO 371/133986 VG1422/12(A).

[72] Commercial Department, Cairo, to Foreign Office, September 5, 1960, PRO FO 371/151001 VG1422/60.

the project the Egyptian government accepted only four bids and took seriously only the two Egyptian bidders. After rejecting tenders submitted by a Swedish conglomerate and a Yugoslavian public sector corporation, it turned to the proposals submitted by two large Egyptian holding companies with a combined capitalization of £E25 million.[73] The lower bid of £E15,799,000 originated from a new firm under the direction of a young Egyptian entrepreneur, Uthman Ahmad Uthman, whose meteoric rise from small businessman to head of a Middle Eastern conglomerate had elevated him to the firmament of Egypt's most powerful capitalists. The second bid of £E27,185,363 came from Egypt's most respected firms and business personages and involved Ahmad Abbud, the Misr Concrete Company, and the Egyptian Contracting Company. Despite Abbud's protestations that Uthman's firm was grossly inexperienced and had not submitted a realistic bid, the government awarded it the contract. Uthman's company completed the work, though not before being nationalized itself.[74]

Textiles

The state's contention that it would limit itself to areas of production where the private sector was not active was tested by textiles, an industry in which private capital and private entrepreneurs, mostly Egyptians, had been entirely dominant. Yet by 1961 all of the large textile factories had been incorporated into the public sector. The first move occurred in 1956–57 with the sequestration of the assets of Bradford Dyers, Calico Printers, and Bleacher's Association, and then their sale to the Economic Organization. The death knell occurred during the implementation of the socialist laws of 1961. By then the major spinning and weaving companies had been nationalized, and even many of the less capital-intensive tricotage and clothing plants. All that remained in private hands were small, unincorporated private firms and partnerships specializing in some of the finishing trades.

Mixed Enterprises: Automobiles and Petroleum

One of the major goals of Egypt's five-year plan was the establishment of an automotive industry. Even though Egypt was not a major importer of vehicles in the post–World War II era, Aziz Sidqi and the planning tech-

[73] *al-Ahram*, May 16, 1959.

[74] Ibid., January 13, 1961; Commercial Department, Cairo, to Foreign Office, February 7, 1961, and February 25, 1961, PRO FO 371/158846 VG1421/7 and VG1421/9; on the career of Uthman Ahmad Uthman, one should consult his autobiography, *Safahat min Tajribati* (Cairo, 1981).

nicians believed that the economy was on the verge of a takeoff in which automobiles would be in great demand. To their minds, an automotive industry would have significant backward and forward economic linkages. It would be the major customer of the Iron and Steel Company, and at the same time it would stimulate an auto parts industry that would produce tires, batteries, headlamps, and a variety of electronic products.

Sidqi assigned a high priority to the automotive industry in the five-year industrial plan. According to his vision, Egypt would commence with the production of trucks and buses and move on to tractors and passenger cars. In the early stages the manufacturing plants in Egypt would simply assemble knocked-down and imported vehicles, but the Egyptian plans called for the local manufacturing content to rise until Egypt employed only locally produced materials in its plants and the industry became thoroughly Egyptian.[75] The government sought an accommodation with Western automotive manufacturers and signed an agreement in early 1959 with the West German firm of Deutz to manufacture trucks and buses. The firm agreed to commence production immediately, with production being confined at the outset to vehicle assembly. The first vehicle was scheduled to come off the assembly line in December 1959.[76]

After signing this agreement, the minister of industry turned his attention to the manufacture of passenger vehicles. He proposed three types: a "people's" car, to be called the Ramses and to cost £E400; a middle-class car; and a luxury vehicle. Multinational firms operating in Egypt were put under pressure to submit bids, and most did, though one firm, Ford of Egypt, admitted that it had little faith in the profitability of the venture.[77] In 1961 the government signed its second automotive agreement, this one with Fiat, for the manufacture of passenger cars.[78] A little later it concluded an agreement with a Yugoslavian public sector firm to produce tractors.[79] The Fiat bid was accepted over twelve others. At the time the agreement was concluded, an Egyptian industrial spokesperson announced that the passenger car industry would mobilize £E6.3 million in equity capital, save £E1,179,000 in hard currency each year, increase the national income by £E1,990,000, and provide employment for 2,000.[80]

The automotive industry was under heavy government pressure to move ahead rapidly. The contract signed with Deutz was originally for an

[75] *al-Ahram*, October 22, 1957.

[76] Ibid., February 4, 1959.

[77] H. E. Jones, Ford International, to J. S. Bugos and Lilley, December 11, 1959, Ford Industrial Archives, AR67–14:1.

[78] *al-Ahram*, April 1, 1961.

[79] J. R. Wraight, Cairo, to K. E. MacKenzie, Board of Trade, April 21, 1961, PRO FO 371/158878 VG1102/10.

[80] *al-Ahram*, April 1, 1961.

eight-stage, eight-year program, starting with the pure assembly of trucks and buses and leading to production using an increasing proportion of local products. When the contract was presented to Sidqi at the Ministry of Industry, he shortened the time frame to five years. Nasser further reduced the schedule to three years. At the time of the signing of the document, the signatories from the German firm and the Egyptian Nasr manufacturing group were aware that the targets could not be met.[81] The effort to establish an automotive industry witnessed a "total breakdown of planned performance."[82]

The oil sector, an ideological and political battleground during the 1950s, retained its mixture of foreign capital and public enterprise into the 1960s. Yet the Egyptian political elite's ambition to achieve a strong Egyptian position within the oil sector bore fruit in late September 1956, at the height of the Western economic war against Egypt and a month before the British-French-Israeli invasion. The government created the General Petroleum Authority. Endowed with wide-ranging powers, the authority became noticeably interventionist after the conclusion of the war.[83] Under Mahmud Abu Zayid, an outspoken critic of multinational oil companies in Egypt, the capital of the General Petroleum Authority rose from £E1 million in 1957 to £E3 million in 1958 and to £E6 million in 1961.[84]

The Egyptian initiative in the oil sector was intended to break the monopoly exercised by foreign firms in exploration work. In 1957 the state established its own oil exploration company, the Eastern Oil Company, which drew 49 percent of its equity from Egyptian sources, including the General Petroleum Authority, and had as the president of its board Mahmud Yunis, Nasser's leading troubleshooter in the public sector. The remaining 51 percent of the equity capital was subscribed by the International Egyptian Petroleum Company, representing the Belgian company Petrofina, the Italian state oil company, and American oil interests registered in Panama.[85] The ensuing nationalization of the Shell companies in Egypt in 1961 further strengthened the position of the Egyptian government in oil affairs.

Although the state succeeded in creating a strong presence in the oil sector, it did not dominate. Approximately half of Egypt's crude oil came

---

[81] Interview with Adel Gazarin in Cairo, September 12, 1989. Gazarin worked with the Nasr group of companies and was involved in the automotive industry.

[82] Hansen and Nashashibi, *Foreign Trade Regimes*, p. 301.

[83] No. 37, Russell D. Pearson to Department of State, July 18, 1957; Dulles to American Embassy, Cairo, September 28, 1956; and no. 276, Russell D. Pearson to Department of State, October 6, 1956; all in USNA 874.2553.

[84] *Egyptian Gazette*, February 22, 1961.

[85] *al-Ahram*, February 10, 1957; *Middle East Economic Digest* 1, no. 1 (March 8, 1957).

from domestic wells, most of which were owned by foreign firms. Seven fields, all of them along both sides of the Gulf of Suez, accounted for almost all of Egypt's domestic supply. The Ras Gharib field yielded 60 percent of the total domestic output. Until 1961 it was operated by Anglo-Egyptian Oil, as was the once important but declining field at Hurghada. The remaining five fields were in Sinai. Three were operated by Anglo-Egyptian Oil in conjunction with Mobil. Only two producing fields were owned and operated by the state-run Eastern Oil Company of Egypt. Thus, most of the domestic supply came from fields owned and operated by Anglo-Egyptian Oil, and even though the nationalization of Anglo-Egyptian Oil enhanced state power in the oil sector dramatically, the state's decision to allow Shell Oil of London to play a role in the direction of the affairs of the new Nasr Oil Company (formerly Anglo-Egyptian Oil) reduced the state's capacity to determine overall oil policy.[86]

Before nationalizing Anglo-Egyptian Oil, the state-run General Petroleum Authority enticed multinational prospecting firms from America, Germany, and elsewhere into the oil sector. The state hoped these firms would counterbalance the influence of Mobil and Anglo-Egyptian Oil and create a more competitive environment among foreign oil firms. The prospecting efforts of these companies languished, however. Oil companies hesitated to commit large funds in a country that their executives regarded as in the grip of a nationalizing impulse. A director of the American Sahara group wrote that "due to political developments in Egypt the partners making up the Sahara Petroleum Company are coming up with the opinion that their operations in Egypt should be reduced to a minimum consistent with the legal requirements of their concession contract."[87] The Egyptian government was aware of the slowing of exploration efforts, but its prodding yielded few results. Exploration in the oil sector, with its mixture of private and public entities, had come to a standstill because of uncertainty in the political and business climate of the late 1950s.

By the end of 1961, Egypt's public sector had emerged triumphant. The most obvious casualty of the nationalizing movement was the large-scale company. Almost all of the firms of long-standing duration had been absorbed into the public sector. The remaining large corporations drew their equity capital from new foreign investment streams and operated in a few highly specialized sectors where Egyptian technical, managerial, and capital deficiencies were obvious.

Egypt stands out among the decolonizing African societies of the

---

[86] No. 749, Russell Pearson to Department of State, April 6, 1957, USNA 874.2553.

[87] Memorandum of Conversation on Subject of Reduction of Petroleum Drilling Operations in Egypt, July 9, 1957, USNA 874.2553; Memorandum of Conversation with Sahara Petroleum Company in Egypt, March 21, 1957, USNA 874.2553.

1950s for the size of its public sector and for abandoning a development policy that gave high priority to the private sector. Why was the Egyptian private sector so rapidly and unceremoniously swept aside? Which of the three factors identified as influencing decolonization—changes in metropolitan attitudes, shifts in the international balance of power, and resurgent nationalism—was decisive? To oversimplify, in order to make comparisons with Nigeria and Kenya, the shift in the international balance of power and the Egyptian nationalist movement, with its wide definition of national independence, were far more important than any changes in Britain related to retaining imperial predominance in Egypt. Indeed, in the ruling circles in Britain, there was a great reluctance to grant Egypt its nationalist wishes.

In international politics, Egypt profited from its substantial political independence, which was far superior to that enjoyed by any other African colonial territory in the era of decolonization. Freedom of political movement enabled the Egyptian rulers, civilian as well as military, to play the East off against the West in a variety of political and economic negotiations. The military men were less squeamish about turning to the Soviets than their civilian predecessors had been, and their bold policies led Egypt into a tight alliance with the Eastern bloc. The second factor was a powerful nationalist impulse, which did not confine its understanding of independence to the political sphere but aspired to control the economy. Increasingly, the Egyptian nationalists came to regard capitalism as a force for foreign control of Egyptian society. The business community itself failed to combat this impression, being often divided along national lines. The military men represented the culmination of a long-lived and deep-seated nationalist tradition. They intensified the nationalist tendency to seek the economic liberation of the country and to see that goal in the eradication of foreign capital. Nasser himself became the moving force in this nationalist vision from 1954 onward. His personality and worldview shaped Egypt's decisive events at virtually every crucial turning point. To the events of the 1950s (the Czech arms deal, the nationalization of the Suez Canal Company, and the sequestration of foreign property) he brought his own boldness, his resentful form of nationalism, and power aggrandizement onto the political scene at every turn.

The growth of the public sector and the dismantling of the private sector occurred in fits and starts and were driven by events. Ideological considerations were not lacking, however, though the principles espoused by the ruling Egyptian elite were rooted in material circumstances and shaped by strong feelings of resentment.

The Egyptian ruling elite dismantled its private sector in the face of a countervailing Western belief in private enterprise and free markets. To be sure, development strategists from the West argued on behalf of an enhanced role for the state as a planner of economic development and a mobilizer of capital. But state-sponsored projects were not intended to eradicate private business activity. The Egyptian rulers were much taken with Soviet, Yugoslavian, and Indian models of development, which emphasized the economic dynamism of the state.

The unwieldy shape of Egypt's public sector stemmed from its awkward, event-driven creation. Duplication of duties existed, and wasteful competition occurred among the large public organizations. Whenever the government took over private businesses, its officials justified the action on the grounds that the private sector wasted resources, exploited the mass of the people, and brought gain for only a few. Yet, in significant ways, the emergent public sector suffered from the same faults. Public enterprises, like the old business firms, were dominated by a few individuals, just as the old business firms had been. Innumerable interlocking directorates were formed within the government; the power of a top bureaucrat like Aziz Sidqi was every bit as great as that of the business persons the regime had so vociferously condemned. Haykal and Nasser liked to argue that there could be no exploitation of the people from the public sector because the government, as agent of the people, was in charge; but in fact, the few lorded it over the many. Despite reserving positions on the boards of companies and organizations for workers and peasants, these representatives of the people had little say about the operation of Egypt's public sector.

Yet private business firms were not completely eliminated in Nasser's Egypt in the 1960s. Some firms persisted, especially in sectors requiring considerable technical and managerial skills. But even in other parts of the public sector, private interests were able to carve out a place for themselves. At the Filature Nationale des Textiles, one of Egypt's oldest textile firms, Robert and Linus Gasche agreed to stay on to run the company after its absorption into the public sector. Similarly, the Egyptians persuaded Shell Oil to nominate board members to the old Anglo-Egyptian Oil Company after it was nationalized. Uthman Ahmad Uthman, who critized the government for taking his company into the public sector and who saw no resulting gain to the state or the Egyptian economy, nonetheless agreed to stay on as the firm's managing director and gave the enterprise as much attention as he had when he was its majority shareholder. What motivated him was his belief that the company was an extension of his personality and that it would always be so, whether it was in the private or the public sector.[88]

---

[88] Uthman Ahmad Uthman, *Tajribati*, pp. 286 ff.

Part Two

NIGERIA

CHAPTER 6

The Political Economy of Nigeria and the Great Debates, 1945–1951

THE NIGERIA of the immediate postwar era offered striking contrasts with Egypt. Not only did the British regard the country as one of their poorest African colonial possessions, albeit one with undoubted economic potential, but its private sector did not have the solidity and long experience that the Egyptian private sector had. Because of the country's vast geographic size and its ethnic and religious diversity, the territory lacked overarching institutional unities, save those supplied by the colonial overlords. Nigeria had virtually no indigenous, countrywide organizations, even at the elite level. The nationalist movement had yet to crystallize, and labor and peasant organizations were small and regionally oriented.

Nigeria's economic, educational, and commercial deficiencies were glaring in comparison with those of Egypt, or with those of other British tropical colonies, for that matter. Yet these lacks did not prevent the British from regarding the country as Africa's most promising tropical dependency. British officials extolled its large and diverse population, its geographic expanse, and the variety of its natural resources as assets needing only to be yoked to a stable polity and a coherent program of economic development to yield dramatic results. Nonetheless, from the moment of conquest, the British also viewed Nigeria as politically unstable, ever close to the edge of anarchy. To prevent chaos, they sought to forge unshakable and mutually rewarding alliances with local elites. In the turbulent years after World War II these alignments were put to a stern test. Possessing sparse military forces in tropical Africa, the British colonial authorities worried about their capacity to oversee the last stage of colonial rule.

Nigeria's special political problems did not arise solely from the country's 250 separate language groups and its heavy population densities. They also originated in the ethnic mix of a population in which three language communities—Yorubas, Ibos, and Hausa-Fulanis—comprised nearly two-thirds of the total population and vied with each other for political predominance and economic favor. Still, the many millions of other Nigerians, the equivalent of the total population of many other African states, refused to be silenced as the scramble for political and economic position got under way after World War II.

In spite of its extraordinary economic prospects, the British knew Nigeria to be a desperately poor country. An official investigation estimated the per capita income on the eve of World War II at a shocking £2. In 1948 the total national income was thought not to exceed £200 million. By including estimates of subsistence food production and household labor, later calculations were higher, but an estimate made in 1950–51 still placed Nigerian per capita gross domestic product (GDP) at a low £20.[1] The Nigerian economy also had a strong external orientation. Exports contributed one-fifth of the GDP, and imports one-tenth; thus the country's economic stability and prospects for development were directly tied to a world economy over which the country exercised little influence.

The raw materials that linked Nigeria to Western Europe paid for the country's colonial bureaucracy through export and import duties. One-third of Nigeria's governmental revenue was derived from import duties in 1946, another 6 percent from export levies, and a further 7 percent from a cigarette excise. Fully 32 percent of the total recurrent state expenditures went to pay the salaries of administrators.[2] Groundnuts and tin from the North, palm oil and palm kernels mainly from the East, and cocoa from the West made up nearly the entire value of all Nigerian exports in 1938. Since cocoa was the most valuable of Nigeria's exports, the West enjoyed a higher standard of living and educational and infrastructural advantages over the North and East.

Cocoa first began to be exported from West Africa at the end of the nineteenth century. Yet by 1939, of the 720,000 tons of cocoa put into world trade, 60 percent originated in West Africa: 100,000 from Nigeria, 250,000 from the Gold Coast, and 50,000 from the Ivory Coast.[3] Much of the cocoa in western Nigeria was grown on small plots cultivated by as many as 330,000 farmers.[4]

An artificial colonial creation, Nigeria was held together by its civil service, military and police forces, and collaborating elites. By any reckoning, and certainly when compared with its bloated postcolonial successor, the Nigerian colonial state of the postwar era was a skeletal apparatus. In 1951 the senior civil service had a mere 4,600 authorized staff positions, of which only 3,730 were actually filled. Of this number, only 597 were Africans, and though Africans were moving into the senior

[1] A. R. Prest and I. G. Stewart, *The National Income of Nigeria, 1950–51*, Colonial Office Research Studies, no. 11 (London, 1953), p. 81.

[2] No. 2514, Governor to Secretary of State, November 1, 1946, PRO CO 583/285/3023/5.

[3] Colonial Products Committee, Note by the Ministry of Food on Present and Prospective World Supply and Demand for Cocoa, 1947, PRO CO 852/902/5.

[4] R. Johns and A. V. Gibbard, Assessment of Swollen Shoot Disease in Nigeria, 1950, PRO CO 583/309/30585/4B/1950; R. Galletti, R. D. S. Baldwin, and I. O. Dina, *Nigerian Cocoa Farmers* (London, 1956).

ranks at a rate of 140 per year, at that rate full Africanization would not be achieved until 1980.[5]

Nor was this thin administrative veneer well integrated or notably democratic. For reasons of history and ideology, the administration of the North remained virtually separate from the South, linked only through an Executive Council at Lagos on which northern and southern officials sat. Nigeria's Legislative Council was an equally atrophied organ. Established by Governor Hugh Charles Clifford in 1922, it had no northern representation and only four elected members, who were chosen on a restricted franchise by voters in Lagos and Calabar.[6]

Not surprisingly, the Nigerian polity seemed to most British colonial officials a fragile construction, held together by a handful of British political and military officers. The British had no reason to suppose that the Nigerians would be able to unite against their rule, or for that matter had any powerful complaints about how Britain ruled Nigeria. Nonetheless, periodic outbursts against colonial overrule confirmed their fears that anticolonial instincts could be aroused. These were thought to be rooted in violent precolonial cultures rather than genuine grievances against colonial rulers. But they were believed to lie smoldering barely beneath the surface. The Satiru revolt in northern Nigeria in 1906, the Abeokuta protests of 1917, and the Aba women's tax riots of 1929 were cited as evidence of the acute tensions pervading Nigerian society. The British colonial authorities did not deceive themselves that a half-century of what they regarded as benign colonial rule had expunged the population's latent anarchic instincts. The colonial officials believed that the challenges anticipated in the postwar period would put the country's ethnic and religious antagonisms to a severe test. They were especially apprehensive about the many Nigerian soldiers who would have to be reintegrated into civilian society once the war was over.

The colonial instruments of coercion were as limited as the imperial financial resources. The nearest British military forces were located at Gibraltar, except for a small naval squadron based at Freetown.[7] Nigeria's military and police contingents were not large. The West African Frontier Force had responsibility for the four colonial territories of British West Africa. Its numbers had expanded from 8,000 to 150,000 during the war

[5] No. 2594, Governor to Colonial Office, August 22, 1951, PRO CO 554/403. The figure on the senior civil service excluded Colliery and Electricity Corporations personnel but included the railway, post and telegraphs, and the development administrations.

[6] Kalu Ezera, *Constitutional Development in Nigeria: An Analytical Study of Nigeria's Constitution-Making Development and the Historical and Political Factors That Affected Constitutional Change* (Cambridge, 1964), pp. 27–28.

[7] Colonial Office Note on the Likelihood of Disturbances in West and East Africa and Cyprus, January 1, 1949, PRO CO 537/4384.

so that West African soldiers could serve in East Africa, the Middle East, and Burma as well as in West Africa. The force was quickly returned to its prewar figure.[8] Local sensitivities over military expenditures made the establishment of a large fighting force in West Africa impossible. Although the British regarded their contribution of roughly 60 percent of the expenses of the colonial military forces in Nigeria as generous, the £750,000 expenditure required of the Nigerian government irritated Nigeria's colonial critics.[9]

The British had good reason to question their military and policing capabilities, and this perception was undeniably a significant factor in accelerating the timetable for transferring power in the region. To compensate for their thin military presence, the British sought to establish a mobile force that could be moved swiftly from one territory to another. Yet, following the Accra riots in the Gold Coast in 1948, the officer commanding the West African Frontier Force claimed that the troops available to him at the time were inadequate. He warned that "should future disturbances spread simultaneously over 2 or more colonies, as seems not unlikely, colonies involved would not be able to spare troops to reinforce each other."[10] In addition, British military men saw Nigeria as West Africa's most difficult territory to hold. Because of its vast geographic expanse and its heavy population densities, they feared that it could easily turn into a military quagmire if several of its dispersed regions were to rise in revolt. The Nigerian army included only 141 British senior officers, 162 British noncommissioned officers, and 4,277 Africans of other ranks. The central Nigerian police forces were equally small and more Africanized; they contained 111 British officers, 9 African officers, 1,334 noncommissioned African officers, and 4,450 Africans of other ranks.[11]

The sparseness of administrative and military personnel notwithstanding, the Nigerian public sector in general was already a potent administrative force and quite capable of notable expansion if a state-controlled form of economic development gained favor in the postwar years. Over the years, the government had undertaken numerous economic tasks, some for strategic and military reasons and others because of private

[8] Chief Secretary of War Council to Colonial Office, January 28, 1949, PRO CO 537/4989.
[9] J. C. Morgan, Colonial Office Minute, March 6, 1950; Foot to Gorsuch, September 22, 1950; both in PRO CO 537/6379; Secretary of State for Colonies, Draft Memorandum, Report on African Land Forces, November 1949, PRO CO 537/5080.
[10] N. M. S. Irwin, General Officer Commanding in Chief, West African Command, to War Office, July 31, 1948, PRO CO 537/4104.
[11] Colonial Office Note on the Likelihood of Disturbances in West and East Africa and Cyprus, January 1, 1949, PRO CO 537/4384.

sector timidity. The railway, post and telegraph, and ports were the heart of the public sector. The railway, Nigeria's main communication artery until the 1930s, was the largest unit of the governmental bureaucracy.[12] In spite of staff shortages and deteriorating equipment, which had reduced the carrying capacity of the railway by 30 to 40 percent during the war, it was expected to grow in size and importance to be a focal point of Nigeria's postwar development.[13]

Attached to the railway administration was the Enugu colliery, located in the eastern part of the country. Coal had been discovered in 1911, and mining commenced in 1915. Because the railway consumed most of the coal mined in Nigeria, the mining operations at Enugu were originally placed under the general manager of the railways. Not until 1943 did the colliery have its own department, despite the fact that its annual output was nearly a half-million tons. Only after the bloody coal miners' strike of 1949 did the government establish an independent colliery board.[14]

The other large government economic organization, the Electricity Corporation, was not established as a separate branch of the government until 1946. Until that time, the state had separately operated nine different power companies. These firms supplied the major cities of Lagos, Port Harcourt, Kaduna, Enugu, Yola, Zaria, Calabar, Warri, and Jos; the Nigerian Electricity Corporation supplied power to the minefields around Jos. In addition, local "native" authorities looked after the power supply of five additional cities: Abeokuta, Kano, Ibadan, Katsina, and Maiduguri. Pressure to unify these dispersed power suppliers arose when the state drew up comprehensive plans to electrify an additional forty towns and cities. By mid-1946, the total capital involved in the already existing electricity companies was £941,473, and expansion plans called for raising another £2.5 million in capital.[15]

At the same time that the public sector was on the rise, the private sector was well entrenched and heavily capitalized. Traditionally, Nigeria's most successful firms were European-domiciled public and private limited companies with a long history of operations in West Africa. The giant, the United Africa Company, a subsidiary of Lever Brothers, had come into existence in 1929 as a result of the amalgamation of numerous other firms. A mere six or seven firms handled between two-thirds and

---

[12] One can consult the various annual reports of the railway administration. A general overview of the Nigerian parastatals is provided in K. H. Osborne, Colonial Office, to Chief Secretary, British Transport Commission, March 12, 1951, PRO FO 583/302/30046/31/1951.

[13] No. 809, Governor to Colonial Office, August 31, 1945, PRO CO 583/275/30647/2.

[14] *Daily Times*, July 29, 1950; no. 478, E. D. Crowley to Secretary of State, January 2, 1951, USNA 845H. 2552.

[15] No. 9, Richards to Hall, April 10, 1946, PRO CO 852/579/9.

three-quarters of West Africa's import and export trade, valued at £300 to £400 million after World War II; of those few firms the United Africa Company had by far the largest share. Its annual turnover at the close of the war fluctuated between £200 and £300 million.[16] It had £3,278,000 invested in the Nigerian trading sector. Its rivals included John Holt and Company, the Société Commerciale Occidentale Africaine, the Compagnie Française Africaine Occidentale, the United Trading Company, and numerous others.

According to an account written in 1938, the total equity capital of European trading and mining firms operating in Nigeria was £20 million.[17] Certainly those enterprises enjoyed unusual political and economic privileges, which they were determined to defend from nationalist attack. They were entitled to representation on the executive and legislative councils of Nigeria, and for decades they had been free from the tax on companies that was standard elsewhere in Britain and the British empire. Although the Nigerian government had finally introduced a company tax in 1938 and raised it to five shillings on the pound during the war, the firms were determined to see that Nigeria maintained its reputation as a territory possessing tax rates and commercial arrangements that favored the private sector.[18]

Entry of new firms into Nigeria's export-import sector was no easy matter, however. In 1942 the large firms, under the guidance of Frank Samuel of the United Africa Company, organized themselves into the Association of West African Merchants (AWAM). The purpose of AWAM was to eliminate "wasteful" competition and coordinate relations with colonial governments.[19] From the outset, AWAM involved all of the major trading enterprises in West Africa and proved particularly effective in allocating the purchase and export of West Africa's major exports among its members. In the process, it created a two-tiered and much-resented hierarchy of firms. Companies with offices or agents in the United Kingdom and willing to accept full responsibility for their actions

[16] P. T. Bauer, *West African Trade* (Cambridge, 1954), p. 99. For general discussions of the economic issues dealt with in this and subsequent chapters, one should also consult D. K. Fieldhouse, *Merchant Capital and Economic Decolonisation: The United Africa Company, 1929–1987* (Oxford, 1994); and the works of Gerald K. Helleiner, *Peasant Agriculture, Government, and Economic Growth in Nigeria* (Homewood, Ill., 1966); C. Eicher and C. Liedholm, *Growth and Development of the Nigerian Economy* (East Lansing, Mich., 1970); and R. Olufemi Ekundare, *An Economic History of Nigeria, 1860–1960* (New York, 1973).

[17] J. Mars, "Extra-Territorial Enterprises," in *Mining, Commerce, and Finance in Nigeria,* ed. Margery Perham (London, 1948), pp. 52–53.

[18] R. H. Heyworth, Report on Visit to Nigeria, October 2–November 5, 1944, November 18, 1944, Unilever Archives.

[19] Agent at Ibadan, Quarterly Report, September 18, 1944, Holt Papers, f232(ii).

in Nigeria were designated "A" shippers. They were given the largest buying quotas. The quotas of the remaining firms, designated "B" shippers, were kept small.[20]

AWAM was the formal organization of the big trading firms; the Lagos Chamber of Commerce was its primary pressure group. Because of the power of the United Africa Company, the Lagos Chamber represented only the big concerns and excluded smaller merchants. It did so by charging what by Nigerian standards was an expensive £20 annual membership fee and by confining membership to companies and individuals based in Lagos and the Western provinces.[21] At first, only the British American Tobacco Company resisted this big-firm orientation. Its preference for broadening the membership met with little support until 1949, when Holt led a campaign to make the Lagos Chamber "the recognized channel of communication between all commercial interests and the specialized government departments."[22] In order to bring the less heavily capitalized groups and individuals, including African merchants, into the Lagos Chamber, the Holt agent persuaded the other member groups to reduce the annual membership fee to £15. Yet the effort to expand the membership list achieved only limited results.[23] Because most African merchants continued to regard the chamber as an essentially European mercantile organization, only eight of its sixty members were Africans or African concerns in 1949.[24]

Although the great export-import companies were the central business companies in Nigeria's open economy, they were not the only powerful and heavily capitalized European firms operating in Nigeria. Elder Dempster Lines monopolized shipping between West Africa and Europe. From the turn of the century, Elder Dempster had forced all exporters and importers, including even the British Crown agents, into using its ships. Its incentive to shippers was a 10 percent rebate for firms that shipped exclusively on its vessels. It also made it impossible for competitors to break into the trade by adopting aggressive pricing policies whenever a firm challenged its monopoly position.[25] Not content to be the shipping magnate of West Africa, Alfred Jones, the founder of Elder Dempster,

[20] Minutes of Meeting held at the United Africa Company location, Ijebu Ode, June 18, 1942, attended by representatives of Holt, CFAO, Patterson and Zochonis, G. B. Ollivant, and UAC, Holt Papers, f535(ii).

[21] R. W. T. Bateson, Lagos, to Holt, September 23, 1948, Holt Papers, f232(ii).

[22] Gates to Cotgreave, May 26, 1949, Holt Papers, f232(iii).

[23] Cotgreave to Gates, October 31, 1949, Holt Papers, f232(iii).

[24] G. Cotgreave, Lagos, to Gates, June 24, 1949, Holt Papers, f232(iii).

[25] Charlotte Leubuscher, *The West African Shipping Trade, 1909–1959* (Leyden, Netherlands, 1963); P. N. Davies, *The Trade Makers: Elder Dempster in West Africa, 1852–1972* (London, 1973).

also created the Bank of British West Africa in 1894. Along with Barclays, it dominated the Nigerian banking business. In 1945 the Bank of
British West Africa had a nominal capitalization of £1.2 million and deposits totaling £19,271,044.[26] Since the primary purpose of these British
banks operating in Nigeria was to facilitate trade between West Africa
and Europe rather than promote deposit banking, they had only a small
proportion of their assets tied up in loans (7.2 percent) while at the same
time they deposited substantial sums (74 percent of total assets) overseas
with their metropolitan affiliates.[27]

Another field of expatriate business activity was mining, centered
largely in the tin mines around the city of Jos. Although Nigerian metal
occupied fourth place in the value of Nigerian exports in 1938, the country was the fourth biggest mineral exporter in the British colonial territories of Africa, after the Rhodesias and the Gold Coast.[28] Nigerian mining
involved a diverse assemblage of firms of varying capital intensities and
efficiencies. Of the twenty-one largest and most important firms, which
together had a total nominal capital of £3,879,000, three groups predominated: the Anglo-Oriental Group, Latella, and Naraguta.[29] The major concern in the Anglo-Oriental Group was the Amalgamated Tin Mines of
Nigeria, the mining industry's most heavily capitalized firm at £1 million
in nominal capital and its largest producer—7,880 tons out of a total
annual production of 13,228 tons in 1945.[30] Amalgamated Tin Mines enjoyed powerful backing in British business and political circles, notably
the London Nigeria Chamber of Mines, which looked after Nigerian tin
mining interests in Britain. Amalgamated Tin Mines was the largest employer of mining labor, estimated at 30,000 in the mid-1940s. It was
efficiently run, though it had a reputation for insensitivity on social and
labor issues. The same could not be said of the other two groups, Latella
and Naraguta. Neither was well managed or efficient. Both managed to
achieve significant profits during the war because the British Ministry of
Supply purchased all the tin mined in Nigeria at inflated prices.[31]

A Nigerian business stratum was also in the process of forming; unlike
in Kenya, it already had a formidable presence in 1945, much like that
enjoyed by the native-born Egyptian bourgeoisie at the close of World

[26] Bank of British West Africa, *Annual Report*, 1944–45.
[27] W. T. Newlyn and D. C. Rowan, *Money and Banking in British Colonial Africa: A
Study of the Monetary and Banking System of Eight British Territories* (Oxford, 1954), pp.
76 ff.
[28] Perham, ed., *Mining, Commerce, and Finance in Nigeria*, p. 1. See also Bill Freund,
Capital and Labor in the Nigerian Tin Mines (Burnt Mill, Eng., 1981).
[29] W. S. McCann, Report on the Technical Aspects of the Nigerian Royalties, August 23,
1947, PRO CO 537/2098.
[30] London Nigeria Chamber of Mines, Minutes, vol. 2, May 23, 1945.
[31] No. 1340, Governor of Nigeria to Colonial Office, June 17, 1946, PRO CO 852/622/5.

War I. Nigerian entrepreneurs, seeking a place for themselves in the Nigerian economy, saw big European capital as their chief impediment. The leading business figures were persons new to commerce, however, who could not draw on Nigeria's rich commercial traditions of the nineteenth century because this past had been so thoroughly expunged by the colonial economic impact. Nor were the careers of rising merchants and industrialists fully anchored in the business sector, since many pursued activities in agriculture, union life, and politics simultaneously.

The most prominent of the new Yoruba mercantile merchants was T. A. Odutola, an Ijebu Ode–based individual, who, like many of the new entrepreneurs, had risen in the business world as buying agent for Holt and the United Africa Company.[32] By 1943 he had become Holt's largest cocoa buyer, in possession of 3,000 to 4,000 tons of storage space in Lagos.[33] The local Holt representative cultivated Odutola's loyalty and worried about his suspicion of the big firms. "Odutola," he wrote, "was imbued with the idea that the big firms were out to smash the African and drive him out of business here; or, if he became at all powerful, offer to buy him out first. He does today realize that for the European firms to be prosperous the African must be prosperous and that we can help to make him that."[34] Incorporated as Odutola and Sons, the firm was already involved in timber cutting and exporting and eager to become more than an agent of the European firms. Odutola petitioned the state to allow his firm to import textiles and sent numerous industrial projects to its officials.[35]

Although Odutola was arguably the most impressive Yoruba entrepreneur, his singular concentration on business was not commonplace. At Ibadan, for instance, two individuals excelled in the dual, often interchangeable roles of politician and businessman: Adegoke Adelabu and Chief Salame Agbaje. Their careers revealed the interconnectedness of balance sheets and officeholding even at this early date in the decolonizing process. Ibadan's most charismatic and feared politician, Adegoke Adelabu, dominated the city's politics until his untimely death in 1958. Yet he always promoted his business interests as assiduously as he pursued his political goals. A graduate of the Yaba Higher College in Lagos, where he took a three-year course in commerce, he became personal secretary to the district manager of the United Africa Company before discovering that his true metier was politics and that officeholding was the ideal location for furthering business plans.[36]

Chief Salame Agbaje, in contrast, literally obliterated the boundary

[32] Rawlings to Winter, December 4, 1939, Holt Papers, f535(ii).

[33] Cotgreave, Lagos, to others, October 25, 1943, Holt Papers, f535(ii).

[34] Winter to Rawlings, November 30, 1943, Holt Papers, f535(ii).

[35] West African Pilot, November 1, 1946.

[36] Kenneth W. J. Post and George D. Jenkins, The Price of Liberty: Personality and Politics in Colonial Nigeria (Cambridge, 1973), esp. pp. 33–53.

lines between business and politics. Born around 1880 in Lagos, he moved to Ibadan as a youngster in search of wealth and title. These came to him beyond his wildest expectations. Though uneducated, he obtained a high office in the Ibadan local administration and became "a millionaire by local standards."[37] A British commission, set up to investigate charges that the chief had violated customary law and was selfish, ruthless, and tyrannical, described him as a man who had enjoyed much success as "a farmer, transporter, produce buyer, saw mill owner, money-lender, contractor, hardware dealer, manufacturer of mineral water, member of Native Authority, firewood seller, Appellate Court judge, poultry keeper, landlord, copartner in various miscellaneous undertakings for the manufacture of profits. . . . He was the richest man in the division, the owner of the largest number of properties, the greatest industrialist, as well as the most astute intriguer." Yet the commissioners censured him for mixing business with politics, arguing that what Nigeria needed at this juncture was "a George Washington or an Abraham Lincoln and not a Henry Ford or John Pierpont Morgan."[38]

Elsewhere, beyond the confines of Lagos and the cocoa-growing regions of the West, business tycoons were not so abundant, but they were beginning to appear. J. Asaboro supplied rubber to Holt. His worth was valued anywhere from £6,000 to £9,000 in 1946, and he succeeded in having his line of credit raised from £2,000 to £5,000 so that he could become a cocoa buyer in the Ilon area.[39] The leading Ibo businessman of the period, Louis Philip Ojukwu, had already parlayed a trucking business into great wealth, and his mind was bursting with ideas for new commercial and industrial ventures. After their first meeting, Governor John Macpherson characterized Ojukwu as "a man of substance . . . a shrewd, hardheaded person who believes in the present policy of the government."[40] In northern Nigeria, where there was greater continuity with precolonial mercantile traditions, the Dantata family dominated the business activity of Kano city and province, the North's most important groundnut-growing region. Alhassan Dantata had been involved in Kano groundnut commerce from its inception in 1912 until his death in the 1950s. During a lifetime of commerce, in which he amassed a fortune valued at £750,000, he founded a local business firm that erected ground-

---

[37] H. L. M. Butcher, *Report of the Commission of Inquiry into the Allegation of Misconduct against Chief Salame Agbaje, the Otun Balogun of Ibadan, and Allegations of Inefficiency and Maladministration on the Part of the Ibadan District Native Authority* (Lagos, 1951), p. 17.

[38] Ibid., pp. 18, 19–20.

[39] E. W. Pearce to Rawlings, December 1, 1946, Holt Papers, f421B(ii).

[40] Macpherson to Lloyd, June 9, 1950, PRO CO 583/310/30647/1C/4H/1950.

nut collection stations and retail stores all over the North.[41] By the 1950s the Dantatas claimed to be responsible for financing 60 percent of all the licensed buying agents of Kano province and to be doing so with free cash grants.[42]

Nigeria's indigenous mercantile class had received a massive and unexpected boost in its fortunes when, in the 1920s, the geographic reach of the big trading companies began to slow. From the turn of the century the big firms had moved into the Nigerian interior as river and rail transportation opened up the country. The furthermost points for the trading firms were railheads and landing sites. And when the firms elected not to pursue the new road system into the more distant interior, they opened a window of commercial opportunity to Africans, Syrians, and Lebanese to extend the trading frontier and profit from the opening up of new areas.[43]

What most characterized both the Nigerian mercantile elite and the rising Nigerian middle stratum was its fluidity and its occupational and even ethnic uncertainty. Education rather than wealth tended to be seen as the main vehicle of social mobility. There was not yet a strong preference among rising, young, and educated Nigerians for positions in the state sector over those in the private sector. That trend developed in the later colonial and postcolonial eras and stemmed directly from certain of the policies enacted by the British after World War II and then embraced by the Nigerian nationalist elites. The new Nigerians had separated themselves, through education and wealth, from the large mass of poor peasants, petty traders, and unskilled laborers; yet their escape from poverty was a recent development. They struggled mightily not to fall back into the ranks of the poor, for the Nigerian mercantile and professional elites were "for the most part first-generation educated and prosperous men, having emerged from very humble peasant and working class stock and from the most grinding and dehumanizing poverty to which they could not 'with equanimity' contemplate returning."[44]

Thus, by 1945, a diverse, competitive, and unstable business structure existed in Nigeria—one in which non-European business enterprises were beginning to challenge the more heavily capitalized and more influ-

---

[41] Ibrahim L. Bashir, "The Political Economy of an Oligarchy: The Case of Kano's Bourgeoisie," Boston University African Studies Center, Working Papers, no. 89, 1984.

[42] Michael Watts, *Silent Violence: Food, Famine, and Peasantry in Northern Nigeria* (Berkeley, Calif., 1983), p. 258.

[43] Lauren van de Laan, "Modern Inland Transport and the European Trading Firms in Colonial West Africa," *Cahiers d'études Africaines* 21, no. 4 (1981), p. 566.

[44] Larry Diamond, *Class, Ethnicity, and Democracy in Nigeria: The Failure of the First Republic* (London, 1988), p. 34. The interpretation here and throughout draws on Sara Berry, *Fathers Work for Their Sons: Accumulation, Mobility, and Class Formation in an Extended Yoruba Community* (Los Angeles, 1985).

ential European companies. Nigerians had even established a presence in the banking sector, where previously the British had held a monopoly. In 1934 a group of Yoruba businessmen created the National Bank of Nigeria with a view to making loans available to Africans, whom the British banks had routinely ignored.[45]

To be sure, the new businesses of Nigeria could be unruly organizations. They were an investor's nightmare, and they duped many an overseas importer. High-sounding company names, corporate status, and glowing publicity documents often concealed glaring organizational defects. The Nigerian company law should have prevented business fraud of this kind, but Nigeria lacked a large and well-trained staff of inspectors to enforce its commercial regulations. For unsuspecting, easily confused foreign merchants, Nigeria was acquiring a reputation as a country where importing firms could lose money and have no judicial recourse. A group of American timber importers, for instance, learned a bitter lesson about Nigeria's commercial conditions when it imported worthless timbers instead of the mahogany it had contracted for and was then unable to enforce its contract in Nigeria. Its inquiries in the country revealed that the export company it had negotiated with was nothing more than a motley group of petty traders who sold pins and cigarettes in local markets.[46]

Nigeria may have had the appearance of stasis in 1945. Institutionally little had changed since the beginning of the war. But the Nigerian polity and economy were simply being held in check by wartime conditions. Everyone awaited the new arrangements promised for the postwar period. The British hoped to seize the political and economic initiative and were already preparing a full range of plans for implementation once the war was over. They were to be surprised by the strong responses from numerous nongovernmental groups to their restructuring designs.

THE GREAT DEBATES, 1945–1951

As the war in Europe drew to a close, the small British administrative staff in Nigeria turned its attention to postwar Nigeria. The new Nigerian governor, Arthur Richards, from whom the Nigerian nationalists expected much because of his liberalizing endeavors in Jamaica, directed the colonial secretariat in Lagos to develop blueprints to guide the country. Though Richards accorded primacy to political and constitutional matters, so convinced was he that good governance and correct constitutional

---

[45] Newlyn and Rowan, *Money and Banking in British Colonial Africa*, p. 103.
[46] No. 180, Winthrop S. Green to Secretary of State, October 6, 1947, USNA 848L.0172.

arrangements were the key to political stability and economic growth, he also knew that economic matters would impinge at every juncture.

Immediately after World War II all three countries analyzed here entered an intense period of thinking about new political and economic arrangements. The war had forestalled dramatic changes in polity and economy within these African territories. Its conclusion meant that a wide spectrum of questions that had been shelved because of the war required attention. Although there were no guidebooks or treatises on the best strategies for promoting the economic growth of less-developed areas (most frequently referred to as backward countries in the discourse of the period), the emerging consensus was that significant economic transformation had to occur, that the state must play a more meaningful role as planner and mobilizer of resources, and that the innovative energies of the private sector needed to be involved. In Egypt, Nigeria, and Kenya the period from 1945 through 1951 was marked by vigorous economic debates on questions of promoting structural change and income growth. Although each country came to slightly different emphases as a result of their different economic and political legacies and the outcome of the politically charged debates, the overall framework stressing the advantages of mixed public and private sector economies was remarkably alike. What came to distinguish the disparate economic and institutional histories of the countries was the success with which the ruling groups in each country adhered to these original premises or forsook them for other approaches.

The governorship of Arthur Richards (1944–1947) will forever be associated with the constitution of 1947. His predecessor, Bernard Bourdillon, had initiated discussions on the postwar constitution and had brought nationalist leaders into the debate. Despite Richards's experience in the West Indies, the new governor was nonetheless a man of the old colonial school, inspired by Lord Hailey's vision of reform from the top down. He was unsympathetic to the new democratic ideas sweeping through the corridors of the Colonial Office. Although Richards was willing to involve more Africans in the governance of Nigeria and wanted to bring the North and South together, he regarded the old elite of emirs, obas, and chiefs as the country's natural rulers. He was intensely suspicious of electoral politics, which he believed were still unsuited for Africa.

The Richards constitution of 1947 divided Nigeria into three large regions—North, East, and West—because Richards believed that these divisions reflected the irreducible ethnic, religious, and geographic realities of the country; he also desired to retain the North as one single, predominant region, rather than two or possibly three separate provinces. In the North the governor feared that "a Mohammedan bloc—a Pakistan—

[might arise] looking to Cairo rather than Lagos for guidance."[47] Except for elections from Lagos and Calabar, the unofficial representatives of the council were to be appointed by the governor from the ruling classes and the business community.

The Colonial Office's fear that the rising nationalist groups would not regard Richards's proposals as a constitutional "advance" was not wide of the mark. The newly organized National Council for Nigeria and the Cameroons (NCNC), under the dynamic leadership of Nnamdi Azikiwe, complained that it had never been consulted, that the unofficial majorities were a sham, that the legislative body was only advisory, and that no advance in electoral practice had occurred.[48] Although the British officials in Nigeria endeavored to dismiss Azikiwe's challenge by describing Nigerian nationalism as "a two-man show centered in Lagos and inspired by Azikiwe" (the other nationalist referred to was the grand old man of Lagosian politics, Herbert Macaulay), in truth, while Lagos was still the launching pad for Nigeria's major political associations and the location of the new journalism of anticolonialism, cadres of educated and critical Nigerians were forming in the cities of the interior—Ibadan, Abeokuta, and Ijebu Ode in the Southwest; Enugu, Calabar, Onitsha, and Port Harcourt in the Southeast; and even in the distant cities of the North. Nationalist politics, still the preserve of the elites, was endeavoring to broaden its base of support. The nationalist spokespersons found the new constitutional proposals the ideal grounds for bringing new groups into the political debates.

Right from the outset, as well, the nationalist critique had an economic dimension. Richards's critics focused their economic complaints on a group of four ordinances that were intended to enlarge the powers of the colonial state so that it could promote economic development. The nationalist critics feared that these decrees, branded as the four obnoxious ordinances, would allow the state to interfere in areas of activity previously exempt from colonial authority. In reality, the four decrees were designed to give the British Crown the power to acquire land and minerals for the public good and to depose chiefs. Nationalists insisted that these far-reaching powers should not be vested in the British monarchy but should belong to the Nigerian people.[49]

Azikiwe and the NCNC profited handsomely from the outpouring of opposition to the constitution and the decrees. They were able to channel the crescendo of criticisms from groups like the West African Students

[47] Richards to Stanley, July 19, 1944, PRO CO 583/286/30453; Richards to Hall, October 31, 1945, PRO CO 583/265/30037.
[48] Governor of Nigeria to Colonial Office, March 29, 1945, PRO CO 583/268/30453/1.
[49] *West African Pilot*, July 2, 1946, and August 7 and 8, 1947.

Union, the Trade Union Congress of Nigeria, and numerous ethnic unions as a vehicle to spread the party's influence outward from Lagos.[50] Even the North seemed fallow political territory, and the NCNC organized a tour of the main northern cities.[51] Its counterplan to the Richards proposals called for a two-stage, fifteen-year transition from colonial rule to independence and the division of the country into eight "protectorates" consisting of twenty-four provinces.[52]

The NCNC's effort to incorporate all of the strands of anticolonial protest under its own banner had little chance of success even in this heady period of sustained opposition to British overrule. Despite attempts to recruit its leadership widely, the party did not overcome the personal and ethnic rivalries that consistently beset Nigerian elite politics. The rising Northern politician, Abu Bakr Balewa, spurned Azikiwe's offer of a high position in the party, and even approached the British for advice on how to deal with the overture.[53] Azikiwe's NCNC encountered an even sterner challenge from Yoruba intellectuals, who until the arrival of Azikiwe on the Nigerian political scene in 1937 had had Lagosian politics to themselves. The NCNC could not fill the political void created by the decline of the National Youth Movement in Lagos and the West; instead the Yoruba intelligentsia rallied around a rising British-trained barrister, Obafemi Awolowo, whose followers established an all-Yoruba organ called the Egbe Omo Oduduwa (the Association of the Descendants of Oduduwa) in 1947 with a view to fostering unity among "the different tribes of the Yoruba nation," coordinating education and cultural programs, discouraging prejudice, and preserving traditional monarchies.

For the British, the nationalist furor over constitutional reform and the emerging ethnic rivalry meant that the nationalists were prepared to subject all propositions originating from the colonial authorities, whether they were economic or political, to the most intense scrutiny. The stage was thus set for the second great colonial debate—the economic future of Nigeria. Although this discussion was rapidly dispersed into a series of smaller but equally controversial questions, such as industrialization, marketing boards, planning, and the like, all of the individual deliberations revolved around the questions of how to conceive of the Nigerian economy in 1945 and how to view the country's economic prospects.

---

[50] H. O. Davies to Colonel Stanley, April 7, 1945; no. 1112, Governor to Colonial Office, May 25, 1945, enclosing memorandum on constitutional reform in Nigeria by the Trade Union Congress of Nigeria, May 7, 1945; both in PRO CO 583/268/30453/1.

[51] Creasy to Gater, July 18, 1946, PRO CO 583/277/30658.

[52] NCNC to Creech Jones, August 11, 1947, enclosing a memorandum submitted by the delegation of the National Council of Nigeria and the Cameroons to the Secretary of State for Colonies, PRO CO 583/292/30558/2; West African Pilot, September 9, 1947.

[53] Balewa to Captain H. H. Wilkinson, April 26, 1947, PRO CO 583/292/30658/1.

The majority British view at the time was that Nigeria was a deeply impoverished country and that in spite of its large population size and abundant natural resources, it lacked certain key ingredients for economic progress. This school of economic thinkers argued that Nigeria must deal first with basic social, infrastructural, and human resource development before it could undertake programs to promote rapid economic growth. A vocal minority, however, argued that Nigeria's economic potential was so palpable that the country could enjoy spectacular and immediate economic growth once the wartime restraints on trade and investment had been removed.

The British Colonial Office initiated the first of these great economic debates in January 1944 when it requested the Nigerian Secretariat to produce a ten-year development plan.[54] In response, the Nigerian government established a new office in the secretariat called the Development Branch, a technical advisory committee called the Advisory Committee on Economic Development and Social Welfare, and twenty-three smaller development committees in each of the country's provinces.[55] By the end of 1944, the government had completed a draft of its ten-year program, which called for total spending of nearly £55 million, of which £27,300,000 would come from the Colonial Development and Welfare Vote as free grants.[56] The colonial secretary lauded the Nigerian officials for developing a plan that could be used elsewhere "as a model for comprehensive outline development schemes"; yet it was still only a sketch of development, not a comprehensive document.[57] In the opinion of a later commentator, the plan represented little more than "a series of projects which had not been coordinated or related to any overall economic target."[58]

The plan's weaknesses notwithstanding, it fit squarely within the prevailing economic paradigm that the majority of British officials had for Nigeria. It emphasized communications and social services, particularly education and public health, over projects that would produce immediate increases in monetary standards of living. It also extolled the virtues of centralized planning and sought an expanded role for the state in economic affairs while remaining ambiguous about the precise contributions

[54] Andrew Cohen, Colonial Office Minute, January 27, 1944, PRO CO 583/272/30572. On Nigerian development planning, one should consult Toyin Falola, *Development Planning and Decolonization in Nigeria* (Gainesville, Fl., 1996).

[55] Richards to Stanley, January 7, 1944, PRO CO 583/272/30572.

[56] Ibid., September 22, 1944, PRO CO 583/272/30572.

[57] Note of meeting in Secretary of State's Room, November 6, 1944, PRO CO 583/272/30572.

[58] P. N. C. Okigbo, *Nigerian National Development Planning, 1900–1992* (London, 1989), p. 31.

that business would make. Conscious of the poverty and overall economic backwardness of the country, the Nigerian planners argued that infrastructural foundations had to be laid and a healthier and better-educated population created before Nigeria could strive for rapid economic growth. Of the total of £53.2 million of estimated expenditures, not less than £9 million, or 17 percent, was earmarked for education and public health.[59] The contrast with the early Kenyan development plans could not be more marked. There the planners worried about excessive expenditures on social programs, which they described as nonremunerative spending and thought would overwhelm the regular administrative budget. In contrast, the Nigerian bureaucrats believed that they must enhance basic living conditions before they could raise income levels.

Convinced that the new development secretary would become the most important Nigerian official after the governor, the Colonial Office sought to recruit a man "of good background, preferably with a liking for a country life, but not necessarily possessing the full academic qualifications which would be required for permanent appointment."[60] It was prepared to compensate the new official at the same rate as the financial secretary, who received a salary of £1,850 and was delighted when F. E. V. Smith accepted the post. Smith, who was to have inordinate influence on all the immediate postwar economic decisions made in Nigeria, was not a trained economist. Holding a bachelor's degree in science from the University of Bristol, he was attractive to the Colonial Office because of his experience in imperial marketing during the war.[61] He seemed to be in full agreement with the main emphases of the Nigerian development plan. Smith believed that Nigeria's most pressing economic priority was to ameliorate the lot of the common person, whom the new development secretary described as living in an "appalling condition." Further, he cautioned that "spectacular development could not be looked for until the basic necessities of life had been provided. When this was done, the productive capacity of the people as a whole would be improved and could be absorbed into some form of economic development."[62]

Nigeria's distinctive economic plan did not escape searching criticism. The ongoing discussion of economic policies emboldened the Nigerian nationalist critics to attack one of their favorite economic targets, the European business houses, and to blame them for Nigeria's economic

---

[59] Nigeria, *A Ten-Year Plan*, Sessional Paper No. 24 of 1945, especially p. 38.

[60] Extract from Note of a Discussion with the Treasury, November 9, 1944, PRO CO 583/272/30572.

[61] A. H. M. Kirk-Greene, *A Biographical Dictionary of the British Colonial Service, 1939–1966* (London, 1991), p. 332.

[62] Extract from Note of a Discussion with the Treasury, November 9, 1944, PRO CO 583/272/30572.

backwardness. Fidelis A. Ogunshege, an acerbic economic critic who frequently wrote for the *Daily Service* and was assistant secretary of the Nigeria Union of Teachers, worried that £32 million of the £55 million development price tag would have to be raised internally and would prove too heavy a burden for the Nigerian Treasury. Ogunshege demanded that the commercial and mining companies shoulder more of the financial load. He was particularly angered that the United Africa Company would continue to receive royalty payments from the government on minerals taken from the ground when the country desperately needed those funds for economic development and social justice. In his view, foreign firms that had enjoyed a privileged existence in Nigeria should now throw their full weight behind the development effort.[63]

Even while the debate on development priorities was occurring, the Nigerian Secretariat had begun an intensive analysis of the single most important institutional question for the postwar and postcolonial political economy of Nigeria: the marketing of Nigeria's major agricultural exports. Many had thought that the British West Africa–wide marketing board, called the West African Produce Control Board, which had been set up during the war to market West Africa's major exports, would be dissolved in favor of the prewar marketing arrangements once the war was over. But the British government's experience with marketing had persuaded its officials that the government would at least have to maintain some measure of oversight. To begin with, the West African Produce Control Board had learned how difficult it was to gauge the world price for West African commodities, having in earlier buying seasons lost small sums of money or made embarrassingly large surpluses. If a large government organization with access to the most sophisticated economic predictions could not estimate world prices with precision, how then could small cultivators be expected to do so? In the opinion of many British officials, what the West African farmers needed was a buffer, preferably the state rather than self-interested retail firms, to stand between them and the vagaries of the international markets.

The first hint of the government's intentions came with the publication of a parliamentary White Paper in 1944—a document that set in motion a debate that reverberated well beyond the halls of the colonial secretariat in Lagos and drew in all of the private groups whose interests were involved. The 1944 report dealt only with cocoa. It first addressed the question of the large surpluses that the Produce Control Board had accumulated during the war.[64] The profits from the cocoa trade were rising and totaled nearly £4 million by the end of 1943. They had aroused justifiable

---

[63] *Daily Service*, February 26, 1946.
[64] West African Produce Control Board (44), 12, April 5, 1944, PRO CO 852/631/3.

concern in the British Parliament and bitter criticism in the West African press, which demanded their return to African cultivators. The authors of the White Paper recommended that the funds be returned to the governments of the West African territories whence they had originated and that, in the future, any state marketing apparatus that was created be based in West Africa rather than in the British metropole so that it could be responsive to the needs of the West African peoples.[65] Further, the report favored state marketing for cocoa but was uncertain about other commodities. The West African states had the financial resources and technical staff to deal with cocoa but might not have them for other products, for which, in any case, the pressure for government controls was not powerful.[66]

Despite the tentative nature of the conclusions of the White Paper, the report set off a chain of critical responses involving a broad spectrum of interested groups. The earliest attack originated from American manufacturers and importers of West African cocoa, who were fearful that government-run marketing organizations would curtail American entry into the West African trade and raise cocoa prices in world markets. Rockwood, Hershey, and the General Cocoa Company, all American firms, directed complaints to the U.S. State Department and the British Colonial Office. Isaac Witkin, president of the General Cocoa Company and the New York Cocoa Exchange, spoke against "autocratic agencies [marketing boards] in authoritarian states" and pointed out that West African and Brazilian producers already controlled 80 percent of the world product. American diplomatic representatives, pressured by Rockwood, Hershey, and Witkin, met with British colonial officials to express their "general convictions about the innate wickedness of government control in any form."[67]

British commercial and manufacturing interests joined their American colleagues in questioning the efficacy of government marketing. At a meeting at the Colonial Office, Frank Samuel of the United Africa Company asserted that the goal of the colonial governments in West Africa seemed to be "to drive European firms, slowly or quickly, out of the cocoa trade," while the British Federation of Commodity and Allied Trade Associations claimed that state-administered marketing authorities were likely to oppress the farmers more systematically than the trading

[65] *Report on Cocoa Control in West Africa, 1939–43*, House of Commons Sessional Papers, 1943–44, vol. 3, cmd. 6554.

[66] Colonial Office Memorandum, Proposal for Marketing Organizations in Nigeria, November 1944, PRO CO 852/650/4.

[67] E. Melville, British Colonies Supply Mission, to E. Tansley, West African Produce Control Board, November 7, 1944, PRO CO 852/630/4.

firms ever had, since there would be no competitive bidding for supplies.[68] The Cocoa and Chocolate War-Time Association reminded the Colonial Office that its factories in the United Kingdom employed 48,800 and relied on the free flow of produce from West Africa.[69]

The protest was not confined to manufacturers and European exporters. The Produce Buyers Union of Ibadan and western Nigeria, drawing on a long tradition of opposition to governmental controls over cocoa marketing, criticized the idea of a cocoa board, pointing out that the West African Produce Board already had a reputation for underpaying cultivators. In all likelihood, its successor would do the same. These African merchant critics also spoke about "our economic struggle between the capitalist giants and the poor ignorant natives." They complained that the government under the present marketing arrangements paid generous commissions to licensed buyers and allowed the big firms to squeeze the African produce middlemen.[70] Much the same complaint was heard at a meeting held in Glover Hall, Lagos, where S. L. Akintola and Dr. Akinola Maja sponsored a resolution demanding an immediate increase in cocoa prices and the prices of other government-marketed commodities as well as the termination of all marketing controls.[71]

In spite of this barrage of criticisms, the colonial officials in London and West Africa held firm. Colonial marketing experts Eric Tansley and Gerald Creasy were deputed to present the government's case to the American and British firms.[72] Governors Alan Burns in the Gold Coast and Richards in Nigeria also opposed compromise, mainly on political grounds, arguing that the nationalists would use the concession as evidence for their charges that the colonial state was nothing more than an agent for the great European firms.[73] Richards went even further. He described the scheme as "a fundamental development of far-reaching importance to the African producers of export crops" and excoriated the trading firms for attempting to keep most of the profits of the produce

[68] Gerald Creasy, Colonial Office Note, September 26, 1944, PRO CO 852/630/4; E. Mackenzie Hay, Chairman of the British Federation of Commodity and Allied Trade Associations, to Stanley, January 2, 1945; and Memorandum from the British Federation of Commodity and Allied Trade Associations to Colonial Office, February 15, 1945; both in PRO CO 852/596/1.

[69] Cocoa and Chocolate War-Time Association to Colonial Office, January 1945, PRO CO 852/596/1.

[70] Nigeria, Sessional Paper No. 20 of 1939, 2; articles in the *Daily Comet*, May 5, 7, and 8, 1945, found in Holt Papers, f535(ii).

[71] *West African Pilot*, January 15, 1946.

[72] Colonial Office Minute, March 1, 1944; Creasy to Colonial Office, October 11, 1944; both in PRO CO 852/630/4.

[73] Richards to Stanley, February 15, 1945, PRO CO 852/596/2.

trade for themselves. Richards's long-term hope was to replace trading firms with African producer cooperatives, thereby securing the whole of the profits from the produce trade to the farmers.[74] At the Colonial Office, Sydney Caine, the chief adviser on West African economic matters, argued in favor of the boards on the grounds of price stabilization but was unwilling to openly criticize private commercial interests for fear of intensifying opposition to the White Paper.[75]

Although the government did not change its stance, the debate revealed it to be the only group fully committed to state marketing. Even Caine admitted so when he wrote that the White Paper had achieved backing only from members of Parliament with close ties to West African nationalists, Fabian Socialists, and the Aborigines Rights Protection Society in West Africa.[76] The formidable opposition lined up against statutory marketing boards included merchant firms, worried about the erosion of their commercial strength in West Africa; American and British manufacturers, alarmed at the prospect of a few governments in cocoa-producing areas conspiring to raise world prices; and Yoruba mercantile groups, fearful that they would lose their most successful avenue of occupational and economic mobility.

The British colonial administrators remained largely impervious to the widespread criticism of their ideas. In the first place, they harbored the old paternalist views of colonial rulers that they and they alone knew what was best for the Nigerian people, and that they were the true protectors of the Nigerian peasants from their many exploiters. Among the exploiters, in the minds of the colonial bureaucrats, were the great European export-import firms who were thought to have taken more out of Nigeria than they had put into it. In addition, although the groups ranged against state marketing represented a formidable collection—Western cocoa manufacturers, European exporters, and Yoruba merchants and large-scale farmers—they failed to unify their opposition or to present alternative visions to that of state control. The American manufacturers were the most outspoken advocates of the free market and unregulated prices, but in this postwar era of nationalizations in Europe and the heightened economic role of the state in Africa, their laissez-faire demands did not serve as a rallying cry for the opposition groups or undermine the statist enthusiasm of the colonial officials.

In April 1945, the colonial officials received their first encouraging and conciliatory gesture from the big cocoa exporters when L. J. Cadbury,

---

[74] Richards to Creasy, November 21, 1944, PRO CO 852/596/1.
[75] Caine to F. E. V. Smith, December 7, 1944, PRO CO 852/630/4.
[76] Caine, Colonial Office Minute, March 12, 1945, PRO CO 852/596/3.

head of Cadbury Brothers, endorsed the main recommendations of the White Paper.[77] Yet his remarks were inspired as much by the knowledge that the merchant firms were not yet in a position to purchase all of the West African cocoa crop as by a genuine belief in the advantages of statutory marketing organizations. Even a year later, that situation had not changed. At a meeting of the Manchester Chamber of Commerce, delegates agreed that although the old mercantile arrangements of West Africa should be restored as soon as possible the firms still needed another year before they would be ready for full-scale buying.[78]

In 1946 the British government issued a second parliamentary White Paper. This document announced that the governments of Nigeria and the Gold Coast would create separate marketing organizations for cocoa. Each one was to have three to five members appointed by the colonial governor and an advisory committee on which commercial and producer interests would be represented. The primary functions of these boards were spelled out in precise language. They were being established so as to create "a buffer between the producer and the international market which will protect him from short-term fluctuations of world prices and allow him a greater stability of income." Any funds that might accumulate with the marketing boards would be used "as a cushion against short and intermediate term price fluctuations in the world price of cocoa; but it will be within the discretion of the boards to allocate funds at their disposal for other purposes of general benefit to the cocoa producers and the industry, such as research and disease eradication, the encouragement of cooperation, and the provision of other amenities and facilities to producers."[79]

This last statement about the use of surpluses was of the highest importance. The cocoa boards already had large surpluses and were likely to see them grow in a world commodity market of steadily rising prices. Although, then, the report permitted using these funds for more than price stabilization, it was clear that their uses were intended to benefit the cocoa producers and the cocoa industry directly. No wider mandate was authorized. The trading firms were to continue to buy the cocoa on the basis of state-assigned quotas. They would be required to pay the price set each season by the board, but they could pay more if they chose. The state would reimburse firms for expenses and allow a margin for profit.[80]

Although few realized it at the time, the decision to create the market-

[77] *Manchester Guardian*, April 17, 1945.

[78] Manchester Chamber of Commerce, Minutes of Meeting of the Joint West Africa Committee, April 17, 1946.

[79] *Statement on Future Marketing of West African Cocoa, November 1946*, House of Commons Sessional Papers, 1945–46, vol. 20, cmd. 6950.

[80] Ibid.

ing boards had the most profound implications for state–private sector relations and even for the career choices of Nigeria's nascent middle class. State power was elevated at the expense of the private sector. Nigerians aspiring to wealth and power soon came to understand that the locus of power lay in the public sector and not in private business activities, largely because the marketing boards became the most efficient institutions for amassing capital and determining the main directions of the Nigerian economy through their lending and grants in aid. The boards had been established for the purpose of price stabilization, and only secondarily to provide grants in aid to producers. They were also to become deeply involved in Nigerian party and electoral politics, though no one realized it at the time.

Although the nationalists later embraced the marketing boards, realizing that they could use the surpluses to further their own political ends, at this stage they subjected the boards to savage attacks. S. L. Akintola assaulted the boards as a colonial intrusion designed to magnify the power of British bureaucrats at the expense of African producers and traders.[81] Earlier, the editors of the *Daily Service* had worried that "the cocoa industry is not to be free again [and] . . . huge cocoa profits will not return to the farmers."[82] The Oni (ruler) of Ife, one of the two African members of the board, sought to defend the board from these attacks, claiming that the board was scrupulous in protecting African interests and that six of the twelve members of the board's advisory committee were Africans who vigorously represented the interests of exporters, cooperatives, middlemen, and farmers.[83] The Oni's article brought a further nationalist outburst that ridiculed the Oni as a colonial collaborator through whom the British concealed their exploitation of African farmers.[84]

The board also did not gain the support of the cocoa farmers of western Nigeria, in whose interest it had ostensibly been established. Cocoa cultivators were already angry at the government for its misguided swollen shoot campaign, which was in high gear and was intended to eradicate trees infected with the swollen shoot virus. Their general disenchantment with the government made them all the more suspicious of the activities of the cocoa board. Farmers' groups complained bitterly about the huge differential between the local price of cocoa and the world price—at one moment £65 and £255 respectively—and doubted the argument that these funds would be used on their behalf when world market prices declined.[85]

[81] *Daily Service*, December 4, 1947.
[82] Ibid., November 22, 1946.
[83] Ibid., December 4, 1947.
[84] Ibid., December 6, 1947.
[85] *West African Pilot*, February 13, 1948.

The debate over cocoa boards had been initiated because the West African Produce Control Board had accumulated large surpluses. The repatriation of the surplus funds to Nigeria and the Gold Coast was supposed to silence the worriers, but it did not. By the early 1950s, as the balances mushroomed, many different groups laid claim to them. Yet the Nigerian colonial authorities were reluctant to allow the money to be disbursed back into the western region in development schemes or, alternatively, to raise the local price of cocoa. They justified their conservative pricing policies on economic grounds. In truth, however, their fears were overwhelmingly political. They believed that an infusion of large sums of money into the local economy, without an increase in the availability of consumer goods, would produce rapid inflation and intensify political agitation.[86]

To Nigerian producers and middlemen, clamoring for kerosene, cement, corrugated iron sheeting, and textiles, the government stance seemed specious.[87] The main opposition to the board arose from the two most effectively organized producer groups—the National Farmers Union, which was dominated by absentee landlords who lived in Lagos and owned cocoa estates at Agege; and the Maiyegun Society, centered in the Ibadan division. Both groups exploited farmers' discontent with the swollen shoot campaign and opposition to government cocoa pricing policy. They sought a larger role for cultivators on the marketing board itself. The National Farmers Union carried its campaign beyond its base in Lagos and Agege and mobilized support in Ondo, Ilesha, and Ife. It formed an alliance with the Egba Farmers Union.[88] At its annual conference, held at Agege on April 29, 1949, the union demanded African majorities on the cocoa board and the board's advisory committee and asked that the board be fully involved in all discussions concerning the board's surpluses. It also demanded that the local price of cocoa be increased immediately to £160 per ton.[89]

The Nigerian government was forced to raise the local price of cocoa in 1948 to £120 per ton, although its new price was still £50 less than the Farmers Union was requesting.[90] The colonial officials reluctantly also allowed the cocoa board to finance a small number of social and economic projects of special interest to the Yoruba intelligentsia. In 1950–51, under prodding from the Oni of Ife, the cocoa board set aside substantial sums to establish a department of agriculture at the University College, Ibadan, and to underwrite a feasibility study for a new medical

[86] Bloomfield, Colonial Office Minute, February 21, 1948, PRO CO 852/904/1.
[87] No. 1159, Governor to Colonial Office, July 29, 1948, PRO CO 852/904/5.
[88] Extract from Nigerian Political Summary, n.d., PRO CO 852/904/5.
[89] *Daily Service*, May 11, 1949.
[90] Note of a meeting held at the Colonial Office, November 7, 1951, PRO CO 554/522.

college there.[91] These expenditures marked a significant departure in the use of these surpluses, for they represented the first large-scale use of board funds for a broad program of social and economic development.

The decision to use the funds for these purposes provoked a strenuous debate within government circles. Although the creation of an agriculture department at the University college, Ibadan, was rationalized on the grounds of its contribution to the well-being of the cocoa farmers of the West, it was much less easy to make a case for expenditures on a medical college. Most British officials on the board were reluctant to sanction such appropriations, but they felt obliged to endorse the position of the Oni of Ife because of his staunch defense of the board against persistent and widespread criticisms.

Although the Colonial Office and the colonial secretariat in Nigeria were the keenest advocates of statutory marketing, even within their own ranks there were sharp differences of opinion. The divisions became more pronounced as the world price for cocoa increased and large surpluses piled up. P. T. Bauer, a consultant for the Colonial Office, leveled a searing criticism at the boards, which ultimately led him to publish his comprehensive and critical study of marketing and trading in West Africa entitled *West African Trade* (1954). Even before the publication of this work, Bauer challenged the actions of the boards, concluding in an internal Colonial Office memorandum that these bodies, which included oil-seeds as well as cocoa, had mammoth and wholly unanticipated balances totaling £100 million as of October 1950 and were likely to rise to £150 by the end of the buying season. Bauer was concerned that "this [sum] represents an obligation which may never be honored." He noted the huge financial losses being sustained by West African cultivators who received only one-third to two-thirds of what their competitors were obtaining in other parts of the world. In Bauer's view underpricing was grossly immoral and exploitative. "The compulsory savings of the local population are used in effect to subsidize the British economy by investing the balances of the marketing boards in British securities." He did not accept the argument that price limitations prevented destabilizing inflation. The return of the surpluses to the West African producers was just as likely to stimulate local industrialists as to lead to inflation and might even draw consumer goods away from the metropole into the more lucrative West African markets.[92]

Officials at the Colonial Office were unimpressed. They described

---

[91] Minutes of the Sixteenth Meeting of the Nigerian Cocoa Marketing Board, March 28, 1951, PRO CO 852/1150/7.

[92] P. T. Bauer, Memorandum on the Accumulation of Sterling Balances by the Marketing Boards, c. October 1950, PRO CO 537/7626.

Bauer's memorandum as "very confused and somewhat unbalanced."[93] And the publication of his book, *West African Trade*, with its even more reasoned criticism of the marketing boards, also did not cause a stir in official circles, which by then were completely in favor of statutory marketing for West Africa's major agricultural exports. Although, at first, cocoa was the only government-marketed commodity, it was only a matter of time before Nigeria's other major agricultural exports, starting with groundnuts, palm oil, and palm kernels, were added to the list.

A final great economic debate of this period revolved around industrial policy. It pitted the Nigerian colonial bureaucracy, led by its new development secretary, F. E. V. Smith, against the export-import firms, which had become interested in promoting Nigerian industrialization. It demonstrated that firms that had been defeated over the creation of marketing boards could have their way provided that they gained backers within the colonial bureaucracy.

Once the Nigerian colonial officials had established the Department of Commerce and Industry and the Development Corporation, they moved quickly to draw up a set of industrial plans as part of the ten-year plan.[94] F. E. V. Smith emerged as the driving intellectual force in the Nigerian colonial bureaucracy. He articulated the government's vision of small-scale, labor-intensive, indigenous factories and workshops, which he believed should grow organically from Nigerian village industries and which would be the spearhead of industrial progress and employment generation.[95] Smith believed that Nigeria was on the verge of a social and political crisis, aggravated by a burgeoning urban population, most visible and politically explosive in the capital city of Lagos. Only rurally based enterprises, exploiting large labor levies and using local raw materials, would improve rural living conditions and slow the rural exodus. If Nigeria needed large industrial sites in order to benefit from economies of scale, pools of skilled labor, and the easy exchange of manufactures, they should be located in lesser urban areas like Sapele, Onitsha, and the Niger delta rather than Lagos or even Ibadan. Much to be preferred, however, were traditional village craft activities—textile spinning and weaving and mat making.[96]

---

[93] Brown, Memorandum, October 6, 1950, PRO CO 537/7626.

[94] Colonial Office Note, Commercial and Industrial Development, December 7, 1944, PRO CO 583/272/30572.

[95] Nigeria, Memorandum, Marketing, Commercial, and Industrial Development, September 1944; and Nigeria, Memorandum, Assistance to Minor Village and Rural Industries: Application for Free Grant of £12,000, November 16, 1944; both in PRO CO 583/273/30572.

[96] J. F. Winter to H. J. Rawlings, August 27, 1945, Holt Papers, f421 B(ii).

Smith's vision did not win approval outside the Nigerian Secretariat, however. The first voice of discontent came from a British textile firm, V. E. Houghton Ltd, manufacturers, dyers, and calico printers located in Lancashire, which requested permission to explore the textile manufacturing prospects in Nigeria in January 1946. When the Nigerian colonial government objected on the grounds that a modern textile factory would create housing and social problems, offer little additional employment because of its capital intensity, and damage Nigeria's rural weaving industry, Houghton carried its case to the Colonial Office.[97] It also sought and gained the backing of the United Africa Company and Holt, which were themselves assessing the prospects of Nigerian industrialization.[98]

The United Africa Company, already involved in the Nigerian industrial sector through its parent firm, Lever Brothers, had established a soap manufacturing plant at Apapa in the 1920s. By 1945 the West African Soap Company was supplying more than half of the Nigerian soap market.[99] As early as 1944 the UAC representative, A. R. I. Mellor, had indicated to the Colonial Office that his firm was prepared to take part in a variety of local manufacturing endeavors at the conclusion of the war. Even more enthusiastic was Holt, which discussed a long list of industrial ventures with the Nigerian Department of Commerce and Industry in 1946 and made a concrete proposal to establish a brewery with the United Africa Company.[100] The prime movers within the Holt entourage were its Lagos representatives, C. Cotgreave and E. W. Pearce, who could see that industrialization was on the horizon in Nigeria and that the export-import firms, to protect lucrative markets, would have to compete. The Holt men predicted that textiles and oil extraction would prove profitable.[101]

At this juncture, the clashing industrial perspectives of Smith (rurally based, labor intensive) and the British corporations (large scale, capital intensive) were referred to the economic experts at the Colonial Office. From the outset, the most influential members of the official team aligned themselves decisively with the capital-intensive school, arguing that in-

[97] No. 64, Governor of Nigeria to Colonial Office, January 11, 1946, PRO CO 852/574/10.

[98] A. R. I. Mellor, United Africa Company, to Caine, September 6, 1944, PRO CO 583/574/6; J. F. Winter to H. J. Rawlings, August 27, 1945, Holt Papers, f421 B(ii).

[99] Roger H. Heyworth, Lever Brothers, to Caine, March 15, 1945, PRO CO 852/536/3.

[100] Memorandum on Nigerian Brewery, John Holt Company, Merchandise Department, January 24, 1946, Holt Papers, f452 B(ii).

[101] C. Cotgreave to Colonial Office and E. W. Pearce to Rawlings, December 1, 1946, Holt Papers, f421 B(ii). For Nigerian industrialization after World War II, one should consult Peter Kilby, *Industrialization in an Open Economy: Nigeria, 1945–1960* (Cambridge, 1969).

dustrial development, spearheaded by British capital on a big scale, was the only way Nigeria could overcome poverty and foster economic development.[102] W. B. L. Monson at the Colonial Office scorned the programs of the Nigerian government, which he wrote "seem to be the creation of a rustic economy whose passing in this country is lamented over by writers like G. K. Chesterton."[103] Smith bristled at this misrepresentation of his views and predicted with compelling foresight that a capital-intensive formula would produce urban chaos, severe trade deficits, and inefficient industries operating behind high tariff walls.[104]

The outcome of this debate was foreordained, given the climate of opinion of the postwar period and the influence of Holt and the United Africa Company with the Colonial Office. Once Sydney Caine, the person whom all conceded to be the most economically sophisticated at the Colonial Office, had decided in favor of the big industrialists, all that remained was to bring Smith into line. Caine sought "a show down on this [issue]," and in April 1946 he summoned Smith to a meeting in London.[105] In preparation for the meeting, G. H. Hall of the Colonial Office drafted a letter to Governor Richards, which upbraided the Nigerian Secretariat for being "a little too cautious in its attitudes toward proposals for new industrial development, and by setting its requirements too high to run the risk that no development will take place at all." Hall added that while the Colonial Office did not favor "uncontrolled development . . . there is no doubt in my mind that industrial development in itself offers one of the most promising means we can have of raising the general level of prosperity of the people in a country like Nigeria."[106] The meeting of May 29, 1946, confirmed the decision to encourage British-financed and -managed industrialization.[107]

FIRST CHALLENGES TO THE COLONIAL VISION

It may be objected that these "great debates" were far from great in that they involved only a small elite of colonial officials, large business firms, and wealthy Yoruba cocoa farmers and that the final decisions were made by a small elite of colonial officials in London and Lagos. Although the

[102] See Rosa, Minute, January 26, 1946, PRO CO 852/574/10.
[103] Monson, January 31, 1946, PRO CO 852/574/10.
[104] Smith to Dawson, United Africa Company, February 20, 1946, PRO CO 852/574/10.
[105] Trenchard to Richards, March 28, 1946, PRO CO 852/574/10.
[106] G. H. Hall to Richards, April 12, 1946, PRO CO 852/574/10.
[107] Memorandum of Meeting at the Colonial Office with Caine, Williams, Monson, Rosa, and Smith, May 29, 1946, PRO CO 852/574/10.

purview of the debate did not extend broadly (and certainly the wage-earning classes and the peasantry in Nigeria were not taken into the confidence of officialdom), the results of the decisions about general strategies of economic development (whether to stress economic infrastructure at the expense of programs designed to promote immediate economic gain), marketing, and industrialization still had implications for all segments of Nigerian society.

It would not be accurate, however, to suggest that the influence of the subalterns was not reflected in these debates, no matter how indirect or even misconstrued it may have been. In the immediate postwar era, and with increasing force thereafter, radical socialist ideas permeated parts of the nationalist movement, most notably the Zikist movement and trade union activity. Also, a more indigenous business challenge to the state-centered orientation of the colonial state and the power of European business appeared among Yoruba merchants operating in Lagos and the western region.

Zikism

On the left, the Zikist movement sought a completely different resolution to the pressing constitutional and economic questions of the era. Endeavoring to draw together Nigeria's radical anticolonial strands, the Zikists, in alliance with radical trade unionists, sought nothing less than an overturning of the whole colonial economic and political project in favor of an independent and socialist Nigeria. Although the Zikists ultimately failed to forge a grand alliance of the left, their effort kept the pressure on the British rulers of Nigeria and brought concessions in order to keep radicals and moderates apart.[108] The Zikists also failed to advance their challenge beyond campaigns of civil disobedience and nonpayment of taxes, but their call for a more state-centered and egalitarian form of economic development and more rapid decolonization kept an alternative vision before the people.

The Zikists would have fared well had the autocratic Arthur Richards

---

[108] Winthrop S. Jordan to Secretary of State, July 10, 1947, USNA 848L.00. Naturally, anyone writing on this period is indebted to a host of scholars. Especially when writing about political developments, one remains indebted to earlier studies, notably the works of James S. Coleman, *Nigeria: Background to Nationalism* (Berkeley, Calif., 1963); Richard L. Sklar, *Nigerian Political Parties: Power in an Emergent Nation* (Princeton, N.J., 1963); C. S. Whitaker, Jr., *The Politics of Tradition: Continuity and Change in Northern Nigeria, 1946–1966* (Princeton, N.J., 1966); and B. J. Dudley, *Parties and Politics in Northern Nigeria* (London, 1968).

remained governor. His high-handed, nonconsultative ways drove moderates into the arms of the radicals. But his successor, John Macpherson, was a more open and gregarious individual, committed to regaining the political initiative from the radical nationalists by offering timely constitutional concessions to moderate nationalists. Still, Macpherson faced a political test from the Zikists in 1948 when the government decided to bring charges against a group of Zikist leaders, one of whom, Osita Christopher Ogwunna, had delivered a lecture in Lagos on October 27, 1948, entitled "A Call to Revolution."

When the Zikists endeavored to unite labor leaders and discontented Ibadan cocoa farmers, Governor Macpherson believed that he had no alternative but to repress the Zikists, who were said to be infiltrating the police, prison warders, and the West African Frontier Force.[109] Macpherson's crackdown in early 1950 involved police raids on the residences of every major leader of the movement living in Kano, Lagos, Kaduna, Enugu, Gusua, and Aba.[110] It proved altogether disabling to Zikism, for the movement virtually disappeared from Nigerian politics. In assessing the Zikist movement in 1950, the British were undoubtedly correct in concluding that Zikism had failed to unify the radicals and had not succeeded in offering a coherent and persuasive alternative to the colonial program. Unable to attract more than a few hundred members, the movement was hamstrung by lack of funds. Although its primary organ of propaganda, the *Labor Champion*, promulgated a socialist message under its motto, "Toward the Creation of the Socialist Republic," its circulation never exceeded 600 or 700 copies a day.[111]

Organized Labor

Labor agitation also was a prominent feature of the immediate postwar era. Although the general strike of 1945 was only partially successful, it demonstrated how vulnerable Nigeria's open economy was to coordinated efforts by disgruntled railway and port workers. Four years later, in 1949, the worst fears of the British seemed about to be realized as the Zikists, radical trade unionists, and militant nationalists sought to forge an alliance among themselves and with such unlikely partners as cocoa farmers and embittered retail merchants. A bitter and bloody dispute at the Enugu coal mines lit the flames of this anticolonial coalition, spread-

---

[109] No. 4, Macpherson to Creech Jones, January 24, 1950, PRO CO 537/5782.

[110] No. 101, Harris N. Williams to Secretary of State, March 1, 1950; and no. 118, Harris N. Williams to Secretary of State, March 8, 1950; both in USNA 845H.00; see also *Daily Times*, February 28, 1951.

[111] Nigeria, Political Summary no. 33, May 1, 1950, PRO CO 537/5806.

ing disaffection among the peoples of southeastern Nigeria and beyond. This incipient dissident movement threatened Britain's vision of controlled and gradual constitutional reform, coupled with economic growth and diversification under capitalist auspices.

The coal mines of Enugu were an especially explosive arena of labor disorder. The harsh labor conditions in the colliery camps were legendary. Men worked below the surface, minimally equipped and protected, and before World War II they labored without the assistance of a welfare staff.[112] Although the government had eradicated the most obvious abuses of labor, it was nonetheless determined to increase coal production massively as part of the state's commitment to Nigeria's ambitious postwar development plans. The state had assembled a new colliery management team, headed up by L. S. Bracegirdle, whom a colleague described as "a highly qualified technician, an excellent 'manager' from the professional point of view but with next to no knowledge of the understanding and treatment of Ibo labor."[113] The colliery managers set in motion plans to achieve an immediate increase of output from 500,000 tons per year to 1,000,000 tons and a long-term rise to 3 million tons.[114]

Unaware of the long history of bad labor relations at the mines, Bracegirdle was unprepared for the stiff opposition that his speed-up engendered from the Coal Miners Union, which had come under the control of a young and charismatic but inexperienced leader, Okwudili Ojiyi. Ojiyi, secretary general of the union in 1943 at the age of thirty, had worked as a teacher before becoming head of the Coal Miners Union.[115] At its founding in 1940 the union had been a company organization, but because of strained relations between management and the workers, independent men had taken over.[116]

Labor-management relations deteriorated until work slowdowns and a threatened strike in 1949 led to clashes with the police in which twenty-one miners were killed and fifty-one others were wounded. According to the findings of a commission sent to investigate the incident, the colliery management, backed by a group of frightened local colonial administrators, transformed a simple labor dispute into a political challenge by con-

---

[112] David Smock, *Conflict and Control in an African Trade Union: A Study of the Nigerian Coal Miners' Union* (Stanford, Calif., 1969); also see the survey of the history of coal mining in Nigeria in the *Daily Times*, August 23, 1950. The literature on Nigerian trade unions is voluminous. Two overviews of the period covered in this study are Wogu Ananaba, *The Trade Union Movement in Nigeria* (London, 1969); and Robin Cohen, *Labour and Politics in Nigeria, 1945–71* (London, 1974).

[113] H. M. Foot to Forsuch, September 1, 1950, PRO CO 537/5785.

[114] Colliery Department, *Annual Report, 1946–47*, PRO CO 583/286/30425.

[115] Smock, *Conflict and Control*, p. 20; E. Cain to Thornley, January 3, 1951, PRO CO 583/310/30647/15.

[116] Colliery Department, *Annual Report, 1943–44*, PRO CO 583/286/30425.

juring up images of Zikism and communism and then provoked a confrontation with the workers.[117] Whether this charge, disputed by Governor Macpherson, was valid, the result of the bloody clash at Enugu was an outpouring of resentment all over the East. That the disaffection was directed against European influences was made evident by the rioters' attacks against foreign mercantile establishments in Aba, Port Harcourt, Onitsha, and Calabar. At Aba, for instance, looters invaded the G. B. Ollivant premises, and at Port Harcourt Bata Shoes and the store of the export-import firm Compagnie Française Africaine Occidentale (CFAO) suffered damage. The properties of G. B. Ollivant and CFAO at Onitsha also were assaulted, while the nationalist press spread the message that the foreign commercial presence was "vitiating the economic structure of the country."[118]

Although the disturbances did not spread to the West or the North or result in the general, nationwide strike that the eastern agitators called for, the confrontation underscored for the Nigerian colonial officials the precariousness of their position and the weaknesses of their instruments of coercion. As usual, the administrators adopted a two-pronged approach. First, they punished their chief adversaries—the radical union leaders and the Zikists—and second, they appeased the moderates. They were certain that quick action was required because, in the aftermath of the widespread rioting in the East, rival politicians and labor had formed the National Emergency Committee to coordinate protests against the British.[119] The British rounded up more Zikists and brought racketeering charges against the most anti-British and anticapitalist labor leaders. Ojiyi was sentenced to a three-year prison term.[120]

Merchant Protest

Although the Zikists were the most radical and feared of the opposition groups, they did not stand alone. Groups having a larger stake in the colonial economy—farmers and merchants in particular—also protested British economic policies. The center of the protest movement in the immediate postwar years was the western region, where African farmers objected to the swollen shoot eradication campaign and a group of market women, under the leadership of Mrs. F. Ransome-Kuti, agitated

---

[117] Great Britain, Colonial Office, *Report of the Commission of Enquiry into the Disorder of the Eastern Province of Nigeria, 1949* (London, 1950), col. no. 256.

[118] Ibid., p. 45.

[119] *Daily Service*, November 23, 1949.

[120] *West African Pilot*, September 4, 1950.

against a new tax on women.[121] In the view of the British officials, Ransome-Kuti combined a "socialist, anti-colonialist ideology, . . . with a radical feminism."[122] She also attacked the great European mercantile firms for making "fabulous profits at the expense of the already poverty-stricken people."[123]

The western region was the center of a rising mercantile class that agitated against the big European firms, especially the AWAM cartel. The Nigerian Association of African Importers and Exporters, largely Yoruba-dominated, organized the discontent, claiming that state policies favored the big firms and made the entry of smaller African merchants into the commercial sector virtually impossible. They protested the way that the state, through the provision of import and export licenses, solidified the dominance of the great European export-import houses.[124] The association drew together the most prosperous Yoruba merchants; by late 1948 it extended its membership lists beyond the West and boasted of having representatives in Kano, Jos, Maiduguri, Calabar, Onitsha, Benin, Port Harcourt, and Sapele. Its chairman was Issa A. Williams, and its board consisted of T. A. Doherty, Dr. Akinola Maja of the National Bank of Nigeria and the Nigerian Youth Movement, S. O. Gbadamosi, and J. B. Daramola—all men with economic interests in the western region.[125] In support of western regional business activities, the association passed a resolution calling upon its members to conduct their banking business exclusively with the indigenous National Bank of Nigeria.[126]

Ibadan became a focal point of mercantile opposition. In 1947, some 2,000 local traders vowed to have nothing to do with the much-resented system of conditional sales, by which foreign firms obligated local merchants to purchase a large range of unpopular and therefore unsalable items in order to obtain items in high demand. The leaders of the Ibadan protest organized the Committee for the Annihilation of Conditional Sales. Later Anthony S. Agbaje, son of Ibadan's foremost merchant-politician, Chief Salame Agbaje, created the Ibadan Traders Union, which enforced a two-month traders' boycott, and this was followed by a massive, 25,000-person demonstration against the big firms and their Syrian and Lebanese

---

[121] Johns and Gibbard, Assessment of Swollen Shoot Disease in Nigeria, 1950, PRO CO 583/309/30585/4B. On Ransome-Kuti and women's protest activities, one should consult Nina Emma Mba, *Nigerian Women Mobilized: Women's Political Activities in Southern Nigeria, 1900–1965* (Berkeley, Calif., 1982).

[122] Nigerian Secretariat to Cohen, May 13, 1947, PRO CO 583/292/30658/1.

[123] F. Ransome-Kuti to Creech Jones, August 12, 1947, PRO CO 583/293/30658/5.

[124] *West African Pilot*, June 21 and July 9, 1946.

[125] *Daily Service*, May 23 and June 17, 1946.

[126] *West African Pilot*, October 1, 1946.

intermediaries.[127] Only after a delegation consisting of Akinola Maja of the United Front Committee, S. Gbadamosi of the Nigerian Association of African Importers and Exporters, and representatives of the Nigerian Traders Association met to coordinate their protests, did the importing firms increase the supply of textiles to Ibadan.[128] The AWAM companies guaranteed to supply at least £60,000 worth of textile products each year, and the United Africa Company, the chief supplier of Ibadan, pledged to double its quotas for its fifteen primary traders and to designate fifty additional traders to handle the increased volume of business.[129]

In Egypt, Nigeria, and Kenya the years between 1945 and 1952 witnessed an outpouring of discussions on the programs needed to develop their economies. In Egypt, where considerable economic diversification and industrialization had occurred between the two world wars, the ruling elites sought to implement programs designed to move beyond import substitution to the establishment of a capital goods industry and even in time an export-oriented economy. In Kenya, the strong influence of the settlers resulted in a strong productionist orientation in the economic arena—one in which the resident European population was expected to collaborate with multinational, mainly British-based capital to raise the material standard of living. In Nigeria, in contrast, the overriding concern was with the level of poverty that was thought to afflict the vast majority of the population. Before rapid economic change could occur, the government officials believed that basic social welfare concerns, like general education and public health, needed to be attended to. Nonetheless, economic diversification, especially industrial development, was to be achieved largely under the aegis of foreign capital.

The Nigerian economic and political discussions that took place right after World War II—the so-called great debates—produced numerous unanticipated consequences for the British. Far from appeasing the elite nationalists or stealing a march on the aspirations of radical Nigerian groups, the debates galvanized anticolonial complaints. The colonial authorities opted for statutory marketing bodies in the face of powerful indigenous and international criticisms. They were little aware at the time how politically intrusive and economically jarring the marketing boards would be. They also preferred large-scale capital-intensive industrialization, led by British multinationals, to a more rural, cottagelike program. By 1951, however, the old Richards constitution had given way to the new Macpherson constitution, which magnified African electoral powers,

---

[127] *Daily Service*, June 17 and June 19, 1947.
[128] Ibid., June 25, 1947.
[129] Ibid., July 12, 1947.

diminished the power of European business, and was seen by many to be moving Nigeria on a fast path to independence. The economic visions were also adjusted. Although the challenge on the left had been met, the British development perspective based on economic growth through European investment and big European business still had many skeptics.

CHAPTER 7

The Vision Undermined, 1951–1956

IN EACH OF the three countries surveyed here, the second period in the era of decolonization—the early to mid-1950s—witnessed decisive challenges to the prevailing strategies based on mixed economies and a supportive relationship between state and private enterprise. Only in Kenya, however, did the ruling elite manage to deflect criticism from radical groups, and there only because of the determination of the economic elite in the face of a political and military challenge from the Kikuyu underclasses. In contrast, the Egyptian ruling military junta shifted the balance of economic power from the private sector to the state following the British-French-Israeli invasion, and the British economic advisers in Nigeria lost much of their control over crucial economic decisions in their conflictual dealings with ethnic nationalist politicians. They were unable to prevent the subordination of the private sector to the public sector as a result of a rising crescendo of nationalist rhetoric championing public sector initiatives.

The British economic strategy for Nigeria rested on two foundation stones. The first was the indispensability of economic growth for a country mired in poverty but with considerable potential for economic progress. Without rising standards of living, Britain's second and related goal—economic development under the auspices of foreign, preferably British, capital—would in all likelihood not occur because of political instability and political violence. Thus the British officials in Nigeria sought to bring about a gradual transfer of power to Nigerian leaders who shared the British vision of decolonization, and at the same time they endeavored to secure a prominent place in the Nigerian economy for British capital and British joint stock companies. The economic and political visions were thus intimately linked. The half-decade of the early 1950s was to demonstrate just how difficult it was to maintain this political and economic linkage.

The Macpherson constitution of 1951 was intended to be the instrument for realizing Britain's economic and political goals in Nigeria. First, it was supposed to erase the perceived defects of the Richards constitution and win over moderate nationalist opinion. Believing that they had weathered the radical challenges of Zikism and trade union strikes, the

British turned their attention to the implementation of their procapitalist strategy. Their goal became to establish the framework within which private investment, indigenous and foreign alike, could work in alliance with a supportive but not overpowering state that would gradually incorporate African personnel in a controlled transfer of power. These plans required a ready group of Nigerian collaborators, and though the early British efforts met with an unanticipated large measure of success, in the span of a few years the British had to face the unpleasant prospect of dealing with a group of nationalists more radical than suited British aspirations for Nigeria. In the first part of the 1950s the British were to learn that although they had effectively resisted the most radical nationalist challenges, their efforts to find a group willing to support their political and economic vision of controlled decolonization encountered much opposition, mainly owing to the competitive rivalry of the different elite and ethnically based political parties.

Seeking to realize their legislative program for the Nigerian economy, the British brought into the central government Nigerian politicians who favored pro-British and pro-capitalist approaches. At the outset, a group of southern politicians, known for their commitment to political gradualism and capitalist development, came to dominate the polity at Lagos. To be sure, the three most prominent southeastern political figures on whom the British rested their hopes—Okoi Arikpo, Eni Njoku, and A. C. Nwapa—lacked the charisma and popularity of Nnamdi Azikiwe, Okwudili Ojiye, and K. O. Mbadiwe, the frontline men of the National Council of Nigeria and the Cameroons (NCNC). But they possessed estimable educational attainments, in British rather than American universities, and considerable economic sophistication.

Following the 1951 elections, Arikpo, Njoku, and Nwapa were allocated the sensitive federal ministerial portfolios of Commerce and Industries, Mines and Power, and Lands. Of Okoi Arikpo the British wrote: he was "a smart and rather theoretical Ibo who has been to England and wears European clothes." They expected the most of A. C. Nwapa, "an Ibo who is regarded as rather outstanding and has had an English education."[1] Following a meeting with Nwapa in 1952, the colonial secretary wrote that he was "an able and far-sighted man. . . . Whether he has the character to go far or not must remain a matter of conjecture, but he is certainly one of the best African ministers with whom I have talked, and if I had to bet I certainly would prefer to bet that he would go far rather

[1] K. W. Prescott, Overseas and Foreign Office, Bank of England (hereafter B of E), Nigeria, January 14, 1953, B of E OV 68/2.

than that he would fall by the wayside."[2] In the Southwest, the British hoped for similar support from Arthur Prest and the Oni of Ife.[3]

The British strategy for shaping the political economy of Nigeria was not entirely dependent, however, on finding pliant and procapitalist ministers in the South. The North was still the "sheet anchor" of British gradualism—the region where the colonial administrators expected a conservative ruling group to brake the strong southern yearnings for immediate independence and radical economic strategies.[4] The North, though, was not without its sources of worry for the British. An alternative, radical element had emerged in the commercially minded province of Kano, where the Northern Elements Progressive Union (NEPU) had come into existence under the leadership of Aminu Kano. It represented a credible challenge to conservative Fulani authority elsewhere, although it did not allow its alliance with the NCNC to deflect its attention from northern concerns. To the British, Aminu Kano was "not without political courage, if of a provocative and uncouth kind," but they regarded the other NEPU leaders as "a disreputable lot . . . without employment, without inhibitions, without loyalties, and without scruples."[5] The British believed that a cult was forming around Aminu Kano with fascistic tendencies.

Conservative and collaborating Fulani leaders established their political party, the Northern Peoples Congress (NPC), in 1951, and the British colonial officers quickly revealed their intentions to link Britain's colonial fortunes to this organization. While recognizing that the NPC had been formed in haste, largely for defensive purposes so that it could compete in the 1951 elections, it displayed, to their relief, no penchant for transformative economic or political change. Believing that the leaders of the NPC had "lived the soft and sheltered lives of members of the ruling families and had never really had to fight [politically]," the British offered themselves as defenders of the Fulani notables in their struggle with southern nationalists. Of the front-line politicians, the British admired the intellectual Abu Bakr Balewa but had to accept his lesser standing in the party because of his nonaristocratic family status. In contrast, Ahmadu Bello, Sardauna of Sokoto (leader of war, one of the highest offices in the Fulani hierarchy), blended traditional Islamic and Fulani legitimacy with a modern Western education. Although he was astute and energetic, the

---

[2] Note of Colonial Office Interview with Nwapa by the Secretary of State, July 4, 1952, PRO CO 852/1085/8.

[3] No. 676, Macpherson to the Colonial Office, March 24, 1953, PRO CO 554/260.

[4] No. 676, Macpherson to the Colonial Office, March 24, 1953, PRO CO 554/260.

[5] T. B. Williamson to Johnston, January 6, 1955, PRO CO 554/480; Sharwood Smith, Memorandum on the Present Political Situation in the Northern Nigerian Emirates, October 1951, PRO CO 554/235.

British recognized his patent political vulnerabilities. They viewed him as "vain and deplorably susceptible to flattery, and his private life is disreputable to an extent that one day someone may blackmail him."[6] Still his religio-political authority was unchallenged, and since the North, in the new 1951 constitution, had half of the seats in the central Legislative Assembly, the British were confident that their Fulani proxies would be able to moderate the pace of constitutional reform and block radical economic initiatives.[7]

This plausible decolonizing perspective, based on a gradual transfer of power and consensual programs of economic development, began to unravel from the outset, however. The first problem confronting the British arose in connection with violent protest over constitutional changes, local rivalries, and especially the competitive position of the elite-controlled political parties, each aspiring to a national prominence. The government was well aware that its meager military, police, and administrative resources rendered the implementation of unpopular policies problematic. Nigeria experienced endemic violence, punctuated by large outbursts between 1951 and 1956. Protest occurred in Ogoja province in 1954 over educational taxes and had to be suppressed by police action.[8] Most of the cities in the country were cauldrons of political tension between native residents and strangers of the same ethnic communities.[9] Two of Nigeria's premier cities—Ibadan and Onitsha—were always on the verge of political turmoil.[10] Although each of the major political parties had a regional homeland and an ethnic base of support, each also sought to invade the other regions in order to cultivate alliances with minority communities and other disaffected groups. Labor unions were equally disorderly, calling for strikes on the one hand and employing high levels of intimidation internally on the other.[11] Labor organizations aspiring to national prominence themselves became battlegrounds of ethnic tension.[12]

---

[6] T. B. Williamson to Johnston, January 6, 1955, PRO CO 554/480.

[7] B. E. Sharwood Smith to Secretary of State, April 18, 1955, PRO CO 554/1183.

[8] No. 332, Macpherson to Colonial Office, March 3, 1954, and June 16, 1954, PRO CO 554/1233.

[9] No. 1429, Macpherson to Colonial Office, September 7, 1954; and no. 133, Macpherson to Colonial Office, September 18, 1954; both in PRO CO 554/1236; see also no. 8, Governor of Nigeria to Colonial Office, November 11, 1954, PRO CO 554/1237.

[10] See Kenneth W. J. Price and George D. Jenkins, *The Price of Liberty: Personality and Politics in Colonial Nigeria* (Cambridge, 1973); and Richard L. Sklar, *Nigerian Political Parties: Power in an Emergent Nation* (Princeton, N.J., 1963).

[11] Extract of letter from UAC African Personnel Office, October 16, 1952, Ocean Archives, 1908 N5; C. J. Pleass, Nigerian Secretariat, to T. B. Williamson, May 6, 1952, PRO CO 554/583.

[12] See Petition from the Eastern Seamen Group to Komoh, April 3, 1954, Ocean Archives, 1908 N5. The Eastern Seamen complained that the Executive Committee of the

Because of the sparseness of police and military forces, the British overlords carefully weighed political and military consequences before embarking on even small policy changes. They were quick to abandon basic policies when low-level protest gave way to violent confrontations involving loss of life and widespread property damage. The Kano riots of May 1953 seemed to confirm the worst fears of the British about Nigerian instability. They led to the replacement of the Macpherson constitution with a document that, in magnifying regional autonomy, also intensified regional antagonism. The Kano riots were "the first collective outburst between Southern and Northern communities or more correctly between the principal political parties contending for influence or control over the operations of the government of Nigeria."[13] They followed a bitter debate in the central legislature, where northern delegates had opposed a southern motion calling for Nigerian self-government in 1956. The northern delegates, jeered as they left the legislative chambers, harbored a deep resentment against the southern nationalists and used a tour of the North by the Yoruba-dominated Action Group (AG) as revenge. Widespread rioting led ultimately to open warfare in the city of Kano, where large numbers of southern immigrants lived. In five days of murder and pillage at least thirty-six people were killed and more than 240 wounded. The shouting of political slogans on both sides gave proof that the 7,000 persons estimated to be involved had been drawn into the nationalist agendas of the Action Group and the Northern Peoples Congress.[14]

An administrative and military machine so delicately maintained, so vulnerable to political shocks, and so dependent on local partners could also be disrupted by external forces. The British decision to appoint Kwame Nkrumah prime minister in the Gold Coast alarmed the Nigerian colonial elite. Macpherson complained that he had not been consulted and predicted that the Gold Coast constitutional advances would lead to regional secessionist demands in Nigeria. In Macpherson's view the Nigerian constitution of 1951 was ahead of Nigeria's political capabilities. It needed to remain in place for "many years to come, up to the time in fact when the Governor of Nigeria would be in a position to report to the Secretary of State that public opinion throughout Nigeria was so overwhelmingly pro–good government and pro–British ideals, institutions, and practices that he could quite safely advocate complete self-government and that Nigerians themselves would either be able to

---

Nigerian Union of Seamen was dominated by Ijaws and Yorubas and lacked adequate representation from the Ibo and Ibibio work forces.

[13] Bernard Nkemdirun, *Social Change and Political Violence in Colonial Nigeria* (Devon, Eng., 1975), p. 60.

[14] Ibid., p. 93.

fill all the important posts remaining in expatriate hands or more likely would themselves wish to retain Britishers there."[15]

One year later, the Gold Coast—that "persistent canker," in Macpherson's opinion—posed a more severe challenge to Nigeria. The British promise of self-government for the Gold Coast in 1954, despite its justification as the only way to forestall violence there, caused Macpherson intense anguish. He wrote that the metropolitan British government was faced with the choice of using "sanctions against the Gold Coast now or being forced to use sanctions against part or parts of Nigeria slightly later."[16] Macpherson believed that the Nigerian government would have to use force either to bring the North along on a faster pace of constitutional change or coerce the southerners to moderate their demands for immediate self-government. Nonetheless, Macpherson merely extracted a promise from Charles Arden-Clarke, the governor of the Gold Coast, to extend the process of self-government over four or five years. Any further delaying, Arden-Clarke asserted, would necessitate the use of troops and would redound against the good name of Britain throughout Africa.[17]

A more fundamental problem was that the Nigerian administrative and legislative apparatus had begun to crumble, not at first at the federal level where reliable pro-British ministers still held the reins of authority for the British, but rather within the southern regions themselves. There, the divisiveness between ethnic and regional parties and within these parties themselves was palpable. In addition, the British encountered statist approaches to economic growth and reservations about private capital and foreign investment there.

The Macpherson constitution had brought Nigeria its first taste of electoral politics at the regional and national level. Electoral competition pitted the regions against each other and also brought regional economic rivalry into the arena of politics. In July 1951, Obafemi Awolowo, leader of the Action Group, portrayed the NCNC as "an evil which my colleagues and I have pledged ourselves to exterminate not only in the Western Region but eventually from the whole of Nigeria."[18] Azikiwe replied in similarly vitriolic and by then familiar tones, claiming that "the God of Africa has specially created the Ibo nation to lead the children of Africa from the bondage of the ages. Otherwise, it is not fortuitous that the Ibo nation is one of the few remnants of indigenous African nations who are not spoliated by the artificial niceties of Western rationalism."[19]

The rivalry between the AG and the NCNC had an economic dimen-

---

[15] Macpherson to Lloyd, January 8, 1952, PRO CO 554/260.
[16] Macpherson to Colonial Office, March 16, 1953, PRO CO 554/260.
[17] Arden-Clarke to Governor of Nigeria, March 21, 1953, PRO CO 554/260.
[18] *Daily Times*, July 4, 1951.
[19] Ibid., July 20, 1951.

sion of considerable intensity and important long-term economic consequences. The AG used its strong base of support in the wealthier western
region to throw down an economic challenge to the other parties.[20] By
mid-1951, its leaders had issued twenty-three economic papers on such
diverse subjects as agriculture, forestry, industry, education, and public
health, the capstone of which was the paper on education, which promised that the western regional government would introduce a program of
universal, free primary education of eight years for all children between
the ages of five and thirteen.[21] Despite the massive price tag for this
project, the education program was trumpeted as the surest way to advance the economic interests of the West over its eastern and northern
rivals. Although northern and eastern politicians accused the westerners
of using education as a cynical electoral ploy, they were forced to develop competitive education agendas. The AG's economic program had
other ingredients. It favored state controls over important sectors of the
economy and called for the nationalization of private mineral companies
and operators, including the oil prospecting and mining firms.[22]

The AG looked to the marketing boards for funds for its economic
programs. The first step in this direction involved the replacement of the
personnel on the old Western Region Production Development Board
with men loyal to the AG. According to the *Daily Service*, the new board
was intended to be the party's economic agency.[23] Indeed, the party's
nominees constituted a veritable "board within the board"; according to
one British critic, it manifested "the Action Group's typical keen desire
for industrialization, coupled with its suspicion of foreign capital and
expatriate staff." The board quickly promulgated plans to erect cement,
paper, textile, and food processing plants in the West as joint public-
private ventures.[24]

Nigeria's other major parties could ill afford to ignore these economic
challenges, least of all the NCNC, which competed electorally against the
AG all over the South. In the Western House of Assembly, Azikiwe
charged the AG politicians with caring more for the comforts and wealth
of office than for the welfare of the common people. He pointed out how
generously they compensated themselves, with salaries ranging between
£2,000 and £2,500.[25] Left with little alternative, however, the NCNC offered a similar program in the East, promising free compulsory educa-

[20] Ibid., July 18, 1951; *Daily Service*, July 10, 1951.

[21] *Daily Service*, May 10, 1951.

[22] See the file PRO CO 554/598.

[23] *Daily Service*, July 15, 1952.

[24] Ernest Sabben-Clark, Nigerian Secretariat, to N. B. J. Huijsman, Colonial Office,
March 16, 1953, PRO CO 554/366.

[25] Western House of Assembly Debates, *Official Record*, February 21, 1952, p. 123.

tion, free secondary and university training for those with aptitudes, the nationalization of the banks, and limitations on the number of foreigners permitted to serve on the boards of companies domiciled in Nigeria.[26] Although the North responded less aggressively, the regional government there reshuffled the membership of the Northern Production Development Board so as to include more NPC representation.[27]

At the federal level, the British were at first spared these regional rivalries and the more radical statist and populist discourse that reverberated through the regional parliaments. Here, relying on the support of conservative African politicians, the British undertook to enact legislation that supported the private sector and foreign investment. The minister of finance, Eric Himsworth, developed a conventional, procapitalist strategy, in keeping with British economic priorities. Himsworth was the typical colonial economic architect of the postwar era—the amateur who possessed a wellspring of common sense and drew upon a lifetime of experience in colonial economic and financial affairs. His budget statement for 1952, laying out the economic and fiscal policies that the British hoped would guide Nigeria during the next decade, stood in marked contrast to the ambitious and state-centered formulas taking shape at the regional level. The finance minister stressed the continuing poverty of the country and reminded legislators that a country with a gross national product of a mere £350,000,000, or £12 per person, could not expect immediate economic progress. He contended that Nigeria's most glaring deficiency was its lack of long-term capital for development.

Nigeria had but three traditional sources of capital, none of which, according to Himsworth, was capable of generating large investable funds. First, the London money market could not offer more than £20 million because other colonial and commonwealth territories were also making large demands on it. Second, the government's own burgeoning surpluses, including those belonging to the marketing boards, had binding restrictions on their use. A large portion of these funds was earmarked for statutory corporations—the railways, the coal corporation, and the electricity corporation—while the marketing board surpluses, standing at £70 to £80 million, had to be kept liquid to protect producers' interests and secure price stabilization. Himsworth's view on marketing board accumulations was already at variance with the perspective being developed by the AG and NCNC, whose leaders were demanding to use the money for development. The third source, the savings of private individuals and companies in Nigeria, was insignificant in a country as poor as Nigeria.

[26] *West African Pilot*, January 9, 1952.
[27] Ernest Sabben-Clark, Nigerian Secretariat, to N. B. J. Huijsman, Colonial Office, March 16, 1953, PRO CO 554/366.

Under such austere economic circumstances, Himsworth concluded that an economic breakthrough could occur only if Nigeria succeeded in attracting foreign capital by convincing potential investors and foreign corporations that Nigeria's prospects for long-term development were rosy.

The primary task of the Nigerian government, then, was to develop an environment that would attract foreign investors. Although Himsworth was prepared to use some of the marketing board surpluses for agricultural development, he expected private, mainly foreign capital to be the engine of industrial progress. Admitting that "the people of this country are looking forward to an improvement in their general well being," Himsworth concluded, "We shall have to send out a call to overseas capital to come into Nigeria and help us."[28]

In Nigeria's nationalistically charged environment, Himsworth's concrete proposals for promoting development elicited strong criticism. His legislation to encourage foreign investors did not have an easy passage through the Nigerian Parliament; another one of his economic proposals, a law to regulate banking, was so clearly directed against indigenous Nigerian bankers that it exposed the whole of the British economic strategy to the charge of bias. No matter how well intentioned the British program was, it had the effect of focusing the nationalist assault on economic issues. Ultimately, it led to Himsworth's resignation and to a lessening of foreign investor optimism about the country.

Himsworth's two most important pieces of legislation designed to foster foreign investment were the Aid to Pioneer Industries Bill and the Lead-Zinc Mining Ordinance. The first provided taxation relief to firms willing to invest in industries favored by the government; the second offered a large mining concession in the East to a foreign firm. The goal of the Pioneer Industries Bill was to alleviate investors' fears of nationalization by permitting firms to build up liquid assets quickly and repatriate them easily so that no nationalistically minded government would be tempted to seize the funds or the firms. In introducing the bill, the minister of commerce and industry, A. C. Nwapa, argued that "Nigeria cannot take her rightful place in the world if she continues to depend solely on agriculture as the mainstay of her economy."[29] Much the same note was struck in the subsequent debate on the Lead-Zinc Mining Ordinance, which offered an exclusive 402 square mile prospecting license in Ogoja province to the British-based Mines Development Syndicate. The prospecting license was to run for five years and would give the firm the right to explore for a long list of designated minerals. A mining license would be granted for any minerals discovered during the prospecting

[28] Nigeria, House of Representatives, *Debates*, March 20, 1952, pp. 339 ff.
[29] Ibid., April 7, 1952, p. 981.

stage. The license was to run for thirty years and was renewable for an additional thirty years. The only minerals exempted from the prospecting concession were radioactive minerals, diamonds, and coal.[30]

These two pieces of legislation came under savage attack from nationalist groups in Nigeria. Although the Pioneer Industries Bill ultimately passed with a vote of seventy-four to eighteen in the central legislature, it was the subject of no fewer than forty amendments. The most vocal opponents of both ordinances were Mbonu Ojike of the NCNC and Awolowo and Anthony Enahoro of the AG, each of whom believed that the bills were excessively generous to foreign investors and would advantage foreign capitalists at the expense of the Nigerian business elite. Awolowo and Enahoro refused to be bound by these laws and warned of the possibility that an independent socialist government would repudiate the legislation.[31] The nationalist assault on the Pioneer Industries Bill was broad and principled. Awolowo argued that the passage of the bill just before political independence would set aside huge portions of the industrial sector for foreign business interests at a time when Nigeria's indigenous industrialist class was not yet ready to compete. An Awolowo supporter, Oluwole Awokoya, claimed that "the indiscriminate invitation of foreign capital is not only voluntary economic enslavement but also national suicide," and a headline of the *Daily Service* announced: "British Government Substitutes Economic for Political Imperialism in the Colonies."[32] The NCNC's chief nationalist organ, the *West African Pilot*, was not far behind, warning of "the economic yoke with which Nigeria is being saddled by the existing foreign firms—all these point to the fact that unregulated foreign capital will only make good the loss sustained through our political advancement."[33]

Awolowo revealed himself to be the most astute and acerbic economic commentator in the federal Nigerian House of Representatives during these debates—a man alive to the economic implications of decolonization and hardly a devotee of the slogan "seek ye first the political kingdom" that was reverberating through the Gold Coast at the time. While conceding the importance of industrialization to the future economic progress of Nigeria, Awolowo argued that "Nigeria's industrial progress should not be achieved by issuing invitations to foreigners to come in a

[30] See the file PRO CO 537/7059 for the correspondence relating to the concession; no. 163, Governor's Deputy to Colonial Office, October 13, 1951, PRO CO 537/7059; no. 2403, Macpherson to Lyttleton, June 10, 1952, PRO CO 554/493, for the final documents. The debate over the bill is to be found in Nigeria, House of Representatives, *Debates*, April 4, 1952, pp 903 ff.

[31] *Daily Service*, March 18, 1952.

[32] Ibid., March 19, 22, and 26, 1952.

[33] *West African Pilot*, April 1, 1952.

large number into this country to exploit its resources but by allowing Africans . . . to embark upon the industrialization of their country." He feared that Himsworth's programs would "open the gate of this country to a flood of foreign investment," and he predicted that the Pioneer Industries Bill, if rigorously implemented, would accelerate the rural exodus, bring a host of expatriate technicians to the country, produce food shortages, and allow unscrupulous individuals to dominate the labor unions. Already foreigners dominated soap manufacturing, beer brewing, municipal transport, and tire retreading, and unless the flow of foreign investment were reversed Nigeria would simply be "throwing off political bondage in exchange for economic stranglehold."[34]

Awolowo, Enaharo, and Awokoya—Himsworth's most outspoken critics—believed that the vehicle for capital formation in Nigeria and industrialization should be the marketing board funds rather than foreign capital. These men also favored a larger degree of state ownership of business firms. Awokoya wanted the state to own 51 percent of all pioneer industries; he also favored a series of planning boards to determine industrial siting, wages, and prices.

The debate in the parliamentary buildings was carried forward in the press and proved highly consequential for Nigeria's economic future. Not only did Himsworth, certainly an able and economically talented minister, feel compelled to resign, but the American Smelting Company, which was to provide technical advice to the Mines Development Syndicate on the Ogoja project, withdrew from the venture. In explaining its decision to back out, R. F. Goodwin, vice president of the American Smelting Company, claimed that the firm had numerous technical reservations about the project, especially after the production estimates were revised downward from 500 tons per day to 300 tons. But Goodwin also cited the firm's growing fear of "the continued spread of nationalism in Africa."[35] The latter explanation so unsettled T. B. Williamson at the Colonial Office that he drafted a strong memorandum that he proposed sending to all of the colonial governors in British Africa. The memorandum warned that "if the rot is to be stopped and overseas capital not frightened off West Africa altogether, African leaders in responsible positions will have to make it abundantly clear and give proof that in West Africa (a) Abadan [Iran's nationalization of Anglo-Iranian Oil] will not be repeated and (b) that attempts to seek constitutional advance by violence are things of the past." His colleagues at the Colonial Office demurred at

---

[34] Nigeria, House of Representatives, *Debates*, March 15, 1952, pp. 105–6.

[35] R. F. Goodwin, Vice President of the American Smelting Company, to W. J. C. Richards, Mines Development Syndicate, December 17, 1952, PRO CO 554/495; no. 383, Robert W. Ross to Secretary of State, May 17, 1952, USNA 845H.2543.

sending the note on the grounds that it would seem a rebuke to the very Nigerian ministers, especially the eastern triad of Njoku, Arikpo, and Nwapa, who had fought so ably and ultimately successfully for Himsworth's policies.[36]

The third piece of economic legislation, that which dealt with Nigerian banking, brought nationalist outrage to a fever pitch. The nationalists now seemed to have conclusive proof that the British were using their political power in the last stage of colonial rule to discriminate in favor of British-based capital at the expense of local entrepreneurs. Nigerian producers, merchants, and nationalists, like their counterparts elsewhere in the colonial world, had long since discovered that the foreign bank was the bedrock of the imperial economic system. They had concluded that colonial authority could not be ended without challenging the supremacy of the colonial banks. Already in 1933 a group of Yoruba merchants had created the first indigenous bank, the National Bank of Nigeria, and subsequently other local banks came into being: the Agbonmagbe Bank in 1945; the African Continental Bank in 1947; and the Nigerian Farmers and Commercial Bank also in 1947. Between February 1951 and May 1952, as the British readied their banking ordinance and Nigerian business persons hastened to found banks before this restrictive legislation took effect, Nigerians founded an additional eighteen banks.[37]

Nigerian banks filled an important, though precarious niche in the colonial economy. By lending to persons unable to obtain funds from the British banks, they spread the money economy into the distant locations of Nigeria, where it had scarcely penetrated. But in doing so, they placed a high proportion of their assets in loans and encountered liquidity difficulties. These banks also sought a wide geographic spread so as to attract depositors and borrowers beyond the reach of the British banks.[38] And their nationalist appeal should not be minimized. Azikiwe, founder of the African Continental Bank, claimed that he established his bank in defiance of the British banks and because the Bank of British West Africa had refused him a loan when he desperately needed it.[39]

This spate of bank creations worried the British bureaucrats, who were convinced that the country was "trying to do too much too fast."[40] The British banking experts believed that only one Nigerian bank was conducting its business on sound fiscal lines—the National Bank of Nigeria.

[36] T. B. Williamson, Memorandum, January 1, 1953, PRO CO 554/495.

[37] Charles V. Brown, *The Nigerian Banking System* (Evanston, Ill., 1966), pp. 24 ff.

[38] For one of the most perceptive analyses of the banking structure in Nigeria, one should read T. A. B. Conley, Overseas and Foreign Office, B of E, December 19, 1952, "Native and British Banks in Nigeria," B of E OV 68/2.

[39] *West African Pilot*, July 2, 1956.

[40] W. J. Jackson, B of E, to Hulland, May 22, 1950, PRO CO 852/1080/3.

The others were said to use pitifully inadequate amounts of paid-up capital to project vaulting financial aspirations. The paid-up capital of the African Continental Bank (with authorized capital of £50,000) was only £250; that of the Nigerian Farmers and Commercial Bank (with authorized capital of £300,000) was £13,194; and that of the National Bank of Nigeria (with authorized capital of £250,000) was £37,144.[41]

At first the British saw no easy way to check the growth of the local banks, and they foresaw fiscal crises sweeping through the indigenous banking sector. Regulating the liquidity ratios of banks, their reserve funds, and their banking procedures would require an inspectorate that was beyond the means of the country. But soon the British realized that banks could be regulated by controlling them at the point of their entry into the Nigerian financial sector and that this could be done without even having to disturb existing British banks.

Nationalist pressures to transfer the surpluses of the marketing boards from the established British banks to the new Nigerian firms put additional pressure on the British to regulate the banks. Although there was a degree of validity to the nationalists' contention that the British opposition to the fund transfers was to protect British business and to ensure that Nigeria's large sterling surpluses remained in Britain as a bulwark of the British currency, the British had a patent duty to prevent inexperienced banks from squandering the treasure of the country's producing classes.[42] Up until 1951, the cocoa board had invested all of its funds in the Bank of British West Africa (75 percent) and Barclays Bank (25 percent). British officials had not opposed the placement of £20,000 in marketing board funds in the National Bank of Nigeria, the country's best-capitalized indigenous bank. But they clearly trembled at the precedent and insisted that the funds be deposited only in proportion to the use that licensed buying agents were making of the National Bank.[43] When, however, the weakly capitalized and not well run Pan Nigerian Bank and the Merchants Bank, both based in the West, demanded similar financial support, the British officials rushed through the new legislation.[44]

The banking ordinance of May 1952 made obtaining a banking license the prerequisite for opening a bank in Nigeria. Though the terms were minimal and seemed easy to achieve—£25,000 in paid-up capital, prohibitions against unsecured loans, creation of reserve funds, and issuance of

[41] No. 1890, Governor to Colonial Office, August 16, 1950, PRO CO 852/1080/3.

[42] Minutes of the 14th Meeting of the Nigerian Cocoa Marketing Board, July 27, 1950, PRO CO 852/1150/6.

[43] Minutes of the 16th Meeting of the Nigerian Cocoa Marketing Board, March 28, 1951, PRO CO 852/1150/3.

[44] Minutes of the 19th Meeting of the Nigerian Cocoa Marketing Board, March 10, 1952, PRO CO 852/1150/8.

quarterly statements and annual balance sheets—they were sufficiently demanding in the Nigerian context to limit the formation of new banks to three between 1952 and 1963 and to force most of the banks already in existence and given three years to conform to the law to make sweeping changes.[45]

As the banking legislation moved toward passage in the Nigerian House of Representatives, the Nigerian business community mounted a campaign intended to demonstrate that the British were dominating the Nigerians economically. The Nigerian banking leaders created an organization, known as the Association of African Banks, which included representatives of the Nigerian Farmers and Commercial Bank, the African Continental Bank, the Agbonmagbe Bank, the Nigerian Standard Bank, and the National Bank of Nigeria, to represent their position with the colonial authorities. Forty-two Nigerian banking representatives met in Lagos to coordinate their positions and to protest discriminatory British attitudes toward foreign and domestic capital.[46] The business groups objected to the far-reaching powers being assumed by the financial secretary to license Nigerian banks and demanded that the Nigerian government create a banking oversight organization on which Nigerian banking nominees were represented. For the first time, economic nationalists, led by K. O. Mbadiwe of the NCNC, proposed to detach Nigeria's financial institutions from the metropole and to establish a Nigerian central bank and an autonomous Nigerian currency.[47]

Although the nationalists accused the British of pursuing selfish aims in the passage of the banking ordinance and were alarmed at the plethora of criminal charges being brought against Nigerian banking executives, in reality, British officials in Nigeria preferred to move cautiously in dealing with the Nigerian banks. They were mindful of nationalist sensitivities and feared a political explosion if they pursued an aggressive policy. The Nigerian financial secretary, A. R. W. Robertson, expressed the government's reserve when, in the midst of a confidential investigation into the affairs of the National Bank of Nigeria, he wrote: "Only under the most drastic circumstances should any action be taken under the Banking Ordinance on political grounds. As you know, political considerations have crept in at all stages."[48]

Of the many economic and financial changes made under the regime of Governor Macpherson, none would appear to have been more crucial, at

---

[45] Brown, *The Nigerian Banking System*, p. 25; *West African Pilot*, March 4, 1952.

[46] *West African Pilot*, March 7, 1952.

[47] Nigeria, House of Representatives, *Debates*, April 9, 1952, pp. 1172 ff.

[48] A. R. W. Robertson, Financial Secretary's Office, Lagos, to E. Melville, Colonial Office, January 9, 1954, PRO CO 554/1142.

least from the comparative perspective, than the resignation of Himsworth. Although Himsworth had succeeded in enacting his economic program, he had aroused such a storm of protest that he had to leave the country, and his successors at the Ministry of Finance were compelled to be much more conciliatory to nationalist sensibilities in their economic enactments. Himsworth's resignation can easily be compared with the appointment of new Egyptian technocrats beholden to Nasser in 1955 and 1956 as a moment that represented the transfer of decision making in the economic sphere from the technocrats to Nasser. The contrast with Kenya is also striking, for here, as we shall see, Ernest Vasey's continued tenure at the Ministry of Finance during the Mau Mau war ensured that economic considerations were given as much weight as political concerns.

It was not coincidental that crucial appointments in economic and financial ministries occurred in all three of the countries studied here in the mid-1950s. They followed upon nationalist, even at times subalternist, challenges to capitalist and gradualist programs of economic development, which colonial officials and conservative elitist politicians had promulgated. In the middle of the decade Egypt witnessed a broad repudiation of its capitalist strategy; Nigeria a partial rejection; and Kenya, under Vasey's tenure as the minister of finance, a determined defense of capitalism in the face of a severe populist assault in the form of the Mau Mau rebellion.

Although the nationalist challenge to the new federal economic policies had forced Himsworth to resign and had galvanized opposition to British economic programs, the British had nonetheless succeeded in enacting the main legislative proposals designed to strengthen the private sector and the place of foreign capital in it. It was at the regional level, however, especially within the politically troubled eastern region, that Britain's control over the Nigerian political economy began to erode. The crisis in the Southeast could not be confined to that region, however, so interconnected were the nationalist politics throughout the South. As its political repercussions spread from the East to the West, the whole of the British strategy for controlling the pace and the institutions of decolonization were put in jeopardy. The first casualty of this crisis was the fall from power of the South's most reliable pro-British politicians, those men in sympathy with Britain's formulas of economic and political devolution. Longer-term consequences entailed the discarding of the Macpherson constitution and the emergence of even more strident and mutually destructive ethnic and personal rivalries.

Nigeria's first large-scale internal crisis was almost surely destined to occur in the East and to involve the NCNC. Ever since the end of World War II, the NCNC, in its aspiration to be a truly national party, had sought bases of support in all regions. It had achieved more success than it might have expected, as evidenced by its electoral triumphs in the East in 1951 and its strong minority position in the West in that election. But its ballot box success had come at the expense of party discipline and ideological coherence. Its effort to accommodate a wide spectrum of political and economic opinion and to balance strong ethnic, local, and personal rivalries had left it fragmented internally. Following the elections of 1951, the party's fragmentation became transparent.

The NCNC parliamentary leaders from the East—Nwapa, Njoku, and Arikpo—represented the conservative branch of the party. They were decidedly procapitalist, welcomed foreign investment, and were eager to work with the British.[49] They favored giving the Macpherson constitution a trial period. The British admired these men and believed that their positions in the central government were essential for the implementation of pro-British policies. Thus the British were alarmed at the growing opposition to Nwapa, Njoku, and Arikpo from more nationalist-minded NCNC members who opposed the Macpherson constitution and demanded immediate and extensive constitutional changes. Ideological and personal splits became unbridgeable when party delegates, meeting at a special NCNC convention called at Jos in mid-December 1952, voted to expel Nwapa, Njoku, and Arikpo from the party and to demand their resignations as ministers, as well as the resignations of all the regional ministers in the East.[50] When the central and regional ministers refused to follow party dictates, however, a full-fledged constitutional crisis could not be averted. As government in the East ground to a halt, the lieutenant governor, Clement Pleass, had to employ his reserve political powers to enact an appropriation bill so that the day-to-day administration could continue.[51]

Nigeria's political paralysis did not stop in the East, however. It was carried up to the national level when on March 31, 1953, Anthony Enahoro of the AG introduced a motion into the central House of Representatives demanding self-government for Nigeria in 1956. Although this motion enjoyed widespread support from the southern delegates, it terrified the northern representatives. The effort of these men to amend the motion caused the AG ministers to resign from the cabinet and left the central Ministry entirely in the hands of NPC men and the three repudiated eastern leaders. At the center and in the East, then, the Nigerian polity had ceased to function; the British believed that they now had no alternative, short of ruling directly, but to reform the 1951 constitution. To this end, they called the leading Nigerian politicians to a constitutional conference in London in

[49] *Daily Times*, October 11, 1952.
[50] *West African Pilot*, December 16, 1952.
[51] Ibid., January 30, February 4, and March 2, 1953.

July and August 1953. They were convinced that Nigeria needed massive doses of regionalism to appease ethnic antagonisms.

The decision to alter the Macpherson constitution and to hold new elections distressed the conservative, pro-British Nigerian politicians and marked a decisive turning point in British policies. Njoku retired from active political life to take up an appointment as lecturer in botany at the University College, Ibadan. Reluctantly, Nwapa agreed to campaign but feared the vituperation of Azikiwe's oratory, which was sure to be directed against him. Arikpo also ran but believed that the Nigerian polity had changed radically. He complained to his British backers that there was now "no place . . . for constructive politicians."[52] Although these men organized a new political party, the National Independence Party (NIP), to challenge the NCNC for the East, they seemed well aware that their brand of gradualism had become outmoded. Despite the NIP's appeal in the non-Ibo areas of Ogoja, Calabar, and Rivers province, the party was no match electorally for the dynamism of Azikiwe and his lieutenants.

The London constitutional conference of July–August 1953 involved delegations from Nigeria's major political parties, including NEPU and NIP. Following their deliberations, the British promulgated a new constitution, designed to come into effect in the next year. It allowed even more regionalism than its predecessor, while retaining northern dominance in the central legislature. It vested residual political powers in the regions rather than at the center. The federal legislature was to have 184 seats, of which 92 came from the North, 42 from the East, 42 from the West, 2 from Lagos, and 6 from the Cameroons. Although the British had opposed the self-government motion introduced in the central legislature in 1953, the secretary of state for colonies now announced that any region requesting self-government in 1956 would be granted it. Azikiwe had at first boycotted the London convention, then attended reluctantly. He was so buoyed by the secretary's pledge, however, that he proclaimed on his return to Nigeria that the British had handed Nigeria its independence on "a platter of gold."[53]

These constitutional advances, with their promise of regional autonomy in three years, brought renewed protests from British business groups in Nigeria. Deprived of their special seats in the central Parliament by the new constitution, the business leaders met to discuss new strategies for defending their interests. Representatives of Shell and Unilever approached the Colonial Office with a suggestion for establishing a

---

[52] No. 1180, Macpherson to Colonial Office, May 17, 1953, PRO CO 554/261.

[53] *Report by the Conference on the Nigerian Constitution, August 1953*, House of Commons Sessional Papers, 1952–53, vol. 8, cmd. 8934; *Daily Times*, August 28, 1953.

pressure group on the model of the India, Burma, and Pakistan Association that had so successfully protected the British economic stake in South Asia during and after the British transfer of power there. Although the Colonial Office was encouraging, it advised the company executives not to revive the Association of West African Merchants (AWAM) and warned them that until anglophone West Africa was fully independent, colonial administrators could not be too closely associated with business groups.[54]

John Holt and Company made an additional effort at organizing the British West African mercantile groups. Conceding that AWAM could not be resuscitated and that the Nigerian chambers of commerce were "unwieldy and slow moving . . . and matters which can be discussed by the chambers are to some extent limited by their constituencies," the Holt agents stressed that the big firms should look beyond the Colonial Office and place more resources with locally based and well-organized pressure groups. Bates of Holt proposed a reorganization of AWAM through the incorporation of all British firms engaged in business on the West African coast, including for the first time banks, insurance companies, shipping firms, and motor transport companies as well as the export-import companies.[55] This flurry of activity reflected the anxiety that the new constitution aroused among the business community in the face of a rapidly changing Nigeria.

The elections of 1954, so crucial for the British strategy of reasserting control over the devolution of economic and political power, were bitterly disappointing to the British. In the federal elections held in the East, the NCNC won thirty-two of the forty-two seats and easily held off the challenge from the Nigerian Independence Party. It also secured twenty-three seats in the western federal elections.[56] As victor in the East and the West, the NCNC was entitled to nominate six of the ten federal ministers despite having fewer seats than the NPC in the federal House of Representatives.[57] This time the NCNC did not nominate men eager to implement Britain's go-slow economic and political programs. The northern ministers—Balewa, Muhammadu Ribadu, and Muhammadu Inuwa Wada—were hardly a sufficient counterweight to the NCNC men: Mbadiwe, R. A. Njoku, Kolawole Balogun, and Adegoke Adelabu.[58] The regional elections ran true to form, with Azikiwe winning in the East, Awolowo in the West, and the Sardauna in the North. The fact that each one of the three Nigerian party leaders elected to remain in his regional house rather

[54] Colonial Office Minute, July 19, 1954, PRO CO 554/848.

[55] Geoffrey Bates, Draft Memorandum, 1954, Holt Papers, f232(v).

[56] Sklar, *Nigerian Political Parties*, p. 35.

[57] No. 21, Macpherson to Colonial Office, November 14, 1954, PRO CO 554/1178.

[58] *West African Pilot*, January 6, 1955.

than going to the center reflected the changing locus of power from Lagos to Ibadan, Enugu, and Kaduna and was bound to sharpen the regional competitions.

The 1954 constitution did not merely pit region against region for electoral and political preeminence. It also spurred the regional economic competition that had appeared in the early 1950s and diminished the power of the economic program that the British had so carefully crafted at the center. The West had initiated regional economic rivalry when it laid down its educational challenge in 1951–52. Buoyed by its electoral fortunes, the NCNC embraced this challenge by dispatching Azikiwe and the businessman-politician, Louis Ojukwu, on an economic mission to the United States and Western Europe. Ostensibly intended to promote Western investor interest in the East, the mission also stressed the East's economic and fiscal autonomy from the rest of the federation.

At the completion of the tour, the mission issued a seventy-eight-page report, entitled *The Economic Rehabilitation of the Eastern Region*, that recommended the use of marketing board surpluses to accelerate economic change.[59] The document outlined a five-year development program for the East, based on floating a £35 million loan from external and internal sources. It also called upon the government to found iron, steel, paper, textile, chemical, vegetable, cement, and oil refining industries.[60] Shortly after the publication of the report, the eastern regional government created statutory corporations for five industries: pharmaceuticals, tourism, printing, cinema, and information services.[61]

A further consequence of the report was the establishment of the Nigerian Engineering and Manufacturing Company Ltd, a private firm with an authorized share capital of £100,000. Although the company was juridically located in the private sector, it was expected to have a close relationship with the eastern regional government. Its purpose was to foster import-substituting industries along the lines first recommended by its young chairman and managing director, Nwankwo Chukwuemeka, in a book entitled *The Industrialization of Nigeria*. The firm included on its board of directors virtually all of the East's most prominent business persons, including the ubiquitous Louis Ojukwu.[62] The company's first project, a joint venture cement factory near Abakaliki, provided a clear example of the kind of public-private sector cooperation that the firm and the eastern government wanted. It involved equity contributions of £1,275,000 from the federal government, £500,000 from the Eastern Re-

---

[59] Ibid., May 13, 1955.

[60] *Daily Times*, July 29, 1955.

[61] Ibid., April 4, 1955.

[62] Ibid.; and Eastern Region of Nigeria, *The Economic Rehabilitation of the Eastern Region of Nigeria*, 1955.

gional Production Development Board, £100,000 from the eastern regional government, and £125,000 from the Tunnel Portland Cement Company and F. L. Smidth. Its goal was to produce 100,000 tons of cement per year.[63]

The American-educated Chukwuemeka represented a new breed in the Nigerian business community—one that interjected American New Deal economic ideas into the debate. Formerly an associate professor of mechanical engineering at Howard University, Chukwuemeka believed that the East could accelerate its economic development, "animated by a revolutionary concept of the role of government in business enterprise." He favored "statutory corporations and limited liability public companies for the purposes of economic development in the Eastern Region," and he described private enterprise as "too mercenary and profit seeking" to promote the welfare of all. Acknowledging a debt to the American New Deal, Chukwuemeka compared the newly founded Eastern Regional Finance Corporation to the Reconstruction Finance Corporation in the United States and cited the Tennessee Valley Authority as a model for salutary government involvement in economic affairs.[64] So optimistic was he about the East's Finance Corporation that he persuaded the eastern regional government to place £2 million in marketing board funds with it.

To implement what Azikiwe called his brand of "socialism," the eastern regional government replaced the old Eastern Regional Production Development Board with a more activist Eastern Regional Development Board.[65] The new body was empowered to enter into partnerships with private individuals and firms as well as make loans and was expected to be a major force for economic transformation.[66] The eastern government justified the Eastern Regional Finance Corporation as a vehicle "to expand our economy by stimulating and diversifying investments in order to achieve an equilibrium in the interests of producers and consumers."[67]

The aggressive eastern economic program did not go unnoticed or unchallenged. In the West, the politicians hurried their plans for universal primary education, which were estimated to require a capital expenditure of £5.2 million and teacher training expenditures of £1,005,000. Along with a projected expansion in secondary education, technical schools, and the university college, Ibadan, the total capital cost was projected at

[63] *West African Pilot*, August 24, 1955.

[64] Eastern Region of Nigeria, *The Economic Rehabilitation of the Eastern Region of Nigeria*, p. 4 and passim.

[65] *West African Pilot*, May 7, 1955.

[66] Ibid., March 2 and 3, 1955.

[67] Ibid., May 7, 1955; Budget Speech by the Eastern Regional Minister of Finance, Mbonu Ojike, in Nigeria, Eastern House of Assembly, *Debates*, March 14, 1956, pp. 27–35.

£9,731,000, with recurrent costs scheduled to increase from £3 million to £6 million by 1959.[68] To pay for these heavy expenses Awolowo raised the capitation tax in the West from 6d (pence) to 10s (shillings) 6d.[69]

At this point the southern rivalry reverberated back and forth between the regions; the NCNC could not disregard either such a striking educational project or the western region's five-year development plan, which carried a total price tag of £110,600,000 for the period 1955–1960.[70] Although the funding of comparable projects in the East might even bankrupt the region, the NCNC leadership concluded that it had no alternative. Azikiwe's attack against the AG program, claiming that its five-year plan placed "more emphasis on the comforts of civil servants and high public officials vis a vis the happiness, welfare, and convenience of the taxpayers," was purely a stalling tactic.[71] Southern regional economic competition had been joined once the eastern politicians readied their own educational program and a five-year development plan.

What finally made the regional economic rivalry the most decisive element in the evolving political economy of Nigeria was the decision in late 1954 to regionalize the marketing boards. Until that time, the boards had been organized on the basis of commodities rather than regions, and thus the large surpluses were not directly under the control of the regional governments. Nor were the surpluses seen as endowments belonging to the regions.[72] The new constitution, by establishing the regions as the fount of final authority, made the regionalization of the marketing bodies unavoidable.

In September 1954 each regional legislature enacted a law establishing a single marketing board in its region. The legislative debates offered a last, albeit fleeting and hopeless opportunity to warn of the harmful consequences of such a change and to restate the purposes for which the boards had been established in the first place. In the North, still insulated from much of the political and economic competition tearing at the fabric of southern society, the minister of local industries, Abba Habib, favored the regionally based boards on the grounds that they would protect cultivators and ensure that the gains belonging to farmers would "get back to

---

[68] Nigeria, Western House of Assembly Debates, *Official Record*, July 30, 1952, pp. 462–70.

[69] *Daily Times*, January 26, 1953.

[70] The three regional five-year plans are contained in Western Region of Nigeria, *Report on the Development of the Western Region of Nigeria, 1955–60*; Nigeria, Northern Region, *Policy for Development, 1955–56*; and Nigeria, Eastern Region, *Outline of the Development Plan, 1955–60*.

[71] *Daily Times*, January 31, 1953.

[72] To be sure, the pressure to treat the commodities regionally, with the West insisting on access to cocoa surpluses and the North on groundnut surpluses, was constant. See Awolowo's demands to use cocoa surpluses in the *West African Pilot*, April 5, 1952.

the producer either in the form of cash or in the form of development contributions to prosperity." Habib promised that any "profit" that the board itself might make "[would not] be treated as a tax on the farmer. The profit belongs to the farmer, and it is our opinion that the marketing board which decides how this profit shall be spent must have an independent existence."[73]

Critics of the new economic directions in the South did not have such a sanguine view of board surpluses and were worried about abuses. In the South funds had already been allocated to promote general economic development and were being described as a tax on producers. The most impassioned participants in the debate were those who worried about the changing purposes and the mounting evidence that the funds were also being channeled into political institutions and even being employed for personal enrichment. In the Western House of Assembly, E. N. Ekwuyasi reminded the legislators that the money turned over to the western regional marketing board still belonged to the cocoa farmers and that the government was not justified in using the money as it liked, even to benefit all the people living in the West. Ekwuyasi predicted that the board would become comfortable making "grants to any institution, society or scheme whatsoever which in the opinion of the board is likely to be of benefit to the people or the Western Region," and he stressed that the marketing boards needed to be "primarily instruments of price stabilization."[74] His final caution that the change in the marketing board location would "offer ample opportunity for making grants to political parties" was taken further in a forceful statement by Chief Edah, who praised the British for having run the boards in an efficient and bureaucratic way "that was not fraught with nepotism and favoritism."[75] The critics were fighting a rear-guard and losing battle, however: since the date of their establishment the boards had moved steadily away from price stabilization and producer benefit purposes toward an interest in general developmental questions and even the well-being of the political parties.

At this critical juncture in the debate, the World Bank lent its authority to an expanded vision for marketing board surpluses. The bank insisted that the boards confine themselves to setting quality standards, fixing producer prices, and purchasing and marketing crops, eschewing all other economic functions, but it also counseled board members to view with favor the allocation of a portion of their surpluses to development pro-

---

[73] Nigeria, Northern House of Assembly, *Debates*, September 8, 1954, pp. 100–101.

[74] Nigeria, Western House of Assembly Debates, *Official Record*, September 2, 1954, pp. 10–11.

[75] Ibid., p. 27.

jects. It pointed out that the existing reserves were already large enough to cover any foreseeable fluctuations in world prices, and though £25 million of the reserve should at all times be kept in a fully liquid form, at least £40 million, constituting the second line reserve, could safely be loaned to spur economic growth.[76]

The World Bank's imprimatur marked the final and definitive evolution of board purposes. Established in the face of the opposition of all interested groups in Nigeria, except for the government bureaucrats, their original intention to secure price stabilization was doomed in a world economy of rising commodity prices and limited imports from the sterling area. The British decision to restrict local commodity prices and to allow surpluses to accumulate, driven by fears of inflation and political turmoil, tempted the competing nationalist groups to use the funds to advance the economic and political agendas of their regions. The marketing boards came to supersede all other sources of investment funding and elevated the influence of the government over the business community.

Once the marketing boards had been regionalized, the regional governments created finance corporations to oversee the investment of surpluses in projects of regional economic development. By the mid-1950s the reserves were massive. Those belonging to the old cocoa marketing board and destined to go to the West stood at £28,088,589 at the end of fiscal year 1953–54. The groundnut reserves, bound for the North, were £20,155,720 at the end of the 1953 buying season; and the palm oil marketing board surplus of £17,500,000 in 1954 was dispersed £10,750,000 to the eastern region, £6,470,000 to the West, and £280,000 to the North.[77]

The fear that the regionalization of the boards would lead to the misuse of funds for political purposes, corrupting political life and removing economic decision making from private actors, was based on considerable evidence of an already dangerous degree of corruption and statism at all levels of the Nigerian polity. Although it is difficult to assess the validity of the charge that Nigerian politics were suffused with venality, since the evidence came from so many biased observers, British and Nigerian alike, by the mid-1950s a plethora of commissions had catalogued widespread abuses of office that could scarcely be ignored. The hardest-hitting report was the inquiry into the Lagos Town Council, which concluded that corruption ran "like a brightly colored thread through the tangled skein of the Council's administration."[78] But there were comparable, al-

[76] International Bank for Reconstruction and Development, *The Economic Development of Nigeria* (Baltimore, Md., 1955), p. 88.

[77] See the annual reports of each of the commodity marketing boards from the last year of their existence published by the Nigerian government.

[78] Bernard Storey, *Report of the Commission of Inquiry into the Administration of the Lagos Town Council* (Lagos, 1953), p. 49.

beit less detailed reports, describing nepotistic and improper political activity at Port Harcourt, Onitsha, Enugu, and Ibadan.

The eastern region, the focus of British worries about corruption, in time became the test case for slowing or perhaps even halting the pace of change toward independence and the predominance of the state over private capital. In the view of the British officials the eastern regional government had completely outstripped the other regional governments in its political venality. As a consequence, Governor Clement Pleass was adamantly opposed to any promises of self-government. He argued that the regional and national politicians had yet to demonstrate a capacity to rule themselves. In a series of graphic, confidential notes to officials in London, he described the pervasive maladministration sweeping through the East.[79]

Alarmed by the East's political malfeasance, the government created the Ikpeazu Commission to document the corruption in the East and then investigated Azikiwe's African Continental Bank. Even before the Ikpeazu Commission had completed its work, however, the colonial secretary in London, alerted by Pleass's savage depictions of eastern peculation, decided upon a full-scale internal review of Nigeria's political evolution. The colonial secretary, Alan Lennox-Boyd, indicated his willingness to suspend his promise of regional self-government in 1956 if conditions warranted. As part of the review, he asked the new governor general, James Robertson, to assess the political and security implications that suspension would pose. Lennox-Boyd was prepared, subject to Robertson and Pleass's advice, to withdraw the self-government pledge for a minimum of two to three years or until the East or any other region had demonstrated a higher level of competence.[80]

British decolonization plans in Nigeria were linked once again to imperfectly and hastily conducted assessments of the country's political tranquillity and Britain's military capabilities. True to form, the British authorities in Nigeria doubted their capacity to deal with heightened levels of protest. After consulting his political officers and military men, Robertson wrote that the withdrawal of the pledge was likely to result in noncooperation from eastern ministers and lead to political disturbances in the East, the West, and Lagos. Robertson expected the NCNC to vie with the AG in anti-British rhetoric. British troops might have to be flown in to garrison the country's major cities so that units of the West African Frontier Force could be released for duty in the interior. In Robertson's view, the security problem had the potential to be "more serious than any recently undertaken," including Malaya and Kenya, because of Nigeria's enormous geographic expanse and Britain's thin political staff.

[79] See the file PRO CO 554/1226.
[80] T. I. K. Lloyd to J. Robertson, July 25, 1955, PRO CO 554/1181.

"We should be committing ourselves to an endless internal security operation in an area and with a population larger than any in similar operations elsewhere and with no clear ideal of what result we hoped to secure
at the end of it." Robertson concluded that the British must honor the
1953 promise in favor of self-government. The promise had been extended "to people who, even though their performance since has been
worse than anyone feared, were not substantially different then from what
they are today. The promise was made and I fear that we shall have to
stick to it."[81]

The regional governors also did not wish a return to direct colonial
rule. Pleass, the most pessimistic of the group and the official who had
opposed self-government most vehemently, anticipated wholesale ministerial resignations and a government boycott if the British reneged. Cyni-
cally, he argued that it would be better for the Nigerian people to vent
their anger on an independent African government than on the British. In
his view, no single region of Nigeria was fit to govern itself, and the
country "will be quite unfitted, nor do the great majority of the people
desire self-government."[82] But, along with Robertson, he believed that the
outside world, unaware of the high levels of political corruption in
Nigeria, would not understand suspending a solemn promise or tolerate
coercing the people.[83] The colonial secretary had to be content, then, with
lecturing Azikiwe on the need for clean and honest government.[84] In a
meeting that took place in November 1955, Lennox-Boyd warned Azikiwe that "it was improper to encourage hopes of better things when the
means to provide them might not be forthcoming."[85]

The decision to allow the pledge of self-government to stand did not
halt inquiries into political corruption or keep the authorities from noting
the ways that peculation was spreading into the business sector. Although
the Ikpeazu investigation had to be aborted, it led directly to the inquiry
concerning the African Continental Bank, which proved to be a defining
moment in Nigeria's postwar politics. Not only did the final report reveal
a destructive meshing of public and private arenas, but it poisoned relations between the AG and the NCNC for years to come, obliterating any
chances of a political alliance between the two political associations.

Azikiwe's African Continental Bank was more than a financial institution. It was a symbol of regional and national pride. Naturally, the colonial authorities were hesitant to investigate such a visible instrument of
eastern political and financial power, and they did so only after consult-

<hr />

[81] J. W. Robertson to Thomas Lloyd, August 7, 1955, PRO CO 554/1181.
[82] C. Pleass to Thomas Lloyd, August 6, 1955, PRO CO 554/1181.
[83] J. W. Robertson to Thomas Lloyd, August 7, 1955, PRO CO 554/1181.
[84] Note of Meeting, October 4, 1955, PRO CO 554/1181.
[85] Alan Lennox-Boyd, Note, November 10, 1955, PRO CO 554/1181.

ing the colonial secretary in London. Lennox-Boyd sanctioned the inquiry even at "the risk of riots and the protracted hostility of the government" on the grounds that "the Colonial Office now regards the African Continental Bank affair as providing the last opportunity before regional independence to inject some understanding of financial rectitude etc. into the government of the Eastern Region."[86] J. B. Loynes at the Bank of England, after meeting with Colonial Office officials in London, wrote that "the extent of public corruption in the Eastern Region is said to be so vast that even an investigation solely into the administration of the African Continental Bank's affairs may uncover a great deal of mud."[87]

The African Continental Bank was the centerpiece of Azikiwe's family of twelve companies, possessing a combined nominal capital of £614,000 in the early 1950s. Of this total the African Continental Bank itself held £250,000.[88] After having purchased the shares of Tunubu Property Ltd in 1944 for £250, Azikiwe founded the African Continental Bank on October 29, 1947.[89] Although the bank had a grace period of three years to bring itself into conformity with the new banking ordinance passed in May 1952, it struggled to meet the requirements of the law well into 1955. The British granted the license only after the newly constituted Eastern Regional Finance Corporation purchased £877,000 of the bank's equity stock and deposited £2 million of its own funds with the bank. Previously, the bank's liquidity ratio had been so far below a defensible standard that licensing had seemed out of the question. Azikiwe's critics were quick to protest the use of regional funds to rescue the bank. They called repeatedly for an investigation of the bank's affairs, its ties with Azikiwe and the NCNC, and the circumstances surrounding the placing of eastern regional funds at its disposal. Responding to these demands, the colonial government of Nigeria designated Appellate Judge Stafford Foster-Sutton to conduct an enquiry of the matter.

Azikiwe did not ignore this assault on his integrity. He counterattacked, stoking the flames of anti-British banking sentiment by introducing a motion into the eastern regional Assembly that accused the Bank of British West Africa of attempting "to create monopoly in banking throughout the Federation of Nigeria" and by calling on the eastern government to conduct an investigation of the bank's affairs. The ensuing report demonstrated the links between British banks in West Africa and British colonial power. It singled out the numerous directors of the Bank of British West Africa who had served at one time or another in the West

---

[86] J. B. Loynes, Nigeria, Eastern Region, July 7, 1956, B of E Archives OV 68/3.
[87] J. B. Loynes, Memorandum, July 16, 1956, B of E Archives OV 68/3.
[88] No. 262, A. W. Childs to Secretary of State, January 14, 1952, USNA 745H.00.
[89] *Daily Times*, November 1, 1956.

African colonial service, and noted, as well, the significant equity positions that powerful metropolitan banks like Lloyds, Westminster, and the Standard Bank of South Africa had in the Bank of British West Africa.[90]

The Foster-Sutton report was published as a British parliamentary paper.[91] Overall, although it found numerous irregularities in the bank's activities and criticized Azikiwe for blurring the lines between politics and business, it conceded Azikiwe's nationalist fervor in creating the bank and found no actionable offenses against the bank's officials. But the commission's close examination of the affairs of the bank did reveal alarming intrusions of politics into banking affairs. These ranged from offering concessionary lending rates to political and financial backers like A. G. Leventis and the Zik enterprises themselves; granting unsecured and vague loans to important businessmen-politicians—Louis Ojukwu and Ugochukwu, in particular; and allowing individual shareholders, especially Azikiwe himself, his family members, and his cohort of companies, to be dilatory in subscribing in full the shares they owned while requiring full payment from the Eastern Regional Finance Corporation for all of its shareholdings.[92]

The Foster-Sutton report, the criminal proceedings initiated earlier against banking executives in connection with the banking ordinance, and much scattered information revealed a business sector thoroughly honeycombed with corruption, politically enmeshed, and run by individuals painfully inexperienced in corporate ways. Evidence abounded that those few individuals who earlier had seemed on the verge of entrepreneurial breakthroughs and corporate successes—men like Louis Ojukwu—had found their energies diverted into politics. In addition to directing the Ojukwu Transport Company Ltd and serving on the board of the multinational construction company Costain of West Africa, Ojukwu served on the boards of the Nigerian Coal Corporation and the African Continental Bank and seemed always at the right hand of the leading NCNC politicians.[93]

Ojukwu was well aware of the distorting effect of these political pressures. In poignant testimony to the Foster-Sutton tribunal he pleaded for a strict separation of public and private domains. "I have been," he as-

---

[90] Nigeria, Eastern Region, *Banking Monopoly in Nigeria*, 1956.

[91] Nigeria, Tribunal of Inquiry, *Report into Allegations Reflecting on the Official Conduct of the Premier of the Eastern Region of Nigeria*, January 1957, Great Britain, House of Commons Sessional Papers, 1955–57, vol. 10, cmd. 51.

[92] The general criticisms and some of the specifics may be found in the parliamentary paper previously cited. Of considerable interest, as well, was the published report compiled by a British firm of chartered accountants, Deloitte, Plenda, Griffiths, and Company, which was sent to the financial secretary of Nigeria on September 10, 1956. B of E Archives OV 68/4.

[93] *Daily Times*, April 14, 1954.

serted, "a critic of government even in the Federal House. I told government that they cannot be the government and be businessmen. The only thing I would like government to do is to encourage African people to get on their way and later on withdraw. I will never like government to interfere in business. In fact, I will not like to share a company with government. It is just like a lion and a lamb sharing business."[94] Similarly, in the West, the leading Yoruba business personality, T. A. Odutola, was compelled to look to the AG for business support. In 1950 he secured a governmental concession for the Omo Sawmills Company of Nigeria and created a joint Nigerian-British venture with an issued capital of £250,000 to exploit the 429 square mile forest reserves his firm was granted in Ijebu province. Odutola allied with a West African timber group, William Mallinson and Sons Ltd, and the Colonial Development Corporation.[95] He also sought government protection for his primary company, the Odutola Tire Company, against J. N. Zarpas and Company, a Lagos bus firm, known ruefully to competitors and antagonists as "the octopus" because of the owner's eagerness to take over as much of the Nigerian transportation sector as he could.[96]

Elsewhere, Nigerian businesses were riddled with managerial incompetence, unchecked greed and graft, and failed, often grandiose projects. The passage of the banking act emboldened the government to expose the fraudulence threatening the whole of this sector and to charge numerous individuals with criminal behavior. Directors of the Standard Bank of Nigeria were accused of stealing depositors' funds, and the Nigerian Farmers and Commercial Bank sought protection from the judicial authorities by going into liquidation.[97] Although its chief executive, A. S. Coker, called the closing of the Farmers and Commercial Bank a "national calamity" and blamed the British banking community for the action, his suicide three years later suggested that the criminal charges being brought against him were likely to be sustained in a court of law.[98] By the end of 1953, one and a half years after the banking ordinance had come into existence, twelve local banks had gone out of operation. Only six banks had been licensed (the Bank of British West Africa, Barclays, the British and French Bank, the Merchants Bank, the National Bank of Nigeria, and the Agbonmagbe Bank), and seven others were endeavoring to qualify for a license, including the African Continental Bank.[99]

[94] *West African Pilot*, October 11, 1956.

[95] M. A. Wills, Economic Department, April 17, 1952, PRO CO 554/673.

[96] *Daily Service*, April 2, 1952.

[97] *Daily Times*, November 1, 1952.

[98] Ibid., December 13, 1952, and January 12, 1955; *West African Pilot*, November 11, 1952.

[99] JCH, Report by the Banking Officer on the Banking Position in Nigeria as of October 31, 1953, B of E Archives OV 68/2.

In other sectors of the indigenous business community, usually under less governmental scrutiny, similar difficulties could be observed. The large export-import houses began to question the loyalty and integrity of their licensed buying agents and reduced their exposure in this area as many irregularities came to light. The Cadbury company reported theft in its local buying branches, and the board of directors in Britain expressed alarm at "the large sums which had to be written off as bad debts."[100] The local Cadbury manager in Nigeria believed that "the temptation to make money dishonestly and 'get rich quickly' is a general feature of the Nigerian scene both in the political and business spheres. This is a shocking state of affairs for a country now moving rapidly towards political self determination and I sometimes wonder how all this will end up. There can be no sound future for a country so riddled with rascality."[101] He added that one of the company's most trusted agents, a man who had worked there for twenty years, had recently absconded with £7,000 in company funds, and stocks in a storage area had been adulterated. Similar problems afflicted the United Africa Company, which made cash advances for the 1955–56 buying season totaling £369,500 against securities of £82,417, thus placing at risk £286,783.[102] The Cadbury manager claimed that fault lay with a "system which places such heavy sums of money in jeopardy regularly each year and which so actively contributes towards adverse trading results here in Nigeria."[103]

The big firms' bad fortune was the Nigerian small merchants' opportunity. As the European companies continued their retreat from licensed buying, Nigerian merchants flocked into this sector. They had much to offer, a fact that a UAC agent conceded when he reported that the Nigerian buyers were on the rise because "their methods of business are far less centralized and organized and their overheads accordingly lower than those of the [big] merchants." Employing "staccato buying and selling at very low margins of profit," small buyers were able to offer higher prices and to put the large companies on the defensive.[104]

To a large extent the maladministration and corruption that were sweeping through the business world of Nigeria derived from the gross inexperience of Nigerian business persons. Testimony given to the Foster-Sutton tribunal revealed that numerous corporate directors were not

[100] Cadbury Board Minutes, July 1, 1953, and March 4, 1954, Cadbury Archives.

[101] Manager's Report to the Directors, Cadbury Minutes, October 31, 1956, Cadbury Archives.

[102] A. M. C. Bayley, Assistant General Manager, to Nigerian Department, United Africa Company, London, September 6, 1955, UAC Archives, safe 3, shelf 3, folder 24.

[103] Manager's Report to the Directors, Cadbury Minutes, October 31, 1956, Cadbury Archives.

[104] Report by R. H. Horsley, April–June 1958, Unilever Archives.

aware of their appointments and that even when aware routinely missed board meetings.[105] When Ojukwu saw his name on the letterhead of the Nigerian Engineering and Manufacturing Company, he ordered it removed because he had never been approached about serving on the board. Ojukwu was not, however, entirely scrupulous in discharging the corporate obligations he had agreed to. He could not recall whether he had attended crucial African Continental Bank meetings, even though the bank's records indicated that he had collected a director's fee for being there. In testimony to the Foster-Sutton tribunal, Azikiwe reported that it was common for shareholders to hold back full payments for their shares in the belief that government surpluses would be available to meet the equity needs of new enterprises.[106] In the same vein, Akinola Williams, a chartered accountant interviewed by the Foster-Sutton commission, argued that Nigeria's most glaring corporate need was for old-fashioned, well-trained corporate secretaries—those individuals who ran firms on a day-to-day basis and whose contributions to the Nigerian business culture had been greatly magnified since firms began seeking to raise funds from widely dispersed shareholders and to involve small investors in their future. Unfortunately, in Williams's opinion, only one such well-qualified corporate secretary existed in all of Nigeria—a man whom the African Continental Bank had the good sense to hire.[107]

The first half of the 1950s was disappointing to the architects of Britain's colonial policies in Nigeria. Although the British had repulsed the radical challenge to their political and economic policies, they failed to rally the elite ethnic politicians to their program. By 1956, with the Macpherson constitution abrogated and corruption being discovered in every corner of the polity, the British concluded that the ethnic nationalists had succeeded in accelerating the pace of constitutional change beyond what the British officials in Nigeria and Britain deemed appropriate. Nationalists engaged in cutthroat economic competition that undercut the vision of a capitalist development strategy. Marketing board surpluses were the major nationalist preoccupation, drawing energy and attention away from the private sector into the political arena. Although Nigeria ostensibly remained committed to a procapitalist formula of development, market freedom and entrepreneurial autonomy were giving way to pressures for an expanding public sector.

By the mid-1950s the Nigerian elite had not broken with foreign capital as their Egyptian counterparts had. Nor had the Nigerian politicians

[105] *West African Pilot*, October 11, 1956.
[106] Ibid., November 1, 1956.
[107] Ibid., October 29, 1956.

become champions of socialist strategies as was occurring in Egypt. But the aggressively procapitalist stance of Himsworth had been repudiated, if not legislatively, then practically. State funds had come to be seen as the primary source of economic transformation.

As the British officials viewed the polity and economy, they saw corruption everywhere. But they felt powerless to root it out or even to slow the pace of political change in light of their discoveries. The second half of the decade witnessed an inexorable march to political independence, full of optimistic public pronouncements about Nigeria's rosy future, only occasionally dampened by despairing statements, usually uttered in private conversations, about a blighted polity and sluggish economy.

CHAPTER 8

The Road to Independence, 1957–1960

IN 1957 THE WESTERN and eastern regional governments gained their self-government, and in the following year the northern politicians demanded that self-government be granted to them in 1959, with a complete termination of colonial jurisdiction to follow by 1960. The final tactic available to the British for delaying the transfer of power—the proclivity of the northern elite to prefer colonial rule over independence—abruptly disappeared; the British had no alternative but to succumb to this accelerated timetable for political independence.

As soon as the main groups in Nigeria learned of the decision to grant independence in 1960, all of them—those close to the centers of power and those more removed, including the business community, organized labor, leaders of the political parties, and organized peasant associations—began to jockey for position. Still, despite the political turmoil of these years, which occasionally exploded into open conflict and always simmered on the surface during election contests, the main economic and political tendencies that had emerged in the decade after World War II were intensified rather than shattered. The autonomy of the private business world was further eroded. To be precise, the marketing boards and the development and finance corporations linked to them, despite declining prices for Nigeria's main agricultural exports, became more deeply politicized. The large, mainly British-based business enterprises were forced from many of their most prized activities because of nationalist pressures, and the rising local bourgeoisie found itself increasingly reliant on the whim of the politicians. Nigeria entered the era of independence far more quickly than any of the British colonial officials had believed possible. It had an overheated polity, deep antagonisms separating its political leaders and political parties, and a private sector suffused with politics.

The final years leading up to independence were so intensely politicized that Nigeria's major indigenous business groups could not remain out of the political fray. Not only were the resources of the regional statutory boards put at the disposal of political parties for the purpose of ensuring electoral success, but the political parties themselves, especially Obafemi Awolowo's Action Group (AG), with its grand national strategy, extolled statist economic policies, redistributive socialist programs, and aversion to foreign capital. The electoral campaigns themselves featured debates about development strategies that often alarmed foreign investors. The AG's efforts to achieve a nationwide following involved a wide-ranging assault on foreign capital and even alarmed some of the western region business groups.

Between 1957 and 1960 mass electoral politics came to Nigeria with a vengeance. From a country that had never had direct national elections, Nigerians hurtled into universal adult suffrage; it was in full force by the regional elections of 1956–57, except in the North, where universal male suffrage was delayed until the federal election of 1959.[1] Because the electorate had expanded so rapidly, electoral outcomes were unpredictable, and the political parties threw all of their ideological, personal, and financial resources into the election campaigns. Two sets of elections framed the period: the regional elections of 1956–57 and the final federal election of 1959, and the influence of those intense electoral contests was not confined to the political sector. The campaigns left a profound impact on Nigeria's business groups, as well. The yoking of the private and public arenas became complete. With control over the instruments of colonial power set to pass to Nigerian political leaders, any boundary lines that had seemed to exist in earlier eras were rudely demolished.

The most decisive of the regional electoral struggles occurred in the East in 1957. Reeling from revelations of corruption and maladministration, the East witnessed a veritable referendum on Nnamdi Azikiwe's leadership. Although his party, the National Council of Nigeria and the Cameroons (NCNC) survived the election, winning sixty-four of the eighty-four seats in the eastern regional House of Assembly, the triumph was not decisive enough to quash the challenges to Azikiwe's leadership. Indeed, the election results encouraged the AG, which had supplanted the United National Independence Party (UNIP) as the major regional opposition party, to entertain visions of future electoral successes in the East and prepared it to employ all of its resources in hopes of winning outright the critical 1959 election—the last one before the conferral of independence.[2] Until the regional elections, only the NCNC's claims to national status had seemed credible. But by exploiting the rising political consciousness of the Midwest, the non-Ibo East, and the middle-belt North, the AG discovered a forceful national strategy.[3] In contrast, the election reduced the NCNC to "increasingly an Ibo party," or so the British governor of the East concluded as he saw the eastern Executive Council fall under virtual Ibo domination.[4] This ethnic narrowness was more pro-

---

[1] Richard L. Sklar, *Nigerian Political Parties: Power in an Emergent Nation* (Princeton, N.J., 1963) p. 32.

[2] *Daily Times*, March 1, 1957; *Daily Service*, March 23, 1957.

[3] *Daily Service*, March 23, 1957.

[4] Governor Stapledon observed that the Executive Council of the East had eleven Ibos

nounced than even the governor recognized. Of the eight new ministers in Azikiwe's eastern government, five came from Azikiwe's home base in Onitsha province.

During the elections the AG exploited the fears of non-Ibo peoples, particularly those living in the states of Calabar, Ogoja, and Rivers (COR). Its so-called COR strategy paid handsome dividends in those areas, where AG and UNIP together won eighteen of thirty-five seats in the 1957 elections. Awolowo concluded that his party would be able to capture enough votes in the East and the North to become the majority party at independence. He began to reorient the party's platform and strategy accordingly.

Several developments strengthened Awolowo's conviction to press on with this all-out national strategy. The first was a belief that the Northern People's Congress (NPC) and NCNC coalition that dominated the federal government following the 1957 elections would prove durable and would seek to deprive the Action Group of power at the center.[5] Second, Awolowo saw a declining probability for any alliance of the AG and the NCNC. The two southern political parties had for too long battled each other for preeminence, and their struggles had left an enduring legacy of dislike. Awolowo also realized that by championing the COR movement he was exposing the Achilles heel of the NCNC and was sure to arouse the antagonism of Azikiwe and his lieutenants. To be sure, the NCNC favored the creation of additional states, but it viewed the AG proposal to found a COR state in the East, a midwestern state in the West, and a middle-belt state in the North as nothing short of a cynical political maneuver to catapult the party to majority status in Nigeria.[6]

Awolowo's vaulting ambitions led him to adopt a more socialist and anti–foreign capital stance than the other two parties. Seeking a broad appeal to the Nigerian intelligentsia of all regions, the western leader coupled his socialist pronouncements with a commitment to build Nigeria's most modern political party. Inviting a London-based American public relations firm, Patrick Dolan and Associates, to equip his party with the full panoply of American campaigning techniques for the 1959 electoral contest, he set his party on a collision course with the NCNC and the NPC.[7] His bold vision aroused massive support as well as massive resentment all over the country, even within his own party.

Awolowo's bid to turn the Action Group into a national party, capable of electoral successes in each of the regions, had large implications for

---

and four non-Ibos following the 1957 election; the previous council had been evenly split between Ibos and non-Ibos. No. 9, Robert Stapledon to Secretary of State, March 26, 1957, PRO CO 554/2128.

[5] *Daily Times*, August 31, 1957; *Daily Service*, August 31, 1957.

[6] *Daily Times*, May 31, 1957.

[7] No. 1035, Fred L. Hadsel to Department of State, October 30, 1958, USNA 745H.00.

the private sector and for the relations between private capital and the state. Ideologically, Awolowo sought to take maximum advantage of a vague socialist program and hoped that he could appeal to the rising young educated elements across the federation, without at the same time frightening off the local business classes, especially the wealthy Yoruba mercantile and industrial groups, who were still the prime financial supporters of his party. The Awolowo forces directed their intellectual assault at European capital, often described as monopolistic. The western region premier made frequent references in campaign speeches to his opposition to "foreign monopoly in any field of industrial venture," to which Awolowo usually added, "by this I mean we must not allow a foreign investor to go it alone."[8]

Indicative of the AG statist orientation was the decision of the Lagos Town Council to nationalize the Zarpas bus lines, not because their services were inefficient but because they were thought inadequate for Lagos's expanding population.[9] No doubt this takeover pleased the young intellectual fire-brands of the party who had nicknamed the Zarpas firm "the octopus" and had denounced the practice of allowing nonnative Nigerians to own Nigeria's vital public services. Yet the AG hardly risked losing the support of the Yoruba business classes. The party's program was designed to pry the private sector from the hands of foreign capital and to increase the opportunities for local business.

Although the NCNC, too, had a left-wing, quasi-socialist bloc, which originally crystallized in the Zikist movement and was later revived in the Zikist National Vanguard, the main core of the NCNC embraced private business, including foreign capital. Part of its predilection for private capital dated from the Azikiwe-Ojukwu economic mission to the United States and Western Europe, which bore fruit in the lead-zinc mining concession and the grant of a large piece of land to the Dunlop rubber company. But another factor was the increasingly attractive prospect that oil would soon be exported from the East and that, according to the formulas for regional revenue allocation, the East would be the largest beneficiary of the oil exports. Predictably, the NCNC opposed the AG's frequent calls for state control over the mining sector, including oil, and endeavored to create a favorable business climate for the two multinational oil firms working in the region—Shell-BP and Mobil Oil.[10]

Awolowo's national political strategy assumed the eventual political fragmentation of his NCNC and NPC opponents. The experience of the late 1950s encouraged the AG leadership in its belief that the two parties

[8] *Daily Service*, October 14, 1957.
[9] Ibid., April 16, 1957.
[10] *West African Pilot*, January 29, 1957.

were declining in popularity. And the NCNC, always a loose coalition of diverse groups and antagonistic personalities, was unable to check its fissiparous tendencies in 1957 and 1958.[11] First, a new radical group, the Zikist National Vanguard, arrived on the scene to contest the 1957 regional elections. It questioned the loyalty of top NCNC leaders, notably K. O. Mbadiwe, Kola Balogun, and H. O. Davies.[12] Azikiwe despaired at the inner turmoil to the point that he complained openly at the Aba party convention that the party lacked all discipline.[13] An even more debilitating blow occurred when Adegoke Adelabu, the NCNC's most charismatic leader in the West, died in an automobile accident. Remembered as "the life and soul of his party, the NCNC opposition in the region," Adelabu best represented the NCNC's aspirations to national, not exclusively eastern and Ibo status.[14] Shortly after his death, the *West African Pilot* warned that the party was "losing ground and popularity" and noted that it had once controlled eleven of the twenty-four political divisions in the West but now dominated only seven.[15]

A crucial ingredient of the western strategy to become undisputed political master of Nigeria was a form of economic warfare waged against the two other regions; it was based on the greater economic resources and potential of the West. For years the western politicians had championed an expansive social program for their region, not merely to solidify their hold on the West but also to put financial pressure on the other regions. By 1958 this policy had fostered much of the political instability that beset the East and led to acrimony within the NCNC. The NCNC's efforts to introduce its own program of universal primary education, in imitation of the program being implemented amidst much fanfare in the West, had brought the eastern government to the brink of insolvency.

In spite of Colonial Office prodding and the heart-to-heart chat that Colonial Secretary Lennox-Boyd had arranged with Azikiwe, the East's unrealistic financial plans and its penchant for maladministration and corruption had continued apace. In 1956 the eastern regional government announced that it would spend £90 million over the next five years on a series of development projects. Universal primary education, a university at Nsukka, extensive road construction, industrialization, and filtered water supplies headed the list. The centerpiece of the effort was a scheme of universal primary education, publicized as the surest way to regional

---

[11] Ibid., May 12, 1958.

[12] Sklar, *Nigerian Political Parties*, pp. 403–5; *Daily Times*, November 1, 1957.

[13] *Daily Times*, October 29, 1957.

[14] Note by M. G. Smith for JIC, April 11, 1958, PRO CO 554/2126.

[15] *West African Pilot*, May 12, 1958.

prosperity and a rising standard of living.[16] Already by the end of 1957, before the program of expenditures was even half way to completion, however, spending on education alone had escalated to £5.5 million and was consuming 42 percent of regular revenues. Of this amount, the primary education component was costing £4 million. At this rate the eastern region would face bankruptcy within a few years.[17]

Once again, the East assumed an unwanted prominence in British colonial thinking. The regional governor, Robert Stapledon, much like his predecessor, Clement Pleass, feared that "a public showdown" would be required to bring state spending into line with state revenues. He complained that the eastern regional cabinet had overreached "in its too ardent pursuit of social services and especially of universal primary education."[18] Stapledon and the governor general, J. W. Robertson, initiated conversations with Prime Minister Balewa about federal intervention, preferring some immediate overt action to a hands-off, "let it rip" approach that might result later in governmental paralysis and a need to call in police and even military units to enforce order.[19] As usual, the British officials drew back from the prospect of coercing the Nigerian nationalists, especially those enjoying the kind of popularity that Azikiwe seemed to have.[20]

No such draconian measures were required, however. Azikiwe and his lieutenants sensed the impending political and financial turmoil. Privately, Azikiwe confided to colleagues: "Thank God we did not, as we intended to do, institute a national health service as well," adding, "I wish we and the West had the courage to tell the people the truth about the impossibility of financing the UPE [universal primary education]."[21] In the eastern House of Assembly the minister of finance, Dr. S. E. Imoke, publicly admitted the mistake of launching UPE "full scale." He gained the House's assent for a more gradual phase-in of the program.[22] In addition, the eastern government decided to introduce registration fees for all children attending school and to require family tuition payments for students in standards five and six.[23] The eastern House of Assembly may well have understood the need for these changes, but not all of the people

[16] No. 1, Governor of the Eastern Region to the Secretary of State, January 28, 1957, PRO CO 554/1929.

[17] No. 33, Robert Stapledon to C. G. Eastwood, December 23, 1957, PRO CO 554/2128; *Daily Times*, February 12, 1958.

[18] *Daily Times*, February 12, 1958.

[19] No. 37, Stapledon to C. G. Eastwood, December 31, 1957, PRO CO 554/2128.

[20] No. 40, J. S. Macpherson to R. Stapledon, January 14, 1958, PRO CO 554/2128.

[21] No. 67, Extract from Eastern Nigeria, Dispatch no. 9, January 29, 1958, PRO CO 554/2129.

[22] Nigeria, Eastern Region, House of Assembly, *Debates*, February 13, 1958, p. 166.

[23] *Daily Times*, January 27, 1958.

in the East agreed, for widespread rioting, led by women, occurred in Owerri and other parts of the East when the government attempted to implement the new policies.[24]

Nor was the North immune from pressures for social and economic betterment. In a letter forwarded to the Colonial Office, Ahmadu Bello wrote of the North's need for £30 million to £40 million in development funds to keep pace with the southern regions. He warned that if the North were limited to £15 or £20 million, as the British Colonial Office was proposing, the government of the region "will be under heavy pressure to invest the greater part of it in social services, especially education, and there will be consequent danger of economic stagnation." Mindful of how responsive the officials in London were to worries about political stability, the Sardauna concluded his plea by stating, "Although, at present, we may appear to be an island of tranquility in a disturbed continent, this political stability can only be preserved if we maintain our economic momentum."[25]

The Sardauna's reference to the political condition of the North brought the issue of colonial coercion once again to the fore. The British had done nothing to strengthen their capacity to intimidate a reluctant or resistant population, even as Nigeria moved closer to political independence. If anything, the military and police were more fragile political organizations than they had been a decade earlier because of a rising ethnic consciousness within them. The Nigerian army still numbered 8,000 men. It had only a small African officer corps—a mere forty-one out of 300.[26] The British ruled out a military coup for the foreseeable future, although they were aware that top officers as well as the rank and file had become increasingly politicized.[27] The police numbered a mere 21,200 and consisted of 8,000 regular police, 6,000 special constables, 1,200 western region local government police, and 6,000 northern region Native Authority police.[28] A colonial territory that had been lightly policed and administered since conquest, Nigeria had changed little in the

[24] No. 74, Stapledon to C. G. Eastwood, March 15, 1958, PRO CO 554/2129.

[25] No. 24, alhaji Ahmadu Bello, Sardauna of Sokoto, to J. D. R. Tilney, MP, October 26, 1959, PRO CO 554/1930. Officials at the Colonial Office suspected that one of their own northern advisers, H. A. S. Johnston, had written the letter on the Sardauna's behalf. In their view, Johnston had "made it his particular aim to try to bring pressure to bear on Her Majesty's Government from all quarters to provide Northern Nigeria with considerable amounts of capital both before and after independence." A. N. Galsworthy, Note, December 1, 1959, PRO CO 554/1930.

[26] No. 20, J. K. Emmerson to Department of State, July 21, 1959, USNA 745H.00.

[27] No. 434, Theo. C. Adam, Consul General, to Department of State, May 5, 1959, USNA 745H.5.

[28] No. 310, J. K. Emmerson to Department of State, November 11, 1959, USNA 745H.00.

postwar period. The British officials on the spot were acutely aware of this tradition and recognized that they could not impose unwanted policies on politicians or hostile populations without calling in British troop reinforcements—a prospect that no senior British officials could contemplate with equanimity.

The vulnerability of the British position, the sense of having already lost the political initiative, and even a degree of fatalism on the part of frontline nationalist politicians had become evident by the last years of imperial rule in Nigeria. Nowhere were these sentiments more clearly revealed than in a conversation between Ralph Grey, the deputy governor general of Nigeria, and Abu Bakr Balewa, the federal prime minister. Balewa's request for full independence by April 1960 stunned and disappointed the British. It convinced Grey that "the real power to determine the pace of events has in fact passed from us to the local people and that attempts to persuade them to a slower pace would be misunderstood and merely result in a loss of good will."[29] Speculating on why a person like Balewa would opt for independence when a few years previously he had threatened a northern invasion of the South if the British withdrew, Grey concluded that Balewa and his fellow workers in the NPC had been caught up in the euphoria of the independence movements sweeping the continent. Grey reported Balewa as saying, "Quite frankly I know that we are going to have trouble after independence. Personally, in my own heart, I know that this country is not ready for it. But we will have to be ready to deal with the trouble, and it is no use Britain saying that we cannot have independence because we shall not be 100 percent efficient and 100 percent trouble free." The deputy governor general added his own gloss on Balewa's comments. Balewa "knew that his country was years away from being ready for independence, but he was a politician, he had accepted the office of Prime Minister charged with the task of securing independence by April 2, 1960, and he must do all that he could to achieve that or he would consider that he had personally failed those who trusted him."[30]

The federal election of 1959, the last one before independence, was bitterly contested. Although its most obvious impact was on the aspirations of the parties and their leaders, it left an indelible imprint on the private sector, confirming its subordination to the political arena and forcing the business community to become involved in politics. The Action Group plunged into the fray with unbridled passion, determined to use its ideological and financial advantages to win a majority of the national votes. Awolowo was the party's driving force. The British concluded that

[29] No. 11, Ralph Grey to John Macpherson, June 24, 1958, PRO CO 554/1548.
[30] No. 13, Ralph Grey to C. G. Eastwood, July 9, 1958, PRO CO 554/1548.

he had become "obsessed with the externals of power."[31] He boasted that his party would win at least 174 seats in the federal Parliament and would not need to form a coalition if the other parties proved obdurate.[32] He was said to recite the following incantation on waking and before going to bed:

> I affirm that by the Grace of God, the Action Group shall win 200 seats in the federal election. . . . I also affirm that by the grace of God I, Obafemi Awolowo, will be Prime Minister of the Federation of Nigeria at the conclusion of the said federal election. . . . Jesus says, 'All things whatsoever ye pray and ask for, believe that ye have received them already and ye have them.' I, therefore, believe quite firmly that the Action Group shall undoubtedly win 200 seats in the following election, and that as a result, I, Obafemi Awolowo, will become Prime Minister of the Federation of Nigeria. I thank God Almighty in advance for granting the object of my desire.[33]

But Awolowo did not leave matters entirely to divine intervention. Exploiting the wealth of the West and his vaunted political machine, he carried his ethnically sensitive and vaguely socialist message to the North and East. On the advice of his American consultants, Dolan and Associates, he opened a dialogue with the American diplomats, not in order to enlist their support in the campaign but to ensure their acceptance after he had won the election. He informed the American consul general that he expected the AG to take ninety seats in the North, fifty in the West, and twenty-five in the East and, then, with his solid 165 supporters in the federal Parliament to bring lesser parties, like NEPU, to his side.[34]

Awolowo's strategy of appealing to minority groups in each region was bound to stir ethnic rivalries and arouse suspicions. Aware of their growing political influence in Nigeria's divided polity and the dangers of being left out of power, the minorities chose to remain silent no longer. The British criticized Awolowo for this "readiness to use tribal passions apparently without troubling about what they may lead to" and believed that ethnic consciousness was "causing considerable resentment and the danger of serious disorder."[35] Acutely sensitive to the volatile political climate that was evident in the outpouring of popular sentiment following Adelabu's death, the British noted that the communities of Nigeria were "subjected almost continuously to violent and extravagant political propa-

[31] No. 119, Rankine to C. G. Eastwood, May 8, 1959, PRO CO 554/2127.
[32] No. 167, J. K. Emmerson to Department of State, September 11, 1959, USNA 745H.00.
[33] K. W. J. Post and M. Vickers, *Structure and Conflict in Nigeria, 1960–1966* (London, 1973), pp. 66–67.
[34] No. 295, J. K. Emmerson to Department of State, November 5, 1959, USNA 745H.00.
[35] E(114), G. W. Bell to James Robertson, March 4, 1959, PRO CO 554/1864.

ganda, with all its African manifestations of the personality cult, by two parties [AG and NCNC] bitterly opposed to each other, and [here] you have a situation which can easily become explosive."[36]

Crucial to Awolowo's formula for electoral success was a populist economic and social program that could be disseminated through the country. The AG's fourteen-point election manifesto stressed the party's commitment to a welfare state and elaborated on its program in more detail than its competitors.[37] Acknowledging their indebtedness to the Beveridge Plan of the United Kingdom, the drafters of the AG document promised the Nigerian population a system of old-age pensions, disability payments, unemployment compensation, maternity benefits, and widows' benefits.[38] Although Awolowo confided to his American friends that he expected the AG's ideas to take root among the *talakawa* (Hausa peasants), it was more likely that the eastern and northern intellectuals were the intended target.[39]

Not satisfied with a socially conscious state, Awolowo's Action Group also favored an economically interventionist state, bordering on socialism. The manifesto spoke of the need for "a high rate of capital investment both in public and private sectors of the national economy in accordance with an overall state plan."[40] The party welcomed foreign investment but only "on terms favorable to Nigeria and her people." Specifically, foreign investors should "not seek to make excessive profits, interfere in our politics by backing one political party against another, or adopt corrupt practices in securing contracts."[41]

Nigeria's political parties were elite organizations. They drew their support from a socioeconomic stratum of the educated and financially privileged. Yet Awolowo's electoral démarche opened a latent ideological division between his party and its chief competitors. The NCNC and NPC chose not to take up the challenge. The NCNC manifesto emphasized the themes of liberal democracy, human rights, and education. It was silent on many economic matters, though it disputed the Action Group's statement on fuel and power on the grounds that the AG's position augured a full-fledged program of nationalization. In contrast, the NCNC praised foreign capital and even had kind words for the most reviled British multinationals—the oil companies; the UAC; and the shipping cartel, West African Conference Shipping Lines. It predicted

[36] No. 41, John Rankine, Governor, Western Region, to Alan Lennox-Boyd, April 9, 1958, PRO CO 554/2126.

[37] *West African Pilot*, June 8, 1959.

[38] *Daily Times*, August 8, 1959.

[39] No. 295, J. K. Emmerson to Department of State, November 5, 1959, USNA 745H.00.

[40] *Daily Times*, August 8, 1959.

[41] Ibid., November 6, 1959.

that AG policies would drive foreign investors away.[42] The NPC document, drafted by the inner core of the northern elite—Balewa, Ribadu, Wada, Bida, Sule, and Bello—reflected their deep political and economic conservatism. They proposed strengthening the links between independent Nigeria and Britain.[43]

The 1959 election results proved an immense political setback to Awolowo, though they did not force him to renounce his grand strategy. Not only did his party fail to win the 174 seats that he had predicted, but the party came in third with 73 seats behind the triumphant NPC (142 seats) and the NCNC (81 seats). Despite running the largest number of candidates (282 to 170 for the NPC, 160 for NEPU, and 143 for the NCNC) and spending lavishly on each delegate, the AG won only 39 seats in the East and North.[44] The NCNC's internal bickering notwithstanding, the party captured more seats in the West than the AG could manage in the East. The NCNC also won every single Ibo seat. Confining its efforts entirely to the North, the NPC won all but five seats in what the U.S. consulate called "the Holy North"—that is, the states of Kano, Katsina, North Bauchi, Sokoto, and Bornu. Only in the middle belt did the AG's appeal to minority fears bring a significant electoral result. There the party garnered twenty-four seats, but the NPC held its own by winning forty-six of the remaining forty-eight seats.[45] Still Awolowo refused to abandon his approach, pointing out to critics that the party had the largest number of votes, over 2 million, or 30 percent of the total cast, and arguing that at the next federal election, when the population had learned more of the AG's policies, it could succeed.[46]

Much as Awolowo had predicted, the NCNC agreed to form a coalition government with the NPC, and once this alignment had been sealed the British announced their willingness to confer independence on the government in 1960. The AG was relegated to the role of the opposition—a position that intensified Awolowo's socialist and radical preferences and his desire to highlight the ideological differences between his party and the others. In reality, an AG alliance with either the NPC or the NCNC was unthinkable in 1959 or 1960, so aggressive had been its electioneering and so derogatory Awolowo's comments about his political adversaries.[47]

Nevertheless, the election left confusion and bitterness within the Action Group and plagued the party thereafter. Awolowo was dismayed that

---

[42] *West African Pilot*, August 31, 1959.

[43] *Daily Times*, August 8, 1959.

[44] Ibid., December 11, 1959.

[45] No. 394, J. K. Emmerson to Secretary of State, December 23, 1959, USNA 745H.00.

[46] No. 401, J. K. Emmerson to Department of State, December 24, 1959, USNA 745H.00.

[47] *Daily Times*, December 23, 1959.

his superior political organization and the immense expenditure on the campaign had yielded such a dismal result. The British estimated that the party had spent between £2,000 and £3,000 per candidate, and perhaps as much as £1 million overall. Yet the party took only 49 percent of the vote in its home region and managed to lose seats in Ibadan, Badagry, Ife, Ilesha, Iwo, Egbe, and Omo, not to mention almost all of the Bini-speaking area.[48]

Awolowo's response was to gather around him the younger, more radical members of the party and to issue a new programmatic battle cry, called "democratic socialism." This broadside deepened the party's commitment to minority representation and gave heightened prominence to the party's demands for the nationalization of foreign capital. Although the new emphases had a surefire appeal to leftists throughout the federation, they also alienated the conservative, probusiness element of the party. A party crisis was in the offing and was made more likely as the AG's prospects for holding power at the center diminished.[49]

The strident electioneering and the populist campaign rhetoric had the most disabling effects on private business, foreign and domestic alike. First, each party had accorded the highest priority to succeeding in the 1959 election, and thus each expected the closest cooperation from its business backers. An even closer interpenetration between business and politics ensued. Nowhere were these tendencies more pronounced than in the western region. Ever since the publication of the Foster-Sutton report, exposing the financial irregularities in the East, the NCNC had demanded a similar investigation of the western region. That opportunity arose in 1962 when the federal government appointed a three-person committee, chaired by Justice G. B. A. Coker and assisted by J. O. Kassum and Akintola Williams, to inquire into the workings of the western regional government bodies, particularly the western regional marketing board, and to account for that body's expenditure of the large sums that it had once had at its disposal. Those who had wanted a report condemning the Action Group could hardly have been happier with the Coker commission's findings. The overarching conclusion of the investigation was that although the marketing board had behaved in a fiscally responsible and proper way until 1957, thereafter it had come under heavy pressure from the top AG leadership. Not only had it conspired to make its considerable resources available to the party but it had also distorted and subordinated the economy to the polity.

The funds that the western marketing board had available were indeed considerable: £43,547,189 as the West's allocation from the old produce

[48] No. 3, J. D. Rankine to Secretary of State, February 29, 1960, PRO CO 554/2292.
[49] Post and Vickers, *Structure and Conflict in Nigeria*, pp. 67–68.

marketing board surpluses in 1954 and additional funds realized between 1954 and 1959.[50] The Coker commission conceded that the marketing board had used a large proportion of these funds, something in the neighborhood of £31,000,000, to promote economic growth in the West. Not so, however, the large sums that were made available to two supposedly private firms—the National Investment and Properties Company and the Cooperative Bank of Western Nigeria—which were said to be mere conduits for the transfer of funds to the AG's political apparatus. The commission also found a systematic bias in favor of business groups in which AG interests were strongly represented, most notably the National Bank of Nigeria, the Agbonmagbe Bank, the Merchants Bank, and Messrs Arab Brothers (Motor) Ltd. These groups were supported financially because of their political affiliation and were also expected to make their own resources available to the party for its political campaigns.

Of the National Investment and Properties Company, the commission affirmed that it had been "formed for the main purpose of providing funds for the Action Group."[51] It also stated that the investments made in the company "were all imprudent . . . and constituted a most flagrant breach of trust . . . by which the peoples of the Western Region have been robbed of the financial benefits to which they are entitled from the Western Regional Marketing Board."[52] The commissioners condemned the marketing board for depositing large sums in the indigenous banks of the region without examining their books or securing adequate representation on their boards. It singled out Awolowo as the driving force for diverting funds to political ends. It was he who funneled funds to the National Investment and Properties Company and nominated its highly politicized board of directors. "His scheme," the report averred, "was to build around him with money an empire in which dominance would be maintained by him by the power of the money which he had given out."[53] Finally, the commission identified Alfred Rewane, head of the Western Nigerian Development Corporation, the Nigersol Construction Company, and the Nigerian Water Resources Development Company Ltd, as Awolowo's chief agent in creating this dependent financial world.[54]

That the Coker commissioners were correct in criticizing the western politicians for squandering the wealth of the cocoa farmers was undeniable. Only two of the numerous industrial projects supported by marketing board funds had paid a dividend by the end of 1961. At the same time,

---

[50] Nigeria, *Report of Coker Commission of Inquiry into the Affairs of Certain Statutory Corporations in Western Nigeria* (Lagos, 1962), vol. 1, p. 9.

[51] Ibid., p. 27.

[52] Ibid., p. 36.

[53] Ibid., p. 39.

[54] Ibid., p. 20.

the marketing board, originally created to ensure cocoa price stability, had liquid cash assets of only £1,761 at the end of September 1961.[55]

THE PRIVATE SECTOR IN A NATIONALIST ENVIRONMENT

Advocates of the private sector did not stand by idly as independence approached, the nationalist momentum accelerated, and the state encroached ever more aggressively on their turf. Yet their efforts to make the private sector less dependent on the whims of the state could hardly be called successful. Indeed, the frequent struggles between foreign and indigenous capital only strengthened the tendency for the state to intervene in sectors of the private sector traditionally reserved to business persons. Throughout the half-decade leading up to independence, foreign investors were on the defensive. They endeavored to secure a future role for themselves by encouraging Nigerians to take up shares in their companies, by forming joint ventures with local firms, and by finding niches for themselves in the local economy where they were safe from nationalist attack. Still, by 1960 foreign capital no longer occupied the dominant economic position that it had enjoyed throughout the classical colonial period.

A first step designed to enhance the autonomy of the private sector in competition with the state for investment capital was to stimulate local savings and investment through the creation of a stock exchange. Not until 1959 had any serious thought been given to establishing a local market for the trading of corporate securities. A Nigerian securities market had lagged behind other African countries because so much of Nigeria's development and equity capital was mobilized through the marketing boards. But the disadvantages of relying so completely on the state became obvious as the marketing board funds began to decline. In 1959 the government created a committee to advise on ways to establish a stock market in Lagos.[56] The committee came to a quick and shocking realization that Nigeria, despite its long history of commercial contact with the West, was entirely devoid of public limited-liability companies. Of the 845 companies incorporated in Nigeria at the time, ninety-two were subsidiaries of overseas firms. Only approximately a dozen of the remaining 753 firms were public companies and thus capable of having their shares traded on a share market. The rest were partnerships or private limited-liability companies, restricted by their terms of incorporation in the number of shareholders that they were permitted. Altogether, the

---

[55] Ibid., pp. 9 and 20.
[56] Nigeria, *Report of the Committee Appointed to Advise on Ways and Means of Fostering a Share Market in Nigeria* (Lagos, 1959).

total value of the shares issued by the public limited-liability companies, though not all paid up, was £24,168,104, of which only £7,498,858 was held by residents of Nigeria. In short, Nigeria had no tradition of corporate investing.

Nor for that matter had the state achieved any success in raising loans locally for any of its purposes. Between the end of World War II and 1959 the one and only effort to float a state loan locally occurred in 1946 when the government offered a £300,000 loan to the local investing public. Although the issue was oversubscribed by £549,000, the state regarded the effort as unsatisfactory because it met its goal only by pressuring the British banks in Nigeria, the African administrative agencies, and the government's own pension funds to take up those parts of the loan that had been set aside for individual investors. So disappointed was the government that it never went back to the local population with another issue.[57]

One week before independence a group of private businessmen opened the first stock exchange of Nigeria in Lagos. They had been encouraged by the fact that a few firms had succeeded in raising equity capital locally. The Nigerian Cement Company at Nkalagu, most of whose share capital belonged to the federal government, led the way.[58] It made a public offering of £174,898 and was delighted when the offering was oversubscribed by £30,000.[59] In the next year (1960) two foreign firms made shares available to local investors. In May, the British American Tobacco Company offered £100,000 of ordinary stock in its local affiliate. The response was overwhelming—2,111 applications totaling £300,000—and so the board agreed to increase the capital of the local firm by £200,000.[60] John Holt announced that it would bring together all of its Nigerian affiliates in one holding company, John Holt Investment Company of Nigeria, and, as a first step in the gradual Nigerianization of this firm, would offer £200,000 worth of shares to Nigerian investors. The new John Holt Investment Company of Nigeria, before its formal establishment, had acquired a controlling interest or strong minority position in Nigerian Breweries, Costain of West Africa, Holt's Nigerian Tanneries, Crittall-Hope, Thomas Watt and Son, P. S. Mandrides and Company, Asbestos Cement Products, and the Investment Company of Nigeria.[61]

These were small steps toward stimulating private shareholding in Nigeria. They did not presage a large-scale Nigerianization of the busi-

---

[57] No. 1, Governor General, Nigeria, to Secretary of State, February 26, 1959, PRO CO 554/1698.

[58] *Daily Times*, June 19, 1959.

[59] Ibid., March 23, 1959.

[60] Ibid., July 15, 1960; *West African Pilot*, May 6 and July 15, 1960.

[61] *West African Pilot*, February 17 and August 26, 1960; *Daily Times*, August 26, 1960.

ness sector—an outcome that was far from the minds of these firms. The companies were seeking protection from nationalist critics and an opportunity to tap new sources of wealth. Yet, at independence, only the oil sector had succeeded in attracting new investment funds, which were coming entirely from the outside. The British alone invested £15 million in the Nigerian oil sector in 1958 and 1959. All of the other sectors combined increased by a mere £4 million, almost all of which was reinvested profits.[62]

The accelerating march toward independence intensified nationalist criticism of the power of the great British joint stock companies over the Nigerian economy and led to only partially successful responses. By 1960 the three areas in which foreign firms had always played such a dominant role—banking, shipping, and trading—had undergone profound changes.

Banking

A first sector that had always concerned nationalists was banking. Nigerian business persons and politicians had a substantial record in the banking sector and were determined to ensure a strong place for their nationalists in banking and finance. A high priority was accorded to strengthening the indigenous banks already in existence but established on shaky foundations. The NCNC was determined to reorganize the financially troubled African Continental Bank and to make it capable of protecting the interests of Nigerian producers and promoting new investment opportunities. In response to efforts to reform the bank, Price Waterhouse dispatched a team of accountants to the eastern regional government to investigate the bank's accounts and make recommendations about its future. Its auditors discovered that the financial position in the branch banks was on the whole reasonable, but the same could not be said for the central Lagos branch, "where the management was inept and almost wholly political in character." The accounting firm found that the board of directors of the bank met only once each year and rubber-stamped the actions of the managing director. Given such an appalling level of supervision, the investigators were not surprised that the central managers had squandered no less than £370,000 of the bank's funds, of which at least £200,000 had been lost on the Azikiwe companies alone.[63] Reluctantly, the British officials accepted Azikiwe's suggestion that the eastern regional government purchase those shares of the bank still in

[62] No. 8, L. Pliatzky, CRO, to D. Center, BOT, December 21, 1960, PRO DO 35/10463.
[63] Bank of England (hereafter B of E), Memorandum, African Continental Bank, July 1, 1958, B of E Archives OV 68/5.

private hands and turn the bank into an eastern region state bank. The British were upset that the chief beneficiaries of the government's take-over would be Azikiwe, his friends, and his family of companies, since all of them held shares in the bank.[64]

From the 1930s, Nigerian nationalists and business persons had been endeavoring to eliminate the monopoly powers of British banking and the British government (through the West African Currency Board) over the Nigerian financial sector. Their first efforts had resulted in the creation of commercial banks, like the National Bank of Nigeria and the African Continental Bank, which, through the depositing of state funds, came to occupy a large position in the financial sector, without, however, funda-mentally undercutting the power of Barclays and the Bank of British West Africa. Thus, it was hardly surprising that in 1952 an NCNC eco-nomic nationalist, K. O. Mbadiwe, proposed the creation of a central bank for Nigeria. In his speech, delivered in the federal House of Repre-sentatives, he described a central bank as "a nerve center which channels . . . industrialization," and added that a Nigerian state bank would loosen the British hold on the Nigerian economy, establish a separate currency, and promote local business activity.[65]

British officials reacted hostilely. Not only did Britain possess large sterling balances belonging to Nigeria but British officials also wanted to protect the preeminence of the two British commercial banks there. Yet a nationalist groundswell compelled them to send a financial expert to ad-vise on the viability of a central bank for Nigeria.[66] The man whom the Colonial Office and the Bank of England chose, J. L. Fisher, was ideal from their point of view. He was not on record as opposing African central banks, but privately he was committed to doing whatever his su-periors in London wanted. Before agreeing to undertake the assignment, he said he would go, "provided we [the Bank of England] also told him the conclusions we should wish to endorse." Fisher even admitted to being quite able to marshal arguments on either side of the question, but he reassured the officials at the Bank of England that he was sympathetic to their view because "neither the financial mechanisms required nor the mentality and outlook are forthcoming. . . . Africa is not fitted or ready for such complex institutions and incapable of manning, using, or sus-taining them."[67] C. F. Cobbold, governor of the Bank of England, wrote to John Harlech, head of the Bank of British West Africa, and Julian Crossley, head of Barclays, DCO, the two banking institutions most di-

[64] J. B. Loynes, Nigeria, Eastern Region, April 11, 1957, B of E Archives OV 68/4.

[65] Nigeria, House of Representatives, *Debates*, March 21, 1952, p. 377.

[66] WJJ, Overseas and Foreign Office, Bank of England, Nigeria, July 17, 1952, B of E Archives OV 68/2.

[67] Memorandum by DHB, July 17, 1952, B of E Archives OV 68/12.

rectly involved in Nigerian banking, asking them to make their facilities in Nigeria available to Fisher.

The Fisher report, characterized at the Colonial Office as "a hasty and in some respects almost a frivolous document," did not silence Nigerian demands for a central bank.[68] To be sure, the basic conclusion of the report was that the time was not yet ripe for such an institution. But Fisher's suggestions, no doubt based on his conversations with Nigerian business persons, that Nigeria should be accorded greater fiscal autonomy, that the West African Currency Board had outlived its usefulness, and that radical changes in Nigeria's financial institutions were inevitable, were not what the officials at the Colonial Office, the Treasury, and the Bank of England had expected to read.[69]

If the Fisher report did not dampen nationalist enthusiasms for a central bank and a separate Nigerian currency, the next major financial report left the British little alternative but to embrace such changes. In 1954 the World Bank, having undertaken a comprehensive investigation of the Nigerian economy, submitted an advance copy of its findings to British officials in London for comment. The economic experts at the Colonial Office and the Bank of England were shocked and even outraged to read in the section on banking that the World Bank authorities recommended the creation of a Nigerian central bank. Believing that they had repulsed the demands for such an institution through the Fisher mission, British officials felt that the World Bank had betrayed them. Their first reaction was to ask the bank officials to amend the report. They sent Fisher to recount the familiar arguments against a central bank, but Fisher's pleas were swept aside. In the opinion of the World Bank officials, nationalist opinion in Nigeria was unanimous in favor of a central bank. The issue was no longer whether to have such an institution but under what auspices it would be established. The World Bank mission believed that it would not get off to a good start without British oversight. At the outset, however, the World Bank recommended that the new organ be given a severely limited range of duties. It foresaw an institution that would issue Nigeria's currency, serve as the principal depositor of government and parastatal funds, buy and sell government securities as they became more widely deployed in the Nigerian economy, and accept the deposits of Nigeria's commercial banks. And the World Bank officials wanted the Nigerian bank to be in place and operating under expert outside guidance well before Nigeria became independent.[70]

[68] H. T. Bourdillon, Note, January 28, 1953, PRO CO 554/691.

[69] Nigeria, *Report on the Central Bank* (Lagos, 1952).

[70] E. Melville, Colonial Office, to J. Fisher, April 16, 1954; ALR, Nigeria: IBRD Report, May 4, 1954, B of E Archives OV 68/3.

The Colonial Office and the Bank of England were forced to bow to the World Bank, though they remained unconvinced. They still believed the centralizing of such large funds in a single indigenous bank "to be unsound and to have dangerous potentialities."[71] They were also intensely suspicious of American business influence lurking behind the World Bank, and they were convinced that the establishment of a central bank in Nigeria held "danger for sterling and for the management of the money and gilt-edged markets here if Nigeria (or any other colony at a similar stage of development) were to be started on the wrong road."[72] Fearing that leaks would reveal their opposition and inflame nationalist opinion against them, they stopped requesting changes in the text of the mission volume. They vowed, however, never again to give the World Bank such a free hand in Britain's colonial territories.

Their fears notwithstanding, the British were determined that the new central bank of Nigeria, if it were to come into being, would operate with British ideas, practices, and personnel. In an internal memorandum, one British official wrote that the Bank of England must "give every assistance in regard to the establishment of an institution suited to Nigeria's needs. Such assistance could be given both in drafting of statutes and in finding suitable personnel."[73] With that end in view, the Bank of England sent yet another of its financial experts, J. B. Loynes, to draft the guiding document for the new bank. Loynes was assured a free hand in Nigeria since, in the opinion of the financial experts in London, no official there, British or Nigerian, had any knowledge of the subject.[74]

The Loynes report, published in 1957, established the foundations for the Nigerian central bank. Recognizing that the Nigerians felt constrained by the rigidities of the West African Currency Board and insisted on their own currency, Loynes nonetheless reminded his readers that a central bank in Nigeria would not at first be able to exercise all of the powers normally associated with central banks because of Nigeria's long history as a dependent colonial economy. Specifically, he pointed out that because the big banks of Nigeria had no liquidity problems and enjoyed the backing of financially solid metropolitan firms, they did not require nor would they profit from close supervision from a central bank. Second, Nigeria still had no securities market and was unlikely to have one for many years. Thus Nigeria's central bank would not be required to over-

---

[71] A. K. Potter, Bank of England, Draft letter to E. Melville, Colonial Office, June 24, 1954, B of E Archives OV 68/2.

[72] AMS, B of E, Memorandum on draft letter to Playfair on the Nigerian Mission Report, November 12, 1954, B of E Archives OV 68/3.

[73] ALR, Overseas and Foreign Office, B of E, Nigeria: IBRD Report, November 5, 1954, B of E Archives OV 68/3.

[74] J. B. Loynes, Nigeria, A State Bank, April 9, 1956, B of E Archives OV 68/3.

see a local money market. While recognizing the natural desire among the Nigerian people to separate their own currency from that of their former colonial power, Loynes recommended moving slowly in detaching the two currencies. In the early stages of the bank's existence there was more to be said for a par exchange rate between sterling and the Nigerian currency than fluctuating rates. Loynes also recommended that the central bank hold large and liquid sterling reserves as backing for its national currency. Although these arrangements might seem to do little to address the traditional nationalist complaint that the Nigerian currency had no life of its own and was tied mechanistically to sterling, Loynes pointed out that the large government and marketing board funds gave the Nigerian monetary system great flexibility.[75]

In introducing the bill to establish a central bank, the federal minister of finance, Festus S. Okotie-Eboh, extolled its benefits. The new central bank would issue Nigeria's new currency; loosen the financial ties that bound Nigeria's currency to sterling; enable a closer regulation of commercial banks operating in the country, including even the big British banks; foster the development of a local money market; and oversee programs of economic growth.[76]

The Central Bank of Nigeria commenced its operations, as the World Bank had wanted, under the most methodical supervision from the Bank of England. Its first governor, Roy P. Fenton, a former adviser of the Bank of England, was handpicked by the British and maintained close ties with the Bank of England during his tenure in Nigeria. In addition, the bank operated under a set of extremely conservative, self-imposed fiscal requirements. It was required to retain a high degree of liquidity— at least 60 percent of the currency issued and 35 percent of the demand deposits during the first five years of its existence. After that period it was allowed to reduce liquidity to 40 percent of all of the bank's outstanding liabilities.[77]

Yet the new central bank marked still another step in the expansion of the role of the state and the delinking of the British and Nigerian economies. In spite of the fact that the new central bank had close ties with the Bank of England, Nigeria had acquired a separate currency and a financial institution that, in theory if not always in practice, exercised supervisory powers over the private banking sector. Not every interested Nigerian business and nationalist group shared this optimistic view of the financial future of the country. Numerous Nigerians complained that the

[75] Nigeria, *Report by J. B. Loynes on the Establishment of a Nigerian Central Bank, the Introduction of a Nigerian Currency, and Other Associated Matters* (Lagos, 1957).

[76] Nigeria, House of Representatives, *Debates*, March 17, 1958, vol. 2, pp. 847 ff.

[77] No. 46, Ralph H. Hunt, Consul General, to Department of State, August 1, 1958, USNA 845.10.

top positions in the bank had been given to Bank of England nominees, and they worried that the bank would make life difficult for Nigeria's two leading commercial banks: the African Continental Bank and the National Bank of Nigeria. To be sure, the new central bank supplanted the old West African Currency Board, and its equity capital of £1.5 million was held entirely by the federal government. But Nigerian economic sophisticates realized that by introducing these changes before independence had occurred the British had ensured a continuation of Nigeria's traditional, pro-British fiscal policies and the ties with sterling.[78]

Shipping

Similarly, the British shipping lines, led by the monopolist Elder Dempster, endeavored to protect their position against rising nationalist protests. In shipping, the nationalist complaint was strident. A number of Nigerian business groups had threatened entry into the shipping sector, only to be deterred by the large capital requirement, estimated at £4.5 million, to start up even a modest firm.[79] But when the western regional and eastern regional governments initiated conversations with the Zim Israel Navigation Company, which was already involved in operating the Black Star Line in Ghana, conservative, pro–foreign business forces in Nigeria began to act.[80]

The federal minister of transport, R. A. Njoku, took the lead. He argued that shipping was a national economic activity and should not be devolved into regional hands. He proposed, instead, to establish a national line, using federal surpluses. Recognizing Nigeria's lack of technical competence, he recommended that the Nigerians, while holding a majority of the shares in the company, merge with a strong, experienced ocean liner company. To the astonishment of Nigerian nationalists, Njoku invited Elder Dempster and its affiliate, Palm Lines, to take up this minority position and to provide the technical and managerial oversight for the Nigerian National Shipping Line. The new firm was to begin with three ships. The board reflected the mixed capital of its originators: its chairman was Louis P. Ojukwu; the other members were Peter Daramola, the acting director of commerce and industry, L. K. Anja, the financial counselor to the Gloko Native Administration; John H. Joyce, chairman of Elder Dempster; A. E. Hoffman, managing director of Palm Lines; and

[78] No. 47, Ralph H. Hunt, Consul General, to Department of State, August 1, 1958, USNA 845.10.

[79] No. 1, Extract from Minutes of the Fourth Meeting of the National Economic Council, January 30, 1958, PRO CO 554/1683.

[80] No. 3, Governor General to Secretary of State, July 23, 1958, PRO CO 554/1683.

A. E. Muirhead, a director at Elder Dempster. The first issue of capital was for £400,000. The federal government took 26 percent, the Nigerian Produce Marketing Board 25 percent, and the remaining 49 percent was divided between Elder Dempster and Palm Lines.[81]

National complaint was immediate and vociferous. Nationalists were incensed that the federal government would allow Nigeria's most formidable, and to many its most exploitative, foreign shippers to occupy a dominant position in the new company. They were not impressed with Njoku's argument that the government had considered fourteen proposals before accepting the Elder Dempster and Palm Lines merger.[82] According to the *West African Pilot*, the merger turned the Nigerian National Shipping Line into little more than "an appendage of the mighty Conference Lines"—a criticism that took on added credibility when the Nigerian National Shipping Line agreed not to compete with the Conference Lines in pricing and volume arrangements.[83] The nationalists also rejected Njoku's defense that the agreement was the only way the firm could guarantee a reasonable tonnage for its operations in its start-up period.[84] The *Daily Service* ridiculed the company, pointing out that its three ships would carry a mere 50,000 tons per year, only 2.5 percent of the total volume of Nigeria's exports and imports.[85]

A Yoruba businessman, P. J. Osoba, organized much of the protest against the new company. Osoba was a timber exporter whose timber often rotted at the docks because of inadequate shipping capacity; he was also interested in establishing his own independent shipping line.[86] The founding of the new federal company entirely undercut his project. As subsequent judicial inquiries revealed, a desperate and illegal financial gamble underlay Osoba's vigorous protest. As managing director of the insecurely established Merchants Bank in Lagos, Osoba had taken £35,000 of a £100,000 deposit made by the Western Nigerian Development Corporation to purchase an ocean liner, the *Empress of Nigeria*, for his new enterprise. Osoba's brief entry into the highly competitive shipping sector was destined for failure. Not only was he brought up on charges of embezzlement, but his company never came into being.[87]

Although the nationalist press believed that Elder Dempster and Palm

---

[81] No. 28, Governor General's Deputy to Secretary of State, July 9, 1959, PRO CO 554/1683.

[82] *West African Pilot*, December 20, 1958; *Daily Times*, July 8, 1959.

[83] *West African Pilot*, April 27, 1959; *Daily Times*, April 27, 1959.

[84] *Daily Times*, July 8, 1959.

[85] *Daily Service*, May 7, 1959; Ocean Archives, 2247.

[86] *West African Pilot*, February 15, 1957.

[87] *Daily Times*, December 22, 1959.

Lines had blocked the creation of a genuinely autonomous nationalist company, the shareholders and major backers of Elder Dempster believed that their firm had conceded too much to the Nigerians. John Joyce, head of Elder Dempster, took infinite care in defending his decision to invest in the new Nigerian firm. In a letter to Mallock Brown, chairman of Shipping of the United Kingdom, he conceded, "Our company is naturally apprehensive regarding the proposed West African lines, but we should be much more concerned at the probable repercussions if any attempt at intervention [from your side] were made."[88] Joyce was well aware that although the Nigerian National Shipping Line posed little immediate threat to the West African Conference Lines, its plans to expand the capital of the firm and to increase the fleet size from three to ten ships would put it in a position to do without Elder Dempster and Palm Lines.[89] In defending the deal to the stockholders, Joyce wrote of the need to "ensure stability in the trade and also ensure the minimum damage to the existing trade."[90] He pointed out that Elder Dempster had defeated Zim Israel Navigation's attempt to create a shipping company entirely free from the Conference Lines.[91]

Elder Dempster's severest critic was Leif Hoegh, a Danish shipping executive as well as a shareholder in Elder Dempster. Hoegh demanded that Elder Dempster keep its assistance to the new Nigerian firm to a minimum. "We presuppose," he wrote to Joyce, "that the Nigerian venture is kept within narrow limits and that a possible further appetite is staggered. . . . We take it for granted that you will not help the Nigerians to run their ships so that the mistakes they make in the field will in all fairness have to be [their own]."[92] But Joyce disagreed. He believed that by cooperating with the new firm Elder Dempster could prevent "some inferior line" from using "political means or their very big cargo potential to give their own line a better chance than the rest of us."[93] As independence approached, Joyce's policy of inclusion seemed to have proved itself. All of the shippers operating out of Nigeria—the traditional ones, like Elder Dempster, Palm Lines, the Holland West African Line, the Woermann Line, and the Guinea Gulf Line, as well as the new lines, like the Nigerian National Shipping Line and the Black Star Line—were

[88] No. E(4), John Joyce, Elder Dempster Lines, to Mallock Brown, Chairman of Shipping of the United Kingdom, March 9, 1959, PRO CO 554/1684.

[89] *Daily Times*, June 20, 1958.

[90] J. H. Joyce to Hoegh, January 20, 1958, Ocean Archives, 2247.

[91] Record of Meeting in Liverpool, November 3, 1958, Ocean Archives, 2247.

[92] Leif Hoegh of Leif Hoegh and Company, Oslo, to Joyce, January 28, 1958, Ocean Archives, 2247.

[93] Joyce to Hoegh, February 4, 1958, Ocean Archives, 2247.

members of the West African Conference conglomerate. Price and volume competition had been avoided.[94]

Export-Import

Although banking and shipping were not forced to make major accommodations to nationalist and local bourgeois agitation as independence approached, the same was not true for the great export-import firms. The problems that had beset these companies since the end of World War II— decline in their share of agricultural export buying, peculation in local branches, and the rise of aggressive local competitors—continued apace. The response of the great trading firms was markedly different from that of the British banks and shipping lines, however. Rather than defending market share and co-opting local competitors, as the bankers and shippers had done, they elected to move out of the areas of severest business competition and to specialize in commercial and manufacturing activities where they enjoyed clear comparative advantages.

The first and most obvious change for the great trading firms was their retreat from produce buying. As its business losses mounted, Cadbury continued to withdraw from cocoa buying, focusing on a single lucrative market where it exercised close administrative supervision. By confining its buying to the Agege-Ilaro region, Cadbury reduced its losses from £31,881 in 1956 to £5,290 in 1957.[95] Yet the Cadbury executives did not withdraw entirely from Nigeria. They wanted to have some influence in government circles, and they valued their independent sources of information on the local cocoa crop.[96]

The United Africa Company undertook a similar consolidation in its produce-buying operations. First, the firm closed down produce-buying activities in the Calabar area because of the heavy losses there, which totaled £30,000 in the 1958–59 season.[97] But Calabar was only the start. In early 1962, the chairman of the United Africa Company, J. B. Davies, announced that the firm was no longer engaged in buying agricultural exports in the East and West of Nigeria, though it retained a foothold in the North.[98]

[94] Letter from Elder Dempster Representative in Hamburg to A. E. Muirhead, July 23, 1959, Ocean Archives, 2046.

[95] Cadbury Board Minutes, April 10, 1957.

[96] Cadbury Board Minutes, January 23, 1957.

[97] United Africa Company, London, Minutes of Meeting, July 23, 1959, UAC Archives, safe 3, shelf 3, file 21.

[98] Memorandum by J. B. Davies, Chairman of UAC, Nigeria, February 6, 1962, UAC Archives, safe 3, shelf 3, file 15.

Not only were the big trading firms pulling out of produce buying, they were also transforming their role as distributors of consumer goods. In the classical colonial period, UAC and other firms sold any product that local populations wanted to buy, without having a commitment to particular product lines. According to A. H. Smith, a UAC official, the traditional UAC organization in West Africa was "essentially defensive, to catch the trade as and where it arose." Consequently, the big firms had a wide spread of trading posts and were "prepared to deal in any and every commodity in order to have the broadest base for its trading posts."[99] Each trading post carried a comprehensive range of merchandise, with an emphasis on basic staples such as flour, gin, cement, cigarettes, and soap. But after the war, as consumer demand grew and became more sophisticated, greater scope existed for marketing skills and the interests of manufacturers and merchants began to diverge. By 1963 that transition seemed complete, as one of the United Africa Company officials, G. J. Cole, reported after a trip through West Africa: "The United African Company as a general merchandising business has in fact ceased to exist in Nigeria."[100]

Ceasing to be produce buyers and withdrawing from the field of general merchandising—the two primary activities of the big trading firms up to World War II—did not mean extinction. But it did entail a massive redirection of energies and capital. The United Africa Company devolved what remained of its general merchandising to its subsidiary, G. B. Ollivant, and then focused its own merchandising on a few lines, for which it advertised heavily and provided follow-up servicing. By the late 1950s and early 1960s, its two most lucrative subsidiaries were the Kingsway department stores dotted around the Nigerian urban landscape, and Niger Motors, specializing in the sale and servicing of cars and trucks.[101] Increasingly, new firms entered Nigeria to distribute their own manufactures and forced the trading companies to give up the merchandising of their lines. In the lucrative soap and detergent field, once thoroughly dominated by the United Africa Company, the American manufacturer Colgate Palmolive had made significant inroads.[102] The general merchandisers had also been driven entirely out of petroleum and tobacco prod-

---

[99] United Africa Group, Review by A. H. Smith at the Directors Conference, November 7, 1958, Unilever Archives.

[100] Report to the Directors Conference (UAC), February 22, 1963, by G. J. Cole on his visit to Nigeria with A. H. Smith, Unilever Archives.

[101] No. 30, Redeployment, text of talk given to UAC managers on April 6, 1965, in UAC House, London, UAC Archives, safe 4, top shelf, folder 8.

[102] Report from Nigeria, June 1960, Unilever Archives.

ucts distribution by locally based Shell–British Petroleum, Mobil Oil, and the British American Tobacco Company.[103]

The big trading companies were also compelled to become manufacturers rather than lose local markets. Holt and the United Africa Company led the way. Although Lever Brothers had set up its first factory in Nigeria in the 1920s, the Apapa Soap Company, it was not until the 1950s that the trading firms considered manufacturing a necessary and potentially profitable undertaking. Their innovations were entirely defensive, intended to keep a lucrative market away from potential local competitors, and they caught the right moment for import-substituting industrialization in textiles, cement, and asbestos.[104] By 1960, Lever Brothers and the United Africa Company held all or part of the equity capital of the Nigerian Breweries, Nigerian Plastics and Company, the West African Portland Cement Company, and Raleigh Bicycles, Nigeria. The proportion of UAC capital devoted to industrial operations had risen steadily from 21 percent in 1954–55 to 58 percent in 1963–64.[105] Holt was not far behind.

Alive to nationalist pressures, these foreign firms also sought Nigerian equity investment and brought a small number of Nigerian businessmen onto their boards. They started to Africanize their firms, although the proportion of African employees in the United Africa Company—19 percent in July 1957, for example—was pitifully small. Much of the pressure to Africanize came from a dawning realization of vulnerability to nationalist attack. The United Africa Company feared that immigration laws and quotas "in the hands of an ill-disposed government . . . could be an extremely dangerous weapon as they [the nationalist government] would be in a position to kill our business at any time."[106]

By the time of the independence celebrations in December 1960, Nigeria seemed to have achieved the blend of public and private economic initiatives that the major political and economic leaders in the era of decolonization had favored. But the Nigerian economic institutions were more form than substance. Just as in the political sphere, where the appearance of a smoothly functioning multiparty democracy was belied by underlying realities of ethnic hatred, corruption, and electoral fraud, so in the

---

[103] Memorandum by J. B. Davies, Chairman of UAC, Nigeria, February 6, 1962, UAC Archives, safe 3, shelf 3, file 15.

[104] Peter Kilby, *Industrialization in an Open Economy: Nigeria, 1945–1960* (Cambridge, 1969), p. 54.

[105] Information Division of Unilever, "The Soap Company—Forty Years of Service to Nigeria, March, 1964," Unilever Archives.

[106] Report to the Directors Conference (UAC), February 22, 1963, by G. J. Cole on his visit to Nigeria with A. H. Smith, Unilever Archives.

economic arena the institutional setting was profoundly flawed. Here the state exercised a suffocating influence over large-scale private capital. It had successfully subordinated the indigenous business elite to its purposes and had forced many of the businessmen-politicians who had emerged after World War II to choose politics over business. As for the still-powerful British-based banking, shipping, and trading conglomerates, they too felt the pressure of nationalism and an enhanced and often antagonistic state. The British banks were still powerful as a result of the 1953 banking law, which halted the mushroom-like growth of indigenous banks. They were also cheered by Britain's preeminence in the new Nigerian Central Bank, although they foresaw the growing influence of this institution over the whole financial sector.

Similarly, the shipping conglomerate Elder Dempster protected itself by forming an alliance with national investors and by placing the Nigerian National Shipping Line, funded in part through marketing board surpluses, within the framework of the Conference Shipping Lines. The large export-import houses had made the largest shift, exiting not so gracefully from the no-longer-profitable trading world and entering the arena of manufacturing.

Nigeria had not traversed as long an institutional distance as Egypt, where large-scale private economic activity came to a halt. A full state takeover of the economy had never been a possibility while the country was under British jurisdiction. Nor was there any politician, even among the radical populists, including Awolowo, who sought such far-reaching change. But the intrusion of the state into most economic sectors, mainly through control over marketing surpluses, was not only continuous but also economically and financially distorting. Electoral success counted for more than carefully crafted economic development.

Why had the Nigerian economy moved so decisively to state predominance, well beyond the policy vision first enunciated by the colonial authorities and embraced by most of the nationalist leaders in the period immediately after World War II? At the level of elite politics two factors proved decisive. The first was the decision to create statutory marketing boards for Nigeria's major export crops; in the era of surging world prices for primary products, the boards were endowed with surpluses far beyond what anyone had anticipated at the time. Faute de mieux, these organizations became the primary source of capital accumulation, far better endowed than any of the large-scale business firms operating in the country. The second factor was the accelerating pace of decolonization, which intensified the electoral struggles of the predominantly elite and ethnic parties. Parties exploited their regional financial resources for political purposes.

Nonelite groups played their own role in hurrying decolonization along. The colonial rulers feared worker and radical discontent and believed that the prospect of anticolonial challenges would become greater if there were prolonged pauses in the transfer of power. The British colonial authorities were acutely aware of their own policing and military limitations. One of the reasons that they retained marketing board surpluses was their fear that the distribution of wealth among the people would lead to inflation and stir up political and social turmoil. For their part, the ethnic politicians attempted to broaden their appeal to the Nigerian populace and reached out for electoral support from the young, newly educated, organized labor, and organized farming groups. Their appeals were populist. They emphasized free education, rising standards of living, and enhanced employment opportunities. The programmatic efforts in those areas stretched the resources of the regional governments and cast the private sector in a subordinate role. Thus Nigeria entered the era of independence with a business sector weakened and in disarray.

In numerous ways, the Nigerian nationalists failed to separate their economy from the metropole. Most disappointing of all, given the near agreement among British colonial officials and Nigerian nationalists about the virtues of indigenous industrialization, industrial progress in this decade and a half was greatly attenuated and largely dominated by foreign capital. Four industries accounted for 40 percent of industrial output and 21 percent of industrial employment by the time of independence. These were cigarettes, beer, cement, and textiles, in each of which foreign capital had a strong presence.[107] Most dismaying of all, the Nigerian government's effort, trumpeted so vigorously in the Pioneer Industries Bill, had yielded a weak harvest. On March 31, 1958, only four pioneer industries existed: Kaduna Textiles, Nigerian Plastics, the Nigerian Cement Company, and the Nigerian Tarpaulin Manufacturing Company. Other industrial projects were on the drawing board but had yet to appear, most notably in the fields of asbestos, chemicals, fertilizers, automobile batteries, sacks and bags, glue, rubber products, and metal goods.[108]

According to the economic correspondent of the *Daily Times*, Nigeria suffered from an excess of nationalist enthusiasm and a dearth of practical projects. This comment, made about the National Engineering and Manufacturing Company (NEMCO) of the East, the brainchild of the Azikiwe-Ojukwu economic mission to the United States, held true for many of the indigenous investments. The *Daily Times* added: "It is all nationalism—diverted into the wrong channels. . . . NEMCO now seems

---

[107] Kilby, *Industrialization in an Open Economy*, p. 81.

[108] No. 173, John K. Emmerson to Department of State, USNA, October 20, 1958, 845H.19.

to be taking its place in the queue among the monuments of Nigerian nationalism—monuments, indeed."[109]

The marketing boards had also evolved dramatically. Originally, they were justified on the grounds of price stabilization and were seen as a protection for Nigerian peasants from the exploitative aspirations of the great import-export houses and as intermediaries between Nigeria's producers and outside consumers. But their mammoth surpluses had turned them into a source of political infighting. With the regionalization of Nigerian politics and the rise of regionally based parties, control over the surpluses and their use to favor one's supporters and block one's opponents became almost routine. More important for the well-being of the private sector, a career in government came to seem far more promising to young Nigerians than entry into the precarious world of business.

[109] *Daily Times*, April 18, 1958.

Part Three

KENYA

CHAPTER 9

Development and the Kenyan Private Sector, 1945–1952

THE ECONOMIC and political future of Kenya was a complex and clouded issue in 1945 and remained so until the very moment of independence. Certainly no colonial administrator believed the country ready for political independence or economic autonomy in 1945, and few at that time would have deemed it possible to achieve that result by 1963. The political economy of Kenya reflected the colony's racial hierarchy and historical legacy, especially in contrast to the political economies of Egypt and Nigeria. To begin with, Kenya's large-scale private sector had a relatively large number of limited liability companies (in Nigeria, a few giants dominated export-import, financial, and shipping activities) and was well positioned for political action.

Kenya was in effect a white man's colony, despite the small size of its European population, which was estimated at 23,384 in 1945; the Asian population was roughly 100,000 and the African population more than 5 million. The private sector was, however, dominated by European and Asian capital and almost entirely devoid of African participation. Confined to their reserves or working outside for state and private sector organizations, the African peoples of Kenya occupied only the lower occupational rungs in the private and government worlds.

Nonetheless, the African populations in the densely populated areas and areas where most Europeans lived, such as the coast, the central highlands, and the Lake Nyanza area, had begun to organize themselves for political action. As it was in Nigeria, nationalist politics was still overwhelmingly elite-focused and ethnically organized, and labor groups were only in the early stages of organized activity. Still, labor had the same power it had in Nigeria: at the chokepoints of the economy, notably at the port of Mombasa and the capital city of Nairobi. Although the collision between African ethnic nationalism and settler predominance was hardly expected in colonial quarters, it began to gather strength in the immediate postwar years. The Mau Mau dispute that erupted into prominence in 1952 put the whole of the political economy of Kenya under challenge. The colonial government had to suppress the rebellion militarily and also ensure that African militancy did not undermine the essential elements of the development strategy and the place of the private sector in decolonizing Kenya.

These African challenges were distant rumblings in 1945, however. At war's end, European economic and social dominance seemed well entrenched. Seventy-two percent of the value of Kenya's exports in 1946 came from its four main agricultural crops (coffee, tea, sisal, and pyrethrum), virtually all of which were produced on European-run estates in the highlands.[1] All phases of life in Kenya were racially segregated. The different communities lived, socialized, and were educated separately. Landholding was allocated according to race. The so-called European highlands, encompassing 16,700 square miles or 10,688,000 acres, were available only to European landowners, according to long-standing precedent and numerous official proclamations. The government had indicated before the war its intention to bring in an additional 150 to 250 European settler families, and Governors Henry Moore and Philip Mitchell were fully committed to this goal. The African agricultural areas, organized in reserves, encompassed some 31,000,000 acres.[2]

Although the European settlers had much to be optimistic about as the war drew to a close, the colonial government of Kenya was filled with a sense of dread and foreboding about the future. Colonial officials saw the mass of African peoples living in the reserves as squatters on European estates; in Kenya's burgeoning urban population they saw land hunger and poverty driving the population to political protest. African economic and social dislocation was worsening and far from easy to remedy. The Kamba locations in the Machakos district, all of the Kikuyu districts, and the heavily populated areas around Lake Nyanza inhabited by the Luo- and Abaluhya-speaking peoples bore witness to economic decline and mounting political anger. Colonial administrators were aware that prewar efforts to deal with economic distress, like the notorious destocking campaign carried out in the Kamba reserve in 1938, had succeeded only in intensifying anticolonial resentment. The Machakos district of the Kamba-speaking peoples caused deep concern. An economic survey conducted in 1946 indicated that although the stock-carrying capacity of the reserve was 47,000, the actual number of livestock was closer to 150,000.[3] Colin Maher, the director of agriculture and one of the individuals who had attempted to destock the Kamba reserve before the war, claimed that the

---

[1] Colonial Office, *Annual Report for Kenya*, 1946, pp. 42–43.

[2] C. W. W. Greenridge, Secretary, Anti-Slavery and Aborigines Protection Society, to Stanley, May 5, 1944, PRO CO 533/537/6.

[3] Memorandum on Machakos Reserve for Submission to Harold Tempany, March 26, 1946, PRO CO 533/556/6.

locations he visited in 1945 were in worse condition than they had been in 1938.[4]

Elsewhere, the picture was the same. The African locations of Central and Nyanza provinces were thought to have an excess of 170,000 families.[5] N. Humphrey's studies of Kikuyu families living in the overcrowded Nyeri district indicated similar distress.[6] Yet acute suffering within the African agricultural regions did not dispose the ruling European groups, either settlers or colonial officials, to look to European areas as a safety valve for African peoples. The occasional effort to persuade European land trust committees to lease land to African farmers aroused intense opposition.[7] The accepted approach to the problems of overcrowding and soil deterioration was the "reconditioning" of reserves; the encouragement of efficient African farmers, even possibly the grant of individual landholding rights; and the development of employment-generating secondary industries. Governor Mitchell believed that such an approach would solve the problem of the reserves, which he, in an optimistic moment, believed would not become acute for "some years."[8]

Another administrative concern was African squatter labor. Tensions had been building for decades between African squatters and European landowners, even though Europeans had once welcomed Africans onto their estates as a cheap form of labor. As the Europeans began to impose their view of the squatting relationship on Africans, antagonisms intensified. Governor Moore estimated the number of squatters at 200,000, a number that was considerably higher than the figure quoted officially.[9] And the squatters were not politically passive. They refused to sign labor contracts on Lord Delamere's Soysambu estate and elsewhere, and a group of them living at Olenguruone perfected techniques of opposition that were widely admired and copied.[10]

The influx of large numbers of Africans into the cities produced a final

---

[4] No. 76, Mitchell to Stanley, June 9, 1946, enclosing report of C. Maher, Director of Agriculture, March 15, 1945, PRO CO 533/537/2.

[5] G. M. Roddam, Director of Agriculture, Kenya, to Geoffrey Clay, Colonial Office, February 25, 1952, PRO CO 822/192.

[6] See the essays of N. Humphrey in *Memorandum on Policy in Native Lands*, ed. H. E. Lambert and P. Wyn Harris (Nairobi, 1945).

[7] See the debate in the Kenya Legislative Council, *Debates*, vol. 27, Part 1, July 23, 1947, pp. 17 ff.

[8] No. 193, Mitchell to Lyttleton, November 16, 1951, PRO CO 822/147/1.

[9] No. 174, Moore to Stanley, October 24, 1944, PRO CO 533/537/6.

[10] E. M. Hyde Clarke, Labor Commissioner to Chief Secretary, September 17, 1946, PRO FO 533/549/4. There are many good general studies on African squatters. One should begin with Frank Furedi, *The Mau Mau War in Perspective* (London, 1989); and Tabitha Kanogo, *Squatters and the Roots of Mau Mau* (London, 1987).

reason for alarm among colonial officials. Worries about urban political action were realized in the Mombasa strike of 1947 that threatened to become a colonywide general strike. Mombasa was a tinder box of labor discontent. Its African population had mushroomed from 55,000 in 1939 to more than 100,000 in 1947.[11] Here, too, the government's answer was development planning, with an emphasis on a high-wage permanent work force.[12] Until this new industrialization began to yield results, however, the government was prepared to deal with urban employment in harsh ways. In 1949 the state enacted an ordinance compelling persons without work in the cities to register with a labor exchange office, where they were to be advised of labor opportunities. If the unemployed individuals refused to accept the work offered them, they would be required to participate in a work training program, go into paid national employment, or return to their home areas.[13]

The growth of the cities brought with it an African labor force that began to create the first African trade unions.[14] Concerned about the destabilizing potential of a labor movement, the Kenya government promoted Western-style labor unions that they hoped would develop under the tutelage of British labor leaders and focus on "bread and butter" issues. Although the African labor movement in Kenya had founded only three unions by 1946, the colonial administrators regarded the emerging African labor leaders with hostility. Chege Kibachia, who put together the most effective African labor union at the time—the African Workers Federation—was banished to the Rift Valley after the Mombasa strike of 1947.[15] Of even greater concern to the colonial authorities was the Indian labor leader, Makhan Singh, an avowed Marxist. In 1948 he became the organizing force behind Kenya's labor federation, the East African Trade Union Congress. Like the other labor organizations across the country, it was chronically short of funds and inexpertly administered, but the labor movement was sufficiently worrisome to the colonial officials that they

[11] Anthony Clayton and Donald Savage, *Government and Labor in Kenya, 1895–1973* (London, 1974), p. 274; H. S. Booker and N. M. Deverell, Report on the Economic and Social Background to the Labour Dispute, April 1947, PRO CO 533/545/4.

[12] See Frederick Cooper, *On the African Waterfront: Urban Disorder and the Transformation of Work in Colonial Mombasa* (New Haven, Conn., 1987); Kenya, Information Office, *The Housing of Africans*, 1946, p. 13.

[13] No. 39, Mitchell to Creech Jones, April 11, 1949, PRO CO 533/556/9.

[14] On the trade union movement in Kenya, one should refer to Richard Sandbrook, *Proletarians and African Capitalism: The Kenya Case, 1962–1970* (Cambridge, 1975); Richard Sandbrook and Robin Cohen, eds., *The Development of an African Working Class* (London, 1975); and Alice Amsden, *International Firms and Labour in Kenya, 1945–1970* (London, 1971).

[15] See the file PRO CO 533/544/5.

arrested Singh and deported him to the distant location of Lokitaung. He remained in detention until 1960.[16]

All of these factors—deterioration of African reserves, growth of squatter numbers, tension between squatters and European farmers, urbanization, and labor agitation—undergirded the thinking of the colonial administration of Kenya as it devised economic plans for the postwar period. A heated debate occurred over the most effective methods of promoting economic growth—whether to encourage agricultural expansion, whether to stress European areas or African reserves, and whether to diversify the economy and stimulate local industries. Even more hotly debated was the issue of the role of the state in promoting economic growth. The one area of consensus within the elite was a sense of urgency about economic development—a belief that without economic progress Kenya would be unable to avert political and social turmoil.

The debate on development raged between 1945 and 1952, coinciding with the governorship of Philip Mitchell. Mitchell arrived in Kenya with a wealth of African experience, having previously served in Tanganyika and Uganda.[17] Although he was said to share the Labour Party's interest in sponsoring Afrocentric policies, he was, if nothing else, a colonial racist of the old school. His vision of the future of Kenya, which he liked to characterize as multiracial, was impregnated with stereotypical racial ideas from an earlier era. In his view, Kenya would remain a colonial possession for the foreseeable future, stratified along racial lines. Although he favored more intermingling of the communities, he expected the European contribution, official and settler, to remain dominant.

At the core of Mitchell's approach to Kenya's future was a deeply held belief that wide disparities in cultural attitudes demarcated the racial communities of the country. The political life of Kenya, he recognized, had been organized on a communal and racial basis. "Whatever may be the theoretical objections to that, I think that at this stage it is wise and wholesome that it should be so." The African populations must be subordinate to the Europeans and the incorporation of Africans into Kenya's electoral life, he believed, to be well off in the future, "unless a very restricted franchise is adopted."[18] The Europeans fully deserved their commanding economic and political position. As regards their possession of large tracts of land in the highlands, Mitchell was sure that the Europeans made more efficient use of the land than African and Asian com-

[16] Colonial Office Minute by E. Parry, January 12, 1950, PRO CO 533/561/14.
[17] See David Throup, *Economic and Social Origins of Mau Mau, 1945–53* (London, 1987), pp. 33–62.
[18] PEM 32/45, Mitchell to Creasy, August 29, 1945, PRO CO 533/537/14.

munities did. While admitting African needs for additional land and hoping to lease fringe areas of the highlands to land-hungry African communities, Mitchell was unabashed in his defense of European control over the highlands. African population density "does not alter the fact that the land we have made is our land by right—by right of achievement," he asserted.[19]

Mitchell was a political gradualist. He foresaw the mixing of populations and the devolution of power to local groups occurring over a long time period. "For as far ahead as it is worth thinking now, the British, whether in Great Britain or Africa, have got to provide what has been described as the steel framework of the building. . . . The guardian in the collective sense must in some degree include all the British living in East Africa, for it would be disastrous to drive them [European settlers] back upon a narrow and selfish concentration upon their communal and sectarian interests, which would then inevitably involve hostility between them and the native tribes." He scoffed at ideas concerning "the end of colonialism or the desire for national freedom" and reminded his critics that East Africa at the turn of the century had been in a primitive state, possessing no harbor, no roads, no railway, and no wheeled transportation. The deadline for the political autonomy in Kenya "such as that of Southern Rhodesia based on an electoral principle which all the communities and His Majesty's Government and Parliament would accept is so far distant as to be out of the picture for us today."[20]

If Mitchell admired European achievement and patronized African peoples, he was contemptuous of the Asian contributions to East African progress. To his mind, the Asians suffered from a persecution complex, and he compared them to the Jews of Eastern Europe. He described the Asians as clinging in an aloof way to their communal traditions, weighed down with corruption.

Not surprisingly, given this racist orientation, Mitchell endeavored to expand the number of European settler families and associate them closely with the governance of the country. He reaffirmed the prewar plans to bring a new wave of settlers to the country, and he established two separate settlement schemes, one for European emigrants of substantial means (£1,500 to £2,000 in assets) who therefore required little governmental assistance, and a tenancy settlement program designed for families of lesser wealth (£700 to £800 in assets) to whom the state would provide financial support.[21] The program itself was not as successful as Mitchell hoped. The unassisted part attracted almost no one, and

---

[19] No. 537, Mitchell to Colonial Office, July 1, 1946, PRO CO 533/549/2.
[20] PEM 11/48, Mitchell to Creech Jones, December 11, 1948, PRO CO 533/540/4.
[21] Colonial Office Note, February 10, 1945, PRO CO 533/534/10.

the tenancy scheme brought far fewer families than the target number of 500. Yet the settler population increased during Mitchell's governorship.[22]

Mitchell's program for preventing African protest was two-pronged. Its first dimension, political reform, was hopelessly out of date, based as it was on devolving more power on the European settlement community. Among his numerous political reforms, the one that most antagonized the Asian and African populations was his elevation of F. W. Cavendish-Bentinck, Kenya's most prominent settler farmer and an elected member of the Legislative Council, to be head of the powerful Department of Agriculture, Animal Husbandry, and Natural Resources and member of the governing Executive Council. The appointment brought an outpouring of discontent from Asian and African communities. A. B. Patel, the leading Indian member in the Legislative Council, much admired by the British, opposed Mitchell's entire scheme, contending that the changes enlarged the powers of the Europeans at the expense of others. Of Cavendish-Bentinck, Patel said, "He has perfectly fixed views on many important questions which are pro-European and definitely against the views held by Indians, Arabs, and Africans."[23] Pritam went even further, claiming that Cavendish-Bentinck was dedicated "to see[ing] that the Indians are eliminated from all walks of life."[24]

The second prong of Mitchell's attack on social and economic problems was economic and far more progressive. Believing that widespread economic progress was the only sure way to prevent political protest, Mitchell created the autonomous Development and Reconstruction Authority, possessing its own budget and under the direction of the chief secretary. The new Development and Reconstruction Authority would obtain its funds externally from loans and wherever possible grants-in-aid, though it was also expected to receive a modest annual contribution from Kenya's ordinary revenue, projected at £300,000 per year. All income was earmarked for long-term, income-generating development projects. Mitchell portrayed the Development and Reconstruction Authority as the final antidote to African lawlessness, land deterioration, squatter despair, rural landlessness, and urban unemployment.[25]

Mitchell wanted the new Development and Reconstruction Authority to consist of three high-ranking personages. He designated the chief secretary as head of the authority; he also appointed the director of the East African Railways and Harbors because he expected the expansion of the transportation system to be crucial to Kenya's economic progress; his

[22] Kenya, Land Utilization and Settlement, *A Statement of Government Policy* (Nairobi, 1945), PRO CO 533/534/11.

[23] Kenya, Legislative Council, *Debates*, July 18, 1945, pp. 41–42.

[24] Ibid., p. 140.

[25] No. 141, Mitchell to Colonial Office, February 28, 1945, PRO CO 533/537/14.

third appointment was Alfred Vincent, an important Kenyan businessman and political personage, director of the Motor Mart Corporation (an automobile distributing agency), and an oft-elected member of the Legislative Council from Nairobi. Vincent's appointment reassured the European business community, who presumed that the private sector would accordingly play an instrumental role in Kenya's development program. But it aroused the antipathy of Asian leaders, who saw the selection of Vincent as further evidence of the devolution of power to Europeans.

The immediate postwar years, then, were full of feverish planning efforts. With the Development and Reconstruction Authority in place, the Kenyan government authorities began to debate development priorities and the mechanisms by which economic goals would be realized. Thus, in Kenya, as in Nigeria and Egypt, a series of debates took place within the confines of the ruling official and nonofficial elites. These discussions revealed the power splits within the elite group and made clear the degree of worry that the elite had about the capacity of lower classes to disrupt the polity. In contrast to Nigeria and Egypt, the ruling groups in Kenya in 1945 believed that they were not under great pressure from African groups to dissolve foreign capital; yet within the colonial bureaucracy itself, there were some well-positioned individuals who favored a powerful and interventionist role for the state in economic affairs. Their vision encountered opposition from Governor Mitchell and well-organized business groups, who wanted private capital to be the engine of economic change and who favored productionist strategies of economic development rather than programs that stressed socially conscious policies.

As the war drew to a close, the state bureaucrats who favored a statist approach to economic problems, most notably H. H. Storey and Charles Lockhart, both of whom had served on the East African Industrial Council during the war, began to promote an "evolution toward a limited industrialization." Lockhart and Storey were deeply committed to the public sector and dubious of the private sector's capacity to generate structural economic change. Storey, for one, thought East Africa so lacking in natural resources as to require an ironclad alliance between big government and big business. Although he believed that some rural industries might come into existence, "few can be expected to compete with the larger-scale factory to which we must look for major developments." Storey saw a bright future in East Africa for food processing, textiles, cement, ceramics, fertilizers, sisal processing, and a heavy chemical industry and wanted the government to play a leading role in their creation.[26]

---

[26] Memorandum by H. H. Storey to East African Industrial Council, November 6, 1944, PRO CO 582/579/1.

Besides industrialization, another emphasis stemming from wartime exigencies was economic planning. H. Thorley Dyer, an adviser on town planning to the Kenyan government, was particularly enamored of the planning concept. In his view, "This process of planning must obtain in all modern countries if they are to avoid the *waste* and *muddle* that has characterized the laissez-faire growth of industrial and agrarian communities alike" (emphasis added). Citing the Tennessee Valley Authority, the Ruhr industrial complex, and the five-year plans of the Soviet Union as successful cases of planning, he recommended that Kenya establish "a large development fund repayable over a long period at a low rate of interest."[27]

As laid out in British-ruled Africa, development plans customarily employed a time frame of ten years, concentrated almost exclusively on government activities rather than private sector initiatives, and were concerned with how to raise funds rather than how to overcome deficiencies in goods and manpower. The Kenyan development plan, published in 1946, was typical of such colonial plans. Its overarching goal was "to increase the national income of Kenya in the shortest space of time so as to raise as quickly as possible the standard of living of the majority of inhabitants."[28] It called for the expenditure of £15.58 million between 1946 and 1955, with the bulk of the funds devoted to soil conservation, agricultural rehabilitation, education, public health, water supplies, and rail and harbor modernization.[29] Unlike Nigeria's development plans, where the emphasis was squarely on health, education, and social and economic infrastructure and where economic gains were not expected to occur immediately, the Kenya plan was expected to yield quick and tangible material improvements that would spread throughout the colonial population.

Between 1946 and the outbreak of Mau Mau, the government moved steadily ahead to implement the plan. As it did, it revised the costs upward. By 1952 the total price tag had grown to £41.5 million, of which £18 million had already been expended and £23.5 million was scheduled to be spent between 1952 and 1955.[30] No doubt £41.5 million spread over ten years was an inadequate sum for tackling the accumulating social and economic problems that undergirded Mau Mau. But these amounts were significant sums. Nearly all of the funds were to be raised externally,

[27] Development and Reconstruction Authority, Technical Organization for Physical Planning in Kenya, Memorandum on Recommendations by H. Thorley, Adviser on Town Planning, to the Governor of Kenya, February 1946, PRO CO 533/552/2.

[28] Kenya, *Interim Report on Development* (Nairobi, 1945), p. 4, PRO CO 533/536/2.

[29] Preliminary Note on Postwar Development by Mitchell, January 15, 1945, PRO CO 533/536/4.

[30] No. 182/52, Mitchell to Lyttleton, January 29, 1952, PRO CO 822/301.

mostly from the London money market. By 1950 the Development and Reconstruction Authority was spending £3 to £4 million per year.[31] Kenya's success in obtaining a loan of £6 million in 1952 made its administrators confident of being able to raise the remainder of the funds and filled them with optimism about the political and economic future of the country.[32] Yet, at the very moment that the 1952 loan was being finalized, Kenya was plunged into the Mau Mau war.

Advocates of the private sector were skeptical about development planning in general and especially critical of any proposals that elevated the power of the state at their expense. Two critical issues occupied their attention in this period; and their resolution in favor of the private sector proved altogether decisive in curbing the influence of public sector advocates and affirming the primacy of the private sector in the Kenyan development effort. The two issues were the sources of capital investment and the role of the state in fostering new industries. The business community in Kenya began its quarrel with state officials over how much of the development effort should be paid for out of local taxation and how much from foreign sources. For years, taxation policy had pitted the government against the European and Asian settler communities, and when the Kenyan government proposed to spend massively on development projects the tax question became an even bigger battle between the government and leaders of the Asian and European communities. In nearly every budgetary session of the Legislative Council between 1945 and 1952 the administration and the "unofficials" clashed over taxation. The European and Asian unofficials complained that the panoply of taxes—the income tax, company tax, and excess profits tax—burdened the most dynamic members of Kenyan society and inhibited investment and development.[33] Using their power in the Legislative Council, European and Asian unofficials persuaded the administration to bring in a South African official to conduct an inquiry and make recommendations. The controversial Plewman report recommended in favor of the private interests, calling on the state to reduce direct and indirect taxes and to rely on externally raised loans for its development program.[34]

The second issue in the Kenyan development debate—the degree of state intervention in an evolving economy—also pitted European and Asian business leaders and settler agriculturalists against the proponents of an enlarged state. The Labour Party's accession to power in Britain in

[31] Rankine to Griffiths, March 16, 1950, PRO CO 533/562/5.

[32] Kenya, Legislative Council, *Debates*, vol. 37, May 10, 1950, pp. 53 ff.

[33] See the minutes of the General Meetings of the Nairobi Chamber of Commerce, vol. 13, November 19, 1946, and January 21, 1947.

[34] See the file PRO CO 533/539/1 for the Wood and Plewman reports; and no. 163, Rankine to Creech Jones, December 1, 1948, PRO CO 822/124/9.

1945 and its broad program of nationalization provided intellectual and political support for the state bureaucrats who championed heavy state involvement and who were suspicious of laissez-faire capitalism.

This debate commenced with the publication in 1945 of a British government policy statement on mining in colonial territories. This brief document, intended primarily as a general guide to mining policy, expounded a more general perspective on the virtues of state enterprises and the defects of private enterprises in bringing material benefits to the rank and file of colonial populations.[35] Issued by a party favoring nationalized industries at home and carrying criticisms of the intentions and benefits of private enterprise, the colonial paper aroused intense suspicion among organized business groups in colonial territories, even in colonies like Kenya that did not have a large mining sector. The business community there regarded the document as a statement of general economic purpose from the Labour Party and a threat to the autonomy of all colonial business firms. The Kenyan business groups responded with alacrity to the challenge of the colonial paper. In the Management Committee of the Nairobi Chamber of Commerce, Nairobi's leading business figures condemned the policy and called on the larger chamber to pass a resolution against it.[36] In the full meeting of the Nairobi Chamber of Commerce, not only did the members criticize the paper, but they recorded their opposition to any effort to nationalize colonial industries. One speaker worried about state enterprises evolving "into vast welfare organizations for indigenous populations" and argued in favor of "free enterprise to the full." A few of the delegates defended the paper on the grounds that some industries could be run more effectively by the state—public utilities as well as mines—but a final vote of thirty to five against the colonial paper revealed the widespread opposition of the business elite of Nairobi to any nationalization program.[37]

The debate in Parliament and the press over the colonial paper prefigured a series of very specific battles in which private sector advocates sought to repulse the efforts of the state to take over key economic sectors and to become the leading edge of economic transformation. In the process, the Asian and European business groups also endeavored to root out the most determined public sector advocates from the colonial bureaucracy and replace them with individuals sympathetic to the business community. In striking contrast to Nigeria, where by 1952 the public sector had become a dynamic force as a result of the creation of the

---

[35] Great Britain, Colonial Office, Colonial Paper no. 206 (London, 1945).

[36] Minutes of the Management Committee of the Nairobi Chamber of Commerce, vol. 23, February 19, 1946.

[37] Nairobi Chamber of Commerce, Minutes of Meetings, vol. 13, March 18, 1947.

statutory marketing boards with their huge surpluses, in Kenya the state witnessed a whittling away of its sphere of action.

The first economic issue to be dealt with was the provision of electrical supplies throughout Kenya. In 1945 all of East Africa obtained its electrical power through a private joint stock company called the East African Power and Lighting Company. East African Power and Lighting had been established in 1922 when Nairobi Electric and Power Lighting Company merged with the Mombasa Power and Lighting Company. In 1924 Balfour, Beatty, and Company, a London-based engineering firm with corporate and consulting interests in public utilities all over the world, became the managers and consulting engineers for the East African utility. Although Balfour, Beatty took no equity position in the company, it exercised direct managerial control over the firm, which was in fact owned by a widely dispersed and ineffective group of shareholders. According to critics, the firm's board paid Balfour, Beatty high fees for its advice and gave large commissions to investment underwriters whenever it increased its equity capital, as it did regularly between 1922 and 1944. During that span the equity capital of East African Power and Lighting rose from £170,000 to £1,056,250.[38]

In addition to having questionable financial policies and heavy financial charges, the firm was run in a cumbersome fashion. It had no fewer than three separate boards of directors—one in Nairobi and two in London, the directors of whom drew large fees. Despite these obstacles East African Power and Lighting had expanded its operation from its base in Nairobi and Mombasa to become a near-monopoly supplier of electricity for Uganda, Tanganyika, and Kenya. Consumer dissatisfaction with the company was rife, reaching a zenith during the latter years of the war. In Kenya the main voices of discontent came from the sisal processing plant owners around Thika and Kiambu. Corporate leaders there complained that the electrical supplies to their companies were unreliable and expensive. E. D. Rutherfoord, head of Swift, Rutherfoord, and Company, a leading sisal processor and one of the large sisal plantation owners in the region, contended that East African Power and Lighting discriminated against the sisal industry. According to an agreement forced on the sisal industry, the power company had the right to disconnect sisal plants during peak usage hours and was obligated to provide electricity only at night. This arrangement, invoked only exceptionally at first, had become the norm by the latter years of the war, with the result that sisal growers and processors had to operate their factories at night. In a letter to the colonial secretary, Oliver Stanley, Rutherfoord catalogued the failings of the firm and took the unusual step of demanding that the East African

[38] Report on East African Power and Lighting Company by A. O. Cosgrove, 1944, PRO CO 533/533/4.

governments nationalize the whole electrical network in the region, citing South Africa as a precedent.[39]

In response to these criticisms, the government of Kenya formed two investigative commissions—the Cosgrove Commission of 1944 and the Westlake Commission of 1947—both of which found massive deficiencies in the generation of electrical power in East Africa. Both reported that the provision of cheap and abundant power was crucial to industrial and agricultural expansion and questioned East African Power and Lighting's capacity to play this role. The first report, written by A. O. Cosgrove, an electrical engineer, took note of the widespread power failures in Nairobi and Mombasa in 1943, criticized the firm for allowing its Mombasa plant to deteriorate, and pointed out that a company that generated most of its power by means of hydroelectric procedures was certain to experience acute shortages during the dry season.[40]

The Westlake report of 1947 was even more censorious. C. R. Westlake reviewed the bad financial arrangements of the earlier decades and the generous fees paid to consultants and board members. He upbraided the firm for placing the interests of its shareholders first, and said that "from the technical point of view the running and general supervision of their plant was an absolute disgrace." Not surprisingly, he called on the three governments of East Africa to nationalize electrical supplies.[41]

Uganda accepted Westlake's recommendation. Under the governorship of John Hall, who was well known in business circles for his suspicion of private capital, the government took over the East African Power and Lighting Company. In Kenya a combination of private sector pressure and administrative preference saved the firm. Leaders of Kenya's private sector rallied the rank and file of the chambers of commerce throughout the country against nationalization. Of critical importance in this campaign was the appointment in 1943 of A. D. J. "Don" Small as head of East African Power and Lighting. A person of energy and resourcefulness, Small promised to put the affairs of the company in order and to raise the necessary capital so that the firm could respond to Kenya's development needs. Realizing the importance of good public relations, Small played a prominent role in the Nairobi business community, often serving as head of the Nairobi Chamber of Commerce. Using his influence in the Nairobi Chamber of Commerce, he persuaded its members to record their opposition to a state takeover of the electrical supplies of the country.[42]

[39] E. D. Rutherfoord of Swift, Rutherfoord, and Company to Stanley, November 6, 1943, PRO CO 533/533/3.

[40] Brief Summary of a Report, March 7, 1944, by A. O. Cosgrove, PRO CO 533/533/4.

[41] Colonial Office Minute by P. A. Carter, April 14, 1947, PRO CO 852/844/1.

[42] Minutes of the Management Committee of the Nairobi Chamber of Commerce, vol. 23, February 19, 1946.

One of the persons Small won over to his side was the Kenya governor, Philip Mitchell. Despite pressure from administrators eager for the state to assume significant responsibilities for the economy, Mitchell rejected pleas to nationalize electrical supplies. In replying to the public sector advocates, he distanced himself from the nationalizing measures being carried out in Britain at the time. He stated that "he could not agree to expropriation of the company as part of a *socialist* policy without a strong technical report" and added that "the Kenya government could not act as though it had just successfully fought a general election" (emphasis added).[43] Mitchell was willing to go no further than the creation of an oversight power board, which, however, did not become a forceful regulatory body until a decade later.[44]

The second pressing state–private sector question was what to do with a cluster of industries that the East African governments had established during World War II in order to manufacture products in short supply in the region. Those industries were eventually overseen by the East African Industrial Management Board, a body that functioned as a corporate holding company entirely in the public sector. Were these companies to remain in the public sector, perhaps to become the leading wedge of a state-driven form of industrialization, or were they to be devolved into private hands as their critics insisted? Certainly the business community viewed the management board as the thin end of a nationalizing effort, all the more so because it was headed by the statist Charles Lockhart. The Kenyan business community was determined to dismantle the board and force the sale or closing of its enterprises.

The threat the East African Industrial Managenent Board posed to the private sector could not be minimized. In the view of its leading advocate, Charles Lockhart, two types of industry were appropriate at this stage of East Africa's industrial progress. One, the processing of raw materials for export, was already well established in private hands and needed little attention. But the other, what he and his colleagues referred to as secondary industries, was in its infancy and capable of considerable expansion. Lockhart believed that the state should play the pioneering role in assisting and perhaps even establishing textile, footwear, pottery, glassware, soap, caustic soda, sulfuric acid, cement, food canning, match, and paint industries.[45]

Private sector representatives were disturbed that the East African In-

[43] No. 20A, Notes on Meeting held at Government House on May 3, 1946, attended by the Governor, Member for Development and Reconstruction, Chief Secretary, Acting Chief Secretary, Financial Secretary, and Postmaster General, KNA State House 4/788.

[44] No. 96, Mitchell to Creech Jones, September 27, 1949, PRO CO 822/148/3.

[45] Minutes of the Third Meeting of the East African Industrial Council, July 25, 1945, PRO CO 852/573/5.

dustrial Management Board already was operating plants in many different sectors, including insecticides, fiber boards, vegetable oils, bricks, pottery, and caustic soda; although none of the plants was large, the industries themselves had significant potential for expansion. The Nairobi Chamber of Commerce organized the opposition. In a meeting in February 1945 its members debated a motion deprecating the activities of the board "in so far as they affect established business by competitive selling and by impinging upon available supplies of materials. . . . The Chamber requests the East African governments to cancel this branch of the East African Management Board's activities."[46] During the discussion L. M. Gibson, chairman of the local manufacturing section of the chamber, complained that the board had promised to confine its activities to research and exploration, the creation of subeconomic projects, and pilot projects and had renounced any intention of running enterprises that the private sector could develop. He was alarmed that the board had entered the edible oil industry, which he claimed had a rosy future for private enterprise.

Although the chamber did not pass the motion, it maintained pressure on the state. In 1947 the East African Industrial Management Board sold off its three most profitable enterprises: the insecticide plant, the fiber board plant, and the vegetable oil plant. Finding no bidders for the other firms, however, the state invited the Colonial Development Corporation of Britain to assist in expanding the remaining plants. By 1949 the East African Industrial Management Board had become East African Industries Ltd, its share capital divided between the government of Kenya (£150,000) and the Colonial Development Corporation (£300,000).[47] The state presented plans to expand the capital of East African Industries to £2 million and to establish factories for the manufacture of edible oils, bricks, and sulfuric acid. These proposals brought renewed protests from the private sector in 1950.[48] The Nairobi Chamber of Commerce restated its complaint that East African Industries was violating earlier promises not to compete with private businesses.[49]

Under pressure, H. L. Adams and V. Maddison, ranking officials at the Ministry of Commerce and Industry, set in motion a search for private investors to buy out the government's stake in East African Industries.[50]

[46] Nairobi Chamber of Commerce, Minutes of the General Meetings, vol. 13, February 20, 1945.

[47] No. 1/1, Minutes of the Board of Directors of East African Industries Ltd, May 16, 1949, KNA MCI 6/445.

[48] No. 102, H. W. Howell to Member for Commerce and Industry, October 13, 1950, KNA MCI 6/445.

[49] Nairobi Chamber of Commerce, Minutes of General Meetings, vol. 14, July 19, 1949.

[50] No. 159, Executive Council of the Ministry of Commerce and Industry, March 9, 1951, KNA MCI 6/445.

Eventually the government persuaded the Unilever Corporation to invest capital and to become the primary shareholder and managing partner of the enterprise, thus bringing to an end this brief experiment in state industrialization.

Not only were these efforts at nationalization defeated, but during Mitchell's tenure as governor, Kenya's development program was forcefully oriented toward the private sector. What surely pleased the business community was that its representatives repulsed the challenge of the public sector advocates—Storey; Troughton, the financial secretary after the war; and Lockhart—and persuaded the government to replace them with persons committed to the private sector, some of whom were even drawn from the business classes themselves.

In 1948 the Kenyan unofficial members in the Legislative Council had pressed the government to create a separate Ministry of Commerce and Industry. They had succeeded in having Arthur Hope-Jones designated as the first head of the new ministry.[51] He remained Kenya's minister of commerce and industry through most of the era of decolonization and was always an energetic supporter of private enterprise. Hope-Jones had acquired an interest in economics as a student at Christ's Church College, Cambridge University, though he had not majored in the subject. During a postgraduate year there he studied under John Maynard Keynes and J. H. Clapham, the economic historian, and at the close of his fellowship year he published a study on English taxation during the Napoleonic era, which contained a flattering introduction from his mentor, Professor Clapham. During World War II he served in the British Ministry of Food and then became an adviser to Anglo-Iranian Oil. Upon moving to Kenya he was attached to the Development and Reconstruction Authority as its first economic and commercial adviser. In the Kenyan Legislative Council his was a steady voice for industrial development. The reward he received for supporting European settler delegates on private sector matters was the leadership of the new Ministry of Commerce and Industry.[52]

Of even greater importance to the private sector as Kenya entered the 1950s was the appointment of Ernest Vasey as minister of finance. Vasey arrived in his new office under troubled circumstances and was to have his hand on Kenya's economic tiller during the whole of the Mau Mau years. Born in 1901 and self-educated, Vasey had emigrated to Kenya in 1935, where he pursued a career in business rather than farming. Drawing on a knowledge of acting, gained in his youth, he became a partner in

[51] Kenya, Legislative Council, *Debates*, vol. 28, January 14, 1948, pp. 818 ff, and vol. 30, July 15, 1948, pp. 91 ff.

[52] No. 22, Extract from Kenya, Legislative Council, *Debates*, November 13, 1945, KNA MCI 4/5.

the playhouse cinema in Nairobi and later the managing director of the New Theatre Ltd, which was described as "the most important motion picture syndicate in British East Africa."[53] As the European community began to recognize his administrative and leadership talents, he rose in the political sphere. Election to the Nairobi Town Council was followed by stints as mayor of the city of Nairobi. In 1945 he entered the Kenyan Legislative Council and remained a member until 1959. From 1949 until 1959 he served on the Executive Council of Kenya.[54]

Vasey was a man of unimpeachable integrity and fierce independent judgment. Although he distanced himself from the settler landowning and farming community, he served on the boards of numerous limited-liability companies and believed that the economic and political future of Kenya could only be salvaged through the effort of large-scale businesses. Despite having no formal training in economics, he proved remarkably adept in finance, and it was in this arena that he made his most decisive contributions to Kenya's political economy. Still, his political preferences were hard to predict. Early in his parliamentary career, he described himself as a socialist, despite membership on the boards of numerous business firms. The British colonial officials in Kenya and Britain admired him for his liberal sentiments, noting that he was one of the first European unofficials to call for power sharing with Africans.[55]

Vasey's multiracialism and willingness to bring Africans and Asians into the political arena did not mean that he was free of the biases common to Europeans at the time. Although later in his life he developed close ties with the Chandaria family, one of the most influential Asian business families, he could be as critical and dismissive of Asian ability as any other European in Kenya. In a conversation he had with Creech Jones, Vasey opined that the only person in the Asian community of Kenya worthy to serve on the Executive Council was A. B. Patel.[56] Vasey believed that he owed his first election to the Legislative Council to the support of European workers and civil servants and not to the favor of the business community, which regarded his economic policies as left-leaning and his political agenda as radical. The British colonial officials agreed, characterizing him as not "a red hot settler."[57]

Vasey's maiden speech in the Legislative Council, delivered on November 27, 1945, revealed a passion for economics and development. He

---

[53] No. 1356, Willard Quincy Stanton to Secretary of State, February 19, 1948, USNA 848T.4061.

[54] See interview with Ernest Vasey, June 21, 1969, conducted by Bruce Berman, Vasey Papers.

[55] Note on Election to Legislative Council, 1945, Vasey Papers.

[56] Creech Jones to Mitchell, November 22, 1948, PRO CO 533/540/4.

[57] Mitchell to Cohen, July 14, 1949, PRO CO 533/540/4.

framed his remarks around Keynesian themes, exhorting the government to build up financial surpluses during times of prosperity so that it could expend them when the economy slowed. He spoke enthusiastically about the new Development and Reconstruction Authority, but he made it clear that this body should draw its fund from external loans, not local taxation, and that the government of Kenya should not hesitate to look beyond the British Treasury and the London money market for financial support.[58]

Vasey entered the Executive Council in Kenya in 1949 as the member for local government but found his milieu when he became member for finance and financial secretary in early 1952. He replaced V. G. Matthews, who resigned after a bitter dispute with unofficial Europeans over the state's fiscal policies.[59] Although Vasey was far from the ideal choice of many unofficials, particularly those from the European agricultural districts, his appointment was viewed as a positive step toward the devolution of power to the European settlers, who at the time controlled two of Kenya's most vital ministries: agriculture and finance. The settlers abated their opposition and passed the budget, but by the time Vasey had settled into his office the Mau Mau uprising was under way, and Kenya faced a whole new set of financial challenges.

By 1952, then, major policy debates had been decided in favor of the private sector in Kenya. This result appears all the more difficult to fathom when compared with Nigeria, where the public sector emerged as a more powerful force after similar debates involving a similar constellation of elite group contestants. Indeed, in Kenya the state bureaucracy had more determined proponents of a statist approach in the form of Lockhart, Thorley, and Storey; and Nigeria had politically more powerful business firms in the United Africa Company, Barclays, the Bank of British West Africa, and Elder Dempster. Nonetheless, the differences stemmed in large measure from the dissimilar structures of power within the ruling elites of the two countries, the intended and unintended consequences of critical policy decisions, and the role that colonized peoples played in shaping the policies of the ruling groups.

To begin, then, with differences in structures of power with the ruling elite, the large-scale Nigerian business community did, of course, have massive financial and political resources, privileged access to state officials, and a seemingly unchallengeable position in the private sector. But state officials and nationalist leaders alike viewed these oligopolies with

---

[58] Kenya, Legislative Council, *Debates*, vol. 23, November 27, 1945, pp. 305 ff.

[59] Kenya, Legislative Council, *Debates*, vol. 48, December 20, 1951, p. 1407; and vol. 49, February 26, 1952, p. 221.

intense suspicion. The large British firms were unable to rally much political and propagandist support for their causes, even within the British colonial bureaucracy of Nigeria. In Kenya, the large-scale firms were not so gigantic and therefore not seen as so threatening. They were unlikely to have an economic stranglehold on the Kenyan economy. Moreover, two influential unofficial groups rallied to the support of large-scale European business in Kenya at critical moments in the policy debates: the Asian community and the settler farmers, largely because of a shared suspicion of the state and a preference for private initiatives. In addition, the advocates of a procapitalist approach found an invaluable and decisive backer in Governor Mitchell and almost no opposition from rising African nationalism, which was virtually silent on all economic matters, except land policy.

Second, the marketing board debate was hardly conceivable in Kenya, given the already extensive influence European farmers had on the various price-setting and marketing agencies of the state. The power of the settlers made it impossible to withhold large sums of money from settler farmers, however much the state might have wanted to pursue such a policy. In contrast, in Nigeria the debate on marketing boards was not at first focused on the accumulation and uses of board surpluses. This development was largely unintended, the result of skyrocketing world prices for Nigeria's primary products. But these surpluses inexorably enhanced the power of the state in relation to private business groups.

Finally, in Nigeria colonial officials believed that state policies, especially in health and education, were vital to diminishing political tensions and the rise of anticolonial sentiments. The perspective of the official mind in Kenya was quite the opposite. There, officialdom, no doubt bowing to settler pressures and ignoring the real challenge that Africans could pose, preferred increased production as the supposed dissolvent of political discontent. British ministers in Kenya were confident that the private sector would be the agent of structural economic transformation and would produce rising standards of living for all segments of the population.

KENYA'S EVOLVING PRIVATE SECTOR

With the political debate about development in the immediate postwar years having been resolved in favor of the private sector, the next question was what kind of a private sector the Kenyan business and government leaders wished to create. As in Nigeria, the overwhelming consensus of the colonial administrators was that it should be dominated by large-scale, limited-liability companies, drawing the bulk of their investment capital and managerial talent from Britain.

Preference for overseas capital originated in the assumption that Kenya lacked a dynamic business elite, well-developed business organizations, and substantial investment capital. Thus, the planners expected that new enterprises would have to come from foreign investment and that the task of the Kenyan state was to make the country attractive to foreign investors. To this end, Kenyan administrators tried to create a generous taxation code and effective protective tariffs. Just after World War II, efforts to raise money locally for a government loan seemed to bear out the assumption that little in the way of risk capital could be generated from within. The British officials were painfully aware that Kenya, unlike the more developed African economies of Egypt and South Africa, had no local money market and only the rudiments of a stock exchange. According to findings of the Nairobi Chamber of Commerce in 1947, only fourteen locally based companies were quoted on Nairobi's primitive local exchange, and in none of them were shares actively traded. In the city of Nairobi only three or four brokers were available to assist investors interested in buying and selling stocks and bonds.[60]

In their preference for British capital, however, the Kenyan planners grossly underestimated the potential of Asian businesses. Their misjudgment stemmed as much from faulty information as from racial prejudice. In the first place, it was difficult for colonial officials to obtain data on Asian enterprises, so self-contained and secretive were they. The typical Asian enterprise was a private, family-based company that kept its own records and published no information on its activities. Asian entrepreneurs eschewed joint stock limited-liability companies, which were favored by European investors and managers, distrusting the very features that attracted Europeans to the joint stock company: widely dispersed bodies of shareholders, annual reports, information about profits and losses, and regular dividend payments. The shares of Asian firms, in contrast, remained in the hands of a few family members, and the profitability of enterprises was known only to an inner circle of trusted individuals, certainly not to government officials. Not surprisingly, the government was inadequately aware of the assets that had accumulated in the Asian business community during the war, and it was taken by surprise when Asian leaders pioneered many of the firms about which the government officials had been most optimistic.

The Plewman report of 1947 purported to give data on the wealth of the different communities; but it badly underestimated Asian wealth. Ac-

---

[60] Nairobi Chamber of Commerce, Minutes of General Meetings, vol. 13, September 2, 1947.

cording to its findings, based on Kenyan tax records, most of Kenya's wealth was in European hands. Persons of European descent paid £7,576,058 in income tax in 1944; non-Europeans paid only £1,280,565. Whereas 155 Europeans living in Kenya had incomes exceeding £2,000 only fifty-six non-Europeans did. The same disparities in wealth were found in the business sector, where 298 resident European firms paid £1,497,391 in taxes and 139 nonresident European firms paid £1,224,061. In contrast, 119 non-European resident companies, mainly Asian companies, paid only £160,332 in taxes and five nonresident non-European firms paid only £10,355. These figures depicted the European element, both individuals and companies, as the basis of Kenya's wealth, with only minor contributions deriving from Asian and African groups.[61]

Although the administrators of Kenya were aware that the Plewman figures had to be used with caution, because underreporting of income was common in Kenya, the government displayed little faith in the business acumen of wealthy Asians. Kenyan government officials believed that Asian capitalists were profligate and that the community had a penchant for investing in unprofitable projects. The government was particularly fearful of what it considered an Asian tendency to pour the resources of the community into a few enterprises where early success had been achieved but where overinvestment would ruin a promising development.

The realities in the Asian business community were altogether different, however. Numerous Asian entrepreneurs emerged in the immediate postwar years, many of them eager to create the secondary industries that the Kenyan government favored. To give but a few examples, the Manji family used wealth accumulated in a bakery business in the interwar period to pioneer a bread baking and confectionery enterprise. The Kohli family imported secondhand soap-making equipment from Germany and established a modern soap industry. Various Indian businessmen participated in an expanding and lucrative beer brewing industry. None of these enterprises received encouragement from the state, however; in some cases they even encountered a hostile administration.

The family destined to play the leading role in Asian manufacturing in Kenya were the Chandarias. In 1914 D. P. Chandaria had emigrated from India to Kenya as a small merchant; between 1940 and 1948, he used the wealth he had amassed in East African commercial ventures to reestablish his family in India. But when this effort to repatriate himself and his business interests failed, Chandaria returned to Kenya. In 1948 he diversified into manufacturing, using a firm he had acquired during the interwar period—the Kenya Aluminum and Industrial Works Com-

---

[61] Appendix O to the Plewman Report, PRO CO 533/539/1.

pany—as his main business vehicle.[62] In the period leading up to Mau Mau, the Chandaria family enterprises engaged in the manufacture of nails and hurricane lamps and made the Kenya Aluminum and Industrial Works East Africa's most important metal rolling plant. Often at loggerheads with the administration and full of complaints against the government for its failure to support his innovations, Chandaria did finally win grudging state admiration. In the midst of a dispute on industrial policy, H. L. Adams at the Ministry of Commerce and Industry admitted that the Kenya Aluminum and Industrial Works was "in fact carrying out [the] most enterprising and far-reaching industrial developments."[63]

The government was even more profoundly pessimistic about the prospects for African capital. The Kenya Register of Companies reported in 1950 that only nineteen African public companies had been registered and had a paid-in capital of £40,444; forty-eight private companies had a paid-in capital of £22,696. The registrar wrote, "There is [not] a single one whose affairs I can honestly describe as satisfactory." Almost all were operating at a loss, and assets were being dissipated in management expenses and salaries.[64] And African business persons did not seem to grasp the legal distinctions between private and public companies and limited and unlimited partnerships. Firms had few shareholders, and directors operated with few checks on them. No doubt there were many more small-scale businesses in African townships and reserves about which the registrar of companies had no information. Yet at this stage no African entrepreneurial class had emerged to compete with large-scale European and Asian capital.

Although prevented from competing with business, the Kenyan state was expected to create the conditions conducive to business success. It offered tariff protection when businesses could demonstrate that foreign competitors were dumping products in the local market. It placed purchasing orders locally whenever possible, and it granted rebates on raw materials when these were used in local industrial processes. No state power was seen as more vital to industrial progress or more useful for encouraging large-scale, British-based capital, however, than industrial licensing.

The concept of licensing had originated during World War II. The East African Industrial Council licensed desperately needed industries in order

---

[62] Robin Murray, "The Chandarias: The Development of a Kenyan Multinational," in *Readings on the Multinational Corporation in Kenya*, ed. Raphael Kaplinsky (Nairobi, 1978).

[63] No. 141, Note by H. L. Adams, January 10, 1952, KNA MCI 6/461.

[64] No. 2, J. F. Spry, Registrar of Companies to Secretary for Commerce and Industry, October 12, 1950, KNA MCI 6/789.

to free them from internal competition and to facilitate their creation. Charles Lockhart, a moving force behind the arrangements, wanted licensing continued after the war. Portraying free-market capitalism as wasteful, Lockhart thought that territories striving for rapid economic progress, social tranquillity, and political equipoise could not afford a full-bore capitalist form of development. Through industrial licensing, the state would guide industrial growth, ensuring that the right kinds of industries were created and the right kind of capital attracted. According to Lockhart's vision, the state would designate key industrial sectors for scheduling and then grant wide-ranging, in some cases monopolistic, powers to those firms deemed most able to bring an industry to a high stage of development. Lockhart believed that where individual businessmen were likely to make errant investment decisions, state officials, with a grasp of the whole economic picture, would not.

In Lockhart's view the scheduling of industrial sectors and the licensing of firms would bring order and planning to the East African economy. It would eliminate deleterious competition. Lockhart had a capacious view of licensing, and he wanted the East African governments to schedule a large number of sectors. He thought that under proper state regulation East Africa could create vigorous industries in tanning, caustic soda, textiles, paper, acid, building board, alcohol, cement, matches, and glass.[65] According to him, the greatest danger came from having "more industrialists with money than ideas." He was especially fearful of the irrationality of Asian business persons. The right kind of industrialist—specifically large-scale, British based capitalists—needed to be protected from "too many spectators ready to join in the game once the performer has shown it to be not dangerous. Hence, the reluctance [of a firm] to embark on any new project without some measure of protection."[66]

Lockhart's industrial licensing program envisaged scheduling almost all of the industrial branches that might prove profitable in East Africa. He also favored limiting production to one or perhaps two carefully selected, well-established foreign corporations. He saw little virtue in allowing a large number of smaller, highly competitive firms to spring up, favoring instead a single overarching business entity, protected from competitors. He admitted in candid moments that an underlying motive for licensing was that the Asian community had a lot of "spare money which they will invest in businesses of all kinds irrespective of the opportunities of market expansion so long as a market is apparently there

---

[65] Minutes of the Meeting of the East African Industrial Council, June 18, 1946, PRO CO 852/573/6.

[66] Colonial Office Memorandum on Industrial Licensing, August 6, 1946, PRO CO 852/573/9.

which is being created by others."[67] His preference for large-scale British capital was evident from his efforts to persuade East African Portland Cement to establish a cement factory, Calico Printers Association a textile complex, and Unilever an oil seeds industry.

The Colonial Office, however, had sharp differences with Lockhart. Its officials pointed out that eliminating competition would result in monopolies, inefficient manufacturers, and overpriced commodities. It would be injurious to consumers.[68] Under its prodding, the East African administrators curtailed the scope of the licensing scheme. Instead of allowing the governments of East Africa to designate a large number of sectors for licensing, London restricted scheduling to two sectors: textiles and pottery.[69] The Colonial Office also attempted to make it difficult for the state to deny a license to a firm in one of the scheduled industries. It stipulated that a prospective firm wishing to establish itself in a sector already scheduled could not be denied a license unless its technical skills were lacking, its access to raw materials inadequate, its failure likely to prejudice the successful development of that industry, or the site unsuitable.[70]

In introducing the licensing bill into the Kenyan Legislative Council in 1948, J. D. Rankine, the chief secretary of the government, went through the usual litany of arguments in favor of the proposal. He contended that laissez-faire approaches did not work in an era of exchange controls and currency shortages and led to "wasteful and unprofitable competition." Still, he asserted, the goal was "removing some of the initial handicaps but not the permanent sheltering from competition." Rankine promised that the powers would be "very sparingly used."[71]

Unofficial opinion was overwhelmingly in support of the bill, and the act passed the Legislative Council by a vote of twenty-six to two, with four abstentions. Vigorous dissent, not surprisingly, came from A. B. Patel, who rightly feared that the powers of the state would be used to favor European capital at the expense of Asian investment. He argued that licensing would produce monopolies and injure the interests of consumers. Hope-Jones and Vasey, the two members of the Legislative Council most committed to European business, could not conceal their disappointment at the extent to which the Colonial Office had weakened Lockhart's ear-

[67] C. Lockhart to S. Caine, April 3, 1947, PRO CO 852/836/1.

[68] Colonial Office Memorandum on Industrial Licensing, August 6, 1946, PRO CO 852/573/9.

[69] Kenya, Legislative Council, *Debates*, vol. 30, July 14, 1948, pp. 65 ff.

[70] N. Harris, East African Industrial Licensing Legislation, March 12, 1951, PRO CO 822/155/9.

[71] Kenya, Legislative Council, *Debates*, vol. 29, March 15, 1948, pp. 79–80.

lier proposals. They supported the bill but called on the government to increase the number of industrial branches eligible for licensing.[72]

Kenya's development program was designed to build upon the substantial position that British capital already enjoyed in Kenya. Before World War II British companies operating in Kenya clustered in financial services, plantation agriculture, and exporting and importing, as befitted an economy oriented to the export of its primary products to Great Britain. At the heart of this export-import economy were three British banks: Barclays Bank; the Standard Bank; and National and Grindlays Bank. They were not primarily banks of deposit, although deposit banking was on the rise during and after World War II. Their main source of profit came from the financing of exports and imports, and to this end they lent money to merchants and cash crop farmers. In 1939 Barclays had fourteen branch banks in Kenya and employed seventy-six European officials and 135 Asian clerks. It had, however, only one African clerk.[73] Despite the growth in African deposit banking after World War II (when accounts belonging to Africans constituted 70,000 of the total of 98,000 in 1960), there were still fewer African staff than Europeans and Asians; of 1,476 at Barclays in 1960, only seventy-nine were Africans.[74] Despite pressures to Africanize, East African banking executives saw more gain in recruiting and training Asian staff. Barclays believed that it already had an impressive cadre of Asian clerks drawn mostly from the Sikh and Goan communities. It sought to attract the more commercially minded Asian groups with a view to capturing a greater proportion of Asian investment.

Even before World War I, Kenya had a large assortment of export-import companies, though this sector was never dominated by a single firm as West Africa was by the United Africa Company. A. Baumann, Smith Mackenzie and Company, and Gailey and Roberts were influential, but by 1945 the import-export firm with the largest capitalization was Mitchell Cotts. Although its share capital was only £668,398 in 1945, it was on the rise; by 1960 this British conglomerate would have eighty associated companies operating in thirty overseas territories and consolidated assets of £20 million.[75]

[72] Ibid., pp. 84 ff.

[73] Report by Brian F. Macdonna, East Africa in Wartime, August 1944, Barclays Bank Archives, M1.1/1–7. For an overview of business and the private sector, one should consult Nicola Swainson, *The Development of Corporate Capitalism in Kenya, 1918–1977* (Berkeley, Calif., 1980).

[74] Report on Visit to South Africa, Rhodesia, and East Africa, February to April 1960, Barclays Bank Archives, M1.1/2.

[75] The Mitchell Cotts Group of Companies, *Annual Report*, 1960.

The European agricultural sector functioning in the highlands of Kenya has often been described as the domain of the yeoman farmer. Yet in dairying and mixed farming as well as plantation crops, most of the larger European estates were run as agribusinesses, with boards of directors and executive officers. Even though the typical coffee estate was not immense, the largest 9 percent of the coffee owners in Kiambu district in the 1940s owned 56 percent of the land. Almost without exception these large estates had been incorporated.[76] Tea and pyrethrum corporations began to appear in the 1920s. Tea was quickly dominated by Brooke Bond and Company, which expanded outward from the Limuru area. Smaller tea planters looked to the Brooke Bond executives for leadership. Brooke Bond had tea plantations in India, Ceylon, and Africa, some 25,000 acres in all in 1951–52 and total corporate assets valued at £26 million.[77] Although tobacco was not grown extensively in Kenya, the government had offered a generous concession to British American Tobacco to cure tobacco grown in the highlands. British American Tobacco had a worldwide capitalization of £92,347,920 in 1950–51.[78] Thus, in spite of Kenya's reputation as a colony for individual farmers, the European agricultural sector, export oriented as well as mixed farming and dairying, increasingly came under the domination of corporations.

Industry and the Private Sector

Although Kenya had only a small industrial base in 1945 and was not projected as the industrial hub for East Africa in the postwar era (that position being accorded to Uganda), the British planners were nonetheless eager to create a sound industrial sector, based on secondary industries, preferably drawing their equity capital from well-known British corporate firms. To many of the officials of the Kenyan government the model firm was the Magadi Soda Company, founded originally in 1904 by the East African Syndicate but taken over in the interwar period by Imperial Chemical Industries. Magadi Soda produced large quantities of soda ash from a concessionary area about 100 miles south of Nairobi.[79] In the postwar period its output was approximately 150,000 tons per year, or one-third of the supply put into world trade. It exported mainly to India

---

[76] Apollo Njonjo, "The Africanization of the 'White Highlands': A Study in Agrarian Class Struggles in Kenya, 1950–1974," Ph.D. thesis, Princeton University, 1978, p. 232.

[77] Brooke Bond, *Annual Report*, 1951–52.

[78] British American Tobacco, *Annual Report*, 1950–51.

[79] C. J. Homewood, Board of Trade, to Darby, Colonial Office, May 21, 1950, PRO CO 533/561/9; Roger Norton, East Africa Office, to A. Hope-Jones, July 28, 1949, KNA Secretariat 1/4/5.

and Japan.[80] Magadi Soda had a large capitalization by Kenya standards (£797,027 in the 1940s), was managed by individuals sent out from the parent company in London, and had a representative of the Kenyan government on its board of directors.[81] The British administrators hoped that they could extend the Magadi model to other sectors of the economy. Here, however, they were to be sorely disappointed.

FOOTWEAR

The manufacturing of all kinds of footwear offered profitable opportunities in Kenya; yet the firm that established its dominance in the postwar era was far from the British ideal. By taking British directors onto its board, however, the Bata Shoe Company circumvented the barriers erected against non-British firms and became one of Kenya's leading secondary industries. Bata shoe manufacturing operations had originated in Ziln, Czechoslovakia, in the second half of the nineteenth century. By the interwar years Bata had opened distributing branches and manufacturing subsidiaries all over the world. From the center of its African operations in South Africa, the firm entered East Africa, where by 1940 it had established thirty-five distributing outlets and a small manufacturing factory at Mombasa. There it produced 4,000 to 5,000 pairs of shoes per week and provided employment to 50 Europeans, 71 Asians, and 125 Africans.[82] Although its capitalization was hardly formidable—a mere £10,000—its managing director, Jan Novosad, had plans to expand production during the war. He envisaged taking over most of the East African market for shoes and wished to move his factory to Nairobi in order to be closer to the markets.[83]

Novosad encountered stiff opposition from British officials. In addition to being a non-British national, Novosad and his Bata firm were believed to be pro-Nazi and even to be secretly aiding the Axis war effort. The Kenyan government erected a series of obstacles against the firm, and finally, after rejecting numerous requests to expand the output of the factory, the government appointed a sequestrator to oversee its affairs.[84] Even when the state could not find evidence of Novosad's aiding the enemy, its officials argued that the Bata plant was inefficiently run and should not be permitted to gain a manufacturing foothold in Kenya. These tactics stymied Bata Shoes until Novosad invited Ernest Vasey to

[80] No. 118, V. A. Maddison Note, July 10, 1951, KNA MCI 6/901.

[81] KNA MCI 6/901.

[82] No. 1A, Managing Director, Bata Company Ltd in South Africa to Commissioner of Customs, Nairobi, January 17, 1940, KNA Secretariat 1/4/8.

[83] No. 22, Maurice W. Ghersie to Chief Secretary, June 13, 1940, KNA Secretariat 1/4/31.

[84] No. 156, Note from E. Vasey, May 12, 1941, KNA Secretariat 1/4/31.

join the board. Vasey's admiration of the company and his confidence in the administrative capacities of Novosad gave the firm for the first time an influential backer who was prepared to defend it from government criticism. In Vasey's opinion, Bata was a company "which, if carefully nursed, may become a valuable secondary industry of this colony and a source of employment to a number of Africans."[85] Vasey missed few opportunities to spread this favorable view of Bata in government circles. Novosad continued to bring influential British business and political figures onto his board and used them to make his case with the government. After the war, Cavendish-Bentinck joined the board. By the 1950s, Bata shoes had made a strong place for itself as both a manufacturing concern and a retail distributor for its own products and those of other firms.[86]

TEXTILES

Among the secondary industries that economic experts favored in East Africa, first place went to textiles. After all of the quarreling over which industries to schedule, only textiles had become fully privileged. Almost the whole gamut of textile production—wool, cotton, and linen—and all of the stages of the production process—spinning, weaving, and finishing—were listed as scheduled. Thus any business person wishing to engage in any of these branches of textile manufacturing was obligated to secure a license from the state.

British officials hoped to attract a large, heavily capitalized and experienced British conglomerate to forge the way in textiles. When the directors of the Calico Printers Association indicated an interest in East Africa, the administrators were delighted. Calico was a Lancashire-based firm that had specialized in the finishing trades in Britain. At the turn of the century Calico had been one of the most heavily capitalized British firms, but it had fallen on hard times in the interwar period. Seeking to arrest its financial decline and to win back overseas markets, it established manufacturing facilities overseas. Its investments outside of Britain had helped to reverse the firm's financial decline, and although the company was no longer as heavily capitalized as other British companies, it remained a leader in Britain's textile sector.

East African officials envisaged East Africa as an economic unit in the early postwar years. In the view of most, Uganda was to be the manufacturing hub of the region. It had abundant and important raw materials,

[85] No. 182B, E. Vasey to W. B. Cummings, Custodian of Enemy Property, November 1, 1941, KNA Secretariat 1/4/31.
[86] See No. 31, M. H. French, East African Hides, Skins, and Leather Controller, to Secretary for Commerce and Industry, April 22, 1949, KNA Secretariat 1/8/1.

including cotton, and cheap and reliable hydroelectric supplies from the Owen Falls dam. Not surprisingly, these officials opted to site the first large-scale textile industry at Jinja in Uganda, from where it was expected to supply all of East Africa. The prospect of entrusting the textile industry to one of Britain's most experienced firms made the British officials willing to grant far-reaching concessions.

Calico officials exploited their strong bargaining position to the utmost. First, they obtained a large equity commitment of £600,000 from the Ugandan government without giving up their own managerial control. The rest of the equity capital came from Calico (£750,000) and Bleacher Associates (£100,000).[87] Second, the Calico executives persuaded the East African Industrial Council to refrain from issuing licenses to other textile manufacturers.[88] They argued that they needed a full five years to install their plant and to put it on a secure technical and financial footing. They feared competition from small Indian enterprises that were trying to create a niche in the East African market. In keeping with their desire to be monopolists, the Calico executives opposed an application submitted by a small Indian-run firm, the Moshi Trading Company, which proposed to produce lines of special interest to the Asian peoples. Claiming that this firm might not confine its manufacturing to these items, the Calico officials pressed the administration into limiting the Moshi Trading Company to producing only the types of cloth shown to Calico and to using no more than twenty looms.[89] Finally, Calico received strong tariff support against Japanese imports on the grounds that Japanese imports would swamp the local market and destroy the profitability of their enterprise.[90]

By the early 1950s, while the five-year license was still running its course, government officials, especially those in Kenya, concluded that they had made a grievous error in conceding so much to Calico. The firm was slow to found its textile complex at Jinja. In the meantime, the prospects for coordinated East African industrial development had dimmed. Officials in Kenya chafed at the injunctions against establishing textile plants in their country. The government's attempt to circumvent the restriction by inviting a Manchester-based British textile industrialist, John Dodd, to take up a license in Kenya failed when Dodd's East African

[87] Minutes of the East African Industrial Council, January 18, 1951, PRO CO 822/157/2.

[88] N. L. Mayle, Colonial Office, to Calico Printers Association, October 20, 1949; and East Africa Industrial Council, Review of Industrial Licensing Policy, July 19, 1949; both in PRO CO 852/836/3.

[89] No. 47, B. Lewis to East African High Commission, June 22, 1950, KNA MCI 6/604.

[90] No. 67, R. de S. Stapledon, Administrator, to H. E. Stacey, Moshi Trading Company, February 14, 1951, KNA MCI 6/605.

Spinning and Weaving Company was unable to attract the necessary capital to erect a plant at Kisumu.[91]

CEMENT

Even though Kenya had imported all of its cement before World War II, its officials regarded the creation of a local cement industry as vital to the country's development agenda. The Kenyan development plan had a large component for public works and construction projects. Even had the state been willing to import all of the necessary supplies of cement, the freighting capacity of East African Railways would not have been large enough to handle the tonnage. British officials were eager for Kenya's traditional cement distributing agencies to take the lead in developing the local cement industry, the most important of which was the East African Portland Cement Company, a British-financed and -run firm. Most of the shares of East African Portland Cement were held by Associated Portland Cement Manufacturers Ltd (Cambridge) and British Portland Cement Manufacturers (Cambridge). At first East African Portland Cement did not disappoint its backers in the government. Its chairman, R. G. Vernon, outlined an ambitious industrial program as the war drew to a close and claimed that his scheme would be "a very notable addition to the secondary industries of the Colony."[92] Vernon, like the Calico Printers executives, however, demanded major concessions, including preferential railway rates, tariff protection, and a government commitment to purchase large quantities of the firm's cement. The Kenya government officials were unable to meet all of these demands, but they remained enthusiastic about the firm. Lockhart hoped that the company would invest £400,000 in a large factory in Kenya.[93]

The Kenya government did not alter its commitment to East African Portland Cement despite unproductive discussions on terms for establishing a plant and attractive proposals from other firms. Kenya Kyanite, under Charles Markham, proposed to create a factory at Kisumu, and a South African firm came forward with a proposal to build a factory at Sultan Hamud.[94] Whenever any of these firms was on the verge of signing an agreement with the government, however, East African Portland Ce-

---

[91] No. 18, Note by H. L. Adams, November 3, 1951, KNA MCI 6/605.

[92] No. 3, R. G. Vernon, Chairman, East African Portland Cement Company, to the Private Secretary of the Government of Kenya, February 9, 1945, KNA State House 4/60.

[93] No. 5, Memorandum on East African Portland Cement Company, February 19, 1945, KNA State House 4/60.

[94] Extract from Minutes of the Meeting of the East African Industrial Council, June 10, 1948, KNA MCI 6/390.

ment renewed its interest in the project.[95] By 1951 four companies were in competition: Industrial Cement from South Africa; Amalgamated Roadstone Company; Kenya Kyanite; and the East African Portland Cement Company.[96] Only when the government was again prepared to grant a license to the South African firm did East African Portland Cement Company finally agree to build a factory at Sultan Hamud, near Kajiado in the Masai reserve.[97] At the same time, another British firm, the British Standard Portland Cement Company, erected a cement factory at Bamburi near Mombasa.[98] Thus, after protracted negotiations, Kenya had created a local cement industry and succeeded in bringing in large-scale British firms that would build plants in areas of high consumption (along the coast and in the highlands).

BREWERIES

The lifting of a colonial restriction on the sale of European-brewed beer in African reserves made the brewing industry one of the fastest growing in postwar Kenya. Two established breweries found themselves in the most favorable position to take advantage of the new marketing opportunities: East African Breweries and Taylors. East African Breweries had been founded in 1922 and became a public limited company with an authorized capital of £80,000 in 1934.[99] Its chief competitor, Taylors, owed its existence to J. W. Taylor, who had emigrated to Kenya as an expert in beer brewing for East African Breweries and then started his own firm. He had expanded the capitalization of the firm in the early postwar years by attracting investment from the British brewing company, Ind, Coope, and Allsopp, and he enhanced the political standing of the firm by adding Ernest Vasey to the board.

Although these two firms had the advantage of experience, capitalization, and distributional networks, they encountered strong competition from a number of smaller, but no less energetic Asian businessmen. A first challenge, from P. Lalo, was defeated, but a more determined effort was made by Shah Veshi Devshi and Company. Each of the Asian enterprises approached the government for support, but with little success.

[95] Note, September 30, 1946; and No. 177, Proposed Manufacture of Cement in Kenya, Note, September 22, 1948; both in KNA MCI 6/390.

[96] No. 369, H. L. Adams, Note, August 29, 1949, KNA MCI 6/390; No. 59, V. A. Maddison, Note, March 5, 1951, KNA MCI 6/391.

[97] No. 144/1, East African Portland Cement Company to Officer in Charge, Masai, January 4, 1952, KNA MCI 6/391.

[98] No. 1, R. Alexander of British Standard Portland Cement Company to Ministry of Finance, January 7, 1952, KNA MCI 6/457.

[99] Kenya Breweries, *Beer in Bora: Sixty Years of Kenya Breweries* (Nairobi, 1982), p. 5.

Vasey wrote to the Ministry of Commerce and Industry to oppose the Indian schemes, reiterating the familiar arguments against excessive competition and the destruction of deserving companies.[100] He and Brian Hobson, chairman of East African Breweries, pleaded with the government to schedule beer brewing on the grounds that there was already a danger of overproduction.[101] But whatever preference the Kenyan officials might have had for protecting settler- and British-based capital, they were unable to persuade the government of Tanganyika to schedule beer brewing.[102] The minister of commerce and industry did, however, write to the chairman of the Mombasa Municipal Board to encourage that body to support East African Breweries. In his note the minister mentioned that Hobson's firm "has the full support of the government and is considered likely to prove of great benefit not only to Kenya, but to the East African territories as a whole as a sound secondary industry and as a source of supply of beer which will help to make us independent of imported supplies."[103]

The government's occasional interventions on behalf of the European companies and its decidedly chilly reception to Asian overtures frightened off most of the Asian businessmen and protected the Kenya market for the two European-run enterprises. East African Breweries took full advantage of the opportunities, entering the African reserves in an aggressive fashion. It recruited African distributors and increased its capitalization at a steady rate by encouraging a wide dispersion of stock among the East African investing public. Its equity capital rose rapidly and made it the most heavily capitalized firm in Kenya.[104] Administrative coolness notwithstanding, Shah Veshi Devshi and Company did finally succeed in establishing the City Brewery Company and became a serious competitor in the Kenya beer brewing industry.[105]

OIL SEEDS AND SOAP

The scheme that most intrigued Lockhart was the creation of a big vegetable oil and oil seeds industry under the auspices of the powerful Unilever Corporation. East Africa, in contrast to West Africa and the Belgian

---

[100] J. W. Taylor to Hope-Jones, January 23, 1950, KNA MCI 6/401.

[101] No. 63, Brian Hobson to H. L. Adams, May 2, 1949, KNA MCI 6/401.

[102] No. 66, H. L. Adams to B. Hobson, May 18, 1949, KNA MCI 6/401.

[103] No. 98, Minister of Commerce and Industry to Chairman of Mombasa Municipal Board, August 30, 1949, KNA MCI 6/401.

[104] Kenya Breweries, *Beer in Bora*, pp. 11 ff.; interview with Brian Hobson, October 31, 1989.

[105] No. 176/1, City Brewery to Commissioner of Customs, East Africa, April 25, 1950, KNA MCI 6/401.

Congo, had never been of importance to Unilever.[106] But with a huge groundnut growing project taking shape in Tanganyika, the Unilever executives were prepared to invest in East Africa. At Lockhart's insistence, a ranking Unilever official, Roger Heyworth, made a fact-finding tour of the region. Lockhart encouraged Unilever to develop a "grand plan" for East African industrialization, including schemes for local manufacturing in which Unilever would play a leading role. Heyworth was excited about the East African prospects. He anticipated rising standards of living in the area and increased consumption of soap, oils, and fats. He noted that the manufacture of those products was still in the hands of Asian businessmen and entrepreneurs, whose technologies were of a very rudimentary nature. Heyworth reported that the soap that was manufactured in East Africa was of poor quality and was produced in numerous underequipped and lightly capitalized workshops.[107] He reported that the plants did not use decorticators and that "seed cleaners, mill beaters, and all the other preparatory machinery are nothing but names to them [the Asian businessmen]."[108] Unilever did not, however, move with the dispatch that Lockhart expected. The firm did not invest any equity capital until just before the outbreak of the Mau Mau rebellion, when it took over a cluster of industries being run by the East African Industrial Management Board.[109] Its subsequent industrial expansion was constrained by the straitened financial and political circumstances brought on by the Mau Mau war.

Over and over, then, British business persons and administrators misjudged the capabilities of Asian capital. Though it was true, as Heyworth indicated, that the locally produced soap was not of high technical quality, what Heyworth failed to note was the drive of the Asian entrepreneurs to establish more modern and efficient plants. The most farsighted of the soap manufacturers was the Kohli family, who had entered Kenya in the 1920s as merchants but who, through a series of happenstances, had started a simple soap manufacturing plant under the name Elephant Soap Company. This company was no different from other Asian firms in this period in that the two Kohli brothers held all of its shares and were opposed to seeking additional capital from other sources. Like similar Asian soap plants (of which there were about twenty-three in 1949), Elephant Soap had no modern machinery, produced soap in vats, used

[106] See W. P. Scott, Report on Visit to Kenya, Uganda, Tanganyika, and Zanzibar, September–October 1935, Unilever Archives.

[107] R. Heyworth to Unilever, November 7, 1945, Unilever Archives.

[108] Report by Roger Heyworth, East Africa as a Market for Locally Manufactured Unilever Products, August 4, 1944, Unilever Archives.

[109] See discussion earlier in this chapter.

wooden stirrers, and burned wood for fuel.[110] But after the war, the elder Kohli toured Germany to learn about modern soap making. He brought a German expert in soap making back to Kenya as well as secondhand equipment.[111] By 1956 he had established a fully automated soap factory, the first of its kind in Kenya, and in spite of governmental obstructionism, his firm began to attract the attention of foreign soap manufacturers, now prepared to sign contracts with local companies to manufacture their products for sale in the East African market.[112]

British officials in Kenya had embarked upon the postwar period with a plan to transform the Kenyan economy. Concerned about political stability and eager to create rising standards of living and new employment opportunities outside of agriculture, they looked to private capital, preferably large-scale, British corporate investment, to establish secondary industries. They did not realize the full extent of their vision before the Mau Mau revolt plunged Kenya into a state of political and economic emergency. The British firms that the experts at the Kenyan Ministries of Commerce and Industry, Finance, and the Treasury placed so much faith in procrastinated or obstructed the implementation of vital projects, often with a view to protecting their export markets. Calico Printers was given a monopoly over textile production but was slow in starting its big textile complex. Unilever did not respond to Lockhart's ideas for a grand industrial scheme, and East African Portland Cement did not invest in local manufacturing until the government of Kenya had offered its concession to a competitor. Colonial planners in Kenya also badly miscalculated Asian enterprise. Believing Asian capitalists to be incapable of identifying profitable and useful investment opportunities, British officials obstructed the efforts of the Chandarias, Kohlis, and Manjis. Yet the Asian business persons prevailed. By 1952, although they had not overcome British prejudice, they had established their firms in many of the industrial sectors that Lockhart and others thought Kenya had the best chance to develop.

[110] No. 113/1, Note, September 13, 1952, KNA Secretariat 2/36.

[111] Interview with Chanda Kohli, Nairobi, November 24, 1989.

[112] No. 41E, H. E. Stacey to Administrator, East Africa High Commission, September 6, 1948, KNA State House 4/68.

CHAPTER 10

Mau Mau and the Private Sector, 1952–1959

THE CHALLENGE to Kenya's development vision, which occurred in roughly the same time frame as the challenges in Egypt and Nigeria, came unequivocally from subaltern communities. Nowhere was the threat to the timetable of decolonization and the agreed-upon formulas of economic growth more rooted in the frustrations and ambitions of the lower segments of African society than within the Aberdare forests and Mt. Kenya, where a small band of disgruntled and dispossessed Kikuyu freedom fighters posed a severe military and political challenge to British authority.

Although the colonial administration in Kenya had feared African protest and violence, the Mau Mau explosion came as a great trauma to the British. It brought far-reaching political changes in Kenya, change that slowed the steady devolution of power into European hands and accelerated transfer of authority to Africans. It did not derail the developmental vision, although it put the development programs and the private sector under heavy financial pressure. In the final analysis, Kenya's economic policies did not need to be adjusted because Mau Mau was too weakly articulated and lacked clear-cut socioeconomic goals. In addition, those individuals in the Kenya elite most responsible for economic matters, in particular Ernest Vasey, the minister of finance from 1952 to 1959, devised fiscal policies that helped to suppress Mau Mau and simultaneously retain investor confidence in Kenya's private sector.

Although Mau Mau continues to elude a definitive historical consensus, it can be agreed that it entailed a buildup of radical opposition to colonial power after World War II and derived its inspiration from discontented African groups. The landless, the squatters, and the urban unemployed rallied around political leaders who had tired of political gradualism. Unfortunately for those critics of colonialism, the administration, under new governor Evelyn Baring, declared Kenya to be in a state of emergency on October 20, 1952, and followed that declaration by rounding up and detaining a large number of African political leaders. The precise relationship of many of the detained individuals to emerging African radicalism was unclear. Certainly some of them espoused a sterner challenge to colonialism than most. But far from eradicating opposition, as its advocates hoped it would, the police action caused power to pass to younger, more irate, and less well educated cadres.

The confrontation between the colonial authorities and the Mau Mau forces may well have been little more than a jacquerie, as Frantz Fanon suggests, or perhaps a protest against the norms of a moral economy, albeit a colonial one, or even a Kikuyu civil war. The administration succeeded in limiting dissidence to the Kikuyu, Embu, and Meru peoples, and it kept the active resisters to small, poorly armed, and poorly led groups, probably numbering no more than 15,000 or 20,000, located in the Aberdare Mountains and the forests around Mt. Kenya. Although these small forces enjoyed widespread support in the reserves and the city of Nairobi at first, they never succeeded in creating an overarching political and military unity or in elaborating a coherent reformist vision. From the start, they were on the defensive, fighting for their lives rather than for new political and economic arrangements.

The leaders in the forests were young men, whom colonial rule had frustrated. Many of them had records of violent behavior. More than likely, they would have been at the forefront of organizations opposed to colonial capitalism and calling for a more equitable, socialist way of life had they had the opportunity to do so. Dedan Kimathi, head of a military band in the Aberdares, only thirty-three years of age, had been expelled from the Church of Scotland Missionary (CSM) station at Tumu Tumu. He had a checkered career that included service in the army, teaching, petty trading, and employment by the Shell Company of East Africa before Mau Mau occurred. The colonial authorities regarded him as a thug and a thief who had continued his criminal practices under the guise of Mau Mau.

His counterpart in the Mt. Kenya area, Waruhiu Itote, known as General China, had a similar though less violent background as a CSM member and an ex-corporal in the King's African Rifles. For men like Itote, who was forced to take an oath of allegiance to Kikuyu values and against colonial rule, and Kimathi, who was an oath taker and giver, the "oathing" of large numbers of Kikuyu provided integration to lives previously in disarray. But oathing never overcame the fragmentary nature of the opposition groups or the varying reasons that men and women congregated in the forests in the first place. Because they were there for a variety of often contradictory motives—some to flee criminal prosecution, others for idealistic motives, still others in search of food, and others at gun point—the efforts to create a defense force or a rudimentary political organization, let alone to adumbrate a vision of a new political economy, was not achieved.

Mau Mau fighters in the forest did march to the goals of land and freedom, and those goals, everyone recognized, could have broad implications for the colonial economy and polity. Yet they remained catchwords, without concrete meaning beyond the vague aspirations originally given them by the proscribed Kenya African Union (KAU), Kenya's main political party after World War II. Indeed, the Mau Mau leaders, rather than seeing themselves as a new force in African politics, separate from the KAU and in rebellion against its failed tactics and goals, revealed themselves in songs and occasional manifestos to be working for the aspirations of the KAU. Their ultimate ambition was to compel the colonial authorities to take KAU programs seriously and to negotiate with its recognized, albeit detained, leaders.[1] Many of the men and women in the forests had been members of the KAU and, before that, the Kikuyu Central Association (KCA), the main anticolonial Kikuyu political party in the 1920s and 1930s. They knew no other set of policies. Dedan Kimathi had been secretary of the Rumuruti and Thomson's Falls branches of the KCA, and Stanley Mathenge, another Aberdare leader and competitor to Kimathi, had been a member of the KAU branch in Nyeri.[2]

Although the direct Mau Mau challenge to Kenya's business community was minimal, two partially successful boycott campaigns showed the potential that economic weapons might have against settled society. From the beginning of the emergency, the Nairobi population participated in a boycott of the foreign-owned and -administered Kenya Bus Service, which transported large numbers of Africans in the capital city. The boycott remained effective for a year and a half, until Operation Anvil removed most of the Kikuyu population from Nairobi. At the time of its greatest activity, it reduced the use of buses by 50 percent and forced the company to discontinue many routes and to run others at a loss.[3] It enabled private African bus companies to come into being and offer alternative services.[4] Another use of economic power occurred in Nairobi, where Kikuyu, Embu, and Meru peoples, encouraged by Mau Mau leaders in the city, refused to patronize shops belonging to peoples of other communities, including other African groups. Hardest hit were non-Kikuyu, African-owned eating houses that formed such a prominent part of the urban landscape.[5]

[1] This observation is taken from the work of Wunyabari O. Maloba, *Mau Mau and Kenya: An Analysis of a Peasant Revolt* (Bloomington, Ind., 1993), pp. 114–33, whose study seems to me full of common sense and good guidance. But anyone reading the brief capsule description of Mau Mau offered here will note an indebtedness to the works of Carl Rosberg and John Nottingham, *The Myth of Mau Mau: Nationalism in Kenya* (Nairobi, 1966); D. L. Barnett and K. Njama, *Mau Mau from Within* (New York, 1966); Tabitha Kanogo, *Squatters and the Roots of Mau Mau, 1905–63* (London, 1987); Frank Furedi, *The Mau Mau War in Perspective* (London, 1989); Bruce Berman and John Lonsdale, *Unhappy Valley: Conflict in Kenya and Africa* (London, 1992); and many others who in their own ways unraveled parts of the Mau Mau puzzle.
[2] No. 704, Baring to Colonial Office, June 6, 1953, PRO CO 822/699.
[3] *East African Standard*, February 10, 1954.
[4] Ibid., April 22, 1954.
[5] Ibid., March 6, 1954.

To leaders of the private sector, these were irritants rather than decisive challenges. Small and Vasey worried about dramatic actions that would frighten foreign investors.[6] They lived in fear of sabotage against the railroad and major commercial and industrial establishments. The fact that none occurred was further evidence of the tentative and defensive nature of the Mau Mau protest. By 1955, the Ministry of Commerce and Industry reported to local business persons and foreign investors that investment levels had remained high since the proclamation of the emergency and that important overseas-based firms like East African Bag and Cordage Company, John Dickinson and Company Ltd, and East African Portland Cement Company were investing large sums in the country, while older industries, like East African Industries, Brooke Bond, Kenya Canners, and Kenya and Aluminum and Industrial Works, were expanding their operations.[7]

If the overt challenge to private business never became serious, the indirect one always was. Suppressing Mau Mau threatened the fiscal stability of the colony, and this jeopardized development programs. The monumental fiscal burdens created by Mau Mau were unappreciated at first. At the beginning, Governor Baring's decision to fly in a battalion of British soldiers from the Suez canal base in Egypt was intended to calm settler fears more than to overpower dissidents. The administration's timetable for quelling opposition was a brief six months. No such easy victory occurred, however, and the struggle with Mau Mau required a panoply of military activities, political reforms, and economic projects, all of which had to be financed and fitted into the framework of the development philosophy based on an active private sector.

Many of the financial problems experienced during the Mau Mau era stemmed from an inadequate understanding of the uprising. In the first place, Mitchell, who wished to leave Kenya, his last colonial posting, with an unblemished record of service to the empire, refused to hear critical accounts of African unrest or even to read local intelligence reports about a rising wave of arson and crime in the Kikuyu districts. His reports to the British Colonial Office reflected his myopia: they portrayed a contented African peasantry. Second, few in the administration and the settler community conceded any legitimacy to the African complaints. Instead, they believed that the violence drew its inspiration from a few demagogic leaders. The colonial governor ordered the arrest and detention of some 138 persons, who were thought to be involved in militant action at three levels in the Mau Mau effort. First was a small group of

---

[6] See the *Kenya Weekly News*, January 30, 1953, pp. 54 ff.

[7] J. H. Marting, Acting Secretary for Commerce and Industry, to Private Secretary, August 2, 1955, KNA State House 4/682.

central planners, prominent among them the members of the Koinange family, who were believed to have ordered the assassination of senior chief Waruhiu, pillar of the colonial administrative system in the Kikuyu reserve. Second were the oath givers in the Kikuyu districts, and third, the so-called thugs who acted as agents in the execution of crimes planned by the leadership.[8] Baring hoped that swift political action would shock the dissidents and bring the opposition movement to an abrupt halt. Only after the removal of these frontline persons did not produce political tranquillity did the governor admit that a more concerted and aggressive military campaign would have to be mounted.

Even after these early measures to suppress the revolt had failed and the British appointed General George Erskine as commander in chief of the Kenya forces to coordinate the military forces, the military men still misunderstood the depth of the opposition facing them.[9] Erskine did not regard Mau Mau as a legitimate political or nationalist expression; in his view he faced "a number of gangs working on their own and with little or no central direction."[10] Like his predecessors he exaggerated the ease and speed of the military operations. Calculating that five zones were affected and that two weeks should suffice to pacify each zone, he set three months as the amount of time the military phase of the operations should take. The military phase was expected to end in October 1953 and was to be followed by a program of civil consolidation. The quick military forays, expected to sow discord and defeatism among the rebel bands, did not. Not even the offer of surrender without penalty undermined the morale of the forest fighters.

Erskine was forced to extend the time frame. March 1954 became the new target date for ending the military phase of the operation.[11] When this date came and went, the British military devised new, more aggressive approaches. Operation Anvil, conceived in March 1954 and put into effect in May 1954, was designed to break the link between the forests and Nairobi by removing nonessential Kikuyu from the capital city. All men with forged identity papers or employment documents, those without papers, people spuriously employed, the unemployed, and people suspected by the colonial administration of subversive activities were to be sent to rehabilitation centers or repatriated to the Kikuyu reserve. In addition, the sweep would affect 20,000 Kikuyu women, most of whom were to be sent back to the Kikuyu land unit.[12]

<hr/>

[8] No. 630, Baring to Colonial Office, October 17, 1952, PRO CO 822/444; Press Handout, October 21, 1952, PRO CO 822/438.

[9] Directive to Commander in Chief, East Africa, May 27, 1953, PRO CO 822/457.

[10] Erskine to Commander of the Imperial General Staff, June 14, 1953, PRO CO 822/693.

[11] Erskine to Harding, September 29, 1953, PRO CO 822/693.

[12] J. O. Moreton to E. B. David, Colonial Office, March 5, 1954, PRO CO 822/796.

Carried out by the Kenya police, Operation Anvil resulted in the detaining of 30,000 men, of whom 19,000 were held for further screening. The denial of Nairobi to the Mau Mau movement and the cordoning off of the forest areas from outside support eventually turned the tide of the military contest against the forests.[13] Little by little the British military forces captured military bands. Although the fighting dragged on for several more years and was a constant irritant to colonial life, the outcome ceased to be in doubt from the beginning of 1955. Yet the British did not remove their military forces at once, and the Kenyan government was not free of British financial subventions until 1959.

The defeat of Mau Mau was inevitable; yet the colonial administration was forced to recognize that there could be no lasting triumph over the African forces of discontent without meaningful adjustments to the political and economic arrangements that Mitchell had put in place between 1945 and 1952. The core of the reformist strategy involved encouraging moderate African groups to play a larger, though still subordinate role in the country's political affairs and to participate more fully in its capitalist, market-oriented economy.

Constitutional reform took center stage first, once the colonial authorities had concluded that moderate Africans would be unable to participate in the colonial economy unless they were given a larger political stake in the country. Although the earliest political reforms following the outbreak of Mau Mau involved increasing the power of the settlers by bringing Michael Blundell, one of their leading spokespersons, into the inner War Council, African political reform followed shortly thereafter.[14] In 1954 the Lyttleton constitution established Kenya's first Council of Ministers, of whom only three were Europeans, two were Asians, and one an African, and promised elections to an enlarged Legislative Council.[15]

The results of the 1956–57 elections could hardly be interpreted as anything less than a full repudiation of the Lyttleton constitution. First came the Asian and European elections in September 1956. The European vote for the fourteen seats allocated to its electorate was crucial. Eight of the fourteen winners were independents who, while refusing to be as critical of Colonial Office direction as the ultraconservative Federal Independence Party, nonetheless were opposed to the idea of multiracialism and ran on the principle of rule by merit (that is, European predominance).[16] Although the right-wing Federal Independence Party, which

---

[13] No. 504, Acting Governor, Kenya, to Colonial Office, May 9, 1954, PRO CO 822/693.

[14] No. 318, Baring to Colonial Office, March 17, 1953, PRO CO 822/440.

[15] Kenya, *Proposals for a Reconstruction of the Government, March 1954*, House of Commons Sessional Papers, vol. 25, cmd. 9103; Memorandum, Establishment and Organization of Departments, April 24, 1954, KNA, State House 4/12.

[16] *East African Standard*, April 12, June 14, and July 10, 1954.

drew its support from European yeoman farmers based in the Rift Valley, did not elect a single one of its candidates, it obtained some 2,000 votes out of the total 12,000 cast, proof that rejectionist sentiments were widespread.[17]

Even more disheartening from the colonial vantage point was the outcome of the African elections. Despite the restricted franchise allowed to African voters and the relatively sparse number of eligible Africans who actually registered to vote (126,508, or approximately one-third of those eligible), the winners were those who had been most outspoken against the government during the election campaign, like Tom Mboya and Oginga Odinga.[18] The platforms of the African delegates did not differ markedly, and the choice for the electorate seemed to be between the representatives who were sympathetic to the government and those who were not. Overall, the electorate supported the colonial critics. Candidates favored increased African representation in Parliament, redress of land grievances, increased educational opportunities for Africans, and an eventual independent African-ruled state. The platforms of the thirty-seven candidates who ran for office were largely silent on fiscal and economic matters. No one espoused a socialist platform and no one called for the nationalization of big business.

Immediately after the announcement of the election results, seven of the eight African elected members signed a petition expressing opposition to the Lyttleton constitution and asserted their unwillingness to accept ministerial office unless the number of elected African members in the Legislative Council was increased immediately from eight to twenty-three.[19] In the face of this united African opposition, the colonial authorities had no choice but to make further constitutional changes. Ever fearful of a revival of Mau Mau and alarmed at reports of a new rebel organization called the Kikuyu Kia Muingi (KKM), operating in the Kikuyu districts, they now also had reports of contacts between Mboya and KKM leaders.[20] Their worst fear was that Mboya would merge rural discontent with the urban-based labor movement to bring about a complete shutdown of the modern sectors of the economy.[21] Thus, even as Mau Mau was being expunged, the administration feared a revival of anticolonial-

[17] Baring to Secretary of State, September 13, 1956, PRO CO 822/799; *East African Standard*, September 22, 1956, and thereafter; and G. F. Engholm, "African Elections in Kenya, March 1957," in W. J. M. Mackenzie and Kenneth Robinson, *Five Elections in Africa: A Group of Electoral Studies* (Oxford, 1960).

[18] No. 436, Edmond Dorsz to Department of State, April 24, 1956, USNA 745R00/4; Kenya, Legislative Council, *Debates*, vol. 68, February 24, 1956, pp. 196 ff.

[19] *East African Standard*, March 19, 1957.

[20] No. 13, Baring to Secretary of State, January 13, 1958, PRO CO 822/1346.

[21] No. 84, Wally to Baring, July 2, 1958, PRO CO 822/1341.

ism of potentially larger and more threatening economic and political proportions. Always, then, the administration worked with the specter of social revolt hanging over its head.

In an effort to appease African moderates and to detach them from the radicals, the new Lennox-Boyd constitution increased the number of elected African seats from eight to fourteen and added twelve special seats—four for Europeans, four for Africans, and four for Asians—to be chosen by the members of the Legislative Council, once elected.[22] The new constitution was intended to be in effect for ten years.

So troubled were the colonial officials and moderate European politicians at the intensity of right-wing European and militant African opposition to the seemingly radical constitutional proposals that Michael Blundell resigned his ministerial position in order to establish a multiracial political party. Established defensively, Blundell's New Kenya Group, descendant of the United Country Party, sought overtly to combat Mboya and the so-called Nkrumah model of decolonization.[23] Under government sponsorship, the New Kenya Group obtained the endorsement of moderate Africans and Asians—men like Musa Amalemba who had been elected to the reserved seats in the Kenyan Parliament and were known to favor multiracialism. Governor Baring put the purpose of the new party candidly in a private note that revealed much about British thinking on African radicalism and moderation: "We have to use Blundell's striking initiative to try to build a counter force to Mboya as he now is."[24] In short, Mboya, who later was to be lionized in the West as a moderate and pro-capitalist force in Kenyan politics, was at this time described as a dangerous and potentially socialist leader.

Blundell's New Kenya Group, a product of Colonial Office vision and moderate European political opinion, advocated a Legislative Council of seventy-eight members elected under a common roll, with fifty-two seats filled by persons of all races and twenty-six seats reserved equally for Europeans and Asians. The franchise requirements were to be restricted

[22] Colonial Office, *Kenya, Proposals for New Constitutional Arrangements, November 1957*, House of Commons Sessional Papers, vol. 24, cmnd. 309, in PRO CO 822/1533.

[23] No. 3, Baring to Secretary of State, November 27, 1957 PRO CO 822/1532; No. 163, Baring to Lennox-Boyd, March 12, 1959, PRO CO 822/1861.

[24] No. 292, Baring to Lord Perth, May 29, 1959, PRO CO 822/1343. It has been customary to portray Mboya as a moderate African nationalist, and no doubt he was. But in the minds of British officialdom throughout the 1950s he was far from that. Margery Perham wrote to Colonial Secretary Lennox-Boyd to argue for Mboya's moderation and to encourage the Colonial Office to support him. Gorell Barnes disputed this characterization at the Colonial Office, noting that "he [Lennox-Boyd] was doubtful, as indeed I am, about the correctness of describing Mr. Mboya as a moderate." No. 302, Margery Perham to Lennox-Boyd, December 1, 1958, PRO CO 822/1426; Comment by W. L. Gorell Barnes, December 3, 1958, PRO CO 822/1426.

so that there would be an equal number of African, Asian, and European voters.[25] As was to be expected, the major African political leaders repudiated the program and demanded universal adult suffrage on a common electoral roll.[26]

Mau Mau threatened the financial stability, the development vision, and the investment climate of Kenya. Perhaps it was because of Mau Mau's threat to Kenya's economy and fiscality that Ernest Vasey's powers within the government as the minister of finance grew by leaps and bounds. Certainly his political dexterity and financial acumen were to be tested over the next seven years, and they were not found wanting. In contrast to Egypt and Nigeria, the exaltation of Vasey's influence within the government ensured that Kenya's critical economic decisions included input from an individual who had sound financial grounding and an agenda to ensure that economic and financial integrity were not sacrificed to political expediency. In Egypt, Nasser's replacement of the early group of economic and financial experts with men who, though well trained economically, were willing agents of the Egyptian autocrat, and in Nigeria, the resignation of Eric Himsworth as the chief financial secretary symbolized the primacy of politics over economics. As Kenya's minister of finance, Vasey saw his primary task as keeping Kenya on a steady fiscal and developmental course and maintaining investor confidence in the economy.

From the outset, the suppression of Mau Mau placed heavy financial burdens on the Kenyan government. The expense of bringing the First Lancashire Fusiliers and the Royal Air Force (RAF) squadrons to Kenya became an immediate charge to the Kenyan exchequer, thus threatening the fiscal stability of Kenya. Vasey calculated the cost to Kenya of the air campaign alone at £9 per hour and was not surprised that by the end of 1952 his government had exhausted an emergency grant of £750,000 set aside by the Legislative Council from government surpluses.[27] It had done so without, however, covering the expenses of the British army and air force.[28] Baring's plea that the British assume the extra military costs brought no reassurances. The prime minister in London merely stated that the British government would stand behind Kenya.[29] The Kenyans cited the precedent of Malaya, but British officials in London countered that argument by pointing out that Malayan insurgency was communist-

---

[25] No. 273A, T. M. Heiser, Colonial Office, Note on a Discussion on August 11, 1959, PRO CO 822/1862.

[26] *Kenya Weekly News*, August 14, 1959.

[27] Gorell Barnes to A. Johnstone, April 27, 1953, PRO CO 822/477.

[28] Kenya, Legislative Council, *Debates*, vol. 53, January 15, 1953, pp. 21–22.

[29] No. 729, Colonial Office to Baring, July 27, 1953, PRO CO 822/477.

inspired and could be dealt with as a Cold War issue. No such larger concern existed in Kenya, where communist ties had not been demonstrated.[30]

In 1952, Vasey saw his first task as protecting the government's financial balances, which were nearly £9 million and earmarked for development and agricultural price supports, from demands made by the Colonial Office and the British Treasury to allocate the funds to pay for the rising military expenses. He succeeded in doing so, arguing to the Colonial Office and the British Treasury that the government's working balances were critical to the financial health of the country and its ability to attract foreign investment. In the first place, the agricultural marketing boards used the funds to guarantee minimum prices for Kenya's main commodities; they could not safely be reduced below £5 or £6 million, in Vasey's estimation. Yet without an infusion of £6 million in 1953, the balances would dip to less than £2 million.[31]

Vasey also succeeded in linking development financing to military success. He averred that the momentum of the development program must be maintained, especially in areas, like housing for Africans in Nairobi, where the improvement of the African condition would undercut the appeal of the dissidents. The development program had budgeted £30 million for the period 1954 to the end of 1956, but here, too, the metropole wished to reduce expenditures to £10 million.[32] Vasey persuaded the British Treasury to offer Kenya an outright grant of £4 million and an interest-free loan of £2 million for 1954 and to earmark another £5 million for expenditures on African agriculture.[33] These agreements restored the government's working balances and provided the development program with the prospect of full financing.

Nonetheless, the government had to make adjustments in its long-term economic goals for Kenya. As part of the agreement to have access to £6 million in loans and grants from Britain, the Kenyan government agreed to undertake a thoroughgoing reappraisal of its development priorities and its system of taxation. First to occur was the development reappraisal. In this area, Vasey favored projects that would yield immediate financial returns, reserving for better times large expenditures on social services. Development funds would be allocated on a priority basis to water projects, agriculture, roads, and industrial development, while expenditures on education and public health were to be held in abeyance.[34]

[30] No. 828, Baring to Colonial Office, July 8, 1953, PRO CO 822/477.

[31] Hall, Colonial Office Memorandum, July 13, 1953, PRO CO 822/477.

[32] E. Vasey, Appreciation of Colony's Financial Position, September 1953, PRO CO 822/477; H. T. Bourdillon to Drake, November 18, 1953, PRO CO 822/477.

[33] Kenya, Legislative Council, *Debates*, vol. 60, April 23, 1954, pp. 14–63.

[34] Kenya, Legislative Council, *Debates*, vol. 58, October 29, 1953, pp. 132 ff.; Baring to Lyttleton, May 23, 1953, PRO CO 822/577.

In the latter areas, Vasey wished merely to "maintain a minimum range of social services at a minimum standard."[35] The stress on the so-called remunerative state expenditures was not new for Kenya (as it would have been for Nigeria), but it strengthened the Kenyan tendency to emphasize economic growth over social justice.

Next came taxation. In Vasey's view, Kenya could not bear a sharp increase in taxation. New and heavy taxes would frighten away foreign capital, slow the pace of economic growth, and undermine the social and economic programs designed to defeat Mau Mau. Still, in the budgetary projections for fiscal year 1954–55 the Kenyan government confronted a huge deficit, calculated at £10 million, much of which stemmed from escalating military costs. Payments to the RAF for its seventeen-month campaign alone totaled £1,750,000, far in excess of the projected £590,000, and Operation Anvil, so effective in breaking the links between Nairobi and the forests, was costing between £36 and £42 per year per detainee.[36]

Although Vasey secured an additional £6 million from Great Britain to cover part of the £10 million deficit, he was left with no alternative but to raise local taxes. He set £2 million as his target figure for increased revenue so as to keep the deficit from growing beyond £2 million.[37] His budget speech for that year, with its array of new taxes, met with stern opposition in the Legislative Council.[38] But Vasey knew that these taxation increases were vital if Kenya hoped to retain the considerable political and financial autonomy that it had enjoyed in the past. In order to increase revenues by 10 percent (from £20 million to £22 million), the minister of finance raised custom duties on numerous items (alcohol and sugar being the most unpopular), placed a 12 1/2 percent export tax on coffee, and doubled the rate of the personal income tax, with a surcharge added for taxpayers with the largest incomes. In addition, the African poll tax was raised, and inhabitants of the Kikuyu, Embu, and Meru land units were assessed a special Mau Mau tax because of their alleged responsibility for causing Mau Mau.[39]

Aware that government revenue would still fall short of its needs, Vasey promoted a project long favored by representatives of the private sector. In 1954, with the advice of businessmen from London, he announced the creation of the Nairobi stock exchange, modeled after the London exchange.[40] Although the Nairobi exchange was designed to facilitate the trading of stocks and bonds of local and foreign companies and the raising of private equity capital, the officials at the Kenyan Min-

[35] Kenya, Legislative Council, *Debates*, vol. 58, October 29, 1953, p. 157.
[36] *East African Standard*, May 15, 1954.
[37] Ibid., April 24, 1954.
[38] Ibid., May 19, 1954.
[39] Kenya, Legislative Council, *Debates*, vol. 60, April 23, 1954, pp. 14–63.
[40] *East African Standard*, July 2, 1954.

istry of Finance also saw it as an instrument for raising domestic capital for state development loans. One of the first issues floated on the new exchange was a £1.5 million loan for the Nairobi city council, which was used primarily to finance the construction of African housing estates. It was quickly oversubscribed.[41]

The government of Kenya continued to receive loans and grants from Britain between 1955 and the end of 1957, but the winding down of the military campaign in 1957 forced it once again to consider ways to become financially self-sufficient. In 1955, emergency costs were running at £1.25 million a month, and Vasey was able to extract funds from Britain to cover most of the budgetary shortfall.[42] For the fiscal year 1955–56, the United Kingdom increased its contribution to £14 million, of which £10 million was in the form of a grant and £4 million an interest-free loan; by the end of that fiscal year, the total metropolitan assistance to Kenya had reached £25 million.[43] Britain provided another substantial tranche in 1956–57 after the effort of the Kenya government to obtain alternative sources of financing in Europe and North America failed.[44]

The vast infusion of British funds made possible the extensive military operations against Mau Mau and sustained the development program as well. These external resources kept the Kenyan economy relatively buoyant, certainly more so than many had believed possible in light of the military and political disturbances. They also generated considerable employment possibilities. Indeed, by the end of 1959 the financial infusion totaled £31,000,000, of which £25,000,000 came in the form of a grant and £6,050,000 came as an interest-free loan, repayable in twenty-eight years.[45]

Yet the fiscal year of 1957–58 loomed ominously for Kenya because the British government was no longer willing to cover Kenya's deficits. The next several years proved the most difficult of Vasey's tenure at the Ministry of Finance, and ended, in 1959, with his resignation from official and parliamentary life in Kenya. Vasey was under few illusions about the financial prospects at the time or the likelihood that his policies would enjoy widespread support in the Parliament and the press. In 1957–58, the United Kingdom had reduced its financial assistance from £8 million to £3 million and expressed its expectation that Kenya be self-supporting in the next fiscal years. Vasey was also aware that he would

[41] Ibid., July 17, 1954.

[42] Ibid., January 14, 1955.

[43] Ibid., February 24, 1955; Kenya, Legislative Council, *Debates*, vol. 64, February 23, 1955, pp. 273–77.

[44] A. F. Kirby, General Manager, East African Railways and Harbors, to Commissioner of Transport, June 19, 1956, KNA CS1/16/29.

[45] Kenya, Legislative Council, *Debates*, vol. 79, February 18, 1959, pp. 16–22.

face a new and more critical constellation of political forces in the Kenyan Parliament, including the first elected African delegates; those worries proved well founded. Odinga and Mboya, for instance, scrutinized the Kenyan development projects for 1957 and found them wanting from the African perspective. Mboya complained about the skewed income levels and contended that Vasey's development vision was "aimed at enriching the rich and leaving the poor where they are." He claimed to favor socialist prescriptions for development over the government's capitalist orientation.[46]

By 1958 the opposition to Vasey had reached new heights. Previously, parliamentary delegates had deferred to their minister of finance because of his success in extracting funds from London. But as those funds diminished, his critics were emboldened to unleash their complaints. An often arrogant and opinionated man who had bloodied those with the audacity to attack him in the Legislative Council, Vasey became the object of retaliation. Humphrey Slade complained that he, too, had advanced training in economics but that his fiscal suggestions were ridiculed. Vasey's most dogged parliamentary opponent, Reginald S. Alexander, believed that his own expertise in fiscal and economic matters was second to none. The confrontations between those two strong-willed men produced a level of verbal and intellectual tension never before seen in debates over economic and financial matters in the colony. Vasey's last three budgets, 1957–58 through 1959–60, sparked animated discussion in the Legislative Council and led Alexander and his supporters to demand the naming of a special commissioner to inquire into Kenya's fiscal policies.[47]

The attack on Vasey was only partly personal. It also stemmed from differences over who would dictate the colony's economic policies—whether it would be a liberal appointed to a cabinet office by the governor (Vasey) or persons enjoying the approval of unofficial European groups. The actual differences between Vasey and Alexander on most economic issues were barely discernible. The things Alexander wanted—more money for development, reduction of the burden of personal and corporate taxation, and alternative sources of foreign funds—were precisely the things Vasey had succeeded in getting.[48] But Vasey's political positions offended important European political leaders in Kenya. Because he was without a political following (although his support within the Asian and African communities was on the rise), he found himself vulnerable to European challengers. When Vasey, in a moment of candor

---

[46] Ibid., vol. 72, part 1, April 9–17, 1957, pp. 22–359.
[47] Ibid., vol. 76, part 2, June 17, 1958, pp. 1938 ff.
[48] Ibid., part 1, May 1, 1958, pp. 74 ff.

yet political folly, remarked that an African majority was inevitable in Kenya, he became a political outcast within the European community—a man who was viewed as a traitor to the settler cause.[49] From that moment, his political future in Kenya was sealed.

Vasey's next-to-last budget (1958–59) brought discontent to a head. Confronted with the withdrawal of British financing, the minister of finance introduced a series of tax hikes. One of the new taxes, the undistributed corporate profits levy, led to an outpouring of discontent, particularly from the business community, which to that point had been his strongest European supporter. The tax was intended to close a tax loophole on groups and individuals who were turning themselves into corporations in order to escape the personal income tax. According to the new law, a corporate entity was allowed to plow back only 20 percent of its profits into the firm; any excess was taxed at the regular company rate. Vasey contended that the law protected corporations that had genuine capital expansion programs and applied only to individuals and small groups who used incorporation to evade taxation.[50] Either because the law was inexpertly drafted or because of Vasey's growing unpopularity, the undistributed profits tax drove a wedge between the private sector and the government of Kenya. The ordinarily supportive Nairobi Chamber of Commerce organized much of the opposition, devoting so many sessions to this one issue that a member complained that little else found its way onto the agenda.[51]

One of the most important consequences of combatting Mau Mau was the government's decision to encourage African capital accumulation and the emergence of a propertied African middle class. Reversing a half-century position toward African producers, the colonial administration undertook to encourage private initiative and free markets in the reserves, though it did so in ways that revealed profound ambivalence. To be sure, the administration did little to promote African commerce, which was still insignificant in relationship to European and Asian business. Its goal was to facilitate private landowning and capital growth among progressive African farmers in the sections of Kenya where commercialized agriculture had begun to take root, most notably the Kikuyu, Luo, and Abaluyha land units and the Machakos district of the Kamba land unit.

Previously, the colonial rulers had wanted to shield African reserves from what were considered the corrosive effects of capital, justifying

---

[49] BBC Television Interview, March 1958, PRO CO 822/1309.

[50] Kenya, Legislative Council, *Debates*, vol. 76, part 1, May 7, 1958, p. 273.

[51] Nairobi Chamber of Commerce, Minutes of the General Meetings, May 19, 1958, and January 26, 1959.

their stance on the grounds that Africans were communalists who did not recognize private property and eschewed acquisitiveness. Believing that the most effective way to administer these societies was through traditional rulers and customary law and practice, British officials resisted demands to recognize individual land rights. In the 1930s, for example, when aspiring Kikuyu cultivators, fearful of the alienation of land in the Kikuyu land unit, asked the government to issue land deeds to them, the government demurred.

The postwar demands for full production throughout the British empire meant that the African reserves in Kenya had to be more than labor-supplying areas for European farms. They had to increase their own agricultural production. In addition, the trauma of Mau Mau intensified the search for political moderates and caused the administration to devise policies that would favor an African gentry class. Although the two-volume *Report* of the East Africa Royal Commission, published in 1955, was a confusing and contradictory document, it was cited to justify the cautious procapitalist orientation in the African reserves.

The Royal Commission's main conclusion was that the East African economies had failed to achieve maximum returns on the land because of restrictive landholding regulations. The commissioners depicted the Kenyan policy of reserving lands to ethnic groups as regressive and anti-capitalist, and they placed heavy responsibility on the Kenya Land Commission of 1932–33 for legitimizing tribal units of land and resisting the emergence of private property and prosperous African landowners. In their conclusion the commissioners asserted that "tribal and racial boundaries" must be replaced in favor of individual titles to the land. Even the privileged European highlands had to be opened to efficient farmers of all races, although, mindful of the sensitivity of European opinion on the subject, the commission asked only that non-European cultivators of proven skill be given the right to lease lands in the highlands.[52]

The findings of the Royal Commission hardly came as a surprise. Similar recommendations had appeared in other parts of British Africa at the time. Much of the report was even prefigured in a document issued in 1954 by Kenya's minister of agriculture, R. J. M. Swynnerton. Swynnerton, too, believed that the restrictions on African farming had to be abolished so that the reserves could take their place alongside European agricultural areas as effective units of production. On the basis of his recommendations, the Ministry of Agriculture allocated £5 million over the period 1955 to 1959 to expand the cultivation of cash crops in African units and encourage private property. Through the spread of coffee,

[52] East Africa Royal Commission, *Report*, 1955–56, House of Commons Sessional Papers, vol. 13, cmd. 9475, pp. 50 ff.

tea, sisal, and fruits, some 60,000 African farming families were expected to see their incomes lifted from £10 to £100 or more per year. Similarly, by encouraging more efficient herding, the value of livestock was expected to rise from £2 per cow to £10 or £15.[53] The Swynnerton plan set ambitious target figures for African cash cropping: 71,500 acres of coffee, 48,000 acres of pyrethrum, 12,000 acres of tea, 25,000 acres of pineapples, and 45,000 acres of sugar under cultivation by 1968; in comparison, the 1954 levels were 4,000 acres of coffee, 130 of pyrethrum, 35 of tea, 3,000 of pineapples, and 200 of sugar cane.[54]

Although the government began the immediate implementation of the new private property initiatives within the African areas, the commitment to the new departures did not pervade the colonial administration, where old attitudes were deeply entrenched. Progressive African farmers questioned the government's willingness to change and accused the state of wanting to create a class of yeoman farmers rather than a smaller group of truly market-oriented and profit-seeking expert cultivators. Eliud Mathu complained in the Legislative Council that the administration prevented the most successful African coffee farmers from transforming their estates into plantations on a scale comparable with that of the European coffee farms.[55] In its defense, the ministry actually confirmed Mathu's charge of impeding the spread of a capitalist ethos into the reserves. Spokespersons for the ministry argued that restricting the expansion of African cash cropping was essential in order to ensure the high quality of production and claimed that the only way to limit expansion was to license all cultivators and limit each one to three acres of land and 1,500 trees. Blundell, the minister of agriculture, stated, "We [the Ministry of Agriculture] cannot leave the development of coffee to a few rapacious fellows in the African land units, leaving out the great bulk of the people."[56]

Mau Mau represented a frightening challenge to the government's financial leaders. They feared that Kenya would lose its high financial standing with overseas investors, and they intensified their efforts to attract overseas capital to the Kenyan private sector. The state became even more willing than before to make crucial concessions to foreign corporations. For example, it used an act of Parliament to silence opposition to setting aside land at Bambari for a cement factory, questions having been

[53] Baring to Lyttleton, March 19, 1954, PRO CO 822/963.
[54] Kenya, *A Plan to Intensify the Development of African Agriculture in Kenya* (Nairobi, 1954), p. 10.
[55] Kenya, Legislative Council, *Debates*, vol. 69, June 14, 1956, pp. 1447–87.
[56] Ibid., p. 1470.

raised at the coast about noise and air pollution.[57] A complaint from the East African Tobacco Company, a subsidiary of British American Tobacco, about a government concession to the Kenya Tobacco Company, an undercapitalized competitor in Kenya, was quickly addressed.[58] Government officials warmly endorsed a proposal from the Shell Oil Company to build a large oil refinery at Mombasa. In the Legislative Council debate on a land concession to Shell, the scheme's most energetic backers, Hope-Jones and Vasey, brushed aside worries that the landowners would not be fairly compensated and that the plant would be noisy and cause pollution.[59] Enthralled by the prospect of injecting £40 million of investment capital in the country at such a propitious moment, Vasey exulted about "bringing to this colony a tremendous economic asset which will provide employment for a large number of people in this colony."[60] Although the agreement was not finalized until 1959, when Shell Oil built a £15 million refinery at the coast and created a local subsidiary, the Kenya Oil Company, at no stage in the negotiations did the state consider strengthening the public sector controls over this vital industry.[61]

In 1952 the Kenyan government believed that it had finally reached an agreement with East African Portland Cement Company for the creation of Kenya's second cement plant at Sultan Hamud in the Kajiado district. The project continued to languish, however, until the government made additional concessions.[62] First, Governor Baring promised the firm a long-term lease in the Kajiado district, and next, he assured the firm's executives that he would override any objections that the district officer of Kajiado or the Masai District Council might raise against the agreement.[63] Only then did the East African Portland Cement Company increase its equity capital from £140,000 to £1 million and commence work on the factory.[64] East African Portland Cement obtained a ninety-nine-year lease on the 1,044 acres of land it required for the project. Numerous smaller issues were also settled in its favor, to the disadvantage of the Maasai people, who were forced to accept lesser royalty payments than the district officer and the Masai District Council considered just. The granting

[57] See KNA MCI 6/1456.

[58] No. 167, P. J. Rogers of East African Tobacco Company Ltd, December 1, 1952, KNA MCI 6/444.

[59] Kenya, Legislative Council, *Debates*, vol. 57, October 7, 1953, pp. 20 ff.

[60] Ibid., p. 30.

[61] No. 77, Ad Hoc Committee on Drawbacks of Customs Duties, 33rd Meeting, July 9, 1956, KNA MCI 6/691; *Kenya Weekly News*, September 18, 1959.

[62] No. 47/1, Extract of Letter from C. J. M. Alport, House of Commons, to Frederick Crawford, Government House, Nairobi, February 18, 1954, KNA MCI 6/395.

[63] No. 165/1, N. M. Jensen to Baring, July 16, 1954, KNA MCI 6/395.

[64] Press Handout 32, n.d., but mid-1953, KNA MCI 6/294.

of such a long lease in an area that had an extended history of bitter colonial land disputes underscored how vital the government officials believed foreign investment to be.[65]

Two of the government's most cherished corporate projects were also brought to fruition during the Mau Mau years. The first was the final agreement with Unilever, signed in October 1953, to assume managerial control of East African Industries and develop plans for establishing a chemicals industries in Kenya, beginning with the manufacture of sulfuric acid and caustic soda.[66] Unilever also entered the soap manufacturing sector through its affiliate, East African Industries, investing £416,000 in fixed assets and borrowing £125,000 locally for its working capital.[67]

The second project was the expansion of the Kenya Canners Company, a British firm first established in Kenya in 1948. Kenya Canners became important to the administration after the publication of the Swynnerton report because of its likely contribution to cash crop cultivation in the Kikuyu districts. Kenya Canners derived most of its capital from Pickerings Ltd of the United Kingdom and was headed by the British food processing executive of Pickerings, B. T. West. By 1956 its equity capital was £125,000.[68] West envisaged the establishment of a large-scale canning business in the highlands of Kenya, specializing in the preservation of pineapples and tomatoes and their export to the United Kingdom. He selected Thika as the location for his factory so as to be able to use the production of settler estates in the vicinity. Responding to the new government emphasis on African agriculture, the firm agreed to include African farmers in nearby Kiambu and Fort Hall districts.[69]

The firm, which had languished in its early years and had complained frequently about a lack of government support, now found the state ready to give it every encouragement. To begin with, the government's avowed preference for open competition in this manufacturing sector gave way to unstinting support of Kenya Canners. In 1955 the local British agent of the firm, T. Benson, outlined a scheme of plant expansion involving the expenditure of £250,000 as "the first step in the establishment of a Kenya canning industry for all horticultural products."[70]

---

[65] No. 179, Baring to Lennox-Boyd, August 14, 1954, KNA MCI 6/395.

[66] No. 2, M. Campbell, Secretary of East African Industries, to Member for Commerce and Industry, August 22, 1952, KNA MCI 6/696; J. Hansard, Note on Visit to Kenya, October 3, 1953, Unilever Archives.

[67] Minutes of Meeting of Special Committee with Overseas Committee, November 23, 1954, Unilever Archives.

[68] No. 308/3, Kenya Canners Ltd, September 28, 1956, KNA MCI 6/419.

[69] No. 64, Note by R. O. Hennings, February 28, 1957, KNA MCI 6/420.

[70] No. 91/1, Record of a Meeting Held in the Ministry of Agriculture, June 20, 1955, KNA MCI 6/526.

Kenya Canners did not prosper, however. The export market that the firm envisaged for itself in Britain failed to materialize when Britain was swamped with cheap tinned pineapples from Formosa. Kenya Canners was also beset by numerous manufacturing deficiencies. Rather than see the firm go bankrupt, however, the government provided loans and then allowed the fruit and vegetable growers and the firm to establish a canning board to control marketing and fix prices.[71] In spite of these aids, the firm continued to falter, and it was with considerable relief that the state saw another British-financed firm, the Tanganyika Cotton Company of I. S. Ednie, buy out the interests of Pickering and assume control over Kenya Canners.[72]

Although locally based European investors did not receive the same encouragement that foreign investors did, the colonial government was eager to support domestic capitalists of European backgrounds in this time of trouble. The most seriously afflicted was the business empire of Charles Markham. Markham, who had bid on a cement factory at one stage, was primarily involved in the mining of kyanite, a mineral with a bluish color, used in precision castings and cements. Kenya possessed one of the few kyanite deposits in the world. Kenya's kyanite factory was located at Marka, near the deposits themselves, about 130 miles inland from Mombasa, on the edge of Tsavo National Park. The Kenyan government was eager to develop this secondary industry and looked to Markham to provide the financial and managerial leadership.[73]

Unfortunately, the enterprise had arisen in a haphazard fashion, and Markham was unable to make it efficient. Major financial problems beset Kenya Kyanite by the mid-1950s, and even a government loan of £25,000 and a promise of additional financing of £75,000 did not relieve the pressure. The prospect of bankruptcy alarmed officials at the Ministry of Commerce and Industry, where it was thought that "if . . . all of the plant were sold at knock down prices, this would involve almost the entire loss of the money invested by the Markham family in a pioneering enterprise which was of undoubted economic value to the colony."[74] To prevent outright bankruptcy, the government-run Industrial Development Corporation of Kenya took over the management of the enterprise with a view to selling it to a foreign firm.[75] When Anglo-American of South

[71] No. 131, G. Bursell, Chairman of Thika Pineapple Growers Association and Thika Fruit Growers Cooperative Association, to Executive Director, Industrial Development Corporation, September 5, 1957, KNA MCI 6/420.

[72] *East African Standard*, January 13, 1956.

[73] No. 2, Aide-Mémoire of a Discussion, August 26, 1954, KNA MCI 6/371.

[74] Ibid.

[75] No. 107/1, S. W. Harding, Acting Commissioner of Mines and Geology, to Manager, Anglo-American Corporation of South Africa, July 29, 1955, KNA MCI 6/371.

Africa declined to invest, the state turned to an American firm, New Consolidated Gold Fields, which bought the Markham enterprise.[76] New Consolidated Gold Fields did not succeed, however, in making the enterprise a success.

Although the administration encouraged local European capitalists, the Mau Mau challenge did not cause it to soften its attitude toward Asian capital. Asian businessmen encountered continued administrative suspicion, against which they protested in a steady stream of letters to government officials.[77] The tension between the state and the Asian business community became so acute that successive presidents of the powerful Indian Chamber of Commerce of Nairobi charged the colonial government with violating its commitment to private enterprise in its dealings with Asian concerns.[78]

Instances of state-Asian business tension abounded. The state blocked the sale of a large percentage of shares in the Allsopp's Brewery in East Africa to Asian investors. An Asian request to purchase the Match Company was rejected on the grounds that the firm was located in the highlands, where Asian landowning was disallowed. The state sanctioned the sale only when the new owners agreed to relocate the business at the coast.[79] The Kholi family, owners of the Elephant Soap Company, continued to do battle with the Ministry of Commerce and Industry over drawbacks on imported raw materials and protection against the dumping of foreign soap products on the local market.[80] No doubt the company was remiss in maintaining and presenting the kind of detailed corporate records that the ministry insisted on having. But the drawn-out negotiations (most of which ended in compromises between the ministry and the firm) made long-range financial planning impossible.[81]

The main Indian entrepreneurs in Kenya, the Chandarias, were fairly bursting with new projects and had established themselves as the most

[76] No. 142, G. W. J. Collis of New Consolidated Gold Fields Ltd, to Charles Markham, September 16, 1955, KNA MCI 6/371.

[77] No. 109/1, M. S. Khimasia, Indian Chamber of Commerce, to Ministry of Commerce and Industry, May 1958; no. 107, J. H. Martin, Acting Secretary of the Ministry of Commerce and Industry, to Honorable Secretary, Indian Chamber of Commerce, Nairobi, May 16, 1958, KNA MCI 6/722.

[78] See the speech by President M. S. Khimasia on April 26, 1958, in No. 104/1, and that of President K. P. Shah on March 21, 1959, in no. 115/1; both in KNA MCI 6/722.

[79] No. 156/n, Record of a Meeting at Parliament, March 1, 1956, KNA MCI 6/726.

[80] No. 89, A. M. Craig of Elephant Soap Factory Ltd to the Secretary for Commerce and Industry, August 16, 1955; and no. 110/1, Memorandum, Customs Duty on Tallow and Fatty Acid for Soap Making by Chanan, Singh, and Handa, Advocates for Elephant Soap Factory Ltd, January 6, 1956; both in KNA MCI 6/697.

[81] No. 138, A. M. Craig, Elephant Soap, to Ministry of Commerce and Industry, October 29, 1956, KNA MCI 6/697.

innovative business force in Kenya. The family's major firm, the Kenya Aluminum and Industrial Works, was a private, limited-liability company, the equity capital of which was held almost entirely within the Chandaria family. The government estimated the firm's capital resources at £1 million in 1959; they were composed of buildings worth £200,000, machinery worth £350,000, and the remainder in working capital.[82] Although not the most heavily capitalized company in Kenya, it was assuredly the most industrially prolific. The Chandarias had created an aluminum rolling plant in Kenya that they boasted would shortly become "one of the largest plants of its kind in Africa, able to cater for all the requirements of the market in the manufacturing of aluminum."[83] The company also manufactured hurricane lamps, nails, oil stoves, and galvanized hollowware and enamelware utensils and ran several cereal gristing mills. It had schemes to establish a bicycle firm and, in conjunction with a foreign manufacturer, to create the first iron and steel complex in East Africa.

Given the wide range of new industrial enterprises in which the Chandarias had invested or were contemplating investment, the family looked to the state for support. On occasions too numerous to catalogue, its representatives were involved in arguments with the Ministry of Commerce and Industry over drawbacks, tariff protection, and antidumping legislation against foreign competitors. During one dispute over drawbacks and tariff protection for its hurricane lamps, H. L. Adams of the Ministry of Commerce and Industry complained of growing "weary with reconsideration of these applications," but added that "when all is said and done, they [the Chandarias] are, to a large extent, pioneers and making heavy capital investment in the colony."[84]

The Chandarias' differences with the government came to a head in 1953 when the family asked to have most of the industries in which it was working scheduled and then protected from internal competitors. The firm's executives requested the scheduling of aluminum rolling mills, hurricane lamps, nails, oil stoves, cereal gristing mills, and galvanized hollowware and enamelware utensils.[85] The requests could not have come at a more inopportune time: the colonial authorities in Nairobi and London were on the verge of concluding that scheduling impeded industrial innovation and, if continued, would leave East Africa with a group of inefficient, high-cost firms, able to survive only behind heavy tariff bar-

---

[82] R. P. Chandaria, Director of Kenya Aluminum and Industrial Works, to Ministry of Commerce and Industry, February 25, 1959, KNA State House 4/411.

[83] No. 105, D. P. Chandaria to Secretary for Commerce and Industry, July 16, 1954, KNA MCI 6/694.

[84] No. 23, Note by H. L. Adams, Secretary for Commerce and Industry, October 6, 1953, KNA MCI 6/694.

[85] No. 29, R. P. Chandaria to Hope-Jones, November 10, 1953, KNA MCI 6/462.

riers. Within months of receiving the application, the Ministry of Industry and Commerce had rejected most of the requests.

The ministry did not rule out the scheduling of aluminum rolling and oil stoves, however, and asked R. Chandaria to supply more information.[86] Chandaria could scarcely conceal his disappointment, which was made all the more intense by the government's highly publicized trips to Europe in search of new investment capital. In his letter of complaint he wrote: "I cannot help but compare this very bleak result with the list of industries already scheduled since I understand it is customary for overseas firms who may contemplate starting a local industry to get the industry scheduled automatically by the government." Although his description of the use of scheduling was not entirely accurate, his general observation about the lack of support for his firm and those of other local capitalists was valid. He concluded his critique of government policy with a natural question: "What are government's intentions concerning industry and capital already established here?" He then berated the government by claiming that government officials "regard any request made by foreign industry for assistance genuine and any request made by local industries as suspicious and made with the only object of looting government's good money in any way possible."[87]

Late in the Mau Mau period the Chandarias engaged in another quarrel with the Ministry of Commerce and Industry. They requested government assistance in the establishment of a bicycle factory and asked for the scheduling of the bicycle industry. Again, the ministry balked. As usual, it complained about the firm's failure to provide full information on the industry. Not lost on the Chandaria executives was the fact that the scheduling of a bicycle industry in East Africa would be at the expense of imported British-made bicycles.[88]

The Chandarias did have some leverage with the government, and they used it, as a last resort, to secure the scheduling of their enamelware industry, albeit for a mere two years. Because the firm also had investments in the Belgian Congo, Tanganyika, and Somalia, its executives could threaten to move capital and factories to these countries.[89] Yet the state's support was never more than lukewarm.

In the end, the Chandaria firm did not persuade the ministry to schedule the manufacture of bicycles, but before the dispute came to an end, R. P. Chandaria left the government with an impassioned articulation of the

[86] No. 18, G. P. Henderson, Registrar, Industrial Licenses, Kenya, to Managing Director of Kenya Aluminum and Industrial Works, October 16, 1953, KNA MCI 6/462.

[87] No. 29, R. P. Chandaria to Hope-Jones, November 10, 1953, KNA MCI 6/462.

[88] No. 268, Note by G. P. Henderson, May 3, 1957, KNA MCI 6/462.

[89] No. 49/1, Appendix to no. 49, G. P. Henderson to the Principal, London School of Economics, September 2, 1954, KNA MCI 6/462.

infant industry argument. In answering the charge that his products were expensive, he wrote: "With regard to the question of price, it can be easily understood that to begin with in a country where there is no prime mover available, where raw materials have to be obtained from overseas, where technicians have to be imported and kept at high costs, where labour is unskilled and has to be trained at considerable expense, and where setbacks are inevitable, the cost of the locally manufactured article is bound to be high. But it is only by the commencement of industrial undertakings that progress can be achieved and related industries set up."[90]

Kenya concluded the era of Mau Mau suppression with its finances intact and its private sector unexpectedly vibrant. Capital was still flowing into the economy, and business firms remained optimistic about future earnings. Much less clear, however, was the likely evolution of the polity, and this uncertainty clouded the financial prospects of Kenya. Whether the colonial authorities in London and Nairobi could forge agreements among the most powerful groups in Kenya and work out compromises for the sharing of authority remained in doubt. In the political arena where these disputes were occurring three men dominated the Mau Mau years: Ernest Vasey, Michael Blundell, and Tom Mboya. Their aspirations, and especially their interactions with one another, were likely to determine the political and economic evolution of Kenya after Mau Mau had been suppressed. Yet their relations between 1952 and 1959 did not bode well for the future. Vasey was the European unofficial with the most progressive political views, and he enjoyed a wide following among Asians and Africans. He had no following within his own community, however, and he had been forced to withdraw to Tanganyika by the close of the period. Although his political and social views were far from extreme, his call for conferring power on elected African representatives and his plea to establish model mixed schools were greeted with settler disapproval.[91]

The other prominent settler leader, Michael Blundell, eschewed radical confrontations favored by the extremists and was eager to support the Lyttleton and Lennox-Boyd constitutions. But he did not enjoy the trust of African leaders. He worked comfortably with the conservative, government-nominated African politicians whom the colonial authorities hoped would win favor among the African masses. But more nationalistically minded Africans had consistently defeated these men in elec-

---

[90] No. 225, R. P. Chandaria to Secretary for Commerce and Industry, December 19, 1956, KNA MCI 6/462.

[91] Vasey to Baring, October 23, 1953; Vasey to the Aga Khan, November 26, 1953; Vasey to Havelock, February 11, 1953; and Aide-Mémoire by Vasey, February 3, 1953; all in the Vasey Papers.

toral contests. Although Blundell had come some distance since 1953, when he had demanded an all-white East African Royal Commission and a Colonial Office statement guaranteeing European control over the highlands, he was still a bitter opponent of the Mboya-Odinga vision of Kenya as a purely African country, whose political evolution was to be no different from that of Ghana.[92] And the Colonial Office was not confident of his political astuteness. Its officials worried about his volatile political temperament. A colonial officer in Kenya described Blundell in 1952 as "inexperienced but brilliant, tolerant, popular with Africans but slightly fascist-minded. He could one day be the George Washington of Kenya."[93] The colonial authorities believed that Blundell had moderated his earlier political views and become more realistic, but their concerns had not been totally allayed. As Kenya entered the last stage of its decolonization journey, the prospects of peaceful transition remained in doubt.

To Blundell, the most dangerous of the African political leaders not in detention was Tom Mboya. Most of the British establishment also saw Mboya in this light. Virtually every political action Blundell took in the later Mau Mau years was designed to undercut Mboya's legitimacy. Mboya's fearlessness and his outspokenness in favor of an all-African state, his trade union leadership, and his support among the Americans engendered profound worry among British colonial officials. In reality, foreign investors were ahead of the colonial officials in realizing that Mboya held the meaningful political power, and they played a critical role in altering the settler and Colonial Office stance toward Mboya.

[92] Verbatim Report of Secretary of State and European Elected Members Held at Government House, October 30, 1952, PRO CO 822/460; Report of a Meeting between Secretary of State and European Elected Members, Nairobi, May 18, 1953, PRO CO 822/714.

[93] Teeling to Lyttleton, October 22, 1952, PRO CO 822/438.

CHAPTER 11

Stemming the Flight of Capital, 1960–1963

KENYA ENTERED the third and last phase of the transfer of power, 1960–1963, with its private sector more secure than it was at similar stages in Egypt and Nigeria. Through the efforts of the British military and the financial and political sagacity of Ernest Vasey, the Mau Mau subalternist threat to Britain's development vision had been thwarted. For many of the later commentators on Kenya, then, the final arrangements for the transfer of power to African leaders reflected the success of British decolonizing policies. In contrast to Egypt and Nigeria, a pro-Western successor regime with a relatively intact and healthy private sector came into being in Kenya.

Most of the commentators on the transfer of power in Kenya have described a bargain supposedly struck between moderate African nationalists and multinational capital at the expense of obdurate and reactionary farmers and distressed and radicalized Africans. This bargain, it has been suggested, was cemented with the transfer of vast tracts of land in the formerly European highlands to African farmers. Through this accommodation, it has been argued, the colonial authorities preserved the most dynamic portion of Kenya's agricultural economy—its plantation estates—while sacrificing its least profitable enterprises—the European mixed farms—to African land hunger. In the process, British policy makers protected the private sector, preventing anticapitalist elements from seizing power, and they laid the preconditions for a smooth and procapitalist transfer of authority to moderates.

From this perspective, then, the Kenya story would seem to contrast sharply with that of Egypt and Nigeria, where British plans for ordering the postcolonial evolution were so often ineffective and undermined. The trouble with this interpretation is that it finds order and coherence where little existed. It suggests that the British officials had an understanding of African nationalism and the concerns of business groups in Kenya that a closer examination of the events does not substantiate. Although the British realized the desired outcome for Kenya's decolonization—the preservation of a relatively strong private sector—the final settlement owed more to African and Indian initiatives than to British policies.

The "grand compromise" between moderate nationalists and multinational capital that Britain achieved at independence was far from the purposeful unfolding of an all-encompassing blueprint. It seems closer to developments already described in Egypt and Nigeria. If British capital emerged in a stronger position in Kenya than in the other two polities, the negotiations that protected the interests of foreign capital occurred in an atmosphere of confusion and were marked by surprising turns. The final arrangements were more often the result of unexpected and unpredictable developments than the culmination of a coherent strategy for devolving power to a neocolonial elite. Indeed, the crucial decisions to transfer land from the European-dominated highlands and thus to protect land values were made only at the last minute and only after setting aside significant tenets of the development strategies and fiscal policies that had informed British policy since the end of World War II. And by the date of independence the decolonization settlement was by no means secure. Unlike in Nigeria, the British had succeeded in preserving the autonomy of the private sector; and unlike in Egypt, they had succeeded in neutralizing a spate of socialist rhetoric that marked the immediate aftermath of the Lancaster House Conference of 1960 and the release of Jomo Kenyatta, the supposed leader of Mau Mau, from detention. Those achievements had, in fact, resulted in creating a political economy that Indian businessmen were better able to take advantage of than British-based capital.

On January 12, 1960, Kenya ended its state of emergency.[1] The conclusion of the struggle to defeat Mau Mau enabled the state to terminate many, though not all of the extensive powers it had been using to combat military and political challenges.[2] But despite the conclusion of the fighting, Kenya's private sector and its investors faced their most severe challenge in the postwar era.

The lifting of the emergency compelled the British government once again to review Kenya's political and economic institutions. Although the discussions that took place at Lancaster House in London in 1960 focused on constitutional matters, they also dealt with crucial economic concerns, because their resolution was likely to determine which among the various Kenyan groups vying for power would emerge in the strongest position. Three broad Kenyan political groups took part in the conference: the African Elected Members Organization, who, for the moment, set aside differences that had nearly produced two opposing political parties; and European settlers who were split into two camps.[3] The New Kenya Party of Michael Blundell included among its more than twenty delegates some Africans and Asians and was opposed by the

---

[1] No. 2, Renison to Colonial Office, January 11, 1960, PRO CO 822/1901.

[2] Kenya, Legislative Council, *Debates*, vol. 83, January 4 and 5, 1960, pp. 1224–1307 and 1342 ff.

[3] No. 12, W. F. Coutts, Chief Secretary, Kenya, to Granville Roberts, January 8, 1960, PRO CO 822/2100.

United Party, which bristled at any concession being offered to African nationalist demands. Although represented by only three persons in London, the United Party had widespread European support in Kenya.

The chasm that separated the African delegates from even the most liberal-minded of the Europeans was wide and seemingly unbridgeable. The forceful Tom Mboya demanded an African chief minister, universal adult suffrage, no communal elections, no special seats, and seventy-two single-member constituencies.[4] Colonial Secretary Iain Macleod demurred, insisting that "none of these things can be given."[5] Appalled at the sweep of the African proposals, the European delegates complained that the Africans were not negotiating flexibly. Reginald Alexander and Humphrey Slade, part of the New Kenya Party, threatened a walkout, and Blundell insisted that one man, one vote would swamp the European electorate and lead to political chaos. He and his supporters would accept common roll elections only if a restricted franchise created roughly equal electorates for the three racial communities. The Europeans also demanded reserved seats, preferably chosen communally.[6]

Through Colonial Secretary Macleod's prodding, the differences on political questions were narrowed. This success raised social and economic questions to high prominence, and the entirety of the private sector was brought to the forefront of the debate. The New Kenya Party demanded property guarantees; the African representatives, though willing to accept a bill of rights and to promise sanctity of private property, refused to issue a comprehensive statement on property. Equally conflictual was the issue of education. No European leaders would accept integrated education, and no African could ask for less.[7]

The deep differences on social and economic questions meant that the final Lancaster House accord of 1960 could be no more than a political agreement and that it had to be imposed by the colonial secretary. Thus, it contained no provision about property except for Macleod's assurance that the British government would lend £5 million for land development and allow some of the money to be used for the purchase of European land for sale to African farmers.[8] The New Kenya Party accepted the accord only after Secretary Macleod met separately with Blundell, W. B. Havelock, Slade, Amalemba, and C. B. Madan and reaffirmed his promise of finding funds for land transfers. Macleod also endorsed the party's segregationist stance on education. In contrast, the colonial secretary re-

---

[4] *East African Standard*, March 4, 1960.

[5] I. Macleod to Home Secretary, February 1, 1960, PRO PREM 11/3030.

[6] No. 4, Blundell to Macleod, February 2, 1960, PRO CO 822/2025.

[7] *East African Standard*, February 3 and 18, 1960; Macleod to the Prime Minister, February 20, 1960, PRO PREM 11/3030.

[8] Macleod to Prime Minister, February 20, 1960, PRO PREM 11/3030.

fused to meet with L. R. Briggs, head of the United Party, on the grounds that this party represented something that was "very close to apartheid." He reminded the New Kenya Party delegates how vital it was to defeat "the old fashioned approach of Group Captain Briggs and his United Party."[9]

Although the New Kenya Party accepted the results of the Lancaster House Conference, its members were astonished at the changed climate of opinion in Britain, which they believed had brought about the radical constitutional proposals. In their view, the British were caught up in a mania of decolonization, and the British decision makers were committed without reservation to African political independence. Blundell was distressed by Macleod's rigidities. Expecting to find a sympathetic Conservative government in office, he was shocked by the colonial secretary's position on most political questions; later he described Macleod as "a Tory Radical . . . convinced that a sweeping transfer of power and influence from European to African hands was necessary in Africa . . . not only because he thought that it was wise but also because it was morally right."[10] In Blundell's view, Macleod maneuvered Briggs's small group out of the debate and made the New Kenya Party the right wing at the talks. Blundell found Macleod's proposals "far in advance of anything which we wished to accept," but he and his party agreed to the secretary's proposals on the understanding that "there was plenty of time for education and development of responsible African opinion."[11]

Under the Macleod constitution, Kenya was equipped with a legislative council with sixty-five seats. The governor was permitted, however, to add seats if he thought it necessary. Fifty-three of the sixty-five members were elected on a common roll based on relatively restrictive franchise requirements involving income, education, and age. Twenty of the fifty-three seats were reserved for minority communities: ten for Europeans, eight for Asians, and two for Arabs, the candidates for which would participate in communally based primary elections in which they would need to garner 25 percent of the vote to proceed to the next electoral stage. The remaining twelve seats were "reserved," four for Europeans, four for Africans, and four for Asians. These delegates were to be chosen by the fifty-three elected members of the Parliament. A Council of Ministers was to be composed of twelve persons of whom four were civil servants, four were Africans, three were Europeans, and one was Asian.[12]

[9] Macleod to Macmillan, February 16, 1960, PRO PREM 11/3031.
[10] Michael Blundell, *So Rough a Wind: The Kenya Memoirs of Sir Michael Blundell* (London, 1964), pp. 270–71.
[11] Ibid., p. 272.
[12] *East African Standard*, February 13, 1960.

The 1960 Lancaster House Conference marked a dramatic political departure in Kenya, a true realization of Prime Minister Harold Macmillan's 1960 speech on the wind of change blowing through the African continent. Despite restrictions on the African franchise, the African political advances were breathtaking. To be sure, communal elections were retained, but in a thoroughly attenuated way through the communal primaries and the reserved seats. The constitution made African majority rule inevitable and held little hope that the pace of change would slow. Africans would even have the decisive votes in the final common roll elections, and they outnumbered non-Africans in the Legislative Council by nine, thirty-seven to twenty-eight.

The Lancaster House constitution provoked a storm of protest in Kenya. The United Party of Briggs repudiated it altogether.[13] Its rejectionism received an immense boost in early March 1960 when F. W. Cavendish-Bentinck resigned as speaker of the Legislative Council, arguing that he could no longer support government policy or remain silent. In the *East African Standard*, he sounded a theme that European settlers would repeat on numerous occasions with devastating psychological effect before the decolonization turmoil ended. "In the past, relying with puerile naivete on assurances and understandings arrived at with the United Kingdom or its representatives," Cavendish-Bentinck iterated, "I have been directly or indirectly responsible for encouraging numbers of young people to come here and settle and to make their lives in the country."[14] Cavendish-Bentinck had been member for agriculture and land settlement before he became speaker, and he had also served as chairman of the Land Settlement Board, which had been instrumental in promoting European immigration. The former speaker of the Legislative Council complained that the Lancaster House terms did not guarantee separate educational and health facilities and provided no compensation for European farmers if their land were expropriated. Within two weeks of his resignation Cavendish-Bentinck announced the founding of a new political organ, the Kenya Coalition, which quickly gained the backing of the United Party.[15]

African opinion was similarly unenthusiastic and fragmented about Lancaster House. Although the coastal politician Ronald Ngala endorsed Macleod's proposals, calling them "a tremendous stride in the right direction and . . . a useful instrument in our country's advance to independence," the immediate consequence of the new constitution was the appearance of two rival political parties.[16] On March 27, 1960, at a

---

[13] Ibid., February 15 and 16, 1960.
[14] Ibid., March 9, 1960.
[15] Ibid., March 22 and 23, 1960.
[16] Ibid., March 14, 1960.

conference held at Limuru and attended by the eight African elected members of the Legislative Council and 120 delegates from all over Kenya, the Kenya African National Union (Kanu) came into being.[17] Although the specific purpose for the calling of the Limuru conference was to designate a team to draw up a constitution for the party—a task deputed to Julius Kiano, Mboya, Odinga, J. W. Mureithi, James Nyamweya, and C. M. G. Argwings-Kodhek—a radical nationalist discourse pervaded many of the discussions at the conference.[18]

On June 25, 1960, two months after the formation of Kanu, the Kenya African Democratic Union (Kadu) came into existence. A loose federation of the Kalenjin Political Alliance, the Masai United Front, the Abaluhya Kenya African People's Party, and the Coast African People's Union, it drew its strength from the minority African communities, many of whom, as pastoralists, feared Kikuyu and Luo expansion into their regions. Kadu was more welcoming to non-African groups and less insistent on the release of Kenyatta. It favored a regional polity for Kenya, rather than a unitary state.[19]

Both Kanu and Kadu were elite parties, however. They represented well-off and well-educated Africans. But they were not disciplined and centralized organizations, and within Kanu regional and more radical subgroups were able to compete for control over local branches and agitate in favor of immediate independence and the wholesale distribution of European properties to impoverished Africans. Kanu's strength came from the most dynamic and politicized of the African ethnic communities—the Kikuyu and Luo—and its policy stances spanned a wider spectrum of political and economic opinion than Kadu's.[20] Its left wing did not shy away from socialist rhetoric and endeavored to represent the wishes of the dispossessed. For this reason the European groups distrusted the Kanu politicians and gravitated toward Kadu.

The constitutional concessions granted at Lancaster House stunned the business community of Kenya as thoroughly as they did the European farmers. Almost overnight, Macleod's program produced a crisis in investor confidence. The *East African Standard* reported on March 19, 1960, just days after the conclusion of the Lancaster House Conference, that nearly £900,000 had been transferred out of the country in a week.[21]

---

[17] Ibid., March 28, 1960.

[18] No. 36, W. F. Coutts, Chief Secretary, Kenya, to Granville Roberts, April 2, 1960, PRO CO 822/2025.

[19] See Suzanne Mueller, "Political Parties in Kenya: Pattern of Opposition and Dissent, 1919–1969," Ph.D. thesis, Princeton University, 1972.

[20] See Apollo Njonjo, "The Africanization of the White Highlands," Ph.D. thesis, Princeton University, 1978; and Geoff Lamb, *Peasant Politics* (Lewes, England, 1974).

[21] *East African Standard*, March 19, 1960.

The efforts of the New Kenya Party to put an optimistic gloss on the new constitution were unavailing. By mid-June 1960 securities on the Nairobi stock exchange had declined 12 percent, falling from £120 million at the opening of the year to £106 million.[22] Banks, building societies, and insurance companies—the primary financial institutions of Kenya's private sector—came under severe financial pressure. Already by the end of July 1960 Kenya's main banks reported the movement of more than £5 million in assets to the United Kingdom, and building societies were forced to reject new loan applicants in order to stabilize their liquidity positions.[23] The Kenya Building Society took an overdraft of £500,000 from its overseas affiliate to cover withdrawals; it expected to apply for another £300,000 by year's end. So ravaged were Kenya's finances that the British cabinet, rarely concerned about the finances of specific African colonial territories, met to discuss measures to inspire investor confidence in Kenya. But the cabinet could find no solutions to the problem of capital transfer, estimated at £4,250,000 from the middle of March to early July 1960.[24]

The loss of investor confidence raised the prospect that the multinational enterprises, so carefully cultivated since the end of World War II, might liquidate their investments in Kenya or adopt a go-slow policy there. Reports that Brooke Bond was contemplating cutting back on its commitments in Kenya dismayed officials at the Colonial Office. Brooke Bond was both a major force in the Kenya economy and one of the most closely watched multinational enterprises there. The Colonial Office concluded that if it withdrew from Kenya or reduced its exposure the rest of the business community would question Kenya's economic future. Shortly after the Lancaster House Conference, John Brooke, chairman of Brooke Bond and Company, expressed his reservations about the new constitution and warned the Colonial Office that the firm would have to "consider the present expansion program involving the planting out of over 500 acres of new tea for a year."[25] So troubled was the Colonial Office about this note that Gorell Barnes met with John Brooke and his second in command, T. D. Rutter, to emphasize the importance the Colonial Office attached to the firm's involvement in Kenya and its need to maintain a regular program of agricultural expansion. The meeting was hardly a success, however. The British business executives reiterated their belief that Lancaster House was a "disaster" that could be mitigated only if the

[22] Ibid., June 14, 1960.

[23] No. 22, J. H. Butter, Treasury, Kenya, to A. N. Galsworthy, Colonial Office, July 27, 1960, PRO CO 822/2560.

[24] Kenya, Land Policy, Memorandum by the Secretary of State for Colonies, July 12, 1960, PRO Cab 129.102, Part 1 C(60)110.

[25] J. Brooke to J. C. Rodgers, Colonial Office, March 17, 1960, PRO CO 822/2127.

British government promised an extended transitional period before independence was granted.[26]

Colonial Office discussion with Unilever business executives produced similar results. George Cole and F. Pedler, the Unilever officials, spoke of their alarm at the precipitous march toward independence and counseled the colonial officials to set forth an extended timetable for self-rule.[27] In both discussions the businessmen objected to statements attributed to radical African nationalists, of whom they singled out Odinga, threatening the wholesale and uncompensated seizure of European properties. Only if these provocative statements ceased, they warned, would European investors regard Kenya as a viable investment area.[28]

The financial reaction to the Lancaster House agreement was one of the defining moments in the decolonization of Kenya. Land questions, a resurgence of Mau Mau, and numerous other concerns were thrown into lesser relief when the colonial authorities were faced with the prospect of British businesses' withdrawing from Kenya. The entirety of the economic and developmental strategies so carefully elaborated after 1945 and so skillfully defended by Vasey was seen to be in jeopardy if the contribution from the private sector could not be relied upon. Without the economic growth that private capital was expected to produce, violence was judged to be inevitable, and any smooth transition to African independence, no matter how extended, would be impossible. While colonial officials did not regard themselves as the handmaids of British capital, the financial panic of March 1960 brought them to the realization that they depended on the business community, and especially the continuing investment interest of British-based multinationals, for achieving their political goals. Henceforth, land adjudication, suppression of violence, appeasing right-wing settlers—all these concerns were subordinated to the creation of a healthy business climate. During the transition to formal political independence, British business leaders in Britain and Kenya were accorded a high level of attention; and the major political and economic reforms, including the transfer of vast tracts of land in the European highlands to African farmers, were undertaken with a view to promoting investor confidence in Kenya and stemming the flight of capital.

To reassure British investors, the colonial government in Kenya dispatched its minister of commerce and industry, Hope-Jones, to meet with leading British business personages in London. Hope-Jones, in the last year of his long tenure at the Ministry of Commerce and Industry, was well regarded in metropolitan business circles. During his visit to Britain

[26] No. 6, W. L. Gorell Barnes to W. F. Coutts, June 17, 1960, PRO CO 822/2187.
[27] No. 7, W. L. Gorell Barnes to W. F. Coutts, June 21, 1960, PRO CO 822/2187.
[28] No. 4, W. F. Coutts to W. L. Gorell Barnes, May 30, 1960, PRO CO 822/2187.

he saw representatives of Power Securities, Brooke Bond, British Petroleum, Harrisons and Crossfield, and various banks. He also arranged for Bruce McKenzie, the minister of agriculture, to meet with John Brooke of Brooke Bond and John Loudon of Shell Oil. Although Hope-Jones announced that he was available to any British investor of substance, he believed that his meetings with the top multinational officials would be decisive. In his view, most investors took their cue from these leaders. "The number of people in London who decide investment policy is very limited"; if the confidence of the major business figures could be won, the Kenyan economy would not lack financial support.

Hope-Jones was surprised at how well informed the British business executives were on constitutional matters and the economic prospects of Kenya. Overall, despite their disquietude over the political concessions granted at Lancaster House, he believed that the business leaders in Britain were prepared to accept an "internal government, as opposed to independence, through an African ministry, with the retention of a Governor having reserved powers appointed by the Secretary of State." Only by bringing moderate African opinion into the government did the business persons believe that the nationalist movement would "make the fullest use of expert advice and civil service guidance which, if it is to be effective, business opinion seems to be quite clear must be made available through the British government." Of all of the nationalists, the business executives believed that Tom Mboya might be the one most likely to make "reassuring statements about the place of capital and expatriate 'know-how' in the Kenya of the future." Statements by European settlers or even by the Kenya colonial government were of no value at this stage, in the opinion of the business community: "It is considered that the only statements which carry real weight are those made by the leading African nationalists themselves."[29]

It was within this framework of a transition to African rule, however extended it might be, and declining European investor confidence in Kenya that the state then directed its attention to the most explosive issue in Kenyan politics—the disposition of the so-called European highlands. Virtually every group in Kenya and numerous groups outside the country had strong views on this issue. The differing perspectives ranged from outright African seizure without compensation to full compensation guaranteed by the British government. The task of the Colonial Office and the administrators in Kenya was to find some middle ground that would command widespread support in Kenya and reassure overseas investors. An extraordinarily boisterous Legislative Council debate of May 17, 1960,

---

[29] No. 195, A. Hope-Jones, East African Office, London, to Patrick Renison, September 20, 1960, KNA State House 4/411.

had brought the land question to the fore. On that occasion, one after another of the elected African nationalist leaders rose to challenge Chief Secretary Coutts's statement that Lancaster House promised no expropriation of land except for purposes of general benefit to the country. Mboya contended that the present government could not obligate an independent African government, and Odinga went further, asserting that "the present government, apart from being the agents of imperialism, is not a popular government elected by the people. . . . The African people are not going to sacrifice what they consider to be their rights for the sake of or for trying to make room for capital to come to this country."[30] No elected African expressed himself otherwise; the message to Asian and European businessmen was that a colonial regime could not make binding guarantees in favor of private capital and investment in Kenya.

The European farming community was appalled at the radicalness of these African positions. Its members were the first to express their displeasure at British colonial policies, and they remained the most outspoken and critical throughout the last stage of decolonization.

J. F. Lipscomb, chairman of the Settlement Board, emerged as one of the settlers' most energetic government critics. He claimed to have played the primary role in the emigration to Kenya of 470 new farming families and 600 European managers and assistants since 1945. Lipscomb's career as a mixed farmer in the highlands made him the obvious leader of this group, which sensed that compromises between European landholding interests in the highlands and moderate African nationalist opinion would be at their expense.[31]

A second settler pressure group, the Kenya National Farmers Union representing mainly European mixed farmers, entered the debate, arguing that "security of title" held the key to overall economic development and the free flow of capital to the country.[32] Shortly after the Lancaster House Conference, the Union sent a delegation to London to promote the idea of a British government guarantee against land expropriation in Kenya. The delegation insisted that land guarantees would benefit the whole of Kenya's diverse private sector.

The unresponsiveness of the British colonial authorities to these proposals as well as to the earlier approaches of individual business representatives in London and Nairobi induced British-based capital invested in Kenya to make a more concerted approach to colonial officials. A. D. McWilliams of the Kenya Tea Board made the first overture, writing to

---

[30] Kenya, Legislative Council, *Debates*, vol. 85, May 17, 1960, pp. 654–55.

[31] *East African Standard*, July 8, 1959.

[32] No. 101/1, Speech by Peter Marrian to Annual Conference of KNFU, November 1960, KNA State House 4/384.

Governor Patrick Renison to express "extreme anxiety over the security of land tenure in Kenya once independence is achieved and to remind the Governor that tea represented a total long-term investment of £20 million."[33] By September 1960, following meetings of business executives with colonial officials in London and Nairobi, the British business groups established a committee under the chairmanship of A. J. Leathers with a view to offering a unified big-business stance on Kenya's most pressing political and economic questions. This committee enjoyed the backing of the major plantation industries in Kenya and its leading export-import agencies, including Brooke Bond, James Findlay and Company, Mitchell Cotts, and George Williamson and Company. The committee submitted a memorandum to the governments of Kenya and Britain entitled "The Future of British Investment in Kenya," which in laying out the plans for the decolonization of Kenya and the preservation of the position of large-scale foreign capital in a soon-to-be-independent Kenya revealed the stance of big British business in 1960.

In the first instance, the authors of the memorandum called attention to the loss of business confidence in Kenya, which in their view was caused by fears that land would be expropriated, that the Colonial Office would not oversee the transition to independence, and that Kenya would be granted self-government in a state of unpreparedness. Their concern, however, was less with land than with the overall need to preserve the security of all business assets against any nationalizing and expropriating measures put forward by radical African nationalists. This result could best be achieved by demanding secure titles for all forms of private property. Yet, because African leaders of an independent state could easily repudiate promises made during the colonial period, the authors of the memorandum demanded that contingents of British armed forces remain in the country as guardians of law and order and that guarantees of private property, compensation in the event of the expropriation of property, and an independent judiciary be embedded in the constitution.[34]

The problem with the vision set forth by business was that it clashed with the positions being articulated by various African nationalist groups. Prospects for a compromise seemed poor in the years immediately after the Lancaster Conference of 1960. The Kenya Federation of Labor, an umbrella organization under the leadership of its president, Tom Mboya, mounted the most serious intellectual challenge to the private sector. Espousing a socialist and nationalizing program that Mboya himself did not champion within Kanu, the Kenya Federation of Labor in 1960 urged the government to nationalize key industries and commercial undertakings,

---

[33] McWilliams to Governor, May 18, 1960, PRO CO 822/2172.
[34] L. J. Leathers to I. Macleod, September 9, 1960, PRO CO 822/2179.

including plantations, banking, insurance, and some food processing industries.[35] A set of resolutions passed at a general council meeting of the federation in December 1962 went further, demanding the introduction of currency exchange controls, the implementation of a centrally planned economy, and the establishment of collective farms in the new African settlement areas. It also called for the nationalization of Kenya's coffee, tea, and sugar estates; the seaport of Mombasa; the distribution of gas and electricity supplies; the Kenya Meat Commission; the Upland Bacon Factory; grain milling; the brewing industry; air transportation; banks; insurance companies; and mines.[36]

Kanu itself was not far behind organized labor in assaulting foreign capital. It entered the political fray with its own policy statement, the first of its kind and eagerly awaited. A document full of recommendations for Kenya's most pressing social and economic concerns, the Kanu statement revealed a party riven with factional and ideological splits. It contained a contradictory mixture of moderate and radical propositions. In the early drafting stages, the radical wing of the party had the upper hand and was able to articulate a vision of Kenya transformed in socialist directions. Oginga Odinga supplied the guiding intellectual perspective, drawing on a circle of Marxist advisers to give his views the correct socialist phraseology. The Colonial Office, after securing an early draft of the document, was horrified by the prospect of its publication. F. D. Webber wrote that "the publication of the document will, more than any other single act that he [Chief Secretary Coutts] can think of, undermine the very confidence to which Kanu rightly attach importance."[37] The Kanu document emphasized income distribution and state ownership of Kenya's major enterprises. While conceding a need to attract foreign investment, the authors of the document claimed that the colonial economy had been "distorted" to help settler farmers. They went on to demand "a large degree of participation by the state in the development of the economy" and affirmed the party's belief that "only the state can undertake the extensive measures or reorganization necessary to remove the distortions that have developed under colonialism." Foreign aid would be welcomed only if it came without strings so as not to jeopardize Kanu's "policy of positive neutrality."

The Kanu draft document was even more outspoken on the land issue. Its authors described land as "a canker in the soul" and claimed that there were large tracts of unutilized lands in the highlands that should be made available at once to African farmers. "A few thousand men possess vast

---

[35] *East African Standard*, January 15, 1960.
[36] Ibid., December 4, 1962.
[37] F. D. Webber, Note, September 29, 1960, PRO CO 822/2109.

estates," the document opined, "while across the fence on the other sides, acute land hunger prevails." Each settler was said to possess an average of three and one-half square miles of land while land hunger ravaged African areas. The government's programs for settling Africans on some of these estates were regarded as "insufficient . . . [when] what is needed is a massive scheme to relieve African land hunger."[38]

After securing a copy of the manifesto, the Colonial Office and the government of Kenya were able to use their influence with Kanu moderates to secure emendations. Tom Mboya's role in softening the language of key propositions in the document was a decisive moment in causing the colonial authorities to change their opinion on Mboya and to view him as a moderate whose influence could be employed against the radicalism and Marxist orientation of Odinga within Kanu.

The final published Kanu statement, however, represented no more than an uneasy compromise between moderates and radicals within Kanu. As a concession to Odinga and his leftist supporters, the moderates allowed the radicals to use overtly Marxist language in the introduction. There the document characterized colonial territories as "dumping grounds for capitalist goods" and Kanu as "the vanguard of the movement" leading Kenya to socialism.[39] Through the interventions of James Gichuru, Kiano, Ngala, and Mboya, however, most of the specifics that followed reflected a more market-oriented approach to economic growth.[40] On the all-important land question, Kanu took no position; it promised further study of the question. The manifesto did state, however, that promises made to the settlers by the British government were not binding on Kenyan nationalists. Although Kanu would be willing to compensate for improvements to the land, it could not guarantee full compensation for any land that it might expropriate.[41]

Certainly the statements of the Kenyan left wing had a more powerful socialist and Marxist orientation than those of similar groups in Nigeria and even much of the early rhetoric of the military regime in Egypt. The documents of Kanu and the trade union movement and many of the maiden speeches of African nationalists in the Kenyan Legislative Council put a pall over the Colonial Office, its representatives in Kenya, and European business groups and settlers. All of these European elements approached the last stage of colonial rule with a sense of impending

---

[38] These quotations are taken from a copy of the draft Kanu program sent to the Colonial Office by the government in Kenya. No. 29, Office of the Chief Secretary, Kenya, to J. L. F. Buist, September 26, 1960, PRO CO 822/2109.

[39] No. 47, Department of Intelligence to W. F. Coutts, October 18, 1960, PRO CO 822/2110.

[40] No. 49, Renison to Macleod, October 24, 1960, PRO CO 822/2110.

[41] For the manifesto, see *East African Standard*, November 21, 1960.

doom. No doubt the fright that these propagandistic blasts aroused played a crucial role in making the British groups eager to negotiate in order to defeat radical opinion. Yet in truth, the radicalness of the African elements was more rhetoric than reality whenever it moved beyond the crucial realm of land. Elsewhere it was not rooted in African social and economic realities, for Africans at this stage had almost no presence in the commercial and industrial middle class. They were competitors to Europeans only in the agrarian sphere.

Between 1960 and 1963 the Kenyan economy was under greater investor pressure than it had been even at the height of Mau Mau. Access to land was becoming the defining issue in Kenyan politics and was gradually being recognized as such for the first time by official and unofficial British groups. Land was important not merely because Kenya's wealth was derived from the produce of its fields. British officials were realizing that its programs for economic diversification under the aegis of foreign capital would not extinguish radical African discontent without a political resolution to the land question. The infusion of investment capital was unlikely to occur if there was no agreed-upon resolution to the land question. All of the complicated negotiations over land from 1960 onward took place within this larger political setting. Because the British officials regarded themselves as responsible for the economic fate of Kenya, they shrank from any proposals for the wholesale, uncompensated dispersal of highland estates to African cultivators, not just because such a step would, in their view, destroy the agricultural sector but also because it would drive away the European investors interested in diversifying the Kenyan economy. In contrast, a controlled and widely agreed upon arrangement for the transfer of some lands from European to African hands would bode well for the future stability of Euro-African relations and a pragmatic, procapitalist, independent African regime.

In 1960, then, the British government initiated its first program of land reform involving the European highlands. It did so under the most extreme pressures and divergent expectations. On the one hand, the settlers demanded full compensation for any land redistribution. On the other, the nationalists called for easy access to the land. Facing a plethora of views, the colonial administration turned to its own agricultural experts for advice. The technicians still held firm to the productionist recommendations of the Swynnerton plan and the report of the East Africa Royal Commission, which had stressed the need to increase agricultural productivity, and were silent on the questions of historical land injustices.

Thus, the Colonial Office's 1960 program for land transfers continued to be couched in economic rather than political terms. It stressed the productivity gains to be realized by expanding private property holdings and facilitating individual initiatives. The colonial officials regarded economic growth as the only certain mechanism for dissipating social tensions, alleviating land hunger, and eradicating poverty; they feared that transfers of large segments of European farmland to landless and poverty-stricken Africans would accelerate the withdrawal of foreign capital. In their view, the African unemployed would be able to find work on efficiently managed farms in the highlands and in secondary industries that would grow in conjunction with agricultural advances.[42]

As the Colonial Office began to evaluate land schemes for the highlands, its officials sought more precise data on the place of European capital in the Kenyan economy.[43] Surveys carried out between 1960 and 1962 made clear how deeply dependent the Kenyan economy was on European agriculture and how certain its devastation would be if there were an exodus of European farmers and agricultural capital.[44] Overall, 3,600 European farming units owned some 7.7 million acres, of which 750 units, comprising 3.7 million acres, were in the hands of companies or incorporated individuals. The holdings themselves were divided into three broad groups: 550 plantations, comprising 2 million acres and producing £18.02 million annually, mostly from coffee, tea, sisal, and pyrethrum; 370 livestock ranches of 3.6 million acres producing £4.5 million worth of annual produce; and 2,680 units of mixed farming, covering 2.1 million acres and worth £15.35 million in annual production. The total annual output of European agriculture thus was £37.87 million; in addition, 275,000 Africans were employed on these farms. Of this number, 100,000 worked on European plantations and 175,000 on mixed farms.

Although the mixed European farms were generally recognized to be the least efficient in the European agricultural sector, their contribution to Kenya's economy (£15.35 million in annual production) and African employment (175,000 workers) could hardly be minimized. In contrast, African marketed crop cultivation was estimated at £9.1 million per year, of which £3.4 million was in plantation crops. Allowing for an underreporting of African marketable crops, it was nonetheless undeniable that the African contribution to the marketed agricultural production was small, probably only a little more than 20 percent of the total.[45] The valuation of

[42] No. 31, Colonial Office Memorandum, Kenya Land Settlement: A Possible Scheme, February 1960, PRO CO 822/2175.

[43] No. 12, Acting Governor, Kenya, to Colonial Office, February 12, 1960, PRO CO 822/2175.

[44] As later scholarly evidence for the European contribution to the colonial economy of Kenya, one should consult Paul Mosley, *The Settler Economies: Studies in the Economic History of Kenya and Southern Rhodesia, 1900–1963* (Cambridge, 1983).

[45] The figures here are a composite of the various reports produced between 1960 and 1962. See, in particular, Kenya, Land Policy: Memorandum by Secretary of State for Colo-

all of the European landholding, at 1959 land prices, was £140 million—a figure that bore out the Colonial Office and Treasury's contention that the government of the United Kingdom was in no position to underwrite a full-scale buyout.[46]

The first land reform scheme, enacted in 1960, was small by later standards; yet it was depicted as a major contribution to economic development and only secondarily to land hunger alleviation. Based on Sessional Papers No. 10 of 1958–59 and No. 6 of 1959–60, it was a lineal descendant of the Royal Commission report of 1955 and the Swynnerton plan. First, it sought to convert leaseholding to freeholding all over Kenya as rapidly as possible, and to facilitate land transfers in the highlands and in the African reserves to experienced farmers. Indeed, the British metropolitan government refused even to acknowledge that any funds were being employed to compensate European farmers, so alarmed was it at the prospect of having to purchase the whole of the £140 million of land in the highlands. Instead, metropolitan officials justified the scheme on the grounds of enhanced agricultural productivity. In introducing the land proposals into the Legislative Council in July 1960, Bruce McKenzie, the minister of agriculture in Kenya, asserted that the program had three goals: land development; retention of Kenya's Asian and European farming and nonfarming populations; and partial relief of African pressure on the land.[47] He gave the details for five specific schemes, which ranged from small settlement programs for experienced African farmers to assisted and tenancy schemes. McKenzie portrayed the fifth program as "a new and far-reaching development of the greatest importance."[48] It was targeted at landless and small farmers and was designated the peasant settlement scheme. In this project the government of Kenya would underwrite the purchase of 60,000 acres in the highlands and settle 4,500 families per year over a three-year period. The cost of all five programs would be £14 million, of which £6 million was to be used to purchase land. The remainder was earmarked for farm improvements.

The 1960 land program was expected to commence in areas where a substantial return on investment could be expected. Of the first 60,000 acres, 20,000 acres were to be planted in coffee, 20,000 in pyrethrum,

---

nies, July 12, 1960, PRO Cab 129/102/Part 1 C(60)110; L. R. Maconochie-Welwood of the Kenya Coalition to R. Maulding, Colonial Office, March 7, 1962, enclosing Memorandum on the Kenya Land Problem Presented by the Kenya Coalition Parliamentary Group, PRO CO 822/2390; and Memorandum by the Secretary of State for Colonies: European and Asian Farming in Kenya, March 14, 1962, PRO Cab 129/108.

[46] Kenya, Land Policy, Memorandum by the Secretary of State for Colonies, July 12, 1960, PRO Cab 129/108.

[47] Kenya, Legislative Council, *Debates*, vol. 86, July 20, 1960, pp. 18 ff.

[48] Ibid.

10,000 in high-yielding maize and low-yielding coffee, and 10,000 in tea. In short, the first group of African farmers in the once-exclusive European highlands were expected to participate in Kenya's market-oriented economy from the day they arrived, to increase the agricultural product of the country, and to give a generalized boost to the private sector. For a first-year investment of £8.15 million, of which £5 million was to come from the World Bank and £3.15 from British Exchequer loans, the Kenya Ministry of Agriculture projected an increase of £1.83 million in annual agricultural output and the creation of 16,000 additional agricultural jobs.[49]

In spite of the propaganda surrounding the scheme and the rosy projections of its additions to gross domestic product, neither settler leaders nor African nationalists endorsed the 1960 program. Group Captain Briggs, head of the United Party, said that the effort fell well short of the £30 million guarantee that his party was seeking as the minimum support required to keep farm prices at reasonable levels.[50] For once, Mboya and Odinga found themselves in agreement, contending that the government program was too little and too late. Delamere, voicing the opinion of the Kenya National Farmers Union, also indicated disappointment.[51] Only Ernest Vasey, from across the border in Tanganyika, praised the government scheme.[52]

In answering the criticisms, the government's most respected agricultural officer, R. J. M. Swynnerton, made some dramatic revelations while sounding a note of caution in the Legislative Council. He contended that the state had already reached the limit of the land it could transfer into African hands without adversely affecting agricultural returns. There was, in his view, no large abundance of unutilized or underutilized lands that could be distributed to the African landless to appease land hunger. Fortunately, in his opinion, the present program, if given a chance, could alleviate African unemployment and landlessness. Further land alienations, however, would harm the European mixed farming sector and might even result in the outright dismantling of European mixed farming, thus reducing output from the European area by as much as 50 percent. In Swynnerton's opinion, African nationalists' claims that the European highlands had vast tracts of idle and underutilized land were false and dangerous. According to Ministry of Agriculture surveys, of the 3,661 registered farms, plantations, and ranches in the European highlands, totaling 7,280,000 acres, only 101 farms could be considered underdeveloped or undeveloped. The total acreage of these farms was

[49] Paper by A. H. Long, Overseas Office, B of E, Kenya Land Settlement Scheme, July 28, 1960, B of E Archives OV 74/2.

[50] Kenya, Legislative Council, *Debates*, vol. 86, July 21, 1960, pp. 51 ff.

[51] *East African Standard*, July 21, 1960.

[52] Ibid., July 22, 1960.

193,208, nearly the exact amount of land that the state was prepared to transfer to African farmers.[53]

In early 1961, attention was briefly diverted from the land question so that Kenyans could participate in a new round of elections. The elections, of course, were certain to have a direct bearing on the economic and social policies that the government would need to implement. Each party's election manifesto staked out a position on land, private capital, and the role of the state. The most eagerly awaited election manifesto was that of Kanu, which was promulgated in late November 1960. It was a vaguely worded document and even, in places, contradictory. On the question of land, the party refused to rule out expropriation but promised that some form of compensation would be paid. Parts of the manifesto reflected the Odinga left wing of the party and alarmed the business community. Private enterprise, the manifesto opined, had "made paupers out of workers, driving them to live in crowded slums." Kanu expected the state to play a decisive economic role after independence. But the most specific statement on the crucial boundary lines between private and public economic endeavors was a masterpiece of ambiguity. It stated, "Kanu wants to ensure that the means of production, distribution, and exchange are under the best obtainable system, consistent with the real interests of the country."[54]

The European primaries, held in January 1961, were widely watched and hotly contested. They pitted the gradualists of Blundell and the New Kenya Party against right-wing settlers, who rallied around their spiritual leader, Cavendish-Bentinck and his Kenya Coalition party. Although only Europeans could vote in their own primaries, Africans were not prevented from campaigning, and they did so as energetically as the Europeans. The African political leaders made clear their preference for the New Kenya Party. The Rift Valley primary election was a contest between the leaders of the two parties (Blundell and Cavendish-Bentinck) and aroused much African interest.[55] Mwai Kibaki, for example, toured the Rift Valley areas, openly attacking Cavendish-Bentinck by claiming that he and his party members were using their influence in Kenya to extract a large sum of money from the British government before leaving Kenya. In contrast, he portrayed Michael Blundell and his party as wanting to stay.[56]

The Kenya Coalition (KC) of Cavendish-Bentinck won impressively in the primaries but did not realize its fundamental goal—preventing the

---

[53] Kenya, Legislative Council, *Debates*, vol. 86, July 26, 1960, pp. 189 ff.
[54] *East African Standard*, November 19, 1960.
[55] Ibid., January 4, 1961.
[56] Ibid., January 5, 1961.

New Kenya Party (NKP) candidates from moving to the second and crucial stage of the electoral process. Cavendish-Bentinck overwhelmed Blundell; Charles Markham defeated the independent Peter Marrian; KC candidate C. W. Salter and rightist independent E. L. Howard Williams outpolled the New Kenya Party candidates in Nairobi West; and F. L. Megson of KC defeated W. B. Havelock of NKP for Nairobi Southwest. In all, eight Kenya Coalition candidates won outright in the nine electoral districts in which the party ran candidates. But the party failed to deliver the knockout punch that it so desperately needed, for the only New Kenya Party candidates prevented from entering the common roll elections were E. D. Hughes from Mombasa, A. B. Goord from West Kenya, and L. Campbell from North Kenya. Blundell escaped by a mere 1.7 percent, polling only 26.7 percent of the Rift Valley European primary vote against Cavendish-Bentinck's astonishing 73.07 percent. The primary elections in the European constituencies demonstrated the widespread rejectionist sentiments of the European settlers.[57]

The final elections took place at the end of February. In those elections in which a common roll was employed, the Kenya Coalition candidates did not fare well at all. The ten electoral seats reserved for Europeans were divided among three competing factions. The four victors of the New Kenya Party represented the intellectual leadership of the party: Blundell from the Rift Valley, who with African support defeated Cavendish-Bentinck; A. R. Shaw from Kericho; R. S. Alexander from Nairobi Suburban; and W. B. Havelock from Nairobi Southwest. The Kenya Coalition elected three delegates (Salter from Nairobi, Wellwood from West Kenya, and D. Cole from North Kenya); and three independents won (Cleasby from Mombasa East, Howard-Williams from Nairobi North, and Marrian from Central Province Rural). As for the African elections, while Kanu outpolled Kadu by a vote of 490,000 to 143,000 (out of a total of 890,000 votes cast), it won only seventeen of the thirty-three seats. Kadu took eleven seats, and the remaining five were divided among minority parties, which were most likely to align with Kadu.[58]

After long and intense negotiations, Kadu established a coalition government involving the New Kenya Party (minus Bruce McKenzie, who deemed it impolitic to create a government without the majority African party) and some important Asian and European independents.[59] Although the business community of Kenya vastly preferred a Kadu-European coalition to Kanu rule, the establishment of the coalition did little to reas-

---

[57] Ibid., January 24, 1961.

[58] Ibid., late February and early March 1961.

[59] Macleod, Memorandum on Jomo Kenyatta, March 1961, PRO Prem 11/3413; *East African Standard*, April 1 and 19, 1961.

sure its leaders. The flight of capital and the waning of investor confidence continued apace.

The new African government in Kenya faced a financial crisis in 1961 that had the potential to escalate into an economic catastrophe if not skillfully dealt with. Had the state's financial bureaucrats not prevailed, an irreversible outflow of investment funds could easily have occurred, and some highly regarded and carefully watched multinational enterprises might have elected to leave Kenya. The crisis had its origins in the building societies sector, which, like building societies elsewhere, used funds from depositors to finance home mortgages and home and farm improvements. These firms were vulnerable in times of financial panic, when anxious depositors might wish to reclaim deposits tied up in long-term loans.

Kenya had three major building societies: the Kenya Building Society, operating only in Kenya and loosely linked to the Norwich Union in Britain; the Savings and Loan Society, which operated mainly in Kenya but had branches in Tanganyika and Uganda and was a wholly owned subsidiary of the Pearl Assurance Company of Great Britain; and the First Permanent Building Society, which operated in Northern Rhodesia and Nyasaland as well as throughout East Africa. The most severely troubled of these firms was the First Permanent Building Society, the East African liabilities of which were £4.5 million. Its decline and possible liquidation would not be confined to East Africa but would spread to Central Africa, where a similar transition from colonial rule to political independence was under way. The Colonial Office might insist that the smaller, more Kenya-based building societies find their way through these financial hard times, but it could hardly allow an institution with such a broad African involvement to founder. The failure of the First Permanent Building Society was certain to provoke a run on the other two building societies in Kenya and undermine the government savings bank as well. Just where the shock waves to investor confidence would stop, these officials were unable to predict.[60] When various expedients, like having the metropolitan affiliates extend large credits to their Kenya affiliates, did not succeed, the British Colonial Office was forced to intervene directly. Its officials persuaded the powerful Colonial Development Corporation to take over the First Permanent Building Society and thereby guarantee the security of its depositors' funds.[61]

At the same time that the state was averting the crisis in the financial

[60] Colonial Office Memo, Building Societies in East Africa, July 18, 1961, PRO CO 822/2624.

[61] No. 147, A. N. Galsworthy, Colonial Office, to K. W. S. MacKenzie, Treasury, Kenya, August 14, 1961, PRO CO 822/2624.

sector it was bracing for the political and economic fallout from the release of Jomo Kenyatta in 1961. Despite Governor Renison's foreboding that Kenyatta was "arrogant, dominating, and satanic," the release was accomplished with a minimum of damage to investor confidence, largely because of the many conciliatory statements that Kenyatta made at the time. In particular, he promised that an independent Kenya would not be "a robber government" and denied reports that he had said that no African should purchase lands from Europeans because Africans would be given estates free after independence.[62] But Kenyatta's reassurances did not silence the radical nationalists, who continued to make provocative remarks about European landholding. In particular, Paul Ngei, a leading Kamba politician and a critic of Kikuyu domination of African politics, aligned himself with Odinga in favor of land takeovers without compensation; and Bildad Kaggia, part of the Kanu left wing, counseled African farmers not to purchase land from Europeans because to do so would be to renounce "our landlordship in our own country."[63]

These statements and the continuing appeal of the African dissidents finally led the colonial authorities to conclude that the land reform schemes of 1960 had not "taken the heat out of the land problem."[64] New programs, even massive land transfers, must be considered. Not only had the earlier land transfers failed to assuage African land hunger as Swynnerton and others had hoped they would, but the programs had not covered the large amount of land being offered for sale by European farmers. By early 1961, just six months after the first land acquisition and redistribution programs had gone into effect, European farmers had offered no less than 900,000 acres of land for sale.[65] So dissatisfied were the settlers in the mixed farming areas that they began to carry out threats to let their farms run down.[66]

On the African side, the results of the 1960 reforms were equally disappointing. Although the figures on the number of Africans settled on formerly European estates as a result of the 1960 schemes were impressive by any measuring stick (some 20,000 families on 350,000 acres at a cost of £14 million), the political effects were disappointing.[67] Kenya had not experienced a diminution of pressure from the landless and the unem-

[62] *East African Standard*, September 20, 1961; no. 497, C. J. Hayes, Treasury, to A. N. Galsworthy, Colonial Office, January 22, 1962, PRO CO 822/2182; *East African Standard*, January 23, 1962.

[63] *East African Standard*, January 27, 1962.

[64] No. 321, A. N. Galsworthy, Colonial Office, to C. J. Hayes, Treasury, July 19, 1961, PRO CO 822/2179.

[65] *East African Standard*, January 21, 1961.

[66] Ibid., May 23, 1961.

[67] No. 7, F. D. Webber to Andrew Cohen, May 29, 1962, PRO CO 822/2148.

ployed; expressions of discontent were only intensifying. Nor had the 1960 land transfer restored investor interest in Kenya and stemmed the flight of capital.

Even as discussion on land questions was taking place, the British government prepared for its second Lancaster House Conference on Kenya. Governor Renison and the new colonial secretary, Reginald Maulding, approached the conference with a clear agenda. Renison worried about the radicalism of Odinga, made all the more intense because of reports that Odinga was receiving communist bloc financial support. In Renison's view, the Odinga faction, if it enjoyed Kenyatta's support, would drive Kenya toward "a Kikuyu dictatorship, with strong attachments to communist powers." Renison hoped that at Lancaster House he could encourage Mboya to break his ties with the Kanu left wing and link up with Kadu.[68]

Maulding's concerns were more squarely economic. He feared the power of the so-called ex-detainees in Kanu, whose ascendancy in Kenya could only cause further deterioration of the economy. European agriculture, he averred, was still the bedrock of Kenya's wealth, and the Lancaster House meeting must therefore establish a timetable for independence that had the support of British business and contained inducements to the minority racial communities to remain in Kenya. For Maulding, investor confidence could only be secured by means of a carefully drafted constitution. To be sure, radical nationalists might not be bound by a constitution promulgated in the colonial era, but he thought that embedding a bill of rights, an independent judiciary, and protections against land seizures in the constitution offered Kenya its best chance for political stability and economic growth after independence.[69]

The conference, which opened on February 14, 1962, remained deadlocked after six weeks of intense negotiations. The main differences were no longer between European delegates and African nationalists but between Kanu and Kadu. Kadu demanded a decentralized polity, with the delegation of wide powers to the regions; Kanu favored a unitary state.[70] As intelligence reports began to filter back to London, indicating a sharp deterioration of security in the highlands and a left-wing Kanu effort to destroy the government in Kenya, Maulding opted, as Macleod had in 1960, to impose his own solution on the conference.[71] The Maulding constitution created two houses of Parliament at the center and six regional

[68] No. 294, Renison to W. B. L. Monson, January 31, 1962, PRO CO 822/2238.
[69] Memorandum by the Secretary of State for Colonies on Kenya, February 6, 1962, PRO Cab 129/108 C.(62)22.
[70] Memorandum by the Secretary of State for Colonies, Kenya, Constitutional Conference, March 19, 1962, PRO Cab 129/109.
[71] No. 71, Acting Governor to Colonial Office, March 22, 1962, PRO CO 822/2031.

assemblies; elections were to take place within a year, and following their outcome Kenya would be expected to move swiftly toward internal self-government.[72] In the interim, Kanu and Kadu agreed to form a coalition government, with Ronald Ngala and Jomo Kenyatta having equal status as ministers of state.[73] Thus ended the longest constitutional conference in London to that date—seven weeks and two days in all.

Although Maulding's imposed constitution was intended to calm the African political climate, dissidents continued to undermine the prospects for an orderly transfer of political and economic power. Political excitement reached a high point in late 1962. The colonial courts convicted 736 persons of oathing, belonging to an illegal organization, and the illegal possession of arms; another 1,313 persons were convicted in African courts for similar offenses, though of a lesser degree. Beneath this group of apprehended individuals existed a much larger element of discontented and alienated Africans. Indeed, the British authorities believed that they were now only "containing subversion rather than eradicating it," and they portrayed the most strident dissidents, the Kenya Land Freedom Army (KLFA), as presenting "a real potential threat to [the] future peace of Kenya because its leaders perceive the future in terms of a militant struggle for Kikuyu domination in which they [the KLFA] will dominate the Kikuyu."[74] It was not until 1962, just a year before the British conferred independence, that the mounting fears of ethnic violence in the Rift Valley compelled the colonial authorities in Nairobi and London to view land transfers in political rather than economic terms. Even the agricultural experts in Kenya, who previously measured all programs by their capacity to enhance economic productivity, conceded the buildup of political pressure. They now admitted that programs based entirely on economic criteria would not calm the African population. By the close of the Lancaster House Conference, Colonial Secretary Maulding had already presented to the British cabinet a memorandum outlining the urgency for a far-reaching land settlement scheme.[75]

British officialdom was an entirely reluctant and last-minute convert to what eventually became the million-acre scheme of 1962. As it was first discussed, the program did not even involve those groups whom the colonial authorities had the most faith in—that is, moderate settlers and moderate African nationalists—or for that matter the most aggrieved Africans, the underclasses who were demanding the right to take over the European highlands. It was, in reality, the handiwork of only a few indi-

[72] *East African Standard*, April 3, 1962.

[73] Ibid., April 7, 1962.

[74] No. 131, Renison to Colonial Office, November 29, 1962, PRO CO 822/2026.

[75] Memorandum by the Secretary of State for Colonies, Kenya Constitutional Conference, March 19, 1962, PRO Cab 129/109.

viduals. The landholding negotiations proceeded without direct reference to the leading architects of the New Kenya Party (Blundell and Alexander), but they also ignored the leaders of Kadu (Ngala and Daniel Arap Moi), leaders of independent African parties (such as Paul Ngei), and Kanu moderates (Mboya, Kiano, and Gichuru). Instead, it was the product of narrow and secret Colonial Office and extreme settler negotiations.

The catalyst for the million-acre scheme was none other than R. Maconochie-Welwood, Cavendish-Bentinck's replacement atop the rejectionist Kenya Coalition. In February 1962, Maconochie-Welwood used a meeting with the British foreign secretary, Lord Home, to argue that without large land transfers to Africans Kenya would explode into widespread violence and experience a mass exodus of Europeans.[76] Subsequently, he encouraged other influential settlers to use their ties with British politicians to force the question of Kenya's future to the center of British parliamentary and press discussions. At the height of this settler campaign in Britain, a deputation of backbench Conservative members of Parliament met with Prime Minister Macmillan and presented many of the proposals favored by Kenya's right-wing farmers. Believing that the plantations and ranches were safe from expropriation and not yet besieged by illegal squatters, the backbenchers argued that the mixed farms were under severe pressure, which could only be relieved by a program of massive land transfers. The price tag of a transfer of power, they believed, was not likely to be less than £30 or £35 million, the cost of underwriting land transactions in the highlands, and possibly even more if the whole mixed farming area was involved.[77]

The European farming group had made its approach to the British government at a propitious moment. Secretary Maulding, in the midst of the badly deadlocked Lancaster House meetings, had realized that the strategy of forging a Kadu-Kanu alliance was unlikely to succeed. He too had concluded that land transfers were the only way to keep a core of European farmers in Kenya and to avoid clashes between European farmers and African land grabbers. In his view, a truly massive plan would be "the best way, perhaps the only way, of keeping a good proportion of European farmers in Kenya." His great fear was a "sudden urgent rush to depart" that would lead to "abandoned farms" and "a very serious security risk as all experience shows Africans will move in and in view of competing tribal claims in this area the dangers of serious and widespread bloodshed are very real."[78]

Maulding concurred with the estimate that £30 million would be re-

---

[76] Home, Foreign Office, to Colonial Secretary, February 13, 1962, PRO FO 371/165292.

[77] No. 542, Note for the Record from G. W., Admiralty, to E. M. West, Colonial Office, March 27, 1962, PRO CO 822/2181.

[78] No. 552, Maulding to Henry Brooke, MP, March 30, 1962, PRO CO 822/2181.

quired to finance a large program. In preparation for such an outlay he sent preliminary proposals to the Treasury that met with strong, if predictable opposition. There, H. Brooke worried about this "huge sum of money . . . and [he added], I cannot regard schemes such as have so far been outlined as practical possibilities for the Exchequer on top of something like £30 million a year which is likely to be needed [for other projects] to keep Kenya going on present plans."[79]

At this critical juncture the Kenya Coalition rather than the New Kenya Group or moderate African nationalists again intervened. The Kenya Coalition forwarded to Secretary Maulding an elaborate memorandum on the land question. This document had been prepared by Maconochie-Welwood; Delamere, president of the Kenya National Farmers Union; and C. O. Oates, chairman of the Convention of Farmers Association, and reflected the interests of European mixed farmers. The position they staked out in the memorandum was not markedly different from that which settler leaders had been championing for some years. The difference was that it found a receptive hearing at the Colonial Office.

The settler document opened by conceding that "for political and other reasons a considerable reallocation of land [was needed] . . . and this should take the form of putting Africans on the land." Without land guarantees, European farmers would depart in a disorderly fashion; with guarantees, the authors of the document predicted that as much as 40 or 50 percent of the European population would remain. Specifically, the British government should underwrite the purchase of nearly half of the European mixed farms in the highlands, 1 million acres in all, at a cost of £15 per acre. But the program should also be unlimited in order to avoid European panic and thus should apply to the whole of the 2 million acres of mixed farming. Since the government of Kenya did not have the resources to finance such a large buyout, the British government would have to advance the funds, of which it could expect to reclaim a significant proportion through payments over time from the new African farmers.

The document went on to recommend that the British government extend a loan of £11 million to the government of Kenya to cover start-up costs on the new farms. The memorandum estimated the three-year cost for 1 million acres at £26 million, an amount that could double if all of the European mixed farmers departed. There was a final disturbing prediction in the memorandum: the authors expected that mixed farms transferred to African hands would revert to subsistence agriculture and lead to a loss of agricultural income and employment.[80]

[79] No. 558, H. Brooke, Treasury, to R. Maulding, April 3, 1961, PRO CO 822/2181.

[80] Memorandum from the Kenya Coalition, L. R. Maconochie-Welwood of Kenya Coalition, to R. Maulding, Colonial Office, March 7, 1962, enclosing Memorandum on the

The last observation was easily the most unsettling to British colonial officers. For years they had supported only programs that would lift agricultural productivity, and they had rejected schemes whose main purpose was to relieve political pressure or offer financial incentives to Europeans to sell. The willingness of the colonial authorities to accept the prospect of widespread subsistence agriculture in the highlands indicated how far colonial thinking had evolved since Swynnerton and the Royal Commission. The Kenyan minister of land development, Bruce McKenzie, was prepared to abandon the production and income targets the ministry had set for individual African farmers and to "do the best we can with the available land and people."[81] Experience with the 1960 land transfers had revealed a tendency of even the most carefully selected African cultivators to subdivide their estates and engage in subsistence agriculture. Few of the farmers involved in the 1960 program had by then achieved the increased agricultural output or produced the additional employment on their estates anticipated by the planners. Indeed, most of the new owners were not even able to generate sufficient income to cover expenses and to pay off their loans. Nor had the Ministry of Agriculture found the wide tracts of unused land that the nationalists claimed existed and the cultivation of which would have added immediately to the agricultural product. Yet despite the government's intense dissatisfaction with the 1960 scheme and its belief that new schemes would have the same negative economic consequences, it concluded that large land transfers had become a political necessity.[82]

But were the assumptions and fears of the Colonial Office justified? Did the government of Kenya need a large program, something in the neighborhood of 1 million acres, capable of absorbing 200,000 or even 300,000 Africans, to stem capital flight and promote moderate African opinion? The British Treasury thought not. Its questioning of the underlying assumptions of the project revealed just how uncertain some of the tenets of colonial policy were. To begin with, the Treasury reminded the Colonial Office of its earlier commitment to agricultural efficiency and increased productivity. It queried the officials in Nairobi whether a program that would remove 1 million acres from the market-oriented economy would benefit Kenya, or even for that matter stem the flight of capital. The Treasury reminded the Colonial Office officials whence the

Kenya Land Problem, Presented by the Kenya Coalition Parliamentary Group, PRO CO 822/2390.

[81] No. 569, B. McKenzie, Minister of Land Development, to A. N. Galsworthy, April 16, 1962, PRO CO 822/2182.

[82] No. 571, Colonial Office to Acting Governor, Kenya, April 20, 1962; no. 572, Acting Governor, Kenya, to Colonial Office, April 24, 1962; and K. MacKenzie, Treasury, Kenya, to A. N. Galsworthy, Colonial Office, May 12, 1962; all in PRO CO 822/2182.

pressures for the buyout were coming—the right-wing settler farmers rather than the agribusinesses or the moderate nationalists. Its officials claimed that the new program was little more than a bribe to a small group of well-organized and outspoken European farmers who were exaggerating the prospects of violence in the country for their own interests. The land transfer scheme had originated, the Treasury averred, "from political pressure applied by the European farmers and amounts to a plan which is hardly in practice distinguishable from payment of compensation for any land held by Europeans (or apparently Asians) as and when they choose to leave Kenya or elect to become tenants instead of owners." The Colonial Office had steadfastly refused to make such guarantees in the past out of fear of facilitating the very exodus that they wanted to prevent, and the Treasury saw no compelling reason to question this assumption now.

Officials at the Treasury asked a further crucial question, for which the colonial experts also had no definitive answer. What evidence existed, other than the threats of settlers themselves, that European farmers would leave Kenya in a panic? The opinion of the Treasury, supported by figures on the relatively small number of settlers who had departed or allowed their farms to run down, was that the settlers were bluffing. Europeans would leave Kenya only if expelled. Treasury representatives also questioned whether the terms of a million-acre scheme obligating the independent government of Kenya to repay the loans would be accepted by an ardent nationalist government.[83]

Yet, just as the colonial administrators and military men in Nigeria were unwilling to risk withdrawing the pledge of regional self-government for fear of provoking large-scale violence, so, in Kenya, the British officials were unwilling to face the uncertain yet potentially devastating results of not carrying out massive land transfers. At that propitious moment, extremist settler publicists intensified their campaign. Using their most effective weapon, they encouraged the Association of European Settlement Board Farmers, a group made up of some 227 members out of 320 farming families who had emigrated to Kenya after World War II, to step up their protests in Britain. The association called on the British government to "discharge its obligations to them" and threatened to stop making rent and loan payments.[84]

The Colonial Office ultimately had its way with the Treasury. Using developments in Algeria and the former Belgian Congo, it convinced other metropolitan officials that European flight was not a remote possibility and would be a disaster to the Kenyan economy. In early July 1962

---

[83] No. E/566, Treasury, Memorandum on Kenya Land, May 14, 1962, PRO CO 822/2182.
[84] *East African Standard*, May 14, 1962.

the British cabinet in London endorsed the million-acre resettlment scheme as "the best hope of avoiding in Kenya a situation comparable with that which had arisen in Algeria through the dissatisfaction of European settlers."[85] In the minds of officials at the Colonial Office the project was to dispose "in a controlled way of the fertile land in the highlands as the European farmers sell out, in a way which will not ruin Kenya's economy and equally in a way which will reconcile the various conflicting interests of the tribes themselves who . . . have their various spheres of influence or for one reason or another have 'claims' on this desirable property."[86] The Treasury did insist, however, that the scheme not be described as compensation for land but as land settlement and that the funds lent to the government of Kenya be a first charge on its revenues. The Treasury wanted no precedent that could be invoked anywhere else, at home or abroad, least of all by newly independent African governments casting covetous eyes on European landholdings and businesses.[87]

The final proposal, as agreed to by the British cabinet, encompassed 1 million acres. It was to proceed at a rate of 200,000 acres per year for five years, by which time some 70,000 African families were expected to be settled on the land. Held in abeyance was a second million acres that might follow in the next five years if African land hunger and European desires to leave had not been extinguished. The program was expected to cost £16.55 million, of which the British government would provide £7.5 million in the form of a grant and the remaining £9 million in a loan to the government of Kenya. The average price of the land was expected to be £10 per acre rather than the £15 proposed in the Kenya Coalition memorandum. The British cabinet accepted the plan with few illusions. It did so lest the colonial government "be faced with the well-nigh inescapable necessity of supporting the Kenya economy and budget from collapse." The government at home was not deceived that the plan would improve the economy of Kenya or even eradicate land tensions. The £16.55 million set aside for the program was a large sum, but the cabinet was also aware that it would not suffice for "the purchase of anything like the whole of the vulnerable European mixed farming area."[88]

The million-acre scheme represented a massive shift in the thinking of

---

[85] Memorandum by the Secretary of State for Colonies, Kenya Land Settlement, July 3, 1962, PRO Cab 129/110.

[86] No. 7, F. D. Webber to Andrew Cohen, May 29, 1962, PRO CO 822/2148.

[87] No. 654, C. J. Hayes, Treasury, to A. N. Galsworthy, Colonial Office, July 25, 1962, PRO CO 822/2183.

[88] Memorandum by Secretary of State for Colonies, Kenya: Land Settlement, July 3, 1962, PRO Cab 129/110; speech by B. McKenzie, Minister for Land Development and Water Resources, in Kenya, Legislative Council, *Debates*, vol. 89, June 22, 1962, pp. 810 ff.

Britain's colonial authorities about the economy of Kenya. Previously the British had resisted demands for large buyouts and had looked suspiciously at proposals originating from organized settler farming groups. In 1962, these bureaucrats shifted their ground. They embraced a scheme being touted by the right-wing settler community, and they developed a land buyout program that was likely, even in the most optimistic view, to bring a decline in the agricultural economy. Among the official British groups, only the Treasury held out for the principles that had undergirded the 1960 land transfers.

This volte face in colonial mentality arose not from a new sympathy for European mixed farmers but from a fear of violence with a concomitant liquidation of those bastions of European capital—the plantations, banks, commercial firms, and industries—that the authorities thought would help to smooth the transition to independence and contribute to postcolonial economic development. Yet, as the Treasury insisted, this fear was far from conclusively demonstrated. Thus, as in Nigeria where an untested but palpable apprehension of political violence drove the colonial authorities to concede increasing degrees of autonomy to Nigerian elite politicians, so in Kenya the uncertainty of the colonial officials about the extremist African groups led the state to embrace a massive land transfer program that its financial and agricultural experts had opposed for a long time. The Kenyan colonial officials concluded that they must sacrifice the mixed farming sector of the Kenyan economy to protect other economic sectors. The overall goal remained the same: stemming the flight of European capital and technical expertise. But the means to achieve it required a step that would, in all likelihood, depress a significant portion of the economy in hopes of permitting an escape of political and social tension.

The million-acre program hardly laid to rest the worries about illegal land takeovers and African violence. The scheme was, after all, the handiwork of British officialdom. It was known to draw its inspiration and even to owe its details to the much-resented settler right wing. In the Legislative Council, J. M. Kariuki, emerging as a left-wing spokesman and a voice for discontented Kikuyu peasants, warned that many of the new African holders placed on the lands would be unable to repay their government loans and that the scheme, a first charge on Kenya's revenues, would drain the state Treasury, preventing expenditures on desperately needed social and economic projects. He recommended that peasant occupants of the land form cooperatives or even that the state purchase the land and work it in Soviet-like collectives.[89] Kariuki's criticisms reminded British officials that a nationalist government might simply repu-

---

[89] Kenya, House of Representatives, *Official Record*, July 5, 1963, vol. 1, pp. 678 ff.

diate the agreement on the grounds that it imposed too heavy a financial obligation on a new state. And the announcement of the scheme also did not bring an end to the illegal occupation of land, occurring in many parts of the Rift Valley, particularly by impoverished, land-hungry Kikuyu families. The specter of interethnic violence persisted.

Although the new landholdings were supposed to average seventeen or eighteen acres per family and be economically viable, what occurred was far from that model. It bore out the most pessimistic predictions of Kenya's agricultural experts, who described many of the newly occupied estates as "slum-like subsistence shambas occupied by a number of families with no prospect of the authorized settler being able to pay his way." The circumstances were held to be so bad in parts of Central Province that "a break down in farming" had to be feared.[90] Yet there was no turning back. The program was extended to all of the European farms west and north of the Aberdares, where to that point no invasion of Kikuyu peasant families had occurred. Thus the land reforms carried out between 1960 and the end of 1963 brought small-scale peasant-dominated agriculture into the European highlands. By the end of 1962 there was already well under way a program in which "the peasant farm economy and society . . . moved far into the middle of the former capitalist white highlands, engulfing its periphery and penetrating deep into its core."[91]

In 1963 Kenya prepared for independence. In May, Kanu won the elections, and in September, the last of the constitutional conferences established December 1963 as the end point of colonial rule. The elections focused attention once again on the question of Kenya's political economy. The differences between Kanu and Kadu were obvious, and as far as the private sector was concerned the advantages of Kadu over Kanu were incontrovertible. The Kanu manifesto, as usual, gave free rein to the socialist segment of the party, asserting that the party's principles were "based on socialism which reflected the African way of life."[92] Kanu's opponents, running on regionalism, stressed their receptivity to private enterprise and foreign investment, promised low taxation rates as an inducement to foreign investors, and offered guarantees against nationalization.[93] Kadu attacked Kanu for extravagant and unrealistic electoral promises, arguing that its program to guarantee seven years of free education and free medical services for all was beyond Kenya's capacity. Seven years of free education, the Kadu critics pointed out, would cost £10

---

[90] The Expanded Settlement Scheme, 1963, KNA State House 4/100.

[91] Colin Leys, "Politics in Kenya: The Development of Peasant Society," mimeograph, p. 14. See, also, Christopher Leo, *Land and Class in Kenya* (Toronto, 1984).

[92] *East African Standard*, April 19, 1963.

[93] Ibid., April 24 and 25, 1963.

million.[94] These observations had the support of the business leaders. Even more appealing was the statement of Masinde Muliro, a Kadu politician, that the state would not discriminate against foreign residents as long as they were contributing to the economic progress of the country.[95]

The elections, based on the new constitution, involved a massive number of contests—334 in all. A total of 715 candidates entered the hustings for the 117 seats for the central House of Representatives, the 176 seats in the 6 regional assemblies, and the 41 places in the central Senate. The election results were mixed, much as Kadu had hoped. The Senate was split between the two parties, as were the regional assemblies. Kanu prevailed in the Central, Nyanza, and Eastern Provinces, while Kadu won at the coast, in the Rift Valley, and in Western Province. For the all-important House of Representatives, however, Kanu won a majority and agreed to form the government.[96]

The business communities, European settlers, and representatives of overseas investors watched with considerable apprehension as Kanu formed its first government and made its first statements on economic issues. Those first statments were still sometimes unclear and contradictory. Certainly they did little to reassure the business community that Kanu would support the private sector or accept the constitutional and financial arrangements that the Colonial Office had been seeking to impose on the government of Kenya. The first Kanu cabinet represented the full range of Kanu opinion. Odinga and Mboya were included, and Kenyatta assumed the office of prime minister. The procapitalist orientation that was to characterize the Kenyatta government throughout the late 1960s and 1970s did not become fully evident until Kadu leaders had joined Kanu and the left wing within Kanu had withdrawn from the party.

The last years of colonial rule (1960–1963) were little more than a holding operation as far as investment capital was concerned. The big British-based companies were content to watch the political processes unfold, and the colonial government was relieved if major firms like Brooke Bond did not withdraw from Kenya or cut back sharply on their commitments. The government's infrequent efforts to attract new foreign capital, such as the campaign to persuade Courtauld's of Britain to establish a large paper and pulp factory, met with little success. Hope-Jones, Kenya's chief negotiator with foreign firms, was forced to concede that the adverse political and economic conditions blighted all discussions.[97]

[94] Ibid., May 1, 1963.
[95] Ibid., May 9, 1963.
[96] Ibid., May 28, 1963.
[97] No. 177, Hope-Jones to Renison, July 22, 1960, KNA State House 4/411.

Indian business, in contrast, demonstrated its continuing economic dynamism and proved an exception to the general investment slowdown. No doubt the willingness of Indian business persons to accept risks that others would not tolerate worked to their advantage. In 1954 the governments of East Africa did not renew the Calico Printers Association monopoly over textile production, having concluded that the original concession had impeded the growth of textile manufacturing in Kenya.[98] In the ensuing years, numerous firms arose, many of them owned and managed by Asian capitalists. By early 1960 the Kenya Textile Mills, the African Textile Mills, and the Kenya Rayon Mills all had been granted licenses to manufacture more than a million square yards of textile products. Textile production flourished, even in the uncertain last decolonizing years. A new rayon spinning mill was established at Thika at a cost of £500,000.[99] Its main equity provider was Nath Brothers, which was affiliated with Bhagwanji and Company and which brought two Japanese firms into the company in order to have access to additional capital.[100]

Asian industrialists also expanded into new manufacturing sectors that the government had hoped to reserve for Western capital. Madhvani of Muljibhai Madhvani Company proposed to build a steel mill in the Nairobi area, using scrap metal to manufacture steel reenforcing bars. It was eager to form a conglomerate with Italian Steelworks Manufacturers and the Colonial Development Corporation. The bulk of the firm's equity capital (£511,250) and its overall direction were to come from the Indian business group.[101] Similarly, Sheet Manufacturing Ltd, an Indian family concern of the Shah family, developed plans to erect a steel rolling mill at Mombasa at a cost of £2 million.[102] Not to be left behind, the Chandarias' Kenya Aluminum and Industrial Works Company proposed to invest £1.6 million in a similar project.[103] Thus, as Kenya moved into the independence era, the new steelmaking industry was in Asian hands.

A similar breakthrough occurred in the sugar industry, where the state found few alternatives to Asian industrialists. The three major enterprises in Kenya were Miwani Sugar Mill, licensed to produce 40,000 tons; the Ramisi Sugar Mill at the coast, licensed for 25,000 tons; and a latecomer, the Uganda Sugar Company of M. M. Mehta, a Ugandan industrialist to whom the Ministry of Commerce and Industry offered an industrial li-

---

[98] No. 147/3, Board of Industrial Development, Memorandum, Industrial Licensing, February 27, 1960, KNA MCI 6/89.

[99] *East African Standard*, October 11, 1961.

[100] Ibid., October 17, 1961.

[101] No. 166, Note by V. A. Maddison, Permanent Secretary for the Ministry of Commerce and Industry, June 15, 1960, KNA State House 4/411.

[102] *East African Standard*, April 25, 1963.

[103] Ibid., July 21, 1961.

cense for the construction of a large sugar factory near Kisumu.[104] In addition to these large-scale operations, smaller Asian manufacturers were involved in local sugar production in the Rift Valley Province.

The transfer of power in December 1963 did not boost investor confidence or energize the private sector, as it had promised. The Nairobi Chamber of Commerce awaited definitive indications from the new government of its attitudes toward the private sector. Kenya's political economy remained confused until Kanu's radical wing lost influence. Not until Kanu absorbed most of Kadu at the expense of its left wing, a merger that the Colonial Office had failed to achieve, did the direction of the Kenyan economy begin to clarify. Yet the actions in the years leading up to independence had indicated the likelihood of a probusiness orientation. As the day of independence approached, the statements of most African politicians moderated. Socialist sloganeering was heard less frequently, and the advantages of foreign capital were touted. Most of the political leaders promised compensation in the event of the expropriation of private property. Odinga and Kaggia found themselves in a diminishing minority position. Kanu's acceptance of the World Bank's recommendations suggested that the new government would try to foster investor confidence and strive for political stability, anchored by a strong administrative machine. The report had emphasized the damage to the economy of "a mass exodus of the higher and specialist civil servants, farmers, industrialists, financiers, traders, technicians, and professional people who constitute the bulk of the non-African communities."[105]

Equally promising for the business community were the close ties developing between Kenya's private sector and the state. Many of the former colonial administrators who elected to remain in Kenya when they retired from government service were promptly recruited onto the boards of Kenya's most important corporations. Not only did East African Power and Light, East African Breweries, and the British banks reserve board positions for Hope-Jones, Mitchell, and F. Maddison, a former Kenyan Treasury official, but they also invited educated Africans to join their firms.[106] Prominent among Africans finding places for themselves in the board rooms of big companies was Charles Rubia, who blazed a path for his compatriots by discovering that the most effective route to partici-

[104] Ibid., September 30, 1961; no. 216, Note by A. W. R., November 16, 1960, KNA State House 4/411; and Kenya, House of Representatives, *Official Record*, September 11, 1963, vol. 1, part 1, pp. 1800 ff.

[105] International Bank for Reconstruction and Development, *The Economic Development of Kenya* (Baltimore, Md., 1963), p. 51.

[106] National Christian Council of Kenya, A Working Party, *Who Controls Industry in Kenya?* (Nairobi, 1968).

pation in Kenya's private sector was through inclusion on boards rather than establishing their own firms.[107]

Although the Kenyan nationalists had shed much of the socialist rhetoric that had existed in the mid-1950s, they, like their Egyptian counterparts, had realized the bedrock economic demand of the nationalist cause. From the earliest colonial decades, the Kenyan Africans had agitated for the restoration of their lost lands, and although they did not succeed in "Africanizing" the whole of the "white" highlands, they set in motion a process for the transference of large portions of the area to African ownership. By 1970 no less than 2.5 million of the 3.1 million acres of mixed European farming had been turned over to Africans.

This vast transference of assets, which was not to be minimized even when comparing it with the seismic shift in the ownership of businesses in Egypt, did not, however, bring about the destruction of the private sector in Kenya or force foreign capitalists and investors out of Kenya as it did in Egypt. The contrasting results of asset transfer in the two countries derived, in the first place, from the differing economic goals of the two nationalist movements. Even before World War I, Egyptian nationalists had linked Britain's political domination of their country with its overall economic power. They had been especially troubled by the dominant position of foreign banks, and, with the establishment of Bank Misr in 1920, they had at least created a competitor to the European banking conglomerates. Even as the overweening economic predominance of Europeans gave way to a rising Egyptian bourgeoisie, and even as areas of European privilege were eradicated (through abolition of the Capitulations, Mixed Tribunals, protective tariff restrictions, and the like), the Egyptian nationalists still eyed foreign capital suspiciously. In contrast, save for a few intellectuals lodged in the Kanu left wing and the trade union movement, and a small number who got caught up in the anti-European sentiments of Mau Mau and its successor groups, the Kenyan nationalists had little interest in reducing foreign influence anywhere other than in landowning. Kanu intellectuals used socialist slogans in their propagandist statements, but few were serious about creating a state-dominated economy. And most Kenyan nationalists did not regard the continuing economic influence of foreign capital as robbing the country of its prized political independence.

A second factor that distinguished the economic arrangements in Kenya from those in Egypt (and Nigeria, for that matter) were the British policies themselves, which could not have been more dissimilar. In Kenya the colonial policy makers compromised with and cajoled the na-

---

[107] Gary Wasserman, *Politics of Decolonization: Kenya, Europeans and the Land Issue, 1960–1965* (Cambridge, 1976), p. 40.

tionalists, making timely concessions so as not to intensify radical anti-European sentiments. They systematically sought the support of big business, especially British-based capital. In contrast, in Egypt the chimera of retaining a political and military presence in a strategically important country drove British policy makers to alienate Egyptian nationalists and to ignore business opinion.

The land transfers of the 1960s restored 2.5 million acres to African peoples. Although critics at the time and later blamed the nationalists for paying too high a price for the land, in fact, the British government provided more than one-third of the funds for the land schemes as a grant (£9.7 million). The remainder, approximately £17 million, came in the form of loans from Britain and other outside agencies.[108] However one evaluates these transactions (and the radical nationalists shrieked that the people of Kenya had been forced to buy back what had always belonged to them, while the departing settlers protested that they were unfairly compensated for all of the work that they had put into the estates), in Kenya, as in Egypt, the metropole ended up paying a considerable portion of the economic costs of power transfer. In Egypt, British taxpayers and European investors paid out nearly £25 million for the uncompensated Egyptianization and subsequent nationalization of foreign property. In Kenya, the British government provided roughly £35 million to support the military and the economy during Mau Mau and then to subsidize the land transfers. The glaring difference was that in Kenya British funds were used effectively to protect the larger interests of European investors, while in Egypt the British resources were employed to compensate European investors after they had been driven from the country.

[108] The statistical data are taken from Hans Ruthenberg, *African Agricultural Production Development Policy in Kenya* (New York, 1966). No discussion is undertaken here of whether the expenditure of funds in the highlands was the most efficient allocation of Kenya's resources. Ruthenberg characterizes the expenditure of £26.5 million as "a colossal injection of capital considering the acreage concerned, far in excess of what was spent on high potential African lands under the Swynnerton Plan" (p. 82). He also concludes that while the overall agricultural return would undoubtedly have been higher had this large sum of money gone into the African agricultural areas, there was little choice because of the centrality of the land question and the restoration of the lost land in the nationalist campaign.

Themes and Variations

DURING THE NATIONALIST campaign for the independence of the Gold Coast, Kwame Nkrumah proclaimed that Africans should seek the political kingdom first; his counterpart in Nigeria returning from the constitutional conference in London in 1955 exulted that the British had handed Nigeria its independence on a platter of gold. Both perspectives stressed the primacy of politics and the ease with which independence seemed to be coming. Yet, not long after this prized political independence was achieved, Nkrumah, noting aborted pan-African dreams and failed economic programs, grumbled that political independence had been a sham triumph. Africans, he opined, had exchanged colonial governors and district officers for the chief executive officers of multinational corporations and had discovered what a poor bargain the trade was. In his opinion, neocolonialism, the last stage of imperialism, was an onerous form of economic exploitation, representing the continued enrichment of non-African economic organizations who no longer assumed any responsibility for the impact of their social and economic policies on local populations.

THEMES

By placing economic institutions, economic programs, private-public sector relations, and the modern corporation at the center of the inquiry into the decolonizing narrative, four major (as well as a number of subordinate) uniformities emerge—conclusions that often prove to be at variance with much of the literature on decolonization and nationalism. First, the decolonization experience realized the historical mission and main goals of the nationalist movements of individual African countries. Second, imperialism was not the avatar of capitalism, as suggested by Catherine Coquery-Vidrovitch.[1] Nor were the large-scale modern corporations, whether foreign or locally based, significant actors in the decisions that

[1] Catherine Coquery-Vidrovitch, "De l'impérialisme ancien à l'impérialismé moderne: l'avatar colonial," in *L'impérialisme française d'avant 1914*, ed. J. Bouvier and J. Girault (Paris, 1976), pp. 21–52. Although this article was written some years ago, it is one of the clearest statements of a still respected and widely held point of view.

led to the withdrawal of European power. Often the primary interests of these economic organizations went unheeded. Third, on balance, the use of force had varying effects for Western economic interests in the last stages of colonial suzerainty. Throughout the two decolonizing decades, British officials debated the efficacy of employing their military might. In Egypt and Kenya, they embarked on major military campaigns, which, however, produced dramatically different outcomes for the private sector of the two countries. Fourth, the European departure from Africa proved expensive and at times threatening to the international order and had many reminders of the chaotic and precipitous way in which the Europeans had first partitioned and conquered the African continent and its peoples.

I

Many contemporary African political leaders and intellectuals look back on the era of decolonization as a time of wasted opportunities, regretting the bargains their predecessors struck with the departing European powers. But even a cursory perusal of the historical record would reveal that the decolonization arrangements were far from one-sided and that they realized the most deeply held, long-standing, and consensual goals of the main-line nationalists movements. Indeed, many of the differences that distinguished the economy of Egypt from those of Nigeria and Kenya in 1963 stemmed directly from the nationalist orientations represented in the three countries.

To begin with Egypt, from at least the end of the nineteenth century and perhaps as far back as the latter years of the reign of Muhammad Ali and that of Ismail, Egyptian intellectuals had concluded that political sovereignty by itself did not suffice and that economic power was inextricably linked with foreign political domination. By the turn of the century, a prominent Egyptian nationalist, Tal'at Harb, had set forth a blueprint for liberating the Egyptian economy from British overrule. Harb's founding of Bank Misr in 1920 was intended to endow Egypt with an indigenous bank capable of competing with the great foreign banks, which he rightly regarded as the core of European economic might in the country. He also envisioned the new bank as a vehicle for promoting economic diversification and industrialization.

Awareness of the economic dimensions of imperial rule intensified as the twentieth century unfolded. By the interwar period, the economic aspects of imperialism were well understood by nonelite groups, like the Muslim Brothers and Young Egypt, and targeted for removal. The Egyptian nationalist movement linked the poverty and economic stagnation of the country with the widespread influence of foreign capital. The symbols of European economic privilege were constant reminders of Egypt's economic inferiority. Foreign banks that seemed unwilling to lend for new industrial projects, ginning and shipping conglomerates conspiring to fix prices against Egyptian cultivators, and that emblem of foreign economic and political power, the Suez Canal Company, made obvious the economic strength of foreign capital and persuaded even the most apolitical individuals and the most moderate nationalists, as well as the more extreme nationalists on the right and the left, to embrace a capacious view of sovereignty and to insist on economic independence and political freedom.

At the opposite extreme of this political-economic spectrum was Kenyan nationalism. Almost from the outset of European-African relations, the principal grievances of African peoples were tied to land alienation. As African populations increased and severe overcrowding occurred within the reserves, the colonial state's failure to accommodate African demands for land propelled the nationalist movement toward radical militancy. Other economic issues were so subordinated to land redress as to be little more than ideological pronouncements, taken almost verbatim from socialist propaganda, and posing no realistic threat to European and Asian dominance of the nonagrarian sectors of Kenya.

Although talented Nigerian businessmen had made a discernible place for themselves in the Nigerian political economy by the end of World War II, Nigeria's nationalist activities and programs focused increasingly on political and constitutional advances and ignored the economic aspects of imperial control. Moreover, as state power swelled and the state became the most effective instrument for mobilizing capital, through marketing board surpluses, any prospect that an autonomous Nigerian business elite might come into being and challenge the predominance of European and Syro-Lebanese capital, let alone the commanding position of the state in economic affairs, was severely limited.

II

In "De l'impérialisme ancien à l'impérialisme moderne: l'avatar colonial," Catherine Coquery-Vidrovitch presented late-nineteenth-century colonialism as the creator of the world capitalist system of the late twentieth century. She suggested that the establishment of formal political controls over nearly all of Africa and many new areas in Asia at the end of the nineteenth century, though primarily carried out for political and prestige motives, laid the foundations for capitalist institutions and a capitalist ethos.[2]

Yet if one examines the last stage of the colonial process—the decolonization of African territories—not only did the transfer of power from British to African hands realize much of the historical mission of African nationalism, it also blocked the plans of British business groups already located on the African continent, and for that matter Western capital in general.

Egypt is the most obvious case in point. Geopolitical factors continued to shape the formulation of British policy as they had from the moment Britain invaded and conquered the country. Occupied by Britain to protect the routes to India and magnified in importance with the creation of a huge military base in the Suez Canal area and the increase of vital European shipping through the canal, Egypt represented the political and military keystone of British imperial policy in the Middle East. This policy orientation was maintained even in the face of growing Egyptian nationalism and overt pressure from the usually politically quiescent major business concerns and chambers of commerce to accommodate nationalist demands. The British efforts to force Egypt into an anti-Soviet Cold War alliance led military strategists and political analysts to regard economic and cultural interests as subordinate to geopolitical goals, however unrealistic and grandiose they were.

It was hardly surprising, then, that the decisive rupture in Anglo-Egyptian relations occurred over the Suez Canal Company, which, in addition to being the archetypal institution of European economic and political domination, was the firm most opposed to the termination of Britain's military and political hold on the country. And it was not surprising that the military preparations leading up to the British-French-Israeli invasion of the country, following the Egyptian nationalization of the Suez Canal Company, gave scant consideration to the long-term financial and economic consequences of an invasion. When occasionally the planners addressed economic and financial issues, they were, as usual, prepared to sacrifice Britain's substantial assets in Egypt to their military and political agenda.

Although the British regarded Nigeria as the most promising economic territory in Africa and as a country in which Britain would employ its power to safeguard a privileged position for British capital, in numerous specific decisions British colonial officials sacrificed the interests of British capital to less economic considerations. In truth, the relationship between British government officials and agents of British-based capital had never been completely amicable, even during Nigeria's classical co-

---

[2] Ibid.

lonial period. It was further strained under the pressures of rising nationalism and power transfer. When the twin goals of ensuring political stability and promoting Britain's economic stake in Nigeria were seen to be in conflict, the British rulers opted to promote political tranquillity rather than to buttress British capital.

In a crucial set of decisions made after World War II, the colonial government established government-run marketing boards in the face of opposition from the powerful export-import houses. Although Colonial Office officials in London rejected the local preference for rurally based, locally financed industrial development in favor of large-scale projects under the auspices of British-based multinational capital, these same officials also removed the special legislative powers that foreign investors had enjoyed under the pre–World War II constitutions; they were unwilling to be seen working closely with newly organized British business pressure groups until the transfer of authority had been achieved. Thus, the once-powerful British exporting and importing businesses found themselves compelled to withdraw from their traditional sectors and to take an active part in industrial investments while the British banking and shipping firms, once nearly unchallenged, faced competition from local capitalists and state regulators.

In Kenya, Mau Mau and the even more unsettling transition from British to African rule caused large-scale, mostly foreign capital, to organize with a view to influencing political outcomes. In those tumultuous years, the British colonial administrators were also intensely solicitous of foreign capital, although their efforts to allay alarm were often unavailing. Particularly in the crucial last stage of formal British authority (1960–1963), Hope-Jones's mission to Europe and Britain yielded insignificant results. Multinational investors kept their distance from the Kenyan economy, awaiting a signal from the new African leaders that their investments would be welcomed and protected. Agents of foreign capital were as profoundly distressed as the British Treasury over the radical land redistribution schemes, which they feared would damage the agrarian sector and rob Kenya of its investor-worthiness. With foreign investors largely detached from the politics of Kenya, right-wing settler opinion took over. Its representatives were able to persuade the British cabinet that the only way to avoid an Algerian- and Congolese-like exodus of capital and technical talent was through massive schemes of land redistribution, even if such programs resulted in the peasantization of vast sections of the central highlands. In this politically and economically uncertain setting, only Asian capitalists continued to risk their capital through new investments in the domestic economy.

It might be natural to assume that the obvious beneficiary, if not the prime mover, of the setbacks to British capital was American capital.

Here, the record is unequivocal. American corporations and diplomats did not spur decolonization in tropical Africa. The closest that U.S. diplomats came to taking an active interest in the new economic arrangements of British-controlled tropical Africa occurred in Kenya, where the Asian business community took the lead in attempting to forge an alliance with American investors in the decade immediately after World War II. Asian merchants complained to the U.S. diplomats that they were unable to deal directly with American manufacturers or facilitate American investment in the country. The American consul in Nairobi rallied to their cause, arguing that the British colonial administrators, in league with British business, were employing sterling zone arguments to block any American entry. These protests found little response from American business groups, and finally, all the State Department in Washington did was to lodge a formal but ineffective protest with the British about trade practices. Not even this level of discontent obtained in Nigeria, where U.S. diplomatic agents tended to be as opposed to the Nigerian political leadership as their British counterparts were. There the influence of American capital was negligible.

Egypt should have been a different case altogether. An American multinational presence existed there. Ford, Chrysler, General Motors, Mobil Oil, TWA, Pan Am, National Cash Register, Kodak, and others had growing economic interests in Egypt and were using Egypt as the center of their Middle East activities. In addition, Egypt had left the sterling area in 1947 with the intention of converting sterling into dollars. Although the effort had fallen short of the mark when the British froze sterling, Egypt's trading and investment policies were still designed to favor capital drawn from multiple sources. Yet, because of Egypt's critical military and political importance in the Cold War struggle, political goals took precedence over economic matters even in American policy. When Dulles withdrew U.S., British, and World Bank support for the Aswan High Dam project, he did so without consulting the American business interests that would have been involved in the lucrative construction and electrical contracts of that project. And there was no outpouring of opposition from American business groups at his action.

III

According to Ronald Robinson, "the [British] rulers came to the [bargaining] table with the idea of keeping authority up to the brink of a situation in which they might have to shoot or get out; [African] subjects came with the idea of enlarging their share of power up to the point of getting shot or backing down."[3] This statement implies a rational political and military calculus notably absent from these African narratives. Indeed, it would be difficult to argue that the British used their military superiority consistently, in ways that advanced Britain's long-term economic, cultural, and political stake in Africa. Quite the contrary, their political and military calculations were entirely problematic, if not downright injurious to long-term British goals. The example of Egypt is almost too obvious to recount. There the British failed to use troops when they had them on the ground in large numbers and when British property and lives were being threatened, as they were in early 1952. Yet four and a half years later, the British attempted the monumentally more difficult task of "reconquering" and "recolonizing" a territory where the strength of anti-British nationalist feelings had caused even the most hardened British political and military analysts to conclude that they could not sustain themselves. The reconquest endeavor was an exercise in futility, and it had a predictable outcome: the dissolution of vast economic and cultural ties from nearly a century of intense Anglo-French-Egyptian relations, carried out by a shrewdly opportunistic and deeply resentful group of young Egyptian army officers.

In Nigeria, in striking contrast to Egypt, the British had never been willing to commit large military resources. The territory was occupied on the cheap and administered through systems of indirect rule that were designed to associate African collaborators with British overlords; and the British colonial establishment proved unwilling to use (or to make a rigorous assessment of) its military and police instrumentalities to delay what many believed was an altogether too precipitous transfer of power. A crucial moment occurred in the mid-1950s, when accumulating evidence of corruption, maladministration, and rising ethnic tension (all of which plagued Nigeria in its first decade of independence and led to military coups d'etat and civil war) caused the secretary of state for colonies to call for a political and military evaluation of the impact of a decision to abridge the timetable for independence. The military assessment was a cursory one at best. Indeed, it was little more than a reaffirmation of the well-worn British principle of not resorting to overt force and above all to maintaining the so-called political initiative.

Even in Kenya, where force was employed to suppress Mau Mau dissidents between 1952 and 1957, the specter of new Mau Maus, and especially the unchallenged assumption that European settlers would pull up stakes from Kenya if their economic demands were not met and plunge

[3] Ronald Robinson, "Andrew Cohen and the Transfer of Power in Tropical Africa, 1940–1951," in *Decolonisation and After: The British and French Experience*, ed. W. H. Morris-Jones and Georges Fischer (London, 1980), p. 51.

the country into economic chaos and ethnic warfare, caused the colonial authorities to leap to the conclusion that only a radical land reform scheme would ensure political tranquillity.

IV

The European departure from Africa was precipitous, uncalculated, and on occasion even threatening to international stability. It has more than a few disturbing parallels with the equally precipitous and thoughtless European occupation of Africa. It also proved to be far more costly than any of its advocates thought possible. Just as most of the partition of Africa occurred in little more than the span of a single decade, from 1882 to 1894, and bore the marks of haste and poor preparation, so the withdrawal from Africa occurred in an even shorter period of time, roughly from 1956 when the Sudan achieved its formal independence, to 1963. It had the same imprint of haste, unpreparedness, and disregard for the welfare of the African peoples. In 1945 Britain's statesmen and colonial officials were just giving thought to the timetable and method of power transfer; within a decade those same individuals were writing the new independence constitutions. By then they had dropped their insistence on the attainment of certain standards of preparation for independence, the achievement of educational goals, promising economic prospects, and various other factors that the British had regarded as essential to successful self-rule and good governance.

The withdrawal was rapid; and it was something else that few thought it would be: expensive. Some observers have asserted that the Europeans left Africa because of a clear and compelling economic calculus. The European rulers withdrew, it is claimed, at a time when the burdens of colonial administration were increasing and the economic benefits to Europe were declining. The European imperial states faced heavier military and policing costs in connection with rising African nationalist movements and were for the first time expected to underwrite programs of economic development. A careful perusal of the economic record does not bear out this point. Nowhere in the Egyptian, Nigerian, and Kenyan colonial records is there evidence that the British carried out a careful cost-benefit calculation. In fact, the actual costs of transferring power proved to be much greater than any of the colonial planners could possibly have imagined. In Egypt the British had to compensate British property holders for the assets that the Egyptian state had nationalized, and in Kenya the costs of suppressing Mau Mau and facilitating land transfers were substantial. There, many of the payments took the form of British grants to the government of Kenya.

Finally, just as the partition of Africa had brought Europe close to war on several occasions (at Fashoda in 1898 and over Morocco between 1905 and 1912), so in the British-French-Israeli invasion of Egypt did the United States refuse to support its primary European allies and the Soviet Union threaten to rain down missiles on London and Paris. In short, the transfer of power in Africa was hardly the smooth and graceful transition portrayed in numerous memoirs of the time and subsequently catalogued in many scholarly accounts. The unanticipated costs, the disruption to the international system that occurred in Egypt, and the hasty and often inaccurate political and economic calculations suggest a confusing era in Euro-African relations. The results of decolonization also lend credence to the argument that a great deal was at stake—that a shift in the locus of power was occurring.

V

There was a fifth uniformity, related to periodization and timing, shared by all three of the African territories. To understand the similar chronology of decolonization one must commence with the observation that all three countries entered the post–World War II era embracing the same general perspectives on how best to promote economic development. Despite the significant different colonial legacies of the three countries, the government leaders and economic technocrats in each country embraced what had become in most of Africa at the close of World War II a consensual view on economic development. The main tenets of what would soon be called development economics stressed the role of the state as the creator of the infrastructural and juridical and legislative environment for private investment, the importance of entrepreneurship, and the centrality of foreign investment in countries still too poor to have spawned a large middle class. Much of the literature focused on the place of the state in planning and even in facilitating the mobilization of investment capital, and paid less attention to expectations of the private sector; but private investment, entrepreneurs, and the modern corporation were viewed as equally important, with the state as agent of economic transformation.

This consensus on development was apparent even in Egypt, where it was elaborated forcibly by the civilian rulers and embraced, perhaps opportunistically but nevertheless enthusiastically, by their military replacements. In Nigeria the great debates were entirely concerned with private and public sector boundary lines and the control over Nigeria's trade surpluses. In Kenya a politically nervous colonial government repulsed an effort of well-placed colonial officials to enlarge the economic powers of the state at the expense of the private sector.

The first decade after World War II witnessed the elaboration of this consensual economic vision. It was followed by important challenges in all three countries. The challenges came from groups overlooked in the new economic programs that were likely to bear the weight of these efforts. In Nigeria radical trade unionists joined forces with socialists to oppose unregulated capitalism. At the time of the general strike in 1945 and then in the Enugu coal miners' strike in 1949, segments from the subaltern Nigerian world protested their unfavorable political and economic prospects. Similarly, in Kenya the Mau Mau revolt of the Kikuyu underclasses posed massive financial and military problems for the state and undermined the colonial and settler perspective on Kenya's economic and political future. Only in Egypt did oppressed groups gain entry to power, but even there access came under the auspices of young military officers who, while they had drunk deeply of left- and right-wing ideologies and had sprung from lower social groups, had a pragmatic bent, an awareness of how little prepared they were to govern, and a commitment to the strength and coherence of the military establishment over any ideological preference. In time and under the pressure of international events and internal demands to bring about significant improvements in standards of living, the new Egyptian rulers experimented with more radical economic formulas. They went further than other ruling groups in redrawing the demarcation lines between state and private enterprise.

A third stage in the decolonizing process in these three countries witnessed the implementation of programs to meet the challenges raised in the second stage, including the speeding up of the decolonization time frame. In Egypt, cataclysmic international pressures and events created a wide range of opportunities for the new leaders to overturn the pro-capitalist orientation that was dominant elsewhere and allowed them to draw up a state-centered approach to development that used Soviet models and experts. Key Nigerian groups, particularly the nationalist aspirants to power, found the much-criticized marketing boards a financial and political resource too tempting to resist. Gradually they extended their power over the vast financial resources of the boards and employed their massive sums for outright political purposes. Kenya's essentially conservative fiscal policies, which were the handiwork of Ernest Vasey at the Ministry of Finance, continued in the even more politically and economically insecure climate of the final stage of power transfer, despite Vasey's absence from power and the growing influence of African nationalists.

VARIATIONS

One of the reasons for employing a comparative method is to highlight variations. The political, economic, and institutional narrative of the three decolonizing societies presented here offered perplexing outcomes. Possessing the most developed and politically influential private sector in 1945, Egypt experienced a series of nationalizing shocks. By the early 1960s, when Nasser broadcast his National Charter and carried out a mopping up campaign against the big capitalists, the large-scale private sector had virtually disappeared. In contrast, Kenya, with its supposedly radical and anti-European Mau Mau conflict, completed the decolonizing phase with its business private sector remarkably intact. Kenya not only weathered an ethnically based, anticolonial uprising, the suppression of which drained the military and financial resources of the colony; it also safeguarded the interests of the local entrepreneurial class, enabling it to be the only dynamic and autonomous business group among the three countries by the end of the decolonizing era. In Nigeria, Britain's eagerness to promote economic growth through a combination of private and public sector initiatives brought corruption and a loss of private sector autonomy. The effort to form an indigenous entrepreneurial elite, so promising in 1945, had to be judged a failure by 1960.

In accounting for the different outcomes for the private sectors of Egypt, Nigeria, and Kenya, three factors, in addition to the uniformities sketched above, stand out as significant: the international setting; domestic leadership; and attitudes toward indigenous bourgeoisies.

I

To begin with the international setting, Egypt was decisively involved in the Cold War struggle because of its geopolitical importance; in contrast, Nigeria and Kenya were sheltered from the Cold War by their colonial status. In Egypt the cataclysmic events of the 1950s created unusual political and economic opportunities and intensified nationalist sensitivities that spilled over into the economic arena. The Soviets exploited nationalist suspicions of the West, and the West wasted much of its enormous economic and cultural advantage in trying to implement misguided military and political policies. Indeed, it could be argued that if Dulles had not withdrawn aid for the Aswan dam and the United States had found a way to provide the crucial financial support for a project of essential importance to the Egyptian elite, the Egyptians would never have been able to turn so aggressively against all forms of large-scale private capital. In contrast, colonial Nigeria and Kenya could not interject themselves into the Cold War despite their occasional efforts to do so. British colonial officials sought financial support from the British Treasury for the suppression of Mau Mau, citing the Malaysian precedent, only to be informed that the basis of support in Malaysia was a communist menace, not an ethnic outburst. Similarly, the Nigerian minister of finance complained of Britain's stinginess in providing economic assistance and contended that Nigeria would receive preferential treatment if only it could manufacture a communist threat.

II

Domestic leadership strongly influenced the position of the private sector in the two decades after the war. Control over the major financial and economic ministries—whether by politicians or by technically trained economic figures—was decisive. Egyptian policy moved in radical directions from 1956 onward not simply because of the appointment of Ismail Sidqi as head of the newly established Ministry of Industry. Sidqi was, after all, fully competent in economic matters. His appointment, however, marked Nasser's move into the economic aspects of Egyptian life. Just as Egyptian economic policy after 1956 bore the imprint of Nasser, so Kenya's conservative fiscal policies designed to preserve the pro-Western and capitalist orientation of Kenya owed much to the astuteness of Ernest Vasey. Nasser was a political animal through and through; Vasey was a man of finance and economics. In Egypt, although there were numerous brilliant economic experts in the Ministries of Finance, Industry, Commerce, and Economic Planning—witness the names of Imari, Sidqi, Qaysuni, and Jiritli—these men had to defer to Nasser. Whether Nasser was motivated by a genuine desire to improve the lot of the common folk or by an aggrandizing political impulse is beside the point (although no doubt both factors were at work). The political aspects of his program were of paramount importance.

In contrast, Vasey, who had no political following or party but whose political acuity was widely admired and regarded as indispensable during the Mau Mau struggle, was permitted great autonomy in Kenya; he ensured that fiscal and economic issues got a fair hearing even when radical settler groups and extremist nationalists demanded that the state curtail the private sector. Vasey was ably assisted by a highly professional group of fiscal and economic experts (MacKenzie, Maddison, and the like) whose drafting of annual budgets and preparation for crucial legislative debates were exemplary.

The difficulty facing Nigeria was that no single individual was able to stamp an economic vision on that vast and diverse country. No British financial expert and no nationalist dominated the economic aspects of the debate. As a consequence, Nigeria tended to drift economically as independence approached and to allow its important economic and fiscal questions to become swallowed up in the turmoil of the nationalist electoral struggles.

III

According to Samir Amin, capitalism in Africa, Asia, and Latin America "spreads only to the extent allowed by an international specialization in which the periphery remains passive and . . . has no tendency of its own to become exclusive." Economic innovation in colonial and semicolonial areas occurs only when allowed by "the great absent member of colonial society: the dominant metropolitan bourgeoisie."[4] In reality, domestically based firms and groups encountered their most effective opponents not in the board rooms of European and North American multinational corporations but within African state apparatuses. At first the critics were the British colonial officers of Nigeria and Kenya; later they were military bureaucrats in Egypt and nationalist aspirants to power in Nigeria and Kenya. Only in Kenya, and there only after the state aggrandizing element within the government had been checked, did the officeholders begin to promote the interests of a market economy aggressively. No doubt one of the reasons for this strikingly strong capitalist orientation in Kenya stemmed from the fact that the Kenyan legislature had elected representatives and the Kenyan cabinet drew some of its members from the nonofficial classes. The two most impressive pro-capitalist members of the British cabinet were Vasey and Hope-Jones, whose efforts on behalf of private capital cannot be minimized.

The attitudes of the state toward indigenous bourgeoisies was therefore a third decisive factor in accounting for the differential outcomes. Nasser and his cohort displayed impatience and suspicion of entrepreneurs. They resented the power that foreign business groups had over the economy, and after undercutting foreign capital they soon turned on an already cowering domestic bourgeoisie. A comparable anti-Asian bias, though it undoubtedly simmered below the surface in Kenya, remained submerged because the nationalist leadership did not regard the Asians as economic competitors or as having inordinate political clout. In this arena, too,

---

[4] Samir Amin, *Accumulation on a World Scale: A Critique of the Theory of Underdevelopment*, tr. Brian Pearce (New York, 1974), vol. 1, p. 177, and vol. 2, p. 360.

Vasey in particular was not as disparaging of Asian capital as some of his compatriots. Finally, in Nigeria it became increasingly clear to nationalist contenders that the surest route to wealth and power was through the government bureaucracy rather than commerce, industry, or even agriculture.

Often comparativists find their explanations for economic differences in more easily quantifiable factors than have been explored here. Levels of economic development, gross domestic product per capita, levels of education and literacy, urbanization, and the like are usually highlighted. This study has been about elites, decision making in the economic arena, economic blueprints, and economic and fiscal legislation, because political economies, like national identities, are constructed. They are the outgrowth of the visions of individuals, the debates of formally and informally organized pressure groups, and the interplay of international politics. In the cases examined here, the overarching question has been why ruling elites, the final arbiters of economic policies, either valued private sectors over public enterprises or preferred a statist orientation. To be sure, levels of literacy, education, urbanization, GDP, and other factors influenced the options available to decision makers, and undeniably, over the long run, had a decisive influence on the successes and failures of particular visions. But in the short span of a decade and a half, as colonial influence was receding and nationalist fervor was waxing, personal dynamism, pressure group energy, and class tensions enjoyed primacy.

Although this study has focused on elites and their debates, the voices and influence of the subaltern populations were also influential in shaping policy decisions. The different outcomes stemmed from the greater role of the subaltern in Egypt than in Kenya and Nigeria. Even in Kenya, however, the unemployed, the landless, and the squatters were scarcely out of the calculations of elite groups. The dispossessed did not sit at the negotiating tables and hence had no direct voice in the final resolution of Kenya's land problem and the formulas for independence, but each of the negotiating teams brought its own understanding of those unrepresented groups to the exchanges and sought arrangements that would, at the very least, mollify lower-class grievances. In Nigeria, where there was no outburst comparable to Mau Mau, the fear of an uprising from the lower orders was a factor at every stage of the decolonization process.

Bibliographical Note

I have attempted to reconstruct the narrative of the decolonizing of Egypt, Nigeria, and Kenya from primary sources. In this effort I have not ignored the substantial secondary literature on this subject and these countries, some of which is referred to in the footnotes; but rather than listing all of the books worthy of inclusion in such a bibliography and thus making this work longer than it already is, I chose to limit this bibliography to primary sources.

Archives and Manuscripts

Government archives were my single most important source of information. In London I looked at the Foreign Office materials on Egypt, the Colonial Office files on Nigeria and Kenya, the Premier's Office, the Board of Trade, the War Office, the Treasury, and the Cabinet Papers. The U.S. National Archives in Washington, D.C., were also helpful for providing another perspective on events. The most useful files were those of the Department of State in Washington, but equally valuable for information on economic affairs and business activities were the embassy and consular records from the three countries in the study. The Kenya National Archives (Nairobi) were of considerable value despite the fact that they were apparently severely pruned for the Mau Mau years. For my purposes I found the records of the Kenyan Ministry of Commerce and Industry particularly useful, but there are also important materials in the Kenyan Secretariat, the State House, the Office of the President, the Ministry of Economic Planning and Development, and the Treasury, as well as private collections held in the Kenyan National Archives. These included the private papers of Ernest Vasey, S. V. Cooke, Wilfred B. Havelock, and George Tyson and a few files on Asian business activities.

It had been my hope when I commenced work on this project to make heavy use of the archives, as well as the published materials, of business firms operating in the three countries. I wrote to numerous firms and was given permission to look at many records, but the results were not nearly as exciting as I had hoped. It would appear that firms did not keep their records from this period as carefully as they now seem to be doing. Also, the government archives proved to be more forthcoming on the extent to which business leaders attempted to influence policy. The companies and business organizations that made their records available to me were the Ford Motor Company, Dearborn, Michigan; Mobil Oil, New York City; Shell Oil, London; Barclays Bank, DCO, London; John Holt, Rhodes House Library, Oxford; the Ocean Archives, Liverpool; Unilever, London; the United Africa Company, London; Cadburys, Birmingham; Calico Printers, Manchester; Bradford Dyers, Manchester; the London Chamber of Commerce, and the Nairobi Chamber of Commerce, Rhodes House Library, Oxford. I also read through the annual stockholders' reports and other publications of nearly every firm that was doing business in Egypt, Kenya, and Nigeria.

The Rhodes House collection of colonial materials is deservedly well known, and I used it extensively. In addition to the Holt Papers and the papers of the Nairobi Chamber of Commerce, already noted, it holds the Michael Blundell papers.

The papers of the Bank of England require a special mention, not only because of their accessibility and excellent cataloguing but also because they contain so much of interest to anyone researching financial and economic matters.

The publications of the British, Egyptian, Kenyan, and Nigerian governments were of great value. Various British parliamentary papers dealt with the three African territories that were of such vital interest to Britain in the 1940s and 1950s. The African governments themselves issued a vast range of individual publications as well as ministerial annual reports of obvious relevance to economic matters. One can find a full listing of these state publications in the catalogues of the British Library, the Library of Congress, and the special volumes dedicated to the serial publications of foreign governments, published by the New York Public Library. For my purposes, in trying to obtain an overview of fiscal and economic policies and the supporters and opponents among politically represented groups, I used the records of the Kenyan Legislative Council and all four of the legislative bodies in Nigeria.

The local press was an important source of information on the political economies of all three countries, especially the newspapers and journals that surveyed economic affairs and politics. For Egypt, *al-Ahram* and the *Egyptian Gazette* had the most comprehensive reporting of economic matters. The Egyptian journals that specialized in economic matters, such as *L'Informateur, L'Egypte Industriel*, and the various journals of the chambers of commerce of Alexandria and Cairo, became less and less useful as the Nasser government extended its control over the press in the 1950s. In Kenya, the *East African Standard* and the *Kenya Weekly News* provided the most comprehensive, albeit elite-oriented view of major economic and political developments. The *West African Pilot*, the *Daily Service*, and the *Daily Times* had their own political perspectives, and each was essential for obtaining information on political and economic developments in Nigeria.

Numerous participants in the events of the period have written memoirs, but the most important for my purposes, because they gave the nationalists' point of view on highly controversial events, were those of the Egyptian military men and their civilian supporters. I mention in particular the works of Sadat, Baghdadi, Khalid Muhi al-Din, Neguib, Ahmad Hamrush, Mahmud Riyad, Kamil al-Sharif, Kamal al-Din Rifat, Mahmud Muhammad al-Jawhari, Ali Sabri, Uthman Ahmad Uthman, Abd al-Jalil al-Imari, Amin Huwaydi, and Sayyid Mari, most of which are cited in the footnotes.

Finally, wherever possible I interviewed persons who had participated in these events. I thank them for their willingness to meet with me and give me their perspectives: J. H. E. Allison, Geoffrey W. Bird, Michael Blundell, Manu Chandaria, W. D. Fischer, Abdel Gazarin, Ahmad Hamrush, Peter Harris, Zaki

Hashem, Abdal-Aziz Higazi, Ibrahim Hilmi abd al-Rahman, Brian Hobson, Amin Huwayti, Hasan Ibrahim, Joan Karmali, Chanda Kohli, Ahmad al-Lawzi, Madatally Manji, Frank Martin, Michael McWilliam, Sarwat Muntasir, Robert Ridley, Edward Rodwell, Ismail Sabri, Rodney Searight, Aziz Sidqi, John C. Skett, Said el-Tawil, and Douglas Taylor.

Index

About the Author

ROBERT L. TIGNOR is the Rosengarten Professor of Modern and Contemporary History at Princeton University. He is the author of *Modernization and British Colonial Rule in Egypt, 1882–1914; The Colonial Transformation of Kenya;* and *State, Private Enterprise, and Economic Change in Egypt, 1918–1952*, all published by Princeton University Press.